Programming Windows® Embedded CE 6.0 Developer Reference

Douglas Boling

PUBLISHED BY
Microsoft Press
A Division of Microsoft Corporation
One Microsoft Way
Redmond, Washington 98052-6399

Library of Congress Control Number: 2007934742

Printed and bound in the United States of America.

1 2 3 4 5 6 7 8 9 QWT 2 1 0 9 8 7

Distributed in Canada by H.B. Fenn and Company Ltd.

A CIP catalogue record for this book is available from the British Library.

Microsoft Press books are available through booksellers and distributors worldwide. For further information about international editions, contact your local Microsoft Corporation office or contact Microsoft Press International directly at fax (425) 936-7329. Visit our Web site at www.microsoft.com/mspress. Send comments to mspinput@microsoft.com.

Acquisitions Editor: Ben Ryan
Developmental Editor: Devon Musgrave
Project Editor: Kathleen Atkins
Editorial Production: Abshier House
Technical Reviewer: Rob Miles; Technical Review services provided by Content Master, a member of CM Group, Ltd.

Body Part No. X14-06995

To Nancy Jane

Contents at a Glance

Table of Contents

Part II Windows CE Programming

Acknowledgments

Books are produced by diverse teams of talented people. My name appears on the cover, but countless others were involved in this book's creation. The teams of people who worked on this edition all pushed themselves to the max to complete this revision.

First, there's the talented team at Microsoft Press. Kathleen Atkins is the project leader and editor of all four editions of this book. Kathleen's continued stewardship of this book over the years has provided a level of quality that wouldn't have been possible without her. Devon Musgrave was the content development manager. Ben Ryan was the acquisitions editor for this edition of the book and deserves credit for getting this revision released.

The technical editor was Rob Miles of Content Master. Rob not only caught some potentially embarrassing errors, his British perspective pointed out some of my more "colonial" expressions. Other editoral and production duties were performed by Abshier House.

Thanks also to the various Microsoft development and marketing teams. Over the years, they have tolerated my endless questions. Thanks to Mike Thomson, Chip Schnarel, and Mike Hall for answering questions and providing support to make this book better.

A special thanks goes to my agent, Claudette Moore, and the team at Moore Literary Agency. Claudette handled all the business details, freeing me to deal with the fun stuff.

This edition of *Programming Windows Embedded CE* builds on the foundation of the three earlier editions, so what you read is based on work from a much larger team. In addition to the people already mentioned, other folks from Microsoft Press have helped immensely in the editing and production of the earlier editions of the book. They include Jim Fuchs, Shawn Peck, Brian Johnson, Julie Xiao, Rebecca McKay, Rob Nance, Cheryl Penner, Elizabeth Hansford, and Michael Victor.

My personal support team is headed by my wife, Nancy. Thanks, Nancy, for the support, help, and love. The team also includes our boys, Andy, Sam, and Jake. They make sure I always remember what is important in life. Finally, I acknowledge my parents, Ronald and Jane Boling. They are my role models.

Introduction

I've been working with Microsoft Windows CE for almost as long as it's been in existence. A Windows programmer for many years, I'm amazed by the number of different, typically quite small, systems to which I can apply my Windows programming experience. These Windows CE systems run the gamut from PC-like mini-laptops to cellular phones to embedded devices buried deep in some large piece of industrial equipment. The use of the Win32 API in Windows CE enables tens of thousands of Windows programmers to write applications for an entirely new class of systems. The subtle differences, however, make writing Windows CE code somewhat different from writing for the desktop versions of Windows. It's those differences that I'll address in this book.

Just What Is Windows CE?

Windows CE is the smallest and arguably the most interesting of the Microsoft Windows operating systems. Windows CE was designed from the ground up to be a small, power-efficient operating system with a Win32 subset API. Windows CE extends the Windows API into the markets and machines that can't support the larger footprints of the Windows Vista or even the Windows Embedded XP kernel.

The now-defunct Windows 95/98/Me line was a great operating system for users who needed backward compatibility with MS-DOS and Windows 2.*x* and 3.*x* programs. Although it had shortcomings, that operating system series succeeded amazingly well at this difficult task. The Windows NT/2000/XP/Vista line, on the other hand, is written for the enterprise. It sacrifices compatibility and size to achieve its high level of reliability and robustness.

Windows CE isn't backward compatible with MS-DOS or Windows. Nor is it an all-powerful operating system designed for enterprise computing. Instead, Windows CE is a lightweight, multithreaded operating system with an optional graphical user interface. Its strength lies in its small size, its Win32 subset API, and its multiplatform support.

A Little Windows CE History

To understand the history of Windows CE, you need to understand the differences between the operating system and the products that use it. The Windows CE operating system is developed by a core group of programmers inside Microsoft. Their product is the operating system itself. Other groups, who develop devices such as the Windows Mobile line, use the most appropriate version of Windows CE that's available at the time their product is to be released and add their own code. This dichotomy has created some confusion about how

Windows CE has evolved. Let's examine the history of each, the devices and the operating system itself.

The Devices

The first products designed for Windows CE were handheld "organizer" devices with 480-by-240 or 640-by-240 screens and chiclet keyboards. These devices, dubbed Handheld PCs, were first introduced in late 1996. Fall Comdex 97 saw the release of a dramatically upgraded version of the operating system, Windows CE 2.0, with newer hardware in a familiar form—this time the box came with a 640-by-240 landscape screen, sometimes in color, and a somewhat larger keyboard.

In January 1998 at the Consumer Electronics Show, Microsoft announced two new platforms, the Palm-size PC and the Auto PC. The Palm-size PC was aimed directly at the pen-based organizer market dominated by Palm OS–based systems. The Palm-size PC featured a portrait mode and a 240-by-320 screen, and it used stylus-based input. Unfortunately for Windows CE fans, the public reception of the original Palm-size PC was less than enthusiastic.

Later that year, a new class of mini-laptop–style Windows CE machines with touch-typable keyboards and VGA or Super VGA screens made their appearance. These machines, called H/PC Professionals, provided 10 hours of battery life combined with improved versions of Microsoft's Pocket Office applications. Many of these machines had built-in modems, and some even diverged from the then-standard touch screen, sporting track pads or IBM's TrackPoint devices.

In April 2000, Microsoft introduced the Pocket PC, a greatly enhanced version of the old Palm-size PC. The original Pocket PC used a prerelease of the more full-featured Windows CE 3.0 operating system under the covers. The user interface of the Pocket PC was also different, with a cleaner, 2D look and a revised home page, the Today screen. The most important feature of the Pocket PC, however, was the greatly improved performance of Windows CE. Much work had been done to tune Windows CE for better performance. That improvement, coupled with faster CPUs, allowed the system to run with the zip expected from a pocket organizer. With the Pocket PC, the inevitability of Moore's Law enabled Windows CE devices to cross over the line: the hardware at this point was now capable of providing the computing power that Windows CE required.

The Handheld PC was updated in 2000 to use Windows CE 3.0. Although these systems (dubbed the Handheld PC 2000) weren't a consumer success, they did find a home in the industrial market, where their relative low cost, large screens, and great battery life satisfy a unique niche market.

The Pocket PC was updated in late 2001 with a release named Pocket PC 2002. This release was based on the final released version of Windows CE 3.0 and contained some user interface improvements. An exciting development was the addition of the Pocket PC Phone

Edition, which integrated cellular phone support into a Pocket PC device. These devices combined the functionality of a Pocket PC with the connectivity of a cellular phone, enabling a new generation of mobile but always connected software.

Another group within Microsoft released the Smart Display, a Windows CE .NET 4.1–based system that integrated a tablet form factor device with wireless networking and a base connected to a PC. When the Smart Display is in its base, it's a second monitor; when removed, it becomes a mobile display for the PC. The Smart Display didn't gain much traction, but the remote desktop technology perfected for the device found its way into later versions of Windows CE.

In the spring of 2003, the Pocket PC team released an update of the Pocket PC called the Pocket PC 2003. This system, while not providing much of a change to the user interface, did provide a huge increase in stability and performance because it was based on Windows CE .NET 4.2. The Pocket PC 2003 also added integrated Bluetooth support for those OEMs that chose to include it.

At the same time, Microsoft was working with OEMs to produce cellular phones based on Windows CE. A smattering of these phones, called Smartphones, were released in late 2002 and were initially based on Windows CE 3.0. An upgrade in 2003 moved the Smartphone to Windows CE 4.2 and increased the feature set of the device to include the .NET runtime.

An update to the Pocket PC and Smartphone platforms, called Pocket PC/Smartphone 2003 Second Edition, was released in March 2004. These devices supported different screen resolutions, screen rotation, and updated communication support. These systems continued to be based on a slightly modified Windows CE .NET 4.2 kernel.

In May 2005, the Pocket PC and Smartphone platforms were updated and renamed with the umbrella term, *Windows Mobile*. These new systems took advantage of an updated Windows CE 5 kernel and featured a change from a RAM-based file system to a flash-based file system. This change prevented data loss on the systems due to run-down batteries with a tradeoff of a noticable drop in performance. The platforms updated their multimedia credentials with Windows Media Player 10 and Direct Show capture support. Later updates to this line provided *push e-mail* support.

The Windows Mobile team followed in February 2007 with Windows Mobile 6. Interestingly, this release was based on a tweaked Windows CE 5 kernel, not Windows CE 6, which had been released a few months before. Nomenclature also changed with the Pocket PC now referred to as *Windows Mobile Classic*, the Pocket PC Phone Edition referred to as *Windows Mobile Professional*, and the Smartphone referred to as *Windows Mobile Standard*.

New devices are being introduced all the time. An example is the Zune media device from Microsoft. While not a programmable device like the Pocket PC or Smartphone, the device is based on Windows CE. The power of the Windows CE operating system enables applications that are beyond the capability of systems with simpler operating systems to run on these devices and yet smaller than devices needed to run Windows Vista.

The Operating System

Although these consumer-oriented products made the news, more important development work was going on in the operating system itself. The Windows CE operating system has evolved from the days of 1.0, when it was a simple organizer operating system with high hopes. Starting with Windows CE 2.0 and continuing to this day, Microsoft has released embedded versions of Windows CE that developers can use on their custom hardware. Although consumer platforms such as the Windows Mobile series get most of the publicity, the improvements to the base operating system are what provide the foundation to these new consumer devices.

Windows CE 2.0 was released with the introduction of the Handheld PC 2.0 at Fall Comdex 1997. Windows CE 2.0 added networking support, including Windows standard network functions, a Network Driver Interface Specification (NDIS) miniport driver model, and a generic NE2000 network card driver. Added COM support allowed scripting, although the support was limited to in-proc servers. A display driver model was also introduced that allowed for pixel depths other than the original 2-bits-per-pixel displays of Windows CE 1.0. Windows CE 2.0 was also the first version of the operating system to be released separately from a product such as the H/PC. Developers could purchase the Windows CE Embedded Toolkit (ETK), which allowed them to customize Windows CE to unique hardware platforms. Developers who used the ETK, however, soon found that the goal of the product exceeded its functionality.

With the release of the original Palm-size PC in early 1998, Windows CE was improved yet again. Although Windows CE 2.01 wasn't released in an ETK form, it was notable for its effort to reduce the size of the operating system and applications. In Windows CE 2.01, the C runtime library, which includes functions such as *strcpy* to copy strings, was moved from a statically linked library attached to each EXE and DLL into the operating system itself. This change dramatically reduced the size of both the operating system and the applications themselves.

In August 1998, Microsoft introduced the H/PC Professional with a new version of the operating system, 2.11. Windows CE 2.11 was a service pack update to Windows CE 2.1, which was never formally released. Later in the year, Windows CE 2.11 was released to the embedded community as Microsoft Windows CE Platform Builder version 2.11. This release included support for an improved object store that allowed files in the object store to be larger than 4 MB. This release also added support for a console and a Windows CE version of CMD.exe, the classic MS-DOS–style command shell. Windows CE 2.11 also included Fast IR to support IrDA's 4-MB infrared standard, as well as some specialized functions for IP multicast. An initial hint of security was introduced in Windows CE 2.11: a device could now examine and reject the loading of unrecognized modules.

Windows CE 2.12 was also a service pack release to the 2.1, or *Birch*, release of Windows CE. The big news in this release was a greatly enhanced set of Platform Builder tools that included a graphical front end. The operating system was tweaked with a new notification interface that combined the disparate notification functions. The notification user interface was exposed in the Platform Builder to allow embedded developers to customize the notification dialog boxes. A version of Microsoft's PC-based Internet Explorer 4.0 was also ported to Windows CE as the Genie, or Generic IE control. This HTML browser control complements the simpler but smaller Pocket Internet Explorer. Microsoft Message Queue support was added as well. The "go/no go" security of Windows CE 2.11 was enhanced to include a "go, but don't trust" option. Untrusted modules could run—but not call—a set of critical functions, nor could they modify parts of the registry.

The long-awaited Windows CE 3.0 was finally released in mid-2000. This release followed the April release of the Pocket PC, which used a slightly earlier internal build of Windows CE 3.0. The big news for Windows CE 3.0 was its kernel, which was optimized for better real-time support. The enhanced kernel support includes 256 thread priorities (up from 8 in earlier versions of Windows CE), an adjustable thread quantum, nested interrupt service routines, and reduced latencies within the kernel.

The improvements in Windows CE 3.0 didn't stop at the kernel. A new COM component was added to complement the in-proc COM support available since Windows CE 2.0. This new component included full COM out-of-proc and DCOM support. The object store was also improved to support up to 256 MB of RAM. File size limits within the object store were increased to 32 MB per file. An Add-On Pack for the Platform Builder 3.0 added even more features, including improved multimedia support though a media player control; improved networking support (and XML support) with PPTP, ICS, and remote desktop display support; and a formal introduction of the DirectX API.

The next release of Windows CE involved more than just new features; the name of the product was also changed. Windows CE .NET 4.0, released in early 2001, changed the way virtual memory was organized, effectively doubling the virtual memory space per application. Windows CE .NET 4.0 also added a new driver loading model, services support, a new file-based registry option, Bluetooth, 802.11, and 1394 support. Ironically, while .NET was added to the name, Windows CE .NET 4.0 didn't support the .NET Compact Framework.

Late in 2001, Windows CE 4.1 was a follow-on to Windows CE 4.0, adding IP v6, Winsock 2, a bunch of new supporting applets, and an example Power Manager. Windows CE 4.1 also supports the .NET Compact Framework. The final bits of the .NET Compact Frameworkruntime were released as a quick fix engineering (QFE) package after the operating system shipped.

The second quarter of 2003 saw the release of Windows CE .NET 4.2. This update provided cool new features for OEMs wanting to support Pocket PC applications on embedded systems. The Pocket PC–specific APIs that support menu bars, the soft input panel (SIP), and other shell features were moved to the base operating system. The Explorer shell was rewritten to support namespace extensions. The performance of the kernel was improved by directly supporting hardware paging tables on some CPUs.

In July 2004, Microsoft released Windows CE 5.0. This release focused as much on improved performance as new features. The kernel retained the familiar 32 process and 32 Meg VM limits that had been in place since the Windows CE 1.0. However, the network stack and file system were modified for better performance. The tools set used by OEMs, Platform Builder, was dramatically updated in an attempt to easy porting of the operating system to new hardware. Some of these efforts were successful, others were not as successful in easing the burden on OEMs.

The most significant update to Windows CE since its inception was provided with the release of Windows Embedded 6.0 in November 2006. The kernel of Windows CE 6 was completely rewritten eliminating the 32 process limit and the 32-MB VM limit that had started to burden embedded developers. The new kernel boasts a "limit" of 32K processes and a 2-GB VM space per process. In addition to the new kernel, Windows Embedded CE 6 brought some of the Windows Mobile 5 features such as Direct Show capture, a cellular radio stack, and support for ExFAT, an improved version of the venerable FAT file system.

Because Windows CE is a work in progress, the next version of Windows CE is being developed. I'll be updating my Web site, *www.bolingconsulting.com*, with information about this release as it becomes available.

Why You Should Read This Book

Programming Microsoft Windows CE is written for anyone who will be writing applications for Windows CE. Embedded systems programmers using Windows CE for a specific application, Windows programmers interested in writing or porting an existing Windows application, and even developers of managed code can use the information in this book to make their tasks easier.

The embedded systems programmer, who might not be as familiar with the Win32 API as the Windows programmer, can read the first section of the book to become familiar with Windows programming. Although this section isn't the comprehensive tutorial that can be found in books such as *Programming Windows*, by Charles Petzold, it does provide a base that will carry the reader through the other chapters in the book. It can also help the embedded systems programmer develop fairly complex and quite useful Windows CE programs.

The experienced Windows programmer can use the book to learn about the differences among the Win32 APIs used by Windows CE and the desktop versions of Windows. The differences between Windows CE and the desktop are significant. The small footprint of Windows CE means that many of the overlapping APIs in the Win32 model aren't supported. Some sections of the Win32 API aren't supported at all. On the other hand, because of its unique setting, Windows CE extends the Win32 API in a number of areas that are covered in this text.

Although no .NET Compact Framework material is covered in this edition, the book remains useful for the developer using the .NET Compact Framework. The Compact Framework currently has gaps in its functionality: it requires managed applications to make calls to the operating system to perform certain tasks. The book is a great guide to what's available in the operating system.

The method used by *Programming Windows CE* is to teach by example. I wrote numerous Windows CE example programs specifically for this book. The source for each of these examples is printed in the text. Both the source and the final compiled programs for a number of the processors supported by Windows CE are also provided on the book Web site. In addition, examples that "didn't make the cut" when the final edits were made are also on the Web site.

The examples in this book are all written directly to the API, the so-called "Petzold" method of programming. Since the goal of this book is to teach you how to write programs for Windows CE, the examples avoid using a class library such as MFC, which obfuscates the unique nature of writing applications for Windows CE. Some people would say that the availability of MFC on Windows CE eliminates the need for direct knowledge of the Windows CE API. I believe the opposite is true. Knowledge of the Windows CE API enables more efficient use of MFC. I also believe that truly knowing the operating system also dramatically simplifies the debugging of applications.

What's New in the Fourth Edition

This new edition of the book is updated for the new Windows Embedded 6.0 kernel. Chapters 7, "Memory Management," and 8, "Processes, Modules, and Threads," have been significantly updated to reflect the new kernel. Chapter 9, "The Windows CE File System," includes new topics such as the storage manager while Chapter 11, "Windows CE Databases," is updated to cover the Embedded Database API. Other parts of the book have been updated and freshened with better examples and coverage of new APIs. Other chapters have been reorganized to better present the topics.

Readers familiar with the earlier editions of this book will notice that it is shorter. The decision was made to focus this edition on the core operating system concepts of Windows CE and not on specific devices. Although it would be great to simply grow and grow the book with new material, there are limits to the size of the book. For this edition, I have chosen the best content of the earlier versions while adding and updating the content relevant to today's embedded programmers.

Windows CE Development Tools

This book is written with the assumption that the reader knows C and is at least familiar with Microsoft Windows. All native code development was done with Microsoft Visual Studio 2005. To compile the example programs in this book, you need Visual Studio 2005 and a Windows CE device SDK. The book Web site has a custom SDK that I created that can be used as a programming target. This SDK includes a device emulator so the examples can be tested without the need of accompanying hardware.

To compile and run the examples, you will need Visual Studio 2005 or later. While there are many verisons of Visual Studio, all but the most basic Express editions support device development. After installing Visual Studio and downloading the SDK from the book Web site, simply launch the installer for the SDK. The install process will add a device target labeled ProgWinCE_SDK, and an emulator that will run all the Windows CE–based examples in the book. In addition, the SDK supports compiling for ARM as well as x86 systems. The ARM CPU support is necessary for the emulator while the x86 support is convenient given the abundance of PC-based hardware.

Each example already has a predefined project set up, but you can also choose to create the projects from scratch. For almost all the examples, simply create a Visual C++ Smart Device, Win32 Smart Device project. Select the ProgWinCE_SDK and select an "empty project." The empty project selection prevents Visual Studio from providing its default wizard code. Then create the files from the book and add them to the project. I have designed the examples not to need special project settings. For example, any nondefault library files are included using in-line compiler commands.

Target Systems

You don't need to have a Windows CE target device to experience the sample programs provided by this book because the example SDK provides an emulator target. This emulator comes in handy when you don't have an actual device handy. The emulator runs a version of Windows CE 6.0 inside an ARM emulator, which results in an actual Windows CE operating system runtime executing. Applications should compile to an ARM CPU target to run in the emulator.

You should consider a number of factors when deciding which Windows CE hardware to use for testing. First, if the application is to be a commercial product, you should buy at least one system for each type of target CPU. You need to test against all the target CPUs because, although the source code will probably be identical, the resulting executable will be different in size and so will the memory allocation footprint for each target CPU.

What's on the Web Site

The Web site (*http://www.microsoft.com/mspress/companion/9780735624177*)[1] contains the source code for all the examples in the book. I've also provided project files for Microsoft Visual Studio so that you can open preconfigured projects. In addition, some examples that were in previous editions of the book are now on the Web site exclusively. These include the CtlView example from the "Windows and Controls" chapter and the AlbumDB example from the "Windows CE Databases" chapter.

---

1 We select these URLs so they are easy to remember.

Other Sources

Although I have attempted to make *Programming Microsoft Windows CE* a one-stop shop for Windows CE programming, no one book can cover everything. To learn more about Windows programming in general, I suggest the classic text *Programming Windows* (Microsoft Press, 1998) by Charles Petzold. This is, by far, the best book for learning Windows programming. Charles presents examples that show how to tackle difficult but common Windows problems. To learn more about the Win32 kernel API, I suggest Jeff Richter's *Programming Applications for Microsoft Windows* (Microsoft Press, 1999). Jeff covers the techniques of process, thread, and memory management down to the most minute detail. For learning more about MFC programming, there's no better text than Jeff Prosise's *Programming Windows with MFC* (Microsoft Press, 1999). This book is the "Petzold" of MFC programming and simply a required read for MFC programmers. Unfortunately, these last two books are currently out of print. I advise finding those books on your bookshelf and guard them carefully. You can also seek out friends who have been in the Windows programming business for a number of years; they should have these books. Of course, there is always Amazon and eBay for buying used books.

Support

Every effort has been made to ensure the accuracy of this book and the contents of the sample files on the Web site. Microsoft Press provides corrections and additional content for its books through the World Wide Web at this location:

http:/www.microsoft.com/mspress/support/

If you have problems, comments, or ideas regarding this book or the Web site, please send them to Microsoft Press.

Send e-mail to

mspinput@microsoft.com

Or send postal mail to

Microsoft Press

Attn: *Programming Microsoft Windows CE*, Fourth Edition, Editor

One Microsoft Way

Redmond, WA 98052-6399

Please note that product support is not offered through these mail addresses. For further information regarding Microsoft software support options, please go to *http://support.microsoft.com/directory/* or call Microsoft Support Network Sales at (800) 936-3500.

Visit the Microsoft Press Web Site

You are also invited to visit the Microsoft Press World Wide Web site at the following location:

http://www.microsoft.com/mspress/

You'll find descriptions for the complete line of Microsoft Press books, information about ordering titles, notice of special features and events, additional content for Microsoft Press books, and much more.

You can also find out the latest in Microsoft Windows CE software developments and news from Microsoft Corporation by visiting the following Web site:

http://www.microsoft.com/windows/embedded

Updates and Feedback

No book about Windows CE can be completely current for any length of time. I maintain a Web page, *http://www.bolingconsulting.com/cebook.htm*, where I'll keep a list of errata, along with updates describing any features found in subsequent versions of Windows CE. Check out this page to see information on new versions of Windows CE as they're released.

Although I have striven to make the information in this book as accurate as possible, you'll undoubtedly find errors. If you find a problem with the text or just have ideas about how to make the next version of the book better, please drop me a note at *CEBook@bolingconsulting.com*. I can't promise you that I'll answer all your notes, but I will read every one.

Doug Boling

Tahoe City, California

August 2007

Part I
Windows Programming Basics

Chapter 1

Hello Windows CE

Since the classic *The C Programming Language*, programming books traditionally start with a "hello, world" program. It's a logical place to begin. Every program has a basic underlying structure that, when not obscured by some complex task it was designed to perform, can be analyzed to reveal the foundation shared by all programs running on its operating system.

In this programming book, the "hello, world" chapter covers the details of setting up and using the programming environment. The environment for developing Microsoft Windows CE applications is somewhat different from that for developing standard Microsoft Windows applications because Windows CE programs are written on PCs running Microsoft Windows XP or Windows Vista and debugged mainly on separate Windows CE–based target devices.

While experienced Windows programmers might be tempted to skip this chapter and move on to meatier subjects, I suggest that they—you—at least skim the chapter to note the differences between a standard Windows program and a Windows CE program. A number of subtle and significant differences in both the development process and the basic program skeleton for Windows CE applications are covered in this first chapter.

What Is Different About Windows CE

Windows CE has a number of unique characteristics that make it different from other Windows platforms. First, the systems running Windows CE are most likely not using an Intel x86–compatible microprocessor. Instead, Windows CE runs on four different CPU families: SHx, MIPS, ARM, and x86. Fortunately, the development environment isolates the programmer from almost all of the differences among the various CPUs.

Nor can a Windows CE program be assured of a screen or a keyboard. Windows Mobile devices have screens ranging from 176 by 220 to 800 by 600 pixels. Some of the screens have a landscape orientation, in which the screen is wider than it is tall, while others have portrait orientation, in which the screen is taller than it is wide. An embedded device might not have a display at all. The target devices might not support color. And, instead of a mouse, most Windows CE devices have a touch screen. On a touch-screen device, left mouse button clicks are achieved by means of a tap on the screen, but no obvious method exists for delivering right mouse button clicks. To give you some method of delivering a right click, the Windows CE convention is to tap and hold with the stylus. Although Windows CE has a helper API to detect this tap and hold gesture, it's up to the Windows CE application to interpret this sequence as a right mouse click.

Fewer Resources in Windows CE Devices

The resources of the target devices vary radically across systems that run Windows CE. When writing a standard Windows program, the programmer can make a number of assumptions about the target device, almost always an IBM-compatible PC. The target device will have a hard drive for mass storage and a virtual memory system that uses the hard drive as a swap device to emulate an almost unlimited amount of (virtual) RAM. The programmer knows that the user has a keyboard, a two-button mouse, and a monitor that these days almost assuredly supports 256 colors and a screen resolution of at least 1024 by 768 pixels.

Windows CE programs run on devices that rarely have hard drives for mass storage. The absence of a hard drive means more than just not having a place to store large files. Without a hard drive, virtual RAM can't be created by swapping data to the drive. So Windows CE programs are almost always run in a low-memory environment. Memory allocations can, and often do, fail because of the lack of resources. A Windows CE shell might be designed to terminate a program automatically when free memory reaches a critically low level. This RAM limitation has a surprisingly large impact on Windows CE programs, and is one of the main challenges involved in porting existing Windows applications to Windows CE.

Unicode

One characteristic that a programmer can count on when writing Windows CE applications is Unicode. Unicode is a standard for providing a platform-independent method of defining characters. The Unicode standard provides for representing characters in 8-bit, 16-bit, or 32-bit formats known as UTF8, UTF16, and UTF32, respectively. Windows CE uses UTF16 to represent characters. Unicode allows for fairly simple porting of programs to different international markets. Dealing with Unicode is relatively painless as long as you avoid the dual assumptions made by most programmers that strings are represented in ASCII and that characters are stored in single bytes.

A consequence of a program using UTF16 is that with each character taking up two bytes instead of one, strings are now twice as long. A programmer must be careful making assumptions about buffer length and string length. No longer should you assume that a 260-byte buffer can hold 259 characters and a terminating zero. Instead of the standard *char* data type, you should use the *TCHAR* data type. *TCHAR* is defined to be *char* for ANSI-compatible application development and unsigned short for Unicode-enabled applications for Microsoft Windows 2000, Windows XP, Windows Vista, and Windows CE development. These types of definitions allow source-level compatibility across ASCII-and Unicode-based operating systems.

New Controls

Windows CE includes a number of new Windows controls designed for specific environments. New controls include the menu bar control that provides menu-and toolbar-like functions all on one space-saving line, critical on the smaller screens of Windows CE devices. Other controls have been enhanced for Windows CE. A version of the edit control in Windows CE can be set to automatically capitalize the first letter of a word, great for the keyboardless design of a PDA. Windows CE also supports most of the controls available on desktop versions of Windows. Some of these controls are even more at home on Windows CE devices than on the desktop. For example, the date and time picker control and calendar control assist calendar and organizer applications suitable for handheld devices, such as Windows Mobile–based devices. Other standard Windows controls have reduced function, reflecting the compact nature of Windows CE hardware-specific OS configurations.

Componentization

Another aspect of Windows CE programming to be aware of is that Windows CE can be broken up and reconfigured by Microsoft or by OEMs so that it can be better adapted to a target market or device. Windows programmers usually just check the version of Windows. When they know the version, they can determine what API functions are available. Windows CE, however, can be configured in countless ways.

By far, the most popular configurations of Windows CE today are in the Windows Mobile–based devices. Microsoft defines the specific set of Windows CE components that are present in all Windows Mobile–branded devices. However, some OEMs produce PDA devices that use Windows CE but are not branded as Windows Mobile systems. These devices have a subtly different API from that of the Windows Mobile devices. If you are unaware of this, you can easily write a program that works on one platform but not on another. In embedded platforms, the OEM decides the components to include and can create a Software Development Kit (SDK) specialized for its specific platform. If the OEM is interested in third-party development, it can make available a customized SDK for its device. New platforms are continually being released, with much in common but also with many differences among them. Programmers need to understand the target platform and to have their programs check what functions are available on that particular platform before trying to use a set of functions that might not be supported on that device.

Win32 Subset

Finally, because Windows CE is so much smaller than Windows XP or Windows Vista, it simply can't support all the function calls that its larger cousins do. For example, Windows CE removes some redundant functions supported by its larger cousins necessary for backward compatbility with applications dating back to the days of DOS and Windows 3.x. If Windows CE doesn't support your favorite function, a different function or set of functions will probably work just as well. Sometimes Windows CE programming seems to consist mainly of figuring out ways to implement a feature using the sparse API of Windows CE (if thousands of functions can be called sparse).

Some functional areas in Windows CE might surprise you. For example, Windows CE supports its own Web, FTP, and Telnet servers. Although the Windows CE Web server isn't as powerful as Microsoft's IIS behemoth, it does provide significant functionality, including support for Active Server Pages and for ISAPI filters and extensions. Windows CE also has strong DirectShow support and even a Voice-over IP (VoIP) stack.

It's Still Windows Programming

Although differences between Windows CE and the other versions of Windows do exist, they shouldn't be overstated. Programming a Windows CE application is programming a Windows application. It has the same message loop, the same windows, and for the most part, the same resources and the same controls. The differences don't hide the similarities. One of the key similarities is the tradition of Hungarian notation.

Hungarian Notation

A tradition, and a good one, of almost all Windows programs since Charles Petzold wrote *Programming Microsoft Windows* is Hungarian notation. This programming style, developed years ago by Charles Simonyi at Microsoft, prefixes all variables in the program usually with one or two letters indicating the variable type. For example, a string array named *Name* would instead be named *szName*, with the *sz* prefix indicating that the variable type is a zero-terminated string. The value of Hungarian notation is the dramatic improvement in readability of the source code. Another programmer (or you after not looking at a piece of code for a while) won't have to look repeatedly at a variable's declaration to determine its type. Table 1-1 shows typical Hungarian prefixes for variables.

TABLE 1-1 Hungarian Prefixes for Variables

Variable Type	Hungarian Prefix
Integer	*i* or *n*
Word (16-bit)	*w* or *s*
Double word (32-bit unsigned)	*dw*
Long (32-bit signed)	*l*
Char	*c*
String	*sz*
Pointer	*p*
Long pointer	*lp*
Handle	*h*
Window handle	*hwnd*
Struct size	*cb*

You can see a few vestiges of the early days of Windows. The *lp*, or long pointer, designation refers to the days when, in the Intel 16-bit programming model, pointers were either short (a 16-bit offset) or long (a segment plus an offset). Other prefixes are formed from the abbreviation of the type. For example, a handle to a brush is typically specified as *hbr*. Prefixes can be combined, as in *lpsz*, which designates a long pointer to a zero-terminated string. Most of the structures defined in the Windows API use Hungarian notation in their field names. Although the use of Hungarian notation has fallen out of vogue, I still use this notation when programming my Win32 applications as well throughout this book, and I encourage you to use this notation in your Win32 programs.

Your First Windows CE Application

Enough talk; let's look at your first Windows CE program. Listing 1-1 shows Hello1, a simple Hello World application written for Windows CE.

LISTING 1-1 Hello1, A simple Windows application

Hello1.cpp

```
//======================================================================
// Hello1 - A simple application for Windows CE
//
// Written for the book Programming Windows CE
// Copyright (C) 2007 Douglas Boling
//======================================================================
#include <windows.h>

//
// Program entry point
//
int WINAPI WinMain (HINSTANCE hInstance, HINSTANCE hPrevInstance,
                    LPWSTR lpCmdLine, int nCmdShow) {

    printf ("Hello World\n");
    return 0;
}
```

As you can see, aside from the entry point of the program, the code looks fairly similar to the classic Kernighan and Ritchie version. Starting from just below the comments, you have the line

```
#include <windows.h>
```

which is the root of a vast array of include files that define the Windows CE API, as well as the structures and constants they use.

The entry point of the program is the biggest difference between this program and a standard C program. Instead of the C standard

```
int main (char **argv, int argc)
```

the Windows CE build environment expects the standard Windows entry point,[1] as in

```
int WINAPI WinMain (HINSTANCE hInstance, HINSTANCE hPrevInstance,
                    LPWSTR lpCmdLine, int nCmdShow);
```

Windows CE differs in some ways from the desktop versions of Windows. The first of the four parameters passed, *hInstance*, identifies the specific instance of the program to other applications and to Windows API functions that need to identify the EXE. The *hPrevInstance* parameter is left over from the old Win16 API (Windows 3.1 and earlier). In all Win32 operating systems, including Windows CE, *hPrevInstance* is always 0 and can be ignored.

The *lpCmdLine* parameter points to a Unicode string that contains the text of the command line. Applications launched from Microsoft Windows Explorer usually have no command-line parameters. But in some instances, such as when the system automatically launches a program, the system includes a command-line parameter to indicate why the program was started. The *lpCmdLine* parameter provides us with one of the first instances in which Windows CE differs from the desktop versions of Windows. Under Windows CE, the command-line string is a Unicode string. In all other versions of Windows, the string is always ASCII.

The final parameter, *nCmdShow*, specifies the initial state of the program's main window. It is passed by the parent application, usually Explorer, and is a recommendation of how the application should configure its main window. This parameter might specify that the window be initially displayed as an icon (*SW_SHOWMINIMIZE*), maximized (*SW_SHOWMAXIMIZED*) to cover the entire desktop, or normal (*SW_RESTORE*), indicating that the window is placed on the screen in the standard resizeable state. Other values specify that the initial state of the window should be invisible to the user or that the window should be visible but incapable of becoming the active window. Under Windows CE, the values for this parameter are limited to only three allowable states: normal (*SW_SHOW*), hidden (*SW_HIDE*), and show without activate (*SW_SHOWNOACTIVATE*). Unless an application needs to force its window to a predefined state, this parameter is simply passed without modification to the *ShowWindow* function after the program's main window has been created.

The next line is the only functioning line of the application.

```
printf ("Hello World\n");
```

[1] When you're using the Visual Studio 2005 wizard to create a console application, it appears that a more conventional "argc / argv" entry point is used. Visual Studio does this by linking a different prologue routine and redirecting the application entry point to the custom routine. The prologue routine has the same "WinMain" style entry point and then generates the conventional "argc / argv" parameters and calls the console application's main entry point that is shown in the application template.

Windows CE supports most of the standard C library, including *printf*, *getchar*, and so forth. An interesting aspect of this line is that unlike almost everywhere else in Windows CE, the string is not Unicode but ANSI. There is a logical reason for this. For the C standard library to be compliant with the ANSI standard, *printf* and the other string library functions such as *strcpy* use ANSI strings. Of course, Windows CE supports the Unicode versions of the standard functions such as *wprintf*, *getwchar*, and *wcscpy*.

Finally the program ends with

```
return 0;
```

The value passed in the return line is available to other processes that use the Win32 API *GetExitCodeProcess*.

Building Your First Application

To create Hello1 from scratch on your system, start Microsoft Visual Studio and create a new project by choosing the New Project command on the File menu. Select Visual C++ and then the Smart Device project type in the left-hand tree view pane and Win32 Smart Device Project in the right-hand pane. Type the name and directory for the project in the edit fields at the bottom of the New Project dialog box, as shown in Figure 1-1.

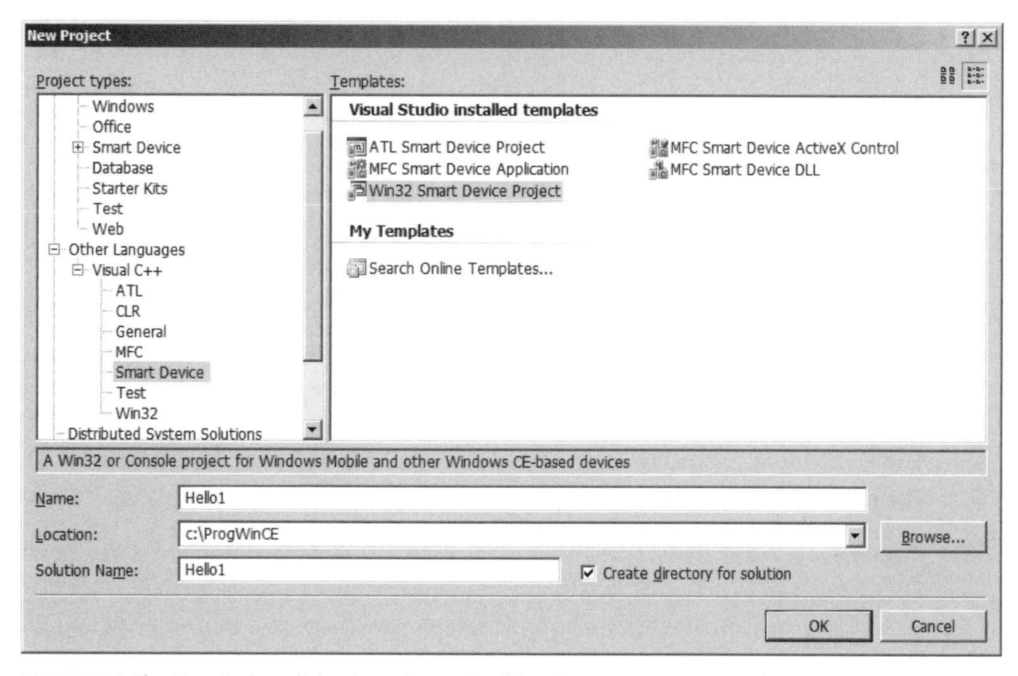

FIGURE 1-1 The New Project dialog box allows Visual Studio 2005 to target Windows CE devices.

Clicking OK displays the Smart Device Project Wizard, which allows you to select the target software development kits (SDKs) and the type of application or DLL to create. The Web site for this book (*http://www.microsoft.com/mspress/companion/9780735624177*) has a custom-built SDK that targets both the Visual Studio 2005 device emulator and a build of Windows CE that runs on a PC. Downloading and installing that SDK on your machine provides the ProgWinCE_SDK target that is selected in Figure 1-2.

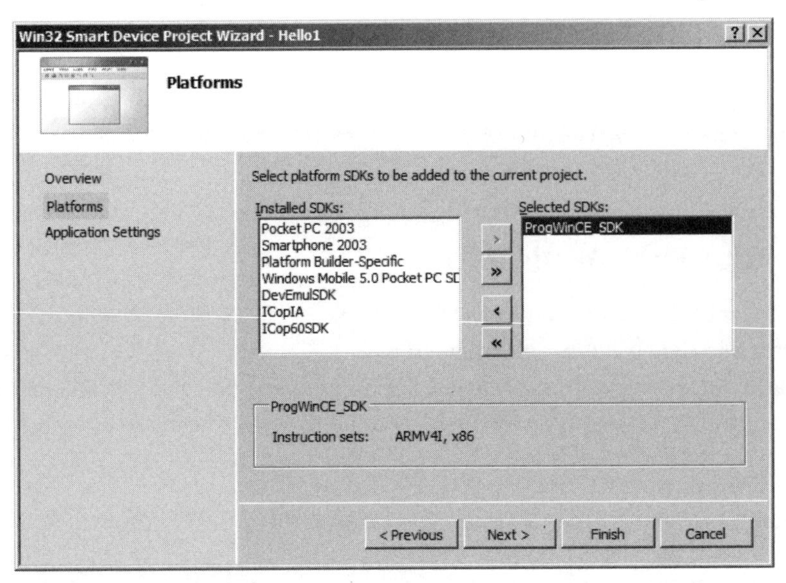

FIGURE 1-2 The Platforms page of the Smart Device ProjectWizard allows selection of one or more target software development kits.

The final page of the Smart Device Project Wizard, the Project Settings page, tells Visual Studio what to create. Your options are Windows Application, Console Application, DLL, or Static Library. For the purposes of this example, and indeed for all the examples in this book, the proper selection is Empty Project, as shown in Figure 1-3.

Now that the project is created, add the file hello1.cpp. Select the Project | Add New Item menu item. Select a C++ file and type the name **Hello1.cpp**. In the blank file, type the text shown in Listing 1-1. Select the ProgWinCE_SDK (ARMV4I) as the target CPU and ProgWinCE_SDK Emulator as the device target. Build the application by selecting the Build | Build Solution menu item.

If you have a Windows CE system available, such as a Windows Mobile device, attach it to the PC the same way you would to sync the contents of the device with the PC. Open Microsoft ActiveSync, and establish a connection between the Windows Mobile device and the PC. While it's not strictly necessary to have the ActiveSync connection to your Windows CE device running (eMbedded Visual C++ is supposed to make this connection automatically),

I've found that having it running makes for a more stable connection between the development environment and the Windows CE system.

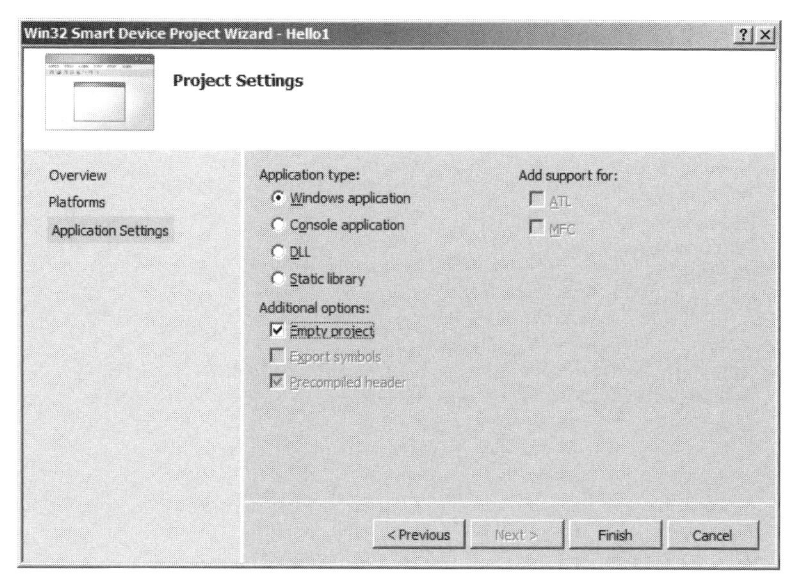

FIGURE 1-3 The Project Settings page allows selection of what to create.

Running the Program

Selecting the Debug | Start without Debugging menu item will cause Visual Studio to launch the Windows CE emulator (if the emulator is the target device), deploy the application, and automatically launch it.

What's Wrong?

When you start Hello1, nothing seems to happen. In the emulator, the program appears to make the screen flash. This is because the program starts, writes to the console, and terminates. Unless you start the program from an already created console, Windows CE creates the console window when Hello1 executes the *printf* statement and closes the console automatically when Hello1 terminates.

On a Windows Mobile device, the application runs, but Windows Mobile devices don't come with support to display the console functions such as the output from *printf*. It's possible to add console support to a Windows Mobile device by adding a driver, console.dll, to the Windows directory of the device. That driver must be written to take input from the driver interface, create a window on the screen, and print the strings. The console driver available in embedded versions of Windows CE does this.

Hello2

Now that you have the basics down, it's time to upgrade Hello1 to something you can at least see. Because many Windows CE systems don't have the console driver, Hello2 creates a message box with the "Hello CE" text instead of using *printf*. Hello2 is shown in Listing 1-2.

LISTING 1-2 Hello2, a simple Windows application using the MessageBox function

Hello2.cpp

```
//======================================================================
// Hello2 - A simple application for Windows CE
//
// Written for the book Programming Windows CE
// Copyright (C) 2007 Douglas Boling
//======================================================================
#include <windows.h>

//
// Program entry point
//
int WINAPI WinMain (HINSTANCE hInstance, HINSTANCE hPrevInstance,
                    LPWSTR lpCmdLine, int nCmdShow) {

    MessageBox (NULL, TEXT ("Hello World"), TEXT ("Hello2"), MB_OK);
    return 0;
}
```

When you compile and run Hello2, you should see a small window like the one shown in Figure 1-4.

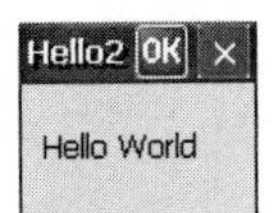

FIGURE 1-4 Hello2 running on a Windows CE desktop

The *MessageBox* function that replaces *printf* provides two features for Hello2. First, and most obvious, it creates a window and places the "Hello World" text in the window. The second feature is that the *MessageBox* function doesn't return until the user closes the message box window. This feature allows Hello2 to continue running until the user closes the window.

The *MessageBox* function is prototyped as

```
int MessageBox (HWND hWnd, LPCTSTR lpText, LPCTSTR lpCaption, UINT uType);
```

The first parameter of *MessageBox* is the handle to the top-level window that is the parent of the message box when it is displayed. For now, leave this parameter *NULL* because Hello2 doesn't have any other windows. The second parameter is the text that appears in the window. Notice that the string passed is couched in the *TEXT* macro, ensuring that it will be compiled as Unicode. The third parameter, *lpCaption*, is the text that will appear in the title bar of the window. The last parameter, *uType*, is a series of flags that specify how the message box appears on the screen. The flags specify the number and type of buttons on the message box; the icon, if any, on the message box; and the settings of style flags for the message box window.

The flags listed in Table 1-2 are valid under Windows CE.

TABLE 1-2 Default Flags

Flags	Button or Icon
For Buttons:	
MB_OK	OK
MB_OKCANCEL	OK and Cancel
MB_RETRYCANCEL	Retry and Cancel
MB_YESNO	Yes and No
MB_YESNOCANCEL	Yes, No, and Cancel
MB_ABORTRETRYIGNORE	Abort, Retry, and Ignore
For Icons:	
MB_ICONEXCLAMATION, MB_ICONWARNING	Exclamation point
MB_ICONINFORMATION, MB_ICONASTERISK	Lower case *i* within a circle
MB_ICONQUESTION	Question mark
MB_YESNO	Yes and No
MB_ICONSTOP, MB_ICONERROR, MB_ICONHAND	Stop sign
MB_DEFBUTTON1	First button
MB_DEFBUTTON2	Second button
MB_DEFBUTTON3	Third button
For Window Styles:	
MB_SETFOREGROUND	Bring the message box to the foreground.
MB_TOPMOST	Make the message box the topmost window.

The return value from *MessageBox* indicates the button clicked by the user. The return values are as follows:

IDOK	OK button pressed
IDYES	Yes button pressed
IDNO	No button pressed
IDCANCEL	Cancel button pressed or Esc key pressed
IDABORT	Abort button pressed
IDRETRY	Retry button pressed
IDIGNORE	Ignore button pressed

MessageBox is a handy function to make an application display a simple but informative dialog box.

One gotcha to look out for here: If you're debugging and recompiling the program, it can't be downloaded again if an earlier version of the program is still running on the target system. That is, make sure Hello2 isn't running on the remote system when you start a new build in Visual Studio, or the autodownload part of the compile process will fail. If this happens, close the application and choose the Build | Deploy Solution menu command in Visual Studio to download the newly compiled file.

Hello2 displays a simple window, but that window is only as configurable as the *MessageBox* function allows. How about showing a window that is completely configurable by the application? Before we can do that, a quick review of how a Windows application really works is in order.

Anatomy of a Windows-Based Application

Windows-based programming is far different from MS-DOS–based or Unix-based programming. An MS-DOS or Unix program uses *getc*-and *putc*-style functions to read characters from the keyboard and write them to the screen whenever the program needs to do so. This is the classic "pull" style used by MS-DOS and Unix programs, which are procedural. A Windows program, on the other hand, uses a "push" model, in which the program must be written to react to notifications from the operating system that a key has been pressed or a command has been received to repaint the screen.

Windows applications don't ask for input from the operating system; the operating system notifies the application that input has occurred. The operating system achieves these notifications by sending *messages* to an application window. All windows are specific instances of a *window class*. Before you go any further, be sure you understand these terms.

The Window

A window is a region on the screen, rectangular in all but the most contrived of cases, that has a few basic parameters, such as position—*x*, *y*, and *z* (a window is over or under other windows on the screen)—visibility, and hierarchy—the window fits into a parent/child window relationship on the system *desktop*, which also happens to be a window.

Every application that displays itself on the desktop has at least one window. In the preceding *Hello2* example, the system created the window for the application when the message box was displayed. The message box is actually composed of two windows: the window that is the message box and the window that contains the Hello World text.

To create a window that is unique to an application, the application must first tell Windows CE some of the basic characteristics of the window to be created. These basic characteristics are shared among all windows of this type, or as Windows refers to it, all windows of a specific *window class*.

The Window Class

Every window created is a specific instance of a window class. A window class is a template that defines a number of attributes common to all the windows of that class. In other words, windows of the same class share the same set of basic attributes.

Windows provides a number of predefined window classes that are used by applications such as the button class seen on the message box in *Hello2*. However, the main window of a Win32 application rarely uses one of the predefiend classes. Instead it defines, or rather *registers*, a unique window class with the system. This class will define items such as the background color of the window, some default styles and most importantly the *window procedure*.

The Window Procedure

The behavior of all windows belonging to a class is defined by the code in its window procedure for that class. The window procedure handles all notifications and requests sent to the window. These notifications are sent either by the operating system, indicating that an event has occurred to which the window must respond, or by other windows querying the window for information.

These notifications are sent in the form of messages. A message is nothing more than a call being made to a window procedure, with a parameter indicating the nature of the notification or request. Messages are sent for events such as a window being moved or resized or to indicate a key press. The values used to indicate messages are defined by Windows. Applications use these predefined constants, such as *WM_CREATE* and *WM_MOVE*, when referring to messages. Because hundreds of messages can be sent, Windows conveniently provides a default processing function to which a message can be passed when no special processing is necessary by the window class for that message.

The Life of a Message

Stepping back for a moment, look at how Windows coordinates all of the messages going to all of the windows in a system. Windows monitors all the sources of input to the system, such as the keyboard, mouse, touch screen, and any other hardware that could produce an event that might interest a window. As an event occurs, a message is composed and directed to a specific window. Instead of Windows directly calling the window procedure, the system imposes an intermediate step. The message is placed in a message queue for the application[2] that owns the window. When the application is prepared to receive the message, it pulls it out of the queue and tells Windows to dispatch that message to the proper window in the application.

If it seems to you that a number of indirections are involved in that process, you're right. You can break it down as follows:

1. An event occurs, so a message is composed by Windows and placed in a message queue for the application that owns the destination window. Events can occur, and therefore messages can be composed, faster than an application can process them. The queue allows an application to process messages at its own rate, although the application had better be responsive, or the user will see some jerkiness in the application. The message queue also allows Windows to set a notification in motion and continue with other tasks without having to be limited by the responsiveness of the application to which the message is being sent.
2. The application removes the message from its message queue and calls Windows back to dispatch the message. While it may seem strange that the application gets a message from the queue and then simply calls Windows back to process the message, there's a method to this madness. Having the application pull the message from the queue allows it to preprocess the message before it asks Windows to dispatch the message to the appropriate window. In a number of cases, the application might call different functions in Windows to process specific kinds of messages.
3. Windows dispatches the message; that is, it calls the appropriate window procedure. Instead of having the application directly call the window procedure, another level of indirection occurs, allowing Windows to coordinate the call to the window procedure with other events in the system. The message doesn't stand in another queue at this point, but Windows might need to make some preparations before calling the window procedure. In any case, the scheme relieves the application of the obligation to determine the proper destination window—Windows does this instead.
4. The window procedure processes the message. All window procedures have the same calling parameters: the handle of the specific window instance being called, the message, and two generic parameters that contain data specific to each message type. The window handle differentiates each instance of a window for the window procedure. The message parameter, of course, indicates the event that the window must react to. The two generic parameters contain data specific to the message being sent. For example, in a *WM_MOVE* message indicating that the window is about to be moved, one of the generic parameters points to a structure containing the new coordinates of the window.

[2] Technically, each thread in a Windows CE application that creates a window has a message queue and it's that thread that must process the message queue. I'll talk about threads later in the book.

Hello3, shown in Listing 1-3, demonstrates all aspects of a Windows program, from registering the window class to the creation of the window to the window procedure. Hello3 has the same entry point, *WinMain*,as the first two examples; but because it creates its own window, it must register a window class for the main window, create the window, and provide a message loop to process the messages for the window.

LISTING 1-3

Hello3

```
//======================================================================
// Hello3 - A simple application for Windows CE
//
// Written for the book Programming Windows CE
// Copyright (C) 2007 Douglas Boling
//======================================================================
#include <windows.h>                 // For all that Windows stuff

LRESULT CALLBACK MainWndProc (HWND, UINT, WPARAM, LPARAM);

//======================================================================
// Program entry point
//
int WINAPI WinMain (HINSTANCE hInstance, HINSTANCE hPrevInstance,
                    LPWSTR lpCmdLine, int nCmdShow) {
    WNDCLASS wc;
    HWND hWnd;
    MSG msg;

    // Register application main window class.
    wc.style = 0;                             // Window style
    wc.lpfnWndProc = MainWndProc;             // Callback function
    wc.cbClsExtra = 0;                        // Extra class data
    wc.cbWndExtra = 0;                        // Extra window data
    wc.hInstance = hInstance;                 // Owner handle
    wc.hIcon = NULL,                          // Application icon
    wc.hCursor = LoadCursor (NULL, IDC_ARROW);// Default cursor
    wc.hbrBackground = (HBRUSH) GetStockObject (WHITE_BRUSH);
    wc.lpszMenuName =  NULL;                  // Menu name
    wc.lpszClassName = TEXT("MyClass");       // Window class name

    if (RegisterClass (&wc) == 0) return -1;

    // Create main window.
```

```
    hWnd = CreateWindowEx(WS_EX_NODRAG,          // Ex style flags
                          TEXT("MyClass"),       // Window class
                          TEXT("Hello"),         // Window title
                          // Style flags
                          WS_VISIBLE | WS_CAPTION | WS_SYSMENU,
                          CW_USEDEFAULT,         // x position
                          CW_USEDEFAULT,         // y position
                          CW_USEDEFAULT,         // Initial width
                          CW_USEDEFAULT,         // Initial height
                          NULL,                  // Parent
                          NULL,                  // Menu, must be null
                          hInstance,             // Application instance
                          NULL);                 // Pointer to create
                                                 // parameters
    if (!IsWindow (hWnd)) return -2;  // Fail code if not created.

    // Standard show and update calls
    ShowWindow (hWnd, nCmdShow);
    UpdateWindow (hWnd);

    // Application message loop
    while (GetMessage (&msg, NULL, 0, 0)) {
        TranslateMessage (&msg);
        DispatchMessage (&msg);
    }
    // Instance cleanup
    return msg.wParam;
}
//======================================================================
// MainWndProc - Callback function for application window
//
LRESULT CALLBACK MainWndProc (HWND hWnd, UINT wMsg, WPARAM wParam,
                              LPARAM lParam) {
    PAINTSTRUCT ps;
    RECT rect;
    HDC hdc;

    switch (wMsg) {
    case WM_PAINT:
        // Get the size of the client rectangle
        GetClientRect (hWnd, &rect);

        hdc = BeginPaint (hWnd, &ps);
        DrawText (hdc, TEXT ("Hello Windows CE!"), -1, &rect,
                  DT_CENTER | DT_VCENTER | DT_SINGLELINE);

        EndPaint (hWnd, &ps);
        return 0;

    case WM_DESTROY:
        PostQuitMessage (0);
        break;
    }
    return DefWindowProc (hWnd, wMsg, wParam, lParam);
}
```

Registering the Window Class

In *WinMain*, Hello3 registers the window class for the main window. Registering a window class is simply a matter of filling out a rather extensive structure describing the class and calling the *RegisterClass* function. *RegisterClass* and the *WNDCLASS* structure are defined as follows:

```
ATOM RegisterClass (const WNDCLASS *lpWndClass);

typedef struct _WNDCLASS {
    UINT style;
    WNDPROC lpfnWndProc;
    int cbClsExtra;
    int cbWndExtra;
    HANDLE hInstance;
    HICON hIcon;
    HCURSOR hCursor;
    HBRUSH hbrBackground;
    LPCTSTR lpszMenuName;
    LPCTSTR lpszClassName;
} WNDCLASS;
```

The parameters assigned to the fields of the *WNDCLASS* structure define how all instances of the main window for Hello3 will behave. The initial field, *style*, sets the class style for the window. In Windows CE, the class styles are limited to the following:

- **CS_GLOBALCLASS** Indicates that the class is global. This flag is provided only for compatibility because all window classes in Windows CE are process global.
- **CS_HREDRAW** Tells the system to force a repaint of the window if the window is sized horizontally.
- **CS_VREDRAW** Tells the system to force a repaint of the window if the window is sized vertically.
- **CS_NOCLOSE** Disables the Close button if one is present on the title bar.
- **CS_PARENTDC** Causes a window to use its parent's device context.
- **CS_DBLCLKS** Enables notification of double-clicks (or double-taps on a touch screen) to be passed to the parent window.

The *lpfnWndProc* field should be loaded with the address of the window's window procedure. Because this field is typed as a pointer to a window procedure, the declaration to the procedure must be defined in the source code before the field is set. Otherwise, the compiler's type checker will flag this line with a warning.

The *cbClsExtra* field allows the programmer to add extra space in the class structure to store class-specific data known only to the application. The *cbWndExtra* field is much handier. This field adds space to the Windows internal structure responsible for maintaining the state of each instance of a window. Instead of storing large amounts of data in the window structure itself, an application should store a pointer to an application-specific structure that contains the data unique to each instance of the window. Under Windows CE, both the *cbClsExtra* and *cbWndExtra* fields must be multiples of 4 bytes.

The *hInstance* field must be filled with the program's instance handle, which specifies the owning process of the window. The *hIcon* field is set to the handle of the window's default icon. For Hello3, however, no icon is supplied, and, unlike other versions of Windows, Windows CE doesn't have any predefined icons that can be loaded.)

Unless the application being developed is designed for a Windows CE system with a mouse, the next field, *hCursor*, must be set to *NULL*. Fortunately, the function call *LoadCursor (IDC_ARROW)* returns *NULL* if the system doesn't support cursors.

The *hbrBackground* field specifies how Windows CE draws the background of the window. Windows uses the *brush*, a small predefined array of pixels, specified in this field to draw the background of the window. Windows CE provides a number of predefined brushes that you can load using the *GetStockObject* function. If the *hbrBackground* field is *NULL*, the window must handle the *WM_ERASEBKGND* message sent to the window telling it to redraw the background of the window. In the case of Hello3, the *WHITE_BRUSH* stock object sets the background to white.

The *lpszMenuName* field must be set to *NULL* because Windows CE doesn't support windows directly having a menu. In Windows CE, menus are provided by menu bar, command bar, or command band controls that the main window can create.

Finally the *lpszClassName* parameter is set to a programmer-defined string that identifies the class name to Windows. Hello3 uses the string *MyClass*.

After the entire *WNDCLASS* structure has been filled out, the *RegisterClass* function is called with a pointer to the *WNDCLASS* structure as its only parameter. If the function is successful, a value identifying the window class is returned. If the function fails, the function returns 0.

Creating the Window

After the window class is successfully registered, the main window can be created. All Windows programmers learn early in their programming lives the *CreateWindow* and *CreateWindowEx* function calls. The prototype for *CreateWindowEx* is as follows:

```
HWND CreateWindowEx (DWORD dwExStyle, LPCTSTR lpClassName,
                     LPCTSTR lpWindowName, DWORD dwStyle,
                     int x, int y, int nWidth, int nHeight,
                     HWND hWndParent, HMENU hMenu,
                     HINSTANCE hInstance, LPVOID lpParam);
```

Although the number of parameters looks daunting, the parameters are fairly logical after you learn them. The first parameter is the extended style flags. The extended style flags supported by Windows CE are as follows:

- **WS_EX_TOPMOST** Window is topmost.
- **WS_EX_WINDOWEDGE** Window has a raised edge.
- **WS_EX_CLIENTEDGE** Window has a sunken edge.
- **WS_EX_STATICEDGE** 3D look for static windows.
- **WS_EX_OVERLAPPEDWINDOW** Combines WS_EX_WINDOWEDGE and WS_EX_CLIENTEDGE.
- **WS_EX_CAPTIONOKBUTTON** Window has an OK button on caption.
- **WS_EX_CONTEXTHELP** Window has help button on caption.
- **WS_EX_NOACTIVATE** Window is not activated when clicked.
- **WS_EX_NOANIMATION** Top-level window will not have exploding rectangles when created nor have a button on the taskbar.
- **WS_EX_NODRAG** Prevents window from being moved.
- **WS_EX_ABOVESTARTUP** Positions a window above the password screen.
- **WS_EX_INK** Prevents screen tap sound when tapping stylus on window.

The *dwExStyle* parameter is the only difference between *CreateWindowEx* and *CreateWindow*. In fact, if you look at the declaration of *CreateWindow* in the Windows CE header files, it's simply a call to *CreateWindowEx* with the *dwExStyle* parameter set to 0.

The second parameter is the name of the window class of which your window will be an instance. In the case of Hello3, the class name is *MyClass*, which matches the name of the class registered in *RegisterClass*.

The next field is referred to as the *window text*. In other versions of Windows, this is the text that would appear on the title bar of a standard window. On most embedded systems, main windows rarely have title bars; this text is used only on the taskbar button for the window. On the Windows Mobile devices, however, this text is shown on the navigation bar at the top of the display. The text is couched in a *TEXT* macro, which ensures that the string will be converted to Unicode under Windows CE.

The style flags specify the initial styles for the window. The style flags are used both for general styles that are relevant to all windows in the system and for class-specific styles, such as those that specify the style of a button or a list box. In this case, all you need to specify is that the window be created initially visible with the *WS_VISIBLE* flag. The supported style flags are as follows:

- **WS_BORDER** The window will have a thin border.
- **WS_CAPTION** The window will have a title bar.
- **WS_CHILD** The window is a child window. The menu parameter will contain the handle of the parent window.
- **WS_DISABLED** The window will not accept any input.
- **WS_DLGFRAME** The window frame looks like the frame of a dialog box.
- **WS_GROUP** Defines the first in a group of control windows. All subsuquent windows will be in this group until another window with the WS_GROUP style is created.
- **WS_HSCROLL** The window is created with a horizonal scroll bar.
- **WS_VSCROLL** The window is created with a vertical scroll bar.
- **WS_OVERLAPPED** The window will have a title bar and a standard border.
- **WS_POPUP** The window is a top-level window owned by the window whose handle is passed in the hMenu parameter.
- **WS_SYSMENU** The window will have a Close box.
- **WS_TABSTOP** When used on a child window in a dialog box, it indicates that the window would like to be in the chain of windows that receives keyboard focus when the Tab key is pressed.
- **WS_THICKFRAME** The window will have a thick border that can be "grabbed" by the mouse or stylus to resize the window.
- **WS_SIZEBOX** Same as WS_THICKFRAME.
- **WS_VISIBLE** The window will be visible to the user if it resides at the top of the z-order.

In addition, all windows in Windows CE are implicitly set to the *WM_CLIPCHILDREN*- and *WS_CLIPSIBLINGS*-style flags.

The next four fields specify the initial position and size of the window. Because most applications under Windows CE are full-screen windows, the size and position fields are set to default values, which are indicated by the *CW_USEDEFAULT* flag in each of the fields. The default value settings create a window that is sized to fit the screen work area. The work area is generally all of the screen not taken up by the shell taskbar. Be careful not to assume any particular screen size for a Windows CE device because different implementations have different screen sizes.

The next field is set to the handle of the parent window. Because this is the top-level window, the parent window field is set to *NULL*. The menu field is also set to *NULL* because Windows CE does not support menus on top-level windows.

The *hInstance* parameter is the same instance handle that was passed to the program. Creation of windows is one case in which that instance handle, saved at the start of the routine, comes in handy. The final parameter is a pointer that can be used to pass data from the *CreateWindow* call to the window procedure during the *WM_CREATE* message. In this example, no additional data needs to be passed, so the parameter is set to *NULL*.

If successful, the *CreateWindow* call returns the handle to the window just created, or it returns 0 if an error occurred during the function. That window handle is then used in the two statements (*ShowWindow* and *UpdateWindow*) just after the error-checking *if* statement. The *ShowWindow* function modifies the state of the window to conform with the state given in the *nCmdShow* parameter passed to *WinMain*. The *UpdateWindow* function forces Windows to send a *WM_PAINT* message to the window that has just been created.

The Message Loop

After the main window has been created, *WinMain* enters the message loop, which is the heart of every Windows application. Hello3's message loop is shown at the top of the next page.

```
while (GetMessage (&msg, NULL, 0, 0)) {
    TranslateMessage (&msg);
    DispatchMessage (&msg);
}
```

The loop is simple: *GetMessage* is called to get the next message in the application's message queue. If no message is available, the call waits, blocking that application's thread until a message is available. When a message is available, the call returns with the message data contained in an *MSG* structure. The *MSG* structure itself contains fields that identify the message, provide any message-specific parameters, and identify the last mouse point recorded before the message was sent. This location information is different depending on if the system has a mouse or a touch panel. On mouse-based systems the point returned is the current mouse position. On touch panel based systems the last mouse point is the last point tapped by the stylus.

The *TranslateMessage* function translates appropriate keyboard messages into a character message. (I'll talk about others of these filter messages, such as *IsDialogMsg*, later.) The *DispatchMessage* function then tells Windows to forward the message to the appropriate window in the application.

This *GetMessage*, *TranslateMessage*, *DispatchMessage* loop continues until *GetMessage* receives a *WM_QUIT* message, which, unlike all other messages, causes *GetMessage* to return 0. As can be seen from the *while* clause, the return value 0 by *GetMessage* causes the loop to terminate.

After the message loop terminates, the program can do little else but clean up and exit. In the case of Hello3, the program simply returns from *WinMain*. The value returned by *WinMain* becomes the return code of the program. Traditionally, the return value is the value in the *wParam* parameter of the last message (*WM_QUIT*). The *wParam* value of *WM_QUIT* is set when that message is sent in response to a *PostQuitMessage* call made by the application.

The Window Procedure

The messages sent or posted to the Hello3 main window are sent to the procedure *MainWndProc*. *MainWndProc*, like all window procedures, is prototyped as follows:

```
LRESULT CALLBACK MainWndProc (HWND hWnd, UINT wMsg, WPARAM wParam,
                              LPARAM lParam);
```

The *LRESULT* return type is actually just a long (a *long* is a 32-bit value under Windows) but is typed this way to provide a level of indirection between the source code and the machine. While you can easily look into the include files to determine the real type of variables that are used in Windows programming, this can cause problems when you attempt to move your code across platforms. Although it can be useful to know the size of a variable type for memory-use calculations, there is no good reason to use (and plenty of reasons not to use) the base-type definitions provided by windows.h.

The *CALLBACK*-type definition specifies that this function is an external entry point into the EXE, necessary because Windows calls this procedure directly. The *CALLBACK*-type definition varies depending on which version of Windows is being targeted, but it typically indicates that parameters are pushed onto the stack in a right-to-left manner.

The first of the parameters passed to the window procedure is the window handle, which is useful when you need to define the specific instance of the window. The *wMsg* parameter indicates the message being sent to the window. This isn't the *MSG* structure used in the message loop in *WinMain*, but a simple, unsigned integer containing the message value. The remaining two parameters, *wParam* and *lParam*, are used to pass message-specific data to the window procedure. The names *wParam* and *lParam* come to us from the Win16 days, when *wParam* was a 16-bit value and *lParam* was a 32-bit value. In Windows CE, as in other Win32 operating systems, both the *wParam* and *lParam* parameters are 32 bits wide.

Hello3 has a traditional window procedure that consists of a switch statement that parses the *wMsg* message ID parameter. The switch statement for Hello3 contains two case statements, one to parse the *WM_PAINT* message and one for the *WM_DESTROY* message. This is about as simple as a window procedure can get.

WM_PAINT

Painting the window, and therefore processing the *WM_PAINT* message, is one of the critical functions of any Windows program. As a program processes the *WM_PAINT* message, the look of the window is achieved. Aside from painting the default background with the brush you specified when you registered the window class, Windows provides no help for processing this message. The lines of Hello3 that process the *WM_PAINT* messages are shown here:

```
case WM_PAINT:
    // Get the size of the client rectangle
    GetClientRect (hWnd, &rect);

    hdc = BeginPaint (hWnd, &ps);
    DrawText (hdc, TEXT ("Hello Windows CE!"), -1, &rect,
              DT_CENTER | DT_VCENTER | DT_SINGLELINE);

    EndPaint (hWnd, &ps);
    return 0;
```

Before the window can be drawn, the routine must determine its size. In a Windows program, a standard window is divided into two areas: the nonclient area and the client area. A window's title bar and its sizing border commonly make up the nonclient area of a window, and Windows is responsible for drawing it. The client area is the interior part of the window, and the application is responsible for drawing that. An application determines the size and location of the client area by calling the *GetClientRect* function. The function returns a *RECT* structure that contains left, top, right, and bottom elements that delineate the boundaries of the client rectangle. The advantage of the client-versus-nonclient area concept is that an application doesn't have to account for drawing such standard elements of a window as the title bar.

Other versions of Windows supply a series of *WM_NCxxx* messages that enable your applications to take over the drawing of the nonclient area. In Windows CE, windows seldom have title bars. Because there's so little nonclient area, the Windows CE team decided not to send the nonclient messages to the window procedure. Instead, the nonclient-area messages are sent directly to the default window procedure.

All drawing performed in a *WM_PAINT* message must be enclosed by two functions: *BeginPaint* and *EndPaint*. The *BeginPaint* function returns an *HDC*, or handle to a device context. A *device context* is a logical representation of a physical display device such as a video screen or a printer. Windows programs never modify the display hardware directly. Instead, Windows isolates the program from the specifics of the hardware with, among other tools, device contexts.

BeginPaint also fills in a *PAINTSTRUCT* structure that contains a number of useful parameters:

```
typedef struct tagPAINTSTRUCT {
    HDC  hdc;
    BOOL fErase;
    RECT rcPaint;
    BOOL fRestore;
    BOOL fIncUpdate;
    BYTE rgbReserved[32];
} PAINTSTRUCT;
```

The *hdc* field is the same handle that's returned by the *BeginPaint* function. The *fErase* field indicates whether the window procedure needs to redraw the background of the window. The *rcPaint* field is a *RECT* structure that defines the client area that needs repainting. Hello3 ignores this field and assumes that the entire client window needs repainting for every *WM_PAINT* message, but this field is quite handy when performance is an issue because only part of the window might need repainting. Windows actually prevents repainting outside the *rcPaint* rectangle, even when a program attempts to do so. The other fields in the structure, *fRestore*, *fIncUpdate*, and *rgbReserved*, are used internally by Windows and can be ignored by the application.

The only painting that takes place in Hello3 occurs in one line of text in the window. To do the painting, Hello3 calls the *DrawText* function. I cover the details of *DrawText* in Chapter 2, "Drawing on the Screen," but if you look at the function it's probably obvious to you that this call draws the string "Hello Windows CE" on the window. After *DrawText* returns, *EndPaint* is called to inform Windows that the program has completed its update of the window.

Calling *EndPaint* also validates any area of the window you didn't paint. Windows keeps a list of areas of a window that are *invalid* (areas that need to be redrawn) and *valid* (areas that are up to date). By calling the *BeginPaint* and *EndPaint* pair, you tell Windows that you've taken care of any invalid areas in your window, whether or not you've actually drawn anything in the window. In fact, you must call *BeginPaint* and *EndPaint*, or validate the invalid areas of the window by other means, or Windows will simply continue to send *WM_PAINT* messages to the window until those invalid areas are validated.

WM_DESTROY

The other message processed by Hello3 is the *WM_DESTROY* message. The *WM_DESTROY* message is sent when a window is about to be destroyed. Because this window is the main window of the application, the application should terminate when the window is destroyed. To make this happen, the code processing the *WM_DESTROY* message calls *PostQuitMessage*. This function places a *WM_QUIT* message in the message queue. The one parameter of this function is the return code value that will be passed back to the application in the *wParam* parameter of the *WM_QUIT* message.

As I've mentioned, when the message loop sees a *WM_QUIT* message, it exits the loop. The *WinMain* function then calls *TermInstance*, which, in the case of Hello3, does nothing but return. *WinMain* then returns, terminating the program.

Hello3 is the classic Windows program. This programming style is sometimes call the Petzold method of Windows programming in homage to the ultimate guru of Windows programming, Charles Petzold. Charles's book *Programming Microsoft Windows* is currently in its fifth edition and is still the best book for learning Windows programming.

I prefer a somewhat different layout of my Windows programs. In a sense, it's simply a method of componentizing the function of a Windows program, which makes it much easier to copy parts of one program to another. In the final example of this chapter, I introduce this programming style along with a few extra features that are necessary for Windows CE applications.

HelloCE

One criticism of the typical SDK style of Windows programming has always been the huge *switch* statement in the window procedure. The *switch* statement parses the message to the window procedure so that each message can be handled independently. This standard structure has the one great advantage of enforcing a similar structure across almost all Windows applications, making it much easier for one programmer to understand the workings of another programmer's code. The disadvantage is that all the variables for the entire window procedure typically appear jumbled at the top of the procedure.

Over the years, I've developed a different style for my Windows programs. The idea is to break up the *WinMain* and *WinProc* procedures into manageable units that can be easily understood and easily transferred to other Windows programs. *WinMain* is broken up into procedures that perform application initialization, instance initialization, and instance termination. Also in *WinMain* is the ubiquitous message loop that's the core of all Windows programs.

I break the window procedure into individual procedures, with each handling a specific message. What remains of the window procedure itself is a fragment of code that simply looks up the message that's being passed to see whether a procedure has been written to handle that message. If so, that procedure is called. If not, the message is passed to the default window procedure.

This structure divides the handling of messages into individual blocks that can be more easily understood. Also, with greater isolation of one message-handling code fragment from another, you can more easily transfer the code that handles a specific message from one program to the next. I first saw this structure described a number of years ago by Ray Duncan in one of his old "Power Programming" columns in *PC Magazine*. Ray is one of the legends in the field of MS-DOS and OS/2 programming. I've since modified the design a bit to fit my needs, but Ray should get the credit for this program structure.

The Code

The source code for HelloCE is shown in Listing 1-4.

LISTING 1-4 The HelloCE program

HelloCE.h

HelloCE.cpp

```
//======================================================================
// HelloCE - A simple application for Windows CE
//
// Written for the book Programming Windows CE
// Copyright (C) 2007 Douglas Boling
//======================================================================
#include <windows.h>                 // For all that Windows stuff
#include "helloce.h"                 // Program-specific stuff

//----------------------------------------------------------------------
// Global data
//
const TCHAR szAppName[] = TEXT("HelloCE");
HINSTANCE hInst;                     // Program instance handle

// Message dispatch table for MainWindowProc
const struct decodeUINT MainMessages[] = {
    WM_PAINT, DoPaintMain,
    WM_DESTROY, DoDestroyMain,
};

//======================================================================
// Program entry point
//
int WINAPI WinMain (HINSTANCE hInstance, HINSTANCE hPrevInstance,
                    LPWSTR lpCmdLine, int nCmdShow) {
    MSG msg;
    int rc = 0;
    HWND hwndMain;

    // Initialize this instance.
    hwndMain = InitInstance (hInstance, lpCmdLine, nCmdShow);
    if (hwndMain == 0) return 0x10;

    // Application message loop
    while (GetMessage (&msg, NULL, 0, 0)) {
        TranslateMessage (&msg);
        DispatchMessage (&msg);
    }
```

```
    // Instance cleanup
    return TermInstance (hInstance, msg.wParam);
}
//----------------------------------------------------------------------
// InitInstance - Instance initialization
//
HWND InitInstance (HINSTANCE hInstance, LPWSTR lpCmdLine, int nCmdShow) {
    WNDCLASS wc;
    HWND hWnd;

    // Save program instance handle in global variable.
    hInst = hInstance;

#if defined(WIN32_PLATFORM_PSPC) || defined(WIN32_PLATFORM_WFSP)
    // If Windows Mobile, only allow one instance of the application
    hWnd = FindWindow (szAppName, NULL);
    if (hWnd) {
        SetForegroundWindow ((HWND)(((DWORD)hWnd) | 0x01));
        return 0;
    }
#endif

    // Register application main window class.
    wc.style = 0;                             // Window style
    wc.lpfnWndProc = MainWndProc;             // Callback function
    wc.cbClsExtra = 0;                        // Extra class data
    wc.cbWndExtra = 0;                        // Extra window data
    wc.hInstance = hInstance;                 // Owner handle
    wc.hIcon = NULL,                          // Application icon
    wc.hCursor = LoadCursor (NULL, IDC_ARROW);// Default cursor
    wc.hbrBackground = (HBRUSH) GetStockObject (WHITE_BRUSH);
    wc.lpszMenuName = NULL;                   // Menu name
    wc.lpszClassName = szAppName;             // Window class name

    if (RegisterClass (&wc) == 0) return 0;

    // Create main window.
    hWnd = CreateWindow (szAppName,           // Window class
                         TEXT("HelloCE"),     // Window title
                         // Style flags
                         WS_VISIBLE | WS_CAPTION | WS_SYSMENU,
                         CW_USEDEFAULT,       // x position
                         CW_USEDEFAULT,       // y position
                         CW_USEDEFAULT,       // Initial width
                         CW_USEDEFAULT,       // Initial height
                         NULL,                // Parent
                         NULL,                // Menu, must be null
                         hInstance,           // Application instance
                         NULL);               // Pointer to create
                                              // parameters
    if (!IsWindow (hWnd)) return 0;  // Fail code if not created.

    // Standard show and update calls
    ShowWindow (hWnd, nCmdShow);
    UpdateWindow (hWnd);
```

```
    return hWnd;
}
//----------------------------------------------------------------------
// TermInstance - Program cleanup
//
int TermInstance (HINSTANCE hInstance, int nDefRC) {
    return nDefRC;
}
//======================================================================
// Message handling procedures for main window
//
//----------------------------------------------------------------------
// MainWndProc - Callback function for application window
//
LRESULT CALLBACK MainWndProc (HWND hWnd, UINT wMsg, WPARAM wParam,
                              LPARAM lParam) {
    INT i;
    //
    // Search message list to see if we need to handle this
    // message.  If in list, call procedure.
    //
    for (i = 0; i < dim(MainMessages); i++) {
        if (wMsg == MainMessages[i].Code)
            return (*MainMessages[i].Fxn)(hWnd, wMsg, wParam, lParam);
    }
    return DefWindowProc (hWnd, wMsg, wParam, lParam);
}
//----------------------------------------------------------------------
// DoPaintMain - Process WM_PAINT message for window.
//
LRESULT DoPaintMain (HWND hWnd, UINT wMsg, WPARAM wParam,
                     LPARAM lParam) {
    PAINTSTRUCT ps;
    RECT rect;
    HDC hdc;

    // Get the size of the client rectangle
    GetClientRect (hWnd, &rect);

    hdc = BeginPaint (hWnd, &ps);
    DrawText (hdc, TEXT ("Hello Windows CE!"), -1, &rect,
              DT_CENTER | DT_VCENTER | DT_SINGLELINE);

    EndPaint (hWnd, &ps);
    return 0;
}
//----------------------------------------------------------------------
// DoDestroyMain - Process WM_DESTROY message for window.
//
LRESULT DoDestroyMain (HWND hWnd, UINT wMsg, WPARAM wParam,
                       LPARAM lParam) {
    PostQuitMessage (0);
    return 0;
}
```

If you look over the source code for HelloCE, you'll see the standard boilerplate for all programs in this book. A few variables defined globally follow the defines and includes. I know plenty of good arguments why no global variables should appear in a program, but I use them as a convenience that shortens and clarifies the example programs in the book. Each program defines an *szAppName* Unicode string to be used in various places in that program. I also use the *hInst* variable a number of places, and I'll mention it when I cover the *InitInstance* procedure. The final global structure is a list of messages along with associated procedures to process the messages. This structure is used by the window procedure to associate messages with the procedure that handles them.

In HelloCE, *WinMain* has two basic functions: it calls *InitInstance* (where the application initialization code is kept), processes the message in the message loop, and calls *TerminateInstance* when the message loop exits. In this program template, *WinMain* becomes a boilerplate routine that almost never changes. In general, the only changes that are made to *WinMain* concern modification of the processing of the message loop to process for keyboard accelerators, watch for modeless dialog box messages, or other tasks.

InitInstance

The main task of *InitInstance* is to register the main window's window class, create the application's main window, and display it in the form specified in the *nCmdShow* parameter passed to *WinMain*. There is also some conditionally compiled code that, if compiled for a Windows Mobile device, prevents more than one instance of the program from running at any one time.

The first task performed by *InitInstance* is to save the program's instance handle *hInstance* in a global variable named *hInst*. The instance handle for a program is useful at a number of points in a Windows application. I save the value here because the instance handle is known, and this is a convenient place in the program to store it.

When running on a Windows Mobile device, HelloCE uses *FindWindow* to see whether another copy of itself is currently running. This function searches the top-level windows in the system looking for ones that match the class name or the window title or both. If a match is found, the window is brought to the foreground with *SetForegroundWindow*. The routine then exits with a zero return code, which causes *WinMain* to exit, terminating the application. Although this book doesn't cover Windows Mobile specific code, the popularity of the devices means that they are often used as Windows CE devices during devlopment. Because so many developers are using Windows Mobile devices, unless otherwise mentioned, all the examples in this book will run on these devices.

These Windows Mobile–specific lines are enclosed in *#if* and *#endif* lines. These lines tell the compiler to include them only if the condition of the *#if* statement is true—in this case, if the constants *WIN32_PLATFORM_PSPC* or *WIN32_PLATFORM_WFSP are* defined. These constants are defined in the Project Settings for the project. A quick look at the C/C++ tab of the Project Properties dialog box shows an entry field for Preprocessor Definitions. In this field, one of the definitions is *$(CePlatform)*, which is a placeholder for a registry value. Deep in the registry, under the key *[HKEY_LOCAL_MACHINE]\Software\Microsoft\Windows CE Tools\SDK*, you can find series of registry keys, one for each target platform installed in Visual Studio 2005. Each key has a value that points to an XML file that contains information about that platform including the definition for the CePlatform. CePlatform is defined differently depending on the target project. For Pocket PC projects, CePlatform is defined as *WIN32_PLATFORM_PSPC*. For Smartphone projects, the value is defined as *WIN32_PLATFORM_WFSP*.

The registering of the window class and the creation of the main window are quite similar to those in the Hello3 example. The only difference is the use of the global string *szAppName* as the class name of the main window class. Each time I use this template, I change the *szAppName* string to match the program name. This keeps the window class names somewhat unique for the different applications, enabling the *FindWindow* code in HelloCE to work.

That completes the *InitInstance* function. At this point, the application's main window has been created and updated. So even before you have entered the message loop, messages have been sent to the main window's window procedure. It's about time to look at this part of the program.

MainWndProc

You spend most of your programming time with the window procedure when you're writing a Windows program. The window procedure is the core of the program, the place where the actions of the program's windows create the personality of the program.

It's in the window procedure that my programming style differs significantly from most Windows programs written without the help of a class library such as MFC. For almost all of my programs, the window procedure is identical to the one previously shown in HelloCE. Before continuing, I repeat: this program structure isn't specific to Windows CE. I use this style for all my Win32 applications, whether they are for Windows XP, Windows Vista, or Windows CE.

This style reduces the window procedure to a simple table lookup function. The idea is to scan the *MainMessages* table defined early in the C++ file for the message value in one of the entries. If the message is found, the associated procedure is then called, passing the original parameters to the procedure processing the message. If no match is found for the message, the *DefWindowProc* function is called. *DefWindowProc* is a Windows function that provides a default action for all messages in the system, which frees a Windows program from having to process every message being passed to a window.

The message table associates message values with a procedure to process it. The table is listed here:

```
// Message dispatch table for MainWindowProc
const struct decodeUINT MainMessages[] = {
    WM_PAINT, DoPaintMain,
    WM_DESTROY, DoDestroyMain,
};
```

The table is defined as a constant, not just as good programming practice, but also because it's helpful for memory conservation. Because Windows CE programs can be executed in place in ROM, data that doesn't change should be marked constant. This allows the Windows CE program loader to leave such constant data in ROM instead of loading a copy into RAM, thus saving precious RAM.

The table itself is an array of a simple two-element structure. The first entry is the message value, followed by a pointer to the function that processes the message. While the functions could be named anything, I'm using a consistent structure throughout the book to help you keep track of them. The names are composed of a *Do* prefix (as a bow to object-oriented practice), followed by the message name and a suffix indicating the window class associated with the table. So *DoPaintMain* is the name of the function that processes *WM_PAINT* messages for the main window of the program.

DoPaintMain and *DoDestroyMain*

The two message-processing routines in HelloCE are *DoPaintMain* and *DoDestroyMain*. They mimic the function of the case clauses in Hello3. The advantage of the separate routines is that the code and their local variables are isolated to the routine. In Hello3's window procedure, the local variables specific to the paint code are bundled at the top of the routine. The encapsulation of the code makes it easy to cut and paste the code into the next application you write.

Running HelloCE

After you've entered the program into Visual Studio and built it, you can execute it remotely from inside VS by choosing Start Without Debugging from the Debug menu or by pressing Ctrl+F5. The program displays the Hello Windows CE text in the middle of an empty window, as shown in Figure 1-5. Tapping on the Close button on the title bar causes Windows CE to send a *WM_CLOSE* message to the window. Although HelloCE doesn't explicitly process the *WM_CLOSE* message, the *DefWindowProc* procedure enables default processing by destroying the main window. As the window is being destroyed, a *WM_DESTROY* message is sent, which causes *PostQuitMessage* to be called.

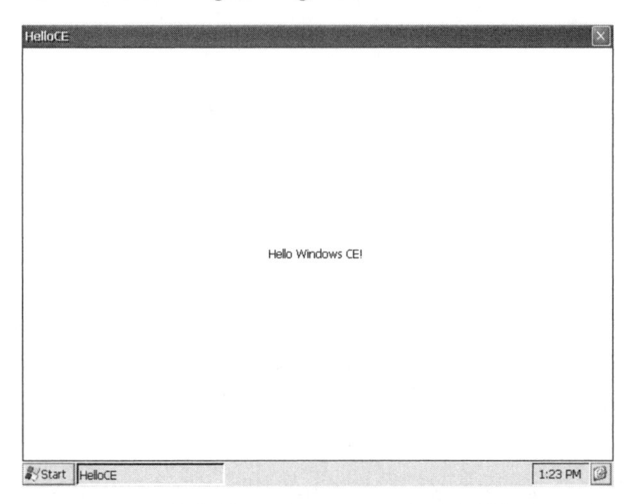

FIGURE 1-5 The HelloCE window on an embedded Windows CE system

As I said, HelloCE is a very basic Windows CE program, but it gives you a skeleton application on which you can build. If you look at the file HelloCE.exe using Explorer, you'll see that the program is represented by a generic icon. When HelloCE is running, the button on the taskbar in Figure 1-5 representing HelloCE has no icon displayed next to the text. Adding a custom icon to a program and how the *DrawText* function works are a couple of the topics I'll address in the next few chapters.

Chapter 2

Drawing on the Screen

In Chapter 1, "Hello Windows CE," the example program HelloCE had one task: to display a line of text on the screen. Displaying that line took only one call to *DrawText*, with Windows CE taking care of such details as the font and its color, the positioning of the line of text inside the window, and so forth. Given the power of a graphical user interface (GUI), however, an application can do much more than simply print a line of text on the screen. It can craft the look of the display down to the most minute of details.

Over the life of the Microsoft Windows operating system, the number of functions available for crafting these displays has expanded dramatically. With each successive version of Windows, functions have been added that extend the tools available to the programmer. As functions were added, the old ones remained, so that even if a function had been superseded by a new function, old programs would continue to run on the newer versions of Windows. The approach in which function after function is piled on while the old functions are retained for backward compatibility was discontinued with the initial version of Windows CE. Because of the requirement to produce a smaller version of Windows, the CE team took a hard look at the Win32 API and replicated only the functions absolutely required by applications written for the Windows CE target market.

One of the areas of the Win32 API hardest hit by this reduction was graphical functions. It's not that you now lack the functions to do the job—it's just that the high degree of redundancy in the Win32 API led to some major pruning of the graphical functions. An added challenge for the programmer is that different Windows CE platforms have subtly different sets of supported APIs. One of the ways in which Windows CE graphics support differs from that of its desktop cousins is that Windows CE doesn't support the different mapping modes available under other implementations of Windows. Instead, the Windows CE device contexts are always set to the *MM_TEXT* mapping mode. Coordinate transformations are also not supported under Windows CE. While these features can be quite useful for some types of applications, such as desktop publishing, their necessity in the Windows CE environment of small portable devices isn't as clear. So when you read about the functions and used in this chapter, remember that some might not be supported on all platforms. So that a program can determine what functions are supported, Windows has always had the *GetDeviceCaps* function, which returns the capabilities of the current graphic device. Throughout this chapter, I'll refer to *GetDeviceCaps* when determining what functions are supported on a given device.

This chapter, like the other chapters in Part I of this book, reviews the drawing features supported by Windows CE. One of the most important facts to remember is that although Windows CE doesn't support the full Win32 graphics API, the functions it does support allow developers to write full-featured graphical applications. Where Windows CE doesn't support a function, you typically can find a workaround. This chapter shows you the functions you can use and how to work around the areas where certain functions aren't supported under Windows CE.

Painting Basics

Historically, Windows has been subdivided into three main components: the kernel, which handles the process and memory management; User, which handles the windowing interface and controls; and the Graphics Device Interface (GDI), which performs the low-level drawing. In Windows CE, User and GDI are combined into the Graphics Windowing and Event Subsystem (GWE). At times, you might hear a Windows CE programmer talk about the GWE. The GWE is nothing really new—just a different packaging of standard Windows parts. In this book, the graphics portion of the GWE is usually referred to under its old name, GDI, to be consistent with standard Windows programming terminology.

But whether you're programming for Windows CE, Windows XP, or Windows Vista, there's more to drawing than simply handling the *WM_PAINT* message. It's helpful to understand just when and why a *WM_PAINT* message is sent to a window.

Valid and Invalid Regions

When, for some reason, an area of a window is exposed to the user, that area, or *region*, as it's referred to in Windows, is marked invalid. When no other messages are waiting in an application's message queue and the application's window contains an invalid region, Windows sends a *WM_PAINT* message to the window. As mentioned in Chapter 1, any drawing performed in response to a *WM_PAINT* message is couched in calls to *BeginPaint* and *EndPaint*. *BeginPaint* actually performs a number of actions. *BeginPaint* starts by hiding the caret—the text entry cursor—if it's displayed. If needed, a *WM_NCPAINT* message is sent directly to the default window procedure.[1] It then aquires a *device context* that is clipped to the invalid region, sends a *WM_ERASEBACKGROUND* message, if needed, to redraw the background, and returns a handle to the device context.

EndPaint, which is called by the application after the drawing is completed, validates the invalid region, releases the device context, and redisplays the caret if necessary. If no other action is performed by a *WM_PAINT* procedure, you must at least call *BeginPaint* and *EndPaint* if only to mark the invalid region as valid.

Alternatively, you can call to *ValidateRect* to blindly validate the region. But no drawing can take place in that case, because an application must have a handle to the device context before it can draw anything in the window.

---

[1] Windows CE supports non-client area messages, but they are sent directly to the default window procedure and therefore are not seen by the window procedure.

Often an application needs to force a repaint of its window. An application should never post or send a *WM_PAINT* message to itself or to another window. Instead, you use the following function:

```
BOOL InvalidateRect (HWND hWnd, const RECT *lpRect, BOOL bErase);
```

Notice that *InvalidateRect* doesn't require a handle to the window's device context, only to the window handle itself. The *lpRect* parameter is the area of the window to be invalidated. This value can be *NULL* if the entire window is to be invalidated. The *bErase* parameter indicates whether the background of the window should be redrawn during the *BeginPaint* call as mentioned earlier. Note that unlike other versions of Windows, Windows CE requires that the *hWnd* parameter be a valid window handle.

Whenever possible, only invalidate the region of the window that needs updating. Passing a *NULL* value for the rectangle parameter in *InvalidateRect* causes the entire window to be redrawn. Because drawing on the screen is one of the slowest actions an application can perform, limiting the drawing results in improved performance.

Device Contexts

A *device context*, often referred to simply as a DC, is a tool that Windows uses to manage access to the display and printer, although I'm covering only the display in this chapter[2]. Also, unless otherwise mentioned, the explanation that follows applies to Windows in general and isn't specific to Windows CE.

Windows applications never write directly to the screen. Instead, they request a handle to a display device context for the appropriate window and then, using the handle, draw to the device context. Windows then arbitrates and manages getting the pixels from the DC to the screen.

BeginPaint, which should be called only in a *WM_PAINT* message, returns a handle to the display DC for the window. An application usually performs its drawing to the screen during the *WM_PAINT* messages. Windows treats painting as a low-priority task, which is appropriate because having painting at a higher priority would result in a flood of paint messages for every little change to the display. Allowing an application to complete all its pending business by processing all waiting messages results in all the invalid regions being painted efficiently at once. Users don't notice the minor delays caused by the low priority of the *WM_PAINT* messages.

Of course, there are times when painting must be immediate. An example of such a time might be when a word processor needs to display a character immediately after its key is

---

[2] This book doesn't cover printing under Windows CE. The techniques for printing are similar to those used on the desktop, which is covered in excellent detail in *Programming Windows*.

pressed. To draw outside a *WM_PAINT* message, the handle to the DC can be obtained using this:

```
HDC GetDC (HWND hWnd);
```

GetDC returns a handle to the DC for the client portion of the window. Drawing can then be performed anywhere within the client area of the window because this process isn't like processing inside a *WM_PAINT* message; there's no clipping to restrict you from drawing in an invalid region.

Windows CE supports another function that can be used to receive the DC. It is

```
HDC GetDCEx (HWND hWnd, HRGN hrgnClip, DWORD flags);
```

GetDCEx allows you to have more control over the device context returned. The new parameter, *hrgnClip*, lets you define the clipping region, which limits drawing to that region of the DC. The *flags* parameter lets you specify how the DC acts as you draw on it. The following flags are supported under Windows CE:

- **DCX_WINDOW** Returns a DC that conforms the the entire window instead of just the client area.
- **DCX_CLIPCHILDREN** Excludes regions of any child windows.
- **DCX_CLIPSIBLINGS** Excludes regions of any sibling windows overlapping the window.
- **DCX_EXCLUDEREGION** Excludes the region indicated by the hrgnClip paramter.
- **DCX_INTERSECTRGN** Defines the clipping region as the intersection of the windows region and the region indicated by hrgnClip.
- **DCX_EXCLUDEUPDATE** Excludes the current update region.
- **DCX_INTERSECTUPDATE** Defines the clipping region as the intersection of the update region and the region defined by hrgnClip.

After the drawing is complete, a call must be made to release the device context:

```
int ReleaseDC (HWND hWnd, HDC hDC);
```

Device contexts are a shared resource, and therefore an application must not hold the DC for any longer than necessary.

While *GetDC* is used to draw inside the client area, sometimes an application needs access to the nonclient areas of a window, such as the title bar. To retrieve a DC for the entire window, make the following call:

```
HDC GetWindowDC (HWND hWnd);
```

As before, the matching call after the drawing is completed for *GetWindowDC* is *ReleaseDC*.

The *DC* functions under Windows CE are identical to the device context functions under the desktop versions of Windows. This should be expected because *DC*s are the core of the Windows drawing philosophy. Changes to this area of the API would result in major incompatibilities between Windows CE applications and their desktop counterparts.

Writing Text

In Chapter 1, the HelloCE example displayed a line of text using a call to *DrawText*. That line from the example is shown here:

```
DrawText (hdc, TEXT ("Hello Windows CE!"), -1, &rect,
          DT_CENTER | DT_VCENTER | DT_SINGLELINE);
```

DrawText is a fairly high-level function that allows a program to display text while having Windows deal with most of the details. The first few parameters of *DrawText* are almost self-explanatory. The handle of the device context being used is passed, along with the text to display couched in a *TEXT* macro, which declares the string as a Unicode string necessary for Windows CE. The third parameter is the number of characters to print, or as is the case here, a -1 indicating that the string being passed is null terminated and Windows should compute the length.

The fourth parameter is a pointer to a *rect* structure that specifies the formatting rectangle for the text. *DrawText* uses this rectangle as a basis for formatting the text to be printed. How the text is formatted depends on the function's last parameter, the formatting flags. These flags specify how the text is to be placed within the formatting rectangle, or in the case of the *DT_CALCRECT* flag, the flags have *DrawText* compute the dimensions of the text that is to be printed. *DrawText* even formats multiple lines with line breaks automatically computed. In the case of HelloCE, the flags specify that the text should be centered horizontally (*DT_CENTER*) and vertically (*DT_VCENTER*). The *DT_VCENTER* flag works only on single lines of text, so the final parameter, *DT_SINGLELINE*, specifies that the text shouldn't be flowed across multiple lines if the rectangle isn't wide enough to display the entire string.

Another way to draw text is by employing the following function:

```
BOOL ExtTextOut (HDC hdc, int X, int Y, UINT fuOptions,
                 const RECT *lprc, LPCTSTR lpString,
                 UINT cbCount, const int *lpDx);
```

The *ExtTextOut* function has a few advantages over *DrawText*. First, *ExtTextOut* tends to be faster for drawing single lines of text. Second, the text isn't formatted inside a rectangle; instead, *x* and *y* starting coordinates are passed, specifying where the text will be drawn. Generally, the point defined by the coordinates is the upper-left corner of the rectangle, but this can be changed with the text alignment settings of the DC. The *rect* parameter that's passed is used as a clipping rectangle or, if the background mode is opaque, the area where the background color is drawn. This rectangle parameter can be *NULL* if you don't want any clipping or opaquing. The next two parameters are the text and the character count. The last parameter, *ExtTextOut*, allows an application to specify the horizontal distance between adjacent character cells.

Windows CE differs from other versions of Windows in having only these two text drawing functions for displaying text. You can emulate most of what you can do with the text functions typically used in other versions of Windows, such as *TextOut* and *TabbedTextOut*, by using either *DrawText* or *ExtTextOut*. This is one of the areas in which Windows CE has broken with earlier versions of Windows, sacrificing backward compatibility to achieve a smaller operating system.

Device Context Attributes

What I haven't mentioned yet about HelloCE's use of *DrawText* is the large number of assumptions the program makes about the DC configuration when displaying the text. Drawing in a Windows device context takes a large number of parameters, such as foreground and background color, and how the text should be drawn over the background as well as the font of the text. Instead of specifying all these parameters for each drawing call, the device context keeps track of the current settings, referred to as *attributes*, and uses them as appropriate for each call to draw to the device context.

Foreground and Background Colors

The most obvious of the text attributes are the foreground and background color. Two functions, *SetTextColor* and *GetTextColor*, allow a program to set and retrieve the current color. These functions work well with both grayscale screens and the color screens supported by Windows CE devices.

To determine how many colors a device supports, use *GetDeviceCaps* as mentioned previously. The prototype for this function is the following:

```
int GetDeviceCaps (HDC hdc, int nIndex);
```

You need the handle to the DC being queried because different DCs have different capabilities. For example, a printer DC would differ from a display DC. The second parameter indicates the capability being queried. In the case of returning the colors available on the device, the *NUMCOLORS* value returns the number of colors as long as the device supports 256 colors or fewer. Beyond that, the returned value for *NUMCOLORS* is -1 and the colors can be returned using the *BITSPIXEL* value, which returns the number of bits used to represent each pixel. This value can be converted to the number of colors by raising 2 to the power of the *BITSPIXEL* returned value, as in the following code sample:

```
nNumColors = GetDeviceCaps (hdc, NUMCOLORS);
if (nNumColors == -1)
    nNumColors = 1 << GetDeviceCaps (hdc, BITSPIXEL);
```

Text Alignment

When displaying text with *ExtTextOut*, the system uses the text alignment of the DC to determine where to draw the text. The text can be aligned both horizontally and vertically, using this function:

```
UINT WINAPI SetTextAlign (HDC hdc, INT fmode);
```

The alignment flags passed to *fmode* are as follows:

- **TA_LEFT** The left edge of the text is aligned with the reference point.
- **TA_RIGHT** The right edge of the text is aligned with the reference point.
- **TA_TOP** The top edge of the text is aligned with the reference point.
- **TA_CENTER** The text is centered horizontally with the reference point.
- **TA_BOTTOM** The bottom edge of the text is aligned with the reference point.
- **TA_BASELINE** The baseline of the text is aligned with the reference point.
- **TA_NOUPDATECP** The current point of the DC is not updated after the ExtTextOut call.
- **TA_UPDATECP** The current point of the DC is updated after the ExtTextOut call.

The reference point in the description refers to the *x* and *y* coordinates passed to the *ExtTextOut* function. For each call to *SetTextAlign*, a flag for vertical alignment and a flag for horizontal alignment can be combined.

Because it might be difficult to visualize what each of these flags does, Figure 2-1 shows the results of each flag. In the figure, the *X* is the reference point.

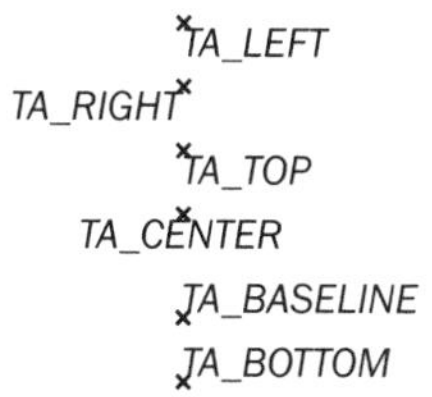

TA_LEFT
TA_RIGHT
TA_TOP
TA_CENTER
TA_BASELINE
TA_BOTTOM

FIGURE 2-1 The relationship between the current drawing point and the text alignment flags

Drawing Mode

Another attribute that affects text output is the background mode. When letters are drawn on the device context, the system draws the letters themselves in the foreground color. The space between the letters is another matter. If the background mode is set to opaque, the space is drawn with the current background color. But if the background mode is set to transparent, the space between the letters is left in whatever state it was in before the text was drawn. While this might not seem like a big difference, imagine a window background filled with a drawing or graph. If text is written over the top of the graph and the background mode is set to opaque, the area around the text is filled, and the background color overwrites the graph. If the background mode is transparent, the text appears as if it had been placed on the graph, and the graph shows through between the letters of the text.

The TextDemo Example Program

The TextDemo program, shown in Listing 2-1, demonstrates the relationships among the text color, the background color, and the background mode.

LISTING 2-1

TextDemo.h

```
//================================================================
// Header file
//
// Written for the book Programming Windows CE
// Copyright (C) 2007 Douglas Boling

//======================================================================
// Returns number of elements
#define dim(x) (sizeof(x) / sizeof(x[0]))

//----------------------------------------------------------------------
// Generic defines and data types
//
struct decodeUINT {                             // Structure associates
    UINT Code;                                  // messages
                                                // with a function.
    LRESULT (*Fxn)(HWND, UINT, WPARAM, LPARAM);
};

//----------------------------------------------------------------------
// Function prototypes
//
HWND InitInstance (HINSTANCE, LPWSTR, int);
int TermInstance (HINSTANCE, int);

// Window procedures
LRESULT CALLBACK MainWndProc (HWND, UINT, WPARAM, LPARAM);
```

```
// Message handlers
LRESULT DoPaintMain (HWND, UINT, WPARAM, LPARAM);
LRESULT DoDestroyMain (HWND, UINT, WPARAM, LPARAM);
```

TextDemo.cpp

```
//======================================================================
// TextDemo - Text output demo
//
// Written for the book Programming Windows CE
// Copyright (C) 2007 Douglas Boling
//======================================================================
#include <windows.h>                 // For all that Windows stuff
#include "TextDemo.h"                // Program-specific stuff

//----------------------------------------------------------------------
// Global data
//
const TCHAR szAppName[] = TEXT ("TextDemo");
HINSTANCE hInst;                     // Program instance handle

// Message dispatch table for MainWindowProc
const struct decodeUINT MainMessages[] = {
    WM_PAINT, DoPaintMain,
    WM_DESTROY, DoDestroyMain,
};
//======================================================================
// Program Entry Point
//
int WINAPI WinMain (HINSTANCE hInstance, HINSTANCE hPrevInstance,
                    LPWSTR lpCmdLine, int nCmdShow) {
    MSG msg;
    int rc = 0;
    HWND hwndMain;

    // Initialize this instance.
    hwndMain = InitInstance (hInstance, lpCmdLine, nCmdShow);
    if (hwndMain == 0)
        return 0x10;

     // Application message loop
    while (GetMessage (&msg, NULL, 0, 0)) {
        TranslateMessage (&msg);
        DispatchMessage (&msg);
    }
    // Instance cleanup
    return TermInstance (hInstance, msg.wParam);
}
//----------------------------------------------------------------------
// InitInstance - Instance initialization
//
```

```
HWND InitInstance (HINSTANCE hInstance, LPWSTR lpCmdLine, int nCmdShow){
    WNDCLASS wc;
    HWND hWnd;

    hInst = hInstance;    // Save handle in global variable.

#if defined(WIN32_PLATFORM_PSPC) || defined(WIN32_PLATFORM_WFSP)
    // If Windows Mobile, allow only one instance of the application.
    hWnd = FindWindow (szAppName, NULL);
    if (hWnd) {
        SetForegroundWindow ((HWND)(((DWORD)hWnd) | 0x01));
        return 0;
    }
#endif
    // Register application main window class.
    wc.style = 0;                             // Window style
    wc.lpfnWndProc = MainWndProc;             // Callback function
    wc.cbClsExtra = 0;                        // Extra class data
    wc.cbWndExtra = 0;                        // Extra window data
    wc.hInstance = hInstance;                 // Owner handle
    wc.hIcon = NULL,                          // Application icon
    wc.hCursor = LoadCursor (NULL, IDC_ARROW);// Default cursor
    wc.hbrBackground = (HBRUSH) GetStockObject (WHITE_BRUSH);
    wc.lpszMenuName =  NULL;                  // Menu name
    wc.lpszClassName = szAppName;             // Window class name

    if (RegisterClass (&wc) == 0) return 0;

    // Create main window.
    hWnd = CreateWindowEx (WS_EX_NODRAG,      // Ex Style flags
                         szAppName,           // Window class
                         TEXT("TextDemo"),    // Window title
                         // Style flags
                         WS_VISIBLE | WS_CAPTION | WS_SYSMENU,
                         CW_USEDEFAULT,       // x position
                         CW_USEDEFAULT,       // y position
                         CW_USEDEFAULT,       // Initial width
                         CW_USEDEFAULT,       // Initial height
                         NULL,                // Parent
                         NULL,                // Menu, must be null
                         hInstance,           // Application instance
                         NULL);               // Pointer to create
                                              // Parameters
    // Return fail code if window not created.
    if ((!hWnd) || (!IsWindow (hWnd))) return 0;

    // Standard show and update calls
    ShowWindow (hWnd, nCmdShow);
    UpdateWindow (hWnd);
    return hWnd;
}
//----------------------------------------------------------------------
// TermInstance - Program cleanup
//
```

```
int TermInstance (HINSTANCE hInstance, int nDefRC) {
    return nDefRC;
}
//======================================================================
// Message handling procedures for MainWindow
//
//----------------------------------------------------------------------
// MainWndProc - Callback function for application window
//
LRESULT CALLBACK MainWndProc (HWND hWnd, UINT wMsg, WPARAM wParam,
                              LPARAM lParam) {
    INT i;
    //
    // Search message list to see if we need to handle this
    // message.  If in list, call procedure.
    //
    for (i = 0; i < dim(MainMessages); i++) {
        if (wMsg == MainMessages[i].Code)
            return (*MainMessages[i].Fxn)(hWnd, wMsg, wParam, lParam);
    }
    return DefWindowProc (hWnd, wMsg, wParam, lParam);
}
//----------------------------------------------------------------------
// DoPaintMain - Process WM_PAINT message for window.
//
LRESULT DoPaintMain (HWND hWnd, UINT wMsg, WPARAM wParam,
                     LPARAM lParam) {
    PAINTSTRUCT ps;
    RECT rect, rectCli;
    HBRUSH hbrOld;
    HDC hdc;
    INT i, cy;
    DWORD dwColorTable[] = {0x00000000, 0x00808080,
                            0x00cccccc, 0x00ffffff};
     TCHAR szHello[] = TEXT ("Hello Windows CE");

    GetClientRect (hWnd, &rectCli);

    hdc = BeginPaint (hWnd, &ps);

    // Get the height and length of the string.
    DrawText (hdc, szHello, -1, &rect,
              DT_CALCRECT | DT_CENTER | DT_SINGLELINE);

    cy = rect.bottom - rect.top + 5;

    // Draw black rectangle on right half of window.
    hbrOld = (HBRUSH)SelectObject (hdc, GetStockObject (BLACK_BRUSH));
    Rectangle (hdc, rectCli.left + (rectCli.right - rectCli.left) / 2,
               rectCli.top, rectCli.right, rectCli.bottom);
    SelectObject (hdc, hbrOld);

    rectCli.bottom = rectCli.top + cy;
    SetBkMode (hdc, TRANSPARENT);
```

```
    for (i = 0; i < 4; i++) {
        SetTextColor (hdc, dwColorTable[i]);
        SetBkColor (hdc, dwColorTable[3-i]);

        DrawText (hdc, szHello, -1, &rectCli, DT_CENTER | DT_SINGLELINE);
        rectCli.top += cy;
        rectCli.bottom += cy;
    }

    SetBkMode (hdc, OPAQUE);
    for (i = 0; i < 4; i++) {
        SetTextColor (hdc, dwColorTable[i]);
        SetBkColor (hdc, dwColorTable[3-i]);

        DrawText (hdc, szHello, -1, &rectCli, DT_CENTER | DT_SINGLELINE);
        rectCli.top += cy;
        rectCli.bottom += cy;
    }
    EndPaint (hWnd, &ps);
    return 0;
}
//----------------------------------------------------------------------
// DoDestroyMain - Process WM_DESTROY message for window.
//
LRESULT DoDestroyMain (HWND hWnd, UINT wMsg, WPARAM wParam,
                       LPARAM lParam) {
    PostQuitMessage (0);
    return 0;
}
```

The meat of TextDemo is in the *DoPaintMain* function. The first call to *DrawText* doesn't draw anything in the device context. Instead, the *DT_CALCRECT* flag instructs Windows to store the dimensions of the rectangle for the text string in *rect*. This information is used to compute the height of the string, which is stored in *cy*. Next, a black rectangle is drawn on the right side of the window. I'll talk about how a rectangle is drawn later in the chapter; it's used in this program to produce two different backgrounds before the text is written. The function then prints out the same string using different foreground and background colors and both the transparent and opaque drawing modes. The result of this combination is shown in Figure 2-2.

The first four lines are drawn using the transparent mode. The second four are drawn using the opaque mode. The text color is set from black to white so that each line drawn uses a different color, while at the same time the background color is set from white to black. In transparent mode, the background color is irrelevant because it isn't used; but in opaque mode, the background color is readily apparent on each line.

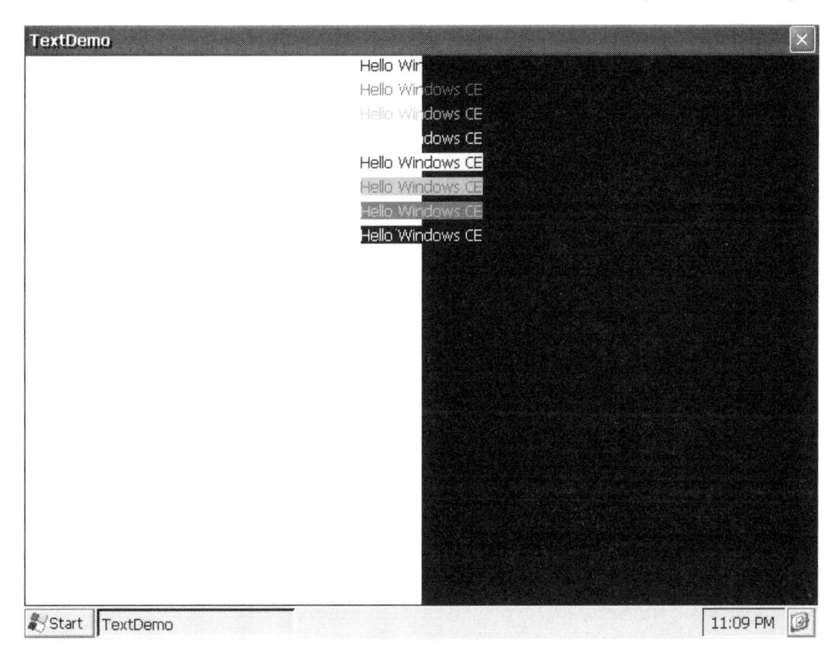

FIGURE 2-2 TextDemo shows how the text color, background color, and background mode relate.

Fonts

If the ability to set the foreground and background colors were all the flexibility that Windows provided, you might as well be back in the days of MS-DOS and character attributes. Arguably, the most dramatic change from MS-DOS is Windows's ability to change the font used to display text. All Windows operating systems are built around the concept of *WYSIWYG*—what you see is what you get—and changeable fonts are a major tool used to achieve that goal.

Two types of fonts appear in all Windows operating systems—*raster* and *TrueType*. Raster fonts are stored as bitmaps, which are small pixel-by-pixel images, one for each character in the font. Raster fonts are easy to store and use, but have one major problem: they don't scale well. Just as a small picture looks grainy when greatly enlarged, raster fonts begin to look blocky as they are scaled to larger and larger sizes.

TrueType fonts solve the scaling problem. Instead of being stored as images, each TrueType character is stored as a description of how to draw the character. The font engine, which is the part of Windows that draws characters on the screen, then takes the description and draws it on the screen in any size needed. A Windows CE system can support either TrueType or raster fonts, but not both. Fortunately, the programming interface is the same for both raster and TrueType fonts, relieving Windows developers from worrying about the font technology in all but the most exacting of applications.

The font functions under Windows CE closely track the same functions under other versions of Windows. Look at the functions used in the life of a font, from creation through selection in a DC and, finally, to deletion of the font. How to query the current font as well as enumerate the available fonts is also covered in the following sections.

Creating a Font

Before an application is able to use a font other than the default font, the font must be created and then selected into the device context. Any text drawn in a DC after the new font is selected into the DC uses the new font.

Creating a font in Windows CE can be accomplished this way:

```
HFONT CreateFontIndirect (const LOGFONT *lplf);
```

This function is passed a pointer to a *LOGFONT* structure that must be filled with the description of the font you want.

```
typedef struct tagLOGFONT {
    LONG lfHeight;
    LONG lfWidth;
    LONG lfEscapement;
    LONG lfOrientation;
    LONG lfWeight;
    BYTE lfItalic;
    BYTE lfUnderline;
    BYTE lfStrikeOut;
    BYTE lfCharSet;
    BYTE lfOutPrecision;
    BYTE lfClipPrecision;
    BYTE lfQuality;
    BYTE lfPitchAndFamily;
    TCHAR lfFaceName[LF_FACESIZE];
} LOGFONT;
```

The *lfHeight* field specifies the height of the font in device units. If this field is 0, the font manager returns the default font size for the font family requested. For most applications, however, you want to create a font of a particular point size. The following equation can be used to convert point size to the *lfHeight* field:

```
lfHeight = -1 * (PointSize * GetDeviceCaps (hdc, LOGPIXELSY) / 72);
```

Here, *GetDeviceCaps* is passed a *LOGPIXELSY* field instructing it to return the number of logical pixels per inch in the vertical direction. The 72 is the number of *points* (a typesetting unit of measure) per inch.

The *lfWidth* field specifies the average character width. Because the height of a font is more important than its width, most programs set this value to 0. This tells the font manager to compute the proper width based on the height of the font. The *lfEscapement* and *lfOrientation* fields specify the angle in tenths of degrees of the baseline of the text and the *x*-axis. The *lfWeight* field specifies the boldness of the font from 0 through 1000, with 400 being a normal font and 700 being bold. The next three fields specify whether the font is to be italic, underline, or strikeout.

The *lpCharSet* field specifies the character set you have chosen. This field is more important in international releases of software, where it can be used to request a specific language's character set. The *lfOutPrecision* field can be used to specify how closely Windows matches your requested font. Among a number of flags available, an *OUT_TT_ONLY_PRECIS* flag specifies that the font created must be a TrueType font. The *lfClipPrecision* field specifies how Windows should clip characters that are partially outside the region being displayed.

The *lfQuality* field is set to one of the following:

- **DEFAULT_QUALITY** Default system quality.
- **DRAFT_QUALITY** Sacrifice quality for speed.
- **CLEARTYPE_QUALITY** Render text using ClearType technology.
- **CLEARTYPE_COMPAT_QUALITY** Render text using ClearType. Use the same spacing as non-ClearType font.

ClearType is a text display technology that provides a sharper look for fonts using the ability to address the individual red, green, and blue LEDs that make up a pixel on a color LCD display. Depending on the system, ClearType might not be supported or it might be enabled for all fonts in the system. For systems that support ClearType but don't enable it globally, using the *CLEARTYPE_QUALITY* or *CLEARTYPE_COMPAT_QUALITY* flags creates a font that is rendered using ClearType. Because ClearType doesn't improve the look of all fonts, test to see whether applying ClearType improves the rendering of your chosen font.

The *lfPitchAndFamily* field specifies the family of the font you want. This field is handy when you need a family such as Swiss, which features proportional fonts without serifs, or a family such as Roman, which features proportional fonts with serifs, but you don't have a specific font in mind. You can also use this field to specify simply a proportional or a monospaced font and allow Windows to determine which font matches the other specified characteristics passed into the *LOGFONT* structure. Finally, the *lfFaceName* field can be used to specify the typeface name of a specific font.

When *CreateFontIndirect* is called with a filled *LOGFONT* structure, Windows creates a logical font that best matches the characteristics provided. To use the font, however, the final step of selecting the font into a device context must be made.

Selecting a Font into a Device Context

You select a font into a DC by using the following function:

```
HGDIOBJ SelectObject (HDC hdc, HGDIOBJ hgdiobj);
```

This function is used for more than just setting the default font; you use this function to select other GDI objects, as you soon see. The function returns the previously selected object (in your case, the previously selected font), which should be saved so that it can be selected back into the DC when you finish with the new font. The line of code looks like the following:

```
hOldFont = (HFONT)SelectObject (hdc, hFont);
```

When the logical font is selected, the system determines the closest match to the logical font from the fonts available in the system. For devices with bitmap fonts, this match could be a fair amount off from the specified parameters. Because of this, never assume that just because you request a particular font, the font returned exactly matches the one you request. For example, the height of the font you asked for might not be the height of the font that's selected into the device context.

Querying a Font's Characteristics

To determine the characteristics of the font that is selected into a device context, a call to

```
BOOL GetTextMetrics (HDC hdc, LPTEXTMETRIC lptm);
```

returns the characteristics of that font. A *TEXTMETRIC* structure is returned with the information and is defined as

```
typedef struct tagTEXTMETRIC {
    LONG tmHeight;
    LONG tmAscent;
    LONG tmDescent;
    LONG tmInternalLeading;
    LONG tmExternalLeading;
    LONG tmAveCharWidth;
    LONG tmMaxCharWidth;
    LONG tmWeight;
    LONG tmOverhang;
    LONG tmDigitizedAspectX;
    LONG tmDigitizedAspectY;
    char tmFirstChar;
    char tmLastChar;
    char tmDefaultChar;
    char tmBreakChar;
    BYTE tmItalic;
    BYTE tmUnderlined;
    BYTE tmStruckOut;
    BYTE tmPitchAndFamily;
    BYTE tmCharSet;
} TEXTMETRIC;
```

The *TEXTMETRIC* structure contains a number of the fields you saw in the *LOGFONT* structure, but this time the values listed in *TEXTMETRIC* are the values of the font selected into the device context. Figure 2-3 shows the relationship of some of the fields to actual characters.

Aside from determining whether you really got the font you wanted, the *GetTextmetrics* call has another valuable purpose—determining the height of the font. Recall that in TextDemo, the height of the line was computed using a call to *DrawText*. Although that method is convenient, it tends to be slow. You can use the *TEXTMETRIC* data to compute this height in a much more straightforward manner. By adding the *tmHeight* field, which is the height of the characters, to the *tmExternalLeading* field, which is the distance between the bottom pixel of one row and the top pixel of the next row of characters, you can determine the vertical distance between the baselines of two lines of text.

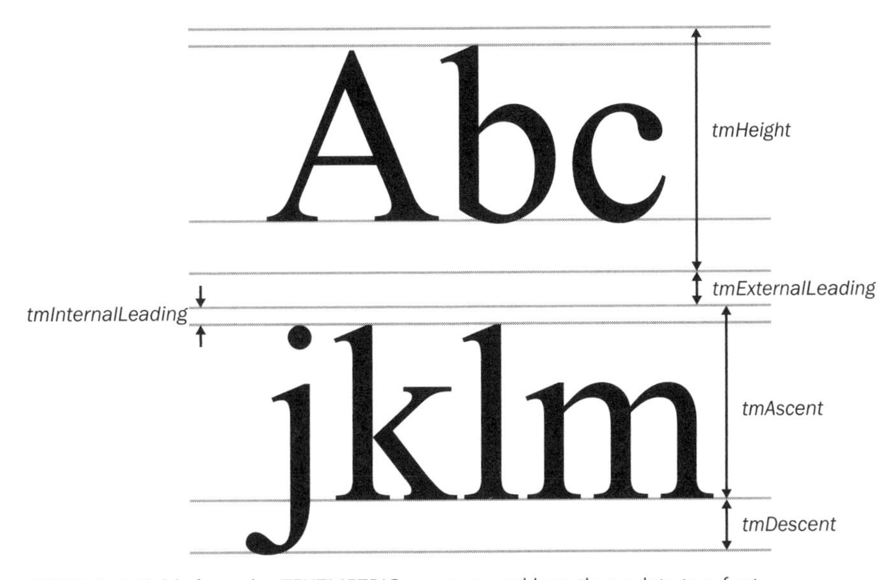

FIGURE 2-3 Fields from the *TEXTMETRIC* structure and how they relate to a font

Although *GetTextMetrics* is great for determining the height of a font, it provides only the average and maximum widths of a font. If more detail is needed for a TrueType font, the function

```
BOOL GetCharABCWidths (HDC hdc, UINT uFirstChar, UINT uLastChar,
                       LPABC lpabc);
```

can be used. *GetCharABCWidths* returns the "ABC" widths of a series of characters delineated by the *uFirstChar* and *uLastChar* parameters. The font examined is the font currently selected in the device context specified by the *hdc* parameter. The ABC structure is defined as follows:

```
typedef struct _ABC {
    int     abcA;
    UINT    abcB;
    int     abcC;
} ABC;
```

The *abcA* field is the distance to add to the current position before drawing the character, or *glyph*. The *abcB* field is the width of the glyph, while the *abcC* field is the distance to add to the current position after drawing the glyph. Both *abcA* and *abcC* can be negative to indicate underhangs and overhangs.

To examine the widths of bitmap fonts, *GetCharWidth32* can be used. It returns an array of character widths for each character in a range of characters.

Destroying a Font

Like other GDI resources, fonts must be destroyed after the program finishes using them. Failure to delete fonts before terminating a program causes what's known as a *resource leak*—an orphaned graphic resource that takes up valuable memory but is no longer owned by an application.

To destroy a font, first deselect it from any device contexts it has been selected into. Do this by calling *SelectObject*. The font passed is the font that was returned by the original *SelectObject* call made to select the font. After the font has been deselected, a call to

```
BOOL DeleteObject (HGDIOBJ hObject);
```

(with *hObject* containing the font handle) deletes the font from the system.

A word of warning: attempting to delete a font, or any GDI object, while it is still selected in a device context will fail. Because most code doesn't check the return code of *DeleteObject*, this creates a classic "leak" situation where an application thinks it has deallocated a resource while in fact it still exists. Leaks will quickly bring a Windows CE system, with its limited memory, to its knees. Take care that all GDI objects are truly deleted as intended.

As you can see from this process, font management is no small matter in Windows. The many parameters of the *LOGFONT* structure might look daunting, but they give an application tremendous power to specify a font exactly.

One problem when dealing with fonts is determining just what types of fonts are available on a specific device. Windows CE devices come with a set of standard fonts, but a specific system might have been loaded with additional fonts by either the manufacturer or the user. Windows CE uses the same font file format as the desktop verisons of Windows, so even after a device is shipped it is possible for developers or even users to add additional fonts. Fortunately, Windows provides a method for enumerating all the available fonts in a system.

Enumerating Fonts

To determine what fonts are available on a system, Windows provides this function:

```
int EnumFontFamilies (HDC hdc, LPCTSTR lpszFamily,
                      FONTENUMPROC lpEnumFontFamProc, LPARAM lParam);
```

This function lets you list all the font families as well as each font within a family. The first parameter is the obligatory handle to the device context. The second parameter is a string to the name of the family to enumerate. If this parameter is null, the function enumerates each of the available families.

The third parameter is something different—a pointer to a function provided by the application. The function is a callback function that Windows calls once for each font being enumerated. The final parameter, *lParam*, is a generic parameter that can be used by the application. This value is passed unmodified to the application's callback procedure.

While the name of the callback function can be anything, the prototype of the callback must match the declaration:

```
int CALLBACK EnumFontFamProc (LOGFONT *lpelf, TEXTMETRIC *lpntm,
                              DWORD FontType, LPARAM lParam);
```

The first parameter passed back to the callback function is a pointer to a *LOGFONT* structure describing the font being enumerated. The second parameter, a pointer to a *textmetric* structure, further describes the font. The font type parameter indicates whether the font is a raster or TrueType font.

The FontList Example Program

The FontList program, shown in Listing 2-2, uses the *EnumFontFamilies* function in two ways to enumerate all fonts in the system.

LISTING 2-2 The FontList program enumerates all fonts in the system

FontList.h

```
//======================================================================
// Header file
//
// Written for the book Programming Windows CE
// Copyright (C) 2007 Douglas Boling
//======================================================================
// Returns number of elements
#define dim(x) (sizeof(x) / sizeof(x[0]))
//----------------------------------------------------------------------
// Generic defines and data types
//
struct decodeUINT {                             // Structure associates
    UINT Code;                                  // messages
                                                // with a function.
    LRESULT (*Fxn)(HWND, UINT, WPARAM, LPARAM);
};

//----------------------------------------------------------------------
```

```
// Program-specific structures
//
#define FAMILYMAX   24
typedef struct {
    int nNumFonts;
    TCHAR szFontFamily[LF_FACESIZE];
} FONTFAMSTRUCT;
typedef FONTFAMSTRUCT *PFONTFAMSTRUCT;

typedef struct {
    INT yCurrent;
    HDC hdc;
} PAINTFONTINFO;
typedef PAINTFONTINFO *PPAINTFONTINFO;

//----------------------------------------------------------------------
// Function prototypes
//
HWND InitInstance (HINSTANCE, LPWSTR, int);
int TermInstance (HINSTANCE, int);

// Window procedures
LRESULT CALLBACK MainWndProc (HWND, UINT, WPARAM, LPARAM);

// Message handlers
LRESULT DoCreateMain (HWND, UINT, WPARAM, LPARAM);
LRESULT DoPaintMain (HWND, UINT, WPARAM, LPARAM);
LRESULT DoDestroyMain (HWND, UINT, WPARAM, LPARAM);
```

FontList.cpp

```
//======================================================================
// FontList - Lists the available fonts in the system
//
// Written for the book Programming Windows CE
// Copyright (C) 2007 Douglas Boling
//======================================================================
#include <windows.h>                 // For all that Windows stuff
#include "FontList.h"                // Program-specific stuff

//----------------------------------------------------------------------
// Global data
//
const TCHAR szAppName[] = TEXT ("FontList");
HINSTANCE hInst;                     // Program instance handle

FONTFAMSTRUCT ffs[FAMILYMAX];
INT sFamilyCnt = 0;

// Message dispatch table for MainWindowProc
```

```
const struct decodeUINT MainMessages[] = {
    WM_CREATE, DoCreateMain,
    WM_PAINT, DoPaintMain,
    WM_DESTROY, DoDestroyMain,
};

//======================================================================
// Program entry point
//
int WINAPI WinMain (HINSTANCE hInstance, HINSTANCE hPrevInstance,
                    LPWSTR lpCmdLine, int nCmdShow) {
    MSG msg;
    int rc = 0;
    HWND hwndMain;

    // Initialize this instance.
    hwndMain = InitInstance (hInstance, lpCmdLine, nCmdShow);
    if (hwndMain == 0)
        return 0x10;
    // Application message loop
    while (GetMessage (&msg, NULL, 0, 0)) {
        TranslateMessage (&msg);
        DispatchMessage (&msg);
    }
    // Instance cleanup
    return TermInstance (hInstance, msg.wParam);
}
//----------------------------------------------------------------------
// InitInstance - Instance initialization
//
HWND InitInstance (HINSTANCE hInstance, LPWSTR lpCmdLine, int nCmdShow) {
    WNDCLASS wc;
    HWND hWnd;

    // Save program instance handle in global variable.
    hInst = hInstance;

#if defined(WIN32_PLATFORM_PSPC) || defined(WIN32_PLATFORM_WFSP)
    // If Windows Mobile, allow only one instance of the application.
    hWnd = FindWindow (szAppName, NULL);
    if (hWnd) {
        SetForegroundWindow ((HWND)(((DWORD)hWnd) | 0x01));
        return 0;
    }
#endif
    // Register application main window class.
    wc.style = 0;                             // Window style
    wc.lpfnWndProc = MainWndProc;             // Callback function
    wc.cbClsExtra = 0;                        // Extra class data
    wc.cbWndExtra = 0;                        // Extra window data
    wc.hInstance = hInstance;                 // Owner handle
    wc.hIcon = NULL,                          // Application icon
    wc.hCursor = LoadCursor (NULL, IDC_ARROW);// Default cursor
    wc.hbrBackground = (HBRUSH) GetStockObject(WHITE_BRUSH);
```

```
    wc.lpszMenuName =  NULL;                    // Menu name
    wc.lpszClassName = szAppName;               // Window class name

    if (RegisterClass (&wc) == 0) return 0;

    // Create main window.
    hWnd = CreateWindowEx (WS_EX_NODRAG,        // Ex style flags
                           szAppName,           // Window class
                           TEXT("Font Listing"),// Window title
                           // Style flags
                           WS_VISIBLE | WS_CAPTION | WS_SYSMENU,
                           CW_USEDEFAULT,       // x position
                           CW_USEDEFAULT,       // y position
                           CW_USEDEFAULT,       // Initial width
                           CW_USEDEFAULT,       // Initial height
                           NULL,                // Parent
                           NULL,                // Menu, must be null
                           hInstance,           // Application instance
                           NULL);               // Pointer to create
                                                // parameters
    // Return fail code if window not created.
    if (!IsWindow (hWnd)) return 0;

    // Standard show and update calls
    ShowWindow (hWnd, nCmdShow);
    UpdateWindow (hWnd);
    return hWnd;
}
//----------------------------------------------------------------------
// TermInstance - Program cleanup
//
int TermInstance (HINSTANCE hInstance, int nDefRC) {
    return nDefRC;
}
//======================================================================
// Font callback functions
//
//----------------------------------------------------------------------
// FontFamilyCallback - Callback function that enumerates the font
// families
//
int CALLBACK FontFamilyCallback (CONST LOGFONT *lplf,
                                 CONST TEXTMETRIC *lpntm,
                                 DWORD nFontType, LPARAM lParam) {
    int rc = 1;

    // Stop enumeration if array filled.
    if (sFamilyCnt >= FAMILYMAX)
        return 0;
    // Copy face name of font.
    lstrcpy (ffs[sFamilyCnt++].szFontFamily, lplf->lfFaceName);
    return rc;
}
//----------------------------------------------------------------------
```

```
// EnumSingleFontFamily - Callback function that enumerates fonts
//
int CALLBACK EnumSingleFontFamily (CONST LOGFONT *lplf,
                                   CONST TEXTMETRIC *lpntm,
                                   DWORD nFontType, LPARAM lParam) {
    PFONTFAMSTRUCT pffs;

    pffs = (PFONTFAMSTRUCT) lParam;
    pffs->nNumFonts++;    // Increment count of fonts in family
    return 1;
}

//----------------------------------------------------------------
// PaintSingleFontFamily - Callback function that draws a font
//
int CALLBACK PaintSingleFontFamily (CONST LOGFONT *lplf,
                                    CONST TEXTMETRIC *lpntm,
                                    DWORD nFontType, LPARAM lParam) {
    PPAINTFONTINFO ppfi;
    TCHAR szOut[256];
    INT nFontHeight, nPointSize;
    HFONT hFont, hOldFont;

    ppfi = (PPAINTFONTINFO) lParam;  // Translate lParam into struct
                                     // pointer.

    // Create the font from the LOGFONT structure passed.
    hFont = CreateFontIndirect (lplf);

    // Select the font into the device context.
    hOldFont = (HFONT)SelectObject (ppfi->hdc, hFont);

    // Compute font size.
    nPointSize = (lplf->lfHeight * 72) /
                 GetDeviceCaps(ppfi->hdc,LOGPIXELSY);

    // Format string and paint on display.
    wsprintf (szOut, TEXT ("%s   Point:%d"), lplf->lfFaceName,
              nPointSize);
    ExtTextOut (ppfi->hdc, 25, ppfi->yCurrent, 0, NULL,
                szOut, lstrlen (szOut), NULL);

    // Compute the height of the default font.
    nFontHeight = lpntm->tmHeight + lpntm->tmExternalLeading;
    // Update new draw point.
    ppfi->yCurrent += nFontHeight;
    // Deselect font and delete.
    SelectObject (ppfi->hdc, hOldFont);
    DeleteObject (hFont);
    return 1;
}
//================================================================
// Message handling procedures for MainWindow
//
```

```
//----------------------------------------------------------------------
// MainWndProc - Callback function for application window
//
LRESULT CALLBACK MainWndProc (HWND hWnd, UINT wMsg, WPARAM wParam,
                              LPARAM lParam) {
    INT i;
    //
    // Search message list to see if we need to handle this
    // message.  If in list, call procedure.
    //
    for (i = 0; i < dim(MainMessages); i++) {
        if (wMsg == MainMessages[i].Code)
            return (*MainMessages[i].Fxn)(hWnd, wMsg, wParam, lParam);
    }
    return DefWindowProc (hWnd, wMsg, wParam, lParam);
}
//----------------------------------------------------------------------
// DoCreateMain - Process WM_CREATE message for window.
//
LRESULT DoCreateMain (HWND hWnd, UINT wMsg, WPARAM wParam,
                      LPARAM lParam) {
    HDC hdc;
    INT i, rc;

    //Enumerate the available fonts.
    hdc = GetDC (hWnd);
    rc = EnumFontFamilies ((HDC)hdc, (LPTSTR)NULL,
        FontFamilyCallback, 0);

    for (i = 0; i < sFamilyCnt; i++) {
        ffs[i].nNumFonts = 0;
        rc = EnumFontFamilies ((HDC)hdc, ffs[i].szFontFamily,
                               EnumSingleFontFamily,
                               (LPARAM)(PFONTFAMSTRUCT)&ffs[i]);
    }
    ReleaseDC (hWnd, hdc);
    return 0;
}
//----------------------------------------------------------------------
// DoPaintMain - Process WM_PAINT message for window.
//
LRESULT DoPaintMain (HWND hWnd, UINT wMsg, WPARAM wParam,
                     LPARAM lParam) {
    PAINTSTRUCT ps;
    RECT rect;
    HDC hdc;
    TEXTMETRIC tm;
    INT nFontHeight, i;
    TCHAR szOut[256];
    PAINTFONTINFO pfi;

    GetClientRect (hWnd, &rect);
```

```
    hdc = BeginPaint (hWnd, &ps);

    // Get the height of the default font.
    GetTextMetrics (hdc, &tm);
    nFontHeight = tm.tmHeight + tm.tmExternalLeading;

    // Initialize struct that is passed to enumerate function.
    pfi.yCurrent = rect.top;
    pfi.hdc = hdc;
    for (i = 0; i < sFamilyCnt; i++) {

        // Format output string, and paint font family name.
        wsprintf (szOut, TEXT("Family: %s   "),
                  ffs[i].szFontFamily);
        ExtTextOut (hdc, 5, pfi.yCurrent, 0, NULL,
                    szOut, lstrlen (szOut), NULL);
        pfi.yCurrent += nFontHeight;

        // Enumerate each family to draw a sample of that font.
        EnumFontFamilies ((HDC)hdc, ffs[i].szFontFamily,
                          PaintSingleFontFamily,
                          (LPARAM)&pfi);
    }
    EndPaint (hWnd, &ps);
    return 0;
}
//----------------------------------------------------------------
// DoDestroyMain - Process WM_DESTROY message for window.
//
LRESULT DoDestroyMain (HWND hWnd, UINT wMsg, WPARAM wParam,
                       LPARAM lParam) {
    PostQuitMessage (0);
    return 0;
}
```

Enumerating the different fonts begins when the application is processing the *WM_CREATE* message in *DoCreateMain*. Here *EnumFontFamilies* is called with the *FontFamily* field set to *NULL*, so that each family is enumerated. The callback function is *FontFamilyCallback*, where the name of the font family is copied into an array of strings.

The remainder of the work is performed during the processing of the *WM_PAINT* message. The *DoPaintMain* function begins with the standard litany of getting the size of the client area and calling *BeginPaint*, which returns the handle to the device context of the window. *GetTextMetrics* is then called to compute the row height of the default font. A loop is then entered in which *EnumerateFontFamilies* is called for each family name that had been stored during the enumeration process in *DoCreateMain*. The callback process for this callback sequence is somewhat more complex than the code seen so far.

The *PaintSingleFontFamily* callback procedure, used in the enumeration of the individual fonts, employs the *lParam* parameter to retrieve a pointer to a *PAINTFONTINFO* structure defined in FontList.h. This structure contains the current vertical drawing position as well as the handle to the device context. By using the *lParam* pointer, FontList avoids having to declare global variables to communicate with the callback procedure.

The callback procedure next creates the font using the pointer to *LOGFONT* that was passed to the callback procedure. The new font is then selected into the device context, while the handle to the previously selected font is retained in *hOldFont*. The point size of the enumerated font is computed using the inverse of the equation mentioned earlier in the chapter. The callback procedure then produces a line of text showing the name of the font family along with the point size of this particular font. Instead of using *DrawText*, the callback uses *ExtTextOut* to draw the string.

After displaying the text, the function computes the height of the line of text just drawn using the combination of *tmHeight* and *tmExternalLeading* that was provided in the passed *TEXTMETRIC* structure. The new font is then deselected using a second call to *SelectObject*, this time passing the handle to the font that was the original selected font. The new font is then deleted using *DeleteObject*. Finally, the callback function returns a nonzero value to indicate to Windows that it is okay to make another call to the *enumerate* callback.

Figure 2-4 shows the Font Listing window. Notice that the font names are displayed in that font and that each font has a specific set of available sizes.

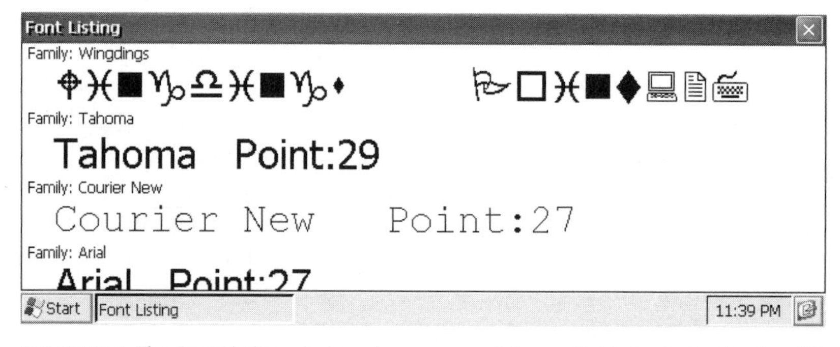

FIGURE 2-4 The Font Listing window shows some of the available fonts for the ProgWinCE Emulator.

Unfinished Business

If you look closely at Figure 2-4, you notice a problem with the display. The list of fonts just runs off the bottom edge of the Font Listing window. The solution for this problem is to add a scroll bar to the window. I'll provide a complete explanation of window controls, including scroll bars, in Chapter 4, "Windows, Controls, and Menus."

Bitmaps

Bitmaps are graphical objects that can be used to create, draw, manipulate, and retrieve images in a device context. Bitmaps are everywhere within Windows, from the little Windows logo on the Start button to the Close button on the title bar. Think of a bitmap as a picture composed of an array of pixels that can be painted onto the screen. Like any picture, a bitmap has height and width. It also has a method for determining what color or colors it uses. Finally, a bitmap has an array of bits that describes each pixel in the bitmap.

Historically, bitmaps under Windows have been divided into two types: *device-dependent bitmaps* (DDBs) and *device-independent bitmaps* (DIBs). DDBs are bitmaps that are tied to the characteristics of a specific DC and can't easily be rendered on DCs with different characteristics. DIBs, on the other hand, are independent of any device, and therefore must carry around enough information so that they can be rendered accurately on any device.

Windows CE contains many of the bitmap functions available in other versions of Windows. The differences include a four-color bitmap format not supported anywhere but on Windows CE and a different method for manipulating DIBs.

Device-Dependent Bitmaps

A device-dependent bitmap can be created with this function:

```
HBITMAP CreateBitmap (int nWidth, int nHeight, UINT cPlanes,
                      UINT cBitsPerPel, CONST VOID *lpvBits);
```

The *nWidth* and *nHeight* parameters indicate the dimensions of the bitmap. The *cPlanes* parameter is a historical artifact from the days when display hardware implemented each color within a pixel in a different hardware plane. For Windows CE, this parameter must be set to 1. The *cBitspPerPel* parameter indicates the number of bits used to describe each pixel. The number of colors is 2 to the power of the *cBitspPerPel* parameter. Under Windows CE, the allowable values are 1, 2, 4, 8, 16, 24, and 32. As I said, the four-color bitmap is unique to Windows CE and isn't supported under other Windows platforms.

The final parameter is a pointer to the bits of the bitmap. Under Windows CE, the bits are always arranged in a packed pixel format; that is, each pixel is stored as a series of bits within a byte, with the next pixel starting immediately after the first. The first pixel in the array of bits is the pixel located in the upper left corner of the bitmap. The bits continue across the top row of the bitmap, then across the second row, and so on. Each row of the bitmap must be double-word (4-byte) aligned. If any pad bytes are required at the end of a row to align the start of the next row, they should be set to 0. Figure 2-5 illustrates this scheme, showing a 126-by-64-pixel bitmap with 8 bits per pixel.

The function

```
HBITMAP CreateCompatibleBitmap (HDC hdc, int nWidth, int nHeight);
```

creates a bitmap whose format is compatible with the device context passed to the function. So if the device context is a four-color DC, the resulting bitmap is a four-color bitmap as well. This function comes in handy when you manipulate images on the screen because it makes it easy to produce a blank bitmap that's directly color compatible with the screen.

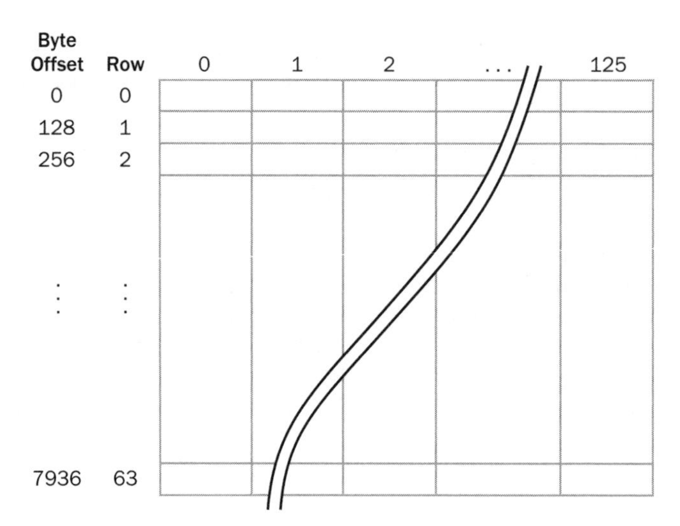

FIGURE 2-5 Layout of bytes within a bitmap

Device-Independent Bitmaps

The fundamental difference between DIBs and their device-dependent cousins is that the image stored in a DIB comes with its own color information. DIB files, with the classic .bmp extension, contain color and layout information that can be directly matched with the information needed to create a DIB in Windows.

In the early days of Windows, it was a rite of passage for a programmer to write a routine that manually read a DIB file and converted the data to a bitmap. These days, the same arduous task can be accomplished with the following function, unique to Windows CE:

```
HBITMAP SHLoadDIBitmap (LPCTSTR szFileName);
```

It loads a bitmap directly from a bitmap file and provides a handle to the bitmap. On the desktop, the same process can be accomplished with *LoadImage* using the *LR_LOADFROMFILE* flag, but this flag isn't supported under the Windows CE implementation of *LoadImage*.

DIB Sections

While Windows CE makes it easy to load a bitmap file, sometimes you must read what is on the screen, manipulate it, and redraw the image back to the screen. This is another case in which DIBs are better than DDBs. While the bits of a device-dependent bitmap are obtainable, the format of the buffer is directly dependent on the screen format. By using a DIB, or more precisely, something called a DIB section, your program can read the bitmap into a buffer that has a predefined format without worrying about the format of the display device.

While Windows has a number of DIB creation functions that have been added over the years, Windows CE carries over only a handful of DIB functions from the desktop versions of Windows. Here is the first of these functions:

```
HBITMAP CreateDIBSection (HDC hdc, const BITMAPINFO *pbmi,
                          UINT iUsage, void *ppvBits,
                          HANDLE hSection, DWORD dwOffset);
```

DIB sections were invented to improve the performance of applications on Windows NT that directly manipulated bitmaps. In short, a DIB section allows a programmer to select a DIB in a device context while still maintaining direct access to the bits that compose the bitmap. To achieve this, a DIB section associates a memory DC with a buffer that also contains the bits of that DC. Because the image is mapped to a DC, other graphics calls can be made to modify the image. At the same time, the raw bits of the DC, in DIB format, are available for direct manipulation. While the improved performance is all well and good on Windows NT, the relevance to the Windows CE programmer is the ease with which an application can work with bitmaps and manipulate their contents.

This call's parameters lead with the pointer to a *BITMAPINFO* structure. The structure describes the layout and color composition of a device-independent bitmap and is a combination of a *BITMAPINFOHEADER* structure and, if necessary, an array of *RGBQUAD* values that represent the palette of colors used by the bitmap.

The *BITMAPINFOHEADER* structure is defined as the following:

```
typedef struct tagBITMAPINFOHEADER{
    DWORD biSize;
    LONG biWidth;
    LONG biHeight;
    WORD biPlanes;
    WORD biBitCount;
    DWORD biCompression;
    DWORD biSizeImage;
    LONG biXPelsPerMeter;
    LONG biYPelsPerMeter;
    DWORD biClrUsed;
    DWORD biClrImportant;
} BITMAPINFOHEADER;
```

As you can see, this structure contains much more information than just the parameters passed to *CreateBitmap*. The first field is the size of the structure and must be filled in by the calling program to differentiate this structure from the similar *BITMAPCOREINFOHEADER* structure that's a holdover from the old OS/2 presentation manager. The *biWidth*, *biHeight*, *biPlanes*, and *biBitCount* fields are similar to their like-named parameters to the *CreateBitmap* call—with one exception. The sign of the *biHeight* field specifies the organization of the bit array. If *biHeight* is negative, the bit array is organized in a top-down format, as is *CreateBitmap*. If *biHeight* is positive, the array is organized in a bottom-up format, in which the bottom row of the bitmap is defined by the first bits in the array. As with the *CreateBitmap* call, the *biPlanes* field must be set to 1.

The *biCompression* field specifies the compression method used in the bit array. Under Windows CE, the allowable flags for this field are *BI_RGB*, indicating that the buffer isn't compressed, and *BI_BITFIELDS*, indicating that the pixel format is specified in the first three entries in the color table. The *biSizeImage* parameter is used to indicate the size of the bit array; when used with *BI_RGB*, however, the *biSizeImage* field can be set to 0, which means that the array size is computed using the dimensions and bits per pixel information provided in the *BITMAPINFOHEADER* structure.

The *biXPelsPerMeter* and *biYPelsPerMeter* fields provide information to accurately scale the image. For *CreateDIBSection*, however, these parameters can be set to 0. The *biClrUsed* parameter specifies the number of colors in the palette that are actually used. In a 256-color image, the palette will have 256 entries, but the bitmap itself might need only 100 or so distinct colors. This field helps the palette manager, the part of Windows that manages color matching, to match the colors in the system palette with the colors required by the bitmap. The *biClrImportant* field further defines the colors that are *really* required as opposed to those that are used. For most color bitmaps, these two fields are set to 0, indicating that all colors are used and that all colors are important.

As I mentioned earlier, an array of *RGBQUAD* structures immediately follows the *BITMAPINFOHEADER* structure if the image is formatted with 8 bits per pixel or less. The *RGBQUAD* structure is defined as follows:

```
typedef struct tagRGBQUAD { /* rgbq */
    BYTE rgbBlue;
    BYTE rgbGreen;
    BYTE rgbRed;
    BYTE rgbReserved;
} RGBQUAD;
```

This structure allows for 256 shades of red, green, and blue. Although almost any shade can be created using this structure, the color that's actually rendered on the device is, of course, limited by what the device can display.

The array of *RGBQUAD* structures, taken as a whole, describe the palette of the DIB. The palette is the list of colors in the bitmap. If a bitmap has a palette, each entry in the bitmap array contains not colors, but an index into the palette that contains the color for that pixel. While redundant on a monochrome bitmap, the palette is quite important when rendering color bitmaps on color devices. For example, a 256-color bitmap has one byte for each pixel, but that byte points to a 24-bit value that represents equal parts red, green, and blue. So while a 256-color bitmap can contain only 256 distinct colors, each of those colors can be one of 16 million colors rendered using the 24-bit palette entry. For convenience in a 32-bit world, each palette entry, while containing only 24 bits of color information, is padded out to a 32-bit-wide entry—hence the name of the data type: *RGBQUAD*.

Of the remaining four *CreateDIBSection* parameters, only two are used under Windows CE. The *iUsage* parameter indicates how the colors in the palette are represented. If the parameter is *DIB_RGB_COLORS*, the bits in the bitmap contain the full RGB color information for each pixel. If the parameter is *DIB_PAL_COLORS*, the bitmap pixels contain indexes into the palette currently selected in the DC. The *ppvBits* parameter is a pointer to a variable that eceives the pointer to the bitmap bits that compose the bitmap image. The final two parameters, *hSection* and *dwOffset*, aren't supported under Windows CE and must be set to 0. Other versions of Windows allow the bitmap bits to be specified by a memory-mapped file. While Windows CE supports memory-mapped files, they aren't supported by *CreateDIBSection*.

Two functions exist to manage the palette of the DIB, as follows:

```
UINT GetDIBColorTable (HDC hdc, UINT uStartIndex,
                       UINT cEntries, RGBQUAD *pColors);
```

and

```
UINT SetDIBColorTable (HDC hdc, UINT uStartIndex,
                       UINT cEntries, RGBQUAD *pColors);
```

For both of these functions, *uStartIndex* indicates the first entry into the palette array to set or query. The *cEntries* parameter indicates how many palette entries to change. The pointer to the *RGBQUAD* array is the array of colors either being set, for *SetDIBColorTable*, or queried, for *GetDIBColorTable*.

Drawing Bitmaps

Creating and loading bitmaps is all well and good, but there's not much point to it unless the bitmaps you create can be rendered on the screen. Drawing a bitmap isn't as straightforward as you might think. Before a bitmap can be drawn in a screen DC, it must be selected into a DC and then copied over to the screen device context. While this process sounds convoluted, there is rhyme to this reason.

The process of selecting a bitmap into a device context is similar to selecting a logical font into a device context; it converts the ideal to the actual. Just as Windows finds the best possible match to a requested font, the bitmap selection process must match the available colors of the device to the colors requested by a bitmap. Only after this is done can the bitmap be rendered on the screen. To help with this intermediate step, Windows provides a shadow type of DC, a *memory device context*.

To create a memory device context, use this function:

```
HDC CreateCompatibleDC (HDC hdc);
```

This function creates a memory DC that's compatible with the current screen DC. Once created, the source bitmap is selected into this memory DC using the same *SelectObject* function you used to select a logical font. Finally, the bitmap is copied from the memory DC to the screen DC using one of the bit functions, *BitBlt* or *StretchBlt*.

The workhorse of bitmap functions is the following:

```
BOOL BitBlt (HDC hdcDest, int nXDest, int nYDest, int nWidth,
             int nHeight, HDC hdcSrc, int nXSrc,  int nYSrc,
             DWORD dwRop);
```

Fundamentally, the *BitBlt* function, pronounced *"bit blit"*, is just a fancy *memcopy* function, but because it operates on device contexts, not memory, it's something far more special. The first parameter is a handle to the destination device context—the DC to which the bitmap is to be copied. The next four parameters specify the location and size of the destination rectangle where the bitmap is to end up. The next three parameters specify the handle to the source device context and the location within that DC of the upper left corner of the source image.

The final parameter, *dwRop*, specifies how the image is to be copied from the source to the destination device contexts. The ROP code defines how the source bitmap and the current destination are combined to produce the final image. The ROP code for a simple copy of the source image is *SRCCOPY*. The ROP code for combining the source image with the current destination is *SRCPAINT*. Copying a logically inverted image, essentially a negative of the source image, is accomplished using *SRCINVERT*. Some ROP codes also combine the currently selected brush into the equation to compute the resulting image. A large number of ROP codes are available—too many for me to cover here. For a complete list, check out the Windows CE programming documentation.

The following code fragment sums up how to paint a bitmap:

```
// Create a DC that matches the device.
hdcMem = CreateCompatibleDC (hdc);

// Select the bitmap into the compatible device context.
hOldSel = SelectObject (hdcMem, hBitmap);

// Get the bitmap dimensions from the bitmap.
GetObject (hBitmap, sizeof (BITMAP), &bmp);

// Copy the bitmap image from the memory DC to the screen DC.
```

```
BitBlt (hdc, rect.left, rect.top, bmp.bmWidth, bmp.bmHeight,
        hdcMem, 0, 0, SRCCOPY);

// Restore original bitmap selection and destroy the memory DC.
SelectObject (hdcMem, hOldSel);
DeleteDC (hdcMem);
```

The memory device context is created, and the bitmap to be painted is selected into that DC. Because you might not have stored the dimensions of the bitmap to be painted, the routine makes a call to *GetObject*. *GetObject* returns information about a graphics object—in this case, a bitmap. Information about fonts and other graphic objects can be queried using this useful function. Next, *BitBlt* is used to copy the bitmap into the screen DC. To clean up, the bitmap is deselected from the memory device context and the memory DC is deleted using *DeleteDC*. Don't confuse *DeleteDC* with *ReleaseDC*, which is used to free a display DC. *DeleteDC* should be paired only with *CreateCompatibleDC*, and *ReleaseDC* should be paired only with *GetDC, GetDCEx,* or *GetWindowDC*.

Instead of merely copying the bitmap, stretch or shrink it using this function:

```
BOOL StretchBlt (HDC hdcDest, int nXOriginDest, int nYOriginDest,
                 int nWidthDest, int nHeightDest, HDC hdcSrc,
                 int nXOriginSrc, int nYOriginSrc, int nWidthSrc,
                 int nHeightSrc, DWORD dwRop);
```

The parameters in *StretchBlt* are the same as those used in *BitBlt*, with the exception that now the width and height of the source image can be specified. Here again, the ROP codes specify how the source and destination are combined to produce the final image. Stretching or shrinking an image is much slower than simply drawing. Whenever possible, use *Bitblt* instead of *StretchBlt*.

Windows CE also has another bitmap function. It is

```
BOOL TransparentImage (HDC hdcDest, LONG DstX, LONG DstY, LONG DstCx,
                       LONG DstCy, HANDLE hSrc, LONG SrcX, LONG SrcY,
                       LONG SrcCx, LONG SrcCy, COLORREF TransparentColor);
```

This function is similar to *StretchBlt*, with two very important exceptions. First, you can specify a color in the bitmap to be the transparent color. When the bitmap is copied to the destination, the pixels in the bitmap that are the transparent color are not copied. The second difference is that the *hSrc* parameter can be either a device context or a handle to a bitmap, which allows you to bypass the requirement to select the source image into a device context before rendering it on the screen. *TransparentImage* is essentially the same function as the desktop's *TransparentBlt* function with the exception that *TransparentBlt* can't directly use a bitmap as the source. Windows CE supports *TransparentBlt* as well, but a quick look at the header files for Windows CE reveals that *TransparentBlt* is simply aliased to *TransparentImage* for Windows CE.

As in other versions of Windows, Windows CE supports two other blit functions: *PatBlt* and *MaskBlt*. The *PatBlt* function combines the currently selected brush with the current image in the destination DC to produce the resulting image. I cover brushes later in this chapter. The *MaskBlt* function is similar to *BitBlt* but encompasses a masking image that provides the ability to draw only a portion of the source image onto the destination DC.

AlphaBlending

Modern GUI operating systems have the ability to draw a bitmap so that it appears semitransparent. In fact, both Apple OS X and Windows Vista use this effect to provide a cool look and feel to their shells. Windows CE also supports this translucent drawing known as *AlphaBlending*. The term *AlphaBlend* comes from the concept of an *alpha channel*. The alpha channel is the fourth property in the pixel of a bitmap that instead of specifying color, specifies the transparency level of that pixel.

The *AlphaBlend* function combines many of the abilities of the other GDI drawing functions such as drawing and stretching, with the added ability to draw bitmaps with a semitransparent look. The prototype for the function is

```
BOOL AlphaBlend (HDC hdcDest, int nXOriginDest, int nYOriginDest,
                 int nWidthDest, int nHeightDest,
                 HDC hdcSrc, int nXOriginSrc, int nYOriginSrc,
                 int nWidthSrc, int nHeightSrc,
                 BLENDFUNCTION blendFunction);
```

The first parameter is the handle of the destination DC followed by the location and size of the destination rectangle. The next five parameters specify the source DC and rectangle for the bitmap. It's the final parameter, *blendFunction*, that is the difference in *AlphaBlend*.

The *BLENDFUNCTION* structure is defined as

```
typedef struct _BLENDFUNCTION {
  BYTE  BlendOp;
  BYTE  BlendFlags;
  BYTE  SourceConstantAlpha;
  BYTE  AlphaFormat;
}BLENDFUNCTION, *PBLENDFUNCTION;
```

The first field, *BlendOp*, must be set to the only flag currently supported, *AC_SRC_OVER*. The *BlendFlags* field must be set to 0. The *SourceConstantAlpha* field is set to a transparency level for the entire source bitmap as it is applied to the destination DC. The resultant formula for a pixel becomes

```
destPixel = (srcPixel * SCA/255) + (destPixel * (1 - SCA/255))
```

where *SCA* is the value in the *SourceConstantAlpha* field.

In addition to a global transparency constant for the bitmap, *AlphaBlend* can also apply a per-pixel transparency effect to the source bitmap. This is accomplished by setting the *AC_SRC_ALPHA* flag in the last field in the *BLENDFUNCTION* structure, *AlphaFormat*. Windows requires that the source bitmap be at least a 32 bit-per-pixel bitmap if the *AC_SRC_ALPHA* flag is set, or the function will fail. Of course alphablending, like transparency, can be quite slow. Don't use these features unless you know that the video hardware is designed to accelerate these operations in hardware.

Lines and Shapes

One of the areas in which Windows CE provides substantially less functionality than other versions of Windows is in the primitive line-drawing and shape-drawing functions. Gone are the *Chord*, *Arc*, and *Pie* functions that created complex circular shapes. Gone, too, are most of the functions using the concept of *current point*. Other than *MoveToEx*, *LineTo*, and *GetCurrentPositionEx*, none of the GDI functions dealing with current point is supported in Windows CE. So drawing a series of connected lines and curves using calls to *ArcTo*, *PolyBezierTo*, and so forth is no longer possible. But even with the loss of a number of graphic functions, Windows CE still provides the essential functions necessary to draw lines and shapes.

Lines

Drawing one or more lines is as simple as a call to

```
BOOL Polyline (HDC hdc, const POINT *lppt, int cPoints);
```

The second parameter is a pointer to an array of *POINT* structures that are defined as the following:

```
typedef struct tagPOINT {
    LONG x;
    LONG y;
} POINT;
```

Each *x* and *y* combination describes a pixel from the upper-left corner of the screen. The third parameter is the number of point structures in the array. So to draw a line from (0, 0) to (50, 100), the code looks like this:

```
POINTS pts[2];

pts[0].x = 0;
pts[0].y = 0;
pts[1].x = 50;
pts[1].y = 100;
PolyLine (hdc, &pts, 2);
```

Another way to draw the same line is to use the *MoveToEx* and *LineTo* functions. They are prototyped as follows:

```
BOOL WINAPI MoveToEx (HDC hdc, int X, int Y, LPPOINT lpPoint);
BOOL WINAPI LineTo (HDC hdc, int X, int Y);
```

To use the functions to draw a line, first call *MoveToEx* to move the current point to the starting coordinates of the line, and then call *LineTo*, passing the ending coordinates. The calls to draw the same line as before using these functions is as follows:

```
MoveToEx (hdc, 0, 0, NULL);
LineTo (hdc, 50, 100);
```

To query the current point, call the following function:

```
WINGDIAPI BOOL WINAPI GetCurrentPositionEx (HDC hdc, LPPOINT pPoint);
```

Just as in the early text examples, these code fragments make a number of assumptions about the default state of the device context. For example, just what does the line drawn between (0, 0) and (50, 100) look like? What is its width and its color, and is it a solid line? All versions of Windows, including Windows CE, allow these parameters to be specified.

Pens

The tool for specifying the appearance of lines and the outline of shapes is called, appropriately enough, a *pen*. A pen is another GDI object and, like the others described in this chapter, is created, selected into a device context, used, deselected, and then destroyed. Among other stock GDI objects, stock pens can be retrieved using the following code:

```
HGDIOBJ GetStockObject (int fnObject);
```

All versions of Windows provide three stock pens, each 1 pixel wide. The stock pens come in three colors: white, black, and null. When you use *GetStockObject*, the call to retrieve one of those pens employs the parameters *WHITE_PEN*, *BLACK_PEN*, and *NULL_PEN*, respectively. Unlike standard graphic objects created by applications, stock objects should never be deleted by the application. Instead, the application should simply deselect the pen from the device context when it's no longer needed.

To create a custom pen under Windows, two functions are available. The first is this:

```
HPEN CreatePen (int fnPenStyle, int nWidth, COLORREF crColor);
```

The *fnPenStyle* parameter specifies the appearance of the line to be drawn. For example, the *PS_DASH* flag can be used to create a dashed line. Windows CE supports only *PS_SOLID-*, *PS_DASH-*, and *PS_NULL*-style flags. The *nWidth* parameter specifies the width of the pen. Finally, the *crColor* parameter specifies the color of the pen. The *crColor* parameter is typed as *COLORREF*, which can be constructed using the *RGB* macro. The *RGB* macro is as follows:

```
COLORREF RGB (BYTE bRed, BYTE bGreen, BYTE bBlue);
```

So to create a solid red pen one pixel wide, the code would look like this:

```
hPen = CreatePen (PS_SOLID, 1, RGB (0xff, 0, 0));
```

The other pen-creation function is the following:

```
HPEN CreatePenIndirect (const LOGPEN *lplgpn);
```

where the logical pen structure *LOGPEN* is defined as

```
typedef struct tagLOGPEN {
    UINT lopnStyle;
    POINT lopnWidth;
    COLORREF lopnColor;
} LOGPEN;
```

CreatePenIndirect provides the same parameters to Windows in a different form. To create the same one-pixel-wide red pen with *CreatePenIndirect*, the code would look like this:

```
LOGPEN lp;
HPEN hPen;
lp.lopnStyle = PS_SOLID;
lp.lopnWidth.x = 1;
lp.lopnWidth.y = 1;
lp.lopnColor = RGB (0xff, 0, 0);

hPen = CreatePenIndirect (&lp);
```

Windows CE devices don't support complex pens such as wide (more than 1 pixel wide) dashed lines. To determine what's supported, your old friend *GetDeviceCaps* comes into play, taking *LINECAPS* as the second parameter. Refer to the Windows CE documentation for the different flags returned by this call.

Shapes

Lines are useful but Windows also provides functions to draw shapes, both filled and unfilled. Here Windows CE does a good job supporting most of the functions familiar to Windows programmers. The *Rectangle*, *RoundRect*, *Ellipse*, and *Polygon* functions are all supported.

Brushes

Before I can talk about shapes such as rectangles and ellipses, I need to describe another GDI object mentioned only briefly before now—a *brush*. A brush is a bitmap, typically 8 by 8 pixels, used to fill shapes. It's also used by Windows to fill the background of a client window. Windows CE provides a number of stock brushes and as well as the ability to create a brush from an application-defined pattern. A number of stock brushes, each a solid color, can be retrieved using *GetStockObject*. Among the brushes available is one for each of the grays of a four-color grayscale display: white, light gray, dark gray, and black.

To create solid-color brushes, the function to call is the following:

```
HBRUSH CreateSolidBrush (COLORREF crColor);
```

The *crColor* parameter specifies the color of the brush. The color is specified using the *RGB* macro.

To create custom pattern brushes, Windows CE supports the Win32 function:

```
HBRUSH CreateDIBPatternBrushPt (const void *lpPackedDIB,
                                UINT iUsage);
```

The first parameter to this function is a pointer to a DIB in *packed* format. This means that the pointer points to a buffer that contains a *BITMAPINFO* structure immediately followed by the bits in the bitmap. Remember that a *BITMAPINFO* structure is actually a *BITMAPINFOHEADER* structure followed by a palette in *RGBQUAD* format, so the buffer contains everything necessary to create a DIB—that is, bitmap information, a palette, and the bits to the bitmap. If the second parameter is set to *DIB_RGB_COLORS*, the palette specified contains *RGBQUAD* values in each entry. For 8-bits-per-pixel bitmaps, the complementary flag *DIB_PAL_COLORS* can be specified, but Windows CE ignores the bitmap's color table.

The *CreateDIBPatternBrushPt* function is more important under Windows CE because the hatched brushes, supplied under other versions of Windows by the *CreateHatchBrush* function, aren't supported under Windows CE. Hatched brushes are brushes composed of any combination of horizontal, vertical, or diagonal lines. Ironically, they're particularly useful with grayscale displays because you can use them to accentuate different areas of a chart with different hatch patterns. You can reproduce these brushes, however, by using *CreateDIBPatternBrushPt* and the proper bitmap patterns. Later in the chapter, the Shapes code example demonstrates a method for creating hatched brushes under Windows CE.

By default, the brush origin is in the upper-left corner of the window. This isn't always what you want. Take, for example, a bar graph where the bar filled with a hatched brush fills a rectangle from (100, 100) to (125, 220). Because this rectangle isn't divisible by 8 (brushes typically being 8 by 8 pixels square), the upper left corner of the bar will be filled with a partial brush that might not look pleasing to the eye.

To avoid this situation, you can move the origin of the brush so that each shape can be drawn with the brush aligned correctly in the corner of the shape to be filled. The function available for this remedy is the following:

```
BOOL SetBrushOrgEx (HDC hdc, int nXOrg, int nYOrg, LPPOINT lppt);
```

The *nXOrg* and *nYOrg* parameters allow the origin to be set between 0 and 7 so that you can position the origin anywhere in the 8-by-8 space of the brush. The *lppt* parameter is filled with the previous origin of the brush so that you can restore the previous origin if necessary.

Rectangles

The rectangle function draws either a filled or a hollow rectangle; the function is defined as the following:

```
BOOL Rectangle (HDC hdc, int nLeftRect, int nTopRect,
                int nRightRect, int nBottomRect);
```

The function uses the currently selected pen to draw the outline of the rectangle and the current brush to fill the interior. To draw a hollow rectangle, select the null brush into the device context before calling *Rectangle*.

The actual pixels drawn for the border are important to understand. Say you're drawing a 5-by-7 rectangle at 0, 0. The function call would look like this:

```
Rectangle (0, 0, 5, 7);
```

Assuming that the selected pen is 1 pixel wide, the resulting rectangle would look like the one shown in Figure 2-6.

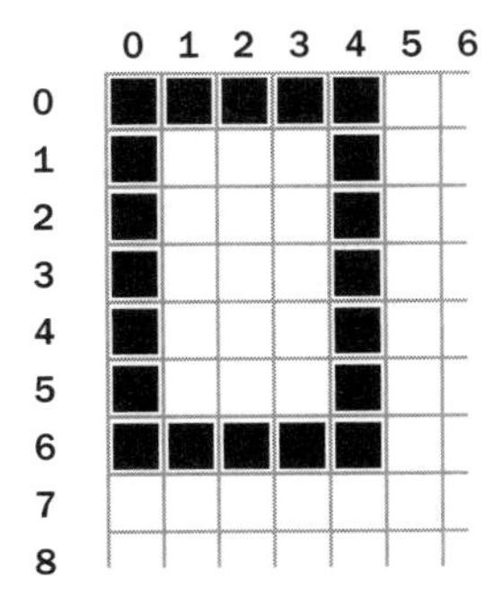

FIGURE 2-6 Magnified view of a rectangle drawn with the *Rectangle* function

Notice how the right edge of the rectangle is actually drawn in column 4 and that the bottom edge is drawn in row 6. This is standard Windows practice. The rectangle is drawn inside the right and bottom boundary specified for the *Rectangle* function. If the selected pen is wider than 1 pixel, the right and bottom edges are drawn with the pen centered on the bounding rectangle. (Other versions of Windows support the *PS_INSIDEFRAME* pen style that forces the rectangle to be drawn inside the frame regardless of the pen width.)

Circles and Ellipses

Circles and ellipses can be drawn with this function:

```
BOOL Ellipse (HDC hdc, int nLeftRect, int nTopRect,
              int nRightRect, int nBottomRect);
```

The ellipse is drawn using the rectangle passed as a bounding rectangle, as shown in Figure 2-7. As with the *Rectangle* function, while the interior of the ellipse is filled with the current brush, the outline is drawn with the current pen.

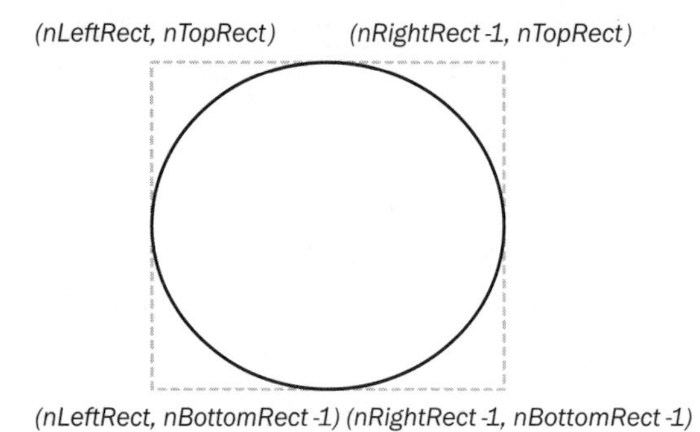

FIGURE 2-7 The ellipse is drawn within the bounding rectangle passed to the *Ellipse* function.

Round Rectangles

The *RoundRect* function,

```
BOOL RoundRect (HDC hdc, int nLeftRect, int nTopRect,
                int nRightRect, int nBottomRect,
                int nWidth, int nHeight);
```

draws a rectangle with rounded corners. The roundedness of the corners is defined by the last two parameters that specify the width and height of the ellipse used to round the corners, as shown in Figure 2-8. Specifying the ellipse height and width enables your program to draw identically symmetrical rounded corners. Shortening the ellipse height flattens out the sides of the rectangle, while shortening the width of the ellipse flattens the top and bottom of the rectangle.

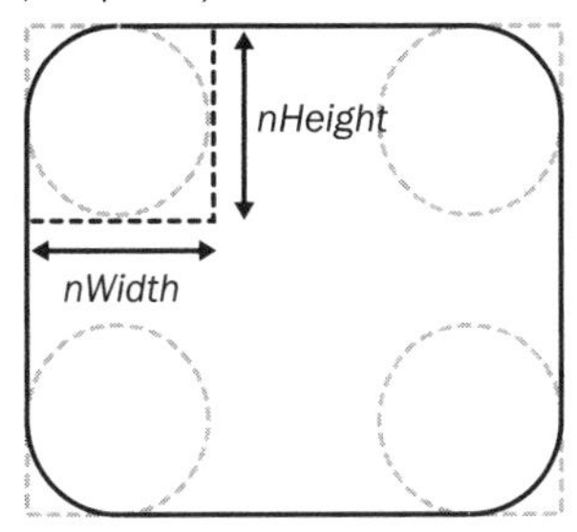

FIGURE 2-8 The height and width of the ellipse define the round corners of the rectangle drawn by *RoundRect*.

Polygons

Finally, the *Polygon* function,

```
BOOL Polygon (HDC hdc, const POINT *lpPoints, int nCount);
```

draws a many-sided shape. The second parameter is a pointer to an array of point structures defining the points that delineate the polygon. The resulting shape has one more side than the number of points because the function automatically completes the last line of the polygon by connecting the last point with the first.

Fill Functions

The preceding functions use a combination of a brush and a pen to draw shapes in the device context. Functions are available to fill areas without dealing with the pen that would normally outline the shape. The first of these functions is as follows:

```
int FillRect (HDC hDC, CONST RECT* lprc, HBRUSH hbr);
```

The parameters of *FillRect* are the handle to the device context, the rectangle to fill, and the brush to fill the rectangle. *FillRect* is a quick and convenient way to paint a solid color or pattern in a rectangular area.

While *FillRect* is convenient, *GradientFill* is cool. *GradientFill* fills a rectangular area that starts on one side with one color and then has a smooth transition to another color on the other side. Figure 2-9 shows a window in which the client area is painted with *GradientFill*. The black-and-white illustration doesn't do the image justice, but even in this figure it's easy to see the smooth nature of the transition.

FIGURE 2-9 A window painted with the *GradientFill* function

The prototype of *GradientFill* looks like this:

```
BOOL GradientFill (HDC hdc, PTRIVERTEX pVertex, ULONG dwNumVertex,
                   PVOID pMesh, ULONG dwNumMesh, ULONG dwMode);
```

The first parameter is the obligatory handle to the device context. The *pVertex* parameter points to an array of *TRIVERTEX* structures, while the *dwNumVertex* parameter contains the number of entries in the *TRIVERTEX* array. The *TRIVERTEX* structure is defined as follows:

```
struct _TRIVERTEX {
    LONG        x;
    Long        y;
    COLOR16     Red;
    COLOR16     Green;
    COLOR16     Blue;
    COLOR16     Alpha;s
} TRIVERTEX;
```

The fields of the *TRIVERTEX* structure describe a point in the device context and an RGB color. The points should describe the upper left and lower right corners of the rectangle being filled. The *pMesh* parameter of *GradientFill* points to a *GRADIENT_RECT* structure defined as follows:

```
struct _GRADIENT_RECT
{
    ULONG UpperLeft;
    ULONG LowerRight;
} GRADIENT_RECT;
```

The *GRADIENT_RECT* structure simply specifies which of the entries in the *TRIVERTEX* structure delineates the upper left and lower right corners. Finally, the *dwNumMesh* parameter of *GradientFill* contains the number of *GRADIENT_RECT* structures, while the *dwMode* structure contains a flag indicating whether the fill should be left to right (*GRADIENT_FILL_RECT_H*) or top to bottom (*GRADIENT_FILL_RECT_V*). The *GradientFill* function is more complex than is apparent because on the desktop, it can also perform a triangular fill that isn't supported by Windows CE. Here's the code fragment that created the window in Figure 2-9:

```
TRIVERTEX vert[2];
GRADIENT_RECT gRect;

vert [0] .x      =  prect->left;
vert [0] .y      =  prect->top;
vert [0] .Red    =  0x0000;
vert [0] .Green  =  0x0000;
vert [0] .Blue   =  0xff00;
vert [0] .Alpha  =  0x0000;

vert [1] .x      =  prect->right;
vert [1] .y      =  prect->bottom;
vert [1] .Red    =  0x0000;
vert [1] .Green  =  0xff00;
vert [1] .Blue   =  0x0000;
vert [1] .Alpha  =  0x0000;

gRect.UpperLeft = 0;
gRect.LowerRight = 1;

GradientFill(hdc,vert,2,&gRect,1,GRADIENT_FILL_RECT_H);
```

The Shapes Example Program

The Shapes program, shown in Listing 2-3, demonstrates a number of these functions. In Shapes, four figures are drawn, each filled with a different brush.

LISTING 2-3 The Shapes program

Shapes.h

```
//================================================================
// Header file
//
// Written for the book Programming Windows CE
// Copyright (C) 2007 Douglas Boling
//======================================================================
// Returns number of elements
#define dim(x) (sizeof(x) / sizeof(x[0]))

//----------------------------------------------------------------------
// Generic defines and data types
//
struct decodeUINT {                             // Structure associates
    UINT Code;                                  // messages
                                                // with a function.
    LRESULT (*Fxn)(HWND, UINT, WPARAM, LPARAM);
};
```

```
//----------------------------------------------------------------------
// Defines used by MyCreateHatchBrush
//
typedef struct {
    BITMAPINFOHEADER bmi;
    COLORREF dwPal[2];
    BYTE bBits[64];
} BRUSHBMP;

#define HS_HORIZONTAL       0       /* ----- */
#define HS_VERTICAL         1       /* ||||| */
#define HS_FDIAGONAL        2       /* \\\\\ */
#define HS_BDIAGONAL        3       /* ///// */
#define HS_CROSS            4       /* +++++ */
#define HS_DIAGCROSS        5       /* xxxxx */

//----------------------------------------------------------------------
// Function prototypes
//
HWND InitInstance (HINSTANCE, LPWSTR, int);
int TermInstance (HINSTANCE, int);

// Window procedures
LRESULT CALLBACK MainWndProc (HWND, UINT, WPARAM, LPARAM);

// Message handlers
LRESULT DoPaintMain (HWND, UINT, WPARAM, LPARAM);
LRESULT DoDestroyMain (HWND, UINT, WPARAM, LPARAM);
```

Shapes.cpp

```
//======================================================================
// Shapes- Brush and shapes demo for Windows CE
//
// Written for the book Programming Windows CE
// Copyright (C) 2007 Douglas Boling
//======================================================================
#include <windows.h>                 // For all that Windows stuff
#include "shapes.h"                  // Program-specific stuff

//----------------------------------------------------------------
// Global data
//
const TCHAR szAppName[] = TEXT ("Shapes");
HINSTANCE hInst;                     // Program instance handle

// Message dispatch table for MainWindowProc
const struct decodeUINT MainMessages[] = {
    WM_PAINT, DoPaintMain,
    WM_DESTROY, DoDestroyMain,
};
```

```
//======================================================================
//
// Program entry point
//
int WINAPI WinMain (HINSTANCE hInstance, HINSTANCE hPrevInstance,
                    LPWSTR lpCmdLine, int nCmdShow) {
    MSG msg;
    HWND hwndMain;

    // Initialize this instance.
    hwndMain = InitInstance(hInstance, lpCmdLine, nCmdShow);
    if (hwndMain == 0)
        return 0x10;

    // Application message loop
    while (GetMessage (&msg, NULL, 0, 0)) {
        TranslateMessage (&msg);
        DispatchMessage (&msg);
    }
    // Instance cleanup
    return TermInstance (hInstance, msg.wParam);
}
//----------------------------------------------------------------------
// InitInstance - Instance initialization
//
HWND InitInstance (HINSTANCE hInstance, LPWSTR lpCmdLine, int nCmdShow){
    WNDCLASS wc;
    HWND hWnd;

    // Save program instance handle in global variable.
    hInst = hInstance;

#if defined(WIN32_PLATFORM_PSPC) || defined(WIN32_PLATFORM_WFSP)
    // If Windows Mobile, allow only one instance of the application.
    hWnd = FindWindow (szAppName, NULL);
    if (hWnd) {
        SetForegroundWindow ((HWND)(((DWORD)hWnd) | 0x01));
        return 0;
    }
#endif
    // Register application main window class.
    wc.style = 0;                             // Window style
    wc.lpfnWndProc = MainWndProc;             // Callback function
    wc.cbClsExtra = 0;                        // Extra class data
    wc.cbWndExtra = 0;                        // Extra window data
    wc.hInstance = hInstance;                 // Owner handle
    wc.hIcon = NULL,                          // Application icon
    wc.hCursor = LoadCursor (NULL, IDC_ARROW);// Default cursor
    wc.hbrBackground = (HBRUSH) GetStockObject (WHITE_BRUSH);
    wc.lpszMenuName =  NULL;                  // Menu name
    wc.lpszClassName = szAppName;             // Window class name

    if (RegisterClass (&wc) == 0) return 0;
    // Create main window.
```

```
    hWnd = CreateWindowEx (WS_EX_NODRAG,         // Ex Style
                           szAppName,            // Window class
                           TEXT("Shapes"),       // Window title
                           WS_VISIBLE,           // Style flags
                           CW_USEDEFAULT,        // x position
                           CW_USEDEFAULT,        // y position
                           CW_USEDEFAULT,        // Initial width
                           CW_USEDEFAULT,        // Initial height
                           NULL,                 // Parent
                           NULL,                 // Menu, must be null
                           hInstance,            // Application instance
                           NULL);                // Pointer to create
                                                 // parameters
    // Return fail code if window not created.
    if (!IsWindow (hWnd)) return 0;

    // Standard show and update calls
    ShowWindow (hWnd, nCmdShow);
    UpdateWindow (hWnd);
    return hWnd;
}
//----------------------------------------------------------------------
// TermInstance - Program cleanup
//
int TermInstance (HINSTANCE hInstance, int nDefRC) {

    return nDefRC;
}
//======================================================================
// Message handling procedures for MainWindow
//

//----------------------------------------------------------------------
// MainWndProc - Callback function for application window
//
LRESULT CALLBACK MainWndProc (HWND hWnd, UINT wMsg, WPARAM wParam,
                              LPARAM lParam) {
    INT i;
    //
    // Search message list to see if we need to handle this
    // message. If in list, call procedure.
    //
    for (i = 0; i < dim(MainMessages); i++) {
        if (wMsg == MainMessages[i].Code)
            return (*MainMessages[i].Fxn)(hWnd, wMsg, wParam, lParam);
    }
    return DefWindowProc (hWnd, wMsg, wParam, lParam);
}
//----------------------------------------------------------------
// MyCreateHatchBrush - Creates hatched brushes
//
HBRUSH MyCreateHatchBrush (INT fnStyle, COLORREF clrref) {
    BRUSHBMP brbmp;
    BYTE *pBytes;
```

```
    int i;
    DWORD dwBits[6][2] = {
        {0x000000ff,0x00000000}, {0x10101010,0x10101010},
        {0x01020408,0x10204080}, {0x80402010,0x08040201},
        {0x101010ff,0x10101010}, {0x81422418,0x18244281},
    };

    if ((fnStyle < 0) || (fnStyle > dim(dwBits)))
        return 0;
    memset (&brbmp, 0, sizeof (brbmp));

    brbmp.bmi.biSize = sizeof (BITMAPINFOHEADER);
    brbmp.bmi.biWidth = 8;
    brbmp.bmi.biHeight = 8;
    brbmp.bmi.biPlanes = 1;
    brbmp.bmi.biBitCount = 1;
    brbmp.bmi.biClrUsed = 2;
    brbmp.bmi.biClrImportant = 2;

    // Initialize the palette of the bitmap.
    brbmp.dwPal[0] = PALETTERGB(0xff,0xff,0xff);
    brbmp.dwPal[1] = PALETTERGB((BYTE)((clrref >> 16) & 0xff),
                                (BYTE)((clrref >> 8) & 0xff),
                                (BYTE)(clrref & 0xff));

    // Write the hatch data to the bitmap.
    pBytes = (BYTE *)&dwBits[fnStyle];
    for (i = 0; i < 8; i++)
        brbmp.bBits[i*4] = *pBytes++;

    // Return the handle of the brush created.
    return CreateDIBPatternBrushPt (&brbmp, DIB_RGB_COLORS);
}
//----------------------------------------------------------------------
// DoPaintMain - Process WM_PAINT message for window.
//
LRESULT DoPaintMain (HWND hWnd, UINT wMsg, WPARAM wParam,
                     LPARAM lParam) {
    PAINTSTRUCT ps;
    RECT rect;
    HDC hdc;
    POINT ptArray[6];
    HBRUSH hBr, hOldBr;
    TCHAR szText[128];

    GetClientRect (hWnd, &rect);
    hdc = BeginPaint (hWnd, &ps);

    // Draw ellipse.
    hBr = (HBRUSH) GetStockObject (DKGRAY_BRUSH);
    hOldBr = (HBRUSH) SelectObject (hdc, hBr);
    Ellipse (hdc, 10, 50, 90, 130);
    SelectObject (hdc, hOldBr);
```

```
    // Draw round rectangle.
    hBr = (HBRUSH) GetStockObject (LTGRAY_BRUSH);
    hOldBr = (HBRUSH) SelectObject (hdc, hBr);
    RoundRect (hdc, 95, 50, 150, 130, 30, 30);
    SelectObject (hdc, hOldBr);

    // Draw hexagon using Polygon.
    hBr = (HBRUSH) GetStockObject (WHITE_BRUSH);
    hOldBr = (HBRUSH) SelectObject (hdc, hBr);
    ptArray[0].x = 192;
    ptArray[0].y = 50;
    ptArray[1].x = 155;
    ptArray[1].y = 75;
    ptArray[2].x = 155;
    ptArray[2].y = 105;
    ptArray[3].x = 192;
    ptArray[3].y = 130;
    ptArray[4].x = 230;
    ptArray[4].y = 105;
    ptArray[5].x = 230;
    ptArray[5].y = 75;

    Polygon (hdc, ptArray, 6);
    SelectObject (hdc, hOldBr);

    hBr = (HBRUSH) MyCreateHatchBrush (HS_DIAGCROSS, RGB (0, 0, 0));
    hOldBr = (HBRUSH) SelectObject (hdc, hBr);
    Rectangle (hdc, 10, 145, 225, 210);
    SelectObject (hdc, hOldBr);
    DeleteObject (hBr);

    SetBkMode (hdc, OPAQUE);
    lstrcpy (szText, TEXT ("Opaque background"));
    ExtTextOut (hdc, 20, 160, 0, NULL,
                szText, lstrlen (szText), NULL);

    SetBkMode (hdc, TRANSPARENT);
    lstrcpy (szText, TEXT ("Transparent background"));
    ExtTextOut (hdc, 20, 185, 0, NULL,
                szText, lstrlen (szText), NULL);

    EndPaint (hWnd, &ps);
    return 0;
}
//----------------------------------------------------------------------
// DoDestroyMain - Process WM_DESTROY message for window
//
LRESULT DoDestroyMain (HWND hWnd, UINT wMsg, WPARAM wParam,
                       LPARAM lParam) {
    PostQuitMessage (0);
    return 0;
}
```

In Shapes, *DoPaintMain* draws the four figures using the different functions discussed earlier. For each of the shapes, a different brush is created, selected into the device context, and, after the shape has been drawn, deselected from the DC. The first three shapes are filled with solid grayscale shades. These solid brushes are loaded with the *GetStockObject* function. The final shape is filled with a brush created with the *CreateDIBPatternBrushPt*. The creation of this brush is segregated into a function called *MyCreateHatchBrush* that mimics the *CreateHatchBrush* function not available under Windows CE. To create the hatched brushes, a black-and-white bitmap is built by filling in a bitmap structure and setting the bits to form the hatch patterns. The bitmap itself is the 8-by-8 bitmap specified by *CreateDIBPatternBrushPt*. Because the bitmap is monochrome, its total size, including the palette and header, is only around 100 bytes. Notice, however, that because each scan line of a bitmap must be double-word aligned, the last three bytes of each 1-byte scan line are left unused.

Finally, the program completes the painting by writing two lines of text into the lower rectangle. The text further demonstrates the difference between the opaque and transparent drawing modes of the system. In this case, the opaque mode of drawing the text might be a better match for the situation because the hatched lines tend to obscure letters drawn in transparent mode. A view of the Shapes window is shown in Figure 2-10.

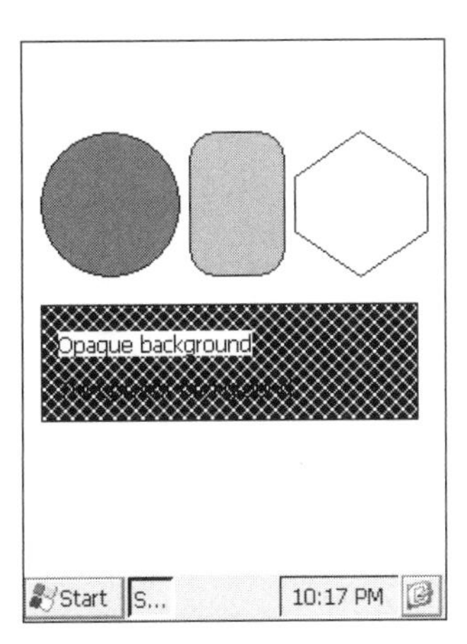

FIGURE 2-10 The Shapes example demonstrates drawing different filled shapes.

To keep things simple, the Shapes example assumes that it's running on at least a 240-pixel-wide display. This allows Shapes to work equally well on all but the smallest of Smartphone screens. I have barely scratched the surface of the abilities of the Windows CE GDI portion of GWE. The goal of this chapter wasn't to provide total presentation of all aspects of GDI programming. Instead, I wanted to demonstrate the methods available for basic drawing and text support under Windows CE. Other chapters in the book extend some of the techniques touched on in this chapter. I talk about these new techniques and newly-introduced functions at the point, generally, where I demonstrate how to use them in code. To further your knowledge, I recommend *Programming Windows*, 5th edition, by Charles Petzold (Microsoft Press, 1998), as the best source for learning about the Windows GDI.

Now that you've looked at output, it's time to turn your attention to the input side of the system—the keyboard and the touch panel.

3 Input: Keyboard, Mouse, and Touch Screen

Traditionally, Microsoft Windows platforms have allowed users two methods of input: the keyboard and the mouse. Windows CE continues this tradition but many systems replace the mouse with a stylus and touch screen. Programmatically, the change is minor because the messages from the stylus are mapped to the mouse messages used in other versions of Windows. A more subtle, but also more important, change from versions of Windows that run on PCs is that a system running Windows CE might have either a tiny keyboard or no keyboard at all. This arrangement makes the stylus input that much more important for Windows CE systems.

The Keyboard

Although keyboards play a lesser role in Windows CE, they're still the best means of entering large volumes of information. Even on systems without a physical keyboard such as some Windows Mobile devices, *soft* keyboards—controls that simulate keyboards on a touch screen—will most likely be available to the user. Given this, proper handling of keyboard input is critical to all but the most specialized of Windows CE applications. Although not much text is devoted to soft keyboards in the book, one point should be made here. To the application, input from a soft keyboard is no different from input from a traditional hard keyboard.

Input Focus

Under Windows operating systems, only one window at a time has the input focus. The focus window receives all keyboard input until it loses focus to another window. The system assigns the keyboard focus using a number of rules, but most often the focus window is the current active window. The active window, you'll recall, is the top-level window, the one with which the user is currently interacting. With rare exceptions, the active window also sits at the top of the Z-order; that is, it's drawn on top of all other windows in the system. In the Explorer, the user can change the active window by pressing Alt+Esc to switch between programs or by tapping on another top-level window's button on the task bar. The focus window is either the active window or one of its child windows.

Under Windows, a program can determine which window has the input focus by calling

```
HWND GetFocus (void);
```

The focus can be changed to another window by calling

```
HWND SetFocus (HWND hWnd);
```

Under Windows CE, the target window of *SetFocus* is limited. The window being given the focus by *SetFocus* must have been created by the thread calling *SetFocus*. An exception to this rule occurs if the window losing focus is related to the window gaining focus by a parent/child or sibling relationship; in this case, the focus can be changed even if the windows were created by different threads.

When a window loses focus, Windows sends a *WM_KILLFOCUS* message to that window informing it of its new state. The *wParam* parameter contains the handle of the window that will be gaining the focus. The window gaining focus receives a *WM_SETFOCUS* message. The *wParam* parameter of the *WM_SETFOCUS* message contains the handle of the window losing focus.

Although it might be stating the obvious, programs shouldn't change the focus window without some input from the user. Otherwise, the user can easily become confused. A proper use of *SetFocus* is to set the input focus to a child window (more than likely a control) contained in the active window. In this case, a window responds to the *WM_SETFOCUS* message by calling *SetFocus* with the handle of a child window contained in the window to which the program wants to direct keyboard messages.

Keyboard Messages

Windows CE practices the same keyboard message processing as its larger desktop relations with a few small exceptions, which I cover shortly. When a key is pressed, Windows sends a series of messages to the focus window, typically beginning with a *WM_KEYDOWN* message. If the key that is pressed represents a character such as a letter or number, Windows follows the *WM_KEYDOWN* with a *WM_CHAR* message. (Some keys, such as function keys and cursor keys, don't represent characters, so *WM_CHAR* messages aren't sent in response to those keys. For those keys, a program must interpret the *WM_KEYDOWN* message to know when the keys are pressed.) When the key is released, Windows sends a *WM_KEYUP* message. If a key is held down long enough for the auto-repeat feature to kick in, multiple *WM_KEYDOWN* and *WM_CHAR* messages are sent for each auto-repeat until the key is released when the final *WM_KEYUP* message is sent. I used the word *typically* to qualify this description because if the Alt key is being held when another key is pressed, the messages just described are replaced by *WM_SYSKEYDOWN*, *WM_SYSCHAR*, and *WM_SYSKEYUP* messages.

For all of these messages, the generic parameters *wParam* and *lParam* are used in mostly the same manner. For *WM_KEYxx* and *WM_SYSKEYxx* messages, the *wParam* value contains the virtual key value, indicating the key being pressed. All versions of Windows provide a level of indirection between the keyboard hardware and applications by translating the scan codes returned by the keyboard into virtual key values. You see a list of the *VK_xx* values and their associated keys in Table 3-1. While the table of virtual keys is extensive, not all keys listed in the table are present on Windows CE devices. For example, function keys, a mainstay on PC keyboards and listed in the virtual key table, aren't present on most Windows CE keyboards. In fact, a number of keys on a PC keyboard are left off the space-constrained Windows CE keyboards.

TABLE 3-1 Virtual Keys

Constant	Value	Keyboard Equivalent
VK_LBUTTON	01	Mouse left button or Stylus tap
VK_RBUTTON	02	Mouse right button[1]
VK_CANCEL	03	Control-break processing
VK_RBUTTON	04	Mouse middle button[1]
--	05–07	Undefined
VK_BACK	08	Backspace key
VK_TAB	09	Tab key
--	0A–0B	Undefined
VK_CLEAR	0C	Clear key
Constant	Value	Keyboard equivalent
VK_RETURN	0D	Enter key
--	0E–0F	Undefined
VK_SHIFT	10	Shift key
VK_CONTROL	11	Ctrl key
VK_MENU	12	Alt key
VK_CAPITAL	14	Caps Lock key
--	15–19	Reserved for Kanji systems
--	1A	Undefined
VK_ESCAPE	1B	Esc key
--	1C–1F	Reserved for Kanji systems
VK_SPACE	20	Spacebar
VK_PRIOR	21	Page Up key
VK_NEXT	22	Page Down key
VK_END	23	End key
VK_HOME	24	Home key
VK_LEFT	25	Left Arrow key
VK_UP	26	Up Arrow key
VK_RIGHT	27	Right Arrow key
VK_DOWN	28	Down Arrow key
VK_SELECT	29	Select key
--	2A	Original equipment manufacturer (OEM)–specific

Constant	Value	Keyboard Equivalent
VK_EXECUTE	2B	Execute key
VK_SNAPSHOT	2C	Print Screen key for Windows 3.0 and later
VK_INSERT	2D	Insert[2]
VK_DELETE	2E	Delete[3]
VK_HELP	2F	Help key
VK_0–VK_9	30–39	0–9 keys
--	3A–40	Undefined
VK_A–VK_Z	41–5A	A through Z keys
VK_LWIN	5B	Windows key
VK_RWIN	5C	Windows key[2]
VK_APPS	5D	
--	5E	Undefined
VK_SLEEP	5F	Sleep key[2]
VK_NUMPAD0-9	60–69	Numeric keypad 0–9 keys
VK_MULTIPLY	6A	Numeric keypad Asterisk (*) key
VK_ADD	6B	Numeric keypad Plus sign (+) key
VK_SEPARATOR	6C	Separator key
VK_SUBTRACT	6D	Numeric keypad Minus sign (-) key
VK_DECIMAL	6E	Numeric keypad Period (.) key
VK_DIVIDE	6F	Numeric keypad Slash mark (/) key
VK_F1–VK_F24	70–87	F1–F24[2]
--	88–8F	Unassigned
VK_NUMLOCK	90	Num Lock[2]
VK_SCROLL	91	Scroll Lock[2]
--	92–9F	Unassigned
VK_LSHIFT	A0	Left Shift[4]
VK_RSHIFT	A1	Right Shift[4]
VK_LCONTROL	A2	Left Control[4]
VK_RCONTROL	A3	Right Control[4]
VK_LMENU	A4	Left Alt[4]
VK_RMENU	A5	Right Alt[4]
VK_BROWSER_BACK	A6	[2]
VK_BROWSER_FORWARD	A7	[2]
VK_BROWSER_REFRESH	A8	[2]
VK_BROWSER_STOP	A9	[2]
VK_BROWSER_SEARCH	AA	[2]
VK_BROWSER_FAVORITES	AB	[2]

Constant	Value	Keyboard Equivalent
VK_BROWSER_HOME	AC	[2]
VK_VOLUME_MUTE	AD	[2]
VK_VOLUME_DOWN	AE	[2]
VK_VOLUME_UP	AF	[2]
VK_MEDIA_NEXT_TRACK	B0	[2]
VK_MEDIA_PREV_TRACK	B1	[2]
VK_MEDIA_STOP	B2	[2]
VK_MEDIA_PLAY_PAUSE	B3	[2]
VK_LAUNCH_MAIL	B4	[2]
VK_LAUNCH_MEDIA_SELECT	B5	[2]
VK_LAUNCH_APP1	B6	[2]
VK_LAUNCH_APP2	B7	[2]
--	B7-B9	Unassigned
VK_SEMICOLON	BA	; key
VK_EQUAL	BB	= key
VK_COMMA	BC	, key
VK_HYPHEN	BD	- key
VK_PERIOD	BE	. key
VK_SLASH	BF	/ key
VK_BACKQUOTE	C0	` key
--	C1–DA	Unassigned[5]
VK_LBRACKET	DB	[key
VK_BACKSLASH	DC	\ key
VK_RBRACKET	DD	] key
VK_APOSTROPHE	DE	' key
VK_OFF	DF	Power button
--	E5	Unassigned
--	E6	OEM-specific
--	E7–E8	Unassigned
--	E9–F5	OEM-specific
VK_ATTN	F6	
VK_CRSEL	F7	
VK_EXSEL	F8	
VK_EREOF	F9	
VK_PLAY	FA	
VK_ZOOM	FB	

Constant	Value	Keyboard Equivalent
VK_NONAME	FC	
VK_PA1	FD	
VK_OEM_CLEAR	FE	

[1] Mouse right and middle buttons are defined but are relevant only on a Windows CE system equipped with a mouse.

[2] Many Windows CE Systems don't have this key

[3] On some Windows CE systems, Delete is simulated with Shift-Backspace

[4] These constants can be used only with *GetKeyState* and *GetAsyncKeyState*.

[5] These codes are used by the application launch keys on systems that have them.

For the *WM_CHAR* and *WM_SYSCHAR* messages, the *wParam* value contains the Unicode character represented by the key. Most often an application can simply look for *WM_CHAR* messages and ignore *WM_KEYDOWN* and *WM_ KEYUP*. The *WM_CHAR* message allows for a second level of abstraction so that the application doesn't have to worry about the up or down state of the keys and can concentrate on the characters being entered by means of the keyboard.

The *lParam* value of any of these keyboard messages contains further information about the pressed key. The format of the *lParam* parameter is shown in Figure 3-1.

The low word, bits 0 through 15, contains the repeat count of the key. On rare occasions, keys on a Windows CE device can be pressed faster than Windows CE can send messages to the focus application. In these cases, the repeat count contains the number of times the key has been pressed. Bit 29 contains the context flag. If the Alt key is held down when the key is pressed, the bit will be set. Bit 30 contains the previous key state. If the key was previously down, this bit is set; otherwise, it's 0. Bit 30 can be used to determine whether the key message is the result of an auto-repeat sequence. Bit 31 indicates the transition state. If the key is in transition from down to up, Bit 31 is set. Bits 16 through 28 are used to indicate the key scan code. In many cases, Windows CE doesn't support this field. However, on some of the newer Windows CE platforms where scan codes are necessary, this field does contain the scan code. You shouldn't plan on the scan code field being available unless you know it's supported on your specific platform.

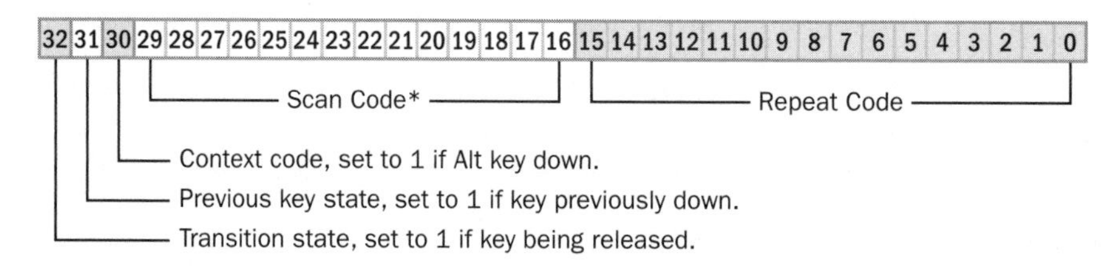

FIGURE 3-1 The layout of the *lParam* value for key messages

One additional keyboard message, *WM_DEADCHAR*, can sometimes come into play. It is sent by the operating system when the pressed key represents a dead character, such as an umlaut, that you want to combine with a character to create a different character. In this case, the *WM_DEADCHAR* message can be used to prevent the text entry point (the caret) from advancing to the next space until the second key is pressed so that you can complete the combined character.

The *WM_DEADCHAR* message has always been present under Windows, but under Windows CE it takes on a somewhat larger role. With the internationalization of the variety of devices that run Windows CE, programmers should plan for, and if necessary use, the *WM_DEADCHAR* message that is so often necessary in foreign language systems.

Keyboard Functions

You'll find useful a few other keyboard state–determining functions for Windows applications. Among the keyboard functions, two are closely related but often confused: *GetKeyState* and *GetAsyncKeyState*.

GetKeyState, prototyped as

```
SHORT GetKeyState (int nVirtKey);
```

returns the up/down state of the shift keys, Ctrl, Alt, and Shift, as well as the Windows key, and indicates whether any of these keys is in a toggled state. If the keyboard has two keys with the same function—for example, two Shift keys, one on each side of the keyboard—this function can also be used to differentiate which of them is being pressed. (Most keyboards have left and right Shift keys, and some include left and right Ctrl and Alt keys.)

You pass to the function the virtual key code for the key being queried. If the high bit of the return value is set, the key is down. If the least significant bit of the return value is set, the key is in a toggled state; that is, it has been pressed an odd number of times since the system started. The state returned is the state at the time the most recent message was read from the message queue, which isn't necessarily the real-time state of the key. An interesting aside: notice that the virtual key label for the Alt key is *VK_MENU*, which relates to the windows convention that the Alt key works in concert with other keys to access various menus from the keyboard.

Note that the *GetKeyState* function is limited under Windows CE to querying the state of the shift keys; Ctrl, Alt, Shift, Numlock, and the Windows key. Under other versions of Windows, *GetKeyState* can determine the state of every key on the keyboard.

To determine the real-time state of a key, use

```
SHORT GetAsyncKeyState (int vKey);
```

As with *GetKeyState*, you pass to this function the virtual key code for the key being queried. The *GetAsyncKeyState* function returns a value subtly different from the one returned by

GetKeyState. As with the *GetKeyState* function, the high bit of the return value is set while the key is being pressed. Like *GetKeyState*, the *GetAsyncKeyState* function can distinguish the left and right Shift, Ctrl, and Alt keys. In addition, by passing the *VK_LBUTTON* virtual key value, *GetAsyncKeyState* determines whether the stylus is currently touching the screen. On systems with a mouse, the VK values; *VK_LBUTTON, VK_MBUTTON, VK_RBUTTON, VK_XBUTTON1, and VK_XBUTTON2* return the state of their respective mouse buttons.

An application can simulate a keystroke using the *keybd_event* function:

```
VOID keybd_event (BYTE bVk, BYTE bScan, DWORD dwFlags,
                  DWORD dwExtraInfo);
```

The first parameter is the virtual key code of the key to simulate. The *bScan* code should be set to *NULL* under Windows CE. The *dwFlags* parameter can have two possible flags: *KEYEVENTF_KEYUP* indicates that the call is to emulate a key up event, while *KEYEVENTF_SILENT* indicates that the simulated key press won't cause the standard keyboard click that you normally hear when you press a key. So to fully simulate a key press, *keybd_event* should be called twice, once without *KEYEVENTF_KEYUP* to simulate a key down, and then once again, this time *with KEYEVENTF_KEYUP* to simulate the key release. When simulating a shift key, specify the specific left or right VK code, as in *VK_LSHIFT* or *VF_RCONTROL*.

A function unique to Windows CE is

```
BOOL PostKeybdMessage (HWND hwnd, UINT VKey,
                       KEY_STATE_FLAGS KeyStateFlags,
                       UINT cCharacters, UINT *pShiftStateBuffer,
                       UINT *pCharacterBuffer );
```

This function sends a series of keys to the specified window. The *hwnd* parameter is the target window. This window must be owned by the calling thread. The *VKey* parameter should be zero. *KeyStateFlags* specifies the key state for all the keys being sent. The *cCharacters* parameter specifies the number of keys being sent. The *pShiftStateBuffer* parameter points to an array that contains a shift state for each key sent, while *pCharacterBuffer* points to the VK codes of the keys being sent. Unlike *keybd_event*, this function doesn't change the global state of the keyboard.

One final keyboard function, *MapVirtualKey*, translates virtual key codes to characters. *MapVirtualKey* in Windows CE doesn't translate keyboard scan codes to and from virtual key codes, although it does so in other versions of Windows. The prototype of the function is the top of the following page.

```
UINT MapVirtualKey (UINT uCode, UINT uMapType);
```

Under Windows CE, the first parameter is the virtual key code to be translated, while the second parameter, *uMapType*, indicates how the key code is translated. *MapVirtualKey* is dependent on the keyboard device driver implementing a supporting function. Some OEMs don't implement this supporting function, so on their systems, *MapVirtualKey* fails.

Testing for the Keyboard

To determine whether a keyboard is even present in the system, you can call

```
DWORD GetKeyboardStatus (VOID);
```

This function returns the *KBDI_KEYBOARD_PRESENT* flag if a hardware keyboard is present in the system. This function also returns a *KBDI_KEYBOARD_ENABLED* flag if the keyboard is enabled. To disable the keyboard, a call can be made to

```
BOOL EnableHardwareKeyboard (BOOL bEnable);
```

with the *bEnable* flag set to *FALSE*. You might want to disable the keyboard in a system for which the keyboard folds around behind the screen; in such a system, a user could accidentally press keys while using the stylus.

The KeyTrac Example Program

The following example program, KeyTrac, displays the sequence of keyboard messages. Programmatically, KeyTrac isn't much of a departure from the earlier programs in the book. The difference is that the keyboard messages described here are all trapped and recorded in an array that's then displayed during the *WM_PAINT* message. For each keyboard message, the message name is recorded along with the *wParam* and *lParam* values and a set of flags indicating the state of the Shift keys. The key messages are recorded in an array because these messages can occur faster than the redraw can occur. Figure 3-2 shows the KeyTrac window after a few keys have been pressed.

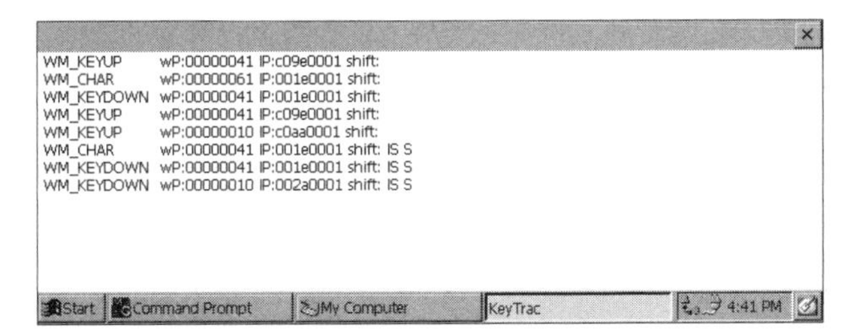

FIGURE 3-2 The KeyTrac window after a Shift+A key combination followed by a lowercase *a* key press

The best way to learn about the sequence of the keyboard messages is to run KeyTrac, press a few keys, and watch the messages scroll down the screen. Pressing a character key such as the *a* results in three messages: *WM_KEYDOWN*, *WM_CHAR*, and *WM_KEYUP*. Holding down the Shift key while pressing the *a* and then releasing the Shift key produces a key-down message for the Shift key followed by the three messages for the *a* key followed by a key-up message for the Shift key. Because the Shift key itself isn't a character key, no *WM_CHAR* message is sent in response to it. However, the *WM_CHAR* message for the *a* key now contains a *0x41* in the *wParam* value, indicating that an uppercase *A* was pressed instead of a lowercase *a*.

Listing 3-1 shows the source code for the KeyTrac program.

LISTING 3-1

KeyTrac.h

```
//======================================================================
// Header file
//
// Written for the book Programming Windows CE
// Copyright (C) 2007 Douglas Boling
//======================================================================
// Returns number of elements
#define dim(x) (sizeof(x) / sizeof(x[0]))

//----------------------------------------------------------------------
// Generic defines and data types
//
struct decodeUINT {                             // Structure associates
    UINT Code;                                  // messages
                                                // with a function.
    LRESULT (*Fxn)(HWND, UINT, WPARAM, LPARAM);
};

//----------------------------------------------------------------------
// Program-specific defines and structures
//
typedef struct {
    UINT wKeyMsg;
    INT wParam;
    INT lParam;
    LPCTSTR pszMsgTxt;
    TCHAR szShift[20];
} MYKEYARRAY, *PMYKEYARRAY;

// Structure to associate messages with text name of message
typedef struct {
    UINT wMsg;
    LPCTSTR pName;
} KEYNAMESTRUCT;

//----------------------------------------------------------------------
// Function prototypes
//
HWND InitInstance (HINSTANCE, LPWSTR, int);
int TermInstance (HINSTANCE, int);

// Window procedures
LRESULT CALLBACK MainWndProc (HWND, UINT, WPARAM, LPARAM);
// Message handlers
LRESULT DoCreateMain (HWND, UINT, WPARAM, LPARAM);
LRESULT DoPaintMain (HWND, UINT, WPARAM, LPARAM);
LRESULT DoKeysMain (HWND, UINT, WPARAM, LPARAM);
LRESULT DoDestroyMain (HWND, UINT, WPARAM, LPARAM);
```

KeyTrac.cpp

```
//======================================================================
// KeyTrac - displays keyboard messages
//
// Written for the book Programming Windows CE
// Copyright (C) 2007 Douglas Boling
//======================================================================
#include <windows.h>                 // For all that Windows stuff
#include <commctrl.h>                // Command bar includes
#include "keytrac.h"                 // Program-specific stuff

// The include and lib files for the Pocket PC are conditionally
// included so that this example can share the same project file.  This
// is necessary since this example must have a menu bar on the Pocket
// PC to have a SIP button.
#if defined(WIN32_PLATFORM_PSPC) || defined(WIN32_PLATFORM_WFSP)
#include <aygshell.h>                // Add Pocket PC includes.
#pragma comment( lib, "aygshell" )   // Link Pocket PC lib for menu bar.
#endif

//----------------------------------------------------------------------
// Global data
//
const TCHAR szAppName[] = TEXT ("KeyTrac");
HINSTANCE hInst;                     // Program instance handle

// Program-specific global data
MYKEYARRAY ka[16];
int nKeyCnt = 0;
int nFontHeight;

// Array associates key messages with text tags
KEYNAMESTRUCT knArray[] = {{WM_KEYDOWN,     TEXT ("WM_KEYDOWN")},
                           {WM_KEYUP,       TEXT ("WM_KEYUP")},
                           {WM_CHAR,        TEXT ("WM_CHAR")},
                           {WM_SYSCHAR,     TEXT ("WM_SYSCHAR")},
                           {WM_SYSKEYUP,    TEXT ("WM_SYSKEYUP")},
                           {WM_SYSKEYDOWN,  TEXT ("WM_SYSKEYDOWN")},
                           {WM_DEADCHAR,    TEXT ("WM_DEADCHAR")},
                           {WM_SYSDEADCHAR, TEXT ("WM_SYSDEADCHAR")}};
// Message dispatch table for MainWindowProc
const struct decodeUINT MainMessages[] = {
    WM_CREATE, DoCreateMain,
    WM_PAINT, DoPaintMain,
    WM_KEYUP, DoKeysMain,
    WM_KEYDOWN, DoKeysMain,
    WM_CHAR, DoKeysMain,
    WM_DEADCHAR, DoKeysMain,
    WM_SYSCHAR, DoKeysMain,
    WM_SYSDEADCHAR, DoKeysMain,
    WM_SYSKEYDOWN, DoKeysMain,
    WM_SYSKEYUP, DoKeysMain,
```

```
    WM_DESTROY, DoDestroyMain,
};

//======================================================================
// Program entry point
//
 int WINAPI WinMain (HINSTANCE hInstance, HINSTANCE hPrevInstance,
                    LPWSTR lpCmdLine, int nCmdShow) {
    MSG msg;
    int rc = 0;
    HWND hwndMain;

    // Initialize this instance.
    hwndMain = InitInstance (hInstance, lpCmdLine, nCmdShow);
    if (hwndMain == 0)
        return 0x10;

    // Application message loop
    while (GetMessage (&msg, NULL, 0, 0)) {
        TranslateMessage (&msg);
        DispatchMessage (&msg);
    }

    // Instance cleanup
    return TermInstance (hInstance, msg.wParam);
}
//----------------------------------------------------------------------
// InitInstance - Instance initialization
//
HWND InitInstance (HINSTANCE hInstance, LPWSTR lpCmdLine, int nCmdShow) {
    WNDCLASS wc;
    HWND hWnd;

#if defined(WIN32_PLATFORM_PSPC) || defined(WIN32_PLATFORM_WFSP)
    // For Windows Mobile devices, allow only one instance of the app
    hWnd = FindWindow (szAppName, NULL);
    if (hWnd) {
        SetForegroundWindow ((HWND)(((DWORD)hWnd) | 0x01));
        return 0;
    }
#endif
    hInst = hInstance;  // Save program instance handle

    // Register application main window class.
    wc.style = 0;                             // Window style
    wc.lpfnWndProc = MainWndProc;             // Callback function
    wc.cbClsExtra = 0;                        // Extra class data
    wc.cbWndExtra = 0;                        // Extra window data
    wc.hInstance = hInstance;                 // Owner handle
    wc.hIcon = NULL,                          // Application icon
    wc.hCursor = LoadCursor (NULL, IDC_ARROW);// Default cursor
    wc.hbrBackground = (HBRUSH) GetStockObject (WHITE_BRUSH);
```

```
    wc.lpszMenuName =  NULL;                      // Menu name
    wc.lpszClassName = szAppName;                 // Window class name

    if (RegisterClass(&wc) == 0) return 0;

    // Create main window.
    hWnd = CreateWindowEx (WS_EX_NODRAG, szAppName, TEXT ("KeyTrac"),
                           WS_VISIBLE | WS_CAPTION | WS_SYSMENU,
                           CW_USEDEFAULT, CW_USEDEFAULT,
                           CW_USEDEFAULT, CW_USEDEFAULT,
                           NULL, NULL, hInstance, NULL);

    // Fail if window not created
    if (!IsWindow (hWnd)) return 0;

    // Standard show and update calls
    ShowWindow (hWnd, nCmdShow);
    UpdateWindow (hWnd);
    return hWnd;
}
//----------------------------------------------------------------------
// TermInstance - Program cleanup
//
int TermInstance (HINSTANCE hInstance, int nDefRC) {
    return nDefRC;
}
//======================================================================
// Message handling procedures for MainWindow
//
//----------------------------------------------------------------------
// MainWndProc - Callback function for application window
//
LRESULT CALLBACK MainWndProc (HWND hWnd, UINT wMsg, WPARAM wParam,
                              LPARAM lParam) {
    INT i;
    //
    // Search message list to see if we need to handle this
    // message. If in list, call procedure.
    //
    for (i = 0; i < dim(MainMessages); i++) {
        if (wMsg == MainMessages[i].Code)
            return (*MainMessages[i].Fxn)(hWnd, wMsg, wParam, lParam);
    }
    return DefWindowProc (hWnd, wMsg, wParam, lParam);
}
//----------------------------------------------------------------------
// DoCreateMain - Process WM_CREATE message for window.
//
LRESULT DoCreateMain (HWND hWnd, UINT wMsg, WPARAM wParam,
                      LPARAM lParam) {
    HDC hdc;
    TEXTMETRIC tm;
```

```
#if defined(WIN32_PLATFORM_PSPC) && (_WIN32_WCE >= 300)
    SHMENUBARINFO mbi;                      // For Pocket PC, create
    memset(&mbi, 0, sizeof(SHMENUBARINFO)); // menu bar so that we
    mbi.cbSize = sizeof(SHMENUBARINFO);     // have a sip button
    mbi.hwndParent = hWnd;
    mbi.dwFlags = SHCMBF_EMPTYBAR;          // No menu
    SHCreateMenuBar(&mbi);
#endif

    // Get the height of the default font.
    hdc = GetDC (hWnd);
    GetTextMetrics (hdc, &tm);
    nFontHeight = tm.tmHeight + tm.tmExternalLeading;
    ReleaseDC (hWnd, hdc);
    return 0;
}
//----------------------------------------------------------------------
// DoPaintMain - Process WM_PAINT message for window.
//
LRESULT DoPaintMain (HWND hWnd, UINT wMsg, WPARAM wParam,
                     LPARAM lParam) {
    PAINTSTRUCT ps;
    RECT rect, rectOut;
    TCHAR szOut[256];
    HDC hdc;
    INT i, j;
    LPCTSTR pKeyText;

    GetClientRect (hWnd, &rect);

    // Create a drawing rectangle for the top line of the window.
    rectOut = rect;
    rectOut.bottom = rectOut.top + nFontHeight;

    hdc = BeginPaint (hWnd, &ps);

    if (nKeyCnt) {
        for (i = 0; i < nKeyCnt; i++) {
            // Create string containing wParam, lParam, and shift data.
            wsprintf (szOut, TEXT ("wP:%08x lP:%08x shift: %s"),
                      ka[i].wParam, ka[i].lParam, ka[i].szShift);

            // Look up name of key message.
            for (j = 0; j < dim (knArray); j++)
                if (knArray[j].wMsg == ka[i].wKeyMsg)
                    break;
            // See if we found the message.
            if (j < dim (knArray))
                pKeyText = knArray[j].pName;
            else
                pKeyText = TEXT ("Unknown");
            // Scroll the window one line.
            ScrollDC (hdc, 0, nFontHeight, &rect, &rect, NULL, NULL);
```

```
            // See if wide or narrow screen.
            if (GetSystemMetrics (SM_CXSCREEN) < 480) {
                // If narrow screen, display info on 2 lines
                ExtTextOut (hdc, 10, rect.top, ETO_OPAQUE, &rectOut,
                            szOut, lstrlen (szOut), NULL);

                // Scroll the window another line.
                ScrollDC(hdc, 0, nFontHeight, &rect, &rect, NULL, NULL);
                ExtTextOut (hdc, 5, rect.top, ETO_OPAQUE, &rectOut,
                            pKeyText, lstrlen (pKeyText), NULL);
            } else {
                // Wide screen, print all on one line.
                ExtTextOut (hdc, 5, rect.top, ETO_OPAQUE, &rectOut,
                            pKeyText, lstrlen (pKeyText), NULL);
                ExtTextOut (hdc, 100, rect.top, 0, NULL,
                            szOut, lstrlen (szOut), NULL);
            }
        }
        nKeyCnt = 0;
    }
    EndPaint (hWnd, &ps);
    return 0;
}
//----------------------------------------------------------------------
// DoKeysMain - Process all keyboard messages for window.
//
LRESULT DoKeysMain (HWND hWnd, UINT wMsg, WPARAM wParam,
                    LPARAM lParam) {

    if (nKeyCnt >= 16) return 0;

    ka[nKeyCnt].wKeyMsg = wMsg;
    ka[nKeyCnt].wParam = wParam;
    ka[nKeyCnt].lParam = lParam;

    // Capture the state of the shift flags.
    ka[nKeyCnt].szShift[0] = TEXT ('\0');

     int siz = dim(ka[nKeyCnt].szShift); //save size of string buffer

    if (GetKeyState (VK_LMENU))
        _tcscat_s (ka[nKeyCnt].szShift, siz, TEXT ("lA "));
    if (GetKeyState (VK_RMENU))
        _tcscat_s (ka[nKeyCnt].szShift, siz, TEXT ("rA "));
    if (GetKeyState (VK_MENU))
        _tcscat_s (ka[nKeyCnt].szShift, siz, TEXT ("A "));
    if (GetKeyState (VK_LCONTROL))
        _tcscat_s (ka[nKeyCnt].szShift, siz, TEXT ("lC "));
    if (GetKeyState (VK_RCONTROL))
        _tcscat_s (ka[nKeyCnt].szShift, siz, TEXT ("rC "));
    if (GetKeyState (VK_CONTROL))
        _tcscat_s (ka[nKeyCnt].szShift, siz, TEXT ("C "));
```

```
    if (GetKeyState (VK_LSHIFT))
        _tcscat_s (ka[nKeyCnt].szShift, siz, TEXT ("lS "));
    if (GetKeyState (VK_RSHIFT))
        _tcscat_s (ka[nKeyCnt].szShift, siz, TEXT ("rS "));
    if (GetKeyState (VK_SHIFT))
        _tcscat_s (ka[nKeyCnt].szShift, siz, TEXT ("S "));

    nKeyCnt++;
    InvalidateRect (hWnd, NULL, FALSE);
    return 0;
}
//----------------------------------------------------------------------
// DoDestroyMain - Process WM_DESTROY message for window.
//
LRESULT DoDestroyMain (HWND hWnd, UINT wMsg, WPARAM wParam,
                       LPARAM lParam) {
    PostQuitMessage (0);
    return 0;
}
```

Here are a few more characteristics of KeyTrac to notice. After each keyboard message is recorded, an *InvalidateRect* function is called to force a redraw of the window and therefore also a *WM_PAINT* message. As I mentioned in Chapter 2, "Drawing on the Screen," a program should never attempt to send or post a *WM_PAINT* message to a window because Windows needs to perform some setup before it calls a window with a *WM_PAINT* message.

Another device context function used in KeyTrac is

```
BOOL ScrollDC (HDC hDC, int dx, int dy, const RECT *lprcScroll,
               const RECT *lprcClip, HRGN hrgnUpdate,
               LPRECT lprcUpdate);
```

which scrolls an area of the device context either horizontally or vertically, but, under Windows CE, not both directions at the same time. The three rectangle parameters define the area to be scrolled, the area within the scrolling area to be clipped, and the area to be painted after the scrolling ends. Alternatively, a handle to a region can be passed to *ScrollDC*. That region is defined by *ScrollDC* to encompass the region that needs painting after the scroll.

Also notice that if the KeyTrac window is covered up for any reason and then reexposed, the message information on the display is lost. This behavior occurs because a device context doesn't store the bit information of the display. The application is responsible for saving any information necessary to completely restore the client area of the screen. Because KeyTrac doesn't save this information, it's lost when the window is covered up.

One last aspect of KeyTrac needs mentioning. In the key message handler, *DoKeysMain*, the program uses *_tcscat_s* to construct the shift strings. The function is a standard string concationation function with a secure twist. The second parameter is the size of the destination string. Windows CE now comes with a secure string library that should be used instead of the old standard string functions. The secure functions provide buffer checking to prevent buffer overrun errors (or attacks) in the code. Although simple example programs such as the ones in this book aren't going to be subject to hordes of hackers attempting to break the code, they are example programs and therefore should show proper coding techniques.

The Mouse and the Touch Screen

Unlike desktop PCs, Windows CE devices don't always have a mouse. Instead, many Windows CE devices have a touch screen and stylus combination. For Windows CE systems that do have a mouse, the programming interface is identical to the desktop.

Mouse Messages

Whenever the mouse cursor moves across the display, the topmost window at that point receives a *WM_MOUSEMOVE* message. If the user clicks the left or right mouse button, the window receives a *WM_LBUTTONDOWN* or *WM_RBUTTONDOWN* message. When the user releases the button, the window receives a *WM_LBUTTONUP* or *WM_RBUTTONUP* message. If the user presses and releases the mouse wheel, the window receives a *WM_MBUTTONDOWN* followed by a *WM_MBUTTONUP* message.

For all of these messages, the *wParam* and *lParam* parameters are loaded with the same values. The *wParam* parameter contains a set of bit flags indicating whether the Ctrl or Shift keys on the keyboard are currently held down. As in other versions of Windows, the Alt key state isn't provided in these messages. To get the state of the Alt key when the message was sent, use the *GetKeyState* function.

The *lParam* parameter contains two 16-bit values that indicate the position on the screen of the tap, or mouse click. The low-order 16 bits contain the *x* (horizontal) location relative to the upper-left corner of the client area of the window, while the high-order 16 bits contain the *y* (vertical) position.

If the user *double-taps*, that is, taps twice on the screen at the same location and within a predefined time, Windows sends a *WM_LBUTTONDBLCLK* message to the double-tapped window, but only if that window's class was registered with the CS_DBLCLKS style. The class style is set when the window class is registered with *RegisterClass*.

You can differentiate between a tap and a double-tap by comparing the messages sent to the window. When a double-tap occurs, a window first receives the *WM_LBUTTONDOWN* and *WM_LBUTTONUP* messages from the original tap. Then a *WM_LBUTTONDBLCLK* is sent followed by another *WM_LBUTTONUP*. The trick is to refrain from acting on a *WM_LBUTTONDOWN* message in any way that precludes action on a subsequent

WM_LBUTTONDBLCLK. This is usually not a problem because single taps usually select an object, while double-tapping launches the default action for the object.

If the user rolls the mouse wheel, the window receives *WM_MOUSEWHEEL* messages. For this message, the contents is the same as the other mouse messages, the horizontal and vertical location of the mouse cursor. The low word of the *wParam* parameter contains the same bit flags indicating the the keys currently held down. The high work of *wParam* contains the distance the wheel was rotated expressed in multiples of a constant *WHEEL_DELTA*. If the value is positive, the rotation is away from the user. A negative value indicates the wheel was rotated back toward the user. The DOIView example in Chapter 4 demonstrates support for the WM_MOUSEWHEEL message.

Working with the Touch Screen

The touch screen and stylus combination might be new to Windows programmers, but fortunately, its integration into Windows CE applications is relatively painless. The best way to deal with the stylus is to treat it as a single-button mouse. The stylus creates the same mouse messages that are provided by the mouse in other versions of Windows and by Windows CE systems that use a mouse. The differences that do appear between a mouse and a stylus are due to the different physical realities of the two input devices.

Unlike a mouse, a stylus doesn't have a cursor to indicate its current position. Therefore, a stylus can't *hover* over a point on the screen in the way that the mouse cursor does. A cursor hovers when a user moves it over a window without pressing a mouse button. This concept can't be applied to programming for a stylus because the touch screen can't detect the position of the stylus when it isn't in contact with the screen.

Another consequence of the difference between a stylus and a mouse is that without a mouse cursor, an application can't provide feedback to the user by means of changes in appearance of a hovering cursor. Touch screen–based Windows CE systems support setting the cursor for one classic Windows method of user feedback. The busy hourglass cursor, indicating that the user must wait for the system to complete processing, is supported under Windows CE so that applications can display the busy hourglass in the same manner as applications running under other versions of Windows.

Stylus Messages

When the user presses the stylus on the screen, the topmost window under that point receives the input focus if it didn't have it before and then receives a *WM_LBUTTONDOWN* message. When the user lifts the stylus, the window receives a *WM_LBUTTONUP* message. Moving the stylus within the same window while it's down causes *WM_MOUSEMOVE* messages to be sent to the window.

Inking

A typical application for a handheld device is capturing the user's writing on the screen and storing the result as *ink*. This process isn't handwriting recognition—simply ink storage. At first pass, the best way to accomplish this would be to store the stylus points passed in each *WM_MOUSEMOVE* message. The problem is that sometimes small CE-type devices can't send these messages fast enough to achieve a satisfactory resolution. Under Windows CE, a function call has been added to assist programmers in tracking the stylus.

```
BOOL GetMouseMovePoints (PPOINT pptBuf, UINT nBufPoints,
                         UINT *pnPointsRetrieved);
```

GetMouseMovePoints returns a number of stylus points that didn't result in *WM_MOUSEMOVE* messages. The function is passed an array of points, the size of the array (in points), and a pointer to an integer that will receive the number of points passed back to the application. Once received, these additional points can be used to fill in the blanks between the last *WM_MOUSEMOVE* message and the current one.

GetMouseMovePoints does have one "gotcha"; it returns points in the resolution of the touch panel, not the screen. This touch panel resolution is generally set at four times the screen resolution, so you need to divide the coordinates returned by *GetMouseMovePoints* by 4 to convert them to screen coordinates. The extra resolution helps programs such as handwriting recognizers.

A short example program, PenTrac, illustrates the difference that *GetMouseMovePoints* can make. Figure 3-3 shows the PenTrac window. Notice the two lines of dots across the window. The top line was drawn using points from *WM_MOUSEMOVE* only. The second line included points that were queried with *GetMouseMovePoints*. The black dots were queried from *WM_MOUSEMOVE*, while the red (lighter) dots were locations queried with *GetMouseMovePoints*.

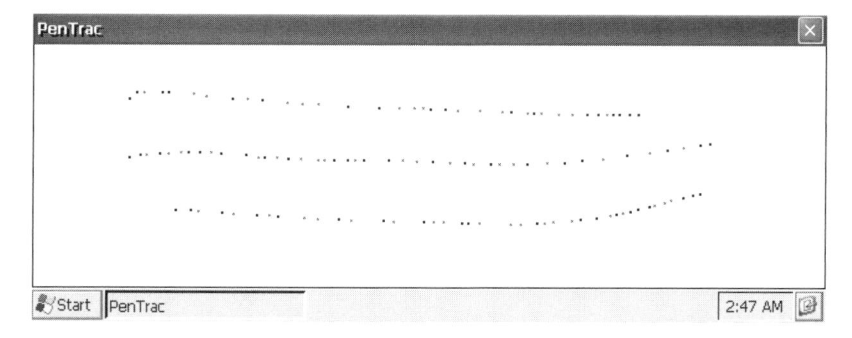

FIGURE 3-3 The PenTrac window showing three lines drawn

The source code for PenTrac is shown in Listing 3-2. The program places a dot on the screen for each *WM_MOUSEMOVE* or *WM_LBUTTONDOWN* message it receives. If the Shift key is held down during the mouse move messages, PenTrac also calls *GetMouseMovePoints* and marks those points in the window in red to distinguish them from the points returned by the mouse messages alone.

PenTrac cheats a little to enhance the effect of *GetMouseMovePoints*. The *DoMouseMain* routine, which handles *WM_MOUSEMOVE* and *WM_LBUTTONDOWN* messages, calls the function *sleep* to kill a few milliseconds. This delay simulates a slow-responding application that might not have time to process every mouse move message in a timely manner.

LISTING 3-2 The PenTrac program

PenTrac.h

```
//======================================================================
// Header file
//
// Written for the book Programming Windows CE
// Copyright (C) 2007 Douglas Boling
//======================================================================
// Returns number of elements.
#define dim(x) (sizeof(x) / sizeof(x[0]))

//----------------------------------------------------------------------
// Generic defines and data types
//
struct decodeUINT {                             // Structure associates
    UINT Code;                                  // messages
                                                // with a function.
    LRESULT (*Fxn)(HWND, UINT, WPARAM, LPARAM);
};

//----------------------------------------------------------------------
// Function prototypes
//
HWND InitInstance (HINSTANCE, LPWSTR, int);
int TermInstance (HINSTANCE, int);

// Window procedures
LRESULT CALLBACK MainWndProc (HWND, UINT, WPARAM, LPARAM);

// Message handlers
LRESULT DoPaintMain (HWND, UINT, WPARAM, LPARAM);
LRESULT DoMouseMain (HWND, UINT, WPARAM, LPARAM);
LRESULT DoDestroyMain (HWND, UINT, WPARAM, LPARAM);
```

PenTrac.cpp

```
//======================================================================
// PenTrac - Tracks stylus movement
//
// Written for the book Programming Windows CE
// Copyright (C) 2007 Douglas Boling
//======================================================================
```

```
#include <windows.h>                  // For all that Windows stuff
#include "pentrac.h"                  // Program-specific stuff

//----------------------------------------------------------------------
// Global data
//
const TCHAR szAppName[] = TEXT ("PenTrac");
HINSTANCE hInst;                      // Program instance handle

// Message dispatch table for MainWindowProc
const struct decodeUINT MainMessages[] = {
    WM_LBUTTONDOWN, DoMouseMain,
    WM_MOUSEMOVE, DoMouseMain,
    WM_DESTROY, DoDestroyMain,
};

//======================================================================
// Program entry point
//
int WINAPI WinMain (HINSTANCE hInstance, HINSTANCE hPrevInstance,
                    LPWSTR lpCmdLine, int nCmdShow) {
    MSG msg;
    int rc = 0;
    HWND hwndMain;

    // Initialize this instance.
    hwndMain = InitInstance (hInstance, lpCmdLine, nCmdShow);
    if (hwndMain == 0)
        return 0x10;

    // Application message loop
    while (GetMessage (&msg, NULL, 0, 0)) {
        TranslateMessage (&msg);
        DispatchMessage (&msg);
    }
    // Instance cleanup
    return TermInstance (hInstance, msg.wParam);
}
//----------------------------------------------------------------------
// InitApp - Application initialization
//
HWND InitInstance (HINSTANCE hInstance, LPWSTR lpCmdLine, int nCmdShow) {
    WNDCLASS wc;
    HWND hWnd;

#if defined(WIN32_PLATFORM_PSPC) || defined(WIN32_PLATFORM_WFSP)
// If Windows Mobile, allow only one instance of the application.
    hWnd = FindWindow (szAppName, NULL);
    if (hWnd) {
        SetForegroundWindow ((HWND)(((DWORD)hWnd) | 0x01));
        return 0;
    }
#endif
    // Save program instance handle in global variable.
```

```
    hInst = hInstance;

    // Register application main window class.
    wc.style = 0;                                // Window style
    wc.lpfnWndProc = MainWndProc;                // Callback function
    wc.cbClsExtra = 0;                           // Extra class data
    wc.cbWndExtra = 0;                           // Extra window data
    wc.hInstance = hInstance;                    // Owner handle
    wc.hIcon = NULL,                             // Application icon
    wc.hCursor = LoadCursor (NULL, IDC_ARROW);// Default cursor
    wc.hbrBackground = (HBRUSH) GetStockObject (WHITE_BRUSH);
    wc.lpszMenuName =  NULL;                     // Menu name
    wc.lpszClassName = szAppName;                // Window class name

    if (RegisterClass (&wc) == 0) return 0;

    // Create main window.
    hWnd = CreateWindowEx (WS_EX_NODRAG, szAppName, TEXT ("PenTrac"),
                         WS_VISIBLE | WS_CAPTION | WS_SYSMENU,
                         CW_USEDEFAULT, CW_USEDEFAULT, CW_USEDEFAULT,
                         CW_USEDEFAULT, NULL, NULL, hInstance, NULL);
    // Return fail code if window not created.
    if (!IsWindow (hWnd)) return 0;

    // Standard show and update calls
    ShowWindow (hWnd, nCmdShow);
    UpdateWindow (hWnd);
    return hWnd;
}
//----------------------------------------------------------------------
// TermInstance - Program cleanup
//
int TermInstance (HINSTANCE hInstance, int nDefRC) {
    return nDefRC;
}
//======================================================================
// Message handling procedures for MainWindow
//

//----------------------------------------------------------------------
// MainWndProc - Callback function for application window
//
LRESULT CALLBACK MainWndProc (HWND hWnd, UINT wMsg, WPARAM wParam,
                              LPARAM lParam) {
    INT i;
    //
    // Search message list to see if we need to handle this
    // message.  If in list, call procedure.
    //
    for (i = 0; i < dim(MainMessages); i++) {
        if (wMsg == MainMessages[i].Code)
            return (*MainMessages[i].Fxn)(hWnd, wMsg, wParam, lParam);
    }
```

```
    return DefWindowProc (hWnd, wMsg, wParam, lParam);
}
//----------------------------------------------------------------------
// DoMouseMain - Process WM_LBUTTONDOWN and WM_MOUSEMOVE messages
// for window.
//
LRESULT DoMouseMain (HWND hWnd, UINT wMsg, WPARAM wParam,
                     LPARAM lParam) {
    POINT pt[64];
    POINT ptM;
    UINT i, uPoints = 0;
    HDC hdc;

    ptM.x = LOWORD (lParam);
    ptM.y = HIWORD (lParam);
    hdc = GetDC (hWnd);
    // If shift and mouse move, see if any lost points.
    if (wMsg == WM_MOUSEMOVE) {
        if (wParam & MK_SHIFT)
            GetMouseMovePoints (pt, 64, &uPoints);

        for (i = 0; i < uPoints; i++) {
            pt[i].x /= 4;  // Convert move pts to screen coords
            pt[i].y /= 4;
            // Covert screen coordinates to window coordinates
            MapWindowPoints (HWND_DESKTOP, hWnd, &pt[i], 1);
            SetPixel (hdc, pt[i].x,   pt[i].y, RGB (255, 0, 0));
            SetPixel (hdc, pt[i].x+1, pt[i].y, RGB (255, 0, 0));
            SetPixel (hdc, pt[i].x,   pt[i].y+1, RGB (255, 0, 0));
            SetPixel (hdc, pt[i].x+1, pt[i].y+1, RGB (255, 0, 0));
        }
    }
    // The original point is drawn last in case one of the points
    // returned by GetMouseMovePoints overlaps it.
    SetPixel (hdc, ptM.x, ptM.y, RGB (0, 0, 0));
    SetPixel (hdc, ptM.x+1, ptM.y, RGB (0, 0, 0));
    SetPixel (hdc, ptM.x, ptM.y+1, RGB (0, 0, 0));
    SetPixel (hdc, ptM.x+1, ptM.y+1, RGB (0, 0, 0));
    ReleaseDC (hWnd, hdc);

    // Kill time to make believe we are busy.
    Sleep(25);
    return 0;
}
//----------------------------------------------------------------------
// DoDestroyMain - Process WM_DESTROY message for window.
//
LRESULT DoDestroyMain (HWND hWnd, UINT wMsg, WPARAM wParam,
                       LPARAM lParam) {
    PostQuitMessage (0);
    return 0;
}
```

Input Focus and Mouse Messages

Here are some subtleties to note about circumstances that rule how and when mouse messages initiated by stylus input are sent to different windows. As mentioned previously, the input focus of the system changes when the stylus is pressed against a window. However, dragging the stylus from one window to the next doesn't cause the new window to receive the input focus. The down tap sets the focus, not the process of dragging the stylus across a window. When the stylus is dragged outside the window, that window stops receiving *WM_MOUSEMOVE* messages but retains input focus. Because the tip of the stylus is still down, no other window receives the *WM_MOUSEMOVE* messages. This is akin to using a mouse and dragging the mouse outside a window with a button held down.

To continue to receive mouse messages even if the stylus moves off its window, an application can call

```
HWND SetCapture (HWND hWnd);
```

passing the handle of the window to receive the mouse messages. The function returns the handle of the window that previously had captured the mouse or *NULL* if the mouse wasn't previously captured. To stop receiving the mouse messages initiated by stylus input, the window calls

```
BOOL ReleaseCapture (void);
```

Only one window can capture the stylus input at any one time. To determine whether the stylus has been captured, an application can call

```
HWND GetCapture (void);
```

which returns the handle of the window that has captured the stylus input or 0 if no window has captured the stylus input—although please note one caveat: *the window that has captured the stylus must be in the same thread context as the window calling the function*. This limitation means that if the stylus has been captured by a window in another application, *GetCapture* still returns 0.

If a window has captured the stylus input and another window calls *GetCapture*, the window that had originally captured the stylus receives a *WM_CAPTURECHANGED* message. The *lParam* parameter of the message contains the handle of the window that gained the capture. You shouldn't attempt to take back the capture by calling *GetCapture* in response to this message. In general, because the stylus is a shared resource, applications should be wary of capturing the stylus for any length of time and should be able to handle gracefully any loss of capture.

Another interesting tidbit: just because a window captures the mouse/stylus, that doesn't prevent a tap on another window from gaining the input focus for that window. You can use other methods for preventing the change of input focus, but in almost all cases, it's better to let the user, not the applications, decide which top-level window should have the input focus.

Right-Button Clicks

When you click the right mouse button on an object in Windows systems, the action typically calls up a context menu, a stand-alone menu displaying a set of choices for what you can do with that particular object. On a system with a mouse, Windows sends *WM_RBUTTONDOWN* and *WM_RBUTTONUP* messages indicating a right-button click. When you use a stylus, you don't have a right button.

Windows CE user interface guidelines specify that a tap-and-hold gesture be used to simulate a right mouse click. The function *SHRecognizeGesture* can be used during the processing of a WM_LBUTTONDOWN message to detect a tap and hold. The function is prototyped as

```
WINSHELLAPI DWORD SHRecognizeGesture(SHRGINFO *shrg);
```

The only parameter is the address of a *SHRGINFO* structure defined as

```
typedef struct tagSHRGI {
    DWORD cbSize;
    HWND hwndClient;
    POINT ptDown;
    DWORD dwFlags;
} SHRGINFO, *PSHRGINFO;
```

The *cbSize* field must be filled with the size of the structure. The *hwndClient* field should be set to the handle of the window that is calling the function. The *ptDown* field is a structure that should be filled with the point where the gesture is being recognized. The *dwFlags* can contain a number of flags. The *SHRG_RETURNCMD* flag causes the function to return *GN_CONTEXTMENU* if the user properly gestures with a tap and hold or zero otherwise. The *SHRG_NOTIFYPARENT* flag causes a *WM_NOTIFY* message to be sent to the parent window if the gesture is properly recognized. Finally, the *SHRG_LONGDELAY* flag requires the user to hold the tap for a longer period of time before the gesture is recognized.

The TicTac1 Example Program

To demonstrate stylus programming, I have written a trivial tic-tac-toe game. The TicTac1 window is shown in Figure 3-4. The source code for the program is shown in Listing 3-3. This program doesn't allow you to play the game against the computer, nor does it determine the end of the game—it simply draws the board and keeps track of the X's and O's. Nevertheless, it demonstrates basic stylus interaction.

FIGURE 3-4 The TicTac1 window

LISTING 3-3 The TicTac1 program

TicTac1.h

```
//======================================================================
// Header file
//
// Written for the book Programming Windows CE
// Copyright (C) 2007 Douglas Boling
//======================================================================
// Returns number of elements
#define dim(x) (sizeof(x) / sizeof(x[0]))
//----------------------------------------------------------------------
// Generic defines and data types
//
struct decodeUINT {                             // Structure associates
    UINT Code;                                  // messages
                                                // with a function.
    LRESULT (*Fxn)(HWND, UINT, WPARAM, LPARAM);
};

//----------------------------------------------------------------------
// Function prototypes
//
HWND InitInstance (HINSTANCE, LPWSTR, int);
int TermInstance (HINSTANCE, int);

// Window procedures
LRESULT CALLBACK MainWndProc (HWND, UINT, WPARAM, LPARAM);

// Message handlers
 LRESULT DoSizeMain (HWND, UINT, WPARAM, LPARAM);
LRESULT DoPaintMain (HWND, UINT, WPARAM, LPARAM);
LRESULT DoLButtonDownMain (HWND, UINT, WPARAM, LPARAM);
LRESULT DoLButtonUpMain (HWND, UINT, WPARAM, LPARAM);
LRESULT DoDestroyMain (HWND, UINT, WPARAM, LPARAM);
```

```
// Game function prototypes
void DrawXO (HDC hdc, HPEN hPen, RECT *prect, INT nCell, INT nType);
void DrawBoard (HDC hdc, RECT *prect);
```

TicTac1.cpp

```
//======================================================================
// TicTac1 - Simple tic-tac-toe game
//
// Written for the book Programming Windows CE
// Copyright (C) 2007 Douglas Boling
//
//======================================================================
#include <windows.h>                    // For all that Windows stuff
#include <commctrl.h>                   // Command bar includes
#include "tictac1.h"                    // Program-specific stuff

//----------------------------------------------------------------------
// Global data
//
const TCHAR szAppName[] = TEXT ("TicTac1");
HINSTANCE hInst;                        // Program instance handle

// State data for game
RECT rectBoard = {0, 0, 0, 0};          // Used to place game board.
RECT rectPrompt;                        // Used to place prompt.
BYTE bBoard[9];                         // Keeps track of X's and O's.
BYTE bTurn = 0;                         // Keeps track of the turn.

// Message dispatch table for MainWindowProc
const struct decodeUINT MainMessages[] = {
    WM_SIZE, DoSizeMain,
    WM_PAINT, DoPaintMain,
    WM_LBUTTONUP, DoLButtonUpMain,
    WM_DESTROY, DoDestroyMain,
};

//======================================================================
//
// Program entry point
//
int WINAPI WinMain (HINSTANCE hInstance, HINSTANCE hPrevInstance,
                    LPWSTR lpCmdLine, int nCmdShow) {
    MSG msg;
    HWND hwndMain;

    // Initialize this instance.
    hwndMain = InitInstance (hInstance, lpCmdLine, nCmdShow);
    if (hwndMain == 0)
        return 0x10;
    // Application message loop
```

```
    while (GetMessage (&msg, NULL, 0, 0)) {
        TranslateMessage (&msg);
        DispatchMessage (&msg);
    }
    // Instance cleanup
    return TermInstance (hInstance, msg.wParam);
}
//----------------------------------------------------------------------
// InitInstance - Instance initialization
//
HWND InitInstance (HINSTANCE hInstance, LPWSTR lpCmdLine, int nCmdShow) {
    WNDCLASS wc;
    HWND hWnd;

    // Save program instance handle in global variable.
    hInst = hInstance;

#if defined(WIN32_PLATFORM_PSPC) || defined(WIN32_PLATFORM_WFSP)
    // If Windows Mobile, allow only one instance of the application.
    hWnd = FindWindow (szAppName, NULL);
    if (hWnd) {
        SetForegroundWindow ((HWND)(((DWORD)hWnd) | 0x01));
        return 0;
    }
#endif
    // Register application main window class.
    wc.style = 0;                             // Window style
    wc.lpfnWndProc = MainWndProc;             // Callback function
    wc.cbClsExtra = 0;                        // Extra class data
    wc.cbWndExtra = 0;                        // Extra window data
    wc.hInstance = hInstance;                 // Owner handle
    wc.hIcon = NULL,                          // Application icon
    wc.hCursor = LoadCursor (NULL, IDC_ARROW);// Default cursor
    wc.hbrBackground = (HBRUSH) GetStockObject (WHITE_BRUSH);
    wc.lpszMenuName =  NULL;                  // Menu name
    wc.lpszClassName = szAppName;             // Window class name

    if (RegisterClass (&wc) == 0) return 0;

    // Create main window.
    hWnd = CreateWindowEx (WS_EX_NODRAG, szAppName, TEXT ("TicTac1"),
                         WS_VISIBLE | WS_CAPTION | WS_SYSMENU,
                         CW_USEDEFAULT, CW_USEDEFAULT,
                         CW_USEDEFAULT, CW_USEDEFAULT,
                         NULL, NULL, hInstance, NULL);
    // Return fail code if window not created.
    if (!IsWindow (hWnd)) return 0;

    // Standard show and update calls
    ShowWindow (hWnd, nCmdShow);
    UpdateWindow (hWnd);
    return hWnd;
}
//----------------------------------------------------------------------
```

```
// TermInstance - Program cleanup
//
 int TermInstance (HINSTANCE hInstance, int nDefRC) {

    return nDefRC;
}
//======================================================================
// Message handling procedures for MainWindow
//
//----------------------------------------------------------------------
// MainWndProc - Callback function for application window
//
LRESULT CALLBACK MainWndProc (HWND hWnd, UINT wMsg, WPARAM wParam,
                              LPARAM lParam) {
    INT i;
    //
    // Search message list to see if we need to handle this
    // message. If in list, call procedure.
    //
    for (i = 0; i < dim(MainMessages); i++) {
        if (wMsg == MainMessages[i].Code)
            return (*MainMessages[i].Fxn)(hWnd, wMsg, wParam, lParam);
    }
    return DefWindowProc(hWnd, wMsg, wParam, lParam);
}
//----------------------------------------------------------------------
// DoSizeMain - Process WM_SIZE message for window.
//
LRESULT DoSizeMain (HWND hWnd, UINT wMsg, WPARAM wParam,
                    LPARAM lParam) {
    RECT rect;
    INT i;
    // Adjust the size of the client rect to take into account
    // the command bar height.
    GetClientRect (hWnd, &rect);

    // Initialize the board rectangle if not yet initialized.
    if (rectBoard.right == 0) {

        // Initialize the board.
        for (i = 0; i < dim(bBoard); i++)
            bBoard[i] = 0;
    }
    // Define the playing board rect.
    rectBoard = rect;
    rectPrompt = rect;
    // Layout depends on portrait or landscape screen.
    if (rect.right - rect.left > rect.bottom - rect.top) {
        rectBoard.left += 20;
        rectBoard.top += 10;
        rectBoard.bottom -= 10;
        rectBoard.right = rectBoard.bottom - rectBoard.top + 10;

        rectPrompt.left = rectBoard.right + 10;
```

```
    } else {
        rectBoard.left += 20;
        rectBoard.right -= 20;
        rectBoard.top += 10;
        rectBoard.bottom = rectBoard.right - rectBoard.left + 10;

        rectPrompt.top = rectBoard.bottom + 10;
    }
    return 0;
}

//----------------------------------------------------------------------
// DoPaintMain - Process WM_PAINT message for window.
//
LRESULT DoPaintMain (HWND hWnd, UINT wMsg, WPARAM wParam,
                     LPARAM lParam) {
    PAINTSTRUCT ps;
    RECT rect;
    HFONT hFont, hOldFont;
    HDC hdc;

    GetClientRect (hWnd, &rect);

    hdc = BeginPaint (hWnd, &ps);

    // Draw the board.
    DrawBoard (hdc, &rectBoard);

    // Write the prompt to the screen.
    hFont = (HFONT)GetStockObject (SYSTEM_FONT);
    hOldFont = (HFONT)SelectObject (hdc, hFont);
    if (bTurn == 0)
        DrawText (hdc, TEXT (« X's turn»), -1, &rectPrompt,
                  DT_CENTER | DT_VCENTER | DT_SINGLELINE);
    else
        DrawText (hdc, TEXT (« O's turn»), -1, &rectPrompt,
                  DT_CENTER | DT_VCENTER | DT_SINGLELINE);

    SelectObject (hdc, hOldFont);
    EndPaint (hWnd, &ps);
    return 0;
}
//----------------------------------------------------------------------
// DoLButtonUpMain - Process WM_LBUTTONUP message for window.
//
LRESULT DoLButtonUpMain (HWND hWnd, UINT wMsg, WPARAM wParam,
                         LPARAM lParam) {
    POINT pt;
    INT cx, cy, nCell = 0;

    pt.x = LOWORD (lParam);
    pt.y = HIWORD (lParam);
    // See if pen on board.  If so, determine which cell.
```

```
    if (PtInRect (&rectBoard, pt)){
        // Normalize point to upper left corner of board.
        pt.x -= rectBoard.left;
        pt.y -= rectBoard.top;

        // Compute size of each cell.
        cx = (rectBoard.right - rectBoard.left)/3;
        cy = (rectBoard.bottom - rectBoard.top)/3;

        // Find column.
        nCell = (pt.x / cx);
        // Find row.
        nCell += (pt.y / cy) * 3;

        // If cell empty, fill it with mark.
        if (bBoard[nCell] == 0) {
            if (bTurn) {
                bBoard[nCell] = 2;
                bTurn = 0;
            } else {
                bBoard[nCell] = 1;
                bTurn = 1;
            }
            InvalidateRect (hWnd, NULL, FALSE);
        } else {
            // Inform the user of the filled cell.
            MessageBeep (0);
            return 0;
        }
    }
    return 0;
}
//----------------------------------------------------------------------
// DoDestroyMain - Process WM_DESTROY message for window.
//
LRESULT DoDestroyMain (HWND hWnd, UINT wMsg, WPARAM wParam,
                       LPARAM lParam) {
    PostQuitMessage (0);
    return 0;
}
//======================================================================
// Game-specific routines
//
//----------------------------------------------------------------------
// DrawXO - Draw a single X or O in a square.
//
void DrawXO (HDC hdc, HPEN hPen, RECT *prect, INT nCell, INT nType) {
    POINT pt[2];
    INT cx, cy;
    RECT rect;

    cx = (prect->right - prect->left)/3;
    cy = (prect->bottom - prect->top)/3;
```

```
    // Compute the dimensions of the target cell.
    rect.left = (cx * (nCell % 3) + prect->left) + 10;
    rect.right = rect.right =  rect.left + cx - 20;
    rect.top = cy * (nCell / 3) + prect->top + 10;
    rect.bottom = rect.top + cy - 20;

    // Draw an X ?
    if (nType == 1) {
        pt[0].x = rect.left;
        pt[0].y = rect.top;
        pt[1].x = rect.right;
        pt[1].y = rect.bottom;
        Polyline (hdc, pt, 2);

        pt[0].x = rect.right;
        pt[1].x = rect.left;
        Polyline (hdc, pt, 2);
    // How about an O ?
    } else if (nType == 2) {
        Ellipse (hdc, rect.left, rect.top, rect.right, rect.bottom);
    }
    return;
}
//----------------------------------------------------------------------
// DrawBoard - Draw the tic-tac-toe board.
//  VK_MENU
void DrawBoard (HDC hdc, RECT *prect) {
    HPEN hPen, hOldPen;
    POINT pt[2];
    LOGPEN lp;
    INT i, cx, cy;

    // Create a nice thick pen.
    lp.lopnStyle = PS_SOLID;
    lp.lopnWidth.x = 5;
    lp.lopnWidth.y = 5;
    lp.lopnColor = RGB (0, 0, 0);
    hPen = CreatePenIndirect (&lp);

    hOldPen = (HPEN)SelectObject (hdc, hPen);

    cx = (prect->right - prect->left)/3;
    cy = (prect->bottom - prect->top)/3;

    // Draw lines down.
    pt[0].x = cx + prect->left;
    pt[1].x = cx + prect->left;
    pt[0].y = prect->top;
    pt[1].y = prect->bottom;
    Polyline (hdc, pt, 2);
    pt[0].x += cx;
    pt[1].x += cx;
    Polyline (hdc, pt, 2);
```

```
    // Draw lines across.
    pt[0].x = prect->left;
    pt[1].x = prect->right;
    pt[0].y = cy + prect->top;
    pt[1].y = cy + prect->top;
    Polyline (hdc, pt, 2);

    pt[0].y += cy;
    pt[1].y += cy;
    Polyline (hdc, pt, 2);

    // Fill in X's and O's.
    for (i = 0; i < dim (bBoard); i++)
        DrawXO (hdc, hPen, &rectBoard, i, bBoard[i]);

    SelectObject (hdc, hOldPen);
    DeleteObject (hPen);
    return;
}
```

The action in TicTac1 is centered around three routines: *DrawBoard*, *DrawXO*, and *DoLButtonUpMain*. The first two perform the tasks of drawing the playing board. The routine that determines the location of a tap on the board (and therefore is more relevant to your current train of thought) is *DoLButtonUpMain*. As the name suggests, this routine is called in response to a *WM_LBUTTONUP* message. The first action to take is to call

```
BOOL PtInRect (const RECT *lprc, POINT pt);
```

which determines whether the tap is even on the game board. The program knows the location of the tap because it's passed in the *lParam* value of the message. The board rectangle is computed when the program starts in *DoSizeMain*. Once the tap is localized to the board, the program determines the location of the relevant cell within the playing board by dividing the coordinates of the tap point within the board by the number of cells across and down.

It was mentioned that the board rectangle was computed during the *DoSizeMain* routine, which is called in response to a *WM_SIZE* message. While it might seem strange that Windows CE supports the *WM_SIZE* message common to other versions of Windows, it needs to support this message because a window is sized frequently: first immediately after it's created, and then each time it's minimized and restored. You might think that another possibility for determining the size of the window would be during the *WM_CREATE* message. The *lParam* parameter points to a *CREATESTRUCT* structure that contains, among other things, the initial size and position of the window. The problem with using those numbers is that the size obtained is the total size of the window, not the size of the client area, which is what we need. Under Windows CE, most windows have no title bar and no border, but some have both, and many have scroll bars, so using these values can cause trouble.

Another reason for the *WM_SIZE* message is that many Windows CE devices have screens that can switch between landscape and portrait orientations. When the screen dimensions change, the system resizes the top-level application windows. This resizing results in a *WM_SIZE* message that gives each application the opportunity to adjust its window contents to fit the new configuration.

So now, with the TicTac1 example, you have a simple program that uses the stylus effectively but isn't complete. To restart the game, you must exit and restart TicTac1. You can't take back a move or have O start first. You need a method for sending these commands to the program. Sure, using keys would work. Another solution would be to create hot spots on the screen that, when tapped, provide the input necessary. Clearly this example needs some extra pieces to make it complete. I've taken the discussion of Windows as far as I can without a more complete discussion of the basic component of the operating system, the windows themselves. It's time to take a closer look at windows, child windows, and controls.

Chapter 4
Windows, Controls, and Menus

Understanding how windows work and relate to each other is the key to understanding the user interface of the Microsoft Windows operating system, whether it be Microsoft Windows XP, Windows Vista, or Microsoft Windows CE. Everything you see on a Windows display is a window. The desktop is a window, the taskbar is a window, even the Start button on the taskbar is a window. Windows are related to one another according to one relationship model or another; they may be in *parent/child*, *sibling*, or *owner/owned* relationships. Windows supports a number of predefined window classes called *controls*. These controls simplify the work of programmers by providing a range of predefined user interface elements as simple as a button or as complex as a multiline text editor. Windows CE supports the same standard set of built-in controls as the other versions of Windows. These built-in controls shouldn't be confused with the complex controls provided by the common control library. Those controls are covered in the next chapter.

Child Windows

Each window is connected via a parent/child relationship scheme. Applications create a main window with no parent, called a *top-level window*. That window might (or might not) contain windows, called *child* windows. A child window is clipped to its parent. That is, no part of a child window is visible beyond the edge of its parent. Child windows are automatically destroyed when their parent windows are destroyed. Also, when a parent window moves, its child windows move with it.

Child windows are programmatically identical to top-level windows. You use the *CreateWindow* or *CreateWindowEx* function to create them, each has a window procedure that handles the same messages as its top-level window, and each can, in turn, contain its own child windows. To create a child window, use the *WS_CHILD* window style in the *dwStyle* parameter of *CreateWindow* or *CreateWindowEx*. In addition, the *hMenu* parameter, unused in top-level Windows CE windows, passes an ID value that you can use to reference the window.

In addition to the parent/child relationship, windows also have an owner/ owned relationship. Owned windows aren't clipped to their owners. However, they always appear "above" (in z-order) the window that owns them. If the owner window is minimized, all windows it owns are hidden. Likewise, if a window is destroyed, all windows it owns are destroyed.

Window Management Functions

Given the windows-centric nature of Windows, it's not surprising that you can choose from a number of functions that enable a window to interrogate its environment so that it might determine its location in the window family tree. To find its parent, a window can call

```
HWND GetParent (HWND hWnd);
```

This function is passed a window handle and returns the handle of the calling window's parent window. If the window has no parent, the function returns *NULL*.

Enumerating Windows

GetWindow, prototyped as

```
HWND GetWindow (HWND hWnd, UINT uCmd);
```

is a multi-use function that allows a window to query its children, owner, and siblings. The first parameter is the window's handle, while the second is a constant that indicates the requested relationship. The *GW_CHILD* constant returns a handle to the first child window of a window. *GetWindow* returns windows in z-order, so the first window in this case is the child window highest in the z-order. If the window has no child windows, this function returns *NULL*. The two constants, *GW_HWNDFIRST* and *GW_HWNDLAST*, return the first and last windows in the z-order. If the window handle passed is a top-level window, these constants return the first and last topmost windows in the z-order. If the window passed is a child window, the *GetWindow* function returns the first and last sibling window. The *GW_HWNDNEXT* and *GW_HWNDPREV* constants return the next lower and next higher windows in the z-order. These constants allow a window to iterate through all the sibling windows by getting the next window, then using that window handle with another call to *GetWindow* to get the next, and so on. Finally, the *GW_OWNER* constant returns the handle of the owner of a window.

Another way to iterate through a series of windows is

```
BOOL EnumWindows (WNDENUMPROC lpEnumFunc, LPARAM lParam);
```

This function calls the callback function pointed to by *lpEnumFunc* once for each top-level window on the desktop, passing the handle of each window in turn. The *lParam* value is an application-defined value, which is also passed to the enumeration function. This function is better than iterating through a *GetWindow* loop to find the top-level windows because it always returns valid window handles. It's possible that a *GetWindow* iteration loop will get a window handle whose window is destroyed before the next call to *GetWindow* can occur. However, because *EnumWindows* works only with top-level windows, *GetWindow* still has a place when a program is iterating through a series of child windows.

Finding a Window

To get the handle of a specific window, use the function

```
HWND FindWindow (LPCTSTR lpClassName, LPCTSTR lpWindowName);
```

This function can find a window either by means of its window class name or by means of a window's title text. This function is handy when an application is just starting up; it can determine whether another copy of the application is already running. All an application has to do is call *FindWindow* with the name of the window class for the main window of the application. Because the first job of almost every application is to create its main window, a *NULL* returned by *FindWindow* indicates that the function can't locate another window with the specified window class—therefore, it's almost certain that another copy of the application isn't running.

You can find the handle to the desktop window by using the function

```
HWND GetDesktopWindow (void);
```

Moving a Window

SetWindowPos is one of those functions used all the time in Windows. It allows the application to move, size, change the z-order of, and even cause the system to redraw the nonclient area of the window. Its prototype is

```
BOOL SetWindowPos (HWND hWnd, HWND hWndInsertAfter, int X, int Y,
                   int cx, int cy, UINT uFlags);
```

The first parameter is the handle of the window that will be changed. The *hWndInsertAfter* parameter optionally allows the function to set the z-order of the window. This parameter can be either a window handle or one of four flags that position the window either at the top or the bottom of the z-order. The flags are shown here:

- **HWND_BOTTOM** The window underneath all windows on the desktop
- **HWND_TOP** The window on top of all windows
- **HWND_TOPMOST** The window to always be placed on top of other windows, even when the window is deactivated
- **HWND_NOTTOPMOST** The window on top of all other nontopmost windows but not marked as a topmost window so that it will be covered when another window is activated

The *X*, *Y*, *cx*, and *cy* parameters optionally specify the position and size of the window. The flags parameter contains one or more flags that describe the task to accomplish. The flags are as follows:

- **SWP_NOMOVE** Don't move the window.
- **SWP_NOSIZE** Don't resize the window.
- **SWP_NOZORDER** Don't set the window's z-order.
- **SWP_NOACTIVATE** If the z-order is set, don't activate the window.
- **SWP_DRAWFRAME** Redraw the nonclient area.
- **SWP_FRAMECHANGED** Recalculate the nonclient area, and then redraw.

Two other flags, *SWP_SHOWWINDOW* and *SWP_HIDEWINDOW*, show and hide the window, but it's easier to call the *ShowWindow* function to show or hide a window. To use *SetWindowPos* to force the frame to be redrawn after the style bits are changed, the call is

```
SetWindowPos (hWnd, 0, 0, 0, 0, 0,
              SWP_NOMOVE | SWP_NOSIZE | SWP_NOZORDER | SWP_FRAMECHANGED);
```

Editing the Window Structure Values

The pair of functions

```
LONG GetWindowLong (HWND hWnd, int nIndex);
```

and

```
LONG SetWindowLong (HWND hWnd, int nIndex, LONG dwNewLong);
```

allow an application to edit data in the window structure for a window. Remember that the *WNDCLASS* structure passed to the *RegisterClass* function has a field, *cbWndExtra*, that controls the number of extra bytes that are to be allocated after the structure. If you allocate extra space in the window structure when the window class is registered, you can access those bytes using the *GetWindowLong* and *SetWindowLong* functions. The data must be allocated and referenced in 4-byte (integer-sized and aligned) blocks. So if a window class was registered with 12 in the *cbWndExtra* field, an application can access those bytes by calling *GetWindowLong* or *SetWindowLong* with the window handle and by setting the values 0, 4, and 8 in the *nIndex* parameter.

GetWindowLong and *SetWindowLong* support a set of predefined index values that allow an application access to some of the basic parameters of a window. Here is a list of the supported values for Windows CE.

- **GWL_STYLE** The style flags for the window
- **GWL_EXSTYLE** The extended style flags for the window

- **GWL_WNDPROC** The pointer to the window procedure for the window
- **GWL_ID** The ID value for the window
- **GWL_USERDATA** An application-usable 32-bit value

Dialog box windows support the following additional values:

- **DWL_DLGPROC** The pointer to the dialog procedure for the window
- **DWL_MSGRESULT** The value returned when the dialog box function returns
- **DWL_USER** An application-usable 32-bit value

Windows CE doesn't support the *GWL_HINSTANCE* and *GWL_HWNDPARENT* values supported by Windows XP and Windows Vista.

Changing the Style Flags

Editing the window structure can be useful in a number of ways. The style bits of a window can be changed after the window is created to change its default actions and look. For example, the title bar of a window can be shown or hidden by toggling the *WS_CAPTION* style bit. After changing any style flag that modifies the look of the window, it's customary to force the system to redraw the nonclient area of the window with a call to *SetWindowPos*. When the *style* or *exstyle* flags are changed, Windows CE sends a *WM_STYLECHANGED* message to the window.

Subclassing a Window

Another use of *SetWindowLong* is to subclass a window. Subclassing a window allows an application to essentially derive an instance of a new window class from a preexisting window class. The classic use for subclassing is to modify the behavior of a window control, such as an edit control.

The process of subclassing is actually quite simple. A window procedure is created that provides only the new functionality required of the subclassed window. A window is then created using the base window class. *GetWindowLong* is called to get and save the pointer to the original window procedure for the window. *SetWindowLong* is then called to set the window procedure for this instance of the window to the new window procedure. The new window procedure then receives the message sent to the window. Any messages not acted upon by the new window procedure are passed on to the old window procedure with the function *CallWindowProc*. The following code shows a window being created and then subclassed. The subclass procedure then intercepts the *WM_LBUTTONDOWN* message and beeps the speaker when the window receives that message.

```
// Prototype of subclass procedure
LRESULT CALLBACK SCWndProc(HWND hWnd, UINT wMsg, WPARAM wParam,
                           LPARAM lParam);
```

```
// Variable that holds the pointer to the original WndProc
WNDPROC lpfnOldProc = 0;
//
// Routine that subclasses the requested window.
//
BOOL SubClassThisWnd (HWND hwndSC) {

    if (lpfnOldProc == 0) {
        // Get and save the pointer to the original window procedure
        lpfnOldProc = (WNDPROC)GetWindowLong (hwndSC, GWL_WNDPROC);

        // Point to new window procedure
        return SetWindowLong (hwndSC, GWL_WNDPROC, (DWORD)SCWndProc);
    }
    return FALSE;
}
//
// Subclass procedure
//
LRESULT CALLBACK SCWndProc(HWND hWnd, UINT wMsg, WPARAM wParam,
                           LPARAM lParam) {
    switch (wMsg) {

    case WM_LBUTTONDOWN:
        MessageBeep(0);
        break;
    }
    return CallWindowProc (lpfnOldProc, hWnd, wMsg, wParam, lParam);
}
```

To un-subclass the window, the program simply calls *SetWindowLong* to set the *WndProc* pointer back to the original window procedure.

Windows Controls

Were it not for the Windows Control library, programming Windows applications would be a slow and arduous process. In addition, every application would have its own look and feel. This would force the user to learn a new way of working with each new application. Fortunately, this scenario is avoided with an assortment of controls that the operating system provides. In short, controls are simply predefined window classes. Each has a custom window procedure supplied by Windows that gives each of these controls a tightly defined user and programming interface.

Working with Controls

Because a control is just another window, it can be created with a call to *CreateWindow* or *CreateWindowEx*. Controls notify their parent window of events via *WM_COMMAND* messages encoding events and the ID and window handle of the control encoded in the parameters of the message.

Like all messages, *WM_COMMAND* contains two generic parameters, *wParam* and *lParam*. For a *WM_COMMAND* message, the high word of *wParam* contains the notification code, the reason for the *WM_COMMAND* message being sent. The low word of *wParam* contains the ID value of the control that sent the message. The ID is a word that's typically defined when the control is created and, to be useful, should be unique among all the sibling windows of the control. The *lParam* value contains the handle of the child window that sent the control. In general, it's easier to track the source of a *WM_COMMAND* message though the control ID rather than the window handle of the control, but both are available in the message. The following code is typical of the first few lines of a *WM_COMMAND* handler:

```
case WM_COMMAND:
    WORD idItem, wNotifyCode;
    HWND hwndCtl;

    // Parse the parameters.
    idItem = (WORD) LOWORD (wParam);
    wNotifyCode = (WORD) HIWORD(wParam);
    hwndCtl = (HWND) lParam;
```

From this point, the *WM_COMMAND* handler typically uses the ID of the control and then uses the notification code to determine why the *WM_COMMAND* message was sent.

Controls can also be configured and manipulated using predefined messages sent to the control. Among other things, applications can set the state of buttons, add items to or delete items from list boxes, and set the selection of text in edit boxes, all by sending messages to the controls. Controls are typically indentified by their ID, but many Windows functions require the handle of the control. The *GetDlgItem* function provides a simple conversion. The function is prototyped as

```
HWND GetDlgItem (HWND hDlg, int nIDDlgItem);
```

The two parameters are the handle of the parent window of the control and the ID value for the control. Although the name implies that the function can be used only in dialog boxes, something discussed in Chapter 6, "Dialog Boxes and Property Sheets," it works quite fine for a control in any window.

Another convenient function you can use to send a message to a control is *SendDlgItemMessage*. This function sends a message to a child window with a specific ID. The prototype of the message is shown here:

```
LONG SendDlgItemMessage (HWND hParent, int nIDChild, UINT Msg,
                         WPARAM wParam, LPARAM lParam);
```

The parameters are similar to those for *SendMessage*. In fact, the following code is functionally identical to that of *SendDlgItemMessage*:

```
LONG SendMessage (GetDlgItem (hParent, nIDChild), Msg, wParam, lParam);
```

The only difference is the convenience of not having to embed the *GetDlgItem* call within *SendMessage*.

There are six predefined window control classes. They are:

- **Button** A wide variety of buttons
- **Edit** A window that can be used to enter or display text
- **List** A window that contains a list of strings
- **Combo** A combination edit box and list box
- **Static** A window that displays text or graphics that a user can't change
- **Scroll bar** A scroll bar not attached to a specific window

Each of these controls has a wide range of function, far too much to cover completely in this chapter. But the following is a quick review of these controls, with a mention at least of the highlights.

Button Controls

Button controls enable several forms of input to the program. Buttons come in many styles, including push buttons, check boxes, and radio buttons. Each style is designed for a specific use—for example, push buttons are designed for receiving momentary input, check boxes are designed for on/off input, and radio buttons allow a user to select one of a number of choices.

Push Buttons

In general, push buttons are used to invoke some action. When a user presses a push button using a stylus, the button sends a *WM_COMMAND* message with a *BN_CLICKED* (for button notification clicked) notify code in the high word of the *wParam* parameter.

Check Boxes

Check boxes display a square box and a label that asks the user to specify a choice. A check box retains its state, either checked or unchecked, until the user clicks it again or the program forces the button to change state. In addition to the standard *BS_CHECKBOX* style, check boxes can come in a three-state style, *BS_3STATE*, that allows the button to be disabled and shown grayed out. Two additional styles, *BS_AUTOCHECKBOX* and *BS_AUTO3STATE*, automatically update the state and look of the control to reflect the checked, the unchecked, and, in the case of the three-state check box, the disabled state.

As with push buttons, check boxes send a *BN_CLICKED* notification when the button is clicked. Unless the check box has one of the automatic styles, it's the responsibility of the application to manually change the state of the button. This can be done by sending a *BM_SETCHECK* message to the button with the *wParam* set to 0 to uncheck the button or 1 to check the button. The three-state check boxes have a third, disabled, state that can be set by means of the *BM_SETCHECK* message with the *wParam* value set to 2. An application can determine the current state using the *BM_GETCHECK* message.

Radio Buttons

Radio buttons allow a user to select from a number of choices. Radio buttons are grouped in a set, with only one item of the set ever being checked at a time. If it's using the standard *BS_RADIOBUTTON* style, the application is responsible for checking and unchecking the radio buttons so that only one is checked at a time. However, like check boxes, radio buttons have an alternative style, *BS_AUTORADIOBUTTON*, that automatically maintains the group of buttons so that only one is checked.

Customizing the Appearance of a Button

You can further customize the appearance of the buttons described so far by using a number of additional styles. The styles, *BS_RIGHT*, *BS_LEFT*, *BS_BOTTOM*, and *BS_TOP*, allow you to position the button text in a place other than the default center of the button. The *BS_MULTILINE* style allows you to specify more than one line of text in the button. The text is flowed to fit within the button. The newline character (\n) in the button text can be used to specifically define where line breaks occur. Windows CE doesn't support the *BS_ICON* and *BS_BITMAP* button styles supported by other versions of Windows.

Owner-Draw Buttons

You can totally control the look of a button by specifying the *BS_OWNERDRAW* style. When a button is specified as owner-draw, its owner window is entirely responsible for drawing the button for all the states in which it might occur. When a window contains an owner-draw button, it's sent a *WM_DRAWITEM* message to inform it that a button needs to be drawn. For this message, the *wParam* parameter contains the ID value for the button and the *lParam* parameter points to a *DRAWITEMSTRUCT* structure defined as

```
typedef struct tagDRAWITEMSTRUCT {
    UINT  CtlType;
    UINT  CtlID;
    UINT  itemID;
    UINT  itemAction;
    UINT  itemState;
    HWND  hwndItem;
    HDC   hDC;
    RECT  rcItem;
    DWORD itemData;
} DRAWITEMSTRUCT;
```

The *CtlType* field is set to *ODT_BUTTON*, while the *CtlID* field, like the *wParam* parameter, contains the button's ID value. The *itemAction* field contains flags that indicate what needs to be drawn and why. The most significant of these fields is *itemState*, which contains the state (selected, disabled, and so forth) of the button. The *hDC* field contains the device context handle for the button window, while the *rcItem* RECT contains the dimensions of the button. The *itemData* field is *NULL* for owner-draw buttons.

As you might expect, the *WM_DRAWITEM* handler contains a number of GDI calls to draw lines, rectangles, and whatever else is needed to render the button. An important aspect of drawing a button is matching the standard colors of the other windows in the system. Because these colors can change, they shouldn't be hard coded. You can query to find out which are the proper colors by using the function

```
DWORD GetSysColor (int nIndex);
```

This function returns an RGB color value for the colors defined for different aspects of windows and controls in the system. Among a number of predefined index values passed in the index parameter, an index of *COLOR_BTNFACE* returns the proper color for the face of a button, while *COLOR_BTNSHADOW* returns the dark color for creating the three-dimensional look of a button.

One function often used in owner-draw buttons is the function

```
BOOL DrawFocusRect (HDC hDC, const RECT* lprc);
```

DrawFocusRect draws a dashed-line rectangle that is used by buttons to indicate they have the focus. The two paramters are the device context handle and a pointer to a RECT structure that delinates the dimensions of the target rectangle.

The Edit Control

The edit control is a window that allows the user to type and edit text. As you might imagine, the edit control is one of the handiest controls in the Windows control pantheon. The edit control is equipped with full editing capability, including cut, copy, and paste interaction with the system clipboard, all without assistance from the application. Edit controls display a single line or, when the *ES_MULTILINE* style is specified, multiple lines of text. The Notepad accessory, provided with the desktop versions of Windows, is simply a top-level window that contains a multiline edit control.

The edit control has a few other features that should be mentioned. An edit control with the *ES_PASSWORD* style displays an asterisk (*) character by default in the control for each character typed; the control saves the real character. The *ES_READONLY* style protects the text contained in the control so that it can be read or copied into the clipboard, but not modified.

The *ES_LOWERCASE* and *ES_UPPERCASE* styles force characters entered into the control to be changed to the specified case.

You can add text to an edit control by using the *WM_SETTEXT* message and retrieve text by using the *WM_GETTEXT* message. Selection can be controlled using the *EM_SETSEL* message. This message specifies the starting and ending characters in the selected area. Other messages allow the position of the caret (the marker that indicates the current entry point in an edit field) to be queried and set. Multiline edit controls contain a number of additional messages to control scrolling as well as to access characters by line and column position.

The List Box Control

The list box control displays a list of text items so that the user might select one or more of the items within the list. The list box stores the text, optionally sorts the items, and manages the display of the items, including scrolling. List boxes can be configured to allow selection of a single item or multiple items, or to prevent any selection at all.

You can add an item to a list box by sending an *LB_ADDSTRING* or *LB_INSERTSTRING* message to the control, passing a pointer to the string to add the *lParam* parameter. The *LB_ADDSTRING* message places the newly added string at the end of the list of items, while *LB_INSERTSTRING* can place the string anywhere within the list of items in the list box. The list box can be searched for a particular item using the *LB_FIND* message.

Selection status can be queried using *LB_GETCURSEL* for single-selection list boxes. For multiple-selection list boxes, *LB_GETSELCOUNT* and *LB_GETSELITEMS* can be used to retrieve the items currently selected. Items in the list box can be selected programmatically using the *LB_SETCURSEL* and *LB_SETSEL* messages.

Starting with Windows CE 6, the list box control supports owner-draw list boxes. To implement an owner-draw list box, use the *LBS_OWNERDRAWFIXED* or *LBS_OWNERDRAWVARIABLE* style flags depending upon whether the items will all be the same height or varying heights. Like owner-draw buttons, the owner window then receives *WM_OWNERDRAW* messages to draw the contents of an individual item in the list box. In addition, the list box sends *WM_MEASUREITEM* messages to query the height of each item—*WM_COMAREITEM* for sorting and *WM_DELETEITEM* to inform the owner that an item was removed from the list box.

Windows CE supports most of the list box functionality available in other versions of Windows with the exception of the *LB_DIR* family of messages. A new style, *LBS_EX_CONSTSTRINGDATA*, is supported under Windows CE. A list box with this style doesn't store strings passed to it. Instead, the pointer to the string is stored, and the application is responsible for maintaining the string. For large arrays of strings that might be loaded from a resource, this procedure can save RAM because the list box won't maintain a separate copy of the list of strings.

The Combo Box Control

The combo box is (as the name implies) a combination of controls—in this case, a single-line edit control and a list box. The combo box is a space-efficient control for selecting one item from a list of many or for providing an edit field with a list of predefined suggested entries. Under Windows CE, the combo box comes in two styles: drop-down and drop-down list. (Simple combo boxes aren't supported.) The drop-down combo box contains an edit field with a button at the right end. Clicking on the button displays a list box that might contain more selections. Clicking on one of the selections fills the edit field of the combo box with the selection. The drop-down list replaces the edit box with a static text control. This allows the user to select from an item in the list but prevents the user from entering an item that's not in the list.

Because the combo box combines the edit and list controls, a list of the messages used to control the combo box strongly resembles a merged list of the messages for the two base controls. *CB_ADDSTRING*, *CB_INSERTSTRING*, and *CB_FINDSTRING* act like their list box cousins. Likewise, the *CB_SETEDITSELECT* and *CB_GETEDITSELECT* messages set and query the selected characters in the edit box of a drop-down or a drop-down list combo box. To control the drop-down state of a drop-down or drop-down list combo box, the messages *CB_SHOWDROPDOWN* and *CB_GETDROPPEDSTATE* can be used.

The Windows CE version of the combo box supports the *CBS_EX_CONSTSTRINGDATA* extended style, which instructs the combo box to store a pointer to the string for an item instead of the string itself. As with the list box *LBS_EX_CONSTSTRINGDATA* style, this procedure can save RAM if an application has a large array of strings stored in ROM because the combo box won't maintain a separate copy of the list of strings.

Static Controls

Static controls are windows that display text, icons, or bitmaps not intended for user interaction. You can use static text controls to label other controls in a window. What a static control displays is defined by the text and the style for the control. Under Windows CE, static controls support the following styles:

- **SS_LEFT** Displays a line of left-aligned text. The text is wrapped, if necessary, to fit inside the control.
- **SS_CENTER** Displays a line of text centered in the control. The text is wrapped, if necessary, to fit inside the control.
- **SS_RIGHT** Displays a line of text aligned with the right side of the control. The text is wrapped, if necessary, to fit inside the control.
- **SS_LEFTNOWORDWRAP** Displays a line of left-aligned text. The text isn't wrapped to multiple lines. Any text extending beyond the right side of the control is clipped.

- **SS_BITMAP** Displays a bitmap. Window text for the control specifies the name of the resource containing the bitmap.
- **SS_ICON** Displays an icon. Window text for the control specifies the name of the resource containing the icon.

Static controls with the *SS_NOTIFY* style send a *WM_COMMAND* message when the control is clicked, enabled, or disabled, although the Windows CE version of the static control doesn't send a notification when it's double-clicked. The *SS_CENTERIMAGE* style, used in combination with the *SS_BITMAP* or *SS_ICON* style, centers the image within the control. The *SS_NOPREFIX* style can be used in combination with the text styles. It prevents the ampersand (&) character from being interpreted as indicating that the next character is an accelerator character.

Windows CE doesn't support static controls that display filled or hollow rectangles such as those drawn with the *SS_WHITEFRAME* or *SS_BLACKRECT* style. Also, Windows CE doesn't support owner-draw static controls.

The Scroll Bar Control

The scroll bar control is a somewhat different beast from the other controls. Scroll bars are typically seen attached to the sides of windows to control the data being viewed in the window. Indeed, other window controls, such as the edit box and the list box, use the scroll bar control internally. Because of this tight relationship to the parent window, the interface of a scroll bar is different from that of the other controls.

Instead of using *WM_COMMAND* messages to report actions, scroll bars use *WM_VSCROLL* and *WM_HSCROLL* messages. *WM_VSCROLL* messages are sent by vertically oriented scroll bars, whereas *WM_HSCROLL* messages are sent by horizontally oriented scroll bars. In addition, instead of something like a *SB_SETPOSITION* message being sent to a scroll bar to set its position, there are dedicated functions to do this. Let's look at this unique interface.

Scroll Bar Messages

A *WM_VSCROLL* message is sent to the owner of a vertical scroll bar any time the user taps on the scroll bar to change its position. A complementary message, *WM_HSCROLL*, is identical to *WM_VSCROLL* but is sent when the user taps on a horizontal scroll bar. For both these messages, the *wParam* and *lParam* assignments are the same. The low word of the *wParam* parameter contains a code indicating why the message was sent. Figure 4-1 shows a diagram of horizontal and vertical scroll bars and how tapping on different parts of the scroll bars results in different messages. The high word of *wParam* is the position of the thumb, but this value is valid only while you process the *SB_THUMBPOSITION* and *SB_THUMBTRACK* codes, which I'll explain shortly. If the scroll bar sending the message is a stand-alone control and not attached to a window, the *lParam* parameter contains the window handle of the scroll bar.

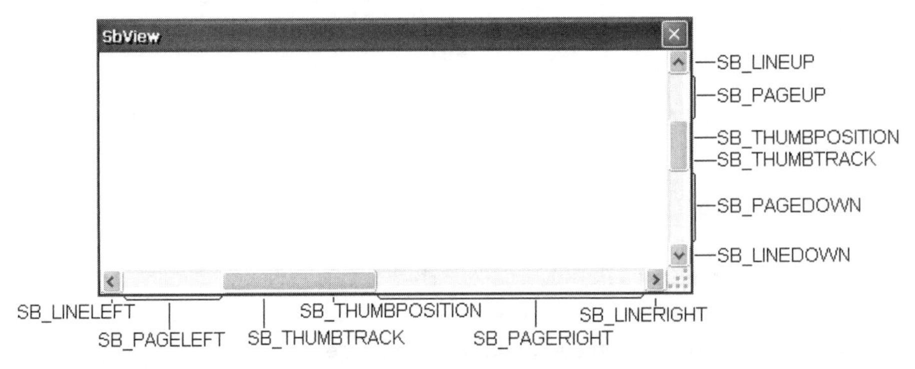

FIGURE 4-1 Scroll bars and their hot spots

The scroll bar message codes sent by the scroll bar allow the program to react to all the different user actions allowable by a scroll bar. The response required by each code is listed in Table 4-1.

The *SB_LINExxx* and *SB_PAGExxx* codes are pretty straightforward. You move the scroll position either a line or a page at a time. The *SB_THUMBPOSITION* and *SB_THUMBTRACK* codes can be processed in one of two ways. When the user drags the scroll bar thumb, the scroll bar sends *SB_THUMBTRACK* code so that a program can interactively track the dragging of the thumb. If your application is fast enough, you can simply process the *SB_THUMBTRACK* code and interactively update the display. If you field the *SB_THUMBTRACK* code, however, your application must be quick enough to redraw the display so that the thumb can be dragged without hesitation or jumping of the scroll bar. This can be a problem on the slower devices that run Windows CE.

TABLE 4-1 Scroll Codes

Codes	Response
For *WM_VSCROLL*	
SB_LINEUP	Program should scroll the screen up one line.
SB_LINEDOWN	Program should scroll the screen down one line.
SB_PAGEUP	Program should scroll the screen up one screen's worth of data.
SB_PAGEDOWN	Program should scroll the screen down one screen's worth of data.
For *WM_HSCROLL*	
SB_LINELEFT	Program should scroll the screen left one character.
SB_LINERIGHT	Program should scroll the screen right one character.
SB_PAGELEFT	Program should scroll the screen left one screen's worth of data.
SB_PAGERIGHT	Program should scroll the screen right one screen's worth of data.

Codes	Response
SB_THUMBTRACK	Programs with enough speed to keep up should update the display with the new scroll position.
SB_THUMBPOSITIO N	Programs that can't update the display fast enough to keep up with the *SB_THUMBTRACK* message should update the display with the new scroll position.
SB_ENDSCROLL	This code indicates that the scroll bar has completed the scroll event. No action is required by the program.
SB_TOP	Program should set the display to the top or left end of the data.
SB_BOTTOM	Program should set the display to the bottom or right end of the data.

If your application (or the system it runs on) is too slow to quickly update the display for every *SB_THUMBTRACK* code, you can ignore the *SB_THUMBTRACK* and wait for the *SB_THUMBPOSITION* code that's sent when the user drops the scroll bar thumb. Then you have to update the display only once, after the user has finished moving the scroll bar thumb.

Configuring a Scroll Bar

To use a scroll bar, an application should first set the minimum and maximum values—the range of the scroll bar, along with the initial position. Windows CE scroll bars, like their desktop cousins, support proportional thumb sizes, which provide feedback to the user about the size of the current visible page compared with the entire scroll range. To set all these parameters, Windows CE applications should use the *SetScrollInfo* function, prototyped as

```
int SetScrollInfo (HWND hwnd, int fnBar, LPSCROLLINFO lpsi, BOOL fRedraw);
```

The first parameter is either the handle of the window that contains the scroll bar or the window handle of the scroll bar itself. The second parameter, *fnBar*, is a flag that determines the use of the window handle. The scroll bar flag can be one of three values: *SB_HORZ* for a window's standard horizontal scroll bar, *SB_VERT* for a window's standard vertical scroll bar, or *SB_CTL* if the scroll bar being set is a stand-alone control. Unless the scroll bar is a control, the window handle is the handle of the window containing the scroll bar. With *SB_CTL*, however, the handle is the window handle of the scroll bar control itself. The last parameter is *fRedraw*, a Boolean value that indicates whether the scroll bar should be redrawn after the call is complete.

The third parameter is a pointer to a *SCROLLINFO* structure, which is defined as

```
typedef struct tagSCROLLINFO {
    UINT cbSize;
    UINT fMask;
    int   nMin;
    int   nMax;
    UINT nPage;
    int   nPos;
    int   nTrackPos;
} SCROLLINFO;
```

This structure allows you to completely specify the scroll bar parameters. The *cbSize* field must be set to the size of the *SCROLLINFO* structure. The *fMask* field contains flags indicating what other fields in the structure contain valid data. The *nMin* and *nMax* fields can contain the minimum and maximum scroll values the scroll bar can report. Windows looks at the values in these fields if the *fMask* parameter contains the *SIF_RANGE* flag. Likewise, the *nPos* field sets the position of the scroll bar within its predefined range if the *fMask* field contains the *SIF_POS* flag.

The *nPage* field allows a program to define the size of the currently viewable area of the screen in relation to the entire scrollable area. This allows a user to have a feel for how much of the entire scrolling range is currently visible. This field is used only if the *fMask* field contains the *SIF_PAGE* flag. The last member of the *SCROLLINFO* structure, *nTrackPos*, isn't used by the *SetScrollInfo* call and is ignored.

The *fMask* field can contain one last flag. Passing an *SIF_DISABLENOSCROLL* flag causes the scroll bar to be disabled but still visible. This is handy when the entire scrolling range is visible within the viewable area and no scrolling is necessary. Disabling the scroll bar in this case is often preferable to simply removing the scroll bar completely.

Those with a sharp eye for detail will notice a problem with the width of the fields in the *SCROLLINFO* structure. The *nMin*, *nMax*, and *nPos* fields are integers and therefore, in the world of Windows CE, are 32 bits wide. On the other hand, the *WM_HSCROLL* and *WM_VSCROLL* messages can return only a 16-bit position in the high word of the *wParam* parameter. If you're using scroll ranges greater than 65,535, use this function:

```
BOOL GetScrollInfo (HWND hwnd, int fnBar, LPSCROLLINFO lpsi);
```

As with *SetScrollInfo*, the flags in the *fnBar* field indicate the window handle that should be passed to the function. The *SCROLLINFO* structure is identical to the one used in *SetScrollInfo*; however, before it can be passed to *GetScrollInfo*, it must be initialized with the size of the structure in *cbSize*. An application must also indicate what data it wants the function to return by setting the appropriate flags in the *fMask* field. The flags used in *fMask* are the same as the ones used in *SetScrollInfo*, with a couple of additions. Now an *SIF_TRACKPOS* flag can be passed to have the scroll bar return its current thumb position. When called during a *WM_xSCROLL* message, the *nTrackPos* field contains the real-time position, while the *nPos* field contains the scroll bar position at the start of the drag of the thumb.

The scroll bar is an unusual control in that it can be added easily to windows simply by specifying the window style flags *WS_VSCROLL* and *WS_HSCROLL*. It's also unusual in that when used this way, the control is placed outside the client area of the window. The reason for this assistance is that scroll bars are commonly needed by applications, so the Windows developers made it easy to attach scroll bars to windows. Now look at the other basic Windows controls. *The DOIView* example, presented later in this chapter, demonstrates how a scroll bar is used when attached to a window.

Controls and Colors

Finally, a word about colors. You can change the background color used by the various controls by fielding the *WM_CTLCOLORxxx* messages. These messages are sent to the parent of a control to ask the parent which colors to use when drawing the control. Each of the controls has a different message. For example, modifying the color of a button by fielding the *WM_CTLCOLORBUTTON* message. Static control background colors are handled by fielding the *WM_CTLCOLORSTATIC* message.

Other controls send different *WM_CTLCOLORxxx* messages so that the colors used to draw them can be modified by the parent window.

Menus

Menus are a mainstay of Windows input. Although each application might have a different keyboard and stylus interface, almost all have sets of menus that are organized in a structure familiar to the Windows user.

Windows CE programs use menus a little differently from other Windows programs, the most obvious difference being that in Windows CE, menus aren't part of the standard top-level window. Instead, menus are attached to a command bar or menu bar control created for the window. Other than this change, the functions of the menu and the way menu selections are processed by the application match the other versions of Windows, for the most part. Because of this general similarity, I give you only a basic introduction to Windows menu management in this section.

Creating a menu is as simple as calling

```
HMENU CreateMenu (void);
```

The function returns a handle to an empty menu. To add an item to a menu, two calls can be used. The first

```
BOOL AppendMenu (HMENU hMenu, UINT fuFlags, UINT idNewItem,
                 LPCTSTR lpszNewItem);
```

appends a single item to the end of a menu. The *fuFlags* parameter is set with a series of flags indicating the initial condition of the item. For example, the item might be initially disabled (thanks to the *MF_GRAYED* flag) or have a check mark next to it (courtesy of the *MF_CHECKED* flag). Almost all calls specify the *MF_STRING* flag, indicating that the *lpszNewItem* parameter contains a string that will be the text for the item. The *idNewItem* parameter contains an ID value that will be used to identify the item when it's selected by the user or to indicate that the state of the menu item needs to be changed.

Another call that can be used to add a menu item is this one:

```
BOOL InsertMenu (HMENU hMenu, UINT uPosition, UINT uFlags,
                 UINT uIDNewItem, LPCTSTR lpNewItem);
```

This call is similar to *AppendMenu*, with the added flexibility that the item can be inserted anywhere within a menu structure. For this call, the *uFlags* parameter can be passed one of two additional flags: *MF_BYCOMMAND* or *MF_BYPOSITION*, which specifies how to locate where the menu item is to be inserted into the menu.

Menus can be nested to provide a cascading effect. To add a cascading menu, or submenu, create the menu you want to attach using

```
HMENU CreatePopupMenu (void);
```

Then use *InsertMenu* or *AppendMenu* to construct the menu, and insert or append the submenu to the main menu using either *InsertMenu* or *AppendMenu* with the *MF_POPUP* flag in the flags parameter. In this case, the *uIDNewItem* parameter contains the handle to the submenu, while *lpNewItem* contains the string that will be on the menu item.

You can query and manipulate a menu item to add or remove check marks or to enable or disable it by means of a number of functions. The function,

```
BOOL EnableMenuItem (HMENU hMenu, UINT uIDEnableItem, UINT uEnable);
```

can be used to enable or disable an item. The flags used in the *uEnable* parameter are similar to the flags used with other menu functions. Under Windows CE, the flag you use to disable a menu item is *MF_GRAYED*, not *MF_DISABLED*. The function

```
DWORD CheckMenuItem (HMENU hmenu, UINT uIDCheckItem, UINT uCheck);
```

can be used to check and uncheck a menu item. Many other functions are available to query and manipulate menu items. Check the SDK documentation for more details.

The following code fragment creates a simple menu structure:

```
hMainMenu = CreateMenu ();

hMenu = CreatePopupMenu ();
AppendMenu (hMenu, MF_STRING | MF_ENABLED, 100, TEXT ("&New"));
AppendMenu (hMenu, MF_STRING | MF_ENABLED, 101, TEXT ("&Open"));
AppendMenu (hMenu, MF_STRING | MF_ENABLED, 101, TEXT ("&Save"));
AppendMenu (hMenu, MF_STRING | MF_ENABLED, 101, TEXT ("E&xit"));

AppendMenu (hMainMenu, MF_STRING | MF_ENABLED | MF_POPUP, (UINT)hMenu,
            TEXT ("&File"));

hMenu = CreatePopupMenu ();
AppendMenu (hMenu, MF_STRING | MF_ENABLED, 100, TEXT ("C&ut"));
AppendMenu (hMenu, MF_STRING | MF_ENABLED, 101, TEXT ("&Copy"));
AppendMenu (hMenu, MF_STRING | MF_ENABLED, 101, TEXT ("&Paste"));
```

```
AppendMenu (hMainMenu, MF_STRING | MF_ENABLED | MF_POPUP,
          (UINT)hMenu, TEXT ("&Edit"));

hMenu = CreatePopupMenu ();
AppendMenu (hMenu, MF_STRING | MF_ENABLED, 100, TEXT ("&About"));

AppendMenu (hMainMenu, MF_STRING | MF_ENABLED | MF_POPUP,
           (UINT)hMenu, TEXT ("&Help"));
```

After a menu is created, it can be displayed with the *TrackPopupMenu* function, prototyped as

```
BOOL TrackPopupMenuEx (HMENU hmenu, UINT uFlags, int x, int y,
                       HWND hwnd, LPTPMPARAMS lptpm);
```

The first parameter is the handle of the menu. The *uFlags* parameter sets the alignment for the menu in relation to the position parameters *x* and *y*. Another flag, *TPM_RETURNCMD*, causes the function to return the ID value of the selected menu item instead of generating a *WM_COMMAND* message. The *hwnd* parameter is the handle to the window that receives all messages relating to the menu, including the resultant *WM_COMMAND* if the user selects a menu item. The final item, *lptpm*, points to a *TPMPARAMS* structure that contains a size value and a rectangle structure. The rectangle structure defines the rectangle on the screen that the menu *shouldn't* cover. This parameter can be null if no exclusion rectangle needs to be specified.

Handling Menu Commands

When a user selects a menu item, Windows sends a *WM_COMMAND* message to the window that owns the menu. The low word of the *wParam* parameter contains the ID of the menu item that was selected. The high word of *wParam* contains the notification code. For a menu selection, this value is always 0. The *lParam* parameter is 0 for *WM_COMMAND* messages sent due to a menu selection. So to act on a menu selection, a window needs to field the *WM_COMMAND* message, decode the ID passed, and act according to the menu item that was selected.

Now that I've covered the basics of menu creation, you might wonder where all this menu creation code sits in a Windows program. The answer is, it doesn't. Instead of dynamically creating menus on the fly, most Windows programs simply load a menu template from a *resource*. To learn more about this, let's spend the remainder of this chapter looking at resources.

Resources

Resources are read-only data segments of an application or a DLL that are linked to the module after it has been compiled. The point of a resource is to give a developer a compiler-independent place for storing content data such as dialog boxes, strings, bitmaps, icons, and yes, menus. Because resources aren't compiled in a program, they can be changed without your having to recompile the application.

You create a resource by building an ASCII file—called a *resource script*—describing the resources. Your ASCII file has the extension RC. You compile this file with a resource compiler, which is provided by every maker of Windows development tools, and then you link it into the compiled executable again using the linker. These days, these steps are masked by a heavy layer of visual tools, but the fundamentals remain the same. For example, Visual Studio creates and maintains an ASCII resource (RC) file even though few programmers directly look at the resource file text any more.

It's always a struggle for the author of a programming book to decide how to approach tools. Some lay out a very high level of instruction, talking about menu selections and describing dialog boxes for specific programming tools. Others show the reader how to build all the components of a program from the ground up, using ASCII files and command-line compilers. Resources can be approached the same way: I could describe how to use the visual tools or how to create the ASCII files that are the basis for the resources. In this book, I stay primarily at the ASCII resource script level since the goal is to teach Windows CE programming, not how to use a particular set of tools. I'll show how to create and use the ASCII RC file for adding menus and the like, but later in the book in places where the resource file isn't relevant, I won't always include the RC file in the listings. The files are, of course, provided with the examples on the book Web site.

Resource Scripts

Creating a resource script is as easy as using Notepad to create a text file. The language used is simple, with C-like tendencies. Comment lines are prefixed by a double slash (//), and files can be included using a *#include* statement.

Following is an example menu template:

```
//
// A menu template
//
ID_MENU MENU DISCARDABLE
BEGIN
    POPUP "&File"
    BEGIN
        MENUITEM "&Open...",                    100
        MENUITEM "&Save...",                    101
        MENUITEM SEPARATOR
        MENUITEM "E&xit",                       120
    END
    POPUP "&Help"
    BEGIN
        MENUITEM "&About",                      200
    END
END
```

The initial *ID_MENU* is the ID value for the resource. Alternatively, this ID value can be replaced by a string identifying the resource. The ID value method provides more compact code, while using a string may provide more readable code when the application loads the resource in the source file. The next word, *MENU*, identifies the type of resource. The menu starts with *POPUP*, indicating that the menu item *File* is actually a pop-up (cascade) menu attached to the main menu. Because it's a menu within a menu, it too has *BEGIN* and *END* keywords surrounding the description of the File menu. The ampersand (&) character tells Windows that the next character should be the key assignment for that menu item. The character following the ampersand is automatically underlined by Windows when the menu item is displayed, and if the user presses the Alt key along with the character, that menu item is selected. Each item in a menu is then specified by the *MENUITEM* keyword followed by the string used on the menu. The ellipsis following the *Open* and *Save* strings is a Windows UI custom indicating to the user that selecting that item displays a dialog box. The numbers following the *Open*, *Save*, *Exit*, and *About* menu items are the menu identifiers. These values identify the menu items in the *WM_COMMAND* message. It's good programming practice to replace these values with equates that are defined in a common include file so that they match the *WM_COMMAND* handler code.

Table 4-2 lists other resource types that you might find in a resource file. The *DISCARDABLE* keyword is optional and tells Windows that the resource can be discarded from memory if it's not in use. The remainder of the menu is couched in *BEGIN* and *END* keywords, although the bracket characters { and } are recognized as well.

TABLE 4-2 Resource Types Allowed by the Resource Compiler[1]

Resource Type	Explanation
MENU	Defines a menu
ACCELERATORS	Defines a keyboard accelerator table
DIALOG	Defines a dialog box template
BITMAP	Includes a bitmap file as a resource
ICON	Includes an icon file as a resource
FONT	Includes a font file as a resource
RCDATA	Defines application-defined binary data block
STRINGTABLE	Defines a list of strings
VERSIONINFO	Includes file version information

Icons

Now that you're working with resource files, it's a trivial matter to modify the icon that the Windows CE shell uses to display a program. Simply create an icon with your favorite icon editor, and add to the resource file an icon statement such as

```
ID_ICON ICON "iconname.ico"
```

[1] The SHMENUBAR resource type used by the Menu Bar control is actually defined as RCDATA inside a wizard-generated include file.

When Windows displays a program in Windows Explorer, it looks inside the .exe file for the first icon in the resource list and uses it to represent the program.

Having that icon represent an application's window is somewhat more of a chore. Windows CE uses a small 16-by-16-pixel icon on the taskbar to represent windows on the desktop. Under the desktop versions of Windows, the *RegisterClassEx* function can be used to associate a small icon with a window, but Windows CE doesn't support this function. Instead, the icon must be explicitly loaded and assigned to the window. The following code fragment assigns a small icon to a window:

```
hIcon = (HICON) SendMessage (hWnd, WM_GETICON, FALSE, 0);
if (hIcon == 0) {
    hIcon = LoadImage (hInst, MAKEINTRESOURCE (ID_ICON1), IMAGE_ICON,
                       16, 16, 0);
    SendMessage (hWnd, WM_SETICON, FALSE, (LPARAM)hIcon);
}
```

The first *SendMessage* call gets the currently assigned icon for the window. The *FALSE* value in *wParam* indicates that you're querying the small icon for the window. If this returns 0, indicating that no icon is assigned, a call to *LoadImage* is made to load the icon from the application resources. The *LoadImage* function can take either a text string or an ID value to identify the resource being loaded. In this case, the *MAKEINTRESOURCE* macro is used to label an ID value to the function. The icon being loaded must be a 16-by-16 icon because under Windows CE, *LoadImage* won't resize the icon to fit the requested size. Also under Windows CE, *LoadImage* is limited to loading icons and bitmaps from resources. Windows CE provides the function *SHLoadDIBitmap* to load a bitmap from a file.

Accelerators

Another resource that can be loaded is a keyboard accelerator table. This table is used by Windows to enable developers to designate shortcut keys for specific menus or controls in your application. Specifically, accelerators provide a direct method for a key combination to result in a *WM_COMMAND* message being sent to a window. These accelerators are different from the Alt+F key combination that, for example, can be used to access a File menu. File menu key combinations are handled automatically as long as the File menu item string is defined with the && character, as in &File. The keyboard accelerators are independent of menus or any other controls, although their assignments typically mimic menu operations, as in pressing Ctrl+O to open a file.

Following is a short resource script that defines a couple of accelerator keys:

```
ID_ACCEL ACCELERATORS DISCARDABLE
BEGIN
    "N", IDM_NEWGAME, VIRTKEY, CONTROL
    "Z", IDM_UNDO,    VIRTKEY, CONTROL
END
```

As with the menu resource, the structure starts with an ID value. The ID value is followed by the type of resource and, again optionally, the *discardable* keyword. The entries in the table consist of the letter identifying the key, followed by the ID value of the command, *VIRTKEY*, which indicates that the letter is actually a virtual key value, followed finally by the *CONTROL* keyword, indicating that Ctrl must be pressed with the key.

Simply having the accelerator table in the resource doesn't accomplish much. The application must load the accelerator table and, for each message it pulls from the message queue, see whether an accelerator has been entered. Fortunately, this is accomplished with a few simple modifications to the main message loop of a program. Here's a modified main message loop that handles keyboard accelerators:

```
// Load accelerator table.
hAccel = LoadAccelerators (hInst, MAKEINTRESOURCE (ID_ACCEL));

// Application message loop
while (GetMessage (&msg, NULL, 0, 0)) {
    // Translate accelerators
    if (!TranslateAccelerator (hwndMain, hAccel, &msg)) {
        TranslateMessage (&msg);
        DispatchMessage (&msg);
    }
}
```

The first difference in this main message loop is the loading of the accelerator table using the *LoadAccelerators* function. Then, after each message is pulled from the message queue, a call is made to *TranslateAccelerator*. If this function translates the message, it returns *TRUE*, which skips the standard *TranslateMessage* and *DispatchMessage* loop body. If no translation was performed, the loop body executes normally.

Bitmaps

Bitmaps can also be stored as resources. Windows CE works with bitmap resources somewhat differently from other versions of Windows. With Windows CE, the call

```
HBITMAP LoadBitmap(HINSTANCE hInstance, LPCTSTR lpBitmapName);
```

loads a read-only version of the bitmap. This means that after the bitmap is selected into a device context, the image can't be modified by other drawing actions in that DC. To load a read/write version of a bitmap resource, use the *LoadImage* function.

Strings

String resources are a good method for reducing the memory footprint of an application while keeping language-specific information out of the code to be compiled. An application can call

```
int LoadString(HINSTANCE hInstance, UINT uID, LPTSTR lpBuffer,
               int nBufferMax);
```

to load a string from a resource. The ID of the string resource is *uID*, the *lpBuffer* parameter points to a buffer to receive the string, and *nBufferMax* is the size of the buffer. To conserve memory, *LoadString* has a unique feature under Windows CE. If *lpBuffer* is *NULL*, *LoadString* returns a read-only pointer to the string as the return value. Simply cast the return value as a pointer and use the string as needed. The length of the string will be located in the word immediately preceding the start of the string. Note that by default the resource compiler removes terminating zeros from string resources. If you want to read string resources directly and have them be zero terminated, invoke the resource compiler with the *–r* command-line switch. Although I'll be covering memory management and strategies for memory conservation in Chapter 7, "Memory Management," one quick note here: it's not a good idea to load a number of strings from a resource into memory. This just uses memory both in the resource and in RAM. If you need a number of strings at the same time, a better strategy might be to use the new feature of *LoadString* to return a pointer directly to the resource itself. As an alternative, you can have the strings in a read-only segment compiled with the program. You lose the advantage of a separate string table, but you reduce your memory footprint.

The DOIView Example Program

The following example, DOIView, demonstrates the use of resources, keyboard accelerators, mouse wheel handling, and pop-up menus. DOIView, short for Declaration of Independence View, displays the United States Declaration of Independence in a window. The text for the program is stored as a series of string resources. DOIView formats the text to fit the application window and uses scroll bars to scroll the text.

Figure 4-3 shows the DOIView window. The keys Ctrl+H and Ctrl+E scroll the document to the start (home) and end of the document. You can tap on the window to display a short menu that allows you to quickly scroll to the start or end of the document as well as end the program. If your Windows CE system supports a mouse with a mouse wheel, DOIView will scroll the window as you move the mouse wheel.[2]

The source for DOIView is shown in Listing 4-1. Notice the inclusion of a third file, DOIView.rc, which contains the resource script for the program. DOIView.rc contains the menu resource, a line to include the icon for the program, and a string table that contains the text to be displayed. Because string resources are limited to 4092 characters, the text is contained in multiple strings.

---

[2] The mouse wheel won't work inside the emulator since the emulator doesn't translate the PC's mouse wheel movement to the software running inside the emulator.

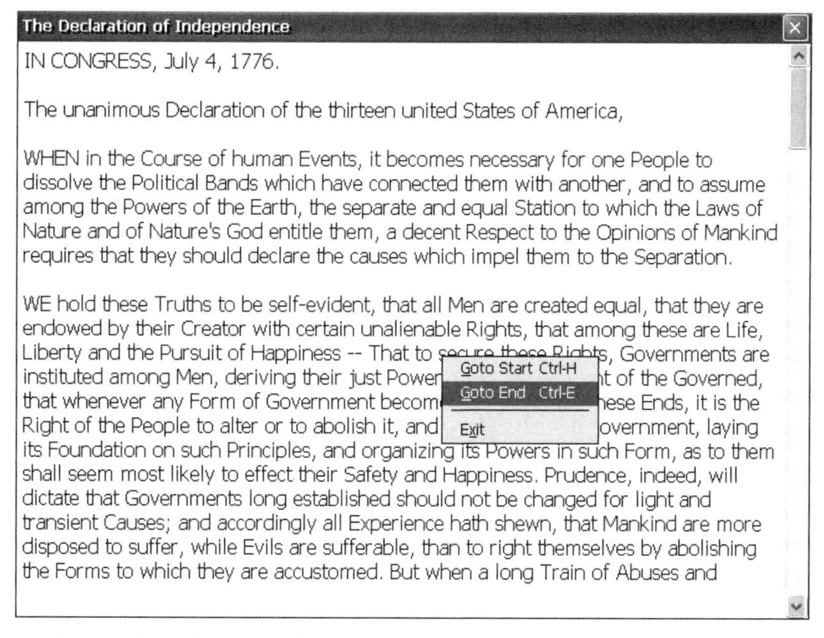

FIGURE 4-2 The DOI View window with the menu displayed

LISTING 4-1 The DOIView program

DOIView.rc

```
//======================================================================
// DOIView - Resource file
//
// Written for the book Programming Windows CE
// Copyright (C) 2007 Douglas Boling
//
//======================================================================
#include "DOIView.h"

//----------------------------------------------------------------------
// Icon
//
ID_ICON ICON "DOIView.ico"

//----------------------------------------------------------------------
// Menu
//
ID_MENU MENU DISCARDABLE
BEGIN
    POPUP "&File"
    BEGIN
        MENUITEM "&Goto Start\tCtrl-H",          IDM_HOME
        MENUITEM "&Goto End\tCtrl-E",            IDM_END
        MENUITEM SEPARATOR
        MENUITEM "E&xit",                        IDM_EXIT
```

```
    END
END
//----------------------------------------------------------------------
// Accelerator table
//
ID_ACCEL ACCELERATORS DISCARDABLE
BEGIN
    "H", IDM_HOME, VIRTKEY, CONTROL
    "E", IDM_END,  VIRTKEY, CONTROL
END
//----------------------------------------------------------------------
// String table
//
STRINGTABLE DISCARDABLE
BEGIN
    IDS_DOITEXT, "IN CONGRESS, July 4, 1776.\012The unanimous \
Declaration of the thirteen united States of America,\012WHEN in the \
Course of human Events, it becomes necessary for one People to \
dissolve the Political Bands which have connected them with another, \
and to assume among the Powers of the Earth, the separate and equal \
Station to which the Laws of Nature and of Nature's God entitle them, \
a decent Respect to the Opinions of Mankind requires that they should \
declare the causes which impel them to the Separation.\012\
WE hold these Truths to be self-evident, that all Men are created \
equal, that they are endowed by their Creator with certain \
unalienable Rights, that among these are Life, Liberty and the Pursuit \
of Happiness -- That to secure these Rights, Governments are \
instituted among Men, deriving their just Powers from the Consent of \
the Governed, that whenever any Form of Government becomes destructive \
of these Ends, it is the Right of the People to alter or to abolish \
it, and to institute new Government, laying its Foundation on such \
Principles, and organizing its Powers in such Form, as to them shall \
seem most likely to effect their Safety and Happiness. Prudence, \
indeed, will dictate that Governments long established should \
not be changed for light and transient Causes; and accordingly all \
Experience hath shewn, that Mankind are more disposed to suffer, while \
Evils are sufferable, than to right themselves by abolishing the Forms \
to which they are accustomed. But when a long Train of Abuses and \
Usurpations, pursuing invariably the same Object, evinces a Design to \
reduce them under absolute Despotism, it is their Right, it is their \
Duty, to throw off such Government, and to provide new Guards for \
their future Security. Such has been the patient Sufferance of these \
Colonies; and \
such is now the Necessity which constrains them to alter their \
former Systems of Government. The History of the present King of Great \
Britain is a History of repeated Injuries and Usurpations, all having \
in direct Object the Establishment of an absolute Tyranny over these \
States. To prove this, let Facts be submitted to a candid World.\012\
HE has refused his Assent to Laws, the most wholesome and \
necessary for the public Good.\012HE has forbidden his Governors to \
pass Laws of immediate and pressing Importance, unless suspended in \
their Operation till his Assent should be obtained; and when so \
suspended, he has utterly neglected to attend to them.\012\
HE has refused to pass other Laws for the Accommodation of large \
```

```
Districts of People, unless those People would relinquish the Right of \
Representation in the Legislature, a Right inestimable to them, and \
formidable to Tyrants only.\012HE has called together Legislative \
Bodies at Places unusual, uncomfortable, and distant from the \
Depository of their public Records, for the sole Purpose of fatiguing \
them into Compliance with his Measures.\012\
HE has dissolved Representative Houses repeatedly, for opposing \
with manly Firmness his Invasions on the Rights of the People.\012HE \
has refused for a long Time, after such Dissolutions, to cause others \
to be elected; whereby the Legislative Powers, incapable of the \
Annihilation, have returned to the People at large for their exercise; \
the State remaining in the mean time exposed to all the Dangers of \
Invasion from without, and the Convulsions within.\012\
HE has endeavoured to prevent the Population of these States; \
for that Purpose obstructing the Laws for Naturalization of Foreigners\
; refusing to pass others to encourage their Migrations hither, and \
raising the Conditions of new Appropriations of Lands.\012HE has \
obstructed the Administration of Justice, by refusing his Assent to \
Laws for establishing Judiciary Powers.\012HE has made Judges \
dependent on his Will alone, for the Tenure of their Offices, and the \
Amount and Payment of their Salaries.\012"

    IDS_DOITEXT1, "HE has erected a Multitude of new Offices, and sent \
hither Swarms of Officers to harrass our People, and eat out their \
Substance.\012HE has kept among us, in Times of Peace, Standing \
Armies, without the consent of our Legislatures.\012HE has affected to \
render the Military independent of and superior to the Civil Power.\012\
HE has combined with others to subject us to a Jurisdiction \
foreign to our Constitution, and unacknowledged by our Laws; giving \
his Assent to their Acts of pretended Legislation:\012FOR quartering \
large Bodies of Armed Troops among us;\012FOR protecting them, by a \
mock Trial, from Punishment for any Murders which they should commit \
on the Inhabitants of these States:\012FOR cutting off our Trade with \
all Parts of the World:\012\
FOR imposing Taxes on us without our Consent:\012FOR depriving \
us, in many Cases, of the Benefits of Trial by Jury:\012FOR \
transporting us beyond Seas to be tried for pretended Offences:\012\
FOR abolishing the free System of English Laws in a neighbouring \
Province, establishing therein an arbitrary Government, and enlarging \
its Boundaries, so as to render it at once an Example and fit \
Instrument for introducing the same absolute Rules into these \
Colonies:\012\
FOR taking away our Charters, abolishing our most valuable Laws, \
and altering fundamentally the Forms of our Governments:\012FOR \
suspending our own Legislatures, and declaring themselves invested \
with Power to legislate for us in all Cases whatsoever.\012HE has \
abdicated Government here, by declaring us out of his Protection and \
waging War against us.\012HE has plundered our Seas, ravaged our \
Coasts, burnt our Towns, and destroyed the Lives of our People.\012\
HE is, at this Time, transporting large Armies of foreign \
Mercenaries to compleat the Works of Death, Desolation, and Tyranny, \
already begun with circumstances of Cruelty and Perfidy, scarcely \
paralleled in the most barbarous Ages, and totally unworthy the Head \
of a civilized Nation.\012HE has constrained our fellow Citizens taken \
```

```
Captive on the high Seas to bear Arms against their Country, to become \
the Executioners of their Friends and Brethren, or to fall themselves \
by their Hands.\012\
HE has excited domestic Insurrections amongst us, and has \
endeavoured to bring on the Inhabitants of our Frontiers, the \
merciless Indian Savages, whose known Rule of Warfare, is an \
undistinguished Destruction, of all Ages, Sexes and Conditions.\012IN \
every stage of these Oppressions we have Petitioned for Redress in the \
most humble Terms: Our repeated Petitions have been answered only by \
repeated Injury. A Prince, whose Character is thus marked by every act \
which may define a Tyrant, is unfit to be the Ruler of a free People. \
NOR have we been wanting in Attentions to our Brittish Brethren. \
We have warned them from Time to Time of Attempts by their Legislature \
to extend an unwarrantable Jurisdiction over us. We have reminded them \
of the Circumstances of our Emigration and Settlement here. We have \
appealed to their native Justice and Magnanimity, and we have conjured \
them by the Ties of our common Kindred to disavow these Usurpations, \
which, would inevitably interrupt our Connections and Correspondence. \
They too have been deaf to the Voice of Justice and of Consanguinity. \
We must, therefore, acquiesce in the Necessity, which denounces our \
Separation, and hold them, as we hold the rest of Mankind, Enemies in \
War, in Peace, Friends.\012"

    IDS_DOITEXT2, "WE, therefore, the Representatives of the UNITED \
STATES OF AMERICA, in GENERAL CONGRESS, Assembled, appealing to the \
Supreme Judge of the World for the Rectitude of our Intentions, do, in \
the Name, and by Authority of the good People of these Colonies, \
solemnly Publish and Declare, That these United Colonies are, and of \
Right ought to be, FREE AND INDEPENDENT STATES; that they are absolved \
from all Allegiance to the British Crown, and that all political \
Connection between them and the State of Great-Britain, is and ought \
to be totally dissolved; and that as FREE AND INDEPENDENT STATES, they \
have full Power to levy War, conclude Peace, contract Alliances, \
establish Commerce, and to do all other Acts and Things which \
INDEPENDENT STATES may of right do. And for the support of this \
Declaration, with a firm Reliance on the Protection of divine \
Providence, we mutually pledge to each other our Lives, our Fortunes, \
and our sacred Honor."
END
```

DOIView.h

```
//======================================================================
// Header file
//
// Written for the book Programming Windows CE
// Copyright (C) 2007 Douglas Boling
//================================================================
// Returns number of elements
#define dim(x) (sizeof(x) / sizeof(x[0]))
```

```
//----------------------------------------------------------------------
// Generic defines and data types
//
struct decodeUINT {                             // Structure associates
    UINT Code;                                  // messages
                                                // with a function.
    LRESULT (*Fxn)(HWND, UINT, WPARAM, LPARAM);
};
struct decodeCMD {                              // Structure associates
    UINT Code;                                  // menu IDs with a
    LRESULT (*Fxn)(HWND, WORD, HWND, WORD);     // function
};
#define    ID_MENU          10
#define    ID_ACCEL         11

#define    IDM_HOME         100
#define    IDM_END          101
#define    IDM_EXIT         102

#define    IDS_DOITEXT      1000                // These IDs must be
#define    IDS_DOITEXT1     1001                // consecutive
#define    IDS_DOITEXT2     1002

//----------------------------------------------------------------------
// Function prototypes
//
int MyScrollWnd (HWND hWnd, int nNewPos);
int ShowContextMenu (HWND hWnd, POINT pt);
LPTSTR WrapString (HDC hdc, LPTSTR pszText, int *pnLen, int nWidth,
                   BOOL *fEOL);

HWND InitInstance (HINSTANCE, LPWSTR, int);
int TermInstance (HINSTANCE, int);

// Window procedures
LRESULT CALLBACK MainWndProc (HWND, UINT, WPARAM, LPARAM);

// Message handlers
LRESULT DoCreateMain (HWND, UINT, WPARAM, LPARAM);
LRESULT DoSizeMain (HWND, UINT, WPARAM, LPARAM);
LRESULT DoCommandMain (HWND, UINT, WPARAM, LPARAM);
LRESULT DoLButtonDownMain (HWND, UINT, WPARAM, LPARAM);
LRESULT DoRButtonDownMain (HWND, UINT, WPARAM, LPARAM);
LRESULT DoMouseWheelMain (HWND, UINT, WPARAM, LPARAM);
LRESULT DoVScrollMain (HWND, UINT, WPARAM, LPARAM);
LRESULT DoPaintMain (HWND, UINT, WPARAM, LPARAM);
LRESULT DoDestroyMain (HWND, UINT, WPARAM, LPARAM);

// Command functions
LPARAM DoMainCommandHome (HWND, WORD, HWND, WORD);
LPARAM DoMainCommandEnd (HWND, WORD, HWND, WORD);
LPARAM DoMainCommandExit (HWND, WORD, HWND, WORD);
```

DOIView.cpp

```
//======================================================================
// DOIView - Demonstrates window scroll bars
//
// Written for the book Programming Windows CE
// Copyright (C) 2007 Douglas Boling
//======================================================================
#include <windows.h>                 // For all that Windows stuff
#include "DOIView.h"                 // Program-specific stuff
#include <aygshell.h>                // Extended shell API

// This line forces the linker to add aygshell.lib to the lib list
#pragma comment( lib, "aygshell" )   // Link for SHRecognizeGesture

//----------------------------------------------------------------------
// Global data
//
const TCHAR szAppName[] = TEXT("DOIView");
HINSTANCE hInst;                     // Program instance handle

// Message dispatch table for MainWindowProc
const struct decodeUINT MainMessages[] = {
    WM_CREATE, DoCreateMain,
    WM_SIZE, DoSizeMain,
    WM_LBUTTONDOWN, DoLButtonDownMain,
    WM_RBUTTONDOWN, DoRButtonDownMain,
    WM_MOUSEWHEEL, DoMouseWheelMain,
    WM_COMMAND, DoCommandMain,
    WM_VSCROLL, DoVScrollMain,
    WM_PAINT, DoPaintMain,
    WM_DESTROY, DoDestroyMain,
};

// Command Message dispatch for MainWindowProc
const struct decodeCMD MainCommandItems[] = {
    IDM_HOME, DoMainCommandHome,
    IDM_END, DoMainCommandEnd,
    IDM_EXIT, DoMainCommandExit,
};

typedef struct {
    LPTSTR pszLine;
    int nLen;
} LINEARRAY, *PLINEARRAY;

#define MAXLINES 1000
LINEARRAY laText[MAXLINES];
int nNumLines = 0;
int nFontHeight = 1;
int nLinesPerPage = 1;
int nMWScroll = -1;
```

```
LPTSTR pszDeclaration;
HFONT hFont;

int nVPos, nVMax;
BOOL fFirst = TRUE;
//======================================================================
// Program entry point
//
int WINAPI WinMain (HINSTANCE hInstance, HINSTANCE hPrevInstance,
                    LPWSTR lpCmdLine, int nCmdShow) {
    MSG msg;
    int rc = 0;
    HWND hwndMain;
    HACCEL hAccel;

    // Initialize this instance.
    hwndMain = InitInstance (hInstance, lpCmdLine, nCmdShow);
    if (hwndMain == 0) return 0x10;

    // Load accelerator table.
    hAccel = LoadAccelerators (hInst, MAKEINTRESOURCE (ID_ACCEL));

    // Application message loop
    while (GetMessage (&msg, NULL, 0, 0)) {
        // Translate accelerators
        if (!TranslateAccelerator (hwndMain, hAccel, &msg)) {
            TranslateMessage (&msg);
            DispatchMessage (&msg);
        }
    }
    // Instance cleanup
    return TermInstance (hInstance, msg.wParam);
}
//----------------------------------------------------------------------
// InitInstance - Instance initialization
//
HWND InitInstance (HINSTANCE hInstance, LPWSTR lpCmdLine, int nCmdShow) {
    WNDCLASS wc;
    HWND hWnd;
    PBYTE pRes, pBuff;
    int nStrLen = 0, i = 0;

    // Save program instance handle in global variable.
    hInst = hInstance;

#if defined(WIN32_PLATFORM_PSPC) || defined(WIN32_PLATFORM_WFSP)
    // For Windows Mobile devices, allow only one instance of the app
    hWnd = FindWindow (szAppName, NULL);
    if (hWnd) {
        SetForegroundWindow ((HWND)(((DWORD)hWnd) | 0x01));
        return 0;
    }
```

```
#endif

    // Load text from multiple string resources into one large buffer
    pBuff = (PBYTE)LocalAlloc (LPTR, 8);
    while (pRes = (PBYTE)LoadString (hInst, IDS_DOITEXT + i++, NULL, 0))
    {
        // Get the length of the string resource
        int nLen = *(PWORD)(pRes-2) * sizeof (TCHAR);
        // Resize buffer
        pBuff = (PBYTE)LocalReAlloc (pBuff, nStrLen + 8 + nLen,
                                     LMEM_MOVEABLE | LMEM_ZEROINIT);
        if (pBuff == NULL) return 0;
        // Copy resource into buffer
        memcpy (pBuff + nStrLen, pRes, nLen);
        nStrLen += nLen;
    }

    *(TCHAR *)(pBuff + nStrLen) = TEXT ('\0');
    pszDeclaration = (LPTSTR)pBuff;

    // Register application main window class.
    wc.style = 0;                             // Window style
    wc.lpfnWndProc = MainWndProc;             // Callback function
    wc.cbClsExtra = 0;                        // Extra class data
    wc.cbWndExtra = 0;                        // Extra window data
    wc.hInstance = hInstance;                 // Owner handle
    wc.hIcon = NULL,                          // Application icon
    wc.hCursor = LoadCursor (NULL, IDC_ARROW);// Default cursor
    wc.hbrBackground = (HBRUSH) GetStockObject (WHITE_BRUSH);
    wc.lpszMenuName =  NULL;                  // Menu name
    wc.lpszClassName = szAppName;             // Window class name

    if (RegisterClass (&wc) == 0) return 0;

    // Create main window.
    hWnd = CreateWindowEx (WS_EX_NODRAG, szAppName,
                           TEXT("The Declaration of Independence"),
                           WS_VSCROLL | WS_VISIBLE | WS_CAPTION |
                           WS_SYSMENU, CW_USEDEFAULT, CW_USEDEFAULT,
                           CW_USEDEFAULT, CW_USEDEFAULT, NULL,
                           NULL, hInstance, NULL);

    if (!IsWindow (hWnd)) return 0;  // Fail code if not created.

    // Standard show and update calls
    ShowWindow (hWnd, nCmdShow);
    UpdateWindow (hWnd);
    return hWnd;
}
//----------------------------------------------------------------------
// TermInstance - Program cleanup
//
int TermInstance (HINSTANCE hInstance, int nDefRC) {
    LocalFree (pszDeclaration);
```

```
    return nDefRC;
}
//======================================================================
// Message handling procedures for main window
//
//----------------------------------------------------------------------
// MainWndProc - Callback function for application window
//
LRESULT CALLBACK MainWndProc (HWND hWnd, UINT wMsg, WPARAM wParam,
                              LPARAM lParam) {
    int i;
    //
    // Search message list to see if we need to handle this
    // message.  If in list, call procedure.
    //
    for (i = 0; i < dim(MainMessages); i++) {
        if (wMsg == MainMessages[i].Code)
            return (*MainMessages[i].Fxn)(hWnd, wMsg, wParam, lParam);
    }
    return DefWindowProc (hWnd, wMsg, wParam, lParam);
}
//----------------------------------------------------------------------
// DoCreateMain - Process WM_CREATE message for window.
//
LRESULT DoCreateMain (HWND hWnd, UINT wMsg, WPARAM wParam,
                      LPARAM lParam) {
    TEXTMETRIC tm;
    HDC hdc = GetDC (hWnd);
    LOGFONT lf;
    HFONT hFontWnd;

    hFontWnd = (HFONT)GetStockObject (SYSTEM_FONT);
    GetObject (hFontWnd, sizeof (LOGFONT), &lf);

    lf.lfHeight = -12 * GetDeviceCaps(hdc, LOGPIXELSY)/ 72;
    lf.lfWeight = 0;
    hFont = CreateFontIndirect (&lf);
    SendMessage (hWnd, WM_SETFONT, (WPARAM)hFont, 0);

    // Get the height of the default font.
    hFontWnd = (HFONT)SelectObject (hdc, hFont);
    GetTextMetrics (hdc, &tm);
    nFontHeight = tm.tmHeight + tm.tmExternalLeading;
    SelectObject (hdc, hFontWnd);
    ReleaseDC (hWnd, hdc);

     // Get the mouse scroll wheel line count.
     SystemParametersInfo (SPI_GETWHEELSCROLLLINES, 0, &nMWScroll, 0);
    return 0;
}
//----------------------------------------------------------------------
// DoSizeMain - Process WM_SIZE message for window.
//
```

```
LRESULT DoSizeMain (HWND hWnd, UINT wMsg, WPARAM wParam,
                    LPARAM lParam) {
    RECT rect;
    HDC hdc = GetDC (hWnd);
    GetClientRect (hWnd, &rect);
    int i = 0, nChars, nWidth;
    LPTSTR pszWndText = pszDeclaration;
    SCROLLINFO si;
    HFONT hFontWnd;
    BOOL fNewLine;

    hFontWnd = (HFONT)SelectObject (hdc, hFont);

    // Compute the line breaks
    nWidth = rect.right - rect.left - 10;
    while (i < MAXLINES){
        pszWndText = WrapString (hdc, pszWndText, &nChars, nWidth,
                                 &fNewLine);
        if (pszWndText == 0)
            break;
        laText[i].pszLine = pszWndText;
        laText[i].nLen = nChars;
        i++;
        if (fNewLine) {
            laText[i].nLen = 0;
            i++;
        }
        pszWndText += nChars;
    }
    nNumLines = i;
    nLinesPerPage = (rect.bottom - rect.top)/nFontHeight;

    // Compute lines per window and total lenght
    si.cbSize = sizeof (si);
    si.nMin = 0;
    si.nMax = nNumLines;
    si.nPage = nLinesPerPage;
    si.nPos = nVPos;
    si.fMask = SIF_ALL;
    SetScrollInfo (hWnd, SB_VERT, &si, TRUE);

    // Clean up
    SelectObject (hdc, hFontWnd);
    ReleaseDC (hWnd, hdc);
    InvalidateRect (hWnd, NULL, TRUE);
    return 0;
}
//----------------------------------------------------------------------
// DoCommandMain - Process WM_COMMAND message for window.
//
LRESULT DoCommandMain (HWND hWnd, UINT wMsg, WPARAM wParam,
                       LPARAM lParam) {
    WORD idItem, wNotifyCode;
    HWND hwndCtl;
```

```
    int  i;

    // Parse the parameters.
    idItem = (WORD) LOWORD (wParam);
    wNotifyCode = (WORD) HIWORD(wParam);
    hwndCtl = (HWND) lParam;

    // Call routine to handle control message.
    for (i = 0; i < dim(MainCommandItems); i++) {
        if (idItem == MainCommandItems[i].Code)
            return (*MainCommandItems[i].Fxn)(hWnd, idItem, hwndCtl,
                                              wNotifyCode);
    }
    return 0;
}
//----------------------------------------------------------------------
// DoLButtonDownMain - Process WM_LBUTTONDOWN message for window.
//
LRESULT DoLButtonDownMain (HWND hWnd, UINT wMsg, WPARAM wParam,
                           LPARAM lParam) {
    POINT pt;
    int rc;

    // Display the menu at the point of the tap
    pt.x = LOWORD (lParam);
    pt.y = HIWORD (lParam);

    SHRGINFO sri;
    sri.cbSize = sizeof (sri);
    sri.dwFlags = 1;
    sri.hwndClient = hWnd;
    sri.ptDown = pt;

    // See if tap and hold
    rc = SHRecognizeGesture (&sri);
    if (rc == 0) return 0;

    // Display the menu at the point of the tap
     ShowContextMenu (hWnd, pt);
    return 0;
}
//----------------------------------------------------------------------
// DoRButtonDownMain - Process WM_RBUTTONDOWN message for window.
//
LRESULT DoRButtonDownMain (HWND hWnd, UINT wMsg, WPARAM wParam,
                           LPARAM lParam) {
    POINT pt;

    // Display the menu at the point of the tap
    pt.x = LOWORD (lParam);
    pt.y = HIWORD (lParam);
     ShowContextMenu (hWnd, pt);
    return 0;
}
```

```
//----------------------------------------------------------------------
// DoMouseWheelMain - Process WM_MOUSEWHEEL message for window.
//
LRESULT DoMouseWheelMain (HWND hWnd, UINT wMsg, WPARAM wParam,
                          LPARAM lParam) {
   // Get the number of clicks the wheel turned
   int nScrollLines = GET_WHEEL_DELTA_WPARAM(wParam) / WHEEL_DELTA;

   // Compute the new position
   int nNewPos = nVPos - nScrollLines;
   // Set the scroll bar and invalidate the window
   MyScrollWnd (hWnd, nNewPos);
   return 0;
}
//----------------------------------------------------------------------
// DoVScrollMain - Process WM_VSCROLL message for window.
//
LRESULT DoVScrollMain (HWND hWnd, UINT wMsg, WPARAM wParam,
                       LPARAM lParam) {
    int nNewPos = nVPos;

    switch (LOWORD (wParam)) {
    case SB_LINEUP:
        nNewPos -= 1;
        break;

    case SB_LINEDOWN:
        nNewPos += 1;
        break;

    case SB_PAGEUP:
        nNewPos -= nLinesPerPage;
        break;

    case SB_PAGEDOWN:
        nNewPos += nLinesPerPage;
        break;

    case SB_THUMBTRACK:
    case SB_THUMBPOSITION:
        nNewPos = HIWORD (wParam);
        break;
    }
     MyScrollWnd (hWnd, nNewPos);
    return 0;
}
//----------------------------------------------------------------------
// DoPaintMain - Process WM_PAINT message for window.
//
LRESULT DoPaintMain (HWND hWnd, UINT wMsg, WPARAM wParam,
                     LPARAM lParam) {
    PAINTSTRUCT ps;
    HFONT hFontOld;
    RECT rect;
```

```
    HDC hdc;
    int i, y = 5;

    GetClientRect (hWnd, &rect);

    hdc = BeginPaint (hWnd, &ps);

   // Select our font
   hFontOld = (HFONT)SelectObject (hdc, hFont);

    // Draw the text
    for (i = nVPos; i < nNumLines; i++) {
        if (y > rect.bottom - nFontHeight - 10)
            break;
        if (laText[i].nLen)
            ExtTextOut (hdc, 5, y, TRANSPARENT, NULL, laText[i].pszLine,
                        laText[i].nLen, NULL);
        y += nFontHeight;
    }
    SelectObject (hdc, hFontOld);
    EndPaint (hWnd, &ps);
    return 0;
}
//----------------------------------------------------------------------
// DoDestroyMain - Process WM_DESTROY message for window.
//
LRESULT DoDestroyMain (HWND hWnd, UINT wMsg, WPARAM wParam,
                       LPARAM lParam) {
    PostQuitMessage (0);
    return 0;
}
//======================================================================
// Command handler routines
//
//----------------------------------------------------------------------
// DoMainCommandHome - Process Program Home command.
//
LPARAM DoMainCommandHome (HWND hWnd, WORD idItem, HWND hwndCtl,
                          WORD wNotifyCode) {
    SCROLLINFO si;
    if (nVPos != 0) {
        nVPos = 0;

        si.cbSize = sizeof (si);
        si.nPos = nVPos;
        si.fMask = SIF_POS;
        SetScrollInfo (hWnd, SB_VERT, &si, TRUE);

        InvalidateRect (hWnd, NULL, TRUE);
    }
    return 0;
}
//----------------------------------------------------------------------
// DoMainCommandEnd - Process End command.
```

```
//
LPARAM DoMainCommandEnd (HWND hWnd, WORD idItem, HWND hwndCtl,
                         WORD wNotifyCode) {
    SCROLLINFO si;
    int nEndPos = nNumLines - nLinesPerPage + 1;

    if (nVPos != nEndPos) {
        nVPos = nEndPos;

        si.cbSize = sizeof (si);
        si.nPos = nVPos;
        si.fMask = SIF_POS;
        SetScrollInfo (hWnd, SB_VERT, &si, TRUE);

        InvalidateRect (hWnd, NULL, TRUE);
    }
    return 0;
}
//----------------------------------------------------------------------
// DoMainCommandExit - Process Program Exit command.
//
LPARAM DoMainCommandExit (HWND hWnd, WORD idItem, HWND hwndCtl,
                          WORD wNotifyCode) {

    SendMessage (hWnd, WM_CLOSE, 0, 0);
    return 0;
}
//----------------------------------------------------------------------
// MyScrollWnd - Adjust the scroll bar and invalidate the window to
// force a repaint at the new top line.
//
int MyScrollWnd (HWND hWnd, int nNewPos) {
    SCROLLINFO si;

     // Check range.
    if (nNewPos < 0)
        nNewPos = 0;
    if (nNewPos > nNumLines-nLinesPerPage+1)
        nNewPos = nNumLines-nLinesPerPage+1;

    // If scroll position changed, update scrollbar and
    // force redraw of window.
    if (nVPos != nNewPos) {
      nVPos = nNewPos;
        si.cbSize = sizeof (si);
        si.nPos = nVPos;
        si.fMask = SIF_POS;
        SetScrollInfo (hWnd, SB_VERT, &si, TRUE);

      // The scrolling is actually done by redrawing the wnd at
      // the new position.  Not very fast but fine in this case.
        InvalidateRect (hWnd, NULL, TRUE);
    }
   return 0;
```

```
}
//----------------------------------------------------------------------
// ShowContextMenu - Display a context menu
//
int ShowContextMenu (HWND hWnd, POINT pt) {
    HMENU hMenuMain, hMenu;

    // Display the menu at the point of the tap
   MapWindowPoints (hWnd, HWND_DESKTOP, &pt, 1);
    pt.x += 5;

    hMenuMain = LoadMenu (hInst, MAKEINTRESOURCE (ID_MENU));
    hMenu = GetSubMenu (hMenuMain, 0);
    TPMPARAMS tpm;
    tpm.cbSize = sizeof (tpm);
    GetClientRect (hWnd, &tpm.rcExclude);
    TrackPopupMenuEx (hMenu, TPM_LEFTALIGN | TPM_TOPALIGN,
                      pt.x, pt.y, hWnd, &tpm);
    DestroyMenu (hMenuMain);
    DestroyMenu (hMenu);
    return 0;
}
//----------------------------------------------------------------------
// WrapString - Determine a length that will fit with a width
//
LPTSTR WrapString (HDC hdc, LPTSTR pszText, int *pnLen, int nWidth,
                   BOOL *fEOL) {
    LPTSTR pszStr, pszStart;
    SIZE Size;

    *fEOL = FALSE;
    *pnLen = 0;

    // Skip to first non-space char
    for (; (*pszText!=TEXT('\0')) && (*pszText<=TEXT (' ')); pszText++);

    pszStart = pszText;

    if (*pszText == 0)
        return 0;

    while (1) {
        pszStr = pszText;
        // Find end of the next word
        for (; (*pszText!=TEXT('\0')) && *pszText>TEXT (' ');pszText++);

        // Get length of the string
        GetTextExtentPoint (hdc, pszStart, pszText - pszStart, &Size);

        if (Size.cx > nWidth)
            break;
        if ((*pszText == TEXT ('\0'))  || (*pszText == TEXT ('\r')) ||
            (*pszText == TEXT ('\n'))) {
```

```
                *fEOL = TRUE;
                pszStr = pszText;
                break;
            }
            // slip past space
            pszText++;
        }
        *pnLen = pszStr - pszStart;
        return pszStart;
    }
```

When the program launches, it reads the string resources into one large buffer. To reduce the memory impact, the string resources are accessed by passing a *NULL* buffer pointer to the *LoadString* function. That causes *LoadString* to return a pointer to the resource in its return value. Note that these strings aren't zero delimited in this case, so DOIView reads the word before the string to get the number of characters. Because the strings are Unicode, the string length is then multiplied by the size of *TCHAR* to get the size of the buffer needed for the string.

The main window of DOIView handles a few extra messages. The *WM_SIZE* handler reformats the text by calling *WrapString*. This routine measures the length of each line by calling *GetTextExtentPoint*. If the length is less than the width of the window, the routine then adds another word to the line and remeasures. This continues until the proper number of words is added to the line to fit within the window.

The *WM_VSCROLL* routine handles the messages from the vertical scroll bar. When the notification is a *SB_PAGEUP* or *SB_PAGEDOWN*, the routine subtracts or adds the number of lines displayed in the window to the current scroll position. The routine then calls *MyScrollWnd*, which moves the scrollbar thumb to the correct position and invaidates the window. The *WM_PAINT* handler then draws the lines of text starting with the top line to be displayed, defined by the new scroll position.

The *WM_LBUTTONDOWN* handler uses the *SHRecognizeGesture* function to determine if the user has performed a successful tap-and-hold gesture to warrant a context menu. If so, the routine calls *ShowContextMenu* to display the menu. The *ShowContextMenu* function loads a menu from a menu resource and calls *TrackPopupMenuEx* to display the menu. The menu has three commands: Home, to scroll to the top of the document; End, to scroll to the bottom; and Exit, which quits the program. DOIView also responds to accelerator keys: Ctrl+H for Home and Ctrl+E for End.

In addition to displaying the context menu with a tap-and-hold of the left mouse button, DOIView also displays the context menu if the right mouse button is clicked on systems that support a mouse. This is accomplished by fielding the *WM_RBUTTONDOWN* message and calling the *ShowContextMenu* routine to display the menu.

The *WM_MOUSEWHEEL* message is also monitored so that the user can use a mouse with a mouse wheel to scroll the document. When *WM_MOUSEWHEEL* is received, the handler looks at the high word of *wParam* to determine the mouse wheel delta. This is converted into the number of clicks the wheel has rotated by dividing by the system-defined constant *WHEEL_DELTA*. The *WM_MOUSEWHEEL* handler then calls *MyScrollWnd* routine to update the window.

This chapter has covered a huge amount of ground, from basic child windows to controls and on to resources and menus. My goal wasn't to teach everything there is to know about these topics. Instead, I've tried to introduce these program elements, provide a few examples, and point out the subtle differences between the way they're handled by Windows CE and the desktop versions of Windows.

Although the Windows controls are useful and quite handy, the next chapter covers the common controls. These controls are a far more powerful, and more complex, set of controls, which Windows CE also supports.

Chapter 5
Common Controls and Windows CE

As Microsoft Windows matured as an operating system, it became apparent that the basic controls provided by Windows were insufficient for the sophisticated user interfaces that users demanded. Microsoft developed a series of additional controls, called common controls, for their internal applications and later made the dynamic-link library (DLL) containing the controls available to application developers. Starting with Microsoft Windows 95 and Microsoft Windows NT 3.5, the common control library was bundled with the operating system (although this didn't stop Microsoft from making interim releases of the DLL as the common control library was enhanced). With each release of the common control DLL, new controls and new features are added to old controls. As a group, the common controls are less mature than the standard Windows controls and therefore show greater differences between implementations across the various versions of Windows. These differences aren't just between Microsoft Windows CE and other versions of Windows, but also between the different desktop versions of Windows. The functionality of the common controls in Windows CE is fairly complete; however, some of the newest features of the common controls are not supported.

It isn't the goal of this chapter to cover in depth all the common controls. That would take an entire book. Instead, only the controls and features of controls the Windows CE programmer most often needs when writing Windows CE applications are covered. The discussion starts with the command bar control and then looks at the month calendar and time and date picker controls. It finishes with an overview of the other common controls supported by Windows CE. By the end of the chapter, you might not know every common control inside and out, but you will be able to see how the common controls work in general. And you'll have the background to look at the documentation and understand the common controls not covered.

Programming Common Controls

Because the common controls are separate from the core operating system, the DLL that contains them must be initialized before any of the common controls can be used. Under all versions of Windows, including Windows CE, you can call the function

```
void InitCommonControls (void);
```

to load the library and register many of the common control classes. This call doesn't initialize the month calendar, time picker, up/down, tooltip, or other newer common controls. To initialize those controls, use the function

```
BOOL InitCommonControlsEx (LPINITCOMMONCONTROLSEX lpInitCtrls);
```

This function allows an application to load and initialize only selected common controls. This function is handy under Windows CE because loading only the necessary controls can reduce the memory impact. The only parameter to this function is a two-field structure that contains a size field and a field that contains a set of flags indicating which common controls should be registered. Table 5-1 shows the available flags and their associated controls.

TABLE 5-1 Flags for Selected Common Controls

Flag	Control classes initialized
ICC_BAR_CLASSES	Toolbar
	Status bar
	Trackbar
	Command bar
ICC_COOL_CLASSES	Rebar
ICC_DATE_CLASSES	Date and time picker Month calendar control
ICC_LISTVIEW_CLASSES	List view Header control
ICC_PROGRESS_CLASS	Progress bar control
ICC_TAB_CLASSES	Tab control
ICC_TREEVIEW_CLASSES	Tree view control
ICC_UPDOWN_CLASS	Up-Down control
ICC_TOOLTIP_CLASSES	Tooltip control
ICC_CAPEDIT_CLASS	Cap edit control

After the common control DLL is initialized, these controls can be treated like any other control. But because the common controls aren't formally part of the Windows core functionality, an additional include file, CommCtrl.h, must be included.

The programming interface for the common controls is similar to that for standard Windows controls. Each of the controls has a set of custom style flags that configure the look and behavior of the control. Messages specific to each control are sent to configure and manipulate the control and cause it to perform actions. One major difference between the standard Windows controls and common controls is that notifications of events or requests for service are sent via *WM_NOTIFY* messages instead of *WM_COMMAND* messages as in the standard controls. This technique allows the notifications to contain much more information than allowed using *WM_COMMAND* message notifications. In addition, the technique allows the *WM_NOTIFY* message to be extended and adapted for each of the controls that use it.

At a minimum, the *WM_NOTIFY* message is sent with *lParam* pointing to an *NMHDR* structure defined as the following:

```
typedef struct tagNMHDR {
    HWND hwndFrom;
    UINT idFrom;
    UINT code;
} NMHDR;
```

The *hwndFrom* field contains the handle of the window that sent the notify message. For property sheets, this is the property sheet window. The *idFrom* field contains the ID of the control if a control is sending the notification. Finally, the code field contains the notification code. While this basic structure doesn't contain any more information than the *WM_COMMAND* message, it's almost always extended, with additional fields appended to it. The notification code then indicates which, if any, additional fields are appended to the notification structure.

One additional difference in programming common controls is that most of the control-specific messages that can be sent to the common controls have predefined macros that make sending the message look as if your application is calling a function. So instead of using an *LVM_INSERTITEM* message to a list view control to insert an item, as in

```
nIndex = (int) SendMessage (hwndLV, LVM_INSERTITEM, 0, (LPARAM)&lvi);
```

an application could just as easily have used the line

```
nIndex = ListView_InsertItem (hwndLV, &lvi);
```

There's no functional difference between the two lines; the advantage of these macros is clarity. The macros themselves are defined in CommCtrl.h along with the other definitions required for programming the common controls. One problem with the macros is that the compiler doesn't perform the type checking on the parameters that normally occurs if the macro is an actual function. This is also true of the *SendMessage* technique, in which the parameters must be typed as *WPARAM* and *LPARAM* types, but at least with messages, the lack of type checking is obvious. All in all, though, the macro route provides better readability. One exception to this system of macros is the calls made to the command bar control and the command bands control. Those controls actually have a number of true functions in addition to a large set of macro-wrapped messages. As a rule, I'll talk about messages as messages, not as their macro equivalents. That should help differentiate a message or a macro from a true function.

The Common Controls

A prime Windows CE target niche—small personal productivity devices—has driven the requirements for the common controls in Windows CE. The frequent need for time and date references for schedule and task management applications has led to inclusion of the date and time picker control and the month calendar control. The small screens of personal productivity devices inspired the space-saving command bar. Mating the command bar with the rebar control that was created for Internet Explorer has produced the command bands control. The command bands control provides even more room for menus, buttons, and other controls across the top of a Windows CE application.

Starting with Windows CE 4.2, the command bar and command bands controls were supplemented with the menu bar control created for Windows Mobile devices. The most apparent difference between the menu bar control and the earlier command bar is that the menu bar snaps to the bottom of the screen instead of the top of the application's window. Functionally, the menu bar is somewhat more limited than the command bands control. However, for applications where compatibility between embedded Windows CE systems and Windows Mobile systems is important, the application should use the menu bar control.

The Command Bar

Briefly, a command bar control combines a menu and a toolbar. This combination is valuable because the combination of a menu and toolbar on one line saves screen real estate on space-constrained Windows CE displays. To the programmer, the command bar looks like a toolbar with a number of helper functions that make programming the command bar a breeze. In addition to the command bar functions, you can also use most toolbar messages when you work with command bars. A window with a command bar is shown in Figure 5-1.

FIGURE 5-1 A window with a command bar control

Creating a Command Bar

You build a command bar in a number of steps, each defined by a particular function. The command bar is created, the menu is added, buttons are added, other controls are added, tooltips are added, and finally, the Close and Help buttons are appended to the right side of the command bar.

You begin the process of creating a command bar with a call to

```
HWND CommandBar_Create (HINSTANCE hInst, HWND hwndParent,
                        int idCmdBar);
```

The function requires the program's instance handle, the handle of the parent window, and an ID value for the control. If successful, the function returns the handle to the newly created command bar control. But a bare command bar isn't much use to the application. It takes a menu and a few buttons to jazz it up.

Command Bar Menus

You can add a menu to a command bar by calling the function:

```
BOOL CommandBar_InsertMenubarEx (HWND hwndCB, HINSTANCE hInst,
                                 LPTSTR pszMenu, int iButton);
```

The first two parameters of this function are the handle of the command bar and the instance handle of the application. The *pszMenu* parameter is either the name of a menu resource or the handle to a menu previously created by the application. If the *pszMenu* parameter is a menu handle, the *hInst* parameter must be *NULL*. The last parameter is the index of the button to the immediate left of the menu. Because the Windows CE guidelines specify that the menu should be at the left end of the command bar, this parameter should be set to 0, which indicates that all the buttons are to the right of the menu.

After a menu is loaded into a command bar, the handle to the menu can be retrieved at any time using

```
HMENU CommandBar_GetMenu (HWND hwndCB, int iButton);
```

The second parameter, *iButton*, is the index of the button to the immediate left of the menu. This mechanism provides the ability to identify more than one menu on the command bar. However, given the Windows CE design guidelines, you should see only one menu on the bar. With the menu handle, you can manipulate the structure of the menu using the many menu functions available.

If an application modifies the menu on the command bar, the application must call

```
BOOL CommandBar_DrawMenuBar (HWND hwndCB, int iButton);
```

which forces the menu on the command bar to be redrawn. Here again, the parameters are the handle to the command bar and the index of the button to the left of the menu. Under Windows CE, you must use *CommandBar_DrawMenuBar* instead of *DrawMenuBar*, which is the standard function used to redraw the menu under other versions of Windows.

Command Bar Buttons

Adding buttons to a command bar is a two-step process and is similar to adding buttons to a toolbar. First, the bitmap images for the buttons must be added to the command bar. Second, the buttons are added, with each of the buttons referencing one of the images in the bitmap list that was previously added.

The command bar maintains its own list of bitmaps for the buttons in an internal image list. Bitmaps can be added to this image list one at a time or as a group of images contained in a long and narrow bitmap. For example, for a bitmap to contain four 16-by-16-pixel images, the dimensions of the bitmap added to the command bar would be 64 by 16 pixels. Figure 5-2 shows this bitmap image layout.

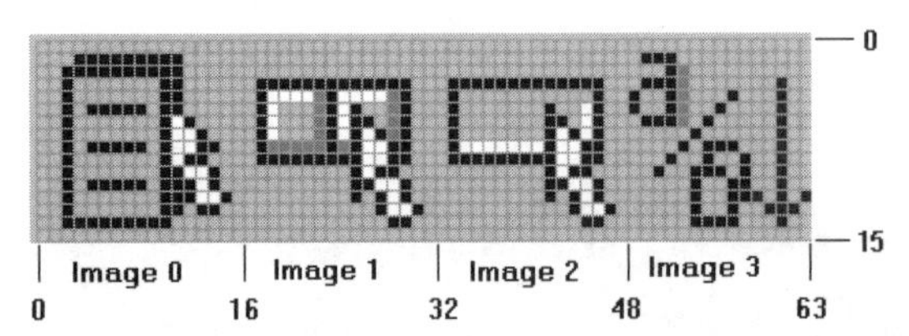

FIGURE 5-2 Layout of a bitmap that contains four 16-by-16-pixel images

Loading an image bitmap is accomplished using

```
int CommandBar_AddBitmap (HWND hwndCB, HINSTANCE hInst, int idBitmap,
                          int iNumImages, int iImageWidth, int iImageHeight);
```

The first two parameters are, as is usual with a command bar function, the handle to the command bar and the instance handle of the executable. The third parameter, *idBitmap*, is the resource ID of the bitmap image. The fourth parameter, *iNumImages*, should contain the number of images in the bitmap being loaded. Multiple bitmap images can be loaded into the same command bar by calling *CommandBar_AddBitmap* as many times as is needed. The last two parameters are the dimensions of the images within the bitmap; set both of these parameters to 16.

Two predefined bitmaps provide a number of images that are commonly used in command bars and toolbars. You load these images by setting the *hInst* parameter in *CommandBar_AddBitmap* to *HINST_COMMCTRL* and setting the *idBitmap* parameter to either *IDB_STD_SMALL_COLOR* or *IDB_VIEW_SMALL_COLOR*. The images contained in these bitmaps are shown in Figure 5-3. There are two groups of bitmaps shown. If the Windows CE system is built with the classic Windows "skin," the top group of bitmaps is used. If the system is built with the XP "skin" the bottom set of bitmaps is used.[1] For each group, the buttons on the top line contain the bitmaps from the standard bitmap, while the second-line buttons contain the bitmaps from the standard view bitmap.

[1] It is also possible to build a Windows CE system with a custom "skin" that uses bitmaps with a different look than either of the two groups shown.

FIGURE 5-3 Images in the standard bitmaps provided by the common control DLL. The top set is used with the classic "skin" while the bottom set is used with the XP "skin."

The index values to these images are defined in CommCtrl.h, so you don't need to know the exact order in the bitmaps.

Referencing Images

The images loaded into the command bar are referenced by their index into the list of images. For example, if the bitmap loaded contains five images, and the image to be referenced is the fourth image into the bitmap, the zero-based index value is 3.

If more than one set of bitmap images is added to the command bar using multiple calls to *CommandBar_AddBitmap*, the images' subsequent lists are referenced according to the previous count of images plus the index into that list. For example, if two calls are made to *CommandBar_AddBitmap* to add two sets of images, with the first call adding five images and the second adding four images, the third image of the second set is referenced with the total number of images added in the first bitmap (5) plus the index into the second bitmap (2), resulting in an index value of 5 + 2 = 7.

After the bitmaps are loaded, the buttons can be added using one of two functions. The first function is this one:

```
BOOL CommandBar_AddButtons (HWND hwndCB, UINT uNumButtons,
                            LPTBBUTTON lpButtons);
```

CommandBar_AddButtons adds a series of buttons to the command bar at one time. The function is passed a count of buttons and a pointer to an array of *TBBUTTON* structures. Each element of the array describes one button. The *TBBUTTON* structure is defined as the following:

```
typedef struct {
    int iBitmap;
    int idCommand;
    BYTE fsState;
    BYTE fsStyle;
    DWORD dwData;
    int iString;
} TBBUTTON;
```

The *iBitmap* field specifies the bitmap image to be used by the button. This is, as I just explained, the zero-based index into the list of images. The second parameter is the command

ID of the button. This ID value is sent via a *WM_COMMAND* message to the parent when a user clicks the button.

The *fsState* field specifies the initial state of the button. The allowable values in this field are the following:

- **TBSTATE_ENABLED** The button is enabled. If this flag isn't specified, the button is disabled and is grayed.
- **TBSTATE_HIDDEN** The button isn't visible on the command bar.
- **TBSTATE_PRESSED** This button is displayed in a depressed state.
- **TBSTATE_CHECKED** The button is initially checked. This state can be used only if the button has the TBSTYLE_CHECKED style.
- **TBSTATE_INDETERMINATE** The button is grayed.

The *fsStyle* field specifies the initial style of the button, which defines how the button acts. The button can be defined as a standard push button, a check button, a drop-down button, or a check button that resembles a radio button but allows only one button in a group to be checked. The possible flags for the *fsStyle* field are the following:

- **TBSTYLE_BUTTON** The button looks like a standard push button.
- **TBSTYLE_CHECK** The button is a check button that toggles between checked and unchecked states each time the user clicks the button.
- **TBSTYLE_GROUP** Defines the start of a group of buttons.
- **TBSTYLE_CHECKGROUP** The button is a member of a group of check buttons that act like radio buttons in that only one button in the group is checked at any one time.
- **TBSTYLE_DROPDOWN** The button is a drop-down list button.
- **TBSTYLE_AUTOSIZE** The button's size is defined by the button text.
- **TBSTYLE_SEP** Defines a separator (instead of a button) that inserts a small space between buttons.

The *dwData* field of the *TBBUTTON* structure is an application-defined value. This value can be set and queried by the application using the *TB_SETBUTTONINFO* and *TB_GETBUTTONINFO* messages. The *iString* field defines the index into the command bar string array that contains the text for the button. The *iString* field can also be filled with a pointer to a string that contains the text for the button.

The other function that adds buttons to a command bar is this one:

```
BOOL CommandBar_InsertButton (HWND hwndCB, int iButton,
                              LPTBBUTTON lpButton);
```

This function inserts one button into the command bar to the left of the button referenced by the *iButton* parameter. The parameters in this function mimic the parameters in *CommandBar_AddButtons* with the exception that the *lpButton* parameter points to a single *TBBUTTON* structure. The *iButton* parameter specifies the position on the command bar of the new button.

Working with Command Bar Buttons

When a user presses a command bar button other than a drop-down button, the command bar sends a *WM_COMMAND* message to the parent window of the command bar. So handling button clicks on the command bar is just like handling menu commands. In fact, because many of the buttons on the command bar have menu command equivalents, it's customary to use the same command IDs for the buttons and the like-functioning menus, thus removing the need for any special processing for the command bar buttons.

The command bar maintains the checked and unchecked state of check and checkgroup buttons. After the buttons are added to the command bar, their states can be queried or set using two messages, *TB_ISBUTTONCHECKED* and *TB_CHECKBUTTON*. (The *TB_* prefix in these messages indicates the close relationship between the command bar and the toolbar controls.) The *TB_ISBUTTONCHECKED* message is sent with the ID of the button to be queried passed in the *wParam* parameter this way:

```
fChecked = SendMessage (hwndCB, TB_ISBUTTONCHECKED, wID, 0);
```

where *hwndCB* is the handle to the command bar containing the button. If the return value from the *TB_ISBUTTONCHECKED* message is nonzero, the button is checked. To place a button in the checked state, send a *TB_CHECKBUTTON* message to the command bar, as in

```
SendMessage (hwndCB, TB_CHECKBUTTON, wID, TRUE);
```

To uncheck a checked button, replace the *TRUE* value in *lParam* with *FALSE*.

Drop-Down Buttons

The drop-down list button is a more complex animal than the standard button on a command bar. The button looks to the user like a button that, when pressed, displays a list of items from which the user can select. To the programmer, a drop-down button is actually a combination of a button and a menu that is displayed when the user clicks the button. Unfortunately, the command bar does little to support a drop-down button except to modify the button appearance to indicate that the button is a drop-down button and to send a special notification when the button is clicked by the user. It's up to the application to display the menu.

The notification of the user clicking a drop-down button is sent to the parent window of the command bar by a *WM_NOTIFY* message with the notification value *TBN_DROPDOWN*.

When the parent window receives the *TBN_DROPDOWN* notification, it must create a pop-up menu immediately below the drop-down button identified in the notification. The menu is filled by the parent window with whatever selections are appropriate for the button. When one of the menu items is selected, the menu sends a *WM_COMMAND* message indicating the menu item picked, and the menu is dismissed. The easiest way to understand how to handle a drop-down button notification is to look at the following procedure that handles a *TBN_DROPDOWN* notification.

```
LRESULT DoNotifyMain (HWND hWnd, UINT wMsg, WPARAM wParam,
                      LPARAM lParam) {
    LPNMHDR pNotifyHeader;
    LPNMTOOLBAR pNotifyToolBar;
    RECT rect;
    TPMPARAMS tpm;
    HMENU hMenu;

    // Get pointer to notify message header.
    pNotifyHeader = (LPNMHDR)lParam;

    if (pNotifyHeader->code == TBN_DROPDOWN) {

        // Get pointer to toolbar notify structure.
        pNotifyToolBar = (LPNMTOOLBAR)lParam;

        // Get the rectangle of the drop-down button.
        SendMessage (pNotifyHeader->hwndFrom, TB_GETRECT,
                     pNotifyToolBar->iItem, (LPARAM)&rect);

        // Convert rect to screen coordinates.  The rect is
        // considered here to be an array of 2 POINT structures.
        MapWindowPoints (pNotifyHeader->hwndFrom, HWND_DESKTOP,
                         (LPPOINT)&rect, 2);

        // Prevent the menu from covering the button.
        tpm.cbSize = sizeof (tpm);
        CopyRect (&tpm.rcExclude, &rect);

        // Load the menu resource to display under the button.
        hMenu = GetSubMenu (LoadMenu (hInst, TEXT ("popmenu")),0);

        // Display the menu.  This function returns after the
        // user makes a selection or dismisses the menu.
        TrackPopupMenuEx (hMenu, TPM_LEFTALIGN | TPM_VERTICAL,
                          rect.left, rect.bottom, hWnd, &tpm);
    }
    return 0;
}
```

After the code determines that the message is a *TBN_DROPDOWN* notification, the first task of the notification handler code is to get the rectangle of the drop-down button. The rectangle is queried so that the drop-down menu can be positioned immediately below the button.

To do this, the routine sends a *TB_GETRECT* message to the command bar with the ID of the drop-down button passed in *wParam* and a pointer to a rectangle structure in *lParam*.

Because the rectangle returned is in the coordinate base of the parent window, and pop-up menus are positioned in screen coordinates, the coordinates must be converted from one basis to the other. You accomplish this using the function

```
MapWindowPoints (HWND hwndFrom, HWND hwndTo,
                 LPPOINT lppoints, UINT cPoints);
```

The first parameter is the handle of the window in which the coordinates are originally based. The second parameter is the handle of the window to which you want to map the coordinates. The third parameter is a pointer to an array of points to be translated; the last parameter is the number of points in the array. In the routine I just showed you, the window handles are the command bar handle and the desktop window handle, respectively.

After the rectangle is translated into desktop coordinates, the pop-up, or context, menu can be created. You do this by first loading the menu from the resource and then displaying the menu with a call to *TrackPopupMenuEx*. If you recall the discussion of *TrackPopupMenuEx* from Chapter 4, "Windows, Controls, and Menus," the *TPMPARAMS* structure contains a rectangle that isn't covered up by the menu when it's displayed. For your purposes, this rectangle is set to the dimensions of the drop-down button so that the button isn't covered by the pop-up menu. The *fuFlags* field can contain a number of values that define the placement of the menu. For drop-down buttons, the only flag needed is *TPM_VERTICAL*. If *TPM_VERTICAL* is set, the menu leaves uncovered as much of the horizontal area of the exclude rectangle as possible. The *TrackPopupMenuEx* function doesn't return until an item on the menu is selected or the menu is dismissed by the user tapping on another part of the screen.

Combo Boxes on the Command Bar

Combo boxes on a command bar are much easier to implement than drop-down buttons. You add a combo box by calling

```
HWND CommandBar_InsertComboBox (HWND hwndCB, HINSTANCE hInst,
                                int iWidth, UINT dwStyle,
                                WORD idComboBox,
                                int iButton);
```

This function inserts a combo box on the command bar to the left of the button indicated by the *iButton* parameter. The width of the combo box is specified, in pixels, by the *iWidth* parameter. The *dwStyle* parameter specifies the style of the combo box. The allowable style flags are any valid Windows CE combo box style and window styles. The function automatically adds the *WS_CHILD* and *WS_VISIBLE* flags when creating the combo box. The *idComboBox* parameter is the ID for the combo box that will be used when *WM_COMMAND* messages are sent notifying the parent window of a combo box event. Experienced Windows programmers will be happy to know that *CommandBar_InsertComboBox* takes care of all the "parenting" problems that occur when a control is added to a standard Windows toolbar. That one function call is all that is needed to create a properly functioning combo box on the command bar.

After a combo box is created, you program it on the command bar the same way you would a stand-alone combo box. Because the combo box is a child of the command bar, you must query the window handle of the combo box by passing the handle of the command bar to *GetDlgItem* with the ID value of the combo box, as in the following code:

```
hwndCombobox = GetDlgItem (GetDlgItem (hWnd, IDC_CMDBAR),
                           IDC_COMBO));
```

However, the *WM_COMMAND* messages from the combo box are sent directly to the parent of the command bar, so handling combo box events is identical to handling them from a combo box created as a child of the application's top-level window.

Other Command Bar Functions

A number of other functions assist in command bar management. The *CommandBar_Height* function returns the height of the command bar and is used in all the example programs that use the command bar. Likewise, the *CommandBar_AddAdornments* function is also used whenever a command bar is used. This function, prototyped as

```
BOOL CommandBar_AddAdornments (HWND hwndCB, DWORD dwFlags,
                               DWORD dwReserved);
```

places a Close button and, if you want, a Help button and an OK button on the extreme right of the command bar. You pass a *CMDBAR_HELP* flag to the *dwFlags* parameter to add a Help button, and you pass a *CMDBAR_OK* flag to add an OK button.

The Help button is treated differently from other buttons on the command bar. When the Help button is pressed, the command bar sends a *WM_HELP* message to the owner of the command bar instead of the standard *WM_COMMAND* message. The OK button's action is more traditional. When you tap it, you send a *WM_COMMAND* message with the control ID *IDOK*. The *CommandBar_AddAdornments* function must be called after all other controls of the command bar have been added.

If your top-level window is resizeable, you must notifiy the command bar of resize during the *WM_SIZE* message by sending a *TB_AUTOSIZE* message to the command bar and then calling

```
BOOL CommandBar_AlignAdornments (HWND hwndCB);
```

The only parameter is the handle to the command bar. A command bar can be hidden by calling

```
BOOL CommandBar_Show (HWND hwndCB, BOOL fShow);
```

The *fShow* parameter is set to *TRUE* to show a command bar and *FALSE* to hide a command bar. The visibility of a command bar can be queried with this:

```
BOOL CommandBar_IsVisible (HWND hwndCB);
```

Finally, a command bar can be destroyed using this:

```
void CommandBar_Destroy (HWND hwndCB);
```

Although a command bar is automatically destroyed when its parent window is destroyed, sometimes it's more convenient to destroy a command bar manually. This is often done if a new command bar is needed for a different mode of the application. Of course, you can create multiple command bars, hiding all but one and switching between them by showing only one at a time, but this isn't good programming practice under Windows CE because all those hidden command bars take up valuable RAM that could be used elsewhere. The proper method is to destroy and create command bars on the fly. You can create a command bar fast enough so that a user shouldn't notice any delay in the application when a new command bar is created.

The CmdBar Example

The CmdBar example demonstrates the basics of command bar operation. On startup, the example creates a bar with only a menu and a Close button. Selecting the different items from the view menu creates various command bars showing the capabilities of the command bar control. The source code for CmdBar is shown in Listing 5-1.

LISTING 5-1

CmdBar.rc

```
//======================================================================
// Resource file
//
// Written for the book Programming Windows CE
// Copyright (C) 2007 Douglas Boling
//======================================================================
#include "windows.h"
#include "CmdBar.h"                      // Program-specific stuff
//----------------------------------------------------------------------
// Icons and bitmaps
//
ID_ICON        ICON    "cmdbar.ico"      // Program icon
DisCross       BITMAP "cross.bmp"        // Disabled button image
DisMask        BITMAP "mask.bmp"         // Disabled button image mask
SortDropBtn    BITMAP "sortdrop.bmp"     // Sort drop-down button image

//----------------------------------------------------------------------
// Menu
//
```

```
ID_MENU MENU DISCARDABLE
BEGIN
    POPUP "&File"
    BEGIN
        MENUITEM "E&xit",                          IDM_EXIT
    END

    POPUP "&View"
    BEGIN
        MENUITEM "&Standard",                      IDM_STDBAR
        MENUITEM "&View",                          IDM_VIEWBAR
        MENUITEM "&Combination",                   IDM_COMBOBAR
    END
END

popmenu MENU DISCARDABLE
BEGIN
    POPUP "&Sort"
    BEGIN
        MENUITEM "&Name",                          IDC_SNAME
        MENUITEM "&Type",                          IDC_STYPE
        MENUITEM "&Size",                          IDC_SSIZE
        MENUITEM "&Date",                          IDC_SDATE
    END
END
```

CmdBar.h

```
//======================================================================
// Header file
//
// Written for the book Programming Windows CE
// Copyright (C) 2007 Douglas Boling
//======================================================================
// Returns number of elements
#define dim(x) (sizeof(x) / sizeof(x[0]))

//----------------------------------------------------------------------
// Generic defines and data types
//
struct decodeUINT {                             // Structure associates
    UINT Code;                                  // messages
                                                // with a function.
    LRESULT (*Fxn)(HWND, UINT, WPARAM, LPARAM);
};
struct decodeCMD {                              // Structure associates
    UINT Code;                                  // menu IDs with a
    LRESULT (*Fxn)(HWND, WORD, HWND, WORD);     // function.
};

//----------------------------------------------------------------------
```

```
// Generic defines used by application
#define  IDC_CMDBAR          1                  // Command band ID
#define  ID_ICON             10                 // Icon resource ID
#define  ID_MENU             11                 // Main menu resource ID
#define  IDC_COMBO           12                 // Combo box on cmd bar ID

// Menu item IDs
#define  IDM_EXIT            101                // File menu
#define  IDM_STDBAR          111                // View menu
#define  IDM_VIEWBAR         112
#define  IDM_COMBOBAR        113
#define  IDM_ABOUT           120                // Help menu
// Command bar button IDs
#define  IDC_NEW             201
#define  IDC_OPEN            202
#define  IDC_SAVE            203
#define  IDC_CUT             204
#define  IDC_COPY            205
#define  IDC_PASTE           206
#define  IDC_PROP            207

#define  IDC_LICON           301
#define  IDC_SICON           302
#define  IDC_LIST            303
#define  IDC_RPT             304
#define  IDC_SNAME           305
#define  IDC_STYPE           306
#define  IDC_SSIZE           307
#define  IDC_SDATE           308
#define  IDC_DPSORT          350

#define  STD_BMPS            (STD_PRINT+1)      // Number of bmps in
                                                // std imglist
#define  VIEW_BMPS           (VIEW_NEWFOLDER+1) // Number of bmps in
                                                // view imglist
//----------------------------------------------------------------------
// Function prototypes
//
HWND InitInstance (HINSTANCE, LPWSTR, int);
int TermInstance (HINSTANCE, int);

// Window procedures
LRESULT CALLBACK MainWndProc (HWND, UINT, WPARAM, LPARAM);

// Message handlers
LRESULT DoCreateMain (HWND, UINT, WPARAM, LPARAM);
LRESULT DoSizeMain (HWND, UINT, WPARAM, LPARAM);
LRESULT DoCommandMain (HWND, UINT, WPARAM, LPARAM);
LRESULT DoNotifyMain (HWND, UINT, WPARAM, LPARAM);
LRESULT DoDestroyMain (HWND, UINT, WPARAM, LPARAM);

// Command functions
LPARAM DoMainCommandExit (HWND, WORD, HWND, WORD);
LPARAM DoMainCommandVStd (HWND, WORD, HWND, WORD);
```

```
LPARAM DoMainCommandVView (HWND, WORD, HWND, WORD);
LPARAM DoMainCommandVCombo (HWND, WORD, HWND, WORD);
```

CmdBar.cpp

```
//======================================================================
// CmdBar - Command bar demonstration
//
// Written for the book Programming Windows CE
// Copyright (C) 2007 Douglas Boling
//======================================================================
#include <windows.h>                 // For all that Windows stuff
#include <commctrl.h>                // Command bar includes
#include "CmdBar.h"                  // Program-specific stuff
//----------------------------------------------------------------------
// Global data
//
const TCHAR szAppName[] = TEXT ("CmdBar");
HINSTANCE hInst;                     // Program instance handle

// Message dispatch table for MainWindowProc
const struct decodeUINT MainMessages[] = {
    WM_CREATE, DoCreateMain,
    WM_SIZE, DoSizeMain,
    WM_COMMAND, DoCommandMain,
    WM_NOTIFY, DoNotifyMain,
    WM_DESTROY, DoDestroyMain,
};

// Command Message dispatch for MainWindowProc
const struct decodeCMD MainCommandItems[] = {
    IDM_EXIT, DoMainCommandExit,
    IDM_STDBAR, DoMainCommandVStd,
    IDM_VIEWBAR, DoMainCommandVView,
    IDM_COMBOBAR, DoMainCommandVCombo,
};

// Standard file bar button structure
const TBBUTTON tbCBStdBtns[] = {
//  BitmapIndex      Command    State        Style        UserData String
    {0,              0,         0,           TBSTYLE_SEP,        0,   0},
    {STD_FILENEW,    IDC_NEW,   TBSTATE_ENABLED,
                                             TBSTYLE_BUTTON,     0,   0},
    {STD_FILEOPEN,   IDC_OPEN,  TBSTATE_ENABLED,
                                             TBSTYLE_BUTTON,     0,   0},
    {STD_FILESAVE,   IDC_SAVE,  TBSTATE_ENABLED,
                                             TBSTYLE_BUTTON,     0,   0},
    {0,                0,       0,           TBSTYLE_SEP,        0,   0},
    {STD_CUT,        IDC_CUT,   TBSTATE_ENABLED,
                                             TBSTYLE_BUTTON,     0,   0},
```

```
    {STD_COPY,        IDC_COPY,  TBSTATE_ENABLED,
                                      TBSTYLE_BUTTON,     0,   0},
    {STD_PASTE,       IDC_PASTE, TBSTATE_ENABLED,
                                      TBSTYLE_BUTTON,     0,   0},
    {0,                0,         0,   TBSTYLE_SEP,        0,   0},
    {STD_PROPERTIES,  IDC_PROP,  TBSTATE_ENABLED,
        TBSTYLE_BUTTON,     0,     0}
};

// Standard view bar button structure
const TBBUTTON tbCBViewBtns[] = {
//  BitmapIndex       Command    State            Style         UserData String
    {0,               0,         0,               TBSTYLE_SEP,        0,   0},
    {VIEW_LARGEICONS, IDC_LICON, TBSTATE_ENABLED | TBSTATE_CHECKED,
                                                  TBSTYLE_CHECKGROUP, 0,   0},
    {VIEW_SMALLICONS, IDC_SICON, TBSTATE_ENABLED,
                                                  TBSTYLE_CHECKGROUP, 0,   0},
    {VIEW_LIST,       IDC_LIST,  0,               TBSTYLE_CHECKGROUP, 0,   0},
    {VIEW_DETAILS,    IDC_RPT,   TBSTATE_ENABLED,
                                                  TBSTYLE_CHECKGROUP, 0,   0},
    {0,               0,         TBSTATE_ENABLED,
                                                  TBSTYLE_SEP,        0,   0},
    {VIEW_SORTNAME,   IDC_SNAME, TBSTATE_ENABLED | TBSTATE_CHECKED,
                                                  TBSTYLE_CHECKGROUP, 0,   0},
    {VIEW_SORTTYPE,   IDC_STYPE, TBSTATE_ENABLED,
                                                  TBSTYLE_CHECKGROUP, 0,   0},
    {VIEW_SORTSIZE,   IDC_SSIZE, TBSTATE_ENABLED,
                                                  TBSTYLE_CHECKGROUP, 0,   0},
    {VIEW_SORTDATE,   IDC_SDATE, TBSTATE_ENABLED,
                                                  TBSTYLE_CHECKGROUP, 0,   0},
    {0,               0,         0,               TBSTYLE_SEP,        0,   0},
};
// Tooltip string list for view bar
const TCHAR *pViewTips[] = {TEXT (""), TEXT ("Large"), TEXT ("Small"),
                            TEXT ("List"), TEXT ("Details"), TEXT (""),
                            TEXT ("Sort by Name"), TEXT ("Sort by Type"),
                            TEXT ("Sort by Size"), TEXT ("Sort by Date"),
};

// Combination standard and view bar button structure
const TBBUTTON tbCBCmboBtns[] = {
//  BitmapIndex       Command    State            Style         UserData String
    {0,               0,         0,               TBSTYLE_SEP,        0,   0},
    {STD_FILENEW,     IDC_NEW,   TBSTATE_ENABLED,
                                                  TBSTYLE_BUTTON,     0,   0},
    {STD_FILEOPEN,    IDC_OPEN,  TBSTATE_ENABLED,
                                                  TBSTYLE_BUTTON,     0,   0},
    {STD_PROPERTIES,  IDC_PROP,  TBSTATE_ENABLED,
                                                  TBSTYLE_BUTTON,     0,   0},
    {0,               0,         0,               TBSTYLE_SEP,        0,   0},
    {STD_CUT,         IDC_CUT,   TBSTATE_ENABLED,
                                                  TBSTYLE_BUTTON,     0,   0},
    {STD_COPY,        IDC_COPY,  TBSTATE_ENABLED,
                                                  TBSTYLE_BUTTON,     0,   0},
```

```
    {STD_PASTE,        IDC_PASTE, TBSTATE_ENABLED,
                                              TBSTYLE_BUTTON,     0,  0},
    {0,                0,         0,          TBSTYLE_SEP,        0,  0},
    {STD_BMPS + VIEW_LARGEICONS,
                       IDC_LICON, TBSTATE_ENABLED | TBSTATE_CHECKED,
                                              TBSTYLE_CHECKGROUP, 0,  0},
    {STD_BMPS + VIEW_SMALLICONS,
                       IDC_SICON, TBSTATE_ENABLED,
                                              TBSTYLE_CHECKGROUP, 0,  0},
    {STD_BMPS + VIEW_LIST,
                       IDC_LIST,  TBSTATE_ENABLED,
                                              TBSTYLE_CHECKGROUP, 0,  0},
    {STD_BMPS + VIEW_DETAILS,
                       IDC_RPT,   TBSTATE_ENABLED,
                                              TBSTYLE_CHECKGROUP, 0,  0},
    {0,                0,         0,          TBSTYLE_SEP,        0,  0},
    {STD_BMPS + VIEW_BMPS,
                       IDC_DPSORT,TBSTATE_ENABLED,
                                              TBSTYLE_DROPDOWN,   0,  0}
};

//======================================================================
// Program entry point
//
int WINAPI WinMain (HINSTANCE hInstance, HINSTANCE hPrevInstance,
                    LPWSTR lpCmdLine, int nCmdShow) {
    HWND hwndMain;
    MSG msg;
    int rc = 0;

    // Initialize application.

    hwndMain = InitInstance (hInstance, lpCmdLine, nCmdShow);
    if (hwndMain == 0) return 0x10;

    // Application message loop
    while (GetMessage (&msg, NULL, 0, 0)) {
        TranslateMessage (&msg);
        DispatchMessage (&msg);
    }
    // Instance cleanup
    return TermInstance (hInstance, msg.wParam);
}
//----------------------------------------------------------------------
// InitInstance - Instance initialization
//
HWND InitInstance (HINSTANCE hInstance, LPWSTR lpCmdLine, int nCmdShow){
    HWND hWnd;
    WNDCLASS wc;
    INITCOMMONCONTROLSEX icex;

#if defined(WIN32_PLATFORM_PSPC) || defined(WIN32_PLATFORM_WFSP)
    // If Windows Mobile, allow only one instance of the application.
```

```
    hWnd = FindWindow (szAppName, NULL);
    if (hWnd) {
        SetForegroundWindow ((HWND)(((DWORD)hWnd) | 0x01));
        return 0;
    }
#endif
    // Register application main window class.
    wc.style = 0;                             // Window style
    wc.lpfnWndProc = MainWndProc;             // Callback function
    wc.cbClsExtra = 0;                        // Extra class data
    wc.cbWndExtra = 0;                        // Extra window data
    wc.hInstance = hInstance;                 // Owner handle
    wc.hIcon = NULL,                          // Application icon
    wc.hCursor = LoadCursor (NULL, IDC_ARROW);// Default cursor
    wc.hbrBackground = (HBRUSH) GetStockObject (WHITE_BRUSH);
    wc.lpszMenuName =  NULL;                  // Menu name
    wc.lpszClassName = szAppName;             // Window class name

    if (RegisterClass (&wc) == 0) return 0;

    // Load the command bar common control class.
    icex.dwSize = sizeof (INITCOMMONCONTROLSEX);
    icex.dwICC = ICC_BAR_CLASSES;
    InitCommonControlsEx (&icex);

    // Save program instance handle in global variable.
    hInst = hInstance;

    // Create main window.
    hWnd = CreateWindow (szAppName, TEXT ("CmdBar Demo"), WS_VISIBLE,
                         CW_USEDEFAULT, CW_USEDEFAULT,
                   CW_USEDEFAULT, CW_USEDEFAULT, NULL, NULL,
                   hInstance, NULL);
    // Return fail code if window not created.
    if (!IsWindow (hWnd)) return 0;

    // Standard show and update calls
    ShowWindow (hWnd, nCmdShow);
    UpdateWindow (hWnd);
    return hWnd;
}
//----------------------------------------------------------------------
// TermInstance - Program cleanup
//
int TermInstance (HINSTANCE hInstance, int nDefRC) {
    return nDefRC;
}
//======================================================================
// Message handling procedures for MainWindow
//----------------------------------------------------------------------
// MainWndProc - Callback function for application window
//
LRESULT CALLBACK MainWndProc (HWND hWnd, UINT wMsg, WPARAM wParam,
                              LPARAM lParam) {
```

```
    int i;
    //
    // Search message list to see if we need to handle this
    // message. If in list, call procedure.
    //
    for (i = 0; i < dim(MainMessages); i++) {
        if (wMsg == MainMessages[i].Code)
            return (*MainMessages[i].Fxn)(hWnd, wMsg, wParam, lParam);
    }
    return DefWindowProc (hWnd, wMsg, wParam, lParam);
}
//----------------------------------------------------------------------
// DoCreateMain - Process WM_CREATE message for window.
//
LRESULT DoCreateMain (HWND hWnd, UINT wMsg, WPARAM wParam,
                      LPARAM lParam) {
    HWND hwndCB;

    // Create a minimal command bar that has only a menu and an
    // exit button.
    hwndCB = CommandBar_Create (hInst, hWnd, IDC_CMDBAR);

    // Insert the menu.
    CommandBar_InsertMenubar (hwndCB, hInst, ID_MENU, 0);

    // Add exit button to command bar.
    CommandBar_AddAdornments (hwndCB, 0, 0);
    return 0;
}
//----------------------------------------------------------------------
// DoSizeMain - Process WM_SIZE message for window.
//
LRESULT DoSizeMain (HWND hWnd, UINT wMsg, WPARAM wParam,
                    LPARAM lParam) {
   // This only needed if the window can be resized
    HWND hwndCB = GetDlgItem (hWnd, IDC_CMDBAR);
   // Tell the command bar to resize itself and reposition Close button.
   SendMessage(hwndCB, TB_AUTOSIZE, 0L, 0L);
   CommandBar_AlignAdornments(hwndCB);

    return 0;
}
//----------------------------------------------------------------------
// DoCommandMain - Process WM_COMMAND message for window.
//
LRESULT DoCommandMain (HWND hWnd, UINT wMsg, WPARAM wParam,
                       LPARAM lParam) {
    WORD idItem, wNotifyCode;
    HWND hwndCtl;
    INT  i;

    // Parse the parameters.
    idItem = (WORD) LOWORD (wParam);
    wNotifyCode = (WORD) HIWORD (wParam);
```

```
    hwndCtl = (HWND) lParam;

    // Call routine to handle control message.
    for (i = 0; i < dim(MainCommandItems); i++) {
        if (idItem == MainCommandItems[i].Code)
            return (*MainCommandItems[i].Fxn)(hWnd, idItem, hwndCtl,
                                              wNotifyCode);
    }
    return 0;
}
//----------------------------------------------------------------------
// DoNotifyMain - Process WM_NOTIFY message for window.
//
LRESULT DoNotifyMain (HWND hWnd, UINT wMsg, WPARAM wParam,
                      LPARAM lParam) {
    LPNMHDR pNotifyHeader;
    LPNMTOOLBAR pNotifyToolBar;
    RECT rect;
    TPMPARAMS tpm;
    HMENU hMenu;

    // Get pointer to notify message header.
    pNotifyHeader = (LPNMHDR)lParam;

    if (pNotifyHeader->code == TBN_DROPDOWN) {

        // Get pointer to toolbar notify structure.
        pNotifyToolBar = (LPNMTOOLBAR)lParam;

        if (pNotifyToolBar->iItem == IDC_DPSORT) {

            // Get the rectangle of the drop-down button.
            SendMessage (pNotifyHeader->hwndFrom, TB_GETRECT,
                         pNotifyToolBar->iItem, (LPARAM)&rect);

            // Convert rect to screen coordinates.  The rect is
            // considered here to be an array of 2 POINT structures.
            MapWindowPoints (pNotifyHeader->hwndFrom, HWND_DESKTOP,
                             (LPPOINT)&rect, 2);

            // Prevent the menu from covering the button.
            tpm.cbSize = sizeof (tpm);
            CopyRect (&tpm.rcExclude, &rect);

            hMenu = GetSubMenu (LoadMenu (hInst, TEXT ("popmenu")),0);
            TrackPopupMenuEx (hMenu, TPM_LEFTALIGN | TPM_VERTICAL,
                              rect.left, rect.bottom, hWnd, &tpm);
        }
    }
    return 0;
}
//----------------------------------------------------------------------
// DoDestroyMain - Process WM_DESTROY message for window.
//
```

```
LRESULT DoDestroyMain (HWND hWnd, UINT wMsg, WPARAM wParam,
                       LPARAM lParam) {
    PostQuitMessage (0);
    return 0;
}
//======================================================================
// Command handler routines
//----------------------------------------------------------------------
// DoMainCommandExit - Process Program Exit command.
//
LPARAM DoMainCommandExit (HWND hWnd, WORD idItem, HWND hwndCtl,
                          WORD wNotifyCode) {

    SendMessage (hWnd, WM_CLOSE, 0, 0);
    return 0;
}
//----------------------------------------------------------------------
// DoMainCommandViewStd - Displays a standard edit-centric command bar
//
LPARAM DoMainCommandVStd (HWND hWnd, WORD idItem, HWND hwndCtl,
                          WORD wNotifyCode) {
    HWND hwndCB;

    // If a command bar exists, kill it.
    if (hwndCB = GetDlgItem (hWnd, IDC_CMDBAR))
        CommandBar_Destroy (hwndCB);

    // Create a command bar.
    hwndCB = CommandBar_Create (hInst, hWnd, IDC_CMDBAR);
    // Insert a menu.
    CommandBar_InsertMenubar (hwndCB, hInst, ID_MENU, 0);

    // Insert buttons.
    CommandBar_AddBitmap (hwndCB, HINST_COMMCTRL, IDB_STD_SMALL_COLOR,
                          STD_BMPS, 0, 0);

    CommandBar_AddButtons (hwndCB, dim(tbCBStdBtns), tbCBStdBtns);

    // Add exit button to command bar.
    CommandBar_AddAdornments (hwndCB, 0, 0);
    return 0;
}
//----------------------------------------------------------------------
// DoMainCommandVView - Displays a standard edit-centric command bar
//
LPARAM DoMainCommandVView (HWND hWnd, WORD idItem, HWND hwndCtl,
                           WORD wNotifyCode) {
    INT i;
    HWND hwndCB;
    TCHAR szTmp[64];
    HBITMAP hBmp, hMask;
    HIMAGELIST hilDisabled, hilEnabled;

    // If a command bar exists, kill it.
```

```
    if (hwndCB = GetDlgItem (hWnd, IDC_CMDBAR))
        CommandBar_Destroy (hwndCB);
    // Create a command bar.
    hwndCB = CommandBar_Create (hInst, hWnd, IDC_CMDBAR);

    // Insert a menu.
    CommandBar_InsertMenubar (hwndCB, hInst, ID_MENU, 0);

    // Insert buttons, first add a bitmap and then the buttons.
    CommandBar_AddBitmap (hwndCB, HINST_COMMCTRL, IDB_VIEW_SMALL_COLOR,
                          VIEW_BMPS, 0, 0);

    // Load bitmaps for disabled image.
    hBmp = LoadBitmap (hInst, TEXT ("DisCross"));
    hMask = LoadBitmap (hInst, TEXT ("DisMask"));

    // Get the current image list and copy.
    hilEnabled = (HIMAGELIST)SendMessage (hwndCB, TB_GETIMAGELIST, 0, 0);
    hilDisabled = ImageList_Duplicate (hilEnabled);
    // Replace a button image with the disabled image.
    ImageList_Replace (hilDisabled, VIEW_LIST, hBmp, hMask);

    // Set disabled image list.
    SendMessage (hwndCB,  TB_SETDISABLEDIMAGELIST, 0,
                 (LPARAM)hilDisabled);

    // Add buttons to the command bar.
    CommandBar_AddButtons (hwndCB, dim(tbCBViewBtns), tbCBViewBtns);

    // Add tooltips to the command bar.
    CommandBar_AddToolTips (hwndCB, dim(pViewTips), pViewTips);

    // Add a combo box between the view icons and the sort icons.
    CommandBar_InsertComboBox (hwndCB, hInst, 75,
                               CBS_DROPDOWNLIST | WS_VSCROLL,
                               IDC_COMBO, 6);
    // Fill in combo box.
    for (i = 0; i < 10; i++) {
        wsprintf (szTmp, TEXT ("Item %d"), i);
        SendDlgItemMessage (hwndCB, IDC_COMBO, CB_INSERTSTRING, -1,
                            (LPARAM)szTmp);
    }
    SendDlgItemMessage (hwndCB, IDC_COMBO, CB_SETCURSEL, 0, 0);

    // Add exit button to command bar.
    CommandBar_AddAdornments (hwndCB, 0, 0);
    return 0;
}
//----------------------------------------------------------------------
// DoMainCommandVCombo - Displays a combination of file and edit buttons
//
LPARAM DoMainCommandVCombo (HWND hWnd, WORD idItem, HWND hwndCtl,
                            WORD wNotifyCode) {
    HWND hwndCB;
```

```
    // If a command bar exists, kill it.
    if (hwndCB = GetDlgItem (hWnd, IDC_CMDBAR))
        CommandBar_Destroy (hwndCB);

    // Create a command bar.
    hwndCB = CommandBar_Create (hInst, hWnd, IDC_CMDBAR);

    // Insert a menu.
    CommandBar_InsertMenubar (hwndCB, hInst, ID_MENU, 0);
    // Add two bitmap lists plus custom bmp for drop-down button.
    CommandBar_AddBitmap (hwndCB, HINST_COMMCTRL, IDB_STD_SMALL_COLOR,
                          STD_BMPS, 0, 0);
    CommandBar_AddBitmap (hwndCB, HINST_COMMCTRL, IDB_VIEW_SMALL_COLOR,
                          VIEW_BMPS, 0, 0);
    CommandBar_AddBitmap (hwndCB, NULL,
                          (int)LoadBitmap (hInst, TEXT ("SortDropBtn")),
                          1, 0, 0);

    CommandBar_AddButtons (hwndCB, dim(tbCBCmboBtns), tbCBCmboBtns);

    // Add exit button to command bar.
    CommandBar_AddAdornments (hwndCB, 0, 0);
    return 0;
}
```

Each of the three command bars created in CmdBar demonstrates different capabilities of the command bar control. The first command bar, created in the routine *DoMainCommandVStd*, creates a vanilla command bar with a menu and a set of buttons. The button structure for this command bar is defined in the array *tbCBStdBtns*, which is defined near the top of CmdBar.cpp.

The second command bar, created in the routine *DoMainCommandVView*, contains two groups of checkgroup buttons separated by a combo box. This command bar also demonstrates the use of a separate image for a disabled button. The list view button, the third button on the bar, is disabled. The image for that button in the image list for disabled buttons is replaced with a bitmap that looks like an X.

The *DoMainCommandVCombo* routine creates the third command bar. It uses both the standard and view bitmap images as well as a custom bitmap for a drop-down button. This command bar demonstrates the technique of referencing the images in an image list that contains multiple bitmaps. The drop-down button is serviced by the *DoNotifyMain* routine, where a pop-up menu is loaded and displayed when a *TBN_DROPDOWN* notification is received.

Other Menu Controls

Over the years, Microsoft has added two other "menu controls" to the operating system that support drop-down menus. The first additional menu control is the Command Bands control. A command bands control is a rebar control that, by default, contains a command bar in each band of the control. The rebar control is a container of controls that the user can drag around the application window. Given that command bands are nothing more than command bars in a rebar control, knowing how to program a command bar is most of the battle when learning how to program the command bands control.

The menu bar control was introduced in the Pocket PC a number of years ago. As mentioned earlier, the menu bar differs from the command bar in that it sits on the bottom of the desktop window, not the top of the application's client window. Not only does the menu bar control look different, but, to the programmer, the menu bar has a vastly different programming interface. The menu bar is actually a top-level window, not a child of the window that creates it. The menu bar is supported on Windows CE for applications that require compatibility with Windows Mobile applications. However, because a menu bar on Windows CE looks significantly different from a menu bar on a Windows Mobile device, the compatibly is only at a programming level, not at a user interface level. Because the menu bar is actually less functional than the command bar or the command bands control, only systems absolutely requiring binary compatibly with Windows Mobile systems should use this control.

The remainder of the chapter covers the highlights of some of the other controls. These other controls are similar to but have somewhat less function than their counterparts under Windows Vista. I'll spend more time on the controls I think you'll need when writing a Windows CE application, starting with the month calendar and the time and date picker controls. These controls have a direct application to the PIM-like applications that are appropriate for many Windows CE systems. I'll also spend some time covering the list view control, concentrating on features of use to Windows CE developers. I'll cover just briefly the remainder of the common controls.

The Month Calendar Control

The month calendar control gives you a handy month-view calendar that can be manipulated by users to look up any month, week, or day as far back as the British adoption of the Gregorian calendar in September 1752. The control can display as many months as will fit into the size of the control. The days of the month can be highlighted to indicate appointments. The weeks can indicate the current week throughout the year. Users can spin through the months by tapping on the name of the month or change years by tapping on the year displayed.

Before using the month calendar control, you must initialize the common control library by calling *InitCommonControlsEx* with the *ICC_DATE_CLASSES* flag. You create the control by calling *CreateWindow* with the *MONTHCAL_CLASS* flag. The style flags for the control are shown here.

- **MCS_MULTISELECT** The control allows multiple selection of days.
- **MCS_NOTODAY** The control won't display today's date under the calendar.
- **MCS_NOTODAYCIRCLE** The control won't circle today's date.

- **MCS_WEEKNUMBERS** The control displays the week number (1 through 52) to the left of each week in the calendar.
- **MCS_DAYSTATE** The control sends notification messages to the parent requesting the days of the month that should be displayed in bold. You use this style to indicate which days have appointments or events scheduled.

Initializing the Control

In addition to the styles just described, you can use a number of messages or their corresponding wrapper macros to configure the month calendar control. You can use an *MCM_SETFIRSTDAYOFWEEK* message to display a different starting day of the week. You can also use the *MCM_SETRANGE* message to display dates within a given range in the control. You can configure date selection to allow the user to choose only single dates or to set a limit to the range of dates that a user can select at any one time. The single/multiple date selection ability is defined by the *MCS_MULTISELECT* style. If you set this style, you use the *MCM_SETMAXSELCOUNT* message to set the maximum number of days that can be selected at any one time.

You can set the background and text colors of the control by using the *MCM_SETCOLOR* message. This message can individually set colors for the different regions within the controls, including the calendar text and background, the header text and background, and the color of the days that precede and follow the days of the month being displayed. This message takes a flag indicating the part of the control to set and a *COLORREF* value to specify the color.

The month calendar control is designed to display months on an integral basis. That is, if the control is big enough for one and a half months, it displays only one month, centered in the control. You can use the *MCM_GETMINREQRECT* message to compute the minimum size necessary to display one month. Because the control must first be created before the *MCM_GETMINREQRECT* can be sent, properly sizing the control is a roundabout process. You must create the control, send the *MCM_GETMINREQRECT* message, and then resize the control using the data returned from the message.

Month Calendar Notifications

The month calendar control has only three notification messages to send to its parent. Of these, the *MCN_GETDAYSTATE* notification is the most important. This notification is sent when the control needs to know what days of a month to display in bold. This is done by querying the parent for a series of bit field values encoded in a *MONTHDAYSTATE* variable. This value is nothing more than a 32-bit value with bits 1 through 31 representing the days 1 through 31 of the month.

When the control needs to display a month, it sends an *MCN_GETDAYSTATE* notification with a pointer to an *NMDAYSTATE* structure defined as the following:

```
typedef struct {
    NMHDR nmhdr;
    SYSTEMTIME stStart;
    int cDayState;
    LPMONTHDAYSTATE prgDayState;
} NMDAYSTATE;
```

The *nmbhdr* field is simply the *NMHDR* structure that's passed with every *WM_NOTIFY* message. The *stStart* field contains the starting date for which the control is requesting information. This date is encoded in a standard *SYSTEMTIME* structure used by all versions of Windows. It's detailed here:

```
typedef struct {
    WORD wYear;
    WORD wMonth;
    WORD wDayOfWeek;
    WORD wDay;
    WORD wHour;
    WORD wMinute;
    WORD wSecond;
    WORD wMilliseconds;
} SYSTEMTIME;
```

For this notification, only the *wMonth*, *wDay*, and *wYear* fields are significant.

The *cDayState* field contains the number of entries in an array of *MONTHDAYSTATE* values. Even if a month calendar control is displaying only one month, it could request information about the previous and following months if days of those months are needed to fill in the top or bottom lines of the calendar.

The month calendar control sends an *MCN_SELCHANGE* notification when the user changes the days that are selected in the control. The structure passed with this notification, *NMSELCHANGE*, contains the newly highlighted starting and ending days. The *MCN_SELECT* notification is sent when the user double-taps on a day. The same *NMSELCHANGE* structure is passed with this notification to indicate the days that have been selected. The DlgDemo example in Chapter 6, "Dialog Boxes and Property Sheets," uses a month calendar control in its property sheet example. A few minutes working with that example amply demonstrates the notification messages sent from the control.

The Date and Time Picker Control

The date and time picker control looks deceptively simple but is a great tool for any application that needs to ask the user to specify a date. Any programmer who has had to parse, validate, and translate a string into a valid system date or time will appreciate this control.

When used to select a date, the control resembles a combo box, which is an edit field with a down-arrow button on the right side. Clicking the arrow, however, displays a month calendar control showing the current month. Selecting a day in the month dismisses the month calendar control and fills the date and time picker control with that date. When you configure it to query for a time, the date and time picker control resembles an edit field with a spin button on the right end of the control.

The date and time picker control has three default formats: two for displaying the date and one for displaying the time. The control also allows you to provide a formatting string so that users can completely customize the fields in the control. The control even lets you insert application-defined fields in the control.

Creating a Date and Time Picker Control

Before you can create the date and time picker control, the common control library must be initialized. If *InitCommonControlsEx* is used, it must be passed an *ICC_DATE_CLASSES* flag. The control is created by using *CreateWindow* with the class *DATETIMEPICK_CLASS*. The control defines the following styles:

- **DTS_LONGDATEFORMAT** The control displays a date in long format, as in Friday, September 14, 2007. The actual long date format is defined in the system registry.
- **DTS_SHORTDATEFORMAT** The control displays a date in short format, as in 9/14/07. The actual short date format is defined in the system registry.
- **DTS_TIMEFORMAT** The control displays the time in a format such as 5:50:28 PM. The actual time format is defined in the system registry.
- **DTS_SHOWNONE** The control has a check box to indicate that the date is valid.
- **DTS_UPDOWN** An up-down control replaces the drop-down button that displays a month calendar control in date view.
- **DTS_APPCANPARSE** Allows the user to directly type text into the control. The control sends a DTN_USERSTRING notification when the user is finished.

The first three styles simply specify a default format string. These formats are based on the regional settings in the registry. Because these formats can change if the user picks different regional settings in the Control Panel, the date and time picker control needs to know when these formats change. The system informs top-level windows of these types of changes by sending a *WM_SETTINGCHANGE* message. An application that uses the date and time picker control and uses one of these default fonts should forward the *WM_SETTINGCHANGE* message to the control if one is sent. This causes the control to reconfigure the default formats for the new regional settings.

The *DTS_APPCANPARSE* style enables the user to directly edit the text in the control. If this isn't set, the allowable keys are limited to the cursor keys and the numbers. When a field, such as a month, is highlighted in the edit field and the user presses the 6 key, the month changes to June. With the *DTS_APPCANPARSE* style, the user can directly type any character in the edit field of the control. When the user has finished, the control sends a *DTN_USERSTRING* notification to the parent window so that the text can be verified.

Customizing the Format

To customize the display format, all you need to do is create a format string and send it to the control using a *DTM_SETFORMAT* message. The format string can be made up of any of the following codes:

```
String        Description
fragment

"d"     One- or two-digit day.
"dd"    Two-digit day. Single digits have a leading zero.
"ddd"   The three-character weekday abbreviation. As in Sun, Mon...
"dddd"  The full weekday name.

"h"     One- or two-digit hour (12-hour format).
"hh"    Two-digit hour (12-hour format). Single digits have a leading zero.
"H"     One- or two-digit hour (24-hour format).
"HH"    Two-digit hour (24-hour format). Single digits have a leading zero.

"m"     One- or two-digit minute.
"mm"    Two-digit minute. Single digits have a leading zero.

"M"     One- or two-digit month.
"MM"    Two-digit month. Single digits have a leading zero.

"MMM"   Three-character month abbreviation.
"MMMM"  Full month name.
"t"     The one-letter AM/PM abbreviation. As in A or P.
"tt"    The two-letter AM/PM abbreviation. As in AM or PM.

"X"     Specifies a callback field that must be parsed by the application.

"y"     One-digit year. As in 1 for 2001.
"yy"    Two-digit year. As in 01 for 2001.
"yyy"   Full four-digit year. As in 2001.
```

Literal strings can be included in the format string by enclosing them in single quotes. For example, to display the string Today is: Saturday, December 2, 2006, the format string would be

```
'Today is: 'dddd', 'MMMM' 'd', 'yyy
```

The single quotes enclose the strings that aren't parsed. That includes the *Today is:* as well as all the separator characters, such as spaces and commas.

The callback field, designated by a series of X characters, provides for the application the greatest degree of flexibility for configuring the display of the date. When the control detects an *X* field in the format string, it sends a series of notification messages to its owner asking what to display in that field. A format string can have any number of *X* fields. For example, the following string has two *X* fields.

```
'Today 'XX' is: ' dddd', 'MMMM' 'd', 'yyy' and is 'XXX' birthday'
```

The number of X characters is used by the application only to differentiate the application-defined fields; it doesn't indicate the number of characters that should be displayed in the fields. When the control sends a notification asking for information about an *X* field, it includes a pointer to the X string so that the application can determine which field is being referenced.

When the date and time picker control needs to display an application-defined *X* field, it sends two notifications: *DTN_FORMATQUERY* and *DTN_FORMAT*. The *DTN_FORMATQUERY* notification is sent to get the maximum size of the text to be displayed. The *DTN_FORMAT* notification is then sent to get the actual text for the field. A third notification, *DTN_WMKEYDOWN*, is sent when the user highlights an application-defined field and presses a key. The application is responsible for determining which keys are valid and modifying the date if an appropriate key is pressed.

The List View Control

The list view control is arguably the most complex of the common controls. It displays a list of items in one of four modes: large icon, small icon, list, and report. The Windows CE version of the list view control supports many, but not all, of the common control library functions released with Internet Explorer 4.0. Some of these functions are a great help in the memory-constrained environment of Windows CE. These features include the ability to manage virtual lists of almost any size, headers that can have images and be rearranged using drag and drop, the ability to indent an entry, and new styles for report mode. The list view control also supports the custom draw interface, which allows a fairly easy way of changing the appearance of the control.

You register the list view control either by calling *InitCommonControls* or by calling an *InitCommonControls* using an *ICC_LISTVIEW_CLASSES* flag. You create the control by calling *CreateWindow* using the class filled with *WC_LISTVIEW*. Under Windows CE, the list view control supports all the styles supported by other versions of Windows, including the *LVS_OWNERDATA* style that designates the control as a virtual list view control.

Styles in Report Mode

In addition to the standard list view styles that you can use when creating the list view, the list view control supports a number of extended styles. This rather unfortunate term doesn't refer to the extended styles field in the *CreateWindowsEx* function. Instead, two messages, *LVM_GETEXTENDEDLISTVIEWSTYLE* and *LVM_SETEXTENDEDLISTVIEWSTYLE*, are used to get and set these extended list view styles. The extended styles supported by Windows CE are listed below.

- **LVS_EX_CHECKBOXES** The control places check boxes next to each item in the control.
- **LVS_EX_HEADERDRAGDROP** The control allows headers to be rearranged by the user using drag and drop.
- **LVS_EX_GRIDLINES** The control draws grid lines around the items in report mode.
- **LVS_EX_SUBITEMIMAGES** The control displays images in the subitem columns in report mode.
- **LVS_EX_FULLROWSELECT** The control highlights the item's entire row in report mode when that item is selected.
- **LVS_EX_ONECLICKACTIVATE** The control activates an item with a single tap instead of requiring a double tap.

Aside from the *LVS_EX_CHECKBOXES* and *LVS_EX_ONECLICKACTIVATE* extended styles, which work in all display modes, these new styles all affect the actions of the list view when in report mode. The effort here clearly has been to make the list view control an excellent control for displaying large lists of data.

Note that the list view control under Windows CE doesn't support other extended list view styles, such as *LVS_EX_INFOTIP*, *LVS_EX_ONECLICKACTIVATE*, *LVS_EX_TWOCLICKACTIVATE*, *LVS_EX_TRACKSELECT*, *LVS_EX_REGIONAL*, or *LVS_EX_FLATSB*, supported in some versions of the common control library.

Virtual List View

The virtual list view mode of the list view control is a huge help for Windows CE devices. In this mode, the list view control tracks only the selection and focus state of the items. The application maintains all the other data for the items in the control. This mode is handy for two reasons. First, virtual list view controls are fast. The initialization of the control is almost instantaneous because all that's required is that you set the number of items in the control. The list view control also gives you hints about what items it will be looking for in the near term. This allows applications to cache necessary data in RAM and leave the remainder of the data in a database or file. Without a virtual list view, an application would have to load an entire database or list of items in the list view when it's initialized. With the virtual list view, the application loads only what the control requires to display at any one time.

The second advantage of the virtual list view is RAM savings. Because the virtual list view control maintains little information on each item, the control doesn't keep a huge data array in RAM to support the data. The application manages what data is in RAM with some help from the virtual list view's cache hint mechanism.

The virtual list view has some limitations. The *LVS_OWNERDATA* style that designates a virtual list view can't be set or cleared after the control has been created. Also, virtual list views don't support drag and drop in large icon or small icon mode. A virtual list view defaults to *LVS_AUTOARRANGE* style, and the *LVM_SETITEMPOSITION* message isn't supported. In addition, the sort styles *LVS_SORTASCENDING* and *LVS_SORTDESCENDING* aren't supported. Even so, the ability to store large lists of items is handy.

To implement a virtual list view, an application needs to create a list view control with an *LVS_OWNERDATA* style and handle these three notifications— *LVN_GETDISPINFO*, *LVN_ODCACHEHINT*, and *LVN_ODFINDITEM*. The *LVN_GETDISPINFO* notification should be familiar to those who have programmed list view controls before. It has always been sent when the list view control needed information to display an item. In the virtual list view, it's used in a similar manner, but the notification is sent to gather all the information about every item in the control.

The virtual list view lets you know what data items it needs using the *LVN_ODCACHEHINT* notification. This notification passes the starting and ending index of items that the control expects to make use of in the near term. An application can take its cue from this set of numbers to load a cache of those items so that they can be quickly accessed. The hints tend to be requests for the items about to be displayed in the control. Because the number of items can change from view to view in the control, it's helpful that the control tracks this instead of having the application guess which items are going to be needed. Because the control often also needs information about the first and last pages of items, it also helps to cache them so that the frequent requests for those items don't clear the main cache of items that will be needed again soon.

The final notification necessary to manage a virtual list view is the *LVN_ODFINDITEM* notification. This is sent by the control when it needs to locate an item in response to a key press or in response to an *LVM_FINDITEM* message.

The CapEdit Control

The CapEdit control is an edit box that capitalizes the first letter in every word in the control. This control is great for edit controls that will receive proper names but are on keyboardless devices, where tapping the Shift key isn't convenient for the user.

To create the CapEdit control, create a window with the *WC_CAPEDIT* class name. Because CapEdit uses the edit control's window procedure for its base function, you can configure the control like an edit control by sending it standard edit control messages. The only message that's unique to this control is *CEM_UPCASEALLWORDS*. If *wParam* isn't 0, the control capitalizes the first letter in every word. Sending this message with *wParam* equal to 0 causes the control to capitalize only the first word in the control.

Other Common Controls

Windows CE supports a number of other common controls available under the desktop versions of Windows. Most of these controls are supported completely within the limits of the capability of Windows CE. Short descriptions of the other supported common controls follow.

The Status Bar Control

The status bar is carried over unchanged from the desktop versions of Windows. General user interface guidelines advise against using this control on devices with small screens but the control is quite useful on devices with larger displays.

The Tab Control

Almost all of the standard tab control features are supported under Windows CE. The tab control features not supported include the *TCS_HOTTRACK* style that highlighted tabs under the cursor and the *TCS_EX_REGISTERDROP* extended style.

The Trackbar Control

The trackbar control gains the capacity for two "buddy" controls that are automatically updated with the trackbar value. The trackbar also supports the custom draw service, providing separate item drawing indications for the channel, the thumb, and the tick marks.

The Progress Bar Control

The progress bar includes support for vertical progress bars and 32-bit ranges. This control also supports the new smooth progression instead of moving the progress indicator in discrete chunks.

The Up-Down Control

The up-down control under Windows CE supports only edit and list box controls for its buddy control.

The Toolbar Control

The Windows CE toolbar supports tooltips differently from the way tooltips are supported by the desktop versions of this control. You add toolbar support for tooltips in Windows CE the same way you do for the command bar, by passing a pointer to a permanently allocated array of strings. The toolbar also supports the transparent and flat styles that are supported by the command bar.

The Tree View Control

The tree view control supports two of the new styles added to the tree view common control: *TVS_CHECKBOXES* and *TVS_SINGLESEL*. The *TVS_CHECKBOXES* style places a check box adjacent to each item in the control. The *TVS_SINGLESEL* style causes a previously expanded item to close up when a new item is selected. The tree view control also supports the custom draw service. The tree view control doesn't support the *TVS_TRACKSELECT* style, which allows you to highlight an item when the cursor hovers over it. The treeview control is demonstrated in the RegView example in Chapter 10, "The Windows CE Registry."

The Animation Control

The animation control enables a program to display video files in the .avi (Audio/Video Interleave) format. The control only supports .avi files without audio. The interface to the control is a simple three messages: *ACM_OPEN*, *ACM_PLAY*, and *ACM_STOP*. *ACM_OPEN* specifys the .avi file or resource to load into the control. *ACM_PLAY* starts the animation, which can be set to start and end at specific frames within the animation and can also be set to loop the animation. To unload an animation, *ACM_OPEN* is sent specifying a file name of *NULL*.

The animation control has some interesting style flags. The *ACS_AUTOPLAY* style tells the control to immediately begin playing the animation as soon as it is loaded. The *ACS_TRANSPARENT* flag tells the control to use the color in the upper-left pixel in the first frame as the transparent color. Any pixel in the animation that contains that color is replaced with the background color for the control.

Care should be taken when using the animation control on Windows CE systems. Most embedded systems are limited by battery life, CPU power, or both. Excessive use of animations in an application needlessly slows the device and drains the battery. While the animation control provides great eye candy, using it may not be the best choice for an embedded system.

Unsupported Common Controls

There are some conmmon controls that Windows CE doesn't support. For example, neither the drag list control nor the hot key control is supported. The hot key control is problematic in that keyboard layouts and key labels, standardized on the PC, vary dramatically on the different hardware that runs Windows CE. And the drag list control isn't that big a loss given the improved power of the report style of the list view control.

The rich edit control is an interesting story. Although not formally supported, Riched20.dll is on Windows CE platforms that have Pocket Word. On these systems, applications can interact with the rich edit control in the same manner as is done on the desktop. To learn how to use the rich edit control, refer to the desktop Windows SDK documentation. The only supported alternative to the rich edit control is the rich ink control supported on Windows Mobile systems. This control provides text and ink input. It also converts Rich Text Format (RTF) and Pocket Word Ink (PWI) files to ASCII text.

Windows CE supports fairly completely the common control library seen under other versions of Windows. The date and time picker, month calendar, and command bar are a great help given the target audience of Windows CE devices.

Now that both the basic window controls and the common controls have been covered, it's time to look at where they're most often used—dialog boxes. Dialog boxes free you from having to create and maintain controls in a window. See how it's done in the next chapter.

Chapter 6

Dialog Boxes and Property Sheets

As discussed in Chapter 4, "Windows, Controls, and Menus," controls can be used to create quite complex user interfaces. The problem, however, is that handling controls at the window level requires a fair amount of code to create and manage the controls, code that you won't find in most Windows applications. Most Windows applications don't manage their child controls manually. Instead, *dialog boxes* are used. Dialog boxes are windows that typically use a predefined window class and a different default window procedure. The combination of the window class and the default window procedure, along with a set of special dialog box creation functions, hides the complexity of creating and managing the control windows.

Dialog boxes (sometimes simply referred to as *dialogs*) query data from the user or present data to the user—hence the term *dialog* box. A specialized form of dialog, named a *property sheet*, allows a program to display multiple but related dialog boxes in an overlapping style; each box or property sheet is equipped with an identifying tab. Property sheets are particularly valuable given the tiny screens associated with many Windows CE devices.

Windows CE also supports a subset of the common dialog library available under Windows Vista. Specifically, Windows CE supports versions of the common dialog boxes File Open, File Save, Color, Font, and Print. These dialogs are somewhat different on Windows CE. They're reformatted to work well with smaller screens and aren't as extensible as their desktop counterparts.

Dialog Boxes

Dialog boxes are windows created by Windows using a template provided by an application. The template describes the type and placement of the controls in the window. The Dialog Manager—the part of Windows that creates and manages dialog boxes—also provides default functionality for switching focus between the controls using the Tab key as well as default actions for the Enter and Esc keys. In addition, Windows provides a default dialog box window class, freeing applications from the necessity of registering a window class for each of the dialog boxes it might create.

Dialog boxes come in two types: *modal* and *modeless*. A modal dialog box prevents the user from using the application until the dialog box is dismissed. For example, the File Open and Print dialog boxes are modal. A modeless dialog box can be used interactively with the remainder of the application. The Find dialog box in Microsoft Word is modeless; the user doesn't need to dismiss it before typing in the main window.

Like other windows, dialog boxes have a window procedure, although the dialog box window procedure is constructed somewhat differently from standard windows procedures. Rather than passing unprocessed messages to the *DefWindowProc* procedure for default processing, a dialog box procedure returns *TRUE* if it processes the message and *FALSE* if it doesn't process the message. Windows supplies a default procedure, *DefDialogProc*, for use in specific cases—that is, for specialized modeless dialog boxes that have their own window classes.

Dialog Box Resource Templates

Most of the time, the description for the size and placement of the dialog box and for the controls is provided via a resource called a *dialog template*. You can create a dialog template in memory, but unless a program has an overriding need to format the size and shape of the dialog box on the fly, loading a dialog template directly from a resource is a much better choice. As is the case for other resources such as menus, dialog templates are contained in the resource (RC) file. The template is referenced by the application using either its name or its resource ID.

Figure 6-1 shows a dialog box. This dialog box will be used as an example throughout the discussion of how a dialog box works.

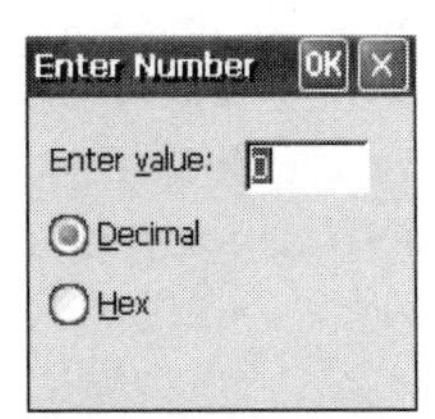

FIGURE 6-1 A simple dialog box

The dialog template for the dialog box in Figure 6-1 is shown here:

```
GetVal DIALOG discardable 10, 10, 90, 70
STYLE  WS_POPUP | WS_VISIBLE | WS_CAPTION | WS_SYSMENU | DS_CENTER
EXSTYLE WS_EX_CAPTIONOKBTN
CAPTION "Enter Number"
BEGIN
    LTEXT "Enter &value:"  IDD_VALLABEL,   5,  10,  40,  12
    EDITTEXT                  IDD_VALUE,  50,  10,  30,  12, WS_TABSTOP
    RADIOBUTTON "&Decimal",     IDD_DEC,   5,  25,  60,  12,
                                                WS_TABSTOP | WS_GROUP
    RADIOBUTTON "&Hex",         IDD_HEX,   5,  40,  60,  12
    LTEXT ""                IDD_ERRMSG,   5,  55,  80,  12
END
```

The syntax for a dialog template follows a simple pattern similar to that for a menu resource. First is the name or ID of the resource followed by the keyword *DIALOG* identifying that what follows is a dialog template. The optional *discardable* keyword is followed by the position and size of the dialog box. The position specified is, by default, relative to the owner window of the dialog box.

The units of measurement in a dialog box aren't pixels but *dialog units*. A dialog unit is defined as one-quarter of the average width of the characters in the system font for horizontal units and one-eighth of the height of one character from the same font for vertical units. The goal is to create a unit of measurement independent of the display technology; in practice, dialog boxes still need to be tested in all display resolutions in which the box might be displayed. You can compute a pixel versus dialog unit conversion using the *GetDialogBaseUnits* function, but you'll rarely find it necessary. The visual tools that come with most compilers these days isolate a programmer from terms such as *dialog units*, but it's still a good idea to know just how dialog boxes are described in an RC file.

The *STYLE* line of code specifies the style flags for the dialog box. The styles include the standard window (*WS_xx*) style flags used for windows as well as a series of dialog (*DS_xx*) style flags specific to dialog boxes. Windows CE supports the following dialog box styles:

- **DS_ABSALIGN** Places the dialog box relative to the upper left corner of the screen instead of basing the position on the owner window.
- **DS_CENTER** Centers the dialog box vertically and horizontally on the screen.
- **DS_MODALFRAME** Creates a dialog box with a modal dialog box frame that can be combined with a title bar and System menu by specifying the WS_CAPTION and WS_SYSMENU styles.
- **DS_SETFONT** Tells Windows to use a nondefault font that is specified in the dialog template.
- **DS_SETFOREGROUND** Brings the dialog box to the foreground after it's created. If an application not in the foreground displays a dialog box, this style forces the dialog box to the top of the Z-order so that the user will see it.

Most dialog boxes are created with at least some combination of the *WS_POPUP*, *WS_CAPTION*, and *WS_SYSMENU* style flags. The *WS_POPUP* flag indicates that the dialog box is a top-level window. The *WS_CAPTION* style gives the dialog box a title bar. A title bar allows the user to drag the dialog box around as well as serving as a site for title text for the dialog box. The *WS_SYSMENU* style causes the dialog box to have a Close button on the right end of the title bar, thus eliminating the need for a command bar control to provide the Close button. Note that Windows CE uses this flag differently from other versions of Windows, in which the flag indicates that a system menu is to be placed on the left end of the title bar.

The *EXSTYLE* line of code specifies the extended style flags for the dialog box. For Windows CE, these flags are particularly important. The *WS_EX_CAPTIONOKBTN* flag tells the dialog manager to place an OK button on the title bar to the immediate left of the Close button. Having both OK and Close (or Cancel) buttons on the title bar saves precious space in dialog boxes that are displayed on the small screens typical of Windows CE devices. The *WS_EX_CONTEXTHELP* extended style places a Help button on the title bar to the immediate left of the OK button. Clicking on this button results in a *WM_HELP* message being sent to the dialog box procedure.

The *CAPTION* line of code specifies the title bar text of the dialog, provided that the *WS_CAPTION* style is specified so that the dialog box has a title bar.

The lines describing the type and placement of the controls in the dialog box are enclosed in *BEGIN* and *END* keywords. Each control is specified either by a particular keyword in the case of commonly used controls, or by the keyword *CONTROL*, which is a generic placeholder that can specify any window class to be placed in the dialog box. The *LTEXT* line of code on the previous page specifies a static left-justified text control. The keyword is followed by the default text for the control in quotes. The next parameter is the *ID* of the control, which must be unique for the dialog box. In this template, the *ID* is a constant defined in an include file that is included by both the resource script and the C or C++ file containing the dialog box procedure.

The next four values are the location and size of the control, in dialog units, relative to the upper-left corner of the dialog box. Following that, any explicit style flags can be specified for the control. In the case of the *LTEXT* line, no style flags are necessary, but as you can see, the *EDITTEXT* and first *AUTORADIOBUTTON* entries each have style flags specified. Each of the control keywords has subtly different syntax. For example, the *EDITTEXT* line doesn't have a field for default text. The style flags for the individual controls deserve notice. The edit control and the first of the two radio buttons have a *WS_TABSTOP* style. The dialog manager looks for controls with the *WS_TABSTOP* style to determine which control gets focus when the user presses the Tab key. In this example, pressing the Tab key results in focus being switched between the edit control and the first radio button.

The *WS_GROUP* style on the first radio button starts a new group of controls. All the controls following the radio button are grouped together, up to the next control that has the *WS_GROUP* style. Grouping auto radio buttons allows only one radio button at a time to be selected.

Another benefit of grouping is that focus can be changed among the controls within a group by exploiting the cursor keys as well as the Tab key. The first member of a group should have a *WS_TABSTOP* style; this allows the user to tab to the group of controls and then use the cursor keys to switch the focus among the controls in the group.

The *CONTROL* statement isn't used in this example, but it's important and merits some explanation. It's a generic statement that allows inclusion of any window class in a dialog box. It has the following syntax:

```
CONTROL "text", id, class, style, x, y, width, height
    [, extended-style]
```

For this entry, the default text and control *ID* are similar to the other statements, but the next field, class, is new. It specifies the window class of the control you want to place in the dialog box. The class field is followed by the style flags and then by the location and size of your control. Finally, the *CONTROL* statement has a field for extended style flags. If you use Visual Studio to create a dialog box and look at the resulting RC file using a text editor, you'll see that it uses *CONTROL* statements as well as the more readable *LTEXT*, *EDITTEXT*, and *BUTTON* statements. There's no functional difference between an edit control created with a *CONTROL* statement and one created with an *EDITTEXT* statement. The *CONTROL* statement is a generic version of the more specific keywords. The *CONTROL* statement also allows inclusion of controls that don't have a special keyword associated with them.

Creating a Dialog Box

Creating and displaying a dialog box is simple; just use one of the many dialog box creation functions. The first two are these:

```
int DialogBox (HANDLE hInstance, LPCTSTR lpTemplate, HWND hWndOwner,
               DLGPROC lpDialogFunc);

int DialogBoxParam (HINSTANCE hInstance, LPCTSTR lpTemplate,
                    HWND hWndOwner, DLGPROC lpDialogFunc,
                    LPARAM dwInitParam);
```

These two functions differ only in *DialogBoxParam*'s additional *LPARAM* parameter, so they are discussed at the same time. The first parameter to these functions is the instance handle of the program. The second parameter specifies the name or ID of the resource containing the dialog template. As with other resources, to specify a resource ID instead of a name requires the use of the *MAKEINTRESOURCE* macro.

The third parameter is the handle of the window that will own the dialog box. The owning window isn't the parent of the dialog box because, were that true, the dialog box would be clipped to fit inside the parent. Ownership means instead that the dialog box is hidden when the owner window is minimized and always appears above the owner window in the z-order.

The fourth parameter is a pointer to the dialog box procedure for the dialog box. I'll describe the dialog box procedure shortly. The *DialogBoxParam* function has a fifth parameter, which is a user-defined value that's passed to the dialog box procedure when the dialog box is to be initialized. This helpful value can be used to pass a pointer to a structure of data that can be referenced when your application is initializing the dialog box controls.

Two other dialog box creation functions create modal dialogs. They are the following:

```
int DialogBoxIndirect (HANDLE hInstance, LPDLGTEMPLATE lpTemplate,
                       HWND hWndParent, DLGPROC lpDialogFunc);
```

```
int DialogBoxIndirectParam (HINSTANCE hInstance,
                            LPCDLGTEMPLATE DialogTemplate, HWND hWndParent,
                            DLGPROC lpDialogFunc, LPARAM dwInitParam);
```

The difference between these two functions and the two previously described is that these two use a dialog box template in memory to define the dialog box rather than using a resource. This allows a program to dynamically create a dialog box template on the fly. The second parameter to these functions points to a *DLGTEMPLATE* structure, which describes the overall dialog box window, followed by an array of *DLGITEMTEMPLATE* structures defining the individual controls.

When any of these four functions is called, the dialog manager creates a modal dialog box using the template passed. The window that owns the dialog box is disabled, and the dialog manager enters its own internal *GetMessage/DispatchMessage* message processing loop; this loop doesn't exit until the dialog box is destroyed. Because of this, these functions don't return to the caller until the dialog box has been destroyed. The *WM_ENTERIDLE* message that's sent to owner windows in other versions of Windows while the dialog box is displayed isn't supported under Windows CE.

If an application wanted to create a modal dialog box with the template shown earlier and pass a value to the dialog box procedure, it might call this:

```
DialogBoxParam (hInstance, TEXT ("GetVal"), hWnd, GetValDlgProc,
                0x1234);
```

The *hInstance* and *hWnd* parameters would be the instance handle of the application and the handle of the owner window. The *GetVal* string is the name of the dialog box template, while *GetValDlgProc* is the name of the dialog box procedure. Finally, *0x1234* is an application-defined value. In this case, it might be used to provide a default value in the dialog box.

Dialog Box Procedures

The final component necessary for a dialog box is the dialog box procedure. As in the case of a window procedure, the purpose of the dialog box procedure is to field messages sent to the window—in this case, a dialog box window—and perform the appropriate processing. In fact, a dialog box procedure is simply a special case of a window procedure, although you should pay attention to a few differences between the two.

The first difference, as mentioned in the previous section, is that a dialog box procedure doesn't pass unprocessed messages to *DefWindowProc*. Instead, the procedure returns *TRUE* for messages it processes and *FALSE* for messages that it doesn't process. The dialog manager uses this return value to determine whether the message needs to be passed to the default dialog box procedure.

The second difference from standard window procedures is the addition of a new message, *WM_INITDIALOG*. Dialog box procedures perform any initialization of the controls during the processing of this message. Also, if the dialog box was created with *DialogBoxParam* or *DialogBoxIndirectParam*, the *lParam* value is the generic parameter passed during the call that created the dialog box. While it might seem that the controls could be initialized during the *WM_CREATE* message, that doesn't work. The problem is that during the *WM_CREATE* message, the controls on the dialog box haven't yet been created, so they can't be initialized. The *WM_INITDIALOG* message is sent after the controls have been created and before the dialog box is made visible, which is the perfect time to initialize the controls.

Here are a few other minor differences between a window procedure and a dialog box procedure. Most dialog box procedures don't need to process the *WM_PAINT* message because any necessary painting is done by the controls or, in the case of owner-draw controls, in response to control requests. Most of the code in a dialog box procedure is responding to *WM_COMMAND* messages from the controls. As with menus, the *WM_COMMAND* messages are parsed by the control ID values. Two special predefined ID values that a dialog box has to deal with are *IDOK* and *IDCANCEL*. *IDOK* is assigned to the OK button on the title bar of the dialog box, while *IDCANCEL* is assigned to the Close button. In response to a click of either button, a dialog box procedure should call

```
BOOL EndDialog (HWND hDlg, int nResult);
```

EndDialog closes the dialog box and returns control to the caller of whatever function created the dialog box. The *hDlg* parameter is the handle of the dialog box, while the *nResult* parameter is the value that's passed back as the return value of the function that created the dialog box.

The difference, of course, between handling the *IDOK* and *IDCANCEL* buttons is that if the OK button is clicked, the dialog box procedure should collect any relevant data from the dialog box controls to return to the calling procedure before it calls *EndDialog*.

A dialog box procedure to handle the *GetVal* template previously described is shown here:

```
//======================================================================
// GetVal Dialog procedure
//
BOOL CALLBACK GetValDlgProc (HWND hWnd, UINT wMsg, WPARAM wParam,
                             LPARAM lParam) {
    TCHAR szText[64];
    int nVal, nBase;
    WORD idItem, wNotifyCode;

    switch (wMsg) {
    case WM_INITDIALOG:
        SetDlgItemInt (hWnd, IDD_VALUE, lParam, FALSE);
        SendDlgItemMessage (hWnd, IDD_VALUE, EM_LIMITTEXT,
                            dim (szText)-1, 0);
        CheckRadioButton (hWnd, IDD_DEC, IDD_HEX, IDD_DEC);
```

```
            return TRUE;

        case WM_COMMAND:
            // Parse the parameters.
            idItem = (WORD) LOWORD (wParam);
            wNotifyCode = (WORD) HIWORD (wParam);

            if ((idItem == IDD_HEX) || (idItem == IDD_DEC) ||
                (idItem == IDOK)) {

                // Get text from edit control.
                GetDlgItemText (hWnd, IDD_VALUE, szText, dim (szText));
                if (SendDlgItemMessage (hWnd, IDD_DEC,
                                BM_GETSTATE, 0, 0) == BST_CHECKED)
                    nBase = 10;
                else
                    nBase = 16;
                // Convert the string to a number.
                if (ConvertValue (szText, nBase, &nVal)  == FALSE) {
                    SetDlgItemText (hWnd, IDD_ERRMSG,
                                    TEXT ("Value not valid"));
                    SendDlgItemMessage (hWnd, IDD_VALUE, EM_SETSEL,
                                        0, -1);
                    return TRUE;
                } else
                    SetDlgItemText (hWnd, IDD_ERRMSG, TEXT (""));

                // Set focus back to the edit control
                SetFocus (GetDlgItem (hWnd, IDD_VALUE));
            }
            switch (LOWORD (wParam)) {

            case IDD_HEX:
                // See if Hex already checked.
                if (nBase == 16)
                    return TRUE;

                // Set new value in hex format
                wsprintf (szText, TEXT ("%X"), nVal);
                SetDlgItemText (hWnd, IDD_VALUE, szText);
                // Set radio button.
                CheckRadioButton (hWnd, IDD_DEC, IDD_HEX, IDD_HEX);
                return TRUE;

            case IDD_DEC:
                // See if Decimal already checked.
                if (nBase == 10)
                    return TRUE;

                // Set new value.
                SetDlgItemInt (hWnd, IDD_VALUE, nVal, FALSE);
                // Set radio button.
                CheckRadioButton (hWnd, IDD_DEC, IDD_HEX, IDD_DEC);
                return TRUE;
           case IDOK:
                EndDialog (hWnd, nVal);
```

```
                break;

            case IDCANCEL:
                EndDialog (hWnd, 0);
                return TRUE;
            }
        break;
        }
        return FALSE;
}
```

This is a typical example of a dialog box procedure for a simple dialog box. The only messages that are processed are the *WM_INITDIALOG* and *WM_COMMAND* messages. The *WM_INITDIALOG* message is used to initialize the edit control using a number passed, via *DialogBoxParam*, through to the *lParam* value. The radio button controls aren't auto radio buttons because the dialog box procedure needs to prevent the buttons from changing if the value in the entry field is invalid. The *WM_COMMAND* message first parses the wParam and lParam parameters and then processes the message depending on the control ID. The *IDOK* and *IDCANCEL* buttons aren't in the dialog box template; as mentioned earlier, those buttons are placed by the dialog manager in the title bar of the dialog box.

Full-Screen Dialog Boxes

Many Windows CE systems, such as Windows Moble systems, have small screens. On these systems, it can be useful to make dialog boxes fit the entire screen. To assist programmers in creating full-size dialog boxes, Windows CE provides a function named *SHInitDialog*. As the name implies, the function should be called during the handling of the *WM_INITDIALOG* message. The function is prototyped as

```
BOOL SHInitDialog (PSHINITDLGINFO pshidi);
```

The function takes a single parameter, a pointer to an *SHINITDLGINFO* structure defined as

```
typedef struct tagSHINITDIALOG{
    DWORD dwMask;
    HWND hDlg;
    DWORD dwFlags;
} SHINITDLGINFO;
```

The *dwMask* field must be set to the single flag currently supported, which is *SHIDIM_FLAGS*. The *hDlg* field should be set to the window handle of the dialog box. The third parameter, *dwFlags*, specifies a number of different initialization options. The *SHIDIF_DONEBUTTON* specifies that the title bar contain an OK button in addition to the Close button in the upper-right corner.

On systems with a touch panel–based or "soft" keyboard, the *SHIDIF_SIPDOWN* flag closes the soft keyboard (SIP) when the dialog is displayed. This flag should be set for informational dialogs that have no text input fields. Note that the absence of this flag doesn't automatically display the SIP. It simply means that the state of the SIP remains unchanged when the dialog box is displayed.

Three other flags can be set in the *dwFlags* field:

- SHIDIF_SIZEDLG
- SHIDIF_SIZEDLGFULLSCREEN
- SHIDIF_FULLSCREENNOMENUBAR

These flags deal with how the dialog box is sized. The *SHIDIF_SIZEDLG* flag tells the system to size the dialog box depending on the state of the SIP. If the SIP is displayed, the dialog box is sized to fit above the SIP. If the SIP is hidden, the dialog box is sized to fit just above the menu bar. If, however, you have a floating SIP, the dialog box doesn't size correctly. The *SHIDIF_SIZEDLGFULLSCREEN* and *SHIDIF_FULLSCREENNOMENUBAR* flags size the dialog box to fit the entire screen regardless of the state of the SIP. The difference between the two flags is that *SHIDIF_FULLSCREENNOMENUBAR* does not leave room for the menu bar at the bottom of the screen.

Modeless Dialog Boxes

I've talked so far about modal dialog boxes that prevent the user from using other parts of the application before the dialog box is dismissed. Modeless dialog boxes, on the other hand, allow the user to work with other parts of the application while the dialog box is still open. Creating and using modeless dialog boxes require a bit more work. For example, you create modeless dialog boxes using different functions than those for modal dialog boxes:

```
HWND CreateDialog (HINSTANCE hInstance, LPCTSTR lpTemplate,
                   HWND hWndOwner, DLGPROC lpDialogFunc);

HWND CreateDialogParam (HINSTANCE hInstance, LPCDLGTEMPLATE lpTemplate,
                        HWND hWndOwner, DLGPROC lpDialogFunc,
                        LPARAM lParamInit);

HWND CreateDialogIndirect (HINSTANCE hInstance,
                           LPCDLGTEMPLATE lpTemplate, HWND hWndOwner,
                           DLGPROC lpDialogFunc);
```

or

```
HWND CreateDialogIndirectParam (HINSTANCE hInstance,
                                LPCDLGTEMPLATE lpTemplate, HWND hWndOwner,
                                DLGPROC lpDialogFunc, LPARAM lParamInit);
```

The parameters in these functions mirror the creation functions for the modal dialog boxes with similar parameters. The difference is that these functions return immediately after creating the dialog boxes. Each function returns 0 if the create fails or returns the handle to the dialog box window if the create succeeds.

The handle returned after a successful creation is important because applications that use modeless dialog boxes must modify their message loop code to accommodate the dialog box. The new message loop should look similar to the following:

```
while (GetMessage (&msg, NULL, 0, 0)) {
    if ((hMlDlg == 0) || (!IsDialogMessage (hMlDlg, &msg))) {
        TranslateMessage (&msg);
        DispatchMessage (&msg);
    }
}
```

The difference from a modal dialog box message loop is that if the modeless dialog box is being displayed, messages should be checked to see whether they're dialog messages. If they're not dialog messages, your application forwards them to *TranslateMessage* and *DispatchMessage*. The code just shown simply checks to see whether the dialog box exists by checking a global variable containing the handle to the modeless dialog box and, if it's not 0, calls *IsDialogMessage*. If *IsDialogMessage* doesn't translate and dispatch the message itself, the message is sent to the standard *TranslateMessage/DispatchMessage* body of the message loop. Of course, this code assumes that the handle returned by *CreateDialog* (or whatever function creates the dialog box) is saved in *hMlDlg* and that *hMlDlg* is set to 0 when the dialog box is closed.

Another difference between modal and modeless dialog boxes is in the dialog box procedure. Instead of using *EndDialog* to close the dialog box, you must call *DestroyWindow* instead. This is because *EndDialog* is designed to work only with the internal message loop processing that's performed with a modal dialog box. Finally, an application usually won't want more than one instance of a modeless dialog box displayed at a time. An easy way to prevent this is to check the global copy of the window handle to see whether it's nonzero before calling *CreateDialog*. To do this, the dialog box procedure must set the global handle to 0 after it calls *DestroyWindow*.

Property Sheets

To the user, a property sheet is a dialog box with one or more tabs across the top that allow the user to switch among different "pages" of the dialog box. To the programmer, a property sheet is a series of stacked dialog boxes. Only the top dialog box is visible; the dialog manager is responsible for displaying the dialog box associated with the tab on which the user clicks. However you approach property sheets, they're invaluable given the limited screen size of Windows CE devices.

Each page of the property sheet, named appropriately a *property page*, is a dialog box template, either loaded from a resource or created dynamically in memory. Each property page has its own dialog box procedure. The frame around the property sheets is maintained by the dialog manager, so the advantages of property sheets come with little overhead to the programmer. Unlike the property sheets supported in other versions of Windows, the property sheets in Windows CE don't support the Apply button. Also, the OK and Cancel buttons for the property sheet are contained in the title bar, not positioned below the pages.

Creating a Property Sheet

Instead of the dialog box creation functions, use this new function to create a property sheet:

```
int PropertySheet (LPCPROPSHEETHEADER lppsph);
```

The *PropertySheet* function creates the property sheet according to the information contained in the *PROPSHEETHEADER* structure, which is defined as the following:

```
typedef struct _PROPSHEETHEADER {
    DWORD dwSize;
    DWORD dwFlags;
    HWND hwndOwner;
    HINSTANCE hInstance;
     union {
        HICON hIcon;
        LPCWSTR pszIcon;
    };
    LPCWSTR pszCaption;
    UINT nPages;
    union {
        UINT nStartPage;
        LPCWSTR pStartPage;
    };
    union {
        LPCPROPSHEETPAGE ppsp;
        HPROPSHEETPAGE FAR *phpage;
    };
    PFNPROPSHEETCALLBACK pfnCallback;
} PROPSHEETHEADER;
```

Filling in this convoluted structure isn't as imposing a task as it might look. The *dwSize* field is the standard size field that must be initialized with the size of the structure. The *dwFlags* field contains the creation flags that define how the property sheet is created, which fields of the structure are valid, and how the property sheet behaves. Some of the flags indicate which fields in the structure are used. (I'll talk about those flags when I describe the other fields.) Two other flags set the behavior of the property sheet. The *PSH_PROPTITLE* flag appends the string "Properties" to the end of the caption specified in the *pszCaption* field. The *PSH_MODELESS* flag causes the *PropertySheet* function to create a modeless property sheet and immediately return. A modeless property sheet is like a modeless dialog box; it allows the user to switch back to the original window while the property sheet is still displayed.

The next two fields are the handle of the owner window and the instance handle of the application. Neither the *hIcon* nor the *pszIcon* field is used in Windows CE, so both fields should be set to 0. The *pszCaption* field should point to the title bar text for the property sheet. The *nStartPage/pStartPage* union should be set to indicate the page that should be initially displayed. This can be selected either by number or by title if the *PSH_USEPSTARTPAGE* flag is set in the *dwFlags* field.

The *ppsp/phpage* union points to either an array of *PROPSHEETPAGE* structures describing each of the property pages or handles to previously created property pages. For either of these, the *nPages* field must be set to the number of entries of the array of structures or page handles. To indicate that the pointer points to an array of *PROPSHEETPAGE* structures, set the *PSH_PROPSHEETPAGE* flag in the *dwFlags* field. I'll describe both the structure and how to create individual pages shortly.

The *pfnCallBack* field is an optional pointer to a procedure that's called with a series of notifications indicating events during creation of the property sheet. The callback function allows applications to fine-tune the appearance of the property sheet. This field is ignored unless the *PSP_USECALLBACK* flag is set in the *dwFlags* field. One place the callback is used is in Windows Mobile applications to place the tabs on the bottom of the property sheet.

The callback procedure should be defined to match the following prototype:

```
UINT CALLBACK PropSheetPageProc (HWND hwnd, UINT uMsg,
                                 LPPROPSHEETPAGE ppsp);
```

The parameters sent back to the application are a handle value documented to be reserved, the notification code in the *uMsg* parameter, and, in some notifications, a pointer to a *PROPSHEETPAGE* structure. The notifications supported in Windows CE are as follows:

- **PSCB_NOPRECREATE** Sent to query if app wants PSCB_PRECREATE notification.
- **PSCB_PRECREATE** Sent just before the property sheet is created.
- **PSCB_INITIALIZED** Sent when the property sheet is initialized.
- **PSCB_GETVERSION** Sent to query the level of support expected by the application.
- **PSCB_GETTITLE** Sent to query property sheet title text.
- **PSCB_GETLINKTEXT** On a Windows Mobile device, sent to query the string to place below the tabbed pages on the property sheet.

Creating a Property Page

As I mentioned earlier, individual property pages can be specified by an array of *PROPSHEETPAGE* structures or an array of handles to existing property pages. Creating a property page is accomplished with a call to the following:

```
HPROPSHEETPAGE CreatePropertySheetPage (LPCPROPSHEETPAGE lppsp);
```

This function is passed a pointer to the same *PROPSHEETPAGE* structure and returns a handle to a property page. *PROPSHEETPAGE* is defined as this:

```
typedef struct _PROPSHEETPAGE {
    DWORD dwSize;
    DWORD dwFlags;
    HINSTANCE hInstance;
    union {
        LPCSTR pszTemplate;
        LPCDLGTEMPLATE pResource;
    };
    union {
        HICON hIcon;
        LPCSTR pszIcon;
    };
    LPCSTR pszTitle;
    DLGPROC pfnDlgProc;
    LPARAM lParam;
    LPFNPSPCALLBACK pfnCallback;
    UINT FAR * pcRefParent;
} PROPSHEETPAGE;
```

The structure looks similar to the *PROPSHEETHEADER* structure, leading with a *dwSize* and a *dwFlags* field followed by an *hInstance* field. In this structure, *hInstance* is the handle of the module from which the resources are loaded. The *dwFlags* field again specifies which fields of the structure are used and how they're used, as well as a few flags specifying the characteristics of the page itself.

The *pszTemplate/pResource* union specifies the dialog box template used to define the page. If the *PSP_DLGINDIRECT* flag is set in the *dwFlags* field, the union points to a dialog box template in memory. Otherwise, the field specifies the name of a dialog box resource. The *hIcon/pszIcon* union isn't used in Windows CE and should be set to 0. If the *dwFlags* field contains a *PSP_USETITLE* flag, the *pszTitle* field points to the text used on the tab for the page. Otherwise, the tab text is taken from the caption field in the dialog box template. The *pfnDlgProc* field points to the dialog box procedure for this specific page, and the *lParam* field is an application-defined parameter that can be used to pass data to the dialog box procedure. The *pfnCallback* field can point to a callback procedure that's called twice—when the page is about to be created and when it's about to be destroyed. Again, like the callback for the property sheet, the property page callback allows applications to fine-tune the page characteristics.

This field is ignored unless the *dwFlags* field contains the *PSP_USECALLBACK* flag. Finally, the *pcRefCount* field can contain a pointer to an integer that stores a reference count for the page. This field is ignored unless the flags field contains the *PSP_USEREFPARENT* flag.

Windows CE supports the *PSP_PREMATURE* flag, which causes a property page to be created when the property sheet that owns it is created. Normally, a property page isn't created until the first time it's shown. This has an impact on property pages that communicate and cooperate with each other. Without the *PSP_PREMATURE* flag, the only property page that's automatically created when the property sheet is created is the page that is displayed first. So at that moment, that first page has no sibling pages to communicate with. Using the *PSP_PREMATURE* flag, you can ensure that a page is created when the property sheet is created, even though it isn't the first page in the sheet. Although it's easy to get overwhelmed by all these structures, simply using the default values and not using the optional fields results in a powerful and easily maintainable property sheet that's also as easy to construct as a set of individual dialog boxes.

After a property sheet is created, the application can add and delete pages. The application adds a page by sending a *PSM_ADDPAGE* message to the property sheet window. The message must contain the handle of a previously created property page in *lParam*; *wParam* isn't used. Likewise, the application can remove a page by sending a *PSM_REMOVEPAGE* message to the property sheet window. The application specifies a page for deletion either by setting *wParam* to the zero-based index of the page selected for removal or by passing the handle to that page in *lParam*.

The following code creates a simple property sheet with three pages. Each of the pages references a dialog box template resource. As you can see, most of the initialization of the structures can be performed in a fairly mechanical fashion.

```
PROPSHEETHEADER psh;
PROPSHEETPAGE psp[3];
int i;
// Initialize page structures with generic information.
memset (&psp, 0, sizeof (psp));      // Zero out all unused values.
for (i = 0; i < dim(psp); i++) {
    psp[i].dwSize = sizeof (PROPSHEETPAGE);
    psp[i].dwFlags = PSP_DEFAULT;      // No special processing needed
    psp[i].hInstance = hInst;          // Instance handle where the
}                                      // dialog templates are located
// Now do the page-specific stuff.
psp[0].pszTemplate = TEXT ("Page1"); // Name of dialog resource for page 1
psp[0].pfnDlgProc = Page1DlgProc;    // Pointer to dialog proc for page 1

psp[1].pszTemplate = TEXT ("Page2"); // Name of dialog resource for page 2
psp[1].pfnDlgProc = Page2DlgProc;    // Pointer to dialog proc for page 2

psp[2].pszTemplate = TEXT ("Page3"); // Name of dialog resource for page 3
psp[2].pfnDlgProc = Page3DlgProc;    // Pointer to dialog proc for page 3
```

```
// Init property sheet header structure.
psh.dwSize = sizeof (PROPSHEETHEADER);
psh.dwFlags = PSH_PROPSHEETPAGE;     // We are using templates, not handles.
psh.hwndParent = hWnd;               // Handle of the owner window
psh.hInstance = hInst;               // Instance handle of the application
psh.pszCaption = TEXT ("Property sheet title");
psh.nPages = dim(psp);               // Number of pages
psh.nStartPage = 0;                  // Index of page to be shown first
psh.ppsp = psp;                      // Pointer to page structures
psh.pfnCallback = 0;                 // We don't need a callback procedure.

// Create property sheet.  This returns when the user dismisses the sheet
// by tapping OK or the Close button.
i = PropertySheet (&psh);
```

While this fragment has a fair amount of structure filling, it's boilerplate code. Everything not defined, such as the page dialog box resource templates and the page dialog box procedures, is required for dialog boxes as well as property sheets. So aside from the boilerplate stuff, property sheets require little, if any, work beyond simple dialog boxes.

Property Page Procedures

The procedures that back up each of the property pages differ in only a few ways from standard dialog box procedures. First, as I mentioned earlier, unless the *PSP_PREMATURE* flag is used, pages aren't created immediately when the property sheet is created. Instead, each page is created and *WM_INITDIALOG* messages are sent only when the page is initially shown. Also, the *lParam* parameter doesn't point to a user-defined parameter; instead, it points to the *PROPSHEETPAGE* structure that defines the page. Of course, that structure contains a user-definable value that can be used to pass data to the dialog box procedure.

Also, a property sheet procedure doesn't field the *IDOK* and *IDCANCEL* control IDs for the OK and Close buttons on a standard dialog box. These buttons instead are handled by the system-provided property sheet procedure that coordinates the display and management of each page. When the OK or Close button is tapped, the property sheet sends a *WM_NOTIFY* message to each sheet notifying it that one of the two buttons has been tapped and that it should acknowledge that it's okay to close the property sheet.

Switching Pages

When a user switches from one page to the next, the dialog manager sends a *WM_NOTIFY* message with the code *PSN_KILLACTIVE* to the page currently being displayed. The dialog box procedure should then validate the data on the page. If it's permissible for the user to change the page, the dialog box procedure should then set the return value of the window structure of the page to *PSNRET_NOERROR* and return *TRUE*. You set the *PSNRET_NOERROR* return field by calling *SetWindowLong* with *DWL_MSGRESULT*, as in the following line of code:

```
SetWindowLong (hwndPage, DWL_MSGRESULT, PSNRET_NOERROR);
```

where *hwndPage* is the handle of the property sheet page. A page can keep focus by returning *PSNRET_INVALID_NOCHANGEPAGE* in the return field. Assuming a page indicates that it's okay to lose focus, the page being switched to receives a *PSN_SETACTIVE* notification via a *WM_NOTIFY* message. The page can then accept the focus or specify another page that should receive the focus.

Closing a Property Sheet

When the user taps the OK button, the property sheet procedure sends a *WM_NOTIFY* with the notification code *PSN_KILLACTIVE* to the page currently being displayed, followed by a *WM_NOTIFY* with the notification code *PSN_APPLY* to each of the pages that has been created. Each page procedure should save any data from the page controls when it receives the *PSN_APPLY* notification code.

When the user clicks the Close button, a *PSN_QUERYCANCEL* notification is sent to the page procedure of the page currently being displayed. All this notification requires is that the page procedure return *TRUE* to prevent the close or *FALSE* to allow the close. A further notification, *PSN_RESET*, is then sent to all the pages that have been created, indicating that the property sheet is about to be destroyed.

Common Dialogs

In the early days of Windows, it was a rite of passage for a Windows developer to write his or her own File Open dialog box. A File Open dialog box is complex—it must display a list of the possible files from a specific directory, allow file navigation, and return a fully justified file name back to the application. While it was great for programmers to swap stories about how they struggled with their unique implementation of a File Open dialog box, it was hard on the users. Users had to learn a different file open interface for every Windows application.

Windows now provides a set of common dialog boxes that perform typical functions, such as selecting a file name to open or save or picking a color. These standard dialog boxes (called *common dialogs*) serve two purposes. First, common dialogs lift from developers the burden of having to create these dialog boxes from scratch. Second, and just as important, common dialogs provide a common interface to the user across different applications. (These days, real Windows programmers reminisce about the pain of COM.)

Windows CE provides five common dialogs: File Open, Save As, Page Setup, Choose Font, and Choose Color. The Font common dialog box isn't supported under Windows CE. The other advantage of the common dialog boxes is that they have a customized look for each platform while retaining the same programming interface. This makes it easy to use, for example, the File Open dialog box on the Windows Mobile devices and embedded versions of Windows CE because the dialog box has the same interface on both systems, even though the look of the dialog box is vastly different on the different platforms. Figure 6-2 shows the File Open dialog box on an embedded Windows CE system; Figure 6-3 shows the File Open dialog box on a Windows Mobile device.

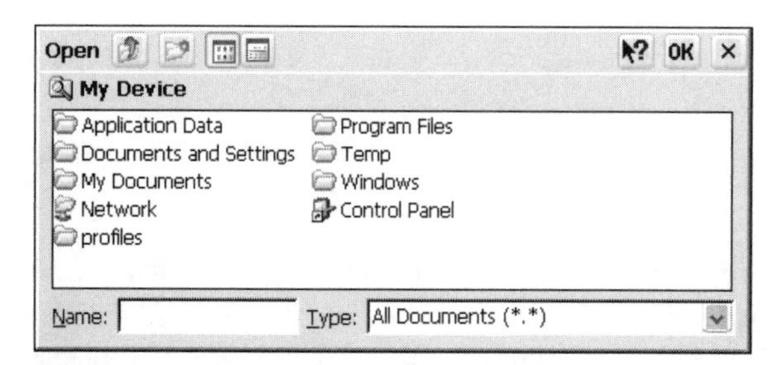

FIGURE 6-2 The File Open dialog box on an embedded Windows CE system

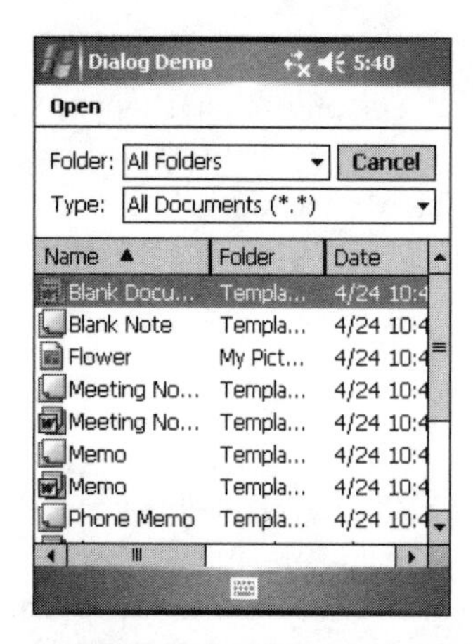

FIGURE 6-3 The File Open dialog box on a Windows Mobile device

Instead of showing you how to use the common dialogs here, I'll let the next example program, DlgDemo, show you. That program demonstrates all four supported common dialog boxes.

The DlgDemo Example Program

The DlgDemo program demonstrates basic dialog boxes, modeless dialog boxes, property sheets, and common dialogs. When you start DlgDemo, it displays a window that shows the *WM_COMMAND* and *WM_NOTIFY* messages sent by the various controls in the dialogs. The different dialogs can be opened using the various menu items. Figure 6-4 shows the Dialog Demo window with the property sheet dialog displayed.

The basic dialog box is a simple "about box" launched by selecting the Help About menu. This dialog uses the *SHInitDialog* function to make the dialog full screen. The property sheet launches by choosing the File Property Sheet menu. The property sheet dialog contains two pages. The first page contains a Month Calendar control. The second page contains a trackbar control and a progress control. The common dialog boxes are launched from the File Open, File Save, File Color, Font, and File Print menu items. The DlgDemo source code is shown in Listing 6-1.

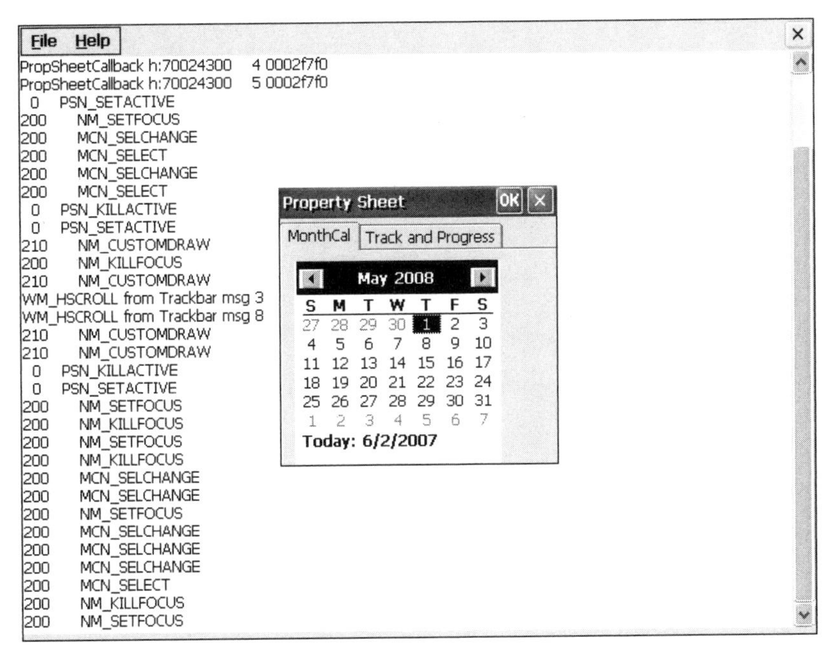

FIGURE 6-4 The Dialog Demo window

LISTING 6-1

DlgDemo.rc

```
//======================================================================
// Resource file
//
// Written for the book Programming Windows CE
// Copyright (C) 2007 Douglas Boling
//======================================================================

#include "windows.h"
#include "DlgDemo.h"                          // Program-specific stuff
#include "commctrl.h"

// Program Icon
ID_ICON       ICON   "DlgDemo.ico"     // Program icon

//----------------------------------------------------------------------
```

```
// Menu, the RC data resource is needed by the menu bar
//
ID_MENU RCDATA MOVEABLE PURE
BEGIN
    ID_MENU, 2,
    -2, 100, TBSTATE_ENABLED, TBSTYLE_DROPDOWN|TBSTYLE_AUTOSIZE,5,0,0,
    -2, 101, TBSTATE_ENABLED, TBSTYLE_DROPDOWN|TBSTYLE_AUTOSIZE,3,0,1
END

ID_MENU MENU DISCARDABLE
BEGIN
    POPUP "&File"
    BEGIN
        MENUITEM "Open...",                    IDM_OPEN
        MENUITEM "Save...",                    IDM_SAVE
        MENUITEM SEPARATOR
        MENUITEM "Color...",                   IDM_COLOR
        MENUITEM "Print...",                   IDM_PRINT
        MENUITEM "Font...",                    IDM_FONT
        MENUITEM SEPARATOR
        MENUITEM "Property Sheet",             IDM_SHOWPROPSHEET
        MENUITEM "Scrollable Dialog",          IDM_SHOWSCROLLABLE
        MENUITEM "Modeless Dialog",            IDM_SHOWMODELESS
        MENUITEM SEPARATOR
        MENUITEM "E&xit",                      IDM_EXIT
    END
    POPUP "&Help"
    BEGIN
        MENUITEM "&About...",                  IDM_ABOUT
    END
END

//----------------------------------------------------------------------
// Property page templates
//
ID_PAGE1 DIALOG discardable 0, 0, 125,  95
CAPTION "MonthCal"
BEGIN
    CONTROL  "", IDC_MONTHCAL, MONTHCAL_CLASS,   WS_VISIBLE,
                                                      5,   5,  95,  95,
END

ID_PAGE2 DIALOG discardable 0, 0, 125,  80
CAPTION "Track and Progress"
BEGIN
    CONTROL  "", IDC_TRACKBAR, TRACKBAR_CLASS, WS_VISIBLE | TBS_AUTOTICKS,
                                                      5,   5, 115,  20,

    CONTROL  "", IDC_PROGRESS, PROGRESS_CLASS,
              WS_BORDER | WS_VISIBLE | PBS_SMOOTH,   5,  30, 115,  20,
END

//----------------------------------------------------------------------
```

```
// Scrollable dialog box template.
//
ScrollDlg DIALOG discardable 20, 10,  90, 50
STYLE  WS_POPUP | WS_CAPTION | WS_SYSMENU | WS_VSCROLL
CAPTION "Scrollable"
BEGIN
    PUSHBUTTON "Button",              IDC_BUTTON,    5,   5,  80,  12,
                                          WS_TABSTOP | BS_NOTIFY
    CHECKBOX "Check Box",             IDC_CHKBOX,    5,  20,  80,  12,
                                          WS_TABSTOP | BS_NOTIFY
    AUTOCHECKBOX "Auto check box"     IDC_ACHKBOX,   5,  35,  80,  12,
                                          WS_TABSTOP
    AUTO3STATE "Auto 3-state box",    IDC_A3STBOX,   5,  50,  80,  12,
                                          WS_TABSTOP
    AUTORADIOBUTTON "Auto radio button 1",
                                      IDC_RADIO1,    5,  65,  80,  12,
                                          WS_TABSTOP | WS_GROUP
    AUTORADIOBUTTON "Auto radio button 2",
                                      IDC_RADIO2,    5,  80,  80,  12
END

//----------------------------------------------------------------------
// Clear list; modeless dialog box template.
//
Clearbox DIALOG discardable 60, 10,  70, 30
STYLE  WS_POPUP | WS_VISIBLE | WS_CAPTION | WS_SYSMENU | DS_MODALFRAME
CAPTION "Clear"
BEGIN
    DEFPUSHBUTTON "Clear Listbox"       IDD_CLEAR,   5,   5,  60,   20
END
//----------------------------------------------------------------------
// About box dialog box template
//
aboutbox DIALOG discardable 10, 10, 132, 45
STYLE  WS_POPUP | WS_CAPTION | WS_SYSMENU | DS_CENTER |
       DS_MODALFRAME
CAPTION "About"
BEGIN
    ICON    ID_ICON                 -1,   5,   5,   0,   0

    LTEXT "DlgDemo - Written for the book Programming Windows \
           CE Copyright 2007 Douglas Boling"
                                    -1,  28,   5, 100,  35
END
```

DlgDemo.h

```
//======================================================================
// Header file
```

```
//
// Written for the book Programming Windows CE
// Copyright (C) 2007 Douglas Boling
//======================================================================
// Returns number of elements
#define dim(x) (sizeof(x) / sizeof(x[0]))

//----------------------------------------------------------------------
// Generic defines and data types
//
struct decodeUINT {                             // Structure associates
    UINT Code;                                  // messages
                                                // with a function.
    LRESULT (*Fxn)(HWND, UINT, WPARAM, LPARAM);
};
struct decodeCMD {                              // Structure associates
    UINT Code;                                  // menu IDs with a
    LRESULT (*Fxn)(HWND, WORD, HWND, WORD);     // function.
};
//----------------------------------------------------------------------
// Generic defines used by application
#define  IDC_CMDBAR          1                  // Command bar ID
#define  IDC_RPTLIST         2                  // ID for report list box
#define  ID_ICON             10                 // Icon resource ID
#define  ID_MENU             11                 // Main menu resource ID

#define  IDM_OPEN            100                // Menu item IDs
#define  IDM_SAVE            101
#define  IDM_COLOR           102
#define  IDM_PRINT           103
#define  IDM_FONT            104
#define  IDM_SHOWPROPSHEET   105
#define  IDM_SHOWSCROLLABLE  106
#define  IDM_SHOWMODELESS    107
#define  IDM_EXIT            108
#define  IDM_ABOUT           110
#define  IDI_BTNICON         120

// Identifiers for the property page resources
#define  ID_PAGE1            50
#define  ID_PAGE2            51

#define  IDC_MONTHCAL        200                 // Page 1 defines

#define  IDC_TRACKBAR        210                 // Page 2 defines
#define  IDC_PROGRESS        211

#define  IDC_BUTTON          300                // Scroll dlg defines
#define  IDC_CHKBOX          301
#define  IDC_ACHKBOX         302
#define  IDC_A3STBOX         303
#define  IDC_RADIO1          304
#define  IDC_RADIO2          305
```

```
// Control IDs for modeless dialog box
#define  IDD_CLEAR          500

// User-defined message to add a line to the window
#define MYMSG_ADDLINE   (WM_USER + 100)

//----------------------------------------------------------------------
// Program-specific structures
//
typedef struct {
    TCHAR *pszLabel;
    DWORD wNotification;
} NOTELABELS, *PNOTELABELS;
//----------------------------------------------------------------------
// Function prototypes
//
HWND InitInstance (HINSTANCE, LPWSTR, int);
int TermInstance (HINSTANCE, int);
void RptMessage (DWORD id, LPTSTR lpszFormat, ...);
LRESULT PrintNotMessage (LPARAM, PNOTELABELS, int);
LRESULT PrintCmdMessage (WPARAM, LPARAM, PNOTELABELS, int);

// Window procedures
LRESULT CALLBACK MainWndProc (HWND, UINT, WPARAM, LPARAM);
// Message handlers
LRESULT DoCreateMain (HWND, UINT, WPARAM, LPARAM);
LRESULT DoCommandMain (HWND, UINT, WPARAM, LPARAM);
LRESULT DoAddLineMain (HWND, UINT, WPARAM, LPARAM);
LRESULT DoDestroyMain (HWND, UINT, WPARAM, LPARAM);
// Command functions
LPARAM DoMainCommandOpen (HWND, WORD, HWND, WORD);
LPARAM DoMainCommandSave (HWND, WORD, HWND, WORD);
LPARAM DoMainCommandColor (HWND, WORD, HWND, WORD);
LPARAM DoMainCommandPrint (HWND, WORD, HWND, WORD);
LPARAM DoMainCommandFont (HWND, WORD, HWND, WORD);
LPARAM DoMainCommandShowProp (HWND, WORD, HWND, WORD);
LPARAM DoMainCommandModeless (HWND, WORD, HWND, WORD);
LPARAM DoMainCommandScrollable (HWND, WORD, HWND, WORD);
LPARAM DoMainCommandExit (HWND, WORD, HWND, WORD);
LPARAM DoMainCommandAbout (HWND, WORD, HWND, WORD);
// Dialog box procedures
BOOL CALLBACK Page1DlgProc (HWND, UINT, WPARAM, LPARAM);
BOOL CALLBACK Page2DlgProc (HWND, UINT, WPARAM, LPARAM);
BOOL CALLBACK AboutDlgProc (HWND, UINT, WPARAM, LPARAM);
BOOL CALLBACK ModelessDlgProc (HWND, UINT, WPARAM, LPARAM);
BOOL CALLBACK ScrollableDlgProc (HWND, UINT, WPARAM, LPARAM);
```

DlgDemo.cpp

```
//======================================================================
// DlgDemo - Dialog box demonstration
```

```
//
// Written for the book Programming Windows CE
// Copyright (C) 2007 Douglas Boling
//======================================================================
#include <windows.h>                 // For all that Windows stuff
#include <commctrl.h>                // Command bar includes
#include <commdlg.h>                 // Common dialog box includes
#include <prsht.h>                   // Property sheet includes

#include "DlgDemo.h"                 // Program-specific stuff
#include <aygshell.h>                // Add extended shell includes
#pragma comment( lib, "aygshell" )   // Link extended shell API

#if defined(WIN32_PLATFORM_PSPC) || defined(WIN32_PLATFORM_WFSP)
#define WINMOBILE 1
#endif
//----------------------------------------------------------------------
// Global data
//
const TCHAR szAppName[] = TEXT ("DlgDemo");
HINSTANCE hInst;                     // Program instance handle
HWND g_hwndMlDlg = 0;                // Handle to modeless dialog box

HINSTANCE hLib = 0;                  // Handle to CommDlg lib
HWND hwndMain;                                                   // Handle to main
window

#ifdef WINMOBILE

typedef BOOL (APIENTRY* LFPRINTDLG) (LPPRINTDLG lppsd);
LFPRINTDLG lpfnPrintDlg = 0;        // Ptr to print common dialog fn

typedef BOOL (APIENTRY* LFCHOOSEFONTPROC) (PVOID);
FARPROC lpfnChooseFontDlg = 0;      // Choose Font

#else

typedef BOOL (APIENTRY* LFPAGESETUPDLG)( LPPAGESETUPDLGW );
LFPAGESETUPDLG lpfnPrintDlg = 0;         // Ptr to print common dialog fn

typedef BOOL (APIENTRY* LFCHOOSEFONTPROC) (LPCHOOSEFONT);
LFCHOOSEFONTPROC lpfnChooseFontDlg = 0;   // Choose Font

#endif

typedef BOOL (APIENTRY* LFCHOOSECOLORPROC) (LPCHOOSECOLOR );
LFCHOOSECOLORPROC lpfnChooseColor = 0;  // Ptr to color common dialog fn


// Message dispatch table for MainWindowProc
const struct decodeUINT MainMessages[] = {
    WM_CREATE, DoCreateMain,
    WM_COMMAND, DoCommandMain,
    MYMSG_ADDLINE, DoAddLineMain,
```

```
    WM_DESTROY, DoDestroyMain,
};

// Command message dispatch for MainWindowProc
const struct decodeCMD MainCommandItems[] = {
    IDM_OPEN, DoMainCommandOpen,
    IDM_SAVE, DoMainCommandSave,
    IDM_SHOWPROPSHEET, DoMainCommandShowProp,
    IDM_SHOWSCROLLABLE, DoMainCommandScrollable,
    IDM_SHOWMODELESS, DoMainCommandModeless,
    IDM_COLOR, DoMainCommandColor,
    IDM_PRINT, DoMainCommandPrint,
    IDM_FONT, DoMainCommandFont,
    IDM_EXIT, DoMainCommandExit,
    IDM_ABOUT, DoMainCommandAbout,
};
//
// Labels for WM_NOTIFY notifications
//
NOTELABELS nlPropPage[] = {{TEXT ("PSN_SETACTIVE  "), PSN_SETACTIVE },
                           {TEXT («PSN_KILLACTIVE «), PSN_KILLACTIVE },
                           {TEXT («PSN_APPLY      «), PSN_APPLY      },
                           {TEXT («PSN_RESET      «), PSN_RESET      },
                           {TEXT («PSN_HELP       «), PSN_HELP       },
                           {TEXT («PSN_WIZBACK    «), PSN_WIZBACK    },
                           {TEXT («PSN_WIZNEXT    «), PSN_WIZNEXT    },
                           {TEXT («PSN_WIZFINISH  «), PSN_WIZFINISH  },
                           {TEXT («PSN_QUERYCANCEL»), PSN_QUERYCANCEL},
                           {TEXT («NM_OUTOFMEMORY «), NM_OUTOFMEMORY },
                           {TEXT («NM_CLICK       «), NM_CLICK       },
                           {TEXT («NM_DBLCLK      «), NM_DBLCLK      },
                           {TEXT («NM_RETURN      «), NM_RETURN      },
                           {TEXT («NM_RCLICK      «), NM_RCLICK      },
                           {TEXT («NM_RDBLCLK     «), NM_RDBLCLK     },
                           {TEXT («NM_SETFOCUS    «), NM_SETFOCUS    },
                           {TEXT («NM_KILLFOCUS   «), NM_KILLFOCUS   },
                           {TEXT («NM_CUSTOMDRAW  «), NM_CUSTOMDRAW  },
                           {TEXT («NM_HOVER       «), NM_HOVER       },
                           {TEXT («NM_NCHITTEST   «), NM_NCHITTEST   },
                           {TEXT («NM_KEYDOWN     «), NM_KEYDOWN     },

};
//======================================================================
// Program entry point
//
int WINAPI WinMain (HINSTANCE hInstance, HINSTANCE hPrevInstance,
                    LPWSTR lpCmdLine, int nCmdShow) {
    MSG msg;
    int rc = 0;

    // Initialize application.
    hwndMain = InitInstance (hInstance, lpCmdLine, nCmdShow);
    if (hwndMain == 0) return 0x10;
```

```
    // Application message loop
    while (GetMessage (&msg, NULL, 0, 0)) {
        // If modeless dialog box is created, let it have
        // the first crack at the message.
        if ((g_hwndMlDlg == 0) ||
            (!IsDialogMessage (g_hwndMlDlg, &msg))) {
            TranslateMessage (&msg);
            DispatchMessage (&msg);
        }
    }
    // Instance cleanup
    return TermInstance (hInstance, msg.wParam);
}
//----------------------------------------------------------------------
// InitInstance - Instance initialization
//
HWND InitInstance (HINSTANCE hInstance, LPWSTR lpCmdLine,
                   int nCmdShow) {
    HWND hWnd;
    WNDCLASS wc;
    INITCOMMONCONTROLSEX iccx;

    // Save program instance handle in global variable.
    hInst = hInstance;

    memset (&iccx, 0, sizeof (iccx));
    iccx.dwSize = sizeof (iccx);
    iccx.dwICC = ICC_DATE_CLASSES | ICC_WIN95_CLASSES | ICC_COOL_CLASSES;
    InitCommonControlsEx (&iccx);

#ifdef WINMOBILE
    // For Windows Mobile devices, allow only one instance of the app
    hWnd = FindWindow (szAppName, NULL);
    if (hWnd) {
        SetForegroundWindow ((HWND)(((DWORD)hWnd) | 0x01));
        return 0;
    }
#endif
    // Register application main window class.
    wc.style = 0;                             // Window style
    wc.lpfnWndProc = MainWndProc;             // Callback function
    wc.cbClsExtra = 0;                        // Extra class data
    wc.cbWndExtra = 0;                        // Extra window data
    wc.hInstance = hInstance;                 // Owner handle
    wc.hIcon = NULL,                          // Application icon
    wc.hCursor = LoadCursor (NULL, IDC_ARROW);// Default cursor
    wc.hbrBackground = (HBRUSH) GetStockObject (WHITE_BRUSH);
    wc.lpszMenuName =  NULL;                  // Menu name
    wc.lpszClassName = szAppName;             // Window class name

    if (RegisterClass (&wc) == 0) return 0;

    // Get the Color and print dialog function pointers.
```

```
    hLib = LoadLibrary (TEXT («COMMDLG.DLL»));
    if (hLib) {
        lpfnChooseColor = (LFCHOOSECOLORPROC)GetProcAddress (hLib,
                                                 TEXT («ChooseColor»));

#ifdef WINMOBILE
        lpfnPrintDlg = (LFPRINTDLG)GetProcAddress (hLib, TEXT («PrintDlg»));
#else
        lpfnPrintDlg = (LFPAGESETUPDLG)GetProcAddress (hLib,
                                                 TEXT («PageSetupDlgW»));
        lpfnChooseFontDlg = (LFCHOOSEFONTPROC)GetProcAddress (hLib,
                                                 TEXT («ChooseFontW»));
#endif

    }
    // Create main window.
    hWnd = CreateWindow (szAppName, TEXT («Dialog Demo»), WS_VISIBLE,
                         CW_USEDEFAULT, CW_USEDEFAULT, CW_USEDEFAULT,
                         CW_USEDEFAULT, NULL, NULL, hInstance, NULL);
    // Return fail code if window not created.
    if (!IsWindow (hWnd)) return 0;

    // Standard show and update calls
    ShowWindow (hWnd, nCmdShow);
    UpdateWindow (hWnd);
    return hWnd;
}
//----------------------------------------------------------------------
// TermInstance - Program cleanup
//
int TermInstance (HINSTANCE hInstance, int nDefRC) {
    if (hLib)
        FreeLibrary (hLib);
    return nDefRC;
}
//======================================================================
// Message-handling procedures for MainWindow
//
//----------------------------------------------------------------------
// MainWndProc - Callback function for application window
//
LRESULT CALLBACK MainWndProc (HWND hWnd, UINT wMsg, WPARAM wParam,
                              LPARAM lParam) {
    INT i;
    //
    // Search message list to see if we need to handle this
    // message. If in list, call procedure.
    //
    for (i = 0; i < dim(MainMessages); i++) {
        if (wMsg == MainMessages[i].Code)
            return (*MainMessages[i].Fxn)(hWnd, wMsg, wParam, lParam);
    }
    return DefWindowProc (hWnd, wMsg, wParam, lParam);
```

```
}
//----------------------------------------------------------------------
// DoCreateMain - Process WM_CREATE message for window.
//
LRESULT DoCreateMain (HWND hWnd, UINT wMsg, WPARAM wParam,
                      LPARAM lParam) {
    HWND hwndChild;
    INT i, nHeight = 0;
    LPCREATESTRUCT lpcs;
    HMENU hMenu;
#ifdef WINMOBILE
    SHMENUBARINFO mbi;                      // For WinMobile, create
    memset(&mbi, 0, sizeof(SHMENUBARINFO)); // menu bar so that we
    mbi.cbSize = sizeof(SHMENUBARINFO);     // have a sip button
    mbi.hwndParent = hWnd;
    mbi.nToolBarId = ID_MENU;
    mbi.hInstRes = hInst;
    SHCreateMenuBar(&mbi);
    hMenu = (HMENU)SendMessage(mbi.hwndMB, SHCMBM_GETSUBMENU, 0, 100);
#else
    // Create a command bar. Add a menu and an exit button.
    HWND hwndCB = CommandBar_Create (hInst, hWnd, IDC_CMDBAR);
    CommandBar_InsertMenubar (hwndCB, hInst, ID_MENU, 0);
    CommandBar_AddAdornments (hwndCB, 0, 0);
    nHeight = CommandBar_Height (hwndCB);
    hMenu = CommandBar_GetMenu (hwndCB, 0);
#endif
    // Convert lParam to pointer to create structure.
    lpcs = (LPCREATESTRUCT) lParam;

    // See color and print functions not found; disable menus.
    if (!lpfnChooseColor)
        EnableMenuItem (hMenu, IDM_COLOR, MF_BYCOMMAND | MF_GRAYED);
    if (!lpfnPrintDlg)
        EnableMenuItem (hMenu, IDM_PRINT, MF_BYCOMMAND | MF_GRAYED);
    if (!lpfnChooseFontDlg)
        EnableMenuItem (hMenu, IDM_FONT, MF_BYCOMMAND | MF_GRAYED);
    //
    // Create report window. Size it so that it fits under
    // the command bar and fills the remaining client area.
    //
    hwndChild = CreateWindowEx (0, TEXT («listbox»),
                         TEXT («»), WS_VISIBLE | WS_CHILD | WS_VSCROLL |
                         LBS_USETABSTOPS | LBS_NOINTEGRALHEIGHT, 0,
                         nHeight, lpcs->cx, lpcs->cy - nHeight,
                         hWnd, (HMENU)IDC_RPTLIST, lpcs->hInstance, NULL);

    // Destroy frame if window not created.
    if (!IsWindow (hwndChild)) {
        DestroyWindow (hWnd);
        return 0;
    }
    // Initialize tab stops for display list box.
    i = 8;
```

```
    SendMessage (hwndChild, LB_SETTABSTOPS, 1, (LPARAM)&i);
    return 0;
}
//----------------------------------------------------------------------
// DoCommandMain - Process WM_COMMAND message for window.
//
LRESULT DoCommandMain (HWND hWnd, UINT wMsg, WPARAM wParam,
                       LPARAM lParam) {
    WORD idItem, wNotifyCode;
    HWND hwndCtl;
    INT  i;

    // Parse the parameters.
    idItem = (WORD) LOWORD (wParam);
    wNotifyCode = (WORD) HIWORD (wParam);
    hwndCtl = (HWND) lParam;

    // Call routine to handle control message.
    for (i = 0; i < dim(MainCommandItems); i++) {
        if (idItem == MainCommandItems[i].Code)
            return (*MainCommandItems[i].Fxn)(hWnd, idItem, hwndCtl,
                                              wNotifyCode);
    }
    return 0;
}
//----------------------------------------------------------------------
// DoAddLineMain - Process MYMSG_ADDLINE message for window.
//
LRESULT DoAddLineMain (HWND hWnd, UINT wMsg, WPARAM wParam,
                       LPARAM lParam) {
    TCHAR szOut[128];
    INT i;

    // If nothing in wParam, just fill in spaces.
    if (wParam == -1) {
        // Print message only.
        wsprintf (szOut, TEXT («%s»), (LPTSTR)lParam);
    } else {
        // If no ID val, ignore that field.
        if (LOWORD (wParam) == 0xffff)
            // Print prop page and message.
            wsprintf (szOut, TEXT («        \t %s»),
                      (LPTSTR)lParam);
        else
            // Print property page, control ID, and message.
            wsprintf (szOut, TEXT («%3d   \t %s»),
                      wParam, (LPTSTR)lParam);
    }
    i = SendDlgItemMessage (hWnd, IDC_RPTLIST, LB_ADDSTRING, 0,
                            (LPARAM)(LPCTSTR)szOut);
    if (i != LB_ERR)
        SendDlgItemMessage (hWnd, IDC_RPTLIST, LB_SETTOPINDEX, i,
                            (LPARAM)(LPCTSTR)szOut);
    return 0;
```

```
}
//----------------------------------------------------------------------
// DoDestroyMain - Process WM_DESTROY message for window.
//
LRESULT DoDestroyMain (HWND hWnd, UINT wMsg, WPARAM wParam,
                       LPARAM lParam) {
    PostQuitMessage (0);
    return 0;
}
//======================================================================
// Command handler routines
//----------------------------------------------------------------------
// DoMainCommandOpen - Process File Open command
//
LPARAM DoMainCommandOpen (HWND hWnd, WORD idItem, HWND hwndCtl,
                          WORD wNotifyCode) {
    OPENFILENAME of;
    TCHAR szFileName [MAX_PATH] = {0};
    const LPTSTR pszOpenFilter = TEXT («All Documents (*.*)\0*.*\0\0»);
    INT rc;

    szFileName[0] = '\0';            // Initialize filename.
    memset (&of, 0, sizeof (of));    // Initialize File Open structure.

    of.lStructSize = sizeof (of);
    of.hwndOwner = hWnd;
    of.lpstrFile = szFileName;
    of.nMaxFile = dim(szFileName);
    of.lpstrFilter = pszOpenFilter;
    of.Flags = 0;

    rc = GetOpenFileName (&of);
    RptMessage (-1, TEXT («GetOpenFileName returned: %x, filename: %s»),
                rc, szFileName);
    return 0;
}
//----------------------------------------------------------------------
// DoMainCommandSave - Process File Save command.
//
LPARAM DoMainCommandSave (HWND hWnd, WORD idItem, HWND hwndCtl,
                          WORD wNotifyCode) {
    OPENFILENAME of;
    TCHAR szFileName [MAX_PATH] = {0};
    const LPTSTR pszOpenFilter = TEXT («All Documents (*.*)\0*.*\0\0»);
    INT rc;

    szFileName[0] = '\0';            // Initialize filename.
    memset (&of, 0, sizeof (of));    // Initialize File Open structure.
    of.lStructSize = sizeof (of);
    of.hwndOwner = hWnd;
    of.lpstrFile = szFileName;
    of.nMaxFile = dim(szFileName);
    of.lpstrFilter = pszOpenFilter;
```

```
    of.Flags = 0;
    rc = GetSaveFileName (&of);

    RptMessage (-1, TEXT («GetSaveFileName returned: %x, filename: %s»),
                rc, szFileName);
    return 0;
}
//----------------------------------------------------------------------
// DoMainCommandColor - Process File Color command.
//
LPARAM DoMainCommandColor (HWND hWnd, WORD idItem, HWND hwndCtl,
                           WORD wNotifyCode) {
    CHOOSECOLOR cc;
    static COLORREF cr[16];
    INT rc;

    // Initialize color structure.
    memset (&cc, 0, sizeof (cc));
    memset (&cr, 0, sizeof (cr));

    cc.lStructSize = sizeof (cc);
    cc.hwndOwner = hWnd;
    cc.hInstance = hInst;
    cc.rgbResult = RGB (0, 0, 0);
    cc.lpCustColors = cr;
    cc.Flags = CC_ANYCOLOR;

    rc = (lpfnChooseColor) (&cc);
    RptMessage (-1, TEXT («Choose Color returned: %x, color: %x»),
                rc, cc.rgbResult);
    return 0;
}
//----------------------------------------------------------------------
// DoMainCommandFont - Process File Font command.
//
LPARAM DoMainCommandFont (HWND hWnd, WORD idItem, HWND hwndCtl,
                          WORD wNotifyCode) {
#ifndef WINMOBILE
    CHOOSEFONT cfd;
    int rc;

    if (lpfnChooseFontDlg == 0)
        RptMessage (-1, TEXT («ChooseFontDlg Not available»));

    // Initialize print structure.
    memset (&cfd, 0, sizeof (cfd));

    cfd.lStructSize = sizeof (cfd);
    cfd.hwndOwner = hWnd;
    cfd.Flags = CF_SCREENFONTS;

    rc = (lpfnChooseFontDlg) (&cfd);
    RptMessage (-1, TEXT («Choose Font returned: %x»), rc);
```

```
#endif
    return 0;
}
//----------------------------------------------------------------------
// DoMainCommandPrint - Process File Print command.
//
LPARAM DoMainCommandPrint (HWND hWnd, WORD idItem, HWND hwndCtl,
                           WORD wNotifyCode) {
    INT rc;
#ifndef WINMOBILE
    PAGESETUPDLG psd;

    // Initialize print structure.
    memset (&psd, 0, sizeof (psd));
    psd.lStructSize = sizeof (psd);
    psd.hwndOwner = hWnd;

    rc = (lpfnPrintDlg) (&psd);
#else
    PRINTDLG pd;
    // Initialize print structure.
    memset (&pd, 0, sizeof (pd));

    pd.cbStruct = sizeof (pd);
    pd.hwndOwner = hWnd;
    pd.dwFlags = PD_SELECTALLPAGES;

    rc = (lpfnPrintDlg) (&pd);
#endif // ifndef WIN32_PLATFORM_PSPC
    RptMessage (-1, TEXT («PrintDlg returned: %x, : %x»),
                rc, GetLastError());
    return 0;
}
//----------------------------------------------------------------------
// PropSheetProc - Function called when Property sheet created
//
int CALLBACK PropSheetProc(HWND hwndDlg, UINT uMsg, LPARAM lParam) {
    HWND hwndTabs;
    DWORD dwStyle;

    RptMessage (-1, TEXT(«PropSheetCallback h:%08x %4d %08x»),
                hwndDlg, uMsg, lParam);

    switch (uMsg)
    {
    case PSCB_INITIALIZED:
        // Get tab control.
        hwndTabs = GetDlgItem (hwndDlg, 0x3020);
        dwStyle = GetWindowLong (hwndTabs, GWL_STYLE);
        SetWindowLong (hwndTabs, GWL_STYLE, dwStyle | TCS_BOTTOM);
        return 0;

    case PSCB_GETTITLE:
        StringCbCopy((LPTSTR)lParam, 256, TEXT («Property Sheet»));
```

```
        return 1;

    case PSCB_GETVERSION:
        return COMCTL32_VERSION;

    // Add a hyperlink line below the tabs.
    case PSCB_GETLINKTEXT:
        StringCbCopy((LPTSTR)lParam, 256, TEXT («Launch the calculator by «)
                TEXT(«tapping <file:\\windows\\calc.exe{here}>.»));
        return 0;
    }
    return 0;
}
//----------------------------------------------------------------------
// DoMainCommandShowProp - Process show property sheet command.
//
LPARAM DoMainCommandShowProp(HWND hWnd, WORD idItem, HWND hwndCtl,
                             WORD wNotifyCode) {
    PROPSHEETPAGE psp[2];
    PROPSHEETHEADER psh;
    INT i;
    // Zero all the property page structures.
    memset (&psp, 0, sizeof (psp));
    // Fill in default values in property page structures.
    for (i = 0; i < dim(psp); i++) {
        psp[i].dwSize = sizeof (PROPSHEETPAGE);
        psp[i].dwFlags = PSP_DEFAULT;
        psp[i].hInstance = hInst;
        psp[i].lParam = (LPARAM)hWnd;
    }
    // Set the dialog box templates for each page.
    psp[0].pszTemplate = MAKEINTRESOURCE (ID_PAGE1);
    psp[1].pszTemplate = MAKEINTRESOURCE (ID_PAGE2);

    // Set the dialog box procedures for each page.
    psp[0].pfnDlgProc = Page1DlgProc;
    psp[1].pfnDlgProc = Page2DlgProc;

    // Initialize property sheet structure.
    psh.dwSize = sizeof (PROPSHEETHEADER);
    psh.dwFlags = PSH_PROPSHEETPAGE;
    psh.hwndParent = hWnd;
    psh.hInstance = hInst;
    psh.pszCaption = TEXT («Property Sheet Demo»);
    psh.nPages = dim(psp);
    psh.nStartPage = 0;
    psh.ppsp = psp;
    psh.pfnCallback = PropSheetProc;
    // On Windows Mobile, make property sheets full screen.
#if WINMOBILE
    psh.dwFlags |= PSH_USECALLBACK | PSH_MAXIMIZE;
#else
    psh.dwFlags |= PSH_USECALLBACK;
#endif
```

```
    // Create and display property sheet.
    PropertySheet (&psh);
    return 0;
}
//----------------------------------------------------------------------
// DoMainCommandModelessDlg - Process the File Modeless menu command.
//
LPARAM DoMainCommandModeless(HWND hWnd, WORD idItem, HWND hwndCtl,
                             WORD wNotifyCode) {

    // Create dialog box only if not already created.
    if (g_hwndMlDlg == 0)
        // Use CreateDialog to create modeless dialog box.
        g_hwndMlDlg = CreateDialog (hInst, TEXT («Clearbox»), hWnd,
                                    ModelessDlgProc);
    return 0;
}
//----------------------------------------------------------------------
// DoMainCommandScrollable - Process the File Scrollable menu command.
//
LPARAM DoMainCommandScrollable(HWND hWnd, WORD idItem, HWND hwndCtl,
                               WORD wNotifyCode) {

    // Create dialog box only if not already created.
    DialogBox (hInst, TEXT («ScrollDlg»), hWnd, ScrollableDlgProc);
    return 0;
}
//----------------------------------------------------------------------
// DoMainCommandExit - Process Program Exit command.
//
LPARAM DoMainCommandExit (HWND hWnd, WORD idItem, HWND hwndCtl,
                          WORD wNotifyCode) {
    SendMessage (hWnd, WM_CLOSE, 0, 0);
    return 0;
}
//----------------------------------------------------------------------
// DoMainCommandAbout - Process the Help About menu command.
//
LPARAM DoMainCommandAbout(HWND hWnd, WORD idItem, HWND hwndCtl,
                          WORD wNotifyCode) {
    // Use DialogBox to create modal dialog box.
    DialogBox (hInst, TEXT («aboutbox»), hWnd, AboutDlgProc);
    return 0;
}
//======================================================================
// Modeless ClearList dialog box procedure
//
BOOL CALLBACK ModelessDlgProc (HWND hWnd, UINT wMsg, WPARAM wParam,
                               LPARAM lParam) {
    switch (wMsg) {
        case WM_COMMAND:
            switch (LOWORD (wParam)) {
                case IDD_CLEAR:
                    // Send message to list box to clear it.
```

```
                SendDlgItemMessage (GetWindow (hWnd, GW_OWNER),
                                    IDC_RPTLIST,
                                    LB_RESETCONTENT, 0, 0);
                return TRUE;

            case IDOK:
            case IDCANCEL:
                // Modeless dialog boxes can't use EndDialog.
                DestroyWindow (hWnd);
                g_hwndMlDlg = 0;  // 0 means dlg destroyed.
                return TRUE;
            }
        break;
    }
    return FALSE;
}
//======================================================================
// About dialog box procedure
//
BOOL CALLBACK AboutDlgProc (HWND hWnd, UINT wMsg, WPARAM wParam,
                           LPARAM lParam) {
    SHINITDLGINFO idi;
    switch (wMsg) {
        case WM_INITDIALOG:
            idi.dwMask = SHIDIM_FLAGS;
            idi.dwFlags = SHIDIF_DONEBUTTON | SHIDIF_SIZEDLGFULLSCREEN |
                          SHIDIF_SIPDOWN;
            idi.hDlg = hWnd;
            SHInitDialog (&idi);
            break;
        case WM_COMMAND:
            switch (LOWORD (wParam)) {
                case IDOK:
                case IDCANCEL:
                    EndDialog (hWnd, 0);
                    return TRUE;
            }
        break;
    }
    return FALSE;
}
//----------------------------------------------------------------------
// PrintCmdMessage - Prints command message data to report window
//
LRESULT PrintCmdMessage (WPARAM wParam, LPARAM lParam,
                        PNOTELABELS lpStruct, int nDim) {
    int i;

    for (i = 0; i < nDim; i++) {
        if (HIWORD (wParam) == lpStruct[i].wNotification) {
            RptMessage (LOWORD(wParam), TEXT(«%s»),
                        lpStruct[i].pszLabel);
            break;
        }
```

```
    }
    if (i == nDim)
        RptMessage (wParam, TEXT(«WM_COMMAND notification: %x»),
                    HIWORD (wParam));
    return 0;
}
//----------------------------------------------------------------------
// PrintNotMessage - Prints notification message data to report window
//
LRESULT PrintNotMessage (LPARAM lParam, PNOTELABELS lpStruct, int nDim) {
    int i;
    LPNMHDR phdr = (NMHDR *)lParam;

    for (i = 0; i < nDim; i++) {
        if (phdr->code == lpStruct[i].wNotification) {
            RptMessage (phdr->idFrom, TEXT(«%s»), lpStruct[i].pszLabel);
            break;
        }
    }
    if (i == nDim)
    {
        // If not in local list, check standard notifications
        for (i = 0; i < sizeof (nlPropPage); i++) {
            if (phdr->code == nlPropPage[i].wNotification) {
                RptMessage (phdr->idFrom, TEXT(«%s»),
                            nlPropPage[i].pszLabel);
                break;
            }
        }
        if (i == sizeof (nlPropPage))
            RptMessage (phdr->idFrom, TEXT («Notify code:%4d»),
                        phdr->code);
    }
    return 0;
}
//----------------------------------------------------------------------
// RptMessage - Add string to the report list box.
//
void RptMessage (DWORD id, LPTSTR lpszFormat, ...) {
    TCHAR szBuffer[512];
    va_list args;

    va_start(args, lpszFormat);
    StringCchVPrintf(szBuffer, dim (szBuffer),lpszFormat, args);
    va_end(args);
    SendMessage (hwndMain, MYMSG_ADDLINE, id,(LPARAM)szBuffer);
}
```

Page1Dlg.cpp

```
//======================================================================
```

```
// Page1DlgProc - Button dialog box window code
//
// Written for the book Programming Windows CE
// Copyright (C) 2007 Douglas Boling
//======================================================================
#include <windows.h>                 // For all that Windows stuff
#include <commctrl.h>                // Common Control includes
#include <prsht.h>                   // Property sheet includes
#include "DlgDemo.h"                 // Program-specific stuff

// Identification strings for various WM_NOTIFY notifications
NOTELABELS nlPage1[] = {{TEXT ("MCN_SELCHANGE    "), MCN_SELCHANGE},
                        {TEXT ("MCN_GETDAYSTATE "), MCN_GETDAYSTATE},
                        {TEXT ("MCN_SELECT       "), MCN_SELECT},
                        {TEXT ("MCN_SELECTNONE   "), MCN_SELECTNONE},
};
//======================================================================
// Page1DlgProc - Page1 dialog box procedure
//
BOOL CALLBACK Page1DlgProc (HWND hWnd, UINT wMsg, WPARAM wParam,
                            LPARAM lParam) {
    switch (wMsg) {

        case WM_INITDIALOG:
            return TRUE;
        //
        // Reflect WM_COMMAND messages to main window.
        //
        case WM_COMMAND:
            PrintCmdMessage (wParam, lParam, NULL, 0);
            return TRUE;

        //
        // Reflect notify message.
        //
        case WM_NOTIFY:
            PrintNotMessage (lParam, nlPage1, sizeof (nlPage1));
            return FALSE;  // Return false to force default processing.
    }
    return FALSE;
}
```

Page2Dlg.cpp

```
///======================================================================
// Page2DlgProc - Button dialog box window code
//
// Written for the book Programming Windows CE
```

```
// Copyright (C) 2007 Douglas Boling
//======================================================================
#include <windows.h>                  // For all that Windows stuff
#include <commctrl.h>                 // Common Control includes
#include <prsht.h>                    // Property sheet includes
#include "DlgDemo.h"                  // Program-specific stuff

//======================================================================
// Page2DlgProc - Button page dialog box procedure
//
BOOL CALLBACK Page2DlgProc (HWND hWnd, UINT wMsg, WPARAM wParam,
                            LPARAM lParam) {
    int i;
    switch (wMsg) {
        case WM_INITDIALOG:
            i = SendDlgItemMessage (hWnd, IDC_TRACKBAR,
                                    TBM_GETRANGEMAX, 0, 0);
            SendDlgItemMessage (hWnd, IDC_PROGRESS,
                                PBM_SETRANGE, 0, MAKELPARAM (0, i));
            return TRUE;
        //
        // Reflect WM_COMMAND messages to main window.
        //
        case WM_COMMAND:
            PrintCmdMessage (wParam, lParam, NULL, 0);
            return TRUE;

        //
        // Reflect notify message.
        //
        case WM_NOTIFY:
            PrintNotMessage (lParam, NULL, 0);
            return FALSE;  // Return false to force default processing.

        //
        // Reflect scroll bar messages that are generated by Trackbar
        //
        case WM_VSCROLL:
            RptMessage (-1, TEXT("WM_VSCROLL from Trackbar msg %d"),
                        LOWORD (wParam));
            return FALSE;

        case WM_HSCROLL:
            RptMessage (-1, TEXT("WM_HSCROLL from Trackbar msg %d"),
                        LOWORD (wParam));

            // Get the position of the trackbar
            i = SendDlgItemMessage (hWnd, IDC_TRACKBAR, TBM_GETPOS, 0, 0);

            // Set the progress bar control
            SendDlgItemMessage (hWnd, IDC_PROGRESS, PBM_SETPOS, i, 0);
            return FALSE;
    }
    return FALSE;
```

```
}
```

ScrollDlg.cpp

```
///======================================================================
// ScrollDlg - Scrollable dialog box window code
//
// Written for the book Programming Windows CE
// Copyright (C) 2007 Douglas Boling
//======================================================================
#include <windows.h>                 // For all that Windows stuff
#include <commctrl.h>                // Common Control includes
#include <prsht.h>                   // Property sheet includes
#include "DlgDemo.h"                 // Program-specific stuff

// Structure labeling the button control WM_COMMAND notifications
NOTELABELS nlBtn[] = {{TEXT ("BN_CLICKED "),      BN_CLICKED },
                      {TEXT ("BN_PAINT   "),      BN_PAINT   },
                      {TEXT ("BN_SETFOCUS "),     BN_SETFOCUS},
                      {TEXT ("BN_KILLFOCUS"),     BN_KILLFOCUS}
};
// Scroll position of dialog
int nVPos = 0;
//======================================================================
// ScrollableDlgProc - Scrollable dialog box procedure
//
BOOL CALLBACK ScrollableDlgProc (HWND hWnd, UINT wMsg, WPARAM wParam,
                                 LPARAM lParam) {
    switch (wMsg) {
        case WM_INITDIALOG:
            return TRUE;
        //
        // Reflect WM_COMMAND messages to main window.
        //
        case WM_COMMAND:
            PrintCmdMessage (wParam, lParam, nlBtn, sizeof(nlBtn));
            // Close dialog for OK or Cancel
            switch (LOWORD (wParam)) {
                case IDOK:
                case IDCANCEL:
                    EndDialog (hWnd, 0);
                    return TRUE;
            }
            return TRUE;
        //
        // Reflect notify message.
        //
        case WM_NOTIFY:
            PrintNotMessage (lParam, NULL, 0);
            return FALSE;  // Return false to force default processing.
```

```
        case WM_VSCROLL:
            {
                int nNewPos = nVPos;
                int nLinesPerPage = 5;

                switch (LOWORD (wParam)) {
                case SB_LINEUP:
                    nNewPos -= 1;
                    break;

                case SB_LINEDOWN:
                    nNewPos += 1;
                    break;

                case SB_PAGEUP:
                    nNewPos -= nLinesPerPage;
                    break;

                case SB_PAGEDOWN:
                    nNewPos += nLinesPerPage;
                    break;

                case SB_THUMBTRACK:
                case SB_THUMBPOSITION:
                    nNewPos = HIWORD (wParam);
                    break;
                }

                // If scroll position changed, Scroll the window and
                // update scrollbar
                if (nVPos != nNewPos) {
                    ScrollWindowEx (hWnd, 0, nVPos - nNewPos, NULL, NULL,
                           NULL, NULL, SW_INVALIDATE | SW_SCROLLCHILDREN);

                    SCROLLINFO si;
                    nVPos = nNewPos;
                    si.cbSize = sizeof (si);
                    si.nPos = nVPos;
                    si.fMask = SIF_POS;
                    SetScrollInfo (hWnd, SB_VERT, &si, TRUE);
                }
            }
            break;
    }
    return FALSE;
}
```

The dialog box procedures for each of the property pages report all *WM_COMMAND* and *WM_NOTIFY* messages back to the main window, where they're displayed in a list box contained in the main window. The property page dialog box procedures are quite simple. They simply reflect the *WM_COMMAND* and *WM_NOTIFY* messages back to the main window. The *Page2DlgProc* also fields the *WM_VSCROLL* and *WM_HSCROLL* messages that are sent from the Trackbar control. When *Page2DlgProc* receives a *WM_HSCROLL* message, it sets the progress control to match the position of the trackbar.

The best way to learn from DlgDemo is to run the program and watch the different *WM_COMMAND* and *WM_NOTIFY* messages that are sent by the controls and the property sheet. Opening the property sheet and switching between the pages results in a flood of *WM_NOTIFY* messages informing the individual pages of what's happening. It's also interesting to note that when the OK button is clicked on the property sheet, the *PSN_APPLY* messages are sent only to property pages that have been displayed.

The menu handlers that display the Print, Font, and Color common dialogs work with a bit of a twist. Because some Windows CE systems don't support these dialogs, DlgDemo can't call the functions directly. That would result in these two functions being implicitly linked at runtime. On systems that did not support these functions, Windows CE wouldn't be able to resolve the implicit links to all the functions in the program, and therefore the program wouldn't be able to load. So instead of calling the functions directly, you explicitly link these functions in *InitApp* by loading the common dialog DLL using *LoadLibrary* and getting pointers to the functions using *GetProcAddress*. If DlgDemo is running on a system that doesn't support one of the functions, the *GetProcAddress* function fails and returns 0 for the function pointer. In *DoCreateMain*, a check is made to see whether these function pointers are 0, and if so, the Print and Color menu items are disabled. In the menu handler functions *DoMainCommandColor*, *DoMainCommandFont*, and *DoMainCommandPrint*, the function pointers returned by *GetProcAddress* are used to call the functions. This extra effort isn't necessary if you know your program will run only on a system that supports a specific set of functions, but every once in a while, this technique comes in handy. Dealing with DLLs is covered in Chapter 8, "Modules, Processes, and Threads."

Windows Mobile devices handle the common print dialog differently. Although they export the function *PageSetupDialog*, the function prototype isn't included in the SDK, and the function returns immediately when called.

One other detail is how this program adapts to Windows Mobile systems. DlgDemo creates a menu bar instead of a command bar when compiled for these systems. This provides a place for the menu as well as exposing the Soft Keyboard button.

In addition, on Windows Mobile systems, *DlgDemo* uses the *PSH_MAXIMIZE* flag when creating the property sheet. This causes the property sheet to expand to fill the full screen. The code in the property sheet callback routine relocates the tabs on the bottom of the sheet instead of the top. While this code also executes on embedded systems, it has no effect. I made these adaptations to demonstrate how to comply with the Windows Mobile user interface guidelines. To place the tabs on the bottom of the sheet and provide the hyperlink text below the pages, DlgDemo provides the property sheet callback function shown here:

```
int CALLBACK PropSheetProc(HWND hwndDlg, UINT uMsg, LPARAM lParam) {

    if (uMsg == PSCB_INITIALIZED) {
        // Get tab control
        HWND hwndTabs = GetDlgItem (hwndDlg, 0x3020);

        DWORD dwStyle = GetWindowLong (hwndTabs, GWL_STYLE);
        SetWindowLong (hwndTabs, GWL_STYLE, dwStyle | TCS_BOTTOM);

    } else if (uMsg ==  PSCB_GETVERSION)
        return COMCTL32_VERSION;
    return 1;
}
```

The source of this rather strange code comes from the MFC source code provided with the Windows Mobile SDK. During the *PSCB_INITIALIZE* notification, the handle of the Tab control of the property sheet is queried using the predefined control ID 0x3020. The style bits of the Tab control are then modified to have the control place the tabs on the bottom instead of the top by setting the *TCS_BOTTOM* style flag.

The function also handles the *PSCB_GETLINKTEXT* notification and returns the following text:

```
TEXT ("Launch the calculator by tapping <file:calc.exe{here}>.")
```

The hyperlink is enclosed in angle brackets <>. The text displayed for the link is enclosed in curly braces {}. When the hyperlink is tapped, the Pocket PC launches calc.exe. The hyperlink can also be a data file such as book1.pxl or memo.pwd.

Dialog boxes and property sheets are quite often the only user interface a Windows CE program has. Although sometimes complex in implementation, the help Windows CE provides in creating and maintaining dialog boxes and property sheets reduces the workload on the program to some extent.

This chapter also marks the end of the introductory section, "Windows Programming Basics." In these first six chapters, I've talked about fundamental Windows programming while also using a basic Windows CE application to introduce the concepts of the system message queue, windows, and messages. I've given you an overview of how to paint text and graphics in a window and how to query the user for input. Finally, I talked about the windows hierarchy, controls, common controls, and dialog boxes. For the remainder of the book, I move from description of the elements common to both Windows CE and the desktop versions of Windows to the unique nature of Windows CE programming. It's time to turn to the operating system itself. Over the next five chapters, I'll cover memory management, processes and threads, the file system, the registry, and databases. These chapters are aimed at the core of the Windows CE operating system.

Part II

Windows CE Programming

Chapter 7
Memory Management

If you have an overriding concern when you write a Microsoft Windows CE program, it should be dealing with memory. A Windows CE machine might have only 16 MB of RAM. This is a tiny amount compared with that of a standard personal computer, which typically needs 512 MB or more. In fact, memory on a Windows CE machine is so scarce that it's sometimes necessary to write programs that conserve memory even to the point of sacrificing the overall performance of the application.

Fortunately, although the amount of memory is small in a Windows CE system, the functions available for managing that memory are fairly complete. Windows CE implements almost the full Win32 memory management API available under Microsoft Windows XP and Windows Vista. Windows CE supports virtual memory allocations, local and separate heaps, and even memory-mapped files.

Like the desktop versions of Windows, Windows CE supports a 32-bit flat address space with memory protection between applications. But because Windows CE was designed for different environments, its underlying memory architecture is different from that of Windows XP or Vista. These differences can affect how you design a Windows CE application. This chapter describes the basic memory architecture of Windows CE. It also covers the different types of memory allocation available to Windows CE programs and how to use each memory type to minimize your application's memory footprint.

Memory Basics

As with all computers, systems running Windows CE have both ROM (read-only memory) and RAM (random access memory). Under Windows CE, however, both ROM and RAM are used somewhat differently than they are in a standard personal computer.[1]

About RAM

The RAM in a Windows CE system, like in all operating systems, is used to store the heaps, stacks, and sometimes the code for the applications. Unlike other operating sysetms, part of the RAM may also be used for the *object store*. The optional object store can be considered something like a permanent virtual RAM disk. Unlike the old virtual RAM disks on a PC, the

---

1 On most systems, this read-only memory is implemented as Flash memory so that the operating system can be updated in the field. I refer to it as ROM here to distinguish it from read/write flash-based drives that are used for file storage.

object store retains the files stored in it even if the system is reset, as long as the system retains the state of the RAM across the reset. This arrangement is the reason some Windows CE systems have a main battery and a backup battery. When the user replaces the main batteries, the backup battery's job is to provide power to the RAM to retain the files in the object store. Even when the user clicks the Reset button, the Windows CE kernel starts up looking for a previously created object store in RAM and uses that store if it finds one.

The boundary between the object store and the program RAM is movable. On systems that support the object store, the user can move the dividing line between object store and program RAM using the System Control Panel applet. Under low-memory conditions, the system asks the user for permission to take some object store RAM to use as program RAM to satisfy an application's demand for more RAM.

When the object store file system is not used, it must be replaced by another file system such as a read-write flash file system or even a simple read-only ROM file system. On these systems, the RAM is dedicated entirely to the program memory.

About ROM

In a personal computer, the ROM is used to store the BIOS (basic input/output system) and is typically 64–128 KB. In a Windows CE system, the ROM can range from 4 to 32 MB and stores the entire operating system, as well as the applications that are bundled with the system. In this sense, the ROM in a Windows CE system is like a small read-only hard drive.

In a Windows CE system, ROM-based programs can be designated as Execute in Place (XIP). That is, they're executed directly from the ROM instead of being loaded into program RAM and then executed. This capability is a huge advantage for small systems in two ways. The fact that the code is executed directly from ROM means that the program code doesn't take up valuable program RAM. Also, because the program doesn't have to be copied into RAM before it's launched, it takes less time to start an application. Programs that aren't in ROM but are contained in the object store, Flash memory storage card, or even a hard drive aren't executed in place; they're copied into the RAM and executed.

About Virtual Memory

Windows CE implements a virtual memory management system. In a virtual memory system, applications deal with virtual memory, which is a separate imaginary address space that might not relate to the physical memory address space that's implemented by the hardware. The operating system uses the memory management unit of the microprocessor to translate virtual addresses to physical addresses in real time.

The key advantage of a virtual memory system is that applications are independent of the physical implementation of the device. Unlike PCs, Windows CE devices vary widely in their hardware implementation. With the applications isloated in a virtual memory environment, hardware designers are free to implement the physical memory architecture best suited for the device.

Paged Memory

Windows, as well as most moden virtual memory-based operating systems use a *paged-based virtual memory system*. In a paged memory system, the smallest unit of memory the microprocessor manages is the *page*. When an application accesses a page, the microprocessor translates the virtual address of the page to a physical page in ROM or RAM. A page can also be tagged so that accessing the page causes an exception. The operating system then determines whether the virtual page is valid and, if so, maps a physical page of memory to the virtual page.

Windows CE systems use a 4096-byte page, the same as the 32-bit implementations of Windows XP and Windows Vista. On some very early systems based on Windows CE 2.12 and earlier, the page size was 1024 bytes. It's safe to assume that these systems are long gone and applications can assume a 4096-byte page size today.

Virtual pages can be in one of three states: *free*, *reserved*, or *committed*. A free page is, as it sounds, free and available to be allocated. A reserved page is a page that has been reserved so that its virtual address can't be allocated by the operating system or another thread in the process. A reserved page can't be used elsewhere, but it also can't be used by the application because it isn't mapped to physical memory. To be mapped, a page must be committed. A committed page has been reserved by an application and has been directly mapped to a physical address.

All that I've just explained is old hat to experienced Win32 programmers. The important thing for the Windows CE programmer is to learn how Windows CE changes the equation. While Windows CE implements most of the same memory API set of its bigger Win32 cousins, the underlying architecture of Windows CE impacts application design. Before diving into the memory architecture of a Windows CE application, let's look at a few of the functions that provide information about the global state of the system memory.

Querying the System Memory

If an application knows the current memory state of the system, it can better manage the available resources. Windows CE implements both the Win32 *GetSystemInfo* and *GlobalMemoryStatus* functions. The *GetSystemInfo* function is prototyped here:

```
VOID GetSystemInfo (LPSYSTEM_INFO lpSystemInfo);
```

It's passed a pointer to a *SYSTEM_INFO* structure defined as

```
typedef struct {
    WORD wProcessorArchitecture;
    WORD wReserved;
    DWORD  dwPageSize;
    LPVOID lpMinimumApplicationAddress;
    LPVOID lpMaximumApplicationAddress;
    DWORD  dwActiveProcessorMask;
    DWORD  dwNumberOfProcessors;
    DWORD  dwProcessorType;
    DWORD  dwAllocationGranularity;
    WORD  wProcessorLevel;
    WORD  wProcessorRevision;
} SYSTEM_INFO;
```

The *wProcessorArchitecture* field identifies the type of microprocessor in the system. The value should be compared with the known constants defined in Winnt.h, such as *PROCESSOR_ARCHITECTURE_INTEL*. Windows CE has extended these constants to include *PROCESSOR_ARCHITECTURE_ARM*, *PROCESSOR_ARCHITECTURE_SHX*, and others. Additional processor constants are added as new CPUs are supported by any of the Win32 operating systems. Skipping a few fields, the *dwProcessorType* field further narrows the microprocessor from a family to a specific microprocessor. Constants for the Hitachi SHx architecture include *PROCESSOR_HITACHI_SH3* and *PROCESSOR_HITACHI_SH4*. The last two fields, *wProcessorLevel* and *wProcessorRevision*, further refine the CPU type. The *wProcessorLevel* field is similar to the *dwProcessorType* field in that it defines the specific microprocessor within a family. The *dwProcessorRevision* field tells you the model and the stepping level of the chip.

The *dwPageSize* field specifies the page size, in bytes, of the microprocessor which these days is always 4096. The *lpMinimumApplicationAddress* and *lpMaximumApplicationAddress* fields specify the minimum and maximum virtual address available to the application. The minimum value is 0x10000 while the maximum value for Windows CE 6 is 0x7FFFFFFF. This high value is quite a change from earlier versions of Windows CE where this value was 0x04000000. The *dwActiveProcessorMask* and *dwNumberOfProcessors* fields are used in systems that support more than one microprocessor. On these systems, the interesting field is *dwNumberOfProcessors,* which indicates how many processors are being used by the operating system. The *dwAllocationGranularity* field specifies the boundaries to which virtual memory regions are rounded. Like the desktop versions of Windows, Windows CE rounds virtual regions to 64 KB boundaries.

A second handy function for determining the system memory state is this:

```
void GlobalMemoryStatus(LPMEMORYSTATUS lpmst);
```

which returns a *MEMORYSTATUS* structure defined as

```
typedef struct {
    DWORD dwLength;
    DWORD dwMemoryLoad;
    DWORD dwTotalPhys;
    DWORD dwAvailPhys;
    DWORD dwTotalPageFile;
    DWORD dwAvailPageFile;
    DWORD dwTotalVirtual;
    DWORD dwAvailVirtual;
} MEMORYSTATUS;
```

The *dwLength* field must be initialized by the application before the call is made to *GlobalMemoryStatus*. The *dwMemoryLoad* field is of dubious value; it makes available a general loading parameter that's supposed to indicate the current memory use in the system. The *dwTotalPhys* and *dwAvailPhys* fields indicate how many pages of RAM are assigned to the program RAM and how many are available. These values don't include RAM assigned to the object store.

The *dwTotalPageFile* and *dwAvailPageFile* fields are used under the desktop versions of Windows to indicate the current status of the paging file. Because paging files aren't supported under Windows CE, these fields are always 0. The *dwTotalVirtual* and *dwAvailVirtual* fields indicate the total and available number of virtual memory pages accessible to the application.

The information returned by *GlobalMemoryStatus* provides confirmation of the memory architecture of Windows CE. Making this call on an embedded Windows CE device with 128 MB of RAM returns the following values:

```
dwMemoryLoad        0x0e          (14)
dwTotalPhys         0x03581000    (56,102,912)
dwAvailPhys         0x02e11000    (48,304,128)
dwTotalPageFile     0
dwAvailPageFile     0
dwTotalVirtual      0x40000000    (1,073,741,824)
dwAvailVirtual      0x3ff80000    (1,073,217,536)
```

The *dwTotalPhys* field indicates that of the 128 MB of RAM in the system, 56 MB is dedicated to the program RAM, of which 48.3 MB is still free. Note that there's no way for an application, using this call, to know that another 54.7 MB of RAM has been dedicated to the object store. To determine the amount of RAM dedicated to the object store, use the function *GetStoreInformation*.

The *dwTotalPageFile* and *dwAvailPageFile* fields are 0, indicating no support for a paging file under Windows CE. The *dwTotalVirtual* field is interesting because it shows a 1024 MB limit on virtual memory that Windows CE enforces on an application. Meanwhile, the *dwAvailVirtual* field indicates that in this application little of that 1 GB of virtual memory is being used.

The 1 GB total virtual memory value is interesting because the advertised amount of virtual address space per application in Windows CE 6 is 2 GB. However, the other 1 GB of an application's virtual memory space is dedicated for specific uses by the operating system and therefore isn't available for memory allocations by the application. Just what these dedicated uses are will be discussed in the following sections.

An Application's Address Space

The virtual space available to an application under Windows CE 6 is a vast improvement over earlier versions of Windows CE, which were limited to 32 MB of usable virtual space per application. In addition to the 1 GB of space available to applications for allocation, another 1 GB is used for specific purposes. A diagram of the 2 GB total application virtual space is shown in Figure 7-1.

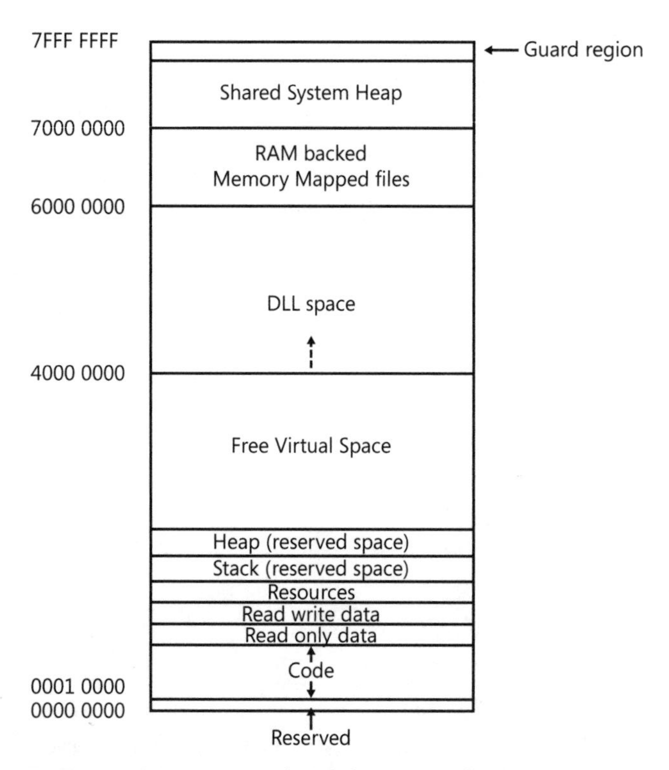

FIGURE 7-1 Memory map of a Windows CE application

As with all 32-bit versions of Windows, the application is mapped to a 64 KB region boundary starting at 0x10000. The lowest 64 KB of the address space for any application is reserved by Windows. The image of the file contains the code along with the static data segments and the resource segments. The actual code pages are not typically loaded in when the application is launched. Instead, each page is loaded on demand as the code in those pages is executed.

The read-only static data segment and the read/write static data areas usually take only a few pages. Each of these segments is page aligned. Like the code, these data segments are committed to RAM only as they're read or written by the application. The resources for the application are loaded into a separate set of pages. The resources are read only and are paged into the RAM only as they're accessed by the application.

The stack for the application's main thread is mapped above the resource segment. The stack segment is easily recognized because the committed pages are at the end of the reserved region, indicative of a stack that grows from higher addresses down. If this application had more than one thread, more than one stack segment would be reserved in the application's address space.

Following the stack is the local heap. The loader reserves a large number of pages, on the order of hundreds of kilobytes, for the heap to grow but commits pages only as necessary to satisfy memory allocations from *malloc*, *new*, or *LocalAlloc* calls. The remaining address space up to the 1 GB boundary is available for allocation by the application for stacks, heaps, direct virtual allocations and for memory-mapped files.

The upper 1 GB of the application's virtual space is used by the operating system for dedicated purposes. The first 512 MB from 0x4000 0000 to 0x5FFF FFFF are used for loading dynamic link libraries (DLLs). Unlike earlier versions of Windows CE, the DLLs are loaded bottom up, from the base address of 0x4000 0000 up to the limit of the region. The address that the DLL is loaded, known as its "base address," is consistent across all applications for a given DLL. So, if a DLL named "Bob.dll" is loaded at address 0x40F6000 in one process, it is loaded at that same address in all other applications. This is consistent with earlier versions of Windows CE; however, because there is so much virtual space available to load DLLs, this isn't the problem it was in earlier versions.

The 255-MB region from 0x6000 0000 to 0x7FF0 0000 is called the *shared system heap*. This region is used for communication between the operating system and the application. The region can be read and written to by the operating system but can only be read by the application. This provides a convenient place for the kernel to place buffers containing data being passed to the application. The final 1 MB of the application address space starting at 0x7FF0 0000 is a "guard region." The system will throw an exception if any thread that accesses that region.

The Different Kinds of Memory Allocation

A Windows CE application has a number of different methods for allocating memory. At the bottom of the memory-management food chain are the *Virtualxxx* functions that directly reserve, commit, and free virtual memory pages. Next comes the heap API. *Heaps* are regions of reserved memory space managed by the system for the application. Heaps come in two flavors: the default local heap automatically allocated when an application is started, and separate heaps that can be manually created by the application. After the heap API is static data—data blocks defined by the compiler and that are allocated automatically by the loader. Finally, you come to the stack, where an application stores variables local to a function.

The one area of the Win32 memory API that Windows CE doesn't support is the global heap. The global heap API, which includes calls such as *GlobalAlloc*, *GlobalFree*, and *GlobalRealloc*, is therefore not present in Windows CE[2]. The global heap is really just a holdover from the Win16 days of Windows 3.*x*. In Win32, the global and local heaps are quite similar. One unique use of global memory, allocating memory for data in the clipboard, is handled by using the local heap under Windows CE.

The key to minimizing memory use in Windows CE is choosing the proper memory-allocation strategy that matches the memory-use patterns for a given block of memory. I'll review each of these memory types and then describe strategies for minimizing memory use in Windows CE applications.

Virtual Memory

Virtual memory is the most basic of the memory types. The system uses calls to the virtual memory API to allocate memory for the other types of memory, including heaps and stacks. The virtual memory API, including the *VirtualAlloc*, *VirtualFree*, and *VirtualReSize* functions, directly manipulates virtual memory pages in the application's virtual memory space. Pages can be reserved, committed to physical memory, and freed using these functions.

Allocating Virtual Memory

Allocating and reserving virtual memory is accomplished using this function:

```
LPVOID VirtualAlloc (LPVOID lpAddress, DWORD dwSize,
                     DWORD flAllocationType,
                     DWORD flProtect);
```

The first parameter to *VirtualAlloc* is the virtual address of the region of memory to allocate. The *lpAddress* parameter is used to identify the previously reserved memory block when you use *VirtualAlloc* to commit a block of memory previously reserved. If this parameter is *NULL*, the system determines where to allocate the memory region, rounded to a 64-KB boundary. The second parameter is *dwSize*, the size of the region to allocate or reserve. While this parameter is specified in bytes, not pages, the system rounds the requested size up to the next page boundary.

The *flAllocationType* parameter specifies the type of allocation. You can specify a combination of the following flags: *MEM_COMMIT*, *MEM_AUTO_COMMIT*, and *MEM_RESERVE*. The *MEM_COMMIT* flag allocates the memory to be used by the program. *MEM_RESERVE* reserves the virtual address space to be later committed. Reserved pages can't be accessed until another call is made to *VirtualAlloc* specifying the region and using the *MEM_COMMIT* flag. The flag *MEM_TOP_DOWN*, which is supported on the desktop and was supported on the earliest versions of Windows CE, is ignored by Windows CE 5 and Windows CE 6.

[2] The function GlobalAlloc exists as a macro in the Windows CE include files. It is simply an alias for LocalAlloc.

The *MEM_AUTO_COMMIT* flag is unique to Windows CE and is quite handy. When this flag is specified, the block of memory is reserved immediately, but each page in the block is automatically committed by the system when it's accessed for the first time. This allows you to allocate large blocks of virtual memory without burdening the system with the actual RAM allocation until the instant each page is first used. The drawback to auto-commit memory is that the physical RAM needed to back up a page might not be available when the page is first accessed. In this case, the system generates an exception.

VirtualAlloc can be used to reserve a large region of memory with subsequent calls committing parts of the region or the entire region. Multiple calls to commit the same region won't fail. This allows an application to reserve memory and then blindly commit a page before it's written to. While this method isn't particularly efficient, it does free the application from having to check the state of a reserved page to see whether it's already committed before making the call to commit the page.

The *flProtect* parameter specifies the access protection for the region being allocated. The different flags available for this parameter are summarized in the following list.

- **PAGE_READONLY** The region can be read. If an application attempts to write to the pages in the region, an access violation will occur.
- **PAGE_READWRITE** The region can be read from or written to by the application.
- **PAGE_EXECUTE** The region contains code that can be executed by the system. Attempts to read from or write to the region will result in an access violation.
- **PAGE_EXECUTE_READ** The region can contain executable code, and applications can also read from the region.
- **PAGE_EXECUTE_READWRITE** The region can contain executable code, and applications can read from and write to the region.
- **PAGE_GUARD** The first access to this region results in a STATUS_GUARD_PAGE exception. This flag should be combined with the other protection flags to indicate the access rights of the region after the first access.
- **PAGE_NOACCESS** Any access to the region results in an access violation.
- **PAGE_NOCACHE** The RAM pages mapped to this region won't be cached by the microprocessor.

The *PAGE_GUARD* and *PAGE_NOCHACHE* flags can be combined with the other flags to further define the characteristics of a page. The *PAGE_GUARD* flag specifies a guard page, a page that generates a one-shot exception when it's first accessed and then takes on the access rights that were specified when the page was committed. The *PAGE_NOCACHE* flag prevents the memory that's mapped to the virtual page from being cached by the microprocessor. This flag is handy for device drivers that share memory blocks with devices using direct memory access (DMA).

Regions versus Pages

Before I go on to talk about the virtual memory API, I need to make a somewhat subtle distinction. Virtual memory is reserved in regions that must align on 64-KB boundaries. Pages within a region can then be committed page by page. You can directly commit a page or a series of pages without first reserving a region of pages, but the page, or series of pages, directly committed will be aligned on a 64-KB boundary. For efficient use of the virtual memory space, it's best to reserve blocks of virtual memory in 64-KB chunks or larger and then commit the pages within the region as needed.

For example, examine the following code fragment:

```
for (i = 0; i < 512; i++)
    pMem[i] = VirtualAlloc (NULL, PAGESIZE, MEM_RESERVE | MEM_COMMIT,
                            PAGE_READWRITE);
```

This code will allocate 512 one-page blocks of virtual memory, but will consume 32 MB of virtual space. On earlier versions of Windows CE, this code would fail due to the limited virtual space available for each process. The code works under Windows CE 6 and later; however, it isn't an efficient use of address space.

A better way to make 512 distinct virtual allocations is to do something like this:

```
// Reserve a region first.
pMemBase = VirtualAlloc (NULL, PAGESIZE * 512, MEM_RESERVE,
                         PAGE_NOACCESS);

for (i = 0; i < 512; i++)
    pMem[i] = VirtualAlloc (pMemBase + (i*PAGESIZE), PAGESIZE,
                            MEM_COMMIT, PAGE_READWRITE);
```

This code first reserves a region; the pages are committed later. Because the region is first reserved, the committed pages aren't rounded to 64 KB boundaries.

While Windows CE 6 has a much larger virtual space per process than earlier versions of the operating system, this simply moves the "limits" of your application to a different place. Windows CE does not support a paging file and therefore is limited to the physical memory available on the device. An application on Windows CE 6 or later may have plenty of virtual memory space but it is still limited by the available RAM on the system. Be sure to check your memory allocations!

Freeing Virtual Memory

You can *decommit*, or free, virtual memory by calling *VirtualFree*. Decommitting a page unmaps the page from a physical page of RAM but keeps the page or pages reserved. The function is prototyped as

```
BOOL VirtualFree (LPVOID lpAddress, DWORD dwSize,
                  DWORD dwFreeType);
```

The *lpAddress* parameter should contain a pointer to the virtual memory region that's to be freed or decommitted. The *dwSize* parameter contains the size, in bytes, of the region if the region is to be decommitted. If the region is to be freed, this value must be 0. The *dwFreeType* parameter contains the flags that specify the type of operation. The *MEM_DECOMMIT* flag specifies that the region will be decommited but will remain reserved. The *MEM_RELEASE* flag both decommits the region if the pages are committed and also frees the region.

All the pages in a region being freed by means of *VirtualFree* must be in the same state. That is, all the pages in the region to be freed must either be committed or reserved. *VirtualFree* fails if some of the pages in the region are reserved while some are committed. To free a region with pages that are both reserved and committed, the committed pages should be decommitted first, and then the entire region can be freed.

Changing and Querying Access Rights

You can modify the access rights of a region of virtual memory, initially specified in *VirtualAlloc*, by calling *VirtualProtect*. This function can change the access rights only on committed pages. The function is prototyped as

```
BOOL VirtualProtect (LPVOID lpAddress, DWORD dwSize,
                     DWORD flNewProtect, PDWORD lpflOldProtect);
```

The first two parameters, *lpAddress* and *dwSize*, specify the block and the size of the region that the function acts on. The *flNewProtect* parameter contains the new protection flags for the region. These flags are the same ones I mentioned when I explained the *VirtualAlloc* function. The *lpflOldProtect* parameter should point to a *DWORD* that will receive the old protection flags of the first page in the region.

The current protection rights of a region can be queried with a call to

```
DWORD VirtualQuery (LPCVOID lpAddress,
                    PMEMORY_BASIC_INFORMATION lpBuffer,
                    DWORD dwLength);
```

The *lpAddress* parameter contains the starting address of the region being queried. The *lpBuffer* pointer points to a *PMEMORY_BASIC_INFORMATION* structure that I'll talk about shortly. The third parameter, *dwLength*, must contain the size of the *PMEMORY_BASIC_INFORMATION* structure.

The *PMEMORY_BASIC_INFORMATION* structure is defined as

```
typedef struct _MEMORY_BASIC_INFORMATION {
    PVOID BaseAddress;
    PVOID AllocationBase;
    DWORD AllocationProtect;
    DWORD RegionSize;
```

```
    DWORD State;
    DWORD Protect;
    DWORD Type;
} MEMORY_BASIC_INFORMATION;
```

The first field of *MEMORY_BASIC_INFORMATION*, *BaseAddress*, is the address passed to the *VirtualQuery* function. The *AllocationBase* field contains the base address of the region when it was allocated using the *VirtualAlloc* function. The *AllocationProtect* field contains the protection attributes for the region when it was originally allocated. The *RegionSize* field contains the number of bytes from the pointer passed to *VirtualQuery* to the end of series of pages that have the same attributes. The *State* field contains the state—free, reserved, or committed—of the pages in the region. The *Protect* field contains the current protection flags for the region. Finally, the *Type* field contains the type of memory in the region. This field can contain the flags *MEM_PRIVATE*, indicating that the region contains private data for the application; *MEM_MAPPED*, indicating that the region is mapped to a memory-mapped file; or *MEM_IMAGE*, indicating that the region is mapped to an EXE or a DLL module.

The best way to understand the values returned by *VirtualQuery* is to look at an example. Say an application uses *VirtualAlloc* to reserve 65,536 bytes (16 pages on a 4 KB page-size machine). The system reserves this 64-KB block at address 0x80000. Later the application commits 28,672 bytes (7 pages) starting 8192 bytes (2 pages) into the initial region. Figure 7-2 shows a diagram of this scenario.

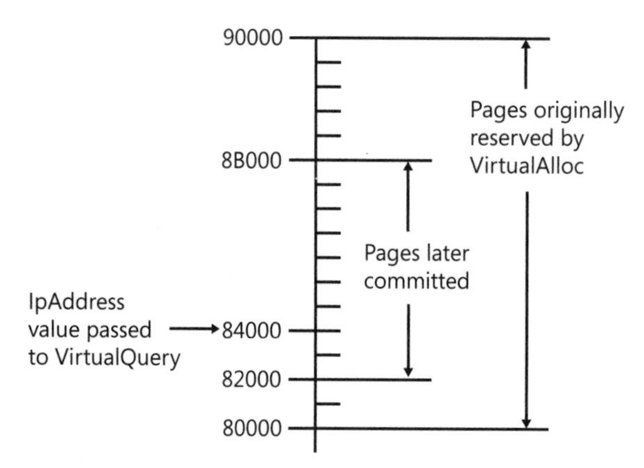

FIGURE 7-2 A region of reserved virtual memory that has nine pages committed

If a call is made to *VirtualQuery* with the *lpAddress* pointer pointing 4 pages into the initial region (address 0x84000), the returned values would be the following:

```
BaseAddress          0x84000
AllocationBase       0x80000
AllocationProtect    PAGE_NOACCESS
RegionSize           0x7000    (28,672 bytes or 7 pages)
State                MEM_COMMIT
Protect              PAGE_READWRITE
Type                 MEM_PRIVATE
```

The *BaseAddress* field contains the address passed to *VirtualQuery*, 0x84000, 16,384 bytes into the initial region. The *AllocationBase* field contains the base address of the original region, while *AllocationProtect* contains *PAGE_NOACCESS*, indicating that the region was originally reserved, not directly committed. The *RegionSize* field contains the number of bytes from the pointer passed to *VirtualQuery*, 0x7000 to the end of the committed pages at 0x8B000. The *State* and *Protect* fields contain the flags indicating the current state of the pages. The *Type* field indicates that the region was allocated by the application for its own use.

The VirtualxxxEx API

Starting with Windows CE 6, the operating system supports the desktop's extended virtual memory API. These functions allow an application to manipulate the memory space of another application. The functions mirror the standard Virtualxxx API. For example, *VirtualAllocEx* performs the same functionality as *VirtualAlloc* but adds a parameter for the handle to the process where the memory is to be allocated. The function is prototyped as:

```
LPVOID VirtualAllocEx (HANDLE hProcess, LPVOID lpAddress,
                       DWORD dwSize, DWORD flAllocationType,
                       DWORD flProtect);
```

The first parameter is the only difference between this function and *VirtualAlloc*. The process handle can be acquired by calling the *OpenProcess* function prototyped as:

```
HANDLE OpenProcess (DWORD fdwAccess, BOOL fInherit, DWORD IDProcess);
```

This function is discussed in detail in Chapter 8, "Modules, Processes, and Threads," but to summarize, the *fdwAccess* parameter is the security rights requested. The *fInherit* paramter must be set to *FALSE*. The final parameter is the ID of the process to open.

The other extended virtual functions are:

```
BOOL VirtualProtectEx (HANDLE hProcess, LPVOID lpAddress,
                       DWORD dwSize, DWORD flNewProtect,
                       PDWORD lpflOldProtect);

DWORD VirtualQueryEx (HANDLE hProcess, LPCVOID lpAddress,
                      PMEMORY_BASIC_INFORMATION lpBuffer,
                      DWORD dwLength);

BOOL VirtualFreeEx (HANDLE hProcess, LPVOID lpAddress,
                    DWORD dwSize, DWORD dwFreeType);
```

As you can see, the functions mirror their original functions with the exception of the process handle as the first parameter.

The memory blocks allocated *VirtualAllocEx* are no different than memory blocks allocated locally by *VirtualAlloc*. Blocks allocated by *VirtualAllocEx* can be released by calling *VirtualFree* (in the process where the allocation occurred, of course). To read and write the blocks allocated in another process, the *ReadProcessMemory* and *WriteProcessMemory* functions can be used.

Of course, there are security implications to *VirtualAllocEx*. The actual security implications reside in *OpenProcess*. While Windows CE 6.0 does not provide any security to prevent other processes from calling *OpenProcess*, you can expect future versions of the operating system to enforce security rights.

Heaps

Clearly, allocating memory on a page basis is inefficient for most applications. To optimize memory use, an application needs to be able to allocate and free memory on a per-byte, or at least a per-32-byte, basis. The system enables allocations of this size through heaps. Using heaps also protects an application from having to deal with the inefficiencies of page-based allocation. An application can simply allocate a block in a heap, and the system deals with the number of pages necessary for the allocation.

As mentioned before, heaps are regions of reserved virtual memory space managed by the system for the application. The system gives you a number of functions that allow you to allocate and free blocks within the heap with a granularity much smaller than a page. As memory is allocated by the application within a heap, the system automatically grows the size of the heap to fill the request. As blocks in the heap are freed, the system looks to see if an entire page is freed. If so, that page is decommitted.

Windows CE supports the allocation of only fixed blocks in the heap. This simplifies the handling of blocks in the heap, but it can lead to the heaps becoming fragmented over time as blocks are allocated and freed. The result can be a heap being fairly empty but still requiring a large number of virtual pages because the system can't reclaim a page from the heap unless it's completely free.

Each application has a default, or local, heap created by the system when the application is launched. Blocks of memory in the local heap can be allocated, freed, and resized using the *LocalAlloc*, *LocalFree*, and *LocalRealloc* functions. An application can also create any number of separate heaps. These heaps have the same properties as the local heap but are managed through a separate set of *Heapxxxx* functions.

The Local Heap

Over the years, the various versions of Windows CE have created local heaps of various sizes. The initial size of the heap isn't critical to the application developer since RAM will only be committed to the heap as needed; and, depending on how the heap is created, the heap is grown when allocations exceed the initial reservation. If an application requests a particular allocation from the local heap, the memory may be allocated outside the heap's reserved block. In addition, growing the heap might require a separate, disjointed address space reserved for the additional space on the heap. Applications shouldn't assume that the local heap is contained in one block of virtual address space. Because Windows CE heaps support only fixed blocks, Windows CE implements only the subset of the Win32 local heap functions necessary to allocate, resize, and free fixed blocks on the local heap.

Allocating Memory on the Local Heap

You allocate a block of memory on the local heap by calling

```
HLOCAL LocalAlloc (UINT uFlags, UINT uBytes);
```

The call returns a value cast as an *HLOCAL*, which is a handle to a local memory block, but because the block allocated is always fixed, the return value can simply be recast as a pointer to the block.

The *uFlags* parameter describes the characteristics of the block. The flags supported under Windows CE are limited to those that apply to fixed allocations. They are the following.

- **LMEM_FIXED** Allocates a fixed block in the local heap. Because all local heap allocations are fixed, this flag is redundant.
- **LMEM_ZEROINIT** Initializes memory contents to 0.
- **LPTR** Combines the LMEM_FIXED and LMEM_ZEROINIT flags.

The *uBytes* parameter specifies the size of the block to allocate in bytes. The size of the block is rounded up. The amount rounded up varies depending on the version of Windows CE. Windows CE 6 rounds up to the next 32-byte boundary.

Freeing Memory on the Local Heap

You can free a block by calling

```
HLOCAL LocalFree (HLOCAL hMem);
```

The function takes the handle to the local memory block and returns *NULL* if successful. If the function fails, it returns the original handle to the block.

Resizing and Querying the Size of Local Heap Memory

You can resize blocks on the local heap by calling

```
HLOCAL LocalReAlloc (HLOCAL hMem, UINT uBytes, UINT uFlag);
```

The *hMem* parameter is the pointer (handle) returned by *LocalAlloc*. The *uBytes* parameter is the new size of the block. The *uFlag* parameter contains the flags for the new block. Under Windows CE, two flags are relevant, *LMEM_ZEROINIT* and *LMEM_MOVEABLE*.

LMEM_ZEROINIT causes the contents of the new area of the block to be set to 0 if the block is grown as a result of this call. The *LMEM_MOVEABLE* flag tells Windows that it can move the block if the block is being grown and there's not enough room immediately above the current block. Without this flag, if you don't have enough space immediately above the block to satisfy the request, *LocalRealloc* will fail with an out-of-memory error. If you specify the *LMEM_MOVEABLE* flag, the handle (really the pointer to the block of memory) might change as a result of the call.

The size of the block can be queried by calling

```
UINT LocalSize (HLOCAL hMem);
```

The size returned will be at least as great as the requested size for the block. As I mentioned earlier, Windows CE rounds the size of a local heap allocation up to the next 32-byte boundary.

Separate Heaps

To avoid fragmenting the local heap, it's better to create a separate heap if you need a series of blocks of memory that will be used for a set amount of time. An example of this is a text editor that might manage a file by creating a separate heap for each file it edits. As files are opened and closed, the heaps are created and destroyed.

Heaps under Windows CE have the same API as those under other Win32 operating systems. The only noticeable difference is the lack of support for the *HEAP_GENERATE_EXCEPTIONS* flag. On the desktop, this flag causes the system to generate an exception if an allocation request can't be accommodated.

Creating a Separate Heap

You create heaps by calling

```
HANDLE HeapCreate (DWORD flOptions, DWORD dwInitialSize,
                   DWORD dwMaximumSize);
```

Under Windows CE, the first parameter, *flOptions*, can be *NULL*, or it can contain the *HEAP_NO_SERIALIZE* flag. By default, Windows heap management routines prevent two threads in a process from accessing the heap at the same time. This serialization prevents the heap pointers that the system uses to track the allocated blocks in the heap from being corrupted. In other versions of Windows, the *HEAP_NO_SERIALIZE* flag can be used if you don't want this type of protection. Under Windows CE, however, this flag is provided only for compatibility, and all heap accesses are serialized.

The other two parameters, *dwInitialSize* and *dwMaximumSize*, specify the initial size and maximum size of the heap. The *dwInitialSize* parameter can be used to force the operating system to commit that many bytes to the heap when it is created. This value is rounded up to the next page size. If *dwInitialSize* is zero, the operating system will default to not committing any RAM. The *dwMaximumSize* value can be used to cap the size of the heap. When set to zero, the operating system initially reserves a region of virtual address space and, if subsequent allocations on the heap exceed this initial reservation, the heap is grown to accommodate the new requests. If *dwMaximumSize* is set, the operating system reserves the specified amount and will commit no more. When the reserved region is filled, subsequent allocation requests will fail. For example, if the *dwMaximumSize* is specified as 100 KB, the heap has 50 KB already allocated, and an application requests a 60 KB block, the allocation will fail with the return code *ERROR_NOT_ENOUGH_MEMORY.* Specifying *dwMaximumSize* also prevents the heap manager from requesting virtual memory outside the heap for very large allocations.

Allocating Memory in a Separate Heap

You allocate memory on the heap using

```
LPVOID HeapAlloc (HANDLE hHeap, DWORD dwFlags, DWORD dwBytes);
```

Notice that the return value is a pointer, not a handle as in the *LocalAlloc* function. As with the local heap, separate heaps always allocate fixed blocks. The first parameter is the handle to the heap returned by the *HeapCreate* call. The *dwFlags* parameter can be one of two self-explanatory values: *HEAP_NO_SERIALIZE* and *HEAP_ZERO_MEMORY.* The final parameter, *dwBytes*, specifies the number of bytes in the block to allocate. The size is rounded up to the next *DWORD*.

Freeing Memory in a Separate Heap

You can free a block in a heap by calling

```
BOOL HeapFree (HANDLE hHeap, DWORD dwFlags, LPVOID lpMem);
```

The only flag allowable in the *dwFlags* parameter is *HEAP_NO_SERIALIZE*. The *lpMem* parameter points to the block to free, while *hHeap* contains the handle to the heap.

Resizing and Querying the Size of Memory in a Separate Heap

You can resize heap allocations by calling

```
LPVOID HeapReAlloc (HANDLE hHeap, DWORD dwFlags, LPVOID lpMem,
                    DWORD dwBytes);
```

The *dwFlags* parameter can be any combination of three flags: *HEAP_NO_SERIALIZE*, *HEAP_REALLOC_IN_PLACE_ONLY*, and *HEAP_ZERO_ MEMORY*. The only new flag here is *HEAP_REALLOC_IN_PLACE_ONLY*, which tells the heap manager to fail the reallocation if the space can't be found for the block without relocating it. This flag is handy if you already have a number of pointers pointing to data in the block and you aren't interested in updating them. The *lpMem* parameter is the pointer to the block being resized, and the *dwBytes* parameter is the requested new size of the block. Notice that the function of the *HEAP_REALLOC_IN_PLACE_ONLY* flag in *HeapReAlloc* provides the opposite function from the one that the *LMEM_MOVEABLE* flag provides for *LocalReAlloc*. *HEAP_REALLOC_IN_PLACE_ONLY* prevents a block from moving that would be moved by default in a separate heap, while *LMEM_MOVEABLE* enables a block to be moved that by default would not be moved in the local heap. *HeapReAlloc* returns a pointer to the block if the reallocation was successful and returns *NULL* otherwise. Unless you specified that the block not be relocated, the returned pointer might be different from the pointer passed in if the block had to be relocated to find enough space in the heap.

To determine the actual size of a block, you can call

```
DWORD HeapSize (HANDLE hHeap, DWORD dwFlags, LPCVOID lpMem);
```

The parameters are as you expect: the handle of the heap; the single, optional flag, *HEAP_NO_SERIALIZE*; and the pointer to the block of memory being checked.

Destroying a Separate Heap

You can completely free a heap by calling

```
BOOL HeapDestroy (HANDLE hHeap);
```

Individual blocks within the heap don't have to be freed before you destroy the heap.

The following heap function is valuable when writing DLLs. The function

```
HANDLE GetProcessHeap (VOID);
```

returns the handle to the local heap of the process calling the DLL. This allows a DLL to allocate memory within the calling process's local heap. All the other heap calls, with the exception of *HeapDestroy*, can be used with the handle returned by *GetProcessHeap*.

Managing a Separate Heap

There are times when an application needs to control the type and location of the memory used by a heap. An example might be where an embedded device has a special type of battery-backed physical memory that the application would like to have managed like a heap. Windows CE has a specialized function that tells the heap manager to call back to the application when the heap needs to allocate, commit, or free virtual memory for the heap. The function is

```
HANDLE CeHeapCreate (DWORD flOptions, DWORD dwInitialSize,
                     DWORD dwMaximumSize, PFN_AllocHeapMem pfnAlloc,
                     PFN_FreeHeapMem pfnFree);
```

The first parameter of *CeHeapCreate* is *flOptions*, which must be 0. The next two parameters mirror the standard *HeapCreate*. The real difference between this call and *HeapCreate* is the addition of the function pointers to custom allocate and free functions. The function pointed to by first of these parameters, *pfnAlloc*, is called when the heap manager needs virtual memory to support an allocation request. This callback function is prototyped as:

```
LPVOID CALLBACK_AllocHeapMem (LPVOID pAddr, DWORD cbSize,
                              DWORD fdwAction, LPDWORD pdwUserData);
```

What an application does when this callback function is called depends on the third parameter, *fdwAction*. This parameter can be one of two self-descriptive values; *MEM_RESERVE* and *MEM_COMMIT*. For a *MEM_RESERVE* call, the *pAddr* value is zero and *cbSize* contains the amount of memory to reserve. The *pdwUserData* parameter points to an application-defined value that can be used for any purpose. When the reserved region is committed, or later freed, this user data value is passed back to the application.

When the callback is called to commit memory, the *pAddr* parameter points to the block of reserved memory to commit. The *cbSize* parameter provides the size of the region to commit, and the *pdwUserData* parameter points to the value set during the reserve callback. For both the reserve and commit actions, the return value for the callback should be a pointer to the memory reserved or committed.

When the heap manager needs to decommit or free memory pages associated with the heap, it calls the function pointed to by the *pfnFree* parameter in *CeHeapCreate*. The free callback function is prototyped as

```
BOOL CALLBACK FreeHeapMem (LPVOID pAddr, DWORD cbSize, DWORD fdwAction,
                           DWORD dwUserData);
```

This function is also called in two situations As with the allocation callback, the reason for the callback is indicated by *fdwAction*. In this case, the operative values are either *MEM_DECOMMIT* or *MEM_FREE*. *MEM_DECOMMIT* is called when the heap manager wants to decommit pages of RAM, while *MEM_FREE* is used to free reserved regions of virtual memory. The *dwUserData* value is the data returned by the application during the calls to the allocation callback for the block that is now being released or decommited.

Although these callbacks talk of reserving, committing, decommitting, and freeing the memory, what actually happens in the callback is under the control of the application. This allows the application to use any memory it controls to satisfy the requests of the heap manager. How these requests are satisfied is up to the application.

The Stack

The stack is the easiest to use (the most self-managing) of the different types of memory under Windows CE. The stack under Windows CE, as in any operating system, is the storage place for temporary variables that are referenced within a function. The operating system also uses the stack to store return addresses for functions and the state of the microprocessor registers during exception handling.

Windows CE manages a separate stack for every thread in the system. By default, each stack in the system is limited to a maximum size of around 56 KB. Each separate thread within one process can grow its stack up to the 56 KB limit. This limit has to do with how Windows CE manages the stack. When a thread is created, Windows CE reserves a 64-KB region for the thread's stack. It then commits virtual pages from the top down as the stack grows. As the stack shrinks, the system, under low-memory conditions, reclaims the unused but still committed pages below the stack. The limit of 56 KB comes from the size of the 64-KB region dedicated to the stack minus the number of pages necessary to guard the stack against overflow and underflow.

For applications that need a larger stack, the maximum size of the stack for the main thread of the application can be specified by a linker switch when an application is linked. When an application creates secondary threads, the maximum size of the stack can be specified in the *CreateThread* call that creates the thread. The same guard pages are applied, but the stack size can be specified up to the space free in the processes' virtual memory space. Note that the size defined for the default stack is also the default size used for all the separate thread stacks. That is, if you specify the main stack to be 128 KB, all other threads in the application have a stack size limit of 128 KB unless you specify a different stack size in each call to *CreateThread*.

One other consideration must be made when you plan how to use the stack in an application. When an application calls a function that needs stack space, Windows CE attempts to commit the pages immediately below the current stack pointer to satisfy the request. If no physical RAM is available, the thread needing the stack space is briefly suspended. If the request can't be granted within a short period of time, an exception is raised. Windows CE goes to great lengths to free the required pages, but if this can't happen the system raises an exception. I'll cover low-memory situations shortly; but for now, just remember that you shouldn't try to use large amounts of stack space in low-memory situations.

Static Data

C and C++ applications have predefined blocks of memory that are automatically allocated when the application loads. These blocks hold statically allocated strings, buffers, and global variables as well as buffers necessary for the library functions that are statically linked with the application. None of this is new to the C programmer, but under Windows CE, these spaces are handy for squeezing the last useful bytes out of RAM.

Windows CE allocates two blocks of RAM for the static data of an application, one for the read/write data and one for the read-only data. Because these areas are allocated on a per-page basis, you can typically find some space left over from the static data up to the next page boundary. The finely tuned Windows CE application can be written to ensure that it has little or no extra space left over. If you have space in the static data area, sometimes it's better to move a buffer or two into the static data area instead of allocating those buffers dynamically.

Another consideration is that if you're writing a ROM-based application, you should move as much data as possible to the read-only static data area. Windows CE doesn't allocate RAM to the read-only area for ROM-based applications. Instead, the ROM pages are mapped directly into the virtual address space. This essentially gives you unlimited read-only space with no impact on the RAM requirements of the application.

The best place to determine the size of the static data areas is to look in the map file that's optionally generated by the linker. The map file is chiefly used to determine the locations of functions and data for debugging purposes, but it also shows the size of the static data if you know where to look. Listing 7-1 shows a portion of an example map file generated by Visual Studio.

LISTING 7-1 The top portion of a map file showing the size of the data segments in an application

```
memtest

Timestamp is 4658889b (Sat May 26 12:20:59 2007)

Preferred load address is 00010000

Start         Length     Name                   Class
0001:00000000 00006100H .text                   CODE
0002:00000000 00000310H .rdata                  DATA
0002:00000310 00000014H .xdata                  DATA
0002:00000324 00000028H .idata$2                DATA
0002:0000034c 00000014H .idata$3                DATA
0002:00000360 000000f4H .idata$4                DATA
0002:00000454 000003eeH .idata$6                DATA
0002:00000842 00000000H .edata                  DATA
0003:00000000 000000f4H .idata$5                DATA
0003:000000f4 00000004H .CRT$XCA                DATA
0003:000000f8 00000004H .CRT$XCZ                DATA
0003:000000fc 00000004H .CRT$XIA                DATA
0003:00000100 00000004H .CRT$XIZ                DATA
0003:00000104 00000004H .CRT$XPA                DATA
0003:00000108 00000004H .CRT$XPZ                DATA
0003:0000010c 00000004H .CRT$XTA                DATA
0003:00000110 00000004H .CRT$XTZ                DATA
0003:00000114 000011e8H .data                   DATA
0003:000012fc 0000108cH .bss                    DATA
0004:00000000 000003e8H .pdata                  DATA
0005:00000000 000000f0H .rsrc$01                DATA
0005:000000f0 00000334H .rsrc$02                DATA
```

```
Address          Publics by Value          Rva+Base      Lib:Object

0001:00000000      _WinMain                 00011000 f   memtest.obj
0001:0000007c      _InitApp                 0001107c f   memtest.obj
0001:000000d4      _InitInstance            000110d4 f   memtest.obj
0001:00000164      _TermInstance            00011164 f   memtest.obj
0001:00000248      _MainWndProc             00011248 f   memtest.obj
0001:000002b0      _GetFixedEquiv           000112b0 f   memtest.obj
0001:00000350      _DoCreateMain            00011350 f   memtest.obj.
§
```

The map file in Listing 7-1 indicates that the EXE has five sections. Section *0001* is the text segment containing the executable code of the program. Section *0002* contains the read-only static data. Section *0003* contains the read/write static data. Section *0004* contains the fix-up table to support calls to other DLLs. Finally, section *0005* is the resource section containing the application's resources, such as menu and dialog box templates.

Examine the *.data*, *.bss*, and *.rdata* lines. The *.data* section contains the initialized read/write data. If you initialize a global variable as in

```
static HINST g_hLoadlib = NULL;
```

the *g_loadlib* variable ends up in the *.data* segment. The *.bss* segment contains the uninitialized read/write data. A buffer defined as

```
static BYTE g_ucItems[256];
```

ends up in the *.bss* segment. The final segment, *.rdata*, contains the read-only data. Static data that you define using the *const* keyword ends up in the *.rdata* segment. An example of this are the structures I use for my message lookup tables, as in the following:

```
// Message dispatch table for MainWindowProc
const struct decodeUINT MainMessages[] = {
    WM_CREATE, DoCreateMain,
    WM_SIZE, DoSizeMain,
    WM_COMMAND, DoCommandMain,
    WM_DESTROY, DoDestroyMain,
};
```

The *.data* and *.bss* blocks are folded into the *0003* section, which, if you add the size of all blocks in the third section, has a total size of 0x2274, or 8820, bytes. Rounded up to the next page size, the read/write section ends up taking three pages, with 3468 bytes not used. So in this example, almost a complete page is unused. Placing a buffer or two in the static data section of the application would be essentially free. The read-only segment, section *0002*, including *.rdata*, ends up being 0x0842, or 2114, bytes, which takes up a single page, with 1982 bytes, almost half a page, wasted.

String Resources

One often-forgotten area for read-only data is the resource segment of your application. While I mentioned a new Windows CE–specific feature of the *LoadString* function in Chapter 4, "Windows, Controls, and Menus," it's worth repeating here. If you call *LoadString* with 0 in place of the pointer to the buffer, the function returns a pointer to the string in the resource segment. An example would be

```
LPCTSTR pString;

pString  = (LPCTSTR)LoadString (hInst, ID_STRING, NULL, 0)
```

The string returned is read only, but it allows you to reference the string without having to allocate a buffer to hold the string. Also, be warned that the string won't be zero terminated unless you have added the *-n* switch to the command line of the resource compiler. However, the word immediately preceding the string contains the length of the string resource.

Selecting the Proper Memory Type

Now that you've looked at the different types of memory, it's time to consider the best use of each. For large blocks of memory, directly allocating virtual memory is best. An application can reserve as much address space but can commit only the pages necessary at any one time. While directly allocated virtual memory is the most flexible memory allocation type, it shifts to you the burden of worrying about page granularity as well as keeping track of the reserved versus committed pages.

The local heap is always handy. It doesn't need to be created and grows as necessary to satisfy a request. Fragmentation is the issue here. Consider that applications on a Windows Mobile device might run for weeks or even months at a time. Many systems don't turn "off" when the power button is pressed; they simply suspend. So when you're thinking about memory fragmentation, don't assume that a user will open the application, change one item, and then close it. A user is likely to start an application and keep it running so that the application is just a quick click away.

The advantage of separate heaps is that you can destroy them when their time is up, nipping the fragmentation problem in the bud. A minor disadvantage of separate heaps is the need to manually create and destroy them.

The static data area is a great place to slip in a buffer or two essentially for free because the page is going to be allocated anyway. The key to managing the static data is to make the size of the static data segments close to, but over the page size of, your target processor. Sometimes it's better to move constant data from the read-only segment to the read/write segment if it saves a page in the read-only segment. The only time you wouldn't do this is if the application is to be burned into ROM. Then the more constant the data is, the better, because it doesn't take up RAM. The read-only segment is handy even for applications loaded from the object store because read-only pages can be discarded and reloaded as needed by the operating system.

The stack is, well, the stack—simple to use and always around. The only considerations are the maximum size of the stack and the problems of enlarging the stack in a low-memory condition. Make sure your application doesn't require large amounts of stack space to shut down. If the system suspends a thread in your application while it's being shut down, the user will more than likely lose data. That won't help customer satisfaction.

Managing Low-Memory Conditions

Even for applications that have been fine-tuned to minimize their memory use, there are going to be times when the system runs very low on RAM. Windows CE applications operate in an almost perpetual low-memory environment. Windows Mobile devices are designed intentionally to run in a low-memory situation. On these devices, applications are not closed until the system needs additional memory. Because of the need to efficiently run in low memory situations, Windows CE offers a number of methods to distribute the scarce memory in the system among the running applications.

The *WM_HIBERNATE* Message

The first and most obvious addition to Windows CE is the *WM_HIBERNATE* message. Windows CE shell sends this message to all top-level windows that have the *WS_OVERLAPPED* style (that is, have neither the *WS_POPUP* nor the *WS_CHILD* style) and have the *WS_VISIBLE* style. These qualifications should allow most applications to have at least one window that receives a *WM_HIBERNATE* message. An exception to this would be an application that doesn't really terminate but simply hides all its windows. This arrangement allows an application a quick start because it only has to show its window, but this situation also means that the application is taking up RAM even when the user thinks it's closed. While this is exactly the kind of application design that should *not* be used under Windows CE, those that are designed this way must act as if they're always in hibernate mode when hidden because they'll never receive a *WM_HIBERNATE* message.

The shell sends *WM_HIBERNATE* messages to the top-level windows in reverse z-order until enough memory is freed to push the available memory above a preset threshold. When an application receives a *WM_HIBERNATE* message, it should reduce its memory footprint as much as possible. This can involve releasing cached data; freeing any GDI objects such as fonts, bitmaps, and brushes; and destroying any window controls. In essence, the application should reduce its memory use to the smallest possible footprint that's necessary to retain its internal state.

If sending *WM_HIBERNATE* messages to the applications in the background doesn't free enough memory to move the system out of a limited-memory state, a *WM_HIBERNATE* message is sent to the application in the foreground. If part of your hibernation routine is to destroy controls on your window, you should be sure that you aren't in the foreground application. Disappearing controls don't give the user a warm and fuzzy feeling.

Memory Thresholds

Windows CE monitors the free RAM in the system and responds differently as less and less RAM is available. As less memory is available, Windows CE first sends *WM_HIBERNATE* messages and then begins limiting the size of allocations possible. Table 7-1 shows the default free-memory levels used by the Explorer shell and the system to trigger low-memory events in the system. Windows CE defines four memory states: normal, limited, low, and critical. The memory state of the system depends on how much free memory is available to the system as a whole.

TABLE 7-1 Memory Thresholds for the Explorer Shell

Event	Free memory	Comments
Limited-memory state	160 KB	Send *WM_HIBERNATE* messages to applications in reverse z-order. Free stack space reclaimed as needed.
Low-memory state	96 KB	Limit virtual allocations to 16 KB. Low- memory dialog displayed.
Critical-memory state	48 KB	Limit virtual allocations to 8 KB.

The effect of these memory states is to share the remaining wealth. First, *WM_HIBERNATE* messages are sent to the applications to ask them to reduce their memory footprint. After an application is sent a *WM_HIBERNATE* message, the system memory levels are checked to see whether the available memory is now above the threshold that caused the *WM_HIBERNATE* messages to be sent. If not, a *WM_HIBERNATE* message is sent to the next application. This continues until all applications have been sent a *WM_HIBERNATE* message.

At this point, the low-memory strategies depend on the shell running. If the Explorer shell is running, the system displays the OOM, the out-of-memory dialog, and requests that the user either select an application to close or reallocate some RAM dedicated to the object store to the program memory. If, after the selected application shuts down or program memory is increased, you still don't have enough memory, the out-of-memory dialog is displayed again. This process repeats until there's enough memory to lift the device above the threshold.

If an application is requested to shut down and it doesn't, the system purges the application after waiting approximately 8 seconds. This is the reason an application shouldn't allocate large amounts of stack space. If the application is shutting down due to low-memory conditions, it's possible that the stack space can't be allocated and the application will be suspended. If this happens after the system has requested that the application close, it could be purged from memory without properly saving its state.

In the low- and critical-memory states, applications are limited in the amount of memory they can allocate. In these states, a request for virtual memory larger than what's allowed is refused even if there's memory available to satisfy the request. Remember that it isn't just virtual memory allocations that are limited; allocations on the heap and stack are rejected if, to satisfy the request, those allocations require virtual memory allocations above the allowable limits.

I should point out that sending *WM_HIBERNATE* messages and automatically closing down applications is performed by the shell. On embedded systems for which the OEM can write its own shell, it is the OEM's responsibility to implement the *WM_HIBERNATE* message and any other memory management techniques. Fortunately, the Microsoft Windows CE Platform Builder provides the source code for the Explorer shell that implements the *WM_HIBERNATE* message.

It should go without saying that applications should check the return codes of any memory allocation call, but because some still don't, I'll say it. *Check the return codes from calls that allocate memory.* There's a much better chance of a memory allocation failing under Windows CE than under the desktop versions of Windows. Applications must be written to react gracefully to rejected memory allocations.

Now that you've seen how Windows CE manages memory, it's time to look at the processes that use that memory and the threads that run in those proceses. And since those processes may have multiple threads, you'll need to know how to coordinate the actions of those threads. All of this is covered in the next chapter, "Modules, Processes, and Threads."

Chapter 8

Modules, Processes, and Threads

Like Windows Vista, Windows CE is a fully multitasking and multithreaded operating system. What does that mean? In this chapter, I'll present a few definitions and then some explanations to answer that question.

Win32 files that contain executable code are called *modules*. Windows CE supports two types of modules: applications, with the EXE extension; and dynamic-link libraries, with the DLL extension. When Windows CE loads an application module, it creates a process.

A *process* is a single instance of an application. If two copies of Microsoft Pocket Word are running, two unique processes are running. Every process has its own, protected address space as described in Chapter 7. Windows CE 6.0 and later allows virtually an unlimited number of processes. Earlier versions of Windows CE enforced a limit of 32 separate processes that can run at any time.

Each process has at least one *thread*. A thread executes code within a process. A process can have multiple threads running "at the same time." I put the phrase *at the same time* in quotes because, in fact, only one thread executes at any instant in time on a single processor. The operating system simulates the concurrent execution of threads by rapidly switching between the threads, alternatively stopping one thread and switching to another.

Modules

The format of Windows CE modules is identical to the PE format used by the desktop versions of Windows. Unlike Windows XP or Windows Vista, Windows CE doesn't support the SYS file format used for device drivers. Instead, Windows CE device drivers are implemented as DLLs.

The difference between an EXE and a DLL is actually quite subtle. The format of the files is identical, save a few bytes in the header of the module. In practice, however, the difference is quite pronounced. When Windows launches an EXE, it creates a separate process space for that module, resolves any imported functions, initializes the proper static data areas, creates a local heap, creates a thread, and then jumps to the entry point of the module.

DLLs, on the other hand, can't be launched independently. The only way a DLL is loaded is by a request from an EXE or another DLL. The request to load a DLL can occur in two ways. The first way is *implicit* loading. In this case, a DLL is loaded automatically when Windows loads an EXE that lists the DLL in its import table. The linker generates the import table when the EXE is linked, and the table contains the list of DLLs and the functions within those DLLs that the EXE might call during the life of the application. When the EXE is loaded, Windows looks at the list of DLLs in the EXE's import table and loads those DLLs into the process space of the application. DLLs also contain import tables. When a DLL is loaded, Windows also looks at the import table of the DLL and loads any DLLs needed by that DLL.

When a DLL is built, it contains zero or more functions it exports. These are the functions that are callable from EXEs or other DLLs. A DLL that has no functions is still useful because it might contain resource data needed by the application.

The other way a DLL can be loaded is through *explicit* loading. In this case, Windows doesn't automatically load the DLL; it's loaded programmatically by the application using one of two calls, *LoadLibrary* or *LoadLibraryEx*.

LoadLibrary is prototyped as

```
HINSTANCE LoadLibrary (LPCTSTR lpLibFileName);
```

The only parameter is the filename of the DLL. If the filename does not have path information, the system searches for DLLs in the following order:

1. The image of the DLL that has already been loaded in memory
2. The directory of the executable loading the library
3. The Windows directory (\Windows)
4. The root directory in the object store (\)
5. The path specified in the *SystemPath* value in *[HKEY_LOCAL_ MACHINE]\Loader*

If the DLL name is a completely specified path name, the search is as follows:

1. The image of the DLL that has already been loaded in memory
2. The completely specified name in the *lpLibFileName* parameter

Notice in all the earlier search sequences that if the DLL has already been loaded into memory, the system uses that copy of the DLL. This behavior is true even if your pathname specifies a different file from the DLL originally loaded. Another peculiarity of *LoadLibrary* is that it ignores the extension of the DLL when comparing the library name with what's already in memory. For example, if Simple.dll is already loaded in memory and you attempt to load the control panel applet Simple.cpl, which under the covers is simply a DLL with a different extension, the system won't load Simple.cpl. Instead, the system returns the handle to the previously loaded Simple.dll.

LoadLibrary returns either an instance handle to the DLL that's now loaded or 0 if for some reason the function couldn't load the library. Calling *GetLastError* will return an error code specifying the reason for the failure.

Once you have the DLL loaded, you get a pointer to a function exported by that DLL by using *GetProcAddress*, which is prototyped as

```
FARPROC GetProcAddress (HMODULE hModule, LPCWSTR lpProcName);
```

The two parameters are the handle of the module and the name of the function you want to get a pointer to. The function returns a pointer to the function, or 0 if the function isn't found. Once you have a pointer to a function, you can simply call the function as if the loader had implicitly linked it.

When you are finished with the functions from a particular library, you need to call *FreeLibrary*, prototyped as

```
BOOL FreeLibrary (HMODULE hLibModule);
```

FreeLibrary decrements the use count on the DLL. If the use count drops to 0 for all processes that had loaded the library, it is removed from memory.

The following routine solves the problem of an application not knowing whether the menu bar API is present on a system.

```
typedef BOOL (WINAPI *SHCREATEMENUBARPROC) (SHMENUBARINFO *pmbi);

fMenuBarCreated = FALSE;

hLib = LoadLibrary (TEXT ("aygshell.dll"));
if (hLib) {
    lpfn = (SHCREATEMENUBARPROC)GetProcAddress (hLib,
                                        TEXT ("SHCreateMenuBar"));
    if (lpfn) {
        memset(&mbi, 0, sizeof(SHMENUBARINFO));
        mbi.cbSize = sizeof(SHMENUBARINFO);
        mbi.hwndParent = hWnd;
        mbi.hInstRes = hInst;
        mbi.nToolBarId = ID_MENU;
        mbi.dwFlags = SHCMBF_HMENU;
        fMenuBarCreated = (*lpfn) (&mbi);
    }
}
if (!fMenuBarCreated) {
    // Create a command bar instead
}
```

In this code, the menu bar is created only if the system supports it. If the library AygShell.dll or the *SHCreateMenuBar* function can't be found, a standard command bar is created.

Windows CE also supports the *LoadLibraryEx* function, prototyped as

```
HMODULE LoadLibraryEx (LPCTSTR lpLibFileName, HANDLE hFile, DWORD dwFlags);
```

The first parameter is the name of the DLL to load. The second parameter, *hFile*, isn't supported by Windows CE and must be set to 0. The last parameter, *dwFlags*, defines how the DLL is loaded. If *dwFlags* contains the flag *DONT_RESOLVE_DLL_REFERENCES*, the DLL is loaded, but any modules the DLL requires are not loaded. In addition, the entry point of the DLL, typically *DllMain*, isn't called. If *dwFlags* contains *LOAD_LIBRARY_AS_DATAFILE*, the DLL is loaded into memory as a data file. The DLL is not relocated or prepared in any way to be called from executable code. However, the handle returned can be used to load resources from the DLL using the standard resource functions such as *LoadString*.

When a DLL is loaded, its entry point, traditionally named *DllMain*, is called. *DllMain* is prototyped as

```
BOOL APIENTRY DllMain( HANDLE hModule, DWORD  ul_reason_for_call,
                       LPVOID lpReserved);
```

In addition to being called when the DLL is first loaded, *DllMain* is also called when it's unloaded or when a new thread is created or destroyed in the process that loads it. The second parameter, *ul_reason_for_call*, indicates the reason for the call to *DllMain*.

DLLs should avoid doing anything more than simple initialization from within *DllMain*. An action such as loading other DLLs or any other action that might load other DLLs can cause problems with the Windows CE loader. This restriction can cause problems for DLLs that have been ported from the desktop versions of Windows because those operating systems are much more tolerant of actions within *DllMain*.

One last DLL function is handy to know about. The function *DisableThreadLibraryCalls* tells the operating system not to send *DLL_THREAD_ ATTACH* and *DLL_THREAD_DETACH* notifications to the DLL when threads are created and terminated in the application. Preventing these notifications can improve performance and reduce the working set of an application because the DLL's *LibMain* isn't called when threads are created and destroyed. The function is prototyped as

```
BOOL DisableThreadLibraryCalls (HMODULE hLibModule);
```

The only parameter is the handle to the DLL identifying the DLL that doesn't want to be notified of the thread events.

Processes

Windows CE diverges from its desktop counterparts in a number of ways. Compared with processes under Windows Vista, Windows CE processes contain much less state information. Because Windows CE doesn't support the concept of a current directory, the individual processes don't need to store that information. Windows CE doesn't maintain a set of environment variables, so processes don't need to keep an environment block. Windows CE doesn't support handle inheritance, so there's no need to tell a process to enable handle inheritance. Because of all this, the parameter-heavy *CreateProcess* function is passed mainly *NULL*s and zeros, with just a few parameters actually used by Windows CE.

Many of the process and thread-related functions are simply not supported by Windows CE because the system doesn't support certain features supported on the desktop. Because Windows CE doesn't support an environment, all the Win32 functions dealing with the environment don't exist in Windows CE. Some functions aren't supported because there's an easy way to work around the lack of the function. For example, *ExitProcess* doesn't exist under Windows CE. But as you might expect, there's a workaround that allows a process to close.

Enough of what Windows CE doesn't do; let's look at what you can do with Windows CE.

Creating a Process

The function for creating a new process is

```
BOOL CreateProcess (LPCTSTR lpApplicationName,
                    LPCTSTR lpCommandLine,
                    LPSECURITY_ATTRIBUTES lpProcessAttributes,
                    LPSECURITY_ATTRIBUTES lpThreadAttributes,
                    BOOL bInheritHandles, DWORD dwCreationFlags,
                    LPVOID lpEnvironment,
                    LPCTSTR lpCurrentDirectory,
                    LPSTARTUPINFO lpStartupInfo,
                    LPPROCESS_INFORMATION lpProcessInformation);
```

Although the list of parameters looks daunting, most of the parameters must be set to *NULL* or 0 because Windows CE doesn't support security or current directories, nor does it handle inheritance. This results in a function prototype that looks more like this:

```
BOOL CreateProcess (LPCTSTR lpApplicationName,
                    LPTSTR lpCommandLine,  NULL, NULL, FALSE,
                    DWORD dwCreationFlags, NULL, NULL, NULL,
                    LPPROCESS_INFORMATION lpProcessInformation);
```

The parameters that remain start with a pointer to the name of the application to launch. As with DLLs, Windows CE's search for the application depends on whether the name is passed with a completely specified path. If so, a module is looked for only in the directory specified by the path. For a module without a completely specified path, the search looks like this:

1. The directory of the executable or DLL launching the process
2. The Windows directory (\Windows)
3. The root directory in the object store (\)
4. The directories in the path specified in the SystemPath value in [HKEY_LOCAL_MACHINE]\Loader

This action is different from the desktop, where *CreateProcess* searches for the executable only if *lpApplicationName* is set to *NULL* and the executable name is passed through the *lp-CommandLine* parameter. In the case of Windows CE, the application name must be passed in the *lpApplicationName* parameter because Windows CE doesn't support the technique of passing a *NULL* in *lpApplicationName* with the application name as the first token in the *lp-CommandLine* parameter.

The *lpCommandLine* parameter specifies the command line that will be passed to the new process. The only difference between Windows CE and the desktop in this parameter is that under Windows CE the command line is always passed as a Unicode string. And as I mentioned previously, you can't pass the name of the executable as the first token in *lpCommandLine.*

The *dwCreationFlags* parameter specifies the initial state of the process after it has been loaded. Windows CE limits the allowable flags to the following:

- **0** Creates a standard process.
- **CREATE_SUSPENDED** Creates the process and then suspends the primary thread.
- **DEBUG_PROCESS** The process being created is treated as a process being debugged by the caller. The calling process receives debug information from the process being launched.
- **DEBUG_ONLY_THIS_PROCESS** When combined with DEBUG_PROCESS, debugs a process but doesn't debug any child processes that are launched by the process being debugged.
- **CREATE_NEW_CONSOLE** Forces a new console to be created.
- **INHERIT_CALLER_PRIORITY** The main thread is created with the same priority as the thread creating the process

The only other parameter of the *CreateProcess* function that Windows CE uses is *lpProcessIn-formation.* This parameter can be set to *NULL*, or it can point to a *PROCESS_INFORMATION* structure that's filled by *CreateProcess* with information about the new process. The *PROCESS_INFORMATION* structure is defined this way:

```
typedef struct _PROCESS_INFORMATION {
    HANDLE hProcess;
    HANDLE hThread;
    DWORD dwProcessId;
    DWORD dwThreadId;
} PROCESS_INFORMATION;
```

The first two fields in this structure are filled with the handles of the new process and the handle of the primary thread of the new process. These handles are useful for monitoring the newly created process, but with them comes some responsibility. Handles are references to data structures maintained by the operating system. As long as a handle is open, Windows

CE must keep that data in memory. When the system creates a process, it creates a handle to that process and the main thread of that process and provides duplicates of those handles in the *PROCESS_INFORMATION* structure. Because there are two copies of each handle it sets the use count for the handles to two. The system can't free the structures associated with the handles until *both* the newly created process has terminated *and* the handles returned in the PROCESS_INFORMATION structure are closed. Failing to close unneeded handles results in a *leak* of that handle. Leaked handles waste memory, and in a low memory environment typical to Windows CE, leaked handles are trouble.

Ideally, if you don't need the process and thread handles, they should be closed immediately following a successful call to *CreateProcess*. However, there are times when the handles are quite useful. I'll describe some good uses for these handles later in this chapter, in the section "Synchronization."

The other two fields in the *PROCESS_INFORMATION* structure are filled with the process ID and primary thread ID of the new process. These ID values aren't handles but simply unique identifiers that can be passed to Windows functions to identify the target of the function. Be careful when using these IDs. If the new process terminates and another new one is created, the system can reuse the old ID values.

Using the create process is simple, as you can see in the following code fragment:

```
TCHAR szFileName[MAX_PATH];
TCHAR szCmdLine[64];
DWORD dwCreationFlags;
PROCESS_INFORMATION pi;
BOOL fSuccess;

lstrcpy (szFileName, TEXT ("pword"));
lstrcpy (szCmdLine, TEXT (""));
dwCreationFlags = 0;

fSuccess = CreateProcess (szFileName, szCmdLine, NULL, NULL, FALSE,
                          dwCreationFlags, NULL, NULL, NULL, &pi);
if (fSuccess) {
    CloseHandle (pi.hThread);
    CloseHandle (pi.hProcess);
}
```

This code launches the Pocket Word application. Because the file name doesn't specify a path, *CreateProcess* will, using the standard Windows CE search path, find pword.exe in the \Windows directory. Because I didn't pass a command line to Pocket Word, I could have simply passed a *NULL* value in the *lpCmdLine* parameter. But I passed a null string in *szCmdLine* to differentiate the *lpCmdLine* parameter from the many other parameters in *CreateProcess* that aren't used. I used the same technique for *dwCreationFlags*. If the call to *CreateProcess* is successful, it returns a nonzero value. The code above checks for this and, if the call was successful, closes the process and thread handles returned in the *PROCESS_INFORMATION* structure. Remember that if you don't need these handles, they should be closed to prevent memory leaks.

Terminating a Process

A process can terminate itself by simply returning from the *WinMain* procedure. For console applications, a simple return from *main* suffices. On Windows CE, the *ExitProcess* function is mapped to *TerminateProcess* discussed below. A better way would be to have the primary thread of the process call *ExitThread*. Under Windows CE, if the primary thread terminates, the process is terminated as well, regardless of what other threads are currently active in the process. The exit code of the process will be the exit code provided by *ExitThread*. You can determine the exit code of a process by calling

```
BOOL GetExitCodeProcess (HANDLE hProcess, LPDWORD lpExitCode);
```

The parameters are the handle to the process and a pointer to a *DWORD* that receives the exit code that was returned by the terminating process. If the process is still running, the return code is the constant *STILL_ACTIVE*.

You can terminate other processes. But while it's possible to do that, you shouldn't be in the business of closing other processes. The user might not be expecting that process to be closed without his or her consent. If you need to terminate a process (or close a process, which is the same thing but a much nicer word), the following methods can be used.

If the process to be closed is one that you created, you can use some sort of interprocess communication to tell the process to terminate itself. This is the most advisable method because you've designed the target process to be closed by another party. Another method of closing a process is to send the main window of the process a *WM_CLOSE* message. This is especially effective on a Windows Mobile device, where applications are designed to respond to *WM_CLOSE* messages by quietly saving their state and closing. Finally, if all else fails and you absolutely must close another process, you can use *TerminateProcess*.

TerminateProcess is prototyped as

```
BOOL TerminateProcess (HANDLE hProcess, DWORD uExitCode);
```

The two parameters are the handle of the process to terminate and the exit code the terminating process will return.

Other Processes

Of course, to terminate another process, you've got to know the handle to that process. You might want to know the handle to a process for other reasons as well. For example, you might want to know *when* the process terminates. Windows CE supports two additional functions that come in handy here (both of which are seldom discussed). The first function is

OpenProcess, which returns the handle of an already running process. *OpenProcess* is prototyped as

```
HANDLE OpenProcess (DWORD dwDesiredAccess, BOOL bInheritHandle,
                    DWORD dwProcessId);
```

Under Windows CE, the first parameter isn't used and should be set to 0. The *bInheritHandle* parameter must be set to *FALSE* because Windows CE doesn't support handle inheritance. The final parameter is the process ID value of the process you want to open.

The other function useful in this circumstance is

```
DWORD GetWindowThreadProcessId (HWND hWnd, LPDWORD lpdwProcessId);
```

This function takes a handle to a window and returns the process ID for the process that created the window. So using these two functions, you can trace a window back to the process that created it.

Two other functions allow you to directly read from and write to the memory space of another process. These functions are

```
BOOL ReadProcessMemory (HANDLE hProcess, LPCVOID lpBaseAddress,
                        LPVOID lpBuffer, DWORD nSize,
                        LPDWORD lpNumberOfBytesRead);
```

and

```
BOOL WriteProcessMemory (HANDLE hProcess, LPVOID lpBaseAddress,
                         LPVOID lpBuffer, DWORD nSize,
                         LPDWORD lpNumberOfBytesWritten);
```

The parameters for these functions are fairly self-explanatory. The first parameter is the handle of the remote process. The second parameter is the base address in the other process's address space of the area to be read or written. The third and fourth parameters specify the name and the size of the local buffer which the data is to be read from or written to. Finally, the last parameter specifies the bytes actually read or written. Both functions require that the entire area being read to or written from must be accessible. Typically, you use these functions for debugging, but there's no requirement that this be their only use. Allocating and freeing memory in other processes can be accomplished with the VirtualxxxEx functions discussed in Chapter 7.

Threads

A thread is, fundamentally, a unit of execution. That is, it has a stack and a processor context, which is a set of values in the CPU internal registers. When a thread is suspended, the registers are pushed onto the thread's stack, the active stack is changed to the next thread to be run, that thread's CPU state is pulled off its stack, and the new thread starts executing instructions.

Threads under Windows CE are similar to threads under the desktop versions of Windows. Each process has a primary thread. Using the functions that I describe below, a process can create any number of additional threads within the process. The only limit to the number of threads in a Windows CE process is the memory and process address space available for the thread's stack.

Threads within a process share the address space of the process. Memory allocated by one thread is accessible to all threads in the process. Threads share the same access rights for handles whether they be file handles, memory object handles, or handles to synchronization objects.

The stack size of the main thread of a process is set by the linker. (The linker switch for setting the stack size in Visual Studio is */stack*.) Secondary threads are created by default with the same stack size as the primary thread, but the default can be overridden when the thread is created.

The System Scheduler

Windows CE schedules threads in a preemptive manner. Threads run for a *quantum*, or time slice. After that time, if the thread hasn't already relinquished its time slice and if the thread isn't a run-to-completion thread, it's suspended and another thread is scheduled to run. Windows CE chooses which thread to run based on a priority scheme. Threads of a higher priority are scheduled before threads of lower priority.

The rules for how Windows CE allocates time among the threads are quite different from other versions of Windows. Windows CE processes don't have a *priority class*. On the desktop, threads are scheduled based on their priority and on the priority class of their parent processe. A Windows Vista process with a higher-priority class has threads that run at a higher priority than threads in a process with a lower-priority class. Threads within a process can refine their priority within a process by setting their relative thread priority.

Because Windows CE has no priority classes, all processes are treated as peers. Individual threads can have different priorities, but the process that the thread runs within doesn't influence those priorities. Also, unlike some of the desktop versions of Windows, the foreground thread in Windows CE doesn't get a boost in priority.

When Windows CE was first developed, the scheduler supported eight priority levels. Starting with Windows CE 3.0, that number was increased to 256 priority levels. However, most applications still use the original (now lowest[1]) eight priority levels. The upper 248 levels are typically used by device drivers or other system-level threads. This doesn't mean that an application can't use the higher levels, but accessing them requires different API calls.

---

1 It is possible for the OEM to set the application priority levels to a different location from the bottom 8 of the 256 system priorities, but this is quite rare.

The eight application priority levels are listed here:

- **THREAD_PRIORITY_TIME_CRITICAL** Indicates 3 points above normal priority
- **THREAD_PRIORITY_HIGHEST** Indicates 2 points above normal priority
- **THREAD_PRIORITY_ABOVE_NORMAL** Indicates 1 point above normal priority
- **THREAD_PRIORITY_NORMAL** Indicates normal priority. All threads are created with this priority
- **THREAD_PRIORITY_BELOW_NORMAL** Indicates 1 point below normal priority
- **THREAD_PRIORITY_LOWEST** Indicates 2 points below normal priority
- **THREAD_PRIORITY_ABOVE_IDLE** Indicates 3 points below normal priority
- **THREAD_PRIORITY_IDLE** Indicates 4 points below normal priority

All higher-priority threads run before lower-priority threads. This means that before a thread set to run at a particular priority can be scheduled, all threads that have a higher priority must be *blocked*. A blocked thread is one that's waiting on some system resource or synchronization object before it can continue. Threads of equal priority are scheduled in a round-robin fashion. Once a thread has voluntarily given up its time slice, is blocked, or has completed its time slice, all other threads of the same priority are allowed to run before the original thread is allowed to continue. If a thread of higher priority is unblocked and a thread of lower priority is currently running, the lower-priority thread is immediately suspended and the higher-priority thread is scheduled. Lower-priority threads can never preempt a higher-priority thread.

There is one exception to the scheduling rules discussed previously: if a low-priority thread owns a resource that a higher-priority thread is waiting on. In this case, the low-priority thread is temporarily given the higher-priority thread's priority to avoid a problem known as a *priority inversion deadlock*, so that it can quickly accomplish its task and free the needed resource.

Although it might seem that lower-priority threads never get a chance to run in this scheme, it works out that threads are almost always blocked, waiting on something to free up before they can be scheduled. Threads are always created at *THREAD_PRIORITY_NORMAL*,[2] so, unless they proactively change their priority level, a thread is usually at an equal priority to most of the other threads in the system. Even at the normal priority level, threads are almost always blocked. For example, an application's primary thread is typically blocked waiting on messages. Other threads should be designed to block waiting on one of the many synchronization objects available to a Windows CE application.

[2] The exception to this rule is the primary thread of a process created with the INHERIT_CALLER_PRIORITY flag.

Never Do This!

What's not supported by the arrangement I just described, or by any other thread-based scheme, is code like the following:

```
while (bFlag == FALSE) {
    // Read new value for flag.
}
// Now do something.
```

This kind of code isn't just bad manners; because it wastes CPU power, it's a death sentence to a battery-powered Windows CE device. To understand why this is important, I need to digress into a quick lesson on Windows CE power management.

Windows CE is designed so that when all threads are blocked, which happens over 90 percent of the time, it calls down to the OEM Abstraction Layer (the equivalent of the BIOS on an MS-DOS machine) to enter a low-power waiting state. Typically, this low-power state means that the CPU is halted; that is, it simply stops executing instructions. Because the CPU isn't executing any instructions, no power-consuming reads and writes of memory are performed by the CPU. At this point, the only power necessary for the system is to maintain the contents of the RAM and light the display. In a well-designed system this low-power mode can reduce power consumption by up to 99 percent of what is required when a thread is running.

As an example of what might happen, consider a Windows Mobile device that is designed to run for 10 hours on a fully charged battery. Given that the system turns itself off after a few minutes of nonuse, this 10 hours translates into weeks of battery life in the device for the user. (I'm basing this calculation on the assumption that the system indeed spends 90 percent or more of its time in its low-power idle state.) Now the user runs a poorly written application containing a thread that spins on a variable instead of blocking. While this application is running, the system will never enter its low-power state. So, instead of 600 minutes of battery time (10 hours × 60 minutes/hour), the system spends 100 percent of its time at full power, resulting in a battery life of slightly over an hour, which means that the battery would be lucky to last a day's normal use. So as you can see, it's good to have the system in its low-power state.

Fortunately, because Windows applications usually spend their time blocked in a call to *GetMessage*, the system power management works by default. However, if you plan on using multiple threads in your application, you must use synchronization objects to block threads while they're waiting. First let's look at how to create a thread, and then I'll dive into the synchronization tools available to Windows CE programs.

Creating a Thread

You create a thread under Windows CE by calling the function *CreateThread*, which is a departure from the desktop versions of Windows in which you're never supposed to call this

API directly. The reason for this change is that on the desktop, calling *CreateThread* doesn't give the C runtime library the chance to create thread-unique data structures. So on the desktop, programmers are instructed to use either of the run-time thread creation functions *_beginthread* or *_beginthreadex*. These functions provide some thread-specific initialization and then call *CreateThread* internally.

In Windows CE, however, the runtime is written to be thread safe and doesn't require explicit thread initialization, so calling *CreateThread* directly is the norm. The function is prototyped as

```
HANDLE CreateThread (LPSECURITY_ATTRIBUTES lpThreadAttributes,
                     DWORD dwStackSize,
                     LPTHREAD_START_ROUTINE lpStartAddress,
                     LPVOID lpParameter, DWORD dwCreationFlags,
                     LPDWORD lpThreadId);
```

As with *CreateProcess*, Windows CE doesn't support a number of the parameters in *CreateThread*, so they are set to *NULL* or 0 as appropriate. For *CreateThread*, the *lpThreadAttributes* parameter isn't supported and must be set to *NULL*. The *dwStackSize* parameter is used only if the *STACK_SIZE_PARAM_IS_A_RESERVATION* flag is set in the *dwCreationFlags* parameter. The size specified in *dwStackSize* is the maximum size to which the stack can grow. Windows CE doesn't immediately commit the full amount of RAM to the stack when the thread is created. Instead, memory is committed only as necessary as the stack grows.

The third parameter, *lpStartAddress*, must point to the start of the thread routine. The *lpParameter* parameter in *CreateThread* is an application-defined value that's passed to the thread function as its only parameter. You can set the *dwCreationFlags* parameter to either 0, *STACK_SIZE_PARAM_IS_A_RESERVATION*, or *CREATE_SUSPENDED*. If *CREATE_SUSPENDED* is passed, the thread is created in a suspended state and must be resumed with a call to *ResumeThread*. The final parameter is a pointer to a *DWORD* that receives the newly created thread's ID value. If the thread ID isn't needed, *lpThreadId* can be set to NULL.

The thread routine should be prototyped this way:

```
DWORD WINAPI ThreadFunc (LPVOID lpArg);
```

The only parameter is the *lpParameter* value, passed unaltered from the call to *CreateThread*. The parameter can be an integer or a pointer. Make sure, however, that you don't pass a pointer to a stack-based structure that will disappear when the routine that called *CreateThread* returns.

If *CreateThread* is successful, it creates the thread and returns the handle to the newly created thread. As with *CreateProcess*, the handle returned should be closed when you no longer need the handle. Following is a short code fragment that contains a call to start a thread and the thread routine.

```
//----------------------------------------------------------------------
//
//
HANDLE hThread1;
DWORD dwThread1ID = 0;
int nParameter = 5;

hThread1 = CreateThread (NULL, 0, Thread2, (PVOID)nParameter, 0,
                         &dwThread1ID);
CloseHandle (hThread1);

//----------------------------------------------------------------------
// Second thread routine
//
DWORD WINAPI Thread2 (PVOID pArg) {

    int nParam = (int) pArg;

    //
    // Do something here.
    // .
    // .
    // .
    return 0x15;
}
```

In this code, the second thread is started with a call to *CreateThread*. The *nParameter* value is passed to the second thread as the single parameter to the thread routine. The second thread executes until it terminates, in this case simply by returning from the routine.

A thread can also terminate itself by calling this function:

```
VOID ExitThread (DWORD dwExitCode);
```

The only parameter is the exit code that's set for the thread. That thread exit code can be queried by another thread using this function:

```
BOOL GetExitCodeThread (HANDLE hThread, LPDWORD lpExitCode);
```

The function takes the handle to the thread (not the thread ID) and returns the exit code of the thread. If the thread is still running, the exit code is *STILL_ACTIVE*, a constant defined as 0x0103. The exit code is set by a thread using *ExitThread* or the value returned by the thread procedure. In the preceding code, the thread sets its exit code to 0x15 when it returns.

All threads within a process are terminated when the process terminates. As I said earlier, a process is terminated when its primary thread terminates.

Setting and Querying Thread Priority

Threads are always created at the priority level *THREAD_PRIORITY_NORMAL*. The thread priority can be changed either by the thread itself or by another thread using one of two functions. The first is

```
BOOL SetThreadPriority (HANDLE hThread, int nPriority);
```

The two parameters are the thread handle and the new priority level. The level passed can be one of the constants described previously, ranging from *THREAD_PRIORITY_IDLE* up to *THREAD_PRIORITY_TIME_CRITICAL*. You must be extremely careful when you're changing a thread's priority. Remember that threads of a lower priority almost never preempt threads of higher priority. So a simple bumping up of a thread one notch above normal can harm the responsiveness of the rest of the system unless that thread is carefully written.

The other function that sets a thread's priority is

```
BOOL CeSetThreadPriority (HANDLE hThread, int nPriority);
```

The difference between this function and *SetThreadPriority* is that this function sets the thread's priority to any of the 256 priorities. Instead of using predefined constants, *nPriority* should be set to a value of 0 to 255, with 0 being highest priority and 255 being the lowest.

A word of caution: *SetThreadPriority* and *CeSetThreadPriority* use completely different numbering schemes for the *nPriority* value. For example, to set a thread's priority to 1 above normal, you could call *SetThreadPriority* with *THREAD_PRIORITY_ABOVE_NORMAL* or call *CeSetThreadPriority* with *nPriority* set to 250 but the constant *THREAD_PRIORITY_ABOVE_NORMAL* defined as 2, not 250. The rule is that you should use the constants for *SetThreadPriority* and the numeric values for *CeSetThreadPriority*. To query the priority level of a thread, call this function:

```
int GetThreadPriority (HANDLE hThread);
```

This function returns the priority level of the thread. You shouldn't use the hard-coded priority levels. Instead, use constants, such as *THREAD_PRIORITY_NORMAL*, defined by the system. This ensures that you're using the same numbering scheme that *SetThreadPriority* uses. For threads that have a priority greater than *THREAD_PRIORITY_TIMECRITICAL*, this function returns the value *THREAD_PRIORITY_TIMECRITICAL*.

To query the priority of a thread that might have a higher priority than *THREAD_PRIORITY_TIMECRITICAL*, call the function

```
int CeGetThreadPriority (HANDLE hThread);
```

The value returned by *CeGetThreadPriority* will be 0 to 255, with 0 being the highest priority possible. Here again, Windows CE uses different numbering schemes for the priority query functions than it does for the priority set functions. For example, for a thread running at normal priority, *GetThreadPriority* would return *THREAD_PRIORITY_NORMAL*, which is defined as the value 3. *CeGetThreadPriority* would return the value 251.

Setting a Thread's Time Quantum

Threads can be individually set with their own *time quantum*. The time quantum is the maximum amount of time a thread runs before it's preempted by the operating system. By default, the time quantum is set to 100 milliseconds, although for embedded systems, the OEM can change this.[3] For example, some Windows Mobile devices use a default quantum of 75 milliseconds, while others use the standard 100-millisecond quantum.

To set the time quantum of a thread, call

```
int CeSetThreadQuantum (HANDLE hThread, DWORD dwTime);
```

The first parameter is the handle to the thread. The second parameter is the time, in milliseconds, of the desired quantum. If you set the time quantum to 0, the thread is turned into a "run-to-completion thread." These threads aren't preempted by threads of their own priority. Obviously, threads of higher priorities preempt these threads.

You can query a thread's time quantum with the function

```
int CeGetThreadQuantum (HANDLE hThread);
```

The first parameter is the handle to the thread. The function returns the current quantum of the thread.

Suspending and Resuming a Thread

You can suspend a thread at any time by calling this function:

```
DWORD SuspendThread (HANDLE hThread);
```

The only parameter is the handle to the thread to suspend. The value returned is the *suspend count* for the thread. Windows maintains a suspend count for each thread. Any thread with a suspend count greater than 0 is suspended. Because *SuspendThread* increments the suspend count, multiple calls to *SuspendThread* must be matched with an equal number of calls to *ResumeThread* before a thread is actually scheduled to run. *ResumeCount* is prototyped as

```
DWORD ResumeThread (HANDLE hThread);
```

[3] In early versions of Windows CE, a thread's time quantum was fixed. Typically, the time quantum was set to 25 milliseconds, although this was changeable by the OEM.

Here again, the parameter is the handle to the thread, and the return value is the previous suspend count. So if *ResumeThread* returns 1, the thread is no longer suspended.

At times, a thread simply wants to kill some time. Because I've already explained why simply spinning in a *while* loop is a very bad thing to do, you need another way to kill time. The best way to do this is to use this function:

```
void Sleep (DWORD dwMilliseconds);
```

Sleep suspends the thread for at least the number of milliseconds specified in the *dwMilliseconds* parameter. Because the scheduler timer has a granularity of 1 millisecond, calls to *Sleep* are accurate to 1 millisecond. On systems based on other versions of Windows, the accuracy of *Sleep* depends on the period of the scheduler timer. It is valid to pass a 0 to *Sleep*. When a thread passes a 0 to *Sleep*, it gives up its time slice but is rescheduled immediately according to the scheduling rules I described previously.

Fibers

Fibers are threadlike constructs that are scheduled within the application instead of by the scheduler. Fibers, like threads, have their own stack and execution context. The difference is that the application must manage and manually switch between a set of fibers so that each one gets the appropriate amount of time to run.

An application creates a fiber by first creating a thread. The thread calls a function to turn itself into a fiber. The thread, now a single fiber, can then create multiple fibers from itself. The operating system schedules all of the fibers as a single thread—the thread that was originally converted to the first fiber. So the system allocates the time scheduled for the original thread to whichever fiber the application chooses. When the application chooses, it can stop a particular fiber and schedule another. This switch is transparent to Windows CE because all it considers is the quantum and the priority of the original thread. Fibers aren't more efficient than a well-designed multithreaded application, but they do allow applications to micromanage the scheduling of code execution within the application.

To create a set of fibers, an application first creates a thread. The thread then calls *ConvertThreadToFiber*, which is prototyped as

```
LPVOID ConvertThreadToFiber  (LPVOID lpParameter);
```

The single parameter is an application-defined value that can be retrieved by the fiber using the macro *GetFiberData*. The value returned is the pointer to the fiber data for this fiber. This value will be used when another fiber wants to schedule this fiber. If the return value is 0, the call failed.

Upon return from the function, the thread is now a fiber. One significant restriction on converting a thread to a fiber is that the thread must use the default stack size for its stack.

If the thread has a different stack size from the main thread in the process, the call to *ConvertThreadToFiber* will fail.

After the original thread has been converted to a fiber, it can spawn additional fibers with the following call:

```
LPVOID CreateFiber (DWORD dwStackSize, LPFIBER_START_ROUTINE lpStartAddress,
                    LPVOID lpParameter);
```

The *dwStackSize* parameter should be set to 0. The *lpStartAddress* parameter is the entry point of the new fiber being created. The final parameter is an application-defined value that is passed to the entry point of the new fiber. The return value from *CreateFiber* is the pointer to the fiber data for this new fiber. This value will be used to switch to the newly created fiber.

The function prototype of the fiber entry point looks similar to the entry point of a thread. It is

```
VOID CALLBACK FiberProc (PVOID lpParameter);
```

The one parameter is the value passed from the *CreateFiber* call. This parameter can also be retrieved by the fiber by calling *GetFiberData*. Note that no return value is defined for the fiber procedure. A fiber procedure should never return. If it does, the system exits the thread that is the basis for all fibers spawned by that thread.

The new fiber does not immediately start execution. Instead, the fiber calling *CreateFiber* must explicitly switch to the new fiber by calling

```
VOID SwitchToFiber (LPVOID lpFiber);
```

The single parameter is the pointer to the fiber data for the fiber to be switched to. When this call is made, the calling fiber is suspended and the new fiber is enabled to run.

The *DeleteFiber* function is used to destroy a fiber. It looks like this:

```
VOID DeleteFiber (LPVOID lpFiber);
```

The single parameter is the pointer to the fiber data of the fiber to destroy. If a fiber calls *DeleteFiber* on itself, the thread is exited and all fibers associated with that thread are also terminated.

It's critical that fibers clean up after themselves. Each fiber should be deleted by another fiber in the set, and then the final fiber can delete itself and properly exit the thread. If the thread is exited without deletion of all fibers, the memory committed to support each of the undeleted fibers will not be freed, resulting in a memory leak for the application.

Fibers are interesting but are they necessary? The short answer is, not really. Fibers were added to Windows CE for two reasons. First, it makes it easier to port applications from Unix style operating systems where something akin to fibers is used frequently. The second reason for adding them was a request from an internal group within Microsoft that wanted to use fibers when they ported their Windows desktop application to Windows CE.

I doubt either of these reasons inspires hoards of developers to start using fibers. There have been groups within Microsoft that have decided for example that fibers are not supported on Windows Mobile devices. Even so, if your system needs fiber support, Windows CE does provide it.

Thread Local Storage

Thread local storage is a mechanism that allows a routine to maintain separate instances of data for each thread calling the routine. This capability might not seem like much, but it has some very handy uses. Take the following thread routine:

```
int g_nGlobal;            // System global variable

int ThreadProc (pStartData) {
    int nValue1;
    int nValue2;

    while (unblocked) {
        //
        // Do some work.
        //
    }
    // We're done now; terminate the thread by returning.
    return 0;
}
```

For this example, imagine that multiple threads are created to execute the same routine, *ThreadProc*. Each thread has its own copy of *nValue1* and *nValue2* because these are stack-based variables and each thread has its own stack. All threads, though, share the same static variable, *g_nGlobal*.

Now imagine that the *ThreadProc* routine calls another routine, *WorkerBee*. As in

```
int g_nGlobal;            // System global variable

int ThreadProc (pStartData) {
    int nValue1;
    int nValue2;
    while (unblocked) {
        WorkerBee();      // Let someone else do the work.
    }
    // We're done now; terminate the thread by returning.
    return 0;
}
```

```
int WorkerBee (void) {
    int nLocal1;
    static int nLocal2;
    //
    // Do work here.
    //
    return nLocal1;
}
```

Now *WorkerBee* doesn't have access to any persistent memory that's local to a thread. *nLocal1* is persistent only for the life of a single call to *WorkerBee*. *nLocal2* is persistent across calls to *WorkerBee* but is static and therefore shared among all threads calling *WorkerBee*. One solution would be to have *ThreadProc* pass a pointer to a stack-based variable to *WorkerBee*. This strategy works, but only if you have control over the routines calling *WorkerBee*. What if you're writing a DLL and you need to have a routine in the DLL maintain a different state for each thread calling the routine? You can't define static variables in the DLL because they would be shared across the different threads. You can't define local variables because they aren't persistent across calls to your routine. The answer is to use thread local storage.

Thread local storage allows a process to have its own cache of values that are guaranteed to be unique for each thread in a process. This cache of values is small because an array must be created for every thread created in the process, but it's large enough if used intelligently. To be specific, the system constant, *TLS_MINIMUM_AVAILABLE*, is defined to be the number of slots in the TLS array that's available for each process. For Windows CE, this value is defined as 64. So each process can have 64 4-byte values that are unique for each thread in that process. For the best results, of course, you must manage those 64 slots well.

To reserve one of the TLS slots, a process calls

```
DWORD TlsAlloc (void);
```

TlsAlloc looks through the array to find a free slot in the TLS array, marks it as *in use*, and then returns an index value to the newly assigned slot. If no slots are available, the function returns -1. It's important to understand that the individual threads don't call *TlsAlloc*. Instead, the process or DLL calls it before creating the threads that will use the TLS slot.

Once a slot has been assigned, each instance of the thread can access its unique data in the slot by calling this function:

```
BOOL TlsSetValue (DWORD dwTlsIndex, LPVOID lpTlsValue);
```

and

```
LPVOID TlsGetValue (DWORD dwTlsIndex);
```

For both of these functions, the TLS index value returned by *TlsAlloc* specifies the slot that contains the data. Both *TlsGetValue* and *TlsSetValue* type the data as a *PVOID*, but the value can be used for any purpose. The advantage of thinking of the TLS value as a pointer is that a thread can allocate a block of memory on the heap and then keep the pointer to that data in the TLS value. This allows each thread to maintain a block of thread-unique data of almost any size.

One other matter is important to thread local storage. When *TlsAlloc* reserves a slot, it zeroes the value in that slot for all currently running threads. All new threads are created with their TLS array initialized to 0 as well. This means that a thread can safely assume that the value in its slot will be initialized to 0. This is helpful for determining whether a thread needs to allocate a memory block the first time the routine is called.

When a process no longer needs the TLS slot, it should call this function:

```
BOOL TlsFree (DWORD dwTlsIndex);
```

The function is passed the index value of the slot to be freed. The function returns *TRUE* if successful. This function frees only the TLS slot. If threads have allocated storage in the heap and stored pointers to those blocks in their TLS slots, that storage isn't freed by this function. Threads are responsible for freeing their own memory blocks.

Synchronization

With multiple threads running around the system, you need to coordinate their activities. Fortunately, Windows CE supports almost the entire extensive set of standard Win32 synchronization objects. The concept of synchronization objects is fairly simple. A thread *waits* on a synchronization object. When the object is signaled, the waiting thread is unblocked and is scheduled (according to the rules governing the thread's priority) to run.

Windows CE doesn't support some of the synchronization primitives supported by the desktop. These unsupported elements include spin locks and waitable timers. The lack of waitable timer support can easily be worked around using other synchronization objects or, for longer-period timeouts, the more flexible Notification API, unique to Windows CE.

One aspect of Windows CE unique to it is that the different synchronization objects don't share the same namespace. This means that if you have an *event* named *Bob*, you can also have a *mutex* named *Bob*. (I'll talk about mutexes later in this chapter.) This naming convention is different from the rule on the desktop, where all kernel objects (of which synchronization objects are a part) share the same namespace. While having the same names in Windows CE is possible, it's not advisable. Not only does the practice make your code incompatible with other versions of Windows, there's no telling whether a redesign of the internals of Windows CE might just enforce this restriction in the future.

Events

The first synchronization primitive I'll describe is the *event object*. An event object is a synchronization object that can be in a *signaled* or *nonsignaled* state. Events are useful to a thread to let it be known that, well, an event has occurred. Event objects can either be created to automatically reset from a signaled state to a nonsignaled state or require a manual reset to return the object to its nonsignaled state. Events can be named and therefore shared across different processes allowing interprocess synchronization.

An event is created by means of this function:

```
HANDLE CreateEvent (LPSECURITY_ATTRIBUTES lpEventAttributes,
                    BOOL bManualReset, BOOL bInitialState,
                    LPTSTR lpName);
```

As with all calls in Windows CE, the security attributes parameter, *lpEventAttributes*, should be set to *NULL*. The second parameter indicates whether the event being created requires a manual reset or will automatically reset to a nonsignaled state immediately after being signaled. Setting *bManualReset* to *TRUE* creates an event that must be manually reset. The *bInitialState* parameter specifies whether the event object is initially created in the signaled or nonsignaled state. Finally, the *lpName* parameter points to an optional string that names the event. Events that are named can be shared across processes. If two processes create event objects of the same name, the processes actually share the same object. This allows one process to signal the other process using event objects. If you don't want a named event, the *lpname* parameter can be set to *NULL*.

To share an event object across processes, each process must individually create the event object. You can't just create the event in one process and send the handle of that event to another process, because handles are specific to a process. To determine whether a call to *CreateEvent* created a new event object or opened an already created object, you can call *GetLastError* immediately following the call to *CreateEvent*. If *GetLastError* returns *ERROR_ALREADY_EXISTS*, the call opened an existing event.

Once you have an event object, you'll need to be able to signal the event. You accomplish this using either of the following two functions:

```
BOOL SetEvent (HANDLE hEvent);
```

or

```
BOOL PulseEvent (HANDLE hEvent);
```

The difference between these two functions is that *SetEvent* doesn't automatically reset the event object to a nonsignaled state. For autoreset events, *SetEvent* is all you need because the event is automatically reset once a thread unblocks on the event. For manual reset events, you must manually reset the event with this function:

```
BOOL ResetEvent (HANDLE hEvent);
```

These event functions sound like they overlap, so let's review. An event object can be created to reset itself or require a manual reset. If it can reset itself, a call to *SetEvent* signals the event object. The event is then automatically reset to the nonsignaled state when *one* thread is unblocked after waiting on that event. In addition, if no threads are waiting on an auto-reset event, the event stays in the signaled state until a thread waits on the event. When the first thread waits on the event, it is immediately signaled, and the event is automatically reset. An event that resets itself doesn't need *PulseEvent* or *ResetEvent*. If, however, the event object was created requiring a manual reset, the need for *ResetEvent* is obvious.

PulseEvent signals the event and then resets the event, which allows *all* threads waiting on that event to be unblocked. So the difference between *PulseEvent* on a manually resetting event and *SetEvent* on an automatic resetting event is that using *SetEvent* on an automatic resetting event frees only one thread to run, even if many threads are waiting on that event. *PulseEvent* frees all threads waiting on that event. Conversely, if no threads are waiting on a manual reset event and *PulseEvent* is called, no threads would be signaled because the event handle typically would return to the unsignaled state before any other thread would get the chance to wait on it.

An application can associate a single *DWORD* value with an event by calling

```
BOOL SetEventData (HANDLE hEvent, DWORD dwData);
```

The parameters are the handle of the event and the data to associate with that event. Any application can retrieve the data by calling

```
DWORD GetEventData (HANDLE hEvent);
```

The single parameter is the handle to the event. The return value is the data previously associated with the event.

You destroy event objects by calling *CloseHandle*. If the event object is named, Windows maintains a use count on the object, so one call to *CloseHandle* must be made for every call to *CreateEvent*.

Waiting...

It's all well and good to have event objects; the question is how to use them. Threads wait on events, as well as on the soon-to-be-described semaphore and mutex, using one of the following functions: *WaitForSingleObject*, *WaitForMultipleObjects*, *MsgWaitForMultipleObjects*, or *MsgWaitForMultipleObjectsEx*. Under Windows CE, the *WaitForMultiple* functions are limited in that they can't wait for all objects of a set of objects to be signaled. These functions support waiting for *one* object in a set of objects being signaled. Whatever the limitations of waiting, I can't emphasize enough that waiting is good. While a thread is blocked with one of these functions, the thread enters an extremely efficient state that takes very little CPU processing power and battery power.

Another point to remember is that the thread responsible for handling a message loop in your application (usually the application's primary thread) shouldn't be blocked by *WaitForSingleObject* or *WaitForMultipleObjects* because the thread can't be retrieving and dispatching messages in the message loop if it's blocked waiting on an object. The function *MsgWaitForMultipleObjects* gives you a way around this problem, but in a multithreaded environment, it's usually easier to let the primary thread handle the message loop and secondary threads handle the shared resources that require blocking on events.

Waiting on a Single Object

A thread can wait on a synchronization object with the function

```
DWORD WaitForSingleObject (HANDLE hHandle, DWORD dwMilliseconds);
```

The function takes two parameters: the handle to the object being waited on and a timeout value. If you don't want the wait to time out, you can pass the value *INFINITE* in the *dwMilliseconds* parameter. The function returns a value that indicates why the function returned. Calling *WaitForSingleObject* blocks the thread until the event is signaled, the synchronization object is abandoned, or the timeout value is reached.

WaitForSingleObject returns one of the following values:

- **WAIT_OBJECT_0** The specified object was signaled.
- **WAIT_TIMEOUT** The timeout interval elapsed, and the object's state remains nonsignaled.
- **WAIT_ABANDONED** The thread that owned a mutex object being waited on ended without freeing the object.
- **WAIT_FAILED** The handle of the synchronization object was invalid.

You must check the return code from *WaitForSingleObject* to determine whether the event was signaled or simply that the timeout had expired. (The *WAIT_ABANDONED* return value will be relevant when I talk about mutexes soon.)

Waiting on Processes and Threads

I've talked about waiting on events, but you can also wait on handles to processes and threads. These handles are signaled when their processes or threads terminate. This allows a process to monitor another process (or thread) and perform some action when the process terminates. One common use for this feature is for one process to launch another and then, by blocking on the handle to the newly created process, wait until that process terminates.

The rather irritating routine that follows is a thread that demonstrates this technique by launching an application, blocking until that application closes, and then relaunching the application:

```
DWORD WINAPI KeepRunning (PVOID pArg) {
    PROCESS_INFORMATION pi;
    TCHAR szFileName[MAX_PATH];
    int rc = 0;

    // Copy the filename.
    StringCchCopy(szFileName, dim(szFileName), (LPTSTR)pArg);
    while (1) {
        // Launch the application.
        rc = CreateProcess (szFileName, NULL, NULL, NULL, FALSE,
                            0, NULL, NULL, NULL, &pi);
        // If the application didn't start, terminate thread.
        if (!rc)
            return -1;
        // Close the new process's primary thread handle.
        CloseHandle (pi.hThread);

        // Wait for user to close the application.
        rc = WaitForSingleObject (pi.hProcess, INFINITE);

        // Close the old process handle.
        CloseHandle (pi.hProcess);

        // Make sure we returned from the wait correctly.
        if (rc != WAIT_OBJECT_0)
            return -2;
    }
    return 0;  //This should never get executed.
}
```

This code simply launches the application using *CreateProcess* and waits on the process handle returned in the *PROCESS_INFORMATION* structure. Notice that the thread closes the child process's primary thread handle and, after the wait, the handle to the child process itself.

Waiting on Multiple Objects

A thread can also wait on a number of events. The wait can end when any one of the events is signaled. The function that enables a thread to wait on multiple objects is this one:

```
DWORD WaitForMultipleObjects (DWORD nCount, CONST HANDLE *lpHandles,
                              BOOL bWaitAll, DWORD dwMilliseconds);
```

The first two parameters are a count of the number of events or mutexes to wait on and a pointer to an array of handles to these events. The *bWaitAll* parameter must be set to *FALSE* to indicate that the function should return if any of the events are signaled. The final parameter is a timeout value, in milliseconds. As with *WaitForSingleObject*, passing *INFINITE* in the timeout parameter disables the timeout. Windows CE doesn't support the use of *WaitForMultipleObjects* to enable waiting for all events in the array to be signaled before returning.

Like *WaitForSingleObject*, *WaitForMultipleObjects* returns a code that indicates why the function returned. If the function returned because of a synchronization object being signaled, the return value will be *WAIT_OBJECT_0* plus an index into the handle array that was passed in the *lpHandles* parameter. For example, if the first handle in the array unblocked the thread, the return code would be *WAIT_OBJECT_0*; if the second handle was the cause, the return code would be *WAIT_OBJECT_0* + 1. The other return codes used by *WaitForSingleObject*—*WAIT_TIMEOUT*, *WAIT_ABANDONED*, and *WAIT_FAILED*—are also returned by *WaitForMultipleObjects* for the same reasons.

Waiting While Dealing with Messages

The Win32 API provides other functions that allow you to wait on a set of objects as well as messages: *MsgWaitForMultipleObjects* and *MsgWaitForMultipleObjectsEx*. These functions are fairly similar, so I'll describe only *MsgWaitForMultipleObjectsEx and then mention where MsgWaitForMultipleObjects fits in.* This function essentially combines the wait function, *MsgW aitForMultipleObjects*, with an additional check into the message queue so that the function returns if any of the selected categories of messages are received during the wait. The prototype for this function is the following:

```
DWORD MsgWaitForMultipleObjectsEx  (DWORD nCount, LPHANDLE pHandles,
                                    DWORD dwMilliseconds,
                                    DWORD dwWakeMasks, DWORD dwFlags);
```

This function has a number of limitations under Windows CE. As with *WaitForMultipleObjects*, *MsgWaitForMultipleObjectsEx* can't wait for all objects to be signaled. Nor are all the *dwWakeMask* flags supported by Windows CE. Windows CE supports the following flags in *dwWakeMask*. Each flag indicates a category of messages that, when received in the message queue of the thread, causes the function to return.

- **QS_ALLINPUT** Any message has been received.
- **QS_INPUT** An input message has been received.
- **QS_KEY** A key up, key down, or syskey up or down message has been received.
- **QS_MOUSE** A mouse move or mouse click message has been received.
- **QS_MOUSEBUTTON** A mouse click message has been received.

- **QS_MOUSEMOVE** A mouse move message has been received.
- **QS_PAINT** A WM_PAINT message has been received.
- **QS_POSTMESSAGE** A posted message, other than those in this list, has been received.
- **QS_SENDMESSAGE** A sent message, other than those in this list, has been received.
- **QS_TIMER** A WM_TIMER message has been received.

The function is used inside the message loop so that an action or actions can take place in response to the signaling of a synchronization object while your program is still processing messages. The *dwFlags* value can be zero, or the flag *MWMO_INPUTAVAILABLE*. This flag causes the function to return if there is a message already in the queue when the funciton is called. If *MWMO_INPUTAVAILABLE* is not set, *MsgWaitForMultipleObjectsEx will wait until a new qualifying message* is added to the queue. The function of *MsgWaitForMultipleObjects is identical to MsgWaitForMultipleObjectsEx with the flags value set to zero.*

The return value is *WAIT_OBJECT_0* up to *WAIT_OBJECT_0* + *nCount* -1 for the objects in the handle array. If a message causes the function to return, the return value is *WAIT_OBJECT_0* + *nCount*. An example of how this function might be used follows. In this code, the handle array has only one entry, *hSyncHandle*.

```
fContinue = TRUE;
while (fContinue) {
    rc = MsgWaitForMultipleObjects (1, &hSyncHandle, FALSE,
                                    INFINITE, QS_ALLINPUT);
    if (rc == WAIT_OBJECT_0) {
        //
        // Do work as a result of sync object.
        //
    } else if (rc == WAIT_OBJECT_0 + 1) {
        // It's a message; process it.
        PeekMessage (&msg, hWnd, 0, 0, PM_REMOVE);
        if (msg.message == WM_QUIT)
            fContinue = FALSE;
        else {
            TranslateMessage (&msg);
            DispatchMessage (&msg);
        }
    }
}
```

Semaphores

Earlier I described the event object. That object resides in either a signaled or a nonsignaled state. Events are synchronization objects that are all or nothing, signaled or nonsignaled. Semaphores, on the other hand, maintain a count. As long as that count is above 0, the semaphore is signaled. When the count is 0, the semaphore is nonsignaled.

Threads wait on semaphore objects as they do events, using *WaitForSingleObject* or *WaitForMultipleObjects*. When a thread waits on a semaphore, the thread is blocked until the count is greater than 0. When another thread releases the semaphore, the count is incremented and the thread blocking on the semaphore returns from the wait function. The maximum count value is defined when the semaphore is created so that a programmer can define how many threads can access a resource protected by a semaphore.

Semaphores are typically used to protect a resource that can be accessed only by a set number of threads at one time. For example, if you have a set of five buffers for passing data, you can allow up to five threads to grab a buffer at any one time. When a sixth thread attempts to access the buffer array protected by the semaphore, it will be blocked until one of the other threads releases the semaphore.

To create a semaphore, call the function

```
HANDLE CreateSemaphore (LPSECURITY_ATTRIBUTES lpSemaphoreAttributes,
                        LONG lInitialCount, LONG lMaximumCount,
                        LPCTSTR lpName);
```

The first parameter, *lpSemaphoreAttributes*, should be set to *NULL*. The parameter *lInitialCount* is the count value when the semaphore is created and must be greater than or equal to 0. If this value is greater than 0, the semaphore will be initially signaled. The *lMaximumCount* parameter should be set to the maximum allowable count value the semaphore will allow. This value must be greater than 0.

The final parameter, *lpName*, is the optional name of the object. This parameter can point to a name or be *NULL*. As with events, if two threads call *CreateSemaphore* and pass the same name, the second call to *CreateSemaphore* returns the handle to the original semaphore instead of creating a new object. In this case, the other parameters, *lInitialCount* and *lMaximumCount*, are ignored. To determine whether the semaphore already exists, you can call *GetLastError* and check the return code for *ERROR_ALREADY_EXISTS*.

When a thread returns from waiting on a semaphore, it can perform its work with the knowledge that only *lMaximumCount* threads or fewer are running within the protection of the semaphore. When a thread has completed work with the protected resource, it should release the semaphore with a call to

```
BOOL ReleaseSemaphore (HANDLE hSemaphore, LONG lReleaseCount,
                       LPLONG lpPreviousCount);
```

The first parameter is the handle to the semaphore. The *lReleaseCount* parameter contains the number by which you want to increase the semaphore's count value. This value must be greater than 0. While you might expect this value to always be 1, sometimes a thread might increase the count by more than 1. The final parameter, *lpPreviousCount*, is set to the address of a variable that will receive the previous resource count of the semaphore. You can set this pointer to *NULL* if you don't need the previous count value.

To destroy a semaphore, call *CloseHandle*. If more than one thread has created the same semaphore, all threads must call *CloseHandle*; or more precisely, *CloseHandle* must be called as many times as *CreateSemaphore* was called before the operating system destroys the semaphore.

Another function, *OpenSemaphore*, is supported on the desktop versions of Windows but not supported by Windows CE. This function is redundant on Windows CE because a thread that wants the handle to a named semaphore can just as easily call *CreateSemaphore* and check the return code from *GetLastError* to determine whether it already exists.

Mutexes

Another synchronization object is the *mutex*. A mutex is a synchronization object that's signaled when it's not owned by a thread and nonsignaled when it *is* owned. Mutexes are extremely useful for coordinating exclusive access to a resource such as a block of memory across multiple threads.

A thread gains ownership by waiting on that mutex with one of the wait functions. When no other threads own the mutex, the thread waiting on the mutex is unblocked and implicitly gains ownership of the mutex. After the thread has completed the work that requires ownership of the mutex, the thread must explicitly release the mutex with a call to *ReleaseMutex*.

To create a mutex, call this function:

```
HANDLE CreateMutex (LPSECURITY_ATTRIBUTES lpMutexAttributes,
                    BOOL bInitialOwner, LPCTSTR lpName);
```

The *lpMutexAttributes* parameter should be set to *NULL*. The *bInitialOwner* parameter lets you specify that the calling thread should immediately own the mutex being created. Finally, the *lpName* parameter lets you specify a name for the object so that it can be shared across other processes. When calling *CreateMutex* with a name specified in the *lpName* parameter, Windows CE checks whether a mutex with the same name has already been created. If so, a handle to the previously created mutex is returned. To determine whether the mutex already exists, call *GetLastError*. It returns *ERROR_ALREADY_EXISTS* if the mutex has been previously created.

Gaining immediate ownership of a mutex using the *bInitialOwner* parameter works only if the mutex is being created. Ownership isn't granted if you're opening a previously created mutex. If you need ownership of a mutex, be sure to call *GetLastError* to determine whether the mutex had been previously committed. If so, call *WaitForSingleObject* to gain ownership of the mutex.

You release the mutex with this function:

```
BOOL ReleaseMutex (HANDLE hMutex);
```

The only parameter is the handle to the mutex.

If a thread owns a mutex and calls one of the wait functions to wait on that same mutex, the wait call immediately returns because the thread already owns the mutex. Because mutexes retain an ownership count for the number of times the wait functions are called, a call to *ReleaseMutex* must be made for each nested call to the wait function.

To close a mutex, call *CloseHandle*. As with events and semaphores, if multiple threads have opened the same mutex, the operating system doesn't destroy the mutex until it has been closed the same number of times that *CreateMutex* was called.

Duplicating Synchronization Handles

Event, semaphore, and mutex handles are process specific, meaning that they can't be passed from one process to another.[4] The ability to name each of these kernel objects makes it easy for each process to "create" an event of the same name, which, as we've seen, simply opens the same event for both processes. There are times, however, when having to name an event is overkill. An example of this situation might be using an event to signal the end of asynchronous I/O between an application and a driver. The driver shouldn't have to create a new and unique event name and pass it to the application for each operation.

The *DuplicateHandle* function exists to avoid having to name events, mutexes, and semaphores all the time. It is prototyped as follows:

```
BOOL DuplicateHandle (HANDLE hSourceProcessHandle, HANDLE hSourceHandle,
                      HANDLE hTargetProcessHandle, LPHANDLE lpTargetHandle,
                      DWORD dwDesiredAccess, BOOL bInheritHandle,
                      DWORD wOptions);
```

The first parameter is the handle of the process that owns the source handle. If a process is duplicating its own handle, it can get this handle by using *GetCurrentProcess*. The second parameter is the handle to be duplicated. The third and fourth parameters are the handle of the destination process and a pointer to a variable that will receive the duplicated handle. The *dwDesiredAccess* parameter is ignored, and the *bInheritHandle* parameter must be *FALSE*. The *dwOptions* parameter must have the flag *DUPLICATE_SAME_ACCESS* set. The parameter can optionally have the *DUPLICATE_CLOSE_SOURCE* flag set, indicating that the source handle should be closed if the handle is successfully duplicated.

Starting with Windows CE 6, DuplicateHandle can duplicate all types of operating system handles including file, process, and thread handles. Earlier versions of Windows CE restricted *DuplicateHandle* to only duplicating event, mutex, and semaphore handles.

[4] In earlier versions of Windows CE, handle sharing across processes was discouraged even though it worked. Starting with Windows CE 6, handles can not be shared across processes.

Critical Sections

Using *critical sections* is another method of thread synchronization. Critical sections are good for protecting sections of code from being executed by two different threads at the same time. Critical sections work by having a thread call *EnterCriticalSection* to indicate that it has entered a critical section of code. If another thread calls *EnterCriticalSection* referencing the same critical section object, it's blocked until the first thread makes a call to *LeaveCriticalSection*. Critical sections can protect more than one linear section of code. All that's required is that all sections of code that need to be protected use the same critical section object. The one limitation of critical sections is that they can only be used to coordinate threads within the same process.

Critical sections are similar to mutexes, with a few important differences. On the downside, critical sections are limited to a single process by means of which mutexes can be shared across processes. But this limitation is also an advantage. Because they're isolated to a single process, critical sections are implemented so that they're significantly faster than mutexes. If you don't need to share a resource across a process boundary, always use a critical section instead of a mutex.

To use a critical section, you first create a critical section handle with this function:

```
void InitializeCriticalSection (LPCRITICAL_SECTION lpCriticalSection);
```

The only parameter is a pointer to a *CRITICAL_SECTION* structure that you define somewhere in your application. Be sure not to allocate this structure on the stack of a function that will be deallocated as soon the function returns. You should also not move or copy the critical section structure. Because the other critical section functions require a pointer to this structure, you'll need to allocate it within the scope of all functions using the critical section. While the *CRITICAL_SECTION* structure is defined in WINBASE.H, an application doesn't need to manipulate any of the fields in that structure. So for all practical purposes, think of a pointer to a *CRITICAL_SECTION* structure as a handle instead of as a pointer to a structure of a known format.

When a thread needs to enter a protected section of code, it should call this function:

```
void EnterCriticalSection (LPCRITICAL_SECTION lpCriticalSection);
```

The function takes as its only parameter a pointer to the critical section structure initialized with *InitializeCriticalSection*. If the critical section is already owned by another thread, this function blocks the new thread and doesn't return until the other thread releases the critical section. If the thread calling *EnterCriticalSection* already owns the critical section, a use count is incremented and the function returns immediately.

If you need to enter a critical section but can't afford to be blocked waiting for that critical section, you can use the function

```
BOOL TryEnterCriticalSection (LPCRITICAL_SECTION lpCriticalSection);
```

TryEnterCriticalSection differs from *EnterCriticalSection* because it always returns immediately. If the critical section was unowned, the function returns *TRUE* and the thread now owns the critical section. If the critical section is owned by another thread, the function returns *FALSE*. This function allows a thread to attempt to perform work in a critical section without being forced to wait until the critical section is free.

When a thread leaves a critical section, it should call this function:

```
void LeaveCriticalSection (LPCRITICAL_SECTION lpCriticalSection);
```

As with all the critical section functions, the only parameter is the pointer to the critical section structure. Because critical sections track a use count, one call to *LeaveCriticalSection* must be made for each call to *EnterCriticalSection* by the thread that owns the section.

Finally, when you're finished with the critical section, you should call

```
void DeleteCriticalSection (LPCRITICAL_SECTION lpCriticalSection);
```

This action cleans up any system resources used to manage the critical section.

Interlocked Variable Access

Here's one more low-level method for synchronizing threads—using the functions for interlocked access to variables. While programmers with multithread experience already know this, I need to warn you that Murphy's Law[5] seems to come into its own when you're using multiple threads in a program. One of the sometimes overlooked issues in a preemptive multitasking system is that a thread can be preempted in the middle of incrementing or checking a variable. For example, a simple code fragment such as

```
if (!i++) {
    // Do something because i was 0.
}
```

can cause a great deal of trouble. To understand why, let's look into how that statement might be compiled. The assembly code for that *if* statement might look something like this:

```
load    reg1, [addr of i]          ;Read variable
add     reg2, reg1, 1              ;reg2 = reg1 + 1
store   reg2, [addr of i]          ;Save incremented var
bne     reg1, zero, skipblk        ;Branch reg1 != zero
```

[5] Murphy's Law: Anything that can go wrong will go wrong. Murphy's first corollary: When something goes wrong, it happens at the worst possible moment.

There's no reason that the thread executing this section of code couldn't be preempted by another thread after the load instruction and before the store instruction. If this happened, two threads could enter the block of code when that isn't the way the code is supposed to work. Of course, I've already described a number of methods (such as critical sections and the like) that you can use to prevent such incidents from occurring. But for something like this, a critical section is overkill. What you need is something lighter.

Windows CE supports the full set of *interlocked* functions from the Win32 API. The first three, *InterlockedIncrement*, *InterlockedDecrement*, and *InterlockedExchange*, allow a thread to increment, decrement, and in some cases optionally exchange a variable without your having to worry about the thread being preempted in the middle of the operation. The other functions allow variables to be added to and optionally exchanged. The functions are prototyped here:

```
LONG InterlockedIncrement(LPLONG lpAddend);

LONG InterlockedDecrement(LPLONG lpAddend);

LONG InterlockedExchange(LPLONG Target, LONG Value);
LONG InterlockedCompareExchange (LPLONG Destination, LONG Exchange,
                                 LONG Comperand);
LONG InterlockedTestExchange (LPLONG Target, LONG OldValue, LONG NewValue);LONG Interlo
ckedExchangeAdd (LPLONG Addend, LONG Increment);
PVOID InterlockedCompareExchangePointer (PVOID* Destination,
                                         PVOID Exchange, PVOID Comperand);
PVOID InterlockedExchangePointer (PVOID* Target, PVOID Value);
```

For the interlocked increment and decrement, the one parameter is a pointer to the variable to increment or decrement. The returned value is the new value of the variable after it has been incremented or decremented. The *InterlockedExchange* function takes a pointer to the target variable and the new value for the variable. It returns the previous value of the variable. Rewriting the previous code fragment so that it's thread safe produces this code:

```
if (!InterlockedIncrement(&i)) {
    // Do something because i was 0.
}
```

The *InterlockedCompareExchange* and *InterlockedTestExchange* functions exchange a value with the target only if the target value is equal to the test parameter. Otherwise, the original value is left unchanged. The only difference between the two functions is the order of the parameters.

InterlockedExchangeAdd adds the second parameter to the *LONG* pointed to by the first parameter. The value returned by the function is the original value before the add operation. The final two functions, *InterlockedCompareExchangePointer* and *InterlockedExchangePointer*, are identical to the *InterlockedCompareExchange* and *InterlockedExchange* functions, but the parameters have been type cast to pointers instead of longs.

Interprocess Communication

Quite often, two Windows CE processes need to communicate. The walls between processes that protect processes from one another prevent casual exchanging of data. The memory space of one process isn't exposed to another process. Handles to files or other objects can't be passed from one process to another. Windows CE doesn't support handle inheritance. Some of the other more common methods of interprocess communication, such as named pipes, are also not supported under Windows CE. However, you can choose from plenty of ways to enable two or more processes to exchange data.

Finding Other Processes

Before you can communicate with another process, you have to determine whether it's running on the system. Strategies for finding whether another process is running depend mainly on whether you have control of the other process. If the process to be found is a third-party application in which you have no control over the design of the other process, the best method might be to use the *FindWindow* function to locate the other process's main window. *FindWindow* can search either by window class or by window title. You can enumerate the top-level windows in the system using *EnumWindows*. You can also use the ToolHelp debugging functions to enumerate the processes running, but this works only when the ToolHelp DLL is loaded on the system, and unfortunately, it generally isn't included, by default, on most systems.

If you're writing both processes, however, it's much easier to enumerate them. In this case, the best methods include using the tools you'll later use in one process to communicate with the other process, such as named mutexes, events, or memory-mapped objects. When you create one of these objects, you can determine whether you're the first to create the object or you're simply opening another object by calling *GetLastError* after another call created the object. And the simplest method might be the best: call *FindWindow*.

The classic case of using *FindWindow* on a Windows Mobile device occurs when an application must determine whether another copy of itself is already running. According to the Windows Mobile guidelines, an application must allow only one copy of itself to run at a time. Following is a code fragment that all the examples in this book use for accomplishing this task:

```
// If Windows Mobile, allow only one instance of the application.
    HWND hWnd = FindWindow (szAppName, NULL);
    if (hWnd) {
        SetForegroundWindow ((HWND)(((DWORD)hWnd) | 0x01));
        return -1;
    }
```

The first statement uses *FindWindow* to find a window class of the same name as the class of the application's main window. Because this call is made before the main window is created in the application, the only way the window could have been found, assuming you're using a unique name for your window class, is for it to have already been created by another copy of your application. An advantage of this technique is that *FindWindow* returns the handle of the main window of the other instance. In the case of a Windows Mobile device, we want to set that instance in the foreground, which is what we do with the subsequent call to *SetForegroundWindow*. Setting the least significant bit of the window handle is a hack of Windows CE that causes the window being activated to be restored if it was in a minimized state.

WM_COPYDATA

After you find your target process, the conversation can begin. If you're staying at the window level, you can simply send a *WM_COPYDATA* message. *WM_COPYDATA* is unique in that it's designed to send blocks of data from one process to another. You can't use a standard user-defined message to pass pointers to data from one process to another because a pointer isn't valid across processes. *WM_COPYDATA* gets around this problem by having the system translate the pointer to a block of data from one process's address space to another's. The recipient process is required to copy the data immediately into its own memory space, but this message does provide a quick-and-dirty method of sending blocks of data from one process to another.

Named Memory-Mapped Objects

The problem with *WM_COPYDATA* is that it can be used only to copy fixed blocks of data at a specific time. Windows CE supports entities referred to as *memory-mapped objects*. These are objects that are backed up by the paging file under other vesions of Windows. Under Windows CE, they are simply areas of virtual memory with only physical RAM to back them up. Without the paging file, these objects can't be as big as they would be on the desktop, but Windows CE does have a way of minimizing the RAM required to back up the memory-mapped object.

Using a named memory-mapped object, two processes can allocate a shared block of memory that's equally accessible to both processes at the same time. You must use named memory-mapped objects so that both processes will be accessing the same block. The system can maintain a proper use count on the object, not freeing it until all processes that opened the block have closed it.

Of course, this level of interaction comes with a price. You need some synchronization between the processes when they're reading and writing data in the shared memory block. The use of named mutexes and named events allows processes to coordinate their actions. Using these synchronization objects requires the use of secondary threads so that the message loop can be serviced, but this isn't an exceptional burden.

You create such a memory-mapped object by calling *CreateFileMapping*. This function is defined as

```
HANDLE CreateFileMapping (HANDLE hFile,
                          LPSECURITY_ATTRIBUTES lpFileMappingAttributes,
                          DWORD flProtect, DWORD dwMaximumSizeHigh,
                          DWORD dwMaximumSizeLow, LPCTSTR lpName);
```

This function creates a file-mapping object and optionally ties the opened file to it. The first parameter for this function is the handle to the opened file. When creating a mapping object without a file, pass the value *INVALID_HANDLE_VALUE*. The security attributes parameter must be set to *NULL* under Windows CE. The *flProtect* parameter should be loaded with the protection flags for the virtual pages that will contain the file data. These flags were described during the discussion of the virtual memory functions in Chapter 7. The maximum size parameters should be set to the expected maximum size of the object. The *lpName* parameter allows you to specify a name for the object. This is handy when you're using a memory-mapped file to share information across different processes. Calling *CreateFileMapping* with the name of an already-opened file-mapping object returns a handle to the object already opened instead of creating a new one.

After a mapping object has been created, a view into the object is created by calling

```
LPVOID MapViewOfFile (HANDLE hFileMappingObject, DWORD dwDesiredAccess,
                      DWORD dwFileOffsetHigh, DWORD dwFileOffsetLow,
                      DWORD dwNumberOfBytesToMap);
```

MapViewOfFile returns a pointer to memory that's mapped to the file. The function takes as its parameters the handle of the mapping object just opened as well as the access rights, which can be *FILE_MAP_READ*, *FILE_MAP_WRITE*, or *FILE_MAP_ALL_ACCESS*. The offset parameters let you specify the starting point within the file that the view starts, while the *dwNumberOfBytesToMap* parameter specifies the size of the view window.

These last three parameters are useful when you're mapping large objects. Instead of attempting to map the file as one large object, you can specify a smaller view that starts at the point of interest in the file. This reduces the memory required because only the view of the object, not the object itself, is backed up by physical RAM.

The following routine creates a 16-MB region by using a memory-mapped file:

```
// Create a 16-MB memory-mapped object.
hNFileMap = CreateFileMapping (INVALID_HANDLE_VALUE, NULL, PAGE_READWRITE,
                               0, 0x1000000, NULL);
 if (hNFileMap)
    // Map in the object.
    pNFileMem = MapViewOfFile (hNFileMap,
                               FILE_MAP_WRITE, 0, 0, 0);
```

The memory object created by this code doesn't actually commit 16 MB of RAM. Instead, only the address space is reserved. Pages are autocommitted as they're accessed. This process allows an application to create a huge, sparse array of pages that takes up only as much physical RAM as is needed to hold the data. At some point, however, if you start reading or writing to a greater number of pages, you'll run out of memory. When this happens, the system generates an exception. I'll talk about how to deal with exceptions later in this chapter. The important thing to remember is that if you really need RAM to be committed to a memory-mapped object, you need to read each of the pages so that the system will commit physical RAM to that object. Of course, don't be too greedy with RAM; commit only the pages you absolutely require.

When you finish with the mapping object, close the view with

```
BOOL UnmapViewOfFile (LPCVOID lpBaseAddress);
```

The only parameter is the pointer to the base address of the view. Next, a call should be made to close the mapping object with a call to *CloseHandle*.

Naming a Memory-Mapped Object

A memory-mapped object can be named by passing a string to *CreateFileMapping*. This isn't the name of a file being mapped. Instead, the name identifies the mapping object being created. In the preceding example, the region was unnamed. The following code creates a memory-mapped object named *Bob*. This name is global so that if another process opens a mapping object with the same name, the two processes will share the same memory-mapped object.

```
// Create a 16-MB memory-mapped object.
hNFileMap = CreateFileMapping ((HANDLE)-1, NULL, PAGE_READWRITE,
                               0, 0x1000000, TEXT ("Bob"));
if (hNFileMap)
    // Map in the object.
    pNFileMem = MapViewOfFile (hNFileMap,
                               FILE_MAP_WRITE, 0, 0, 0);
```

The difference between named and unnamed file mapping objects is that a named object is allocated only once in the system. Subsequent calls to *CreateFileMapping* that attempt to create a region with the same name will succeed, but the function will return a handle to the original mapping object instead of creating a new one. For unnamed objects, the system creates a new object each time *CreateFileMapping* is called.

When you're using a memory-mapped object for interprocess communication, processes should create a named object and pass the name of the region to the second process rather than pass a pointer. While earlier versions of Windows CE could simply pass a pointer to the mapping region from one process to the other, this can't be done on Windows CE 6 and later. Instead, the second process must create a memory-mapped object with the same name as the initial process. Windows knows to pass a pointer to the same region that was opened by the first process. The system also increments a use count to track the number of opens. A named memory-mapped object won't be destroyed until all processes have closed the object. This system assures a process that the object will remain at least until it closes the object itself. The XTalk example, presented later in this chapter, provides an example of how to use a named memory-mapped object for interprocess communication.

Point-to-Point Message Queues

Windows CE supports a method of interprocess communication called *point-to-point message queues*. The Message Queue API, as the name suggests, provides data queues for sending data from one process to another.

To communicate with a message queue, a process or pair of processes creates a message queue for reading and one for writing. A call to create or open a queue can specify only read or write access, not both read and write access. The queue is then opened again for the corresponding write or read access. "Messages" are then written to the queue by using the write handle to the queue. (In this context, a message is simply a block of data with a defined length.) The message can be read by using the read handle to the queue. If a series of messages is written to a queue, they are read in the order they were written in classic first in, first out (FIFO) fashion. When a queue is created, the number and the maximum size of messages are defined for the queue. If the queue is full and a write occurs, the write function will either block (waiting for a free slot in the queue), fail and return immediately, or wait for a specific amount of time before failing and returning. Likewise, read functions can block until a message is in the queue to be read, or they can wait a specific period of time before returning.

In addition, a message can be marked as an "alert" message. Alert messages are sent to the front of the queue so that the next read of the queue will read the alert message regardless of the number of messages that have been waiting to be read. Only one alert message can be in the queue at any one time. If a second alert message is written to the queue before the first one was read, the second alert message replaces the first and the first alert message is lost.

Finally, it's perfectly valid for more than one thread or process to open the same queue for read access or for write access. Point-to-point message queues support multiple readers and multiple writers. This practice allows, for example, one writer process to send messages to mutiple client processes or multiple writer processes to send messages to a single reader process. There is, however, no way to address a message to a specific reader process. When a process, or a thread, reads the queue, it will read the next available message. There is also no way to broadcast a message to multiple readers.

To create a message queue, call this function:

```
HANDLE CreateMsgQueue (LPCWSTR lpszName, LPMSGQUEUEOPTIONS lpOptions);
```

The first parameter is the name of the queue that will be either opened or created. The name is global to the entire system. That is, if one process opens a queue with a name and another process opens a queue with the same name, they open the same queue. The name can be up to *MAX_PATH* characters in length. The parameter can also be set to *NULL* to create an unnamed queue.

The second parameter of *CreateMsgQueue* is a pointer to a *MSGQUEUEOPTIONS* structure defined as follows:

```
typedef MSGQUEUEOPTIONS_OS {
    DWORD dwSize;
    DWORD dwFlags;
    DWORD dwMaxMessages;
    DWORD cbMaxMessage;
    BOOL bReadAccess
} MSGQUEUEOPTIONS;
```

The *dwSize* field must be filled in with the size of the structure. The *dwFlags* parameter describes how the queue should act. The flags supported are *MSGQUEUE_NOPRECOMMIT*, which tells Windows CE not to allocate the RAM necessary to support messages in the queue until the RAM is needed; and *MSGQUEUE_ALLOW_BROKEN*, which allows writes and reads to the queue to succeed even if another call hasn't been made to open the queue for the matching read or write of the message. The *dwMaxMessages* field should be set to the maximum number of messages that are expected to be in the queue at any one time. The *cbMaxMessage* field indicates the maximum size of any single message. Finally, the *bReadAccess* field should be set to *TRUE* if read access is desired for the queue and *FALSE* if write access is desired. A single call to *CreateMsgQueue* can only create the queue for either read or write access.

The function returns the handle to the queue if successful, or *NULL* if the function failed. The handle returned by *CreateMsgQueue* is an event handle that can be waited on with *WaitForSingleObject* and the other related *Wait* functions. The event is signaled when the state of the queue changes, either by a new message being placed in the queue or by an entry in the queue becoming available.

CreateMsgQueue will succeed even if a queue of the same name already exists. *GetLastError* will return *ERROR_ALREADY_EXISTS* if the queue existed before the call to *CreateMsgQueue*.

A previously created message queue can be opened with this function:

```
HANDLE  OpenMsgQueue (HANDLE hSrcProc, HANDLE hMsgQ,
                      LPMSGQUEUEOPTIONS pOptions);
```

The advantage of *OpenMsgQueue* is that the queue doesn't have to be named. The parameters are the process handle of the process that originally opened the message queue. This handle is typically obtained with a call to *OpenProcess*. The second parameter is the handle returned by *CreateMsgQueue*. The last parameter is a pointer to a *MSGQUEUEOPTIONS* structure. The only fields in the *MSGQUEUEOPTIONS* structure examined by the function are the *dwSize* field and the *bReadAccess* field.

To write a message to the queue, the aptly named *WriteMsgQueue* function is used. It is prototyped as follows:

```
BOOL WriteMsgQueue (HANDLE hMsgQ, LPVOID lpBuffer, DWORD cbDataSize,
                    DWORD dwTimeout, DWORD dwFlags);
```

The initial parameter is the write handle to the message queue. The *lpBuffer* parameter points to the buffer containing the message, whereas *cbDataSize* should be set to the size of the message. If *cbDataSize* is greater than the maximum message size set when the queue was created, the call will fail.

The *dwTimeout* parameter specifies the time, in milliseconds, that *WriteMsgQueue* should wait for a slot in the queue to become available before returning. If *dwTimeout* is set to 0, the call will fail and return immediately if the queue is currently full. If *dwTimeout* is set to *INFINITE*, the call will wait until a slot becomes free to write the message. The *dwFlags* parameter can be set to *MSGQUEUE_MSGALERT* to indicate that the message being written is an alert message.

The return value from *WriteMsgQueue* is a Boolean, with *TRUE* indicating success. The function will fail if the queue has not been opened for read access and *MSGQUEUE_ALLOW_BROKEN* was not specified when the queue was created. To determine the reason for failure, call *GetLastError*.

To read a message from the queue, the function *ReadMsgQueue* is used. It's prototyped as follows:

```
BOOL ReadMsgQueue (HANDLE hMsgQ, LPVOID lpBuffer, DWORD cbBufferSize,
                   LPDWORD lpNumberOfBytesRead, DWORD dwTimeout,
                   DWORD* pdwFlags);
```

As with *WriteMsgQueue*, the first two parameters are the handle to the message queue, the pointer to the buffer that, in this case, will receive the message. The *cbBufferSize* parameter should be set to the size of the buffer. If *cbBufferSize* is less than the size of the message at the head of the queue, the read will fail with *ERROR_INSUFFICIENT_BUFFER* returned by a call to *GetLastError*.

The *lpNumberOfBytesRead* parameter should point to a *DWORD* that will receive the size of the message read. The *dwTimeout* parameter specifies how long the function should wait until a message is present in the queue to read. As with *WriteMsgQueue*, passing 0 in this parameter causes *ReadMsgQueue* to fail and return immediately if there is no message in the queue. Passing *INFINITE* in the *dwTimeout* parameter causes the call to wait until there is a message in the queue before returning. The *pdwFlags* parameter should point to a *DWORD* that will receive the flags associated with the message read. The only flag currently defined is *MSGQUEUE_MSGALERT*, which indicates that the message just read was an alert message.

You can query the configuration of a message queue with this function:

```
BOOL GetMsgQueueInfo (HANDLE hMsgQ, LPMSGQUEUEINFO lpInfo);
```

The parameters are the handle to the message queue and a pointer to a *MSGQUEUEINFO* structure defined as follows:

```
typedef MSGQUEUEINFO {
    DWORD dwSize;
    DWORD dwFlags;
    DWORD dwMaxMessages;
    DWORD cbMaxMessage;
    DWORD dwCurrentMessages;
    DWORD dwMaxQueueMessages;
    WORD wNumReaders;
    WORD wNumWriters
} MSGQUEUEINFO;
```

The first few fields in this structure match the *MSGQUEUEOPTIONS* structure used in creating and opening queues. The field *dwSize* should be set to the size of the structure before the call to *GetMsgQueueInfo* is made. The remaining fields are filled in by a successful call to *GetMsgQueueInfo*.

The *dwFlags* field will be set to the queue flags, which are *MSGQUEUE_NOPRECOMMIT* and *MSGQUEUE_ALLOW_BROKEN*. The *dwMaxMessages* field contains the maximum number of messages the queue can contain, while *cbMaxMessage* contains the maximum size of any single message.

The *dwCurrentMessages* field is set to the number of messages currently in the queue waiting to be read. The *dwMaxQueueMessages* field is set to the maximum number of messages that were ever in the queue. The *wNumReaders* field is set to the number of handles opened for read access for the queue, while *wNumWriters* is set to the number of handles opened for write access.

To close a message queue, call this function:

```
BOOL CloseMsgQueue (HANDLE hMsgQ);
```

The single parameter is the handle to the queue. Because queues must be opened at least twice, once for reading and once for writing, this call must be made at least twice per queue.

Message queues are great for interprocess communication because they are fast and they are thread safe. Messages can be almost any size, although for long queues with really huge buffers it might be best to allocate data buffers dynamically by using memory-mapped objects and by using message queues to pass pointers to the large data buffers.

Communicating with Files and Databases

A more basic method of interprocess communication is the use of files or a custom database. These methods provide a robust, if slower, communication path. Slow is relative. Files and databases in the Windows CE object store are slow in the sense that the system calls to access these objects must find the data in the object store, uncompress the data, and deliver it to the process. However, because the object store is based in RAM, you see none of the extreme slowness of a mechanical hard disk that you'd see under the desktop versions of Windows. To improve performance with files in the object store, the *FILE_FLAG_RANDOM_ACCESS* flag should be used. Of course, when using files for communication, make sure the underlying file system *is* the object store. If it's flash based or hard drive based, the performance will be quite slow.

The XTalk Example Program

The following example program, XTalk, uses events, mutexes, and a shared memory-mapped block of memory to communicate among different copies of itself. The example demonstrates the rather common problem of one-to-many communication. In this case, the XTalk window has an edit box with a Send button next to it. When a user taps the Send button, the text in the edit box is communicated to every copy of XTalk running on the system. Each copy of XTalk receives the text from the sending copy and places it in a list box, also in the XTalk window. Figure 8-1 shows two XTalk programs communicating.

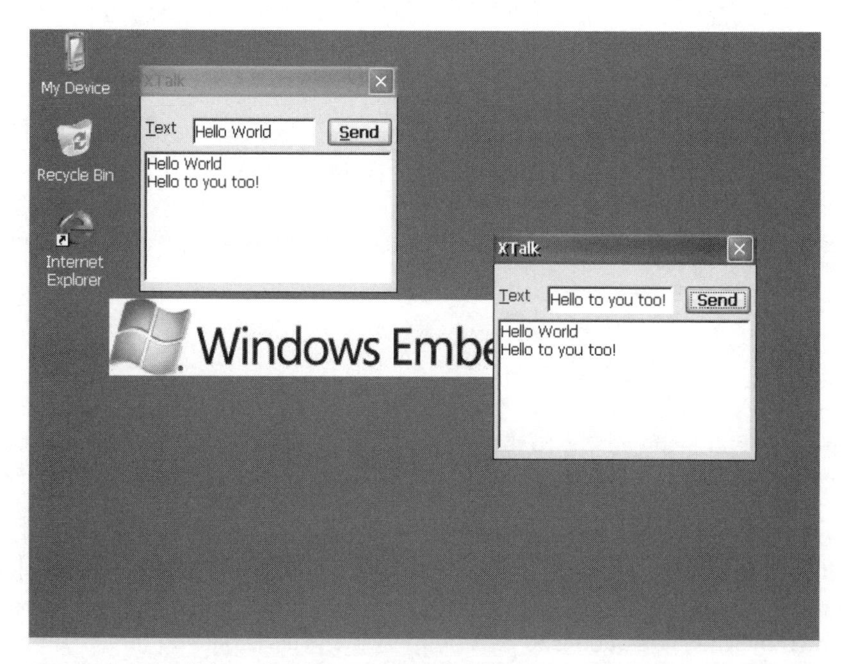

FIGURE 8-1 The desktop showing two XTalk windows

To perform this feat of communication, XTalk uses a named memory-mapped object as a transfer buffer, a mutex to coordinate access to the buffer, and two event objects to indicate the start and end of communication. A third event is used to tell the sender thread to read the text from the edit control and write the contents to the shared memory block. Listing 8-1 shows the source code for XTalk.

LISTING 8-1

XTalk.rc

```
//======================================================================
// Resource file
//
// Written for the book Programming Windows CE
// Copyright (C) 2007 Douglas Boling
//======================================================================
#include "windows.h"
#include "xtalk.h"                            // Program-specific stuff

//----------------------------------------------------------------------
// Icons and bitmaps
//
ID_ICON ICON   "xtalk.ico"                    // Program icon

//----------------------------------------------------------------------
xtalk DIALOG discardable 10, 10, 120, 87
STYLE  WS_OVERLAPPED | WS_VISIBLE | WS_CAPTION | WS_SYSMENU |
       DS_CENTER | DS_MODALFRAME
CAPTION "XTalk"
CLASS "xtalk"
BEGIN
    LTEXT "&Text"                     -1,   2,  10,  20,  12
    EDITTEXT                IDD_OUTTEXT,  25,  10,  58,  12,
                                         WS_TABSTOP | ES_AUTOHSCROLL
    PUSHBUTTON "&Send",    IDD_SENDTEXT,  88,  10,  30,  12, WS_TABSTOP

    LISTBOX                  IDD_INTEXT,   2,  25, 116,  60,
                                         WS_TABSTOP | WS_VSCROLL
END
```

XTalk.h

```
//======================================================================
// Header file
//
// Written for the book Programming Windows CE
// Copyright (C) 2007 Douglas Boling
//======================================================================
// Returns number of elements
#define dim(x) (sizeof(x) / sizeof(x[0]))
```

```
//----------------------------------------------------------------------
// Generic defines and data types
//
struct decodeUINT {                              // Structure associates
    UINT Code;                                   // messages
                                                 // with a function.
 LRESULT (*Fxn)(HWND, UINT, WPARAM, LPARAM);
};
struct decodeCMD {                               // Structure associates
    UINT Code;                                   // menu IDs with a
    LRESULT (*Fxn)(HWND, WORD, HWND, WORD);      // function.
};

//----------------------------------------------------------------------
// Generic defines used by application
#define  ID_ICON            1

#define  IDD_INTEXT         10                   // Control IDs
#define  IDD_SENDTEXT       11
#define  IDD_OUTTEXT        12

#define  MMBUFFSIZE         1024                 // Size of shared buffer
#define  TEXTSIZE           256

// Interprocess communication structure mapped in shared memory
typedef struct {
#if _WIN32_WCE < 0x600
    LONG nAppCnt;
    LONG nReadCnt;
#else
    LONG volatile nAppCnt;
    LONG volatile nReadCnt;
#endif
    TCHAR szText[TEXTSIZE];
} SHAREBUFF, *PSHAREBUFF;

//----------------------------------------------------------------------
// Function prototypes
//
HWND InitInstance (HINSTANCE, LPWSTR, int);
int TermInstance (HINSTANCE, int);

// Window procedures
LRESULT CALLBACK MainWndProc (HWND, UINT, WPARAM, LPARAM);
// Message handlers
LRESULT DoCreateMain (HWND, UINT, WPARAM, LPARAM);
LRESULT DoSetFocusMain (HWND, UINT, WPARAM, LPARAM);
LRESULT DoCommandMain (HWND, UINT, WPARAM, LPARAM);
LRESULT DoDestroyMain (HWND, UINT, WPARAM, LPARAM);

// Command functions
LPARAM DoMainCommandSend (HWND, WORD, HWND, WORD);
LPARAM DoMainCommandExit (HWND, WORD, HWND, WORD);
```

```
// Thread functions
DWORD WINAPI SenderThread (PVOID pArg);
DWORD WINAPI ReaderThread (PVOID pArg);
```

XTalk.cpp

```
//======================================================================
// XTalk - A simple interprocess communication application for Windows CE
//
// Written for the book Programming Windows CE
// Copyright (C) 2007 Douglas Boling
//======================================================================
#include <windows.h>                    // For all that Windows stuff
#include <commctrl.h>                   // Command bar includes
#include "xtalk.h"                      // Program-specific stuff

// The include and lib files for the Windows Mobile are conditionally
// included so that this example can share the same project file. This
// is necessary because this example must have a menu bar on the
// Windows Mobile device to have a SIP button.
#if defined(WIN32_PLATFORM_PSPC) || defined(WIN32_PLATFORM_WFSP)
#include <aygshell.h>                   // Add Pocket PC includes
#pragma comment( lib, "aygshell" )     // Link Pocket PC lib for menu bar
#endif
//----------------------------------------------------------------------
// Global data
//
const TCHAR szAppName[] = TEXT ("xtalk");
HINSTANCE hInst;                        // Program instance handle

HANDLE g_hMMObj = 0;                    // Memory-mapped object
PSHAREBUFF g_pBuff = 0;                 // Pointer to mm object
HANDLE g_hmWriteOkay = 0;               // Write mutex
HANDLE g_hSendEvent = 0;                // Local send event
HANDLE g_hReadEvent = 0;                // Shared read data event
HANDLE g_hReadDoneEvent = 0;            // Shared data read event
HANDLE g_hSendThread = 0;               // Sender thread handle
HANDLE g_hReadThread = 0;               // Sender thread handle

// Message dispatch table for MainWindowProc
const struct decodeUINT MainMessages[] = {
    WM_CREATE, DoCreateMain,
    WM_SETFOCUS, DoSetFocusMain,
    WM_COMMAND, DoCommandMain,
    WM_DESTROY, DoDestroyMain,
};
// Command Message dispatch for MainWindowProc
const struct decodeCMD MainCommandItems[] = {
    IDOK, DoMainCommandExit,
    IDCANCEL, DoMainCommandExit,
    IDD_SENDTEXT, DoMainCommandSend,
```

```
};
//======================================================================
// Program entry point
//
int WINAPI WinMain (HINSTANCE hInstance, HINSTANCE hPrevInstance,
                    LPWSTR lpCmdLine, int nCmdShow) {
    MSG msg;
    int rc = 0;
    HWND hwndMain;

    // Initialize application.
    hwndMain = InitInstance (hInstance, lpCmdLine, nCmdShow);
    if (hwndMain == 0)
        return TermInstance (hInstance, 0x10);

    // Application message loop
    while (GetMessage (&msg, NULL, 0, 0)) {
        if ((hwndMain == 0) || !IsDialogMessage (hwndMain, &msg)) {
            TranslateMessage (&msg);
            DispatchMessage (&msg);
        }
    }
    // Instance cleanup
    return TermInstance (hInstance, msg.wParam);
}
//----------------------------------------------------------------------
// InitInstance - Instance initialization
//
HWND InitInstance (HINSTANCE hInstance, LPWSTR lpCmdLine, int nCmdShow){
    HWND hWnd;
    RECT rect;
    int rc;
    BOOL fFirstApp = TRUE;
    WNDCLASS wc;

    // Save program instance handle in global variable.
    hInst = hInstance;

    // Register application main window class.
    wc.style = 0;                             // Window style
    wc.lpfnWndProc = MainWndProc;             // Callback function
    wc.cbClsExtra = 0;                        // Extra class data
    wc.cbWndExtra = DLGWINDOWEXTRA;           // Extra window data
    wc.hInstance = hInstance;                 // Owner handle
    wc.hIcon = NULL,                          // Application icon
    wc.hCursor = NULL;                        // Default cursor
    wc.hbrBackground = (HBRUSH) (COLOR_BTNFACE + 1);
    wc.lpszMenuName =  NULL;                  // Menu name
    wc.lpszClassName = szAppName;             // Window class name

    if (RegisterClass (&wc) == 0) return 0;

    // Create mutex used to share memory-mapped structure.
    g_hmWriteOkay = CreateMutex (NULL, TRUE, TEXT ("XTALKWRT"));
```

```
rc = GetLastError();
if (rc == ERROR_ALREADY_EXISTS)
    fFirstApp = FALSE;
else if (rc) return 0;

// Wait here for ownership to ensure that the initialization is done.
// This is necessary since CreateMutex doesn't wait.
rc = WaitForSingleObject (g_hmWriteOkay, 2000);
if (rc != WAIT_OBJECT_0)
    return 0;

// Create a file-mapping object.
g_hMMObj = CreateFileMapping (INVALID_HANDLE_VALUE, NULL,
                              PAGE_READWRITE, 0,
                              MMBUFFSIZE, TEXT ("XTALKBLK"));
if (g_hMMObj == 0) return 0;

// Map into memory the file-mapping object.
g_pBuff = (PSHAREBUFF)MapViewOfFile (g_hMMObj, FILE_MAP_WRITE,
                                     0, 0, 0);
if (!g_pBuff)
    CloseHandle (g_hMMObj);

// Initialize structure if first application started.
if (fFirstApp)
    memset (g_pBuff, 0, sizeof (SHAREBUFF));
// Increment app running count. Interlock not needed due to mutex.
g_pBuff->nAppCnt++;

// Release the mutex. We need to release the mutex twice
// if we owned it when we entered the wait above.
ReleaseMutex (g_hmWriteOkay);
if (fFirstApp)
    ReleaseMutex (g_hmWriteOkay);

// Now create events for read, and send notification.
g_hSendEvent = CreateEvent (NULL, FALSE, FALSE, NULL);
g_hReadEvent = CreateEvent (NULL, TRUE, FALSE, TEXT ("XTALKREAD"));
g_hReadDoneEvent = CreateEvent (NULL, FALSE, FALSE,
                                TEXT ("XTALKDONE"));
if (!g_hReadEvent || !g_hSendEvent || !g_hReadDoneEvent)
    return 0;

// Create main window.
hWnd = CreateDialog (hInst, szAppName, NULL, NULL);

// Return fail code if window not created.
if (!IsWindow (hWnd)) return 0;

if (!fFirstApp) {
    GetWindowRect (hWnd, &rect);
    MoveWindow (hWnd, rect.left+10, rect.top+10,
                rect.right-rect.left, rect.bottom-rect.top, FALSE);
}
```

```
    // Create secondary threads for interprocess communication.
    g_hSendThread = CreateThread (NULL, 0, SenderThread, hWnd, 0, NULL);
    g_hReadThread = CreateThread (NULL, 0, ReaderThread, hWnd, 0, NULL);
    if ((g_hSendThread == 0) || (g_hReadThread == 0)) {
        DestroyWindow (hWnd);
        return 0;
    }

    // Standard show and update calls
    ShowWindow (hWnd, nCmdShow);
    UpdateWindow (hWnd);
    return hWnd;
}
//----------------------------------------------------------------------
// TermInstance - Program cleanup
//
int TermInstance (HINSTANCE hInstance, int nDefRC) {

    // Close event handles.
    if (g_hReadEvent)
        CloseHandle (g_hReadEvent);

    if (g_hReadDoneEvent)
        CloseHandle (g_hReadDoneEvent);

    if (g_hSendEvent)
        CloseHandle (g_hSendEvent);

    // Wait for the threads to terminate.  They'll do so when the
    // handles above are closed since the waits will fail.
    if (g_hSendThread) {
        WaitForSingleObject (g_hSendThread, 1000);
        CloseHandle (g_hSendThread);
    }
    if (g_hReadThread) {
        WaitForSingleObject (g_hReadThread, 1000);
        CloseHandle (g_hReadThread);
    }
    // Free memory-mapped object.
    if (g_pBuff) {
        // Decrement app running count.
        InterlockedDecrement (&g_pBuff->nAppCnt);
        UnmapViewOfFile (g_pBuff);
    }
    if (g_hMMObj)
        CloseHandle (g_hMMObj);

    // Free mutex.
    if (g_hmWriteOkay)
        CloseHandle (g_hmWriteOkay);
    return nDefRC;
}
//======================================================================
// Message handling procedures for main window
```

```
//----------------------------------------------------------------------
// MainWndProc - Callback function for application window
//
LRESULT CALLBACK MainWndProc (HWND hWnd, UINT wMsg, WPARAM wParam,
                              LPARAM lParam) {
    int i;
    //
    // Search message list to see if we need to handle this
    // message. If in list, call procedure.
    //
    for (i = 0; i < dim(MainMessages); i++) {
        if (wMsg == MainMessages[i].Code)
            return (*MainMessages[i].Fxn)(hWnd, wMsg, wParam, lParam);
    }
    return DefWindowProc (hWnd, wMsg, wParam, lParam);
}
//----------------------------------------------------------------------
// DoCreateMain - Process WM_CREATE message for window.
//
LRESULT DoCreateMain (HWND hWnd, UINT wMsg, WPARAM wParam,
                      LPARAM lParam) {
#if defined(WIN32_PLATFORM_PSPC) || defined(WIN32_PLATFORM_WFSP)
    SHMENUBARINFO mbi;                        // For Pocket PC, create
    memset(&mbi, 0, sizeof(SHMENUBARINFO)); // menu bar so that we
    mbi.cbSize = sizeof(SHMENUBARINFO);      // have a sip button.
    mbi.hwndParent = hWnd;
    mbi.dwFlags = SHCMBF_EMPTYBAR;           // No menu
    SHCreateMenuBar(&mbi);
#endif
    return 0;
}
//----------------------------------------------------------------------
// DoSetFocusMain - Process WM_SETFOCUS message for window.
//
LRESULT DoSetFocusMain (HWND hWnd, UINT wMsg, WPARAM wParam,
                        LPARAM lParam) {
    SetFocus (GetDlgItem (hWnd, IDD_OUTTEXT));
    return 0;
}
//----------------------------------------------------------------------
// DoCommandMain - Process WM_COMMAND message for window.
//
LRESULT DoCommandMain (HWND hWnd, UINT wMsg, WPARAM wParam,
                       LPARAM lParam) {
    WORD    idItem, wNotifyCode;
    HWND    hwndCtl;
    int     i;

    // Parse the parameters.
    idItem = (WORD) LOWORD (wParam);
    wNotifyCode = (WORD) HIWORD (wParam);
    hwndCtl = (HWND) lParam;

    // Call routine to handle control message.
```

```
    for(i = 0; i < dim(MainCommandItems); i++) {
        if(idItem == MainCommandItems[i].Code)
            return (*MainCommandItems[i].Fxn)(hWnd, idItem, hwndCtl,
                                              wNotifyCode);
    }
    return 0;
}
//----------------------------------------------------------------------
// DoDestroyMain - Process WM_DESTROY message for window.
//
LRESULT DoDestroyMain (HWND hWnd, UINT wMsg, WPARAM wParam,
                       LPARAM lParam) {
    PostQuitMessage (0);
    return 0;
}
//======================================================================
// Command handler routines
//----------------------------------------------------------------------
// DoMainCommandExit - Process Program Exit command.
//
LPARAM DoMainCommandExit (HWND hWnd, WORD idItem, HWND hwndCtl,
                          WORD wNotifyCode) {

    SendMessage (hWnd, WM_CLOSE, 0, 0);
    return 0;
}
//----------------------------------------------------------------------
// DoMainCommandSend - Process Program Send command.
//
LPARAM DoMainCommandSend (HWND hWnd, WORD idItem, HWND hwndCtl,
                          WORD wNotifyCode) {

    SetEvent (g_hSendEvent);
    return 0;
}
//======================================================================
// SenderThread - Performs the interprocess communication
//
DWORD WINAPI SenderThread (PVOID pArg) {
    HWND hWnd;
    int nGoCode, rc;
    TCHAR szText[TEXTSIZE];

    hWnd = (HWND)pArg;
    while (1) {
        nGoCode = WaitForSingleObject (g_hSendEvent, INFINITE);
        if (nGoCode == WAIT_OBJECT_0) {
            SendDlgItemMessage (hWnd, IDD_OUTTEXT, WM_GETTEXT,
                                sizeof (szText), (LPARAM)szText);

            rc = WaitForSingleObject (g_hmWriteOkay, 2000);
            if (rc == WAIT_OBJECT_0) {
                StringCchCopy (g_pBuff->szText, TEXTSIZE, szText);
                g_pBuff->nReadCnt = g_pBuff->nAppCnt;
```

```
                PulseEvent (g_hReadEvent);
                // Wait while reader threads get data.
                while (g_pBuff->nReadCnt)
                    rc = WaitForSingleObject (g_hReadDoneEvent,
                                              INFINITE);
                ReleaseMutex (g_hmWriteOkay);
            }
        } else
            return -1;
    }
    return 0;
}
//======================================================================
// ReaderThread - Performs the interprocess communication
//
DWORD WINAPI ReaderThread (PVOID pArg) {
    HWND hWnd;
    int nGoCode, rc, i;
    TCHAR szText[TEXTSIZE];

    hWnd = (HWND)pArg;
    while (1) {
        nGoCode = WaitForSingleObject (g_hReadEvent, INFINITE);
        if (nGoCode == WAIT_OBJECT_0) {
            i = SendDlgItemMessage (hWnd, IDD_INTEXT, LB_ADDSTRING, 0,
                                    (LPARAM)g_pBuff->szText);
            SendDlgItemMessage (hWnd, IDD_INTEXT, LB_SETTOPINDEX, i, 0);

            InterlockedDecrement (&g_pBuff->nReadCnt);
            SetEvent (g_hReadDoneEvent);
        } else {
            rc = GetLastError();
            wsprintf (szText, TEXT ("rc:%d"), rc);
            MessageBox (hWnd, szText, TEXT ("ReadThread Err"), MB_OK);
        }
    }
    return 0;
}
```

The interesting routines in the XTalk example are the *InitInstance* procedure and the two thread procedures *SenderThread* and *ReaderThread*. The relevant part of *InitInstance* is shown below with the error checking code removed for brevity.

```
// Create mutex used to share memory-mapped structure.
g_hmWriteOkay = CreateMutex (NULL, TRUE, TEXT ("XTALKWRT"));
rc = GetLastError();
if (rc == ERROR_ALREADY_EXISTS)
    fFirstApp = FALSE;
// Wait here for ownership to ensure that the initialization is done.
// This is necessary since CreateMutex doesn't wait.
rc = WaitForSingleObject (g_hmWriteOkay, 2000);
if (rc != WAIT_OBJECT_0)
    return 0;
```

```
// Create a file-mapping object.
g_hMMObj = CreateFileMapping (INVALID_HANDLE_VALUE, NULL,
                              PAGE_READWRITE, 0,
                              MMBUFFSIZE, TEXT ("XTALKBLK"));

// Map into memory the file-mapping object.
g_pBuff = (PSHAREBUFF)MapViewOfFile (g_hMMObj, FILE_MAP_WRITE,
                                     0, 0, 0);

// Initialize structure if first application started.
if (fFirstApp)
    memset (g_pBuff, 0, sizeof (SHAREBUFF));

// Increment app running count. Interlock not needed due to mutex.
g_pBuff->nAppCnt++;

// Release the mutex.  We need to release the mutex twice
// if we owned it when we entered the wait above.
ReleaseMutex (g_hmWriteOkay);
if (fFirstApp)
    ReleaseMutex (g_hmWriteOkay);

// Now create events for read and send notification.
g_hSendEvent = CreateEvent (NULL, FALSE, FALSE, NULL);
g_hReadEvent = CreateEvent (NULL, TRUE, FALSE, TEXT ("XTALKREAD"));
g_hReadDoneEvent = CreateEvent (NULL, FALSE, FALSE,
                                TEXT ("XTALKDONE"));
```

This code is responsible for creating the necessary synchronization objects as well as creating and initializing the shared memory block. The mutex object is created first with the parameters set to request initial ownership of the mutex object. A call is then made to *GetLastError* to determine whether the mutex object has already been created. If not, the application assumes that the first instance of XTalk is running and later will initialize the shared memory block. Once the mutex is created, an additional call is made to *WaitForSingleObject* to wait until the mutex is released. This call is necessary to prevent a late-starting instance of XTalk from disturbing communication in progress. Once the mutex is owned, calls are made to *CreateFileMapping* and *MapViewOfFile* to create a named memory-mapped object. Because the object is named, each process that opens the object opens the same object and is returned a pointer to the same block of memory.

After the shared memory block is created, the first instance of XTalk zeroes out the block. This procedure also forces the block of RAM to be committed because memory-mapped objects by default are autocommit blocks. Then *nAppCnt*, which keeps a count of the running instances of XTalk, is incremented. Finally, the mutex protecting the shared memory is released. If this is the first instance of XTalk, *ReleaseMutex* must be called twice because it gains ownership of the mutex twice—once when the mutex is created and again when the call to *WaitForSingleObject* is made.

Finally, three event objects are created. *SendEvent* is an unnamed event, local to each instance of XTalk. The primary thread uses this event to signal the sender thread that the user has pressed the Send button and wants the text in the edit box transmitted. *ReadEvent* is a named event that tells the other instances of XTalk that there's data to be read in the transfer buffer. *ReadDoneEvent* is a named event signaled by each of the receiving copies of XTalk to indicate that they have read the data.

The two threads, *ReaderThread* and *SenderThread*, are created immediately after the main window of XTalk is created. The code for *SenderThread* is shown here:

```
DWORD WINAPI SenderThread (PVOID pArg) {
    HWND hWnd;
    int nGoCode, rc;
    TCHAR szText[TEXTSIZE];

    hWnd = (HWND)pArg;
    while (1) {
        nGoCode = WaitForSingleObject (g_hSendEvent, INFINITE);
        if (nGoCode == WAIT_OBJECT_0) {
            SendDlgItemMessage (hWnd, IDD_OUTTEXT, WM_GETTEXT,
                                sizeof (szText), (LPARAM)szText);

            rc = WaitForSingleObject (g_hmWriteOkay, 2000);
            if (rc == WAIT_OBJECT_0) {
                lstrcpy (g_pBuff->szText, szText);
                g_pBuff->nReadCnt = g_pBuff->nAppCnt;
                PulseEvent (g_hReadEvent);

                // Wait while reader threads get data.
                while (g_pBuff->nReadCnt)
                    rc = WaitForSingleObject (g_hReadDoneEvent,
                                              INFINITE);
                ReleaseMutex (g_hmWriteOkay);
            }
        }
    }
    return 0;
}
```

The routine waits on the primary thread of XTalk to signal *SendEvent*. The primary thread of XTalk makes the signal in response to a *WM_COMMAND* message from the Send button. The thread is then unblocked, reads the text from the edit control, and waits to gain ownership of the *WriteOkay* mutex. This mutex protects two copies of XTalk from writing to the shared block at the same time. When the thread owns the mutex, it writes the string read from the edit control into the shared buffer. It then copies the number of active copies of XTalk into the *nReadCnt* variable in the same shared buffer and pulses *ReadEvent* to tell the other copies of XTalk to read the newly written data. A manual resetting event is used so that all threads waiting on the event will be unblocked when the event is signaled.

The thread then waits for the *nReadCnt* variable to return to 0. Each time a reader thread reads the data, the *nReadCnt* variable is decremented and the *ReadDone* event signaled. Note that the thread doesn't spin on this variable but uses an event to tell it when to check the variable again. This actually would be a great place to use *WaitForMultipleObjects* and have all reader threads signal when they've read the data, but Windows CE doesn't support the *WaitAll* flag in *WaitForMultipleObjects*.

Finally, when all the reader threads have read the data, the sender thread releases the mutex protecting the shared segment and the thread returns to wait for another send event.

The *ReaderThread* routine is even simpler. Here it is:

```
DWORD WINAPI ReaderThread (PVOID pArg) {
    HWND hWnd;
    int nGoCode, rc, i;
    TCHAR szText[TEXTSIZE];

    hWnd = (HWND)pArg;
    while (1) {
        nGoCode = WaitForSingleObject (g_hReadEvent, INFINITE);
        if (nGoCode == WAIT_OBJECT_0) {
            i = SendDlgItemMessage (hWnd, IDD_INTEXT, LB_ADDSTRING, 0,
                                    (LPARAM)g_pBuff->szText);
            SendDlgItemMessage (hWnd, IDD_INTEXT, LB_SETTOPINDEX, i, 0);

            InterlockedDecrement (&g_pBuff->nReadCnt);
            SetEvent (g_hReadDoneEvent);
        }
    }
    return 0;
}
```

The reader thread starts up and immediately blocks on *ReadEvent*. When it's unblocked, it adds the text from the shared buffer into the list box in its window. The list box is then scrolled to show the new line. After this is accomplished, the *nReadCnt* variable is decremented using *InterlockedDecrement* to be thread safe, and the *ReadDone* event is signaled to tell *SenderThread* to check the read count. After that's accomplished, the routine loops around and waits for another read event to occur.

Exception Handling

Windows CE, along with Visual Studio, supports both Microsoft's standard structured exception handling extensions to the C language (the *__try, __except* and *__try, __finally* blocks) and the ANSI-standard C++ exception handling framework, with keywords such as *catch* and *throw*.

Windows exception handling is complex, and if I were to cover it completely, I could easily write another entire chapter. The following review introduces the concepts to non-Win32 programmers and conveys enough information about the subject for you to get your feet wet.

C++ Exception Handling

The statements, *try*, *catch*, and *throw* are familiar to C++ programmers and work as expected in Windows CE. To use C++ exception handling in a Windows CE C++ application, the application must be compiled with the *–GX* compiler switch. For those not familiar with the operation of these keywords, what follows is a quick introduction. One caution to using C++ exception handling: the component that implements C++ exception handling in Windows CE is optional. Not all systems, including many embedded systems, will have this component in the system. To provide truly cross-platform support for your Windows CE application, don't use C++ exception handling. Instead, use Win32 structured exception handling, which is discussed in the following sections.

Using Exceptions to Report Errors

It's the vogue in programming circles these days to report errors in a function by throwing an exception. Using this scheme, a calling function that doesn't check for errors will have the exception automatically passed on to its calling function. If no function ever checks for the exception, the exception will be passed to the operating system, which will act appropriately on the offending application. Functions that simply report an error code in a return code can't enforce error checking because the lack of verification of the error code isn't automatically reported up the stack chain.

A simple example of the different methods of reporting errors is shown in the following code fragments. In the first code fragment, the failure of *LocalAlloc* in *AddItem* is reported by returning 0. Note how each call to *AddItem* has to be checked to see whether an error occurred in *AddItem*.

```
PMYITEM AddItem (PMYITEM pLast, DWORD dwData) {

    // Allocate the item
    PMYITEM p = (PMYITEM)LocalAlloc (LPTR, sizeof (MYITEM));
    if (p == 0)
        return 0;

    // Link the list
    p->pPrev = pLast;
    if (pLast)  pLast->pNext = p;
    p->dwData = dwData;
    return p;
}

int test (HWND hWnd) {
    PMYITEM pNext;

    pNext = AddItem (NULL, 1);
    if (pNext == NULL)
        return ERROR_CODE;
```

```
    pNext = AddItem (pNext, 2);
    if (pNext == NULL)
        return ERROR_CODE;

    pNext = AddItem (pNext, 3);
    if (pNext == NULL)
        return ERROR_CODE;
    return 0;
}
```

In the following code fragment, *AddItem* throws an exception if the memory allocation fails. Notice how much cleaner the calling routine *test1* looks.

```
PMYITEM AddItem (PMYITEM pLast, DWORD dwData) {

    // Allocate the item
    PMYITEM p = (PMYITEM)LocalAlloc (LPTR, sizeof (MYITEM));
    if (p == 0)
        throw ("failure to allocate item in AddItem");

    // Link the list
    p->pPrev = pLast;
    if (pLast)  pLast->pNext = p;
    p->dwData = dwData;
    return p;
}

int test1 (HWND hWnd) {
    PMYITEM pNext;

    try {
        pNext = AddItem (NULL, 1);
        pNext = AddItem (pNext, 2);
        pNext = AddItem (pNext, 3);
    }
    catch (char * strException) {
        return ERROR_CODE;
    }
    return 0;
}
```

The simple structure of the foregoing routines demonstrates the ease with which C++ exception handling can be added to an application. The *try* keyword wraps code that might generate an exception. The wrapped code includes any routines called from within the *try* block. If an exception is thrown with a string argument, the exception will be caught by the *catch* block in *test1*. What happens if some other exception is thrown? Let's look at the basics of the *try*, *catch*, and *throw* keywords to see.

The *try*, *catch* Block

The basic structure of the exception keywords is demonstrated in the following pseudocode.

```
try
{
    throw (arg of type_t);
}
catch (type_t arg)
{
    // catches all throws with argument of type_t
}
```

Within the *try* block, if an exception is thrown with an argument, the exception will be caught by the *catch* block that has the matching argument. If no *catch* block has a matching argument, the exception is passed to the function that called the code containing the *try* block. If no enclosing *try*, *catch* block is found, the thread is terminated. If no exception occurs within the *try* block, none of the associated *catch* blocks are executed.

For example

```
try
{
    throw (1);
}
```

would be caught if the *try* block had an associated *catch* block with an integer argument such as

```
catch (int nExceptionCode)
{
    // Exception caught!
}
```

The argument doesn't have to be a simple type; it can be a C++ class. It's also permissible to have multiple *catch* blocks, each with a different argument string associated with the *try* block. *Catch* blocks are evaluated in the order they appear in the code. Finally, a *catch* block with ellipsis arguments catches all exceptions within the *try* block.

```
try
{
    throw (1);

    throw ("This is an ascii string");

    throw (CMyException cEx);
}
catch (int nExCode)
{
    // catches all throws with an integer argument
}
catch (char * szExCode)
{
    // catches all throws with a string argument
```

```
}
catch (CMyException cEx)
{
    // catches all throws with a CMyException class argument
}
catch (...)
{
    // catches all exceptions not caught above
}
```

Win32 Exception Handling

Windows CE has always supported the Win32 method of exception handling, using the *__try*, *__except*, and *__finally* keywords. What follows is a brief overview of these statements. In addition, unlike C++ exception handling, Win32 structured exception handling is always supported, regardless of the configuration of the operating system.

The *__try, __except* Block

The *__try, __except* block looks like this:

```
__try {

    // Try some code here that might cause an exception.

}
__except (exception filter) {

    // This code is depending on the filter on the except line.

}
```

Essentially, the *try-except* pair allows you the ability to anticipate exceptions and handle them locally instead of having Windows terminate the thread or the process because of an unhandled exception.

The exception filter is essentially a return code that tells Windows how to handle the exception. You can hard code one of the three possible values or call a function that dynamically decides how to respond to the exception.

If the filter returns *EXCEPTION_EXECUTE_HANDLER*, Windows aborts the execution in the *try* block and jumps to the first statement in the *except* block. This is helpful if you're expecting the exception and you know how to handle it. In the code that follows, the access to memory is protected by a *__try, __except* block.

```
BYTE ReadByteFromMemory (LPBYTE pPtr, BOOL *bDataValid) {
    BYTE ucData = 0;

    *bDataValid = TRUE;
    __try {
```

```
        ucData = *pPtr;
    }
    __except (DecideHowToHandleException ()) {
        // The pointer isn't valid; clean up.
        ucData = 0;
        *bDataValid = FALSE;
    }
    return ucData;
}
int DecideHowToHandleException (void) {
    return EXCEPTION_EXECUTE_HANDLER;
}
```

If the memory read line above wasn't protected by a *__try, __except* block and an invalid pointer was passed to the routine, the exception generated would have been passed up to the system, causing the thread and perhaps the process to be terminated. If you use the *__try, __except* block, the exception is handled locally and the process continues with the error handled locally.

Another possibility is to have the system retry the instruction that caused the exception. You can do this by having the filter return *EXCEPTION_CONTINUE_EXECUTION*. On the surface, this sounds like a great option—simply fix the problem and retry the operation your program was performing. The problem with this approach is that what will be retried isn't the *line* that caused the exception, but *the machine instruction* that caused the exception. The difference is illustrated by the following code fragment that looks okay but probably won't work:

```
// An example that doesn't work...
int DivideIt (int aVal, int bVal) {
    int cVal;
    __try {
        cVal = aVal / bVal;
    }
    __except (EXCEPTION_CONTINUE_EXECUTION) {
        bVal = 1;
    }
    return cVal;
}
```

The idea in this code is noble: protect the program from a divide-by-zero error by ensuring that if the error occurs, the error is corrected by replacing *bVal* with 1. The problem is that the line

```
cVal = aVal / bVal;
```

is probably compiled to something like the following on a MIPS-compatible CPU:

```
lw    t6,aVal(sp)        ;Load aVal
lw    t7,bVal(sp)        ;Load bVal
div   t6,t7              ;Perform the divide
sw    t6,cVal(sp)        ;Save result into cVal
```

In this case, the third instruction, the *div*, causes the exception. Restarting the code after the exception results in the restart beginning with the *div* instruction. The problem is that the execution needs to start at least one instruction earlier to load the new value from *bVal* into the register. The moral of the story is that attempting to restart code at the point of an exception requires knowledge of the specific machine instruction that caused the exception.

The third option for the exception filter is to not even attempt to solve the problem and to pass the exception up to the next, higher, *__try, __except* block in code. The exception filter returns *EXCEPTION_CONTINUE_SEARCH*. Because *__try, __except* blocks can be nested, it's good practice to handle specific problems in a lower, nested, *__try, __except* block and more global errors at a higher level.

Determining the Problem

With these three options available, it would be nice if Windows let you in on why the exception occurred. Fortunately, Windows provides the function

```
DWORD GetExceptionCode (void);
```

This function returns a code that indicates why the exception occurred in the first place. The codes are defined in WINBASE.H and range from *EXCEPTION_ACCESS_VIOLATION* to *CONTROL_C_EXIT*, with a number of codes in between. Another function allows even more information:

```
LPEXCEPTION_POINTERS GetExceptionInformation (void);
```

GetExceptionInformation returns a pointer to a structure that contains pointers to two structures: *EXCEPTION_RECORD* and *CONTEXT*. *EXCEPTION_RECORD* is defined as

```
typedef struct _EXCEPTION_RECORD {
    DWORD ExceptionCode;
    DWORD ExceptionFlags;
    struct _EXCEPTION_RECORD *ExceptionRecord;
    PVOID ExceptionAddress;
    DWORD NumberParameters;
    DWORD ExceptionInformation[EXCEPTION_MAXIMUM_PARAMETERS];
} EXCEPTION_RECORD;
```

The fields in this structure go into explicit detail about why an exception occurred. To narrow the problem down even further, you can use the *CONTEXT* structure. The *CONTEXT* structure is different for each CPU and essentially defines the exact state of the CPU when the exception occurred.

There are limitations on when these two exception information functions can be called. *GetExceptionCode* can be called only from inside an *except* block or from within the exception filter function. The *GetExceptionInformation* function can be called only from within the exception filter function.

Generating Your Own Exceptions

There are times when an application might want to generate its own exceptions. The Win32 method for raising an exception is the function *RaiseException*, prototyped as follows:

```
void RaiseException (DWORD dwExceptionCode, DWORD dwExceptionFlags,
                     DWORD nNumberOfArguments, const DWORD *lpArguments);
```

The first parameter is the exception code, which will be the value returned by *GetExceptionCode* from within the *__except* block. The codes understood by the system are the same codes defined for *GetExceptionCode*, discussed earlier. The *dwExceptionFlags* parameter can be *EXCEPTION_NONCONTINUABLE* to indicate that the exception can't be continued or 0 if the exception can be continued. The last two parameters, *nNumberOfArguments* and *lpArguments*, allow the thread to pass additional data to the exception handler. The data passed can be retrieved with the *GetExceptionInformation* function in the *__except* filter function.

The ***__try, __finally*** Block

Another tool of the structured exception handling features of the Win32 API is the *__try, __finally* block. It looks like this:

```
__try {

    // Do something here.

}
__finally {

    // This code is executed regardless of what happens in the try block.

}
```

The goal of the *__try, __finally* block is to provide a block of code, the *finally* block, that always executes regardless of how the other code in the *try* block attempts to leave the block. Unfortunately, the current Windows CE C compilers don't support leaving the *__try* block by a return or a *goto* statement for many of the CPU types. The Windows CE compilers do support the *__leave* statement that immediately exits the *__try* block and executes the *__finally* block. Using the *__try, __leave, __finally* combination provides a great way for a sequence of code to "leave" the sequence and go straight to the cleanup code if one of the steps fails.

In this chapter, I've covered the basics for how processes and threads are created, how they communicate, and how exceptions are handled. In the next few chapters, I will look at how the Windows CE stores data. Windows CE supports a number of different file systems including a RAM-based file system called the object store. Let's take a look.

Chapter 9
The Windows CE File System

Windows CE provides a fully functional file system stack that supports a variety of file systems and storage media. Unique to Windows CE is a RAM-based file system known as the *object store*. In implementation, the object store more closely resembles a database than it does a file allocation system for a disk. In addition to storing files, the object store can store the Windows CE registry and database volumes. Fortunately for the programmer, most of the unique implementation of the object store is hidden behind standard Win32 functions. In addition to the object store, Windows CE supports a variety of file systems including flash-based solutions and even those quaint rotating, ferromagnetic storage devices known as disk drives.

The Windows CE file API is taken directly from Win32, and for the most part, the API is fairly complete. There are some differences, however, in the Windows CE implementation. The most obvious difference is that Windows CE doesn't use drive letters. Instead, the path of a file is defined from the root of the file system. Different storage volumes, such as partitions of hard drives or separate flash file systems, are represented as directories off the root of the file system.

In addition to the lack of drive letters, the concept of the *current directory*, so important in other versions of Windows, isn't present in Windows CE. Files are specified by their complete path. The command line–based shell, CMD.EXE, maintains its own current directory, but this directory is independent of the file system.

The object store also exposes some additional differences. Execute-in-place files, stored in ROM, appear as files in the object store, but these files can't be opened and read as standard files. The object store format is undocumented, so there is no way to dig underneath the file system API to look at sectors, clusters, or cylinders of data as you could on a FAT-formatted disk.

This chapter covers the Windows CE file system from two perspectives. First, the file system API is discussed, showing how applications read, write, move, and copy files. A section follows on how to manage the various storage devices attached to the system. This section will cover how to talk to the *storage manager*, the part of Windows CE that loads and manages the various file systems and storage devices in the system. But before that, lets look at standard file I/O.

The Windows CE File System API

As should be expected for a Win32-compatible operating system, the file name format for Windows CE is the same as that of its larger counterparts. Filenames have the same *name.ext* format as they do in other Windows operating systems. The extension is the three characters following the last period in the file name and defines the type of file. The file type is used by the shell when determining the difference between executable files and different documents.

Allowable characters in filenames are the same as for the desktop versions of Windows. Windows CE supports long filenames. Filenames and their complete paths can be up to *MAX_PATH* in length, which is currently defined at 260 bytes. However, Windows CE does not support the path prefix sequence "\\?\" to extend the path length longer than *MAX_PATH*. UNC naming convention to reference network servers, as in "\\<server name>\<share name> is supported.

Windows CE files support many of the same attribute flags as other versions of Windows, with a few additions. Attribute flags include the standard read-only, system, hidden, compressed, and archive flags. A few additional flags have been included to support the special RAM/ROM mix of files in the object store.

Standard File I/O

Windows CE supports most of the same file I/O functions found in other Win32 operating systems. The same Win32 API calls, such as *CreateFile*, *ReadFile*, *WriteFile*, and *CloseFile*, are all supported. A Windows CE programmer must be aware of a few differences, however. First of all, the old Win16 standards, *_lread*, *_lwrite*, and *_llseek*, aren't supported. This isn't really a huge problem because all of these functions can easily be implemented by wrapping the Windows CE file functions with a small amount of code. Windows CE does support basic console library functions such as *fprintf* and *printf* for console applications if the console is supported on that configuration.

Windows CE doesn't support the overlapped I/O that's supported under the desktop versions of Windows. Files or devices can't be opened with the *FILE_ FLAG_OVERLAPPED* flag, nor can reads or writes use the overlapped mode of asynchronous calls and returns. Programmers needing this type of functionality can simply create a separate thread to handle the file I/O asynchronous to the main thread of the application.

File operations in Windows CE follow the traditional handle-based methodology used on all modern operating systems. Files are opened by means of a function that returns a handle. Read and write functions are passed the handle to indicate the file to act on. Data is read from or written to the offset in the file indicated by a system-maintained file pointer. Finally, when the reading and writing have been completed, the application indicates this by closing the file handle. Now on to the specifics.

Creating and Opening Files

Creating a file or opening an existing file or device driver is accomplished by means of the standard Win32 function:

```
HANDLE CreateFile (LPCTSTR lpFileName, DWORD dwDesiredAccess,
                   DWORD dwShareMode,
                   LPSECURITY_ATTRIBUTES lpSecurityAttributes,
                   DWORD dwCreationDistribution,
                   DWORD dwFlagsAndAttributes, HANDLE hTemplateFile);
```

The first parameter is the name of the file to be opened or created. The filename should have a fully specified path. Filenames with no path information are assumed to be in the root directory of the object store.

The *dwDesiredAccess* parameter indicates the requested access rights. The allowable flags are *GENERIC_READ* to request read access to the file and *GENERIC_WRITE* for write access. Both flags must be passed to get read/write access. You can open a file with neither read nor write permissions. This is handy if you just want to get the attributes of a device. The *dwShareMode* parameter specifies the access rights that can be granted to other processes. This parameter can be *FILE_SHARE_READ* and/or *FILE_SHARE_WRITE*. The *lpSecurityAttributes* parameter is ignored by Windows CE and should be set to *NULL*.

The *dwCreationDistribution* parameter tells *CreateFile* how to open or create the file. The following flags are allowed:

- **CREATE_NEW** Creates a new file. If the file already exists, the function fails.
- **CREATE_ALWAYS** Creates a new file or truncates an existing file.
- **OPEN_EXISTING** Opens a file only if it already exists.
- **OPEN_ALWAYS** Opens a file or creates a file if it doesn't exist. This differs from CREATE_ALWAYS because it doesn't truncate the file to 0 bytes if the file exists.
- **TRUNCATE_EXISTING** Opens a file and truncates it to 0 bytes. The function fails if the file doesn't already exist.

The *dwFlagsAndAttributes* parameter defines the attribute flags for the file if it's being created in addition to flags in order to tailor the operations on the file. The following flags are allowed under Windows CE:

- **FILE_ATTRIBUTE_NORMAL** This is the default attribute. It's overridden by any of the other file attribute flags.

- **FILE_ATTRIBUTE_READONLY** Sets the read-only attribute bit for the file. Subsequent attempts to open the file with write access will fail.
- **FILE_ATTRIBUTE_ARCHIVE** Sets the archive bit for the file.
- **FILE_ATTRIBUTE_SYSTEM** Sets the system bit for the file indicating that the file is critical to the operation of the system.
- **FILE_ATTRIBUTE_HIDDEN** Sets the hidden bit. The file will be visible only to users who have the View All Files option set in the Explorer.
- **FILE_FLAG_WRITE_THROUGH** Write operations to the file won't be lazily cached in memory.
- **FILE_FLAG_RANDOM_ACCESS** Indicates to the system that the file will be randomly accessed instead of sequentially accessed. This flag can help the system determine the proper caching strategy for the file. On the object store file system, the file will not be compressed.

Windows CE doesn't support a number of file attributes and file flags that are supported under other versions of Windows. The unsupported flags include, but aren't limited to the following: *FILE_ATTRIBUTE_OFFLINE, FILE_FLAG_OVERLAPPED, FILE_FLAG_NO_BUFFERING, FILE_FLAG_SEQUENTIAL_SCAN, FILE_FLAG_ DELETE_ON_CLOSE, FILE_FLAG_BACKUP_ SEMANTICS*, and *FILE_FLAG_POSIX_ SEMANTICS*. On the desktop, the flag *FILE_ATTRIBUTE_ TEMPORARY* is used to indicate a temporary fil;, but, as we'll see later, it's used by Windows CE to indicate a directory that is, in reality, a separate drive or network share.

The final parameter in *CreateFile*, *hTemplate*, is ignored by Windows CE and should be set to 0. *CreateFile* returns a handle to the opened file if the function was successful. If the function fails, it returns *INVALID_HANDLE_VALUE*. To determine why the function failed, call *GetLastError*. If the *dwCreationDistribution* flags included *CREATE_ALWAYS* or *OPEN_ALWAYS*, you can determine whether the file previously existed by calling *GetLastError* to see if it returns *ERROR_ALREADY_EXISTS*. *CreateFile* will set this error code even though the function succeeded.

In addition to opening files and devices, *CreateFile* can open storage volumes such as hard disks and flash cards. To open a volume, pass the name of the volume appended with *\Vol:*. For example, to open a compact flash card volume represented by the directory name *Storage Card*, the call would be as follows:

```
h = CreateFile (TEXT ("\\Storage card\\Vol:"),
                GENERIC_READ|GENERIC_WRITE,
                0, NULL, OPEN_ALWAYS, FILE_ATTRIBUTE_NORMAL, NULL);
```

The handle returned by the *CreateFile* call can be used to pass IO Control (IOCTL) commands to the file system driver that mounted the volume.

Reading and Writing

Windows CE supports the standard Win32 functions *ReadFile* and *WriteFile*; both functions return *TRUE* if successful and *FALSE* otherwise. Reading a file is as simple as calling the following:

```
BOOL ReadFile (HANDLE hFile, LPVOID lpBuffer,
               DWORD nNumberOfBytesToRead,
               LPDWORD lpNumberOfBytesRead, LPOVERLAPPED lpOverlapped);
```

The parameters are fairly self-explanatory. The first parameter is the handle of the opened file to read followed by a pointer to the buffer that will receive the data and the number of bytes to read. The fourth parameter is a pointer to a *DWORD* that will receive the number of bytes that were actually read. Finally, the *lpOverlapped* parameter must be set to *NULL* because Windows CE doesn't support overlapped file operations. As an aside, Windows CE does support multiple reads and writes pending on a device; it just doesn't support the ability to return from the function before the operation completes.

Data is read from the file starting at the file offset indicated by the file pointer. After the read has completed, the file pointer is adjusted by the number of bytes read.

ReadFile won't read beyond the end of a file. If a call to *ReadFile* asks for more bytes than remain in the file, the read will succeed, but only the number of bytes remaining in the file will be returned. This is why you must check the variable pointed to by *lpNumberOfBytesRead* after a read completes to learn how many bytes were actually read. A call to *ReadFile* with the file pointer pointing to the end of the file results in the read being successful, but the number of read bytes is set to 0.

Writing to a file is accomplished with this:

```
BOOL WriteFile (HANDLE hFile, LPCVOID lpBuffer,
                DWORD nNumberOfBytesToWrite,
                LPDWORD lpNumberOfBytesWritten,
                LPOVERLAPPED lpOverlapped);
```

The parameters are similar to *ReadFile*, with the obvious exception that *lpBuffer* now points to the data that will be written to the file. As in *ReadFile*, the *lpOverlapped* parameter must be *NULL*. The data is written to the file offset indicated by the file pointer, which is updated after the write so that it points to the byte immediately beyond the data written.

Moving the File Pointer

The file pointer can be adjusted manually with a call to the following:

```
DWORD SetFilePointer (HANDLE hFile, LONG lDistanceToMove,
                      PLONG lpDistanceToMoveHigh, DWORD dwMoveMethod);
```

The parameters for *SetFilePointer* are the handle of the file;

a signed offset distance to move the file pointer; a second, upper 32-bit, offset parameter; and *dwMoveMethod*, a parameter indicating how to interpret the offset. Although *lDistanceToMove* is a signed 32-bit value, *lpDistanceToMoveHigh* is a pointer to a signed 32-bit value. For file pointer moves of greater than 4 GB, the *lpDistanceToMoveHigh* parameter should point to a *LONG* that contains the upper 32-bit offset of the move. This variable will receive the high 32 bits of the resulting file pointer. For moves of less than 4 GB, simply set *lpDistanceToMoveHigh* to *NULL*. Clearly, for most Windows CE systems, the *lpDistanceToMoveHigh* parameter is a bit excessive, but there are a growing number of Windows CE platforms that need this feature.

The offset value is interpreted as being from the start of the file if *dwMoveMethod* contains the flag *FILE_BEGIN*. To base the offset on the current position of the file pointer, use *FILE_CURRENT*. To base the offset from the end of the file, use *FILE_END* in *dwMoveMethod*.

SetFilePointer returns the file pointer at its new position after the move has been accomplished. To query the current file position without changing the file pointer, simply call *SetFilePointer* with a zero offset and relative to the current position in the file, as shown here:

```
nCurrFilePtr = SetFilePointer (hFile, 0, NULL, FILE_CURRENT);
```

Closing a File

Closing a file handle is a simple as calling

```
BOOL CloseHandle (HANDLE hObject);
```

This generic call, used to close a number of handles, is also used to close file handles. The function returns *TRUE* if it succeeds. If the function fails, a call to *GetLastError* will return the reason for the failure.

Truncating a File

When you have finished writing the data to a file, you can close it with a call to *CloseHandle* and you're done. Sometimes, however, you must truncate a file to make it smaller than it currently is. In the days of MS-DOS, the way to set the end of a file was to make a call to write zero bytes to a file. The file was then truncated at the current file pointer. This won't work in Windows CE. To set the end of a file, move the file pointer to the location in the file where you want the file to end and call:

```
BOOL SetEndOfFile (HANDLE hFile);
```

Of course, for this call to succeed, you need write access to the file. The function returns *TRUE* if it succeeds.

To insure that all the data has been written to a storage device and isn't just sitting around in a cache, you can call this function:

```
BOOL FlushFileBuffers (HANDLE hFile);
```

The only parameter is the handle to the file you want to flush to the disk. Take care not to call this function too frequently. Writing to flash or disk storage is slow, so calling this function excessively can affect system performance.

Getting File Information

A number of calls allow you to query information about a file or directory. To quickly get the attributes knowing only the file or directory name, you can use this function:

```
DWORD GetFileAttributes (LPCTSTR lpFileName);
```

In general, the attributes returned by this function are the same ones that I covered for *CreateFile*, with the addition of the attributes listed here:

- **FILE_ATTRIBUTE_COMPRESSED** The file is compressed.
- **FILE_ATTRIBUTE_INROM** The file is in ROM.
- **FILE_ATTRIBUTE_ROMMODULE** The file is an executable module in ROM formatted for execute-in-place loading. These files can't be opened with CreateFile.
- **FILE_ATTRIBUTE_DIRECTORY** The name specifies a directory, not a file.
- **FILE_ATTRIBUTE_TEMPORARY** When this flag is set in combination with FILE_ATTRIBUTE_DIRECTORY, the directory is the root of a secondary storage device, such as a PC Card, a hard drive, or the network share folder.

The attribute *FILE_ATTRIBUTE_COMPRESSED* is somewhat misleading on a Windows CE device. Files in the RAM-based object store are always compressed, but this flag isn't set for those files. On the other hand, the flag does accurately reflect whether a file in ROM is compressed. Compressed ROM files have the advantage of taking up less space but the disadvantage of not being execute-in-place files.

An application can change the basic file attributes, such as read only, hidden, system, and attribute by calling this function:

```
BOOL SetFileAttributes (LPCTSTR lpFileName, DWORD dwFileAttributes);
```

This function simply takes the name of the file and the new attributes. Note that you can't compress a file by attempting to set its compressed attribute. Under other Windows systems that do support selective compression of files, the way to compress a file is to make a call directly to the file system driver.

A number of other informational functions are supported by Windows CE. All of these functions, however, require a file handle instead of a file name, so the file must have been previously opened by means of a call to *CreateFile*.

File Times

The standard Win32 API supports three file times: the time the file was created, the time the file was last accessed (that is, the time it was last read, written, or executed), and the last time the file was written to. This support, however, is limited to what the underlying file system tracks. Many file systems don't support all three file times. One of the ways to query the file times for a file is to call this function:

```
BOOL GetFileTime (HANDLE hFile, LPFILETIME lpCreationTime,
                  LPFILETIME lpLastAccessTime,
                  LPFILETIME lpLastWriteTime);
```

The function takes a handle to the file being queried and pointers to three *FILETIME* values that will receive the file times. If you're interested in only one of the three values, the other pointers can be set to *NULL*.

When the file times are queried for a file in the object store, Windows CE copies the last write time into all *FILETIME* structures. This goes against Win32 documentation, which states that any unsupported time fields should be set to 0. For the FAT file system used on storage cards, two times are maintained: the file creation time and the last write time. When *GetFileTime* is called on a file on a storage card, the file creation and last write times are returned and the last access time is set to 0.

The *FILETIME* structures returned by *GetFileTime* and other functions can be converted to something readable by calling

```
BOOL FileTimeToSystemTime (const FILETIME *lpFileTime,
                           LPSYSTEMTIME lpSystemTime);
```

This function translates the *FILETIME* structure into a *SYSTEMTIME* structure that has documented day, date, and time fields that can be used. One large caveat is that file times are stored in coordinated universal time format (UTC), also known as Greenwich Mean Time. This doesn't make much difference as long as you're using unreadable *FILETIME* structures, but when you're translating a file time into something readable, a call to

```
BOOL FileTimeToLocalFileTime (const FILETIME *lpFileTime,
                              LPFILETIME lpLocalFileTime);
```

before translating the file time into system time provides the proper time zone translation to the user.

You can manually set the file times of a file by calling

```
BOOL SetFileTime (HANDLE hFile, const FILETIME *lpCreationTime,
                  const FILETIME *lpLastAccessTime,
                  const FILETIME *lpLastWriteTime);
```

The function takes a handle to a file and three times each in *FILETIME* format. If you want to set only one or two of the times, the remaining parameters can be set to *NULL*. Remember that file times must be in UTC time, not local time.

For files in the Windows CE object store, setting any one of the time fields results in all three being updated to that time. If you set multiple fields to different times and attempt to set the times for an object store file, *lpLastWriteTime* takes precedence. Files on storage cards maintain separate creation and last-write times. You must open the file with write access for *SetFileTime* to work.

File Size and Other Information

You can query a file's size by calling

```
DWORD GetFileSize (HANDLE hFile, LPDWORD lpFileSizeHigh);
```

The function takes the handle to the file and an optional pointer to a *DWORD* that's set to the high 32 bits of the file size. This second parameter can be set to *NULL* if you don't expect to be dealing with files over 4 GB. *GetFileSize* returns the low 32 bits of the file size.

I've been talking about these last few functions separately, but an additional function, *GetFile InformationByHandle*, returns all this information and more. The function prototyped as

```
BOOL GetFileInformationByHandle (HANDLE hFile,
                   LPBY_HANDLE_FILE_INFORMATION lpFileInformation);
```

takes the handle of an opened file and a pointer to a *BY_HANDLE_FILE_INFORMATION* structure. The function returns *TRUE* if it was successful.

The *BY_HANDLE_FILE_INFORMATION* structure is defined this way:

```
typedef struct _BY_HANDLE_FILE_INFORMATION {
    DWORD dwFileAttributes;
    FILETIME ftCreationTime;
    FILETIME ftLastAccessTime;
    FILETIME ftLastWriteTime;
    DWORD dwVolumeSerialNumber;
    DWORD nFileSizeHigh;
    DWORD nFileSizeLow;
    DWORD nNumberOfLinks;
    DWORD nFileIndexHigh;
    DWORD nFileIndexLow;
    DWORD dwOID;
} BY_HANDLE_FILE_INFORMATION;
```

As you can see, the structure returns data in a number of fields that separate functions return. I'll talk about only the new fields here.

The *dwVolumeSerialNumber* field is filled with the serial number of the volume in which the file resides. Under Windows CE, the volume refers to disk, partition, or file system, such as the object store or a disk on a local area network. For files in the object store, the volume serial number is 0.

The *nNumberOfLinks* field is used by Windows's NTFS file system and can be ignored under Windows CE. The *nFileIndexHigh* and *nFileIndexLow* fields contain a systemwide unique identifier number for the file. This number can be checked to see whether two different file handles point to the same file. The File Index value is used by the desktop, but Windows CE has a more useful value, the *object ID* of the file, which is returned in the *dwOID* field. The object ID is an identifier that can be used to reference directories, files, databases, and individual database records. Handy stuff.

Memory-Mapped Files

Memory-mapped files give you a completely different method for reading and writing files. With the standard file I/O functions, files are read as streams of data. To access bytes in different parts of a file, the file pointer must be moved to the first byte, the data read, the file pointer moved to the other byte, and then the file read again.

With memory-mapped files, the file is mapped to a region of memory. Then, instead of using *FileRead* and *FileWrite*, you simply read and write the region of memory that's mapped to the file. Updates of the memory are automatically reflected back to the file itself. Setting up a memory-mapped file is a somewhat more complex process than making a simple call to *CreateFile*, but once a file is mapped, reading and writing the file is trivial.

I discussed memory-mapped objects in Chapter 8. Now with just a couple of extra calls, we can use memory-mapped techniques to read and write a file directly.

Memory-Mapped Files

In Windows CE 6 and later, to open a file for memory-mapped access, the file is first opened with a call to *CreateFile* just as when opening a file for standard stream access. In Windows CE 5 and before, a function, unique to Windows CE, is needed to open the file; it's named *CreateFileForMapping*. The prototype for *CreateFileForMapping* is the same as *CreateFile*. Windows CE 6 and later maintain compatibility with the earlier versions of the operating system by defining a macro that maps *CreateFileForMapping* to *CreateFile*.

The handle returned by *CreateFile* can then be passed in the first parameter to *CreateFileMapping*. This function creates a file-mapping object and ties the opened file to it. As with memory-mapped objects, you need to create a view into the object by calling *MapViewOfFile*, which returns a pointer to memory that's mapped to the file. These two functions were covered in the "Interprocess Communication" section of Chapter 8.

As you write to the memory-mapped file, the changes are reflected in the data you read back from the same buffer. When you close the memory-mapped file, the system writes the modified data back to the original file. If you want to have the data written to the file before you close the file, you can use the following function:

```
BOOL FlushViewOfFile (LPCVOID lpBaseAddress,
                      DWORD dwNumberOfBytesToFlush);
```

The parameters are the base address and size of a range of virtual pages within the mapped view that will be written to the file. The function writes only the pages that have been modified to the file.

When you're finished with the memory-mapped file, a little cleanup is required. First a call should be made to *UnmapViewOfFile* to unmap the view to the object. Next, a call should be made to close the mapping object and the file itself. Both these actions are accomplished by means of calls to *CloseHandle*. The first call should be to close the memory-mapped object, and then *CloseHandle* should be called to close the file.

The code fragment that follows shows the entire process of opening a file, creating the file-mapping object, mapping the view, and then cleaning up.

```
HANDLE hFile, hFileMap;
PBYTE pFileMem;
TCHAR szFileName[MAX_PATH];

hFile = CreateFile (szFileName, GENERIC_WRITE, FILE_SHARE_READ, NULL,
                    OPEN_EXISTING, FILE_ATTRIBUTE_NORMAL |
                    FILE_FLAG_RANDOM_ACCESS,0);

if (hFile != INVALID_HANDLE_VALUE) {

    hFileMap = CreateFileMapping (hFile, NULL, PAGE_READWRITE, 0, 0, 0);
    if (hFileMap) {
        pFileMem = (PBYTE)MapViewOfFile (hFileMap, FILE_MAP_WRITE,
                                         0, 0, 0);
        if (pFileMem) {
            //
            // Use the data in the file.
            //

            // Start cleanup by unmapping view.
            UnmapViewOfFile (pFileMem);
        }
        CloseHandle (hFileMap);
    }
    CloseHandle (hFile);
}
```

Navigating the File System

Now that we've seen how files are read and written, let's take a look at how the files themselves are managed in the file system. Windows CE supports most of the convenient file and directory management APIs, such as *CopyFile*, *MoveFile*, and *CreateDirectory*.

File and Directory Management

Windows CE supports a number of functions useful in file and directory management. You can move files using *MoveFile*, copy them using *CopyFile*, and delete them using *DeleteFile*. You can create directories using *CreateDirectory* and delete them using *RemoveDirectory*. While most of these functions are straightforward, I should cover a few intricacies here.

To copy a file, call

```
BOOL CopyFile (LPCTSTR lpExistingFileName, LPCTSTR lpNewFileName,
               BOOL bFailIfExists);
```

The parameters are the name of the file to copy and the name of the destination directory. The third parameter indicates whether the function should overwrite the destination file if one already exists before the copy is made.

When copying a large file, the time for *CopyFile* to return can be disconcerting to the user. Starting with Windows CE 5, *CopyFileEx* is supported. It is prototyped as

```
BOOL CopyFileEx (LPCTSTR lpExistingFileName, LPCTSTR lpNewFileName,
                 LPPROGRESS_ROUTINE lpProgressRoutine, LPVOID lpData,
                 LPBOOL pbCancel, DWORD dwCopyFlags);
```

CopyFileEx accepts a pointer to a callback routine, *lpProgressRoutine*, that is called just before the copy starts and then periodically while the file is being copied. The callback routine allows the application to provide feedback to the user to track the progress of the copy. The other new parameters are *lpData*, which is a user-defined value that is passed to the callback routine, and *pbCancel* which, on return indicates if the file copy was canceled before it was completed. The *dwCopyFlags* parameter accepts one flag, *COPY_FILE_FAIL_IF_EXISTS*, which fails the copy if the destination file already exists.

The callback routine is prototyped as

```
DWORD CALLBACK CopyProgressRoutine (LARGE_INTEGER TotalFileSize,
           LARGE_INTEGER TotalBytesTransferred, LARGE_INTEGER StreamSize,
           LARGE_INTEGER StreamBytesTransferred, DWORD dwStreamNumber,
           DWORD dwCallbackReason, HANDLE hSourceFile,
           HANDLE hDestinationFile, LPVOID lpData);
```

The parameters to the callback routine provide information on the progress of the copy. The *TotalFileSize* parameter is a 64-bit value that indicates the size of the source file. The *TotalBytesTransferred* parameter indicates the number of bytes already copied. For Windows CE, the *StreamSize* and *StreamBytesTransferred* parameters contain the same values as the *TotalFileSize* and *TotalBytesTransferred* parameters, respectively. The *dwStreamNumber* parameter is always set to 1. The *dwCallbackReason* parameter is first set to *CALLBACK_STREAM_SWITCH* on the initial callback made just before the copy is started and then is set to *CALLBACK_CHUNK_FINISHED* for the subsequent calls. The *hSourceFile* and *hDestinationFile* parameters are the open file handles as the copy is taking place. Finally, *lpData* is the value passed in the *CopyFileEx lpData* parameter.

The return value from the callback routine can be one of the four values listed here.

- **PROGRESS_CONTINUE** The copy process should continue.
- **PROGRESS_CANCEL** The copy process is aborted. If the file is partially copied, the destination file is deleted.
- **PROGRESS_STOP** The copy process is aborted. If the file is partially copied, the partially copied destination file remains.
- **PROGRESS_QUIET** Continue the copy process but don't call the callback routine anymore.

Files and directories can be moved and renamed using

```
BOOL MoveFile (LPCTSTR lpExistingFileName, LPCTSTR lpNewFileName);
```

To move a file, simply indicate the source and destination names for the file. The destination file must not already exist. File moves can be made within the object store, from the object store to an external drive, or from an external drive to the object store. *MoveFile* can also be used to rename a file. In this case, the source and target directories remain the same; only the name of the file changes.

MoveFile can also be used in the same manner to move or rename directories. This practice is much faster than calling *CopyFile* because the file system only has to update directory information and not move the file data. The only limitation is that *MoveFile* can't move a directory from one volume to another. For that, *CopyFile* or *CopyFileEx* is needed.

Deleting a file is as simple as calling

```
BOOL DeleteFile (LPCTSTR lpFileName);
```

You pass the name of the file to delete. For the delete to be successful, the file must not be currently open.

You can create and destroy directories using the following two functions:

```
BOOL CreateDirectory (LPCTSTR lpPathName,
                      LPSECURITY_ATTRIBUTES lpSecurityAttributes);
```

and

```
BOOL RemoveDirectory (LPCTSTR lpPathName);
```

CreateDirectory takes the name of the directory to create and a security parameter that should be *NULL* under Windows CE. *RemoveDirectory* deletes a directory. The directory must be empty for the function to be successful.

Creating a Temporary File

At times you will need to create a temporary file. How do you pick a unique filename? You can ask Windows for the name of a temporary file by using the following function:

```
UINT GetTempFileName (LPCTSTR lpPathName, LPCTSTR lpPrefixString,
                      UINT uUnique, LPTSTR lpTempFileName);
```

The first parameter is the path of the temporary file. The second parameter, *lpPrefixString*, is the name prefix. The first three characters of the prefix become the first three characters of the temporary filename. The *uUnique* parameter can be any number you want or 0. If you pass 0, Windows will generate a number based on the system time and use it as the last four characters of the filename. If *uUnique* is 0, Windows guarantees that the filename produced by *GetTempFileName* will be unique. If you specify a value other than 0 in *uUnique*, Windows returns a filename based on that value but doesn't check to see whether the filename is unique. The last parameter is the address of the output buffer to which *GetTempFileName* returns the filename. This buffer should be at least *MAX_PATH* characters (not bytes) in length.

Finding Files

Windows CE supports the basic *FindFirstFile*, *FindNextFile*, *FindClose* procedure for enumerating files that is supported under the desktop versions of Windows. Searching is accomplished on a per-directory basis using template filenames with wild card characters in the template.

Searching a directory involves first passing a file name template to *FindFirstFile*, which is prototyped in this way:

```
HANDLE FindFirstFile (LPCTSTR lpFileName,
                      LPWIN32_FIND_DATA lpFindFileData);
```

The first parameter is the template file name used in the search. This file name can contain a fully specified path if you want to search a directory other than the root. Windows CE has no concept of *Current Directory* built into it; if no path is specified in the search string, the root directory of the file system is searched.

As you would expect, the wild cards for the file name template are ? and *. The question mark (?) indicates that any single character can replace the question mark. The asterisk (*) indicates that any number of characters can replace the asterisk. For example, the search string *\Windows\Alarm?.wav* would return the files \Windows\Alarm1.wav, \Windows\Alarm2.wav, and \Windows\Alarm3.wav. On the other hand, the search string *\Windows*.wav* would return all files in the windows directory that have the WAV extension.

The second parameter of *FindFirstFile* is a pointer to a *WIN32_FIND_DATA* structure, as defined here:

```
typedef struct _WIN32_FIND_DATA {
    DWORD dwFileAttributes;
```

```
    FILETIME ftCreationTime;
    FILETIME ftLastAccessTime;
    FILETIME ftLastWriteTime;
    DWORD nFileSizeHigh;
    DWORD nFileSizeLow;
    DWORD dwOID;
    WCHAR cFileName[ MAX_PATH ];
} WIN32_FIND_DATA;
```

This structure is filled with the file data for the first file found in the search. The fields shown are similar to what we've seen.

If *FindFirstFile* finds no files or directories that match the template file name, it returns *INVALID_HANDLE_VALUE*. If at least one file is found, *FindFirstFile* fills in the *WIN32_FIND_DATA* structure with the specific data for the found file, and returns a handle value that you use to track the current search.

To find the next file in the search, call this function:

```
BOOL FindNextFile (HANDLE hFindFile,
                   LPWIN32_FIND_DATA lpFindFileData);
```

The two parameters are the handle returned by *FindFirstFile* and a pointer to a find data structure. *FindNextFile* returns *TRUE* if a file matching the template passed to *FindFirstFile* is found and fills in the appropriate file data in the *WIN32_FIND_DATA* structure. If no file is found, *FindNextFile* returns *FALSE*.

When you've finished searching, either because *FindNextFile* returned *FALSE* or because you simply don't want to continue searching, you must call this function:

```
BOOL FindClose (HANDLE hFindFile);
```

This function accepts the handle returned by *FindFirstFile*. If *FindFirstFile* returned *INVALID_HANDLE_VALUE*, you shouldn't call *FindClose*.

The following short code fragment encompasses the entire file search process. This code computes the total size of all files in the Windows directory.

```
WIN32_FIND_DATA fd;
HANDLE hFind;
INT nTotalSize = 0;

// Start search for all files in the windows directory.
hFind = FindFirstFile (TEXT ("\\windows\\*.*"), &fd);

// If a file was found, hFind will be valid.
if (hFind != INVALID_HANDLE_VALUE) {

    // Loop through found files.  Be sure to process file
    // found with FindFirstFile before calling FindNextFile.
    do {
```

```
        // If found file is not a directory, add its size to
        // the total.  (Assume that the total size of all files
        // is less than 2 GB.)
        if (!(fd.dwFileAttributes & FILE_ATTRIBUTE_DIRECTORY))
            nTotalSize += fd.nFileSizeLow;

    // See if another file exists.
    } while (FindNextFile (hFind, &fd));

    // Clean up by closing file search handle.
    FindClose (hFind);
}
```

In this example, the Windows directory is searched for all files. If the found "file" isn't a directory; that is, if it's a true file, its size is added to the total. Notice that the return handle from *FindFirstFile* must be checked, not only so that you know whether a file was found, but also to prevent *FindClose* from being called if the handle is invalid.

A more advanced version of the *FindxxxFile* API is *FindFirstFileEx*. The advantage of this function is the added ability to enumerate only directories and even to enumerate the device drivers currently running. The function is prototyped as

```
HANDLE FindFirstFileEx(LPCTSTR lpFileName,
                 FINDEX_INFO_LEVELS fInfoLevelId,
                 LPVOID lpFindFileData, FINDEX_SEARCH_OPS fSearchOp,
                 LPVOID lpSearchFilter, DWORD dwAdditionalFlags);
```

As in *FindFirstFile*, the first parameter, *lpFileName*, specifies the search string. The parameter *fInfoLevelId* must be set to the constant *FindExInfoStandard*. Given that the second parameter must be *FindExInfoStandard*, the third parameter always points to a *WIN32_FIND_DATA* structure. The final two parameters, *lpSearchFilter* and *dwAdditionalFlags*, must be set to 0 on Windows CE.

The fourth parameter, *fSearchOp*, is what differentiates *FindFirstFileEx* from *FindFirstFile* on Windows CE. This parameter can be one of three values: *FindExSearchNameMatch*, *FindExSearchLimitToDirectories*, or *FindExSearchLimitToDevices*. The value *FindExSearchNameMatch* tells *FindFirstFileEx* to act just like *FindFirstFile*, searching for a matching file name. The value *FindExSearchLimitToDirectories* indicates that the function should search only for directories matching the search specification. This search should be slightly faster than repeatedly calling *FindFirstFile* and checking for the directory attribute because this check is done inside the file system, thereby reducing the number of *FindNextFile* calls. The final value, *FindExSearchLimitToDevices*, is the most interesting. It causes the function to search the names of the loaded device drivers to find a matching name. You shouldn't provide a path, with the exception of an optional leading "\".

FindFirstFileEx returns a handle if the search is successful and returns *INVALID_HANDLE_VALUE* if the search fails. When performing a search, use *FindFirstFileEx* in place of *FindFirstFile*. To search for the second and all other files, call *FindNextFile*. When you have completed the search, call *FindClose* to close the handle.

Distinguishing Drives from Directories

As I mentioned at the beginning of this chapter, Windows CE doesn't support the concept of drive letters so familiar to Windows users. Instead, file storage devices such as Compact Flash cards or even hard drives are shown as directories in the root directory. That leads to the question, "How can you tell a directory from a drive?" To do this, you need to look at the file attributes for the directory. Directories that are actually secondary storage devices—that is, they store files in a place other than the root file system—have the file attribute flag *FILE_ATTRIBUTE_TEMPORARY* set. Windows CE also uses this attribute flag for other "nondirectory" directories such as the NETWORK folder. The NETWORK folder lists network shares. So finding storage devices on any version of Windows CE is fairly easy, as is shown in the following code fragment:

```
WIN32_FIND_DATA fd;
HANDLE hFind;
TCHAR szPath[MAX_PATH], szName[MAX_PATH];
ULARGE_INTEGER lnTotal, lnFree;

StringCchCopy(szPath, dim(szPath), TEXT ("\\*.*"));
hFind = FindFirstFile (szPath, &fd);

if (hFind != INVALID_HANDLE_VALUE) {
    do {
        if ((fd.dwFileAttributes & FILE_ATTRIBUTE_DIRECTORY) &&
            (fd.dwFileAttributes & FILE_ATTRIBUTE_TEMPORARY)) {

            StringCchCopy(szName, dim(szName), fd.cFileName);
            StringCchCat(szName, dim(szName), TEXT ("\\Vol:"));
            HANDLE h = CreateFile (szName,
                                   GENERIC_READ|GENERIC_WRITE,
                                   0, NULL, OPEN_EXISTING,
                                   FILE_ATTRIBUTE_NORMAL, NULL);
            if (h != INVALID_HANDLE_VALUE) {
                CloseHandle (h);

                memset (&lnTotal, 0, sizeof (lnTotal));
                memset (&lnFree, 0, sizeof (lnFree));
                // Get the disk space statistics for drive.
                GetDiskFreeSpaceEx (fd.cFileName, NULL, &lnTotal,
                                    &lnFree);
                printf ("External Store %S total %d  Free %d\r\n",
                   fd.cFileName, lnTotal.LowPart, lnFree.LowPart);
            }
        }
    } while (FindNextFile (hFind, &fd));
}
FindClose (hFind);
```

This code uses the find first/find next functions to search the root directory for all directories with the *FILE_ATTRIBUTE_TEMPORARY* attribute set. It then checks to see whether the directory can be opened as a volume. Other directories with the *FILE_ATTRIBUTE_TEMPORARY* flag can't be opened because they don't represent file system volumes.

Notice the call to the following function in the code I just showed you:

```
BOOL GetDiskFreeSpaceEx (LPCWSTR lpDirectoryName,
                         PULARGE_INTEGER lpFreeBytesAvailableToCaller,
                         PULARGE_INTEGER lpTotalNumberOfBytes,
                         PULARGE_INTEGER lpTotalNumberOfFreeBytes);
```

This function provides information about the total size of the drive and the amount of free space it contains. The first parameter is the name of any directory on the drive in question. This doesn't have to be the root directory of the drive. *GetDiskFreeSpaceEx* returns three values: the free bytes available to the caller, the total size of the drive, and the total free space on the drive. These values are returned in three *ULARGE_INTEGER* structures. These structures contain two *DWORD* fields named *LowPart* and *HighPart*. This allows *GetDiskFreeSpaceEx* to return 64-bit values. If you aren't interested in one or more of the fields, you can pass a *NULL* in place of the pointer for that parameter. You can also use *GetDiskFreeSpaceEx* to determine the size of the object store.

Another function that can be used to determine the size of the object store is

```
BOOL GetStoreInformation (LPSTORE_INFORMATION lpsi);
```

GetStoreInformation takes one parameter, a pointer to a *STORE_INFORMATION* structure defined as

```
typedef struct STORE_INFORMATION {
    DWORD dwStoreSize;
    DWORD dwFreeSize;
} STORE_INFORMATION, *LPSTORE_INFORMATION;
```

As you can see, this structure simply returns the total size and amount of free space in the object store.

Dealing with Storage

The file system API just discussed is used by applications to access files regardless of the file system that is storing the file. As Windows CE has matured, the different file systems supported by the operating system have increased from the original object store file system to a variety of file systems from FAT to UDFS to custom flash file systems. Along the way, storage capacity has not just grown, but grown exponentially. These developments have prompted the need for a way to manage these disparate file systems. The Storage Manager, which manages these file systems, provides a series of functions that allow applications to manage file systems and file system volumes.

The Object Store

The default file system, and the original Windows CE file system, is the object store. The object store is equivalent to the hard drive on a Windows CE device. It's a subtly complex file storage system incorporating compressed RAM storage for read/write files and seamless integration with ROM-based files. A user sees no difference between a file in RAM in the object store and those files based in ROM. Files in RAM and ROM can reside in the same directory, and document files in ROM can be opened (although not modified) by the user. In short, the object store integrates the default files provided in ROM with the user-generated files stored in RAM.

To the programmer, the difference between files in the RAM part of the object store and the files based in ROM are subtle. The files in ROM can be detected by a special in-ROM file attribute flag. Execute-in-place (XIP) modules in ROM are marked by an additional ROM-Module attribute indicating their XIP status. XIP files can't be opened using the standard file opening functions such as *CreateFile*. In addition, some files in ROM and almost all files in RAM are compressed and therefore marked with the compressed file attribute.

The object store in Windows CE has some basic limitations. First, the size of the object store is currently limited to 256 MB of RAM. Given the compression features of the object store, this means that the amount of data that the object store can contain is somewhere around 512 MB. Individual files in the object store are limited to 32 MB. These file size limits don't apply to files in secondary storage such as hard drives, SD cards, and CompactFlash cards.

Accessing Volumes With the File API

As just mentioned, it's possible to easily determine which top-level directories are really file system volumes. After you discover an external file system, there are a number of ways to find out information about that volume. The first is to call the function

```
BOOL  CeGetVolumeInfo (LPCWSTR pszRootPath,
                       CE_VOLUME_INFO_LEVEL InfoLevel,
                       LPCE_VOLUME_INFO lpVolumeInfo);
```

The first parameter is the name of the folder representing the volume. The second parameter specifies the information level for the query. The only valid information level is *VolumeInfoLevelStandard*. The final parameter is a pointer to a *CE_VOLUME_INFO* structure defined as

```
typedef  struct _CE_VOLUME_INFO {
    DWORD cbSize;
    DWORD dwAttributes;
    DWORD dwFlags;
    DWORD dwBlockSize;
    TCHAR szStoreName[STORENAMESIZE];
    TCHAR szPartitionName[PARTITIONNAMESIZE];
} CE_VOLUME_INFO;
```

The first field of *CE_VOLUME_INFO* is the size of the structure that should be set before calling *CeGetVolumeInfo*. The *dwAttributes* field contains attribute flags describing the volume. The following list details the possible attribute flags.

- **CE_VOLUME_ATTRIBUTE_READONLY** The volume is read-only.
- **CE_VOLUME_ATTRIBUTE_HIDDEN** The volume is hidden.
- **CE_VOLUME_ATTRIBUTE_REMOVABLE** The volume can be removed.
- **CE_VOLUME_ATTRIBUTE_SYSTEM** All files and directories on the volume are treated as system files and directories.
- **CE_VOLUME_ATTRIBUTE_BOOT** The volume is the boot volume and contains the registry information.

The *dwFlags* field contains even more information about the volume:

- **CE_VOLUME_TRANSACTION_SAFE** The volume transacts actions on the volume allocation structures.
- **CE_VOLUME_FLAG_TRANSACT_WRITE** The volume transacts file write operations.
- **CE_VOLUME_FLAG_WFSC_SUPPORTED** The volume supports "scatter gather" reads and writes.
- **CE_VOLUME_FLAG_LOCKFILE_SUPPORTED** The volume supports the LockFile API.
- **CE_VOLUME_FLAG_NETWORK** The volume is a network share.
- **CE_VOLUME_FLAG_STORE** The volume is backed up by physical storage.
- **CE_VOLUME_FLAG_RAMFS** The volume is a RAM-based file system.
- **CE_VOLUME_FLAG_FILE_SECURITY_SUPPORTED** The volume supports security.
- **CE_VOLUME_FLAG_64BIT_FILES_SUPPORTED** The volume supports files larger than 2 GB.

The *dwBlockSize* field contains the smallest unit of allocation on the storage volume. For example, on a FAT-based file system this is the cluster size of the file system.

The *szStoreName* field contains the name of the block mode device driver for the storage hardware. This is typically something like "DSK1:". The *szPartitionName* is the name of the partition on the storage device. While this partition name can be specified when the drive is partitioned, most partitions are named by default with something like "Part00" and "Part01."

CeGetVolumeInfo returns a wealth of information on the volume. The attribute and flags fields let you find the boot file system, and determine if the file system is RAM based or if it supports the *LockFileEx* function. The final two fields, *szStoreName* and *szPartition*, provide information on the underlying driver support for the volume. We can use these two names with the storage manager to determine even more information.

The Storage Manager

The storage manager provides applications and a method to work with the storage devices and their partitions. Devices and partitions can be opened and queried to determine their size, attributes, and other useful information.

The storage manager also provides the ability to repartition devices as well as formatting devices and partitions. The formatting at this level consists of clearing the partition table, in the case of formatting a device; or setting the partition type, in the case of formatting a partition. Actually placing a file system on a partition is accomplished by the driver for a particular file system.

Opening, Querying a Storage Device

To work with a storage device, we first need to open it. The function to open a device is the appropriately named

```
HANDLE OpenStore (LPCSTR szDeviceName);
```

The only parameter, *szDeviceName*, is the name of the block mode driver, for example, "DSK1:". The return value is a handle that can be used by various other storage manager functions. When you are done with the handle, call *CloseHandle* to close the handle.

Once opened, information about the device can be queried with the function

```
BOOL GetStoreInfo (HANDLE hStore, PSTOREINFO pStoreInfo);
```

The first parameter is the handle returned from *OpenStore*. The second parameter is a pointer to a *STOREINFO* structure that describes the storage device. The *cbSize* field of the *STOREINFO* structure should be set before calling *GetStoreInfo*.

The STOREINFO structure is defined as

```
typedef  struct {
  DWORD cbSize;
  TCHAR szDeviceName[DEVICENAMESIZE];
  TCHAR szStoreName[STORENAMESIZE];
  DWORD dwDeviceClass;
  DWORD dwDeviceType;
  STORAGEDEVICEINFO sdi;
  DWORD dwDeviceFlags;
  SECTORNUM snNumSectors;
  DWORD dwBytesPerSector;
  SECTORNUM snFreeSectors;
  SECTORNUM snBiggestPartCreatable;
  FILETIME ftCreated;
  FILETIME ftLastModified;
  DWORD dwAttributes;
  DWORD dwPartitionCount;
  DWORD dwMountCount;
} STOREINFO, *PSTOREINFO;
```

The rather big *STOREINFO* structure provides some interesting information about the storage device. The *szDeviceName* is the name of the device driver managing the device. The name will be something similar to "DSK1:". The *szStoreName* is a friendly name that can be displayed to users. This is *not* the name of the directory where the device is mounted. The *dwDeviceClass* field can contain either *STORAGE_DEVICE_CLASS_BLOCK* or *STORAGE_DEVICE_CLASS_MULTIMEDIA*. The *dwDeviceType* field has a series of self-explanatory flags in the following list:

- STORAGE_DEVICE_TYPE_PCIIDE
- STORAGE_DEVICE_TYPE_FLASH
- STORAGE_DEVICE_TYPE_ATA
- STORAGE_DEVICE_TYPE_ATAPI
- STORAGE_DEVICE_TYPE_PCCARD
- STORAGE_DEVICE_TYPE_CFCARD
- STORAGE_DEVICE_TYPE_SRAM
- STORAGE_DEVICE_TYPE_DVD
- STORAGE_DEVICE_TYPE_CDROM
- STORAGE_DEVICE_TYPE_USB
- STORAGE_DEVICE_TYPE_DOC
- STORAGE_DEVICE_TYPE_UNKNOWN
- STORAGE_DEVICE_TYPE_REMOVABLE_DRIVE
- STORAGE_DEVICE_TYPE_REMOVABLE_MEDIA

The interesting flags are the removable media and removable drive flags indicating if the storage device or media can be removed from the system. These two flags are combined with one or more device technology flags such as *STORAGE_DEVICE_TYPE_USB* to complete the field. It's possible a device might report more than one device technology flag. For example, an IDE controller might report both the *STORAGE_DEVICE_TYPE_PCIIDE* and *STORAGE_DEVICE_TYPE_ATA* flags.

The *dwDeviceFlags* field contains flags indicating the support for read-only or read/write access to the device. In addition, there are flags to indicate if the device is transacted and if it needs media sense notifications. The *snNumSectors* field is a 64-bit field that contains the total number of sectors on the device. Multiplying this value by the *dwBytesPerSector* field will provide the total capacity of the device. The *snFreeSectors* field contains the number of sectors currently not allocated to a partiton. The *snBiggestPartCreatable* field contains the number of sectors that can be dedicated to a new partition.

The *ftCreated* and *ftLastModified* field contains *FILETIME* values that indicate when the device was initially formatted and when the last partition was created. However, many device drivers do not record these times, and on these devices, the two fields will be zero. The *dwAttributes* field contains the attribute flags for the volume. The possible values are the same flags discussed in the *dwAttribute* field of the *CE_VOLUME_INFO* structure. Finally, the *dwPartitionCount* field contains the number of partitions on the device. The *dwMountCount* indicates the number of the partitions that have been mounted as volumes in the system.

Enumerating Storage Devices

To use *GetStoreInfo* on a storage device, you first have to open the device; to do that you need to know the device name. One method of learning about the storage devices on a system is to enumerate them using the function

```
HANDLE FindFirstStore (PSTOREINFO pStoreInfo);
```

The only parameter to the function is a pointer to a STOREINFO structure. This is the same *STOREINFO* structure just discussed. As with *GetStoreInfo*, the *cbSize* field of this structure should be filled with the size of the structure before the call is made to *FindFirstStore*. If the function returns anything but *INVALID_HANDLE_VALUE*, the *STOREINFO* structure contains information about the first storage device found. To find other storage devices, repeated calls should be made to

```
BOOL FindNextStore (HANDLE hSearch, PSTOREINFO pStoreInfo);
```

The parameters are the handle returned by *FindFirstStore* and a pointer to a *STOREINFO* structure. *FindNextStore* should be called until it returns *FALSE* indicating there are no more storage devices to enumerate. At that point, a call to

```
BOOL FindCloseStore (HANDLE hSearch);
```

should be made to close the store enumeration handle.

Enumerating Partitions

Large storage devices are typically partitioned. As on the desktop, each partition is mounted as a separate volume. Like devices, partitions can be opened if you know the name of the partition. However, it's usually easier to enumerate the partitions on a particular device with the function

```
HANDLE FindFirstPartition (HANDLE hStore, PPARTINFO pPartInfo);
```

The first parameter is the handle of the open storage device. The second is a pointer to a *PARTINFO* structure. I will discuss the *PARTINFO* structure below. At this point, its important to know that the *cbSize* field of this structure should be filled with the size of the structure before the call is made to *FindFirstPartition*. If the function returns a valid handle, the

PARTINFO structure contains information about the first partition found on the device. To enumerate the other partitions, repeated calls should be made to

```
BOOL FindNextPartition (HANDLE hSearch, PPARTINFO pPartInfo);
```

The parameters are the handle returned by *FindFirstPartition* and a pointer to a *PARTINFO* structure. As with *FindNextStore*, *FindNextPartition* should be called until it returns *FALSE* indicating there are no more partitions on the device to enumerate. At that point, a call to

```
BOOL FindClosePartition (HANDLE hSearch);
```

should be made to close the partition enumeration handle.

The *PARTINFO* structure is defined as

```
typedef struct tagPARTINFO
{
    DWORD       cbSize;
    TCHAR       szPartitionName[PARTITIONNAMESIZE];
    TCHAR       szFileSys[FILESYSNAMESIZE];
    TCHAR       szVolumeName[VOLUMENAMESIZE];
    SECTORNUM   snNumSectors;
    FILETIME    ftCreated;
    FILETIME    ftLastModified;
    DWORD       dwAttributes;
    BYTE        bPartType;
} PARTINFO, *PPARTINFO;
```

The *szPartitionName* field contains the name of the partition. As just mentioned, most partitions are named by default with something like "Part00" and "Part01." This is the name that would be used to open a partition with *OpenPartition*. The *szFileSys* field contains the name of the file system driver that is implementing the file system for the partition. For example, the FAT file system DLL is typically named FATFS.DLL in earlier versions of Windows CE and EXFAT.DLL for Windows CE 6. The *szFileSys* field is important, because you will use the DLL in this field when formatting the partition. The *szVolumeName* field contains the string that is the name of the folder that contains the volume. Typical names for this are "Storage Card" or "Hard Disk2."

The *snNumSectors* field contains the size of the partition in sectors. The *ftCreated* and *ftLastModified* fields contain creation and modification times for the partition. Many storage drivers do not keep this information. For these systems, the fields are zero.

The *dwAttributes* field can have the following flags:

- **PARTITION_ATTRIBUTE_READONLY** Partition is read only.
- **PARTITION_ATTRIBUTE_ACTIVE** This is a bootable partition.
- **PARTITION_ATTRIBUTE_BOOT** Same as PARTITION_ATTRIBUTE_ACTIVE.
- **PARTITION_ATTRIBUTE_MOUNTED** Partition is mounted.

The *bPartType* field contains the partition type. The partition type value, like the partition scheme itself, has its roots back in the MS-DOS 3.1 days when it originally defined values indicating primary and extended partition types. As newer versions of DOS and other operating systems, including OS/2, Windows, and various Unix implementations appeared, each added new partition types for its particualar storage format. Ironically, it's variants of the original DOS FAT file system and its partition types that are the lingua franca for storage formats across operating systems today. For Windows CE, these partition types are listed in the registry and provide the file system manager guidance in which file system to load.

Working with Partitions

Creating a partition is accomplished with the function

```
BOOL CreatePartitionEx (HANDLE hStore, LPCTSTR szPartitionName,
                        BYTE bPartType, SECTORNUM snNumSectors);
```

The first parameter is the handle to the open storage device. The *szPartitionName* should be set to the name of the partition. Depending on the device, the partition name may not be kept if the system is restarted. The *bPartType* parameter defines the partition type parameter, which identifies the file system expected to be used when accessing the partition. The *snNumSectors* parameter is a 64-bit parameter that specifies the number of sectors for the partition. The storage device must have enough contiguous unallocated sectors to create the partition.

Deleting a partition can be accomplished with the function

```
BOOL DeletePartition (HANDLE hStore, LPCTSTR szPartitionName);
```

The parameters are the handle to the storage device and the name of the partition.

On a running system, partitions with FAT partition IDs are typically mounted automatically either on boot or when the storage device is inserted. To format a partition or to delete a series of partitions so the device can be repartitioned with differently sized partitions, the partitions need to be unmounted. Partitions are mounted and unmounted with the functions:

```
BOOL MountPartition (HANDLE hPartition);
BOOL DismountPartition (HANDLE hPartition);
```

For both these functions, the only parameter is the handle returned by *OpenPartition.*

Formatting Volumes

One place where the storage manager can't help is in formatting partitions. While there is a *FormatPartition* function, all it does is clear the first sector of the partition. The task of actually formatting a partition so that it can store data is the job of the file system driver that will be using the partition to store data.

The function that will format a partition is

```
DWORD FormatVolume (HANDLE hVolume, PDISK_INFO pdi,
                    PFORMAT_OPTIONS pfo, PFN_PROGRESS pfnProgress,
                    PFN_PROGRESS pfnMessage);
```

The first parameter is the handle to the partition to format. The *pdi* parameter is ignored. The *pfo* parameter points to a *FORMAT_OPTIONS* structure that describes the options for the format. If *pfo* is set to *NULL, FormatVolume* uses the default settings for the format. The *pfnProgress* parameter points to a callback function that will be called to display progress feedback to the user. The final parameter *pfnMessage* points to a callback routine that will be called if there is an error during the format process.

The *FORMAT_OPTIONS* structure is defined as

```
typedef struct _FORMAT_OPTIONS {
    DWORD   dwClusSize;
    DWORD   dwRootEntries;
    DWORD   dwFatVersion;
    DWORD   dwNumFats;
    DWORD   dwFlags;
} FORMAT_OPTIONS *PFORMAT_OPTIONS;
```

Notice that this structure is very FAT-centric. The only file system delivered with Windows CE that can format a partition is FAT. Third parties can provide file system drivers with their own formatting functions. I'll discuss in the next section how this is accomplished. The *dwClusSize* parameter specifies the number of bytes in each cluster on the volume. In FAT, the cluster is the smallest unit of allocation. This value should be zero for a default cluster size or a power of two between 512 and 32768. The *dwRootEntries* field specifies the number of root directory entries to specify for the volume. The *dwFatVersion* field specifies the version of FAT; 12, 16, or 32, to be used when formatting the volume. If this field is zero, the file system will determine which version of FAT to use depending on the size of the partition. The *dwNumFats* field can be set to 1 or 2 to specify the number of FAT tables to be used in the partition. Finally, the *dwFlags* value can be set to the following flags:

- **FATUTIL_FULL_FORMAT** Perform full format, writing to every sector.
- **FATUTIL_FORMAT_TFAT** Format the partition for transacted FAT file system.
- **FATUTIL_DISABLE_MOUNT_CHK** Skip check to see if partition mounted before formatting partition.
- **FATUTIL_SECURE_WIPE** When formatting partiton, attempt to zero out all data on partition, even if a reboot occurs during format.
- **FATUTIL_FORMAT_EXFAT** Format the partition with the extended FAT file system.

In addition to *FormatVolume*, Windows CE also supports *FormatVolumeUI* prototyped as

```
VOID FormatVolumeUI (HANDLE hVolume, HWND hWnd);
```

This function presents a dialog box that provides the ability for the user to select the parameters for the format. The two parameters are the handle of the partition and a window handle that will be the owner window of the dialog box.

Finding the *FormatVolume* API

Unlike almost all the functions I discuss in this chapter, you can't just provide and include file, link to a library file, and directly call *FormatVolume*. The problem is that the location of the code for *FormatVolume* is dependent on the file system being formatted. In addition, there is a bit of a twist to this tale. The FAT file system driver provided with Windows CE uses a separate DLL for the formatting functions. So, if it's FAT that needs to be formatted, a different DLL must be loaded.

To locate the *FormatVolume* call, use the *szFileSys* field of the *PARTINFO* structure. This field names the file system DLL for the partition. If the field contains the string FATFSD.DLL or EXFAT.DLL, then load FATUTIL.DLL instead. If any other file system driver is specified, you should load that DLL. The DLL can be opened with *LoadLibrary*. Once loaded, use *GetProcAddress* to find the *FormatVolume* entry point. *GetProcAddress* will return a pointer to the function that can then be called. This technique of manually loading a DLL and finding an exported function was covered in Chapter 8.

That covers the Windows CE file system. As you can see, very little Windows CE–unique code is necessary when you're working at the file API level. The storage manager, however, is a different story with a series of Windows CE unique calls. Regardless of how it's done, the file system functionality in Windows CE should provide developers with all they will need for dealing with storage at the file or device level. Now let's look at the registry API, where Windows CE follows the Win32 API quite closely.

Chapter 10

The Registry

The registry is a system database used to store configuration information for applications and for Windows itself. The registry as defined by Windows CE is similar but not identical in function and format to the registries under other versions of Windows. In other words, for an application, most of the same registry access functions exist, but the layout of the Windows CE registry doesn't exactly follow the desktop.

As in all versions of Windows, the registry is made up of keys and values. Keys can contain keys or values or both. Values contain data in one of a number of predefined formats. Because keys can contain keys, the registry is distinctly hierarchical. The highest-level keys, the root keys, are specified by their predefined numeric constants. Keys below the root keys and values are identified by their text name. Multiple levels of keys can be specified in one text string by separating the keys with a backslash (\).

To query or modify a value, the key containing the value must first be opened, the value queried or written, and then the key closed. Keys and values can also be enumerated so that an application can determine what a specific key contains. Data in the registry can be stored in a number of different predefined data types. Among the available data types are strings, 32-bit numbers, and free-form binary data.

Registry Organization

The Windows CE registry supports three of the high-level, root, keys seen on other Windows platforms: *HKEY_LOCAL_MACHINE*, *HKEY_CURRENT_USER*, and *HKEY_CLASSES_ROOT*. As with other Windows platforms, Windows CE uses the *HKEY_LOCAL_MACHINE* key to store hardware and driver configuration data, *HKEY_CURRENT_USER* to store user-specific configuration data, and the *HKEY_CLASSES_ROOT* key to store file type matching and OLE configuration data. When Windows CE is operating under a multiuser configuration, the *HKEY_CURRENT_USER* will be specific to the user currently logged in.

As a practical matter, the registry is used by the operating system, drivers, and applications to store state information that needs to be saved across invocations. Applications typically store their current state when they are requested to close and then restore this state when they are launched again. The traditional location for storing data in the registry by an application is obtained by means of the following structure:

```
{ROOT_KEY}\Software\{Company Name}\{Company Product}
```

In this template, *ROOT_KEY* is either *HKEY_LOCAL_MACHINE* for machine-specific data, such as what optional components of an application can be installed on the machine, or *HKEY_CURRENT_USER* for user-specific information, such as the list of the user's last-opened files. Under the *Software* key, the name of the company that wrote the application is used followed by the name of the specific application. For example, Microsoft saves the user settings information for Internet Explorer under the key

```
HKEY_CURRENT_USER\Software\Microsoft\Internet Explorer
```

While this hierarchy is great for segregating registry values from different applications from one another, it's best not to create too deep a set of keys. Because of the way the registry is designed, it takes less memory to store a value than it does a key. Because of this, you should design your registry storage so that it uses fewer keys and more values. To optimize even further, it's more efficient to store more information in one value than to have the same information stored across a number of values.

The window in Figure 10-1 shows the hierarchy of keys used to store data for Internet Explorer. The left pane shows the hierarchy of keys down to the *Settings* key under the Internet Explorer key. In the *Settings* key, four values are stored: Anchor Color, Anchor Color Visited, Background Color, and Text Color. In this case, these values are string values, but they could have been *DWORD*s or other data types.

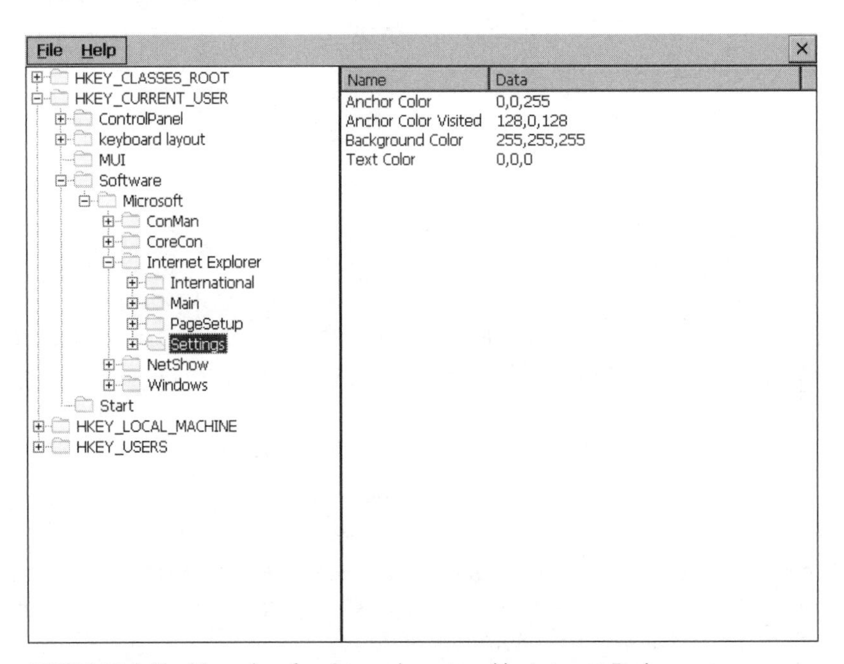

FIGURE 10-1 The hierarchy of registry values stored by Internet Explorer

The Registry API

Now let's turn toward the Windows CE registry API. In general, the registry API provides all the functions necessary to read and write data in the registry as well as enumerate the keys and data store within.

Opening and Creating Keys

You open a registry key with a call to this function:

```
LONG RegOpenKeyEx (HKEY hKey, LPCWSTR lpszSubKey, DWORD ulOptions,
                   REGSAM samDesired, PHKEY phkResult);
```

The first parameter is the key that contains the second parameter, the subkey. This first key must be either one of the root key constants or a previously opened key. The subkey to open is specified as a text string that contains the key to open. This subkey string can contain multiple levels of subkeys as long as each subkey is separated by a backslash. For example, to open the subkey *HKEY_LOCAL_MACHINE\Software\Microsoft\Pocket Word*, an application could either call *RegOpenKeyEx* with *HKEY_LOCAL_MACHINE* as the key and *Software\Microsoft\Pocket Word* as the subkey or open the *Software\Microsoft* key and then make a call with that opened handle to *RegOpenKeyEx*, specifying the subkey *Pocket Word*. Key and value names aren't case specific.

Windows CE ignores the *ulOptions* and *samDesired* parameters. To remain compatible with future versions of the operating system that might use security features, these parameters should be set to 0 for *ulOptions* and *NULL* for *samDesired*. The *phkResult* parameter should point to a variable that will receive the handle to the opened key. The function, if successful, returns a value of *ERROR_SUCCESS* and an error code if it fails.

Another method for opening a key is

```
LONG RegCreateKeyEx (HKEY hKey, LPCWSTR lpszSubKey, DWORD Reserved,
                     LPWSTR lpszClass, DWORD dwOptions,
                     REGSAM samDesired,
                     LPSECURITY_ATTRIBUTES lpSecurityAttributes,
                     PHKEY phkResult, LPDWORD lpdwDisposition);
```

The difference between *RegCreateKeyEx* and *RegOpenKeyEx*, aside from the extra parameters, is that *RegCreateKeyEx* creates the key if it didn't exist before the call. The first two parameters, the key handle and the subkey name, are the same as in *RegOpenKeyEx*. The *Reserved* parameter should be set to 0. The *lpClass* parameter points to a string that contains the class name of the key if it's to be created. This parameter can be set to *NULL* if no class name needs to be specified. The *dwOptions* parameter indicates if the newly created key is to be volatile or nonvolatile. The default is nonvolatile, indicating that the key will persist when the system restarts. To create a volatile key, *dwOptions* should be set to *REG_OPTION_VOLATILE*. The *samDesired* and *lpSecurityAttributes* parameters should be set to *NULL*. The *phkResult* parameter points to the variable that receives the handle to the opened or newly created key. The *lpdwDisposition* parameter points to a variable that's set to indicate whether the key was opened or created by the call. If the key was created, the parameter will be set to *REG_CREATED_NEW_KEY*. If the key previously existed, the value will be *REG_OPENED_EXISTING_KEY*.

Reading Registry Values

You can query registry values by first opening the key containing the values of interest and calling this function:

```
LONG RegQueryValueEx (HKEY hKey, LPCWSTR lpszValueName,
                      LPDWORD lpReserved, LPDWORD lpType,
                      LPBYTE lpData, LPDWORD lpcbData);
```

The *hKey* parameter is the handle of the key opened by *RegCreateKeyEx* or *RegOpenKeyEx*. The *lpszValueName* parameter is the name of the value that's being queried. The *lpType* parameter is a pointer to a variable that receives the variable type. The *lpData* parameter points to the buffer to receive the data, while the *lpcbData* parameter points to a variable that receives the size of the data. If *RegQueryValueEx* is called with the *lpData* parameter equal to *NULL*, Windows returns the size of the data but doesn't return the data itself. This allows applications to first query the size and type of the data before actually receiving it.

Writing Registry Values

You set a registry value by calling

```
LONG RegSetValueEx (HKEY hKey, LPCWSTR lpszValueName, DWORD Reserved,
                    DWORD dwType, const BYTE *lpData, DWORD cbData);
```

The parameters here are fairly obvious: the handle to the open key followed by the name of the value to set. The function also requires that you pass the type of data, the data itself, and the size of the data. The data type parameter is simply a labeling aid for the application that eventually reads the data. Data in the registry is stored in a binary format and returned in that same format. Specifying a different type has no effect on how the data is stored in the registry or how it's returned to the application. However, given the availability of third-party registry editors, you should make every effort to specify the appropriate data type in the registry.

The data types can be one of the following:

- **REG_SZ** A zero-terminated Unicode string
- **REG_EXPAND_SZ** A zero-terminated Unicode string with embedded environment variables
- **REG_MULTI_SZ** A series of zero-terminated Unicode strings terminated by two zero characters

- **REG_DWORD** A 4-byte binary value
- **REG_BINARY** Free-form binary data
- **REG_DWORD_BIG_ENDIAN** A DWORD value stored in big-endian format
- **REG_DWORD_LITTLE_ENDIAN** Equivalent to REG_DWORD
- **REG_LINK** A Unicode symbolic link
- **REG_NONE** No defined type
- **REG_RESOURCE_LIST** A device driver resource list

You can glean a wealth of information about a key by calling this function:

```
LONG RegQueryInfoKey (HKEY hKey, LPWSTR lpszClass, LPDWORD lpcchClass,
                      LPDWORD lpReserved, LPDWORD lpcSubKeys,
                      LPDWORD lpcchMaxSubKeyLen,
                      LPDWORD lpcchMaxClassLen,
                      LPDWORD lpcValues, LPDWORD lpcchMaxValueNameLen,
                      LPDWORD lpcbMaxValueData,
                      LPDWORD lpcbSecurityDescriptor,
                      PFILETIME lpftLastWriteTime);
```

The only input parameter to this function is the handle to a key. The function returns the class of the key, if any, as well as the maximum lengths of the subkeys and values under the key. The last parameter, last write time, is not supported under Windows CE and should be set to *NULL*.

Deleting Keys and Values

You delete a registry key by calling

```
LONG RegDeleteKey (HKEY hKey, LPCWSTR lpszSubKey);
```

The parameters are the handle to the open key and the name of the subkey you plan to delete. For the deletion to be successful, the key must not be currently open. You can delete a value by calling

```
LONG RegDeleteValue (HKEY hKey, LPCWSTR lpszValueName);
```

The function returns 0 to indicate success or a non-zero error code if the function failed to delete the value.

Closing Keys

You close a registry key by calling

```
LONG RegCloseKey (HKEY hKey);
```

When a registry key is closed, Windows CE flushes any unwritten key data to the registry before returning from the call.

Enumerating Registry Keys

In some instances, you'll find it helpful to be able to query a key to see what subkeys and values it contains. You accomplish this with two different functions: one to query the subkeys, another to query the values. The first function

```
LONG RegEnumKeyEx (HKEY hKey, DWORD dwIndex, LPWSTR lpszName,
                   LPDWORD lpcchName, LPDWORD lpReserved,
                   LPWSTR lpszClass, LPDWORD lpcchClass,
                   PFILETIME lpftLastWriteTime);
```

enumerates the subkeys of a registry key through repeated calls. The parameters to pass the function are the handle of the opened key and an index value. To enumerate the first subkey, the *dwIndex* parameter should be 0. For each subsequent call to *RegEnumKeyEx*, *dwIndex* should be incremented to get the next subkey. When there are no more subkeys to be enumerated, *RegEnumKeyEx* returns *ERROR_NO_MORE_ITEMS*.

For each call to *RegEnumKeyEx*, the function returns the name of the subkey and its classname. The last write time parameter isn't supported under Windows CE.

Values within a key can be enumerated with a call to this function:

```
LONG RegEnumValue (HKEY hKey, DWORD dwIndex, LPWSTR lpszValueName,
                   LPDWORD lpcchValueName, LPDWORD lpReserved,
                   LPDWORD lpType, LPBYTE lpData, LPDWORD lpcbData);
```

Like *RegEnumKey*, this function is called repeatedly, passing index values to enumerate the different values stored under the key. When the function returns *ERROR_NO_MORE_ITEMS*, no more values are under the key. *RegEnumValue* returns the name of the values and the data stored in each value, as well as its data type and the size of the data.

Flushing the Registry

Windows CE will flush any changes to the registry to persistent storage when the registry key is closed. However, there may be times when you want to keep a key open but persist the changes immediately. To force a flush of the registry to persistent storage, call the function

```
LONG RegFlushKey (HKEY hKey);
```

The only parameter is the open key handle or one of the predefined keys such as *HKEY_LOCAL_MACHINE*.

A word of warning about *RegFlushKey*: although it may seem important to persist registry changes immediately, excessive calling of *RegFlushKey* can have disastrous effects on the performance of the system. When this function is called, the system may write the entire registry to the persistent store. If the storage technology is slow, which it typically is relative to the other parts of the system, the performance impact is quite noticeable.

Registry Change Notifications

Sometimes it is convenient to know when a registry entry has changed. Monitoring changes in the registry involves a sequence of calls similar to the *FindFirst*, *FindNext*, and *FindClose* call sequence for searching the file system. Add to that a bit of event handling logic, and you can monitor the registry. The process starts with a call to

```
HANDLE CeFindFirstRegChange (HKEY hKey, BOOL bWatchSubTree,
                             DWORD dwNotifyFilter);
```

The parameters of this call start with the handle of the registry key that you want to monitor. This can be an open key handle or one of the top-level keys such as *HKEY_LOCAL_MACHINE*. The *bWatchSubTree* parameter should be set to *TRUE* if you want to be notified for changes for subkeys to the key indicated in the first parameter. The *dwNotifyFilter* specifies what changes are monitored. The possible flags can be a combination of *REG_NOTIFY_CHANGE_NAME* and *REG_NOTIFY_CHANGE_LAST_SET*. The first flag enables monitoring of key changes, while the second enables monitoring of value changes.

The value returned by *CeFindFirstRegChange* is an event handle. The handle will be in a signaled state when a change occurs. To use the handle, the application needs to create a nonuser interface thread; call *CeFindFirstRegChange,* and then call *WaitForSingleObject* on the change handle. The call to *WaitForSingleObject* won't return until the event is signaled, a timeout occurs, or an error occurs. Because this function blocks, it can't be called from a user interface thread that must spend its time in the message loop calling *GetMessage*.

To monitor subsequent changes to the registry, call

```
BOOL CeFindNextRegChange (HANDLE hNotify);
```

The only parameter is the change handle returned from *CeFindFirstRegChange*. After the call to *CeFindNextRegChange*, wait again on the change handle with *WaitForSingleObject*. When you are done monitoring the registry, call the function

```
BOOL CeFindCloseRegChange (HANDLE hNotify);
```

The only parameter is the change notification handle.

The RegView Example Program

The following program is a registry viewer application. It allows a user to navigate the trees in the registry and examine the contents of the data stored. RegView doesn't let you edit the registry, just view it. However, such an extension wouldn't be difficult to make. Listing 10-1 contains the code for the RegView program.

LISTING 10-1

RegView.rc

```
//======================================================================
// Resource file
//
// Copyright (C) 2007 Douglas Boling
//======================================================================
#include "windows.h"
#include "regview.h"                        // Program-specific stuff

//----------------------------------------------------------------------
// Icons and bitmaps
//
ID_ICON ICON   "regview.ico"                // Program icon
ID_BMPS BITMAP "TVBmps.bmp"

//----------------------------------------------------------------------
// Menu
//
ID_MENU MENU DISCARDABLE
BEGIN
    POPUP "&File"
    BEGIN
        MENUITEM "E&xit",                       IDM_EXIT
    END
    POPUP "&Help"
    BEGIN
        MENUITEM "&About...",                   IDM_ABOUT
    END
END
//----------------------------------------------------------------------
// About box dialog template
//
aboutbox DIALOG discardable 10, 10, 135, 40
STYLE  WS_POPUP | WS_VISIBLE | WS_CAPTION | WS_SYSMENU | DS_CENTER |
       DS_MODALFRAME
CAPTION "About"
BEGIN
    ICON  ID_ICON,                     -1,   3,   5,  10,  10
    LTEXT "RegView - Written for the book Programming Windows CE \
           Copyright 2007 Douglas Boling"
                                       -1,  30,   5, 102,  33
END
```

RegView.h

```
//======================================================================
// Header file
//
// Written for the book Programming Windows CE
```

```
// Copyright (C) 2007 Douglas Boling
//======================================================================
// Returns number of elements
#define dim(x) (sizeof(x) / sizeof(x[0]))

//----------------------------------------------------------------------
// Generic defines and data types
//
struct decodeUINT {                             // Structure associates
    UINT Code;                                  // messages
                                                // with a function.
    LRESULT (*Fxn)(HWND, UINT, WPARAM, LPARAM);
};
struct decodeCMD {                              // Structure associates
    UINT Code;                                  // control IDs with a
    LRESULT (*Fxn)(HWND, WORD, HWND, WORD);     // function.
};
struct decodeNotify {                           // Structure associates
    UINT Code;                                  // control IDs with a
    LRESULT (*Fxn)(HWND, UINT, HWND, LPNMHDR);  // notify handler.
};

//----------------------------------------------------------------------
// Generic defines used by application
#define  ID_ICON            1                   // App icon resource ID
#define  ID_BMPS            2                   // Bitmap resource ID
#define  IDC_CMDBAR         10                  // Command band ID
#define  ID_MENU            11                  // Main menu resource ID
#define  ID_TREEV           12                  // Tree view control ID
#define  ID_LISTV           13                  // List view control ID

// Menu item IDs
#define  IDM_EXIT           101                 // File menu
#define  IDM_ABOUT          150                 // Help menu

//----------------------------------------------------------------------
// Function prototypes
//
HWND InitInstance (HINSTANCE, LPWSTR, int);
int TermInstance (HINSTANCE, int);

int EnumChildren (HWND, HTREEITEM, HKEY, LPTSTR, int);
DWORD CountChildren (HKEY, LPTSTR, LPTSTR);
int EnumValues (HWND, HKEY, LPTSTR);
int DisplayValue (HWND, int, LPTSTR, PBYTE, DWORD, DWORD);
int GetTree (HWND, HTREEITEM, HKEY *, TCHAR *, int *);
HTREEITEM InsertTV (HWND, HTREEITEM, TCHAR *, LPARAM, DWORD);
int InsertLV (HWND, int, LPTSTR, LPTSTR);
HWND CreateLV (HWND, RECT *);
HWND CreateTV (HWND, RECT *);

// Window procedures
LRESULT CALLBACK MainWndProc (HWND, UINT, WPARAM, LPARAM);
```

```
// Message handlers
LRESULT DoCreateMain (HWND, UINT, WPARAM, LPARAM);
LRESULT DoSizeMain (HWND, UINT, WPARAM, LPARAM);
LRESULT DoNotifyMain (HWND, UINT, WPARAM, LPARAM);
LRESULT DoCommandMain (HWND, UINT, WPARAM, LPARAM);
LRESULT DoDestroyMain (HWND, UINT, WPARAM, LPARAM);

// Command functions
LPARAM DoMainCommandExit (HWND, WORD, HWND, WORD);
LPARAM DoMainCommandAbout (HWND, WORD, HWND, WORD);

// Notify functions
LPARAM DoMainNotifyTreeV (HWND, UINT, HWND, LPNMHDR);

// Dialog procedures
BOOL CALLBACK AboutDlgProc (HWND, UINT, WPARAM, LPARAM);
```

RegView.cpp

```
//======================================================================
// RegView - Windows CE registry viewer
//
// Written for the book Programming Windows CE
// Copyright (C) 2007 Douglas Boling
//======================================================================
#include <windows.h>                // For all that Windows stuff
#include <commctrl.h>               // Common control includes
#include "RegView.h"                // Program-specific stuff

//----------------------------------------------------------------------
// Global data
//
const TCHAR szAppName[] = TEXT ("RegView");
HINSTANCE hInst;                    // Program instance handle
int nDivPct = 40;                   // Divider setting between windows

// Message dispatch table for MainWindowProc
const struct decodeUINT MainMessages[] = {
    WM_CREATE, DoCreateMain,
    WM_SIZE, DoSizeMain,
    WM_COMMAND, DoCommandMain,
    WM_NOTIFY, DoNotifyMain,
    WM_DESTROY, DoDestroyMain,
};
// Command message dispatch for MainWindowProc
const struct decodeCMD MainCommandItems[] = {
    IDM_EXIT, DoMainCommandExit,
    IDM_ABOUT, DoMainCommandAbout,
};
// Notification message dispatch for MainWindowProc
```

```
const struct decodeNotify MainNotifyItems[] = {
    ID_TREEV, DoMainNotifyTreeV,
};
//======================================================================
//
// Program entry point
//
int WINAPI WinMain (HINSTANCE hInstance, HINSTANCE hPrevInstance,
                    LPWSTR lpCmdLine, int nCmdShow) {
    HWND hwndMain;
    MSG msg;
    int rc = 0;

    // Initialize this instance.
    hwndMain = InitInstance (hInstance, lpCmdLine, nCmdShow);
    if (hwndMain == 0)
        return 0x10;

    // Application message loop
    while (GetMessage (&msg, NULL, 0, 0)) {
        TranslateMessage (&msg);
        DispatchMessage (&msg);
    }
    // Instance cleanup
    return TermInstance (hInstance, msg.wParam);
}
//----------------------------------------------------------------------
// InitInstance - Instance initialization
//
HWND InitInstance (HINSTANCE hInstance, LPWSTR lpCmdLine, int nCmdShow){
    WNDCLASS wc;
    INITCOMMONCONTROLSEX icex;
    HWND hWnd;

    // Save program instance handle in global variable.
    hInst = hInstance;

#if defined(WIN32_PLATFORM_PSPC) || defined(WIN32_PLATFORM_WFSP)
    // For Windows Mobile devices, allow only one instance of the app
    hWnd = FindWindow (szAppName, NULL);
    if (hWnd) {
        SetForegroundWindow ((HWND)(((DWORD)hWnd) | 0x01));
        return 0;
    }
#endif
    // Register application main window class.
    wc.style = 0;                             // Window style
    wc.lpfnWndProc = MainWndProc;             // Callback function
    wc.cbClsExtra = 0;                        // Extra class data
    wc.cbWndExtra = 0;                        // Extra window data
    wc.hInstance = hInstance;                 // Owner handle
    wc.hIcon = NULL,                          // Application icon
    wc.hCursor = LoadCursor (NULL, IDC_ARROW);// Default cursor
```

```
    wc.hbrBackground = (HBRUSH) GetStockObject (WHITE_BRUSH);
    wc.lpszMenuName = NULL;                    // Menu name
    wc.lpszClassName = szAppName;              // Window class name

    if (RegisterClass (&wc) == 0) return 0;

    // Load the command bar common control class.
    icex.dwSize = sizeof (INITCOMMONCONTROLSEX);
    icex.dwICC = ICC_BAR_CLASSES | ICC_TREEVIEW_CLASSES |
                 ICC_LISTVIEW_CLASSES;
    InitCommonControlsEx (&icex);

    // Create main window.
    hWnd = CreateWindow (szAppName, TEXT ("RegView"), WS_VISIBLE,
                         CW_USEDEFAULT, CW_USEDEFAULT, CW_USEDEFAULT,
                         CW_USEDEFAULT, NULL, NULL, hInstance, NULL);
    // Return fail code if window not created.
    if (!IsWindow (hWnd)) return 0;

    // Standard show and update calls
    ShowWindow (hWnd, nCmdShow);
    UpdateWindow (hWnd);
    return hWnd;
}
//----------------------------------------------------------------------
// TermInstance - Program cleanup
//
int TermInstance (HINSTANCE hInstance, int nDefRC) {
    return nDefRC;
}
//======================================================================
// Message handling procedures for MainWindow
//----------------------------------------------------------------------
// MainWndProc - Callback function for application window
//
LRESULT CALLBACK MainWndProc (HWND hWnd, UINT wMsg, WPARAM wParam,
                              LPARAM lParam) {
    int i;
    //
    // Search message list to see if we need to handle this
    // message.  If in list, call procedure.
    //
    for (i = 0; i < dim(MainMessages); i++) {
        if (wMsg == MainMessages[i].Code)
            return (*MainMessages[i].Fxn)(hWnd, wMsg, wParam, lParam);
    }
    return DefWindowProc (hWnd, wMsg, wParam, lParam);
}
//----------------------------------------------------------------------
// DoCreateMain - Process WM_CREATE message for window.
//
LRESULT DoCreateMain (HWND hWnd, UINT wMsg, WPARAM wParam,
                      LPARAM lParam) {
```

```
    HWND hwndCB, hwndChild;
    RECT rect;

    // Create a minimal command bar that has only a menu and an
    // exit button.
    hwndCB = CommandBar_Create (hInst, hWnd, IDC_CMDBAR);
    // Insert the menu.
    CommandBar_InsertMenubar (hwndCB, hInst, ID_MENU, 0);
    // Add exit button to command bar.
    CommandBar_AddAdornments (hwndCB, 0, 0);

    // The position of the child windows will be set in WM_SIZE
    SetRect (&rect, 0, 0, 10, 10);
    // Create the tree view control
    hwndChild = CreateTV (hWnd, &rect);
    if (!IsWindow (hwndChild)) {
        DestroyWindow (hWnd);
        return 0;
    }
    // Create the list view control
    hwndChild = CreateLV (hWnd, &rect);
    // Destroy frame if window not created.
    if (!IsWindow (hwndChild)) {
        DestroyWindow (hWnd);
        return 0;
    }
    // Insert the base keys.
    InsertTV (hWnd, NULL, TEXT ("HKEY_CLASSES_ROOT"),
              (LPARAM)HKEY_CLASSES_ROOT, 1);
    InsertTV (hWnd, NULL, TEXT ("HKEY_CURRENT_USER"),
              (LPARAM)HKEY_CURRENT_USER, 1);
    InsertTV (hWnd, NULL, TEXT ("HKEY_LOCAL_MACHINE"),
              (LPARAM)HKEY_LOCAL_MACHINE, 1);
    InsertTV (hWnd, NULL, TEXT ("HKEY_USERS"),
              (LPARAM)HKEY_USERS, 1);
    return 0;
}
//----------------------------------------------------------------------
// DoSizeMain - Process WM_SIZE message for window.
//
LRESULT DoSizeMain (HWND hWnd, UINT wMsg, WPARAM wParam, LPARAM lParam){
    HWND hwndLV, hwndTV;
    RECT rect, rectLV, rectTV;
    int nDivPos, cx, cy;

    hwndTV = GetDlgItem (hWnd, ID_TREEV);
    hwndLV = GetDlgItem (hWnd, ID_LISTV);

    // Adjust the size of the client rect to take into account
    // the command bar height.
    GetClientRect (hWnd, &rect);
    rect.top += CommandBar_Height (GetDlgItem (hWnd, IDC_CMDBAR));
    cx = rect.right - rect.left;
    cy = rect.bottom - rect.top;
```

```
    // Narrow screens, stack the windows; otherwise, they're side by side.
    if (GetSystemMetrics (SM_CXSCREEN) < GetSystemMetrics (SM_CYSCREEN)){
        nDivPos = (cy * nDivPct)/100;
        SetRect (&rectTV, rect.left, rect.top, cx, nDivPos);
        SetRect (&rectLV, rect.left, nDivPos + rect.top, cx, cy - nDivPos);
    } else {
        nDivPos = (cx * nDivPct)/100;
        SetRect (&rectTV, rect.left, rect.top, nDivPos, cy);
        SetRect (&rectLV, nDivPos, rect.top, cx - nDivPos, cy);
    }
    // The child window positions
    SetWindowPos (hwndTV, NULL, rectTV.left, rectTV.top,
                  rectTV.right, rectTV.bottom, SWP_NOZORDER);
    SetWindowPos (hwndLV, NULL, rectLV.left, rectLV.top,
                  rectLV.right, rectLV.bottom, SWP_NOZORDER);
    return 0;
}
//----------------------------------------------------------------------
// DoCommandMain - Process WM_COMMAND message for window.
//
LRESULT DoCommandMain (HWND hWnd, UINT wMsg, WPARAM wParam,
                       LPARAM lParam) {
    // Parse the parameters.
    WORD idItem = (WORD) LOWORD (wParam);
    WORD wNotifyCode = (WORD) HIWORD (wParam);
    HWND hwndCtl = (HWND) lParam;

    // Call routine to handle control message.
    for (int i = 0; i < dim(MainCommandItems); i++) {
        if (idItem == MainCommandItems[i].Code)
            return (*MainCommandItems[i].Fxn)(hWnd, idItem, hwndCtl,
                                              wNotifyCode);
    }
    return 0;
}
//----------------------------------------------------------------------
// DoNotifyMain - Process WM_NOTIFY message for window.
//
LRESULT DoNotifyMain (HWND hWnd, UINT wMsg, WPARAM wParam,
                      LPARAM lParam) {

    // Parse the parameters.
    UINT idItem = wParam;
    LPNMHDR pHdr = (LPNMHDR) lParam;
    HWND hCtl = pHdr->hwndFrom;

    // Call routine to handle control message.
    for (int i = 0; i < dim(MainNotifyItems); i++) {
        if (idItem == MainNotifyItems[i].Code)
            return (*MainNotifyItems[i].Fxn)(hWnd, idItem, hCtl, pHdr);
    }
    return 0;
}
//----------------------------------------------------------------------
```

```
// DoDestroyMain - Process WM_DESTROY message for window.
//
LRESULT DoDestroyMain (HWND hWnd, UINT wMsg, WPARAM wParam,
                       LPARAM lParam) {
    PostQuitMessage (0);
    return 0;
}
//======================================================================
// Command handler routines
//----------------------------------------------------------------------
// DoMainCommandExit - Process Program Exit command.
//
LPARAM DoMainCommandExit (HWND hWnd, WORD idItem, HWND hwndCtl,
                          WORD wNotifyCode) {

    SendMessage (hWnd, WM_CLOSE, 0, 0);
    return 0;
}
//----------------------------------------------------------------------
// DoMainCommandAbout - Process the Help | About menu command.
//
LPARAM DoMainCommandAbout(HWND hWnd, WORD idItem, HWND hwndCtl,
                          WORD wNotifyCode) {

    // Use DialogBox to create modal dialog box.
    DialogBox (hInst, TEXT ("aboutbox"), hWnd, AboutDlgProc);
    return 0;
}
//======================================================================
// Notify handler routines
//----------------------------------------------------------------------
// DoMainNotifyTreeV - Process notify message for list view.
//
LPARAM DoMainNotifyTreeV (HWND hWnd, UINT idItem, HWND hwndCtl,
                          LPNMHDR pnmh) {
    TCHAR szKey[256];
    HKEY hRoot;
    HTREEITEM hChild, hNext;
    int nMax;

    LPNM_TREEVIEW pNotifyTV = (LPNM_TREEVIEW) pnmh;

    switch (pnmh->code) {
        case TVN_ITEMEXPANDED:
            if (pNotifyTV->action == TVE_COLLAPSE) {
                // Delete the children so that on next open, they will
                // be reenumerated.
                hChild = TreeView_GetChild (hwndCtl,
                                      pNotifyTV->itemNew.hItem);
                while (hChild) {
                    hNext = TreeView_GetNextItem (hwndCtl, hChild,
                                                  TVGN_NEXT);
                    TreeView_DeleteItem (hwndCtl, hChild);
                    hChild = hNext;
```

```
                }
            }
            break;

        case TVN_SELCHANGED:
            nMax = dim(szKey);
            GetTree (hWnd, pNotifyTV->itemNew.hItem, &hRoot,
                     szKey, &nMax);
            EnumValues (hWnd, hRoot, szKey);
            break;

        case TVN_ITEMEXPANDING:
            if (pNotifyTV->action == TVE_EXPAND) {
                nMax = dim(szKey);
                GetTree (hWnd, pNotifyTV->itemNew.hItem, &hRoot,
                         szKey, &nMax);
                EnumChildren (hWnd, pNotifyTV->itemNew.hItem,
                              hRoot, szKey, dim (szKey));
                TreeView_SortChildren (hwndCtl,
                                       pNotifyTV->itemNew.hItem, TRUE);
            }
            break;
    }
    return 0;
}
//----------------------------------------------------------------------
// CreateLV - Create list view control.
//
HWND CreateLV (HWND hWnd, RECT *prect) {
    HWND hwndLV;
    LVCOLUMN lvc;

    // Create report window. Size it so that it fits under
    // the command bar and fills the remaining client area.
    hwndLV = CreateWindowEx (0, WC_LISTVIEW, TEXT (""),
                         WS_VISIBLE | WS_CHILD | WS_VSCROLL |
                         WS_BORDER | LVS_REPORT,
                         prect->left, prect->top,
                         prect->right - prect->left,
                         prect->bottom - prect->top,
                         hWnd, (HMENU)ID_LISTV,
                         hInst, NULL);
    // Add columns.
    if (hwndLV) {
        lvc.mask = LVCF_TEXT | LVCF_WIDTH | LVCF_FMT | LVCF_SUBITEM |
                   LVCF_ORDER;
        lvc.fmt = LVCFMT_LEFT;
        lvc.cx = 120;
        lvc.pszText = TEXT ("Name");
        lvc.iOrder = 0;
        lvc.iSubItem = 0;
        SendMessage (hwndLV, LVM_INSERTCOLUMN, 0, (LPARAM)&lvc);

        lvc.mask |= LVCF_SUBITEM;
```

```
        lvc.pszText = TEXT ("Data");
        lvc.cx = 250;
        lvc.iOrder = 1;
        lvc.iSubItem = 1;
        SendMessage (hwndLV, LVM_INSERTCOLUMN, 1, (LPARAM)&lvc);
    }
    return hwndLV;
}
//----------------------------------------------------------------------
// InitTreeView - Initialize tree view control.
//
HWND CreateTV (HWND hWnd, RECT *prect) {
    HBITMAP hBmp;
    HIMAGELIST himl;
    HWND hwndTV;

    // Create tree view.  Size it so that it fits under
    // the command bar and fills the left part of the client area.
    hwndTV = CreateWindowEx (0, WC_TREEVIEW,
                         TEXT (""), WS_VISIBLE | WS_CHILD | WS_VSCROLL |
                         WS_BORDER | TVS_HASLINES | TVS_HASBUTTONS |
                         TVS_LINESATROOT, prect->left, prect->top,
                         prect->right, prect->bottom,
                         hWnd, (HMENU)ID_TREEV, hInst, NULL);

    if (!IsWindow (hwndTV))
        return 0;

    // Create image list control for tree view icons.
    himl = ImageList_Create (16, 16, ILC_COLOR, 2, 0);
    // Load first two images from one bitmap.
    hBmp = LoadBitmap (hInst, MAKEINTRESOURCE (ID_BMPS));
    ImageList_Add (himl, hBmp, NULL);
    DeleteObject (hBmp);

    TreeView_SetImageList(hwndTV, himl, TVSIL_NORMAL);
    return hwndTV;
}
//----------------------------------------------------------------------
// InsertLV - Add an item to the list view control.
//
int InsertLV (HWND hWnd, int nItem, LPTSTR pszName, LPTSTR pszData) {

    HWND hwndLV = GetDlgItem (hWnd, ID_LISTV);
    LVITEM lvi;
    int rc;

    lvi.mask = LVIF_TEXT | LVIF_IMAGE | LVIF_PARAM;
    lvi.iItem = nItem;
    lvi.iSubItem = 0;
    lvi.pszText = pszName;
    lvi.iImage = 0;
    lvi.lParam = nItem;
```

```
    rc = SendMessage (hwndLV, LVM_INSERTITEM, 0, (LPARAM)&lvi);

    lvi.mask = LVIF_TEXT;
    lvi.iItem = nItem;
    lvi.iSubItem = 1;
    lvi.pszText = pszData;

    rc = SendMessage (hwndLV, LVM_SETITEM, 0, (LPARAM)&lvi);
    return 0;
}
//----------------------------------------------------------------------
// InsertTV - Insert item into tree view control.
//
HTREEITEM InsertTV (HWND hWnd, HTREEITEM hParent, TCHAR *pszName,
                    LPARAM lParam, DWORD nChildren) {
    TV_INSERTSTRUCT tvis;

    HWND hwndTV = GetDlgItem (hWnd, ID_TREEV);
    // Initialize the insertstruct.
    memset (&tvis, 0, sizeof (tvis));
    tvis.hParent = hParent;
    tvis.hInsertAfter = TVI_LAST;
    tvis.item.mask = TVIF_TEXT | TVIF_PARAM | TVIF_CHILDREN |
                     TVIF_IMAGE;
    tvis.item.pszText = pszName;
    tvis.item.cchTextMax = lstrlen (pszName);
    tvis.item.iImage = 1;
    tvis.item.iSelectedImage = 1;
    tvis.item.lParam = lParam;
    if (nChildren)
        tvis.item.cChildren = 1;
    else
        tvis.item.cChildren = 0;

    return TreeView_InsertItem (hwndTV, &tvis);
}
//----------------------------------------------------------------------
// GetTree - Compute the full path of the tree view item.
//
int GetTree (HWND hWnd, HTREEITEM hItem, HKEY *pRoot, TCHAR *pszKey,
             int *pnMax) {
    TV_ITEM tvi;
    TCHAR szName[256];
    HTREEITEM hParent;
    HWND hwndTV = GetDlgItem (hWnd, ID_TREEV);

    memset (&tvi, 0, sizeof (tvi));

    hParent = TreeView_GetParent (hwndTV, hItem);
    if (hParent) {
        // Get the parent of the parent of the...
        GetTree (hWnd, hParent, pRoot, pszKey, pnMax);
```

```
        // Get the name of the item.
        tvi.mask = TVIF_TEXT;
        tvi.hItem = hItem;
        tvi.pszText = szName;
        tvi.cchTextMax = dim(szName);
        TreeView_GetItem (hwndTV, &tvi);

        StringCchCat (pszKey, *pnMax, TEXT ("\\"));
        (*pnMax)--;
        StringCchCat (pszKey, *pnMax, szName);
        (*pnMax) -= lstrlen(szName);
    } else {
        *pszKey = TEXT ('\0');
        szName[0] = TEXT ('\0');
        // Get the name of the item.
        tvi.mask = TVIF_TEXT | TVIF_PARAM;
        tvi.hItem = hItem;
        tvi.pszText = szName;
        tvi.cchTextMax = dim(szName);
        if (TreeView_GetItem (hwndTV, &tvi))
            *pRoot = (HKEY)tvi.lParam;
        else {
            int rc = GetLastError();
        }
    }
    return 0;
}
//----------------------------------------------------------------------
// DisplayValue - Display the data, depending on the type.
//
int DisplayValue (HWND hWnd, int nCnt, LPTSTR pszName, PBYTE pbData,
                  DWORD dwDSize, DWORD dwType) {
    TCHAR szData[512];
    int i, len, len1;

    switch (dwType) {
    case REG_MULTI_SZ:
        len = dim (szData);
        szData[0] = TEXT('\0');
        while ((*pbData != 0) && (len > 0)) {
            len1 = lstrlen ((LPTSTR)pbData);
            if (FAILED (StringCchCat (szData, len, (LPTSTR)pbData)))
                break;
            len -= len1;
            pbData += (len1+1) * sizeof (TCHAR);
            if (*pbData == 0)
                break;
            if (FAILED (StringCchCat (szData, len, TEXT(","))))
                break;
            len--;
        }
        break;
    case REG_EXPAND_SZ:
```

```
    case REG_SZ:
        StringCchCopy (szData, dim (szData), (LPTSTR)pbData);
        break;

    case REG_DWORD:
        wsprintf (szData, TEXT ("%X"), *(int *)pbData);
        break;

    case REG_BINARY:
        szData[0] = TEXT ('\0');
        for (i = 0; i < (int)dwDSize; i++) {
            len = lstrlen (szData);
            wsprintf (&szData[len], TEXT ("%02X "), pbData[i]);
            if (len > dim(szData) - 6)
                break;
        }
        break;
    default:
        wsprintf (szData, TEXT ("Unknown type: %x"), dwType);
    }
    InsertLV (hWnd, nCnt, pszName, szData);
    return 0;
}
//----------------------------------------------------------------------
// EnumValues - Enumerate each of the values of a key.
//
int EnumValues (HWND hWnd, HKEY hRoot, LPTSTR pszKey) {
    int nCnt = 0, rc;
    DWORD dwNSize, dwDSize, dwType;
    TCHAR szName[MAX_PATH];
    BYTE bData[1024];
    HKEY hKey;

    if (lstrlen (pszKey)) {
        if (RegOpenKeyEx (hRoot, pszKey, 0, 0, &hKey) != ERROR_SUCCESS)
            return 0;
    } else
        hKey = hRoot;

    // Clean out list view.
    ListView_DeleteAllItems (GetDlgItem (hWnd, ID_LISTV));

    // Enumerate the values in the list view control.
    nCnt = 0;
    dwNSize = dim(szName);
    dwDSize = dim(bData);
    rc = RegEnumValue (hKey, nCnt, szName, &dwNSize,
                       NULL, &dwType, bData, &dwDSize);

    while (rc == ERROR_SUCCESS) {
        // Display the value in the list view control.
        DisplayValue (hWnd, nCnt, szName, bData, dwDSize, dwType);
```

```
        dwNSize = dim(szName);
        dwDSize = dim(bData);
        nCnt++;
        rc = RegEnumValue (hKey, nCnt, szName, &dwNSize,
                           NULL, &dwType, bData, &dwDSize);
    }
    if (hKey != hRoot)
        RegCloseKey (hKey);
    return 1;
}
//----------------------------------------------------------------------
// CountChildren - Count the number of children of a key.
//
DWORD CountChildren (HKEY hRoot, LPTSTR pszKeyPath, LPTSTR pszKey,
                     int nPathMax) {
    TCHAR *pEnd;
    DWORD dwCnt;
    HKEY hKey;
    size_t dwLen;

    // Safe lstrlen
    if (FAILED(StringCchLength (pszKeyPath, nPathMax, &dwLen)))
        return 0;

    pEnd = pszKeyPath + dwLen;
    StringCchCopy (pEnd, nPathMax - dwLen, TEXT("\\"));
    StringCchCopy (pEnd, nPathMax - dwLen - 1, pszKey);
    if (RegOpenKeyEx(hRoot, pszKeyPath, 0, 0, &hKey) ==
        ERROR_SUCCESS) {
        RegQueryInfoKey (hKey, NULL, NULL, 0, &dwCnt, NULL, NULL, NULL,
                         NULL, NULL, NULL, NULL);
        RegCloseKey (hKey);
    }
    *pEnd = TEXT ('\0');
    return dwCnt;
}
//----------------------------------------------------------------------
// EnumChildren - Enumerate the child keys of a key.
//
int EnumChildren (HWND hWnd, HTREEITEM hParent, HKEY hRoot,
                  LPTSTR pszKey, int nKeyMax) {
    int i = 0, rc;
    DWORD dwNSize;
    DWORD dwCSize;
    TCHAR szName[MAX_PATH];
    TCHAR szClass[256];
    FILETIME ft;
    DWORD nChild;
    HKEY hKey;
    TVITEM tvi;

    // All keys but root need to be opened.
```

```
    if (*pszKey != TEXT('\0')) {
        if (RegOpenKeyEx (hRoot, pszKey, 0, 0, &hKey) != ERROR_SUCCESS) {
            rc = GetLastError();
            return 0;
        }
    } else
        hKey = hRoot;

    dwNSize = dim(szName);
    dwCSize = dim(szClass);
    rc = RegEnumKeyEx (hKey, i, szName, &dwNSize, NULL,
                       szClass, &dwCSize, &ft);
    while (rc == ERROR_SUCCESS) {

        nChild = CountChildren (hRoot, pszKey, szName, nKeyMax);
        // Add key to tree view.
        InsertTV (hWnd, hParent, szName, 0, nChild);
        dwNSize = dim(szName);
        rc = RegEnumKeyEx (hKey, ++i, szName, &dwNSize,
                           NULL, NULL, 0, &ft);
    }
    // If this wasn't the root key, close it.
    if (hKey != hRoot)
        RegCloseKey (hKey);
    // If no children, remove expand button.
    if (i == 0) {
        tvi.hItem = hParent;
        tvi.mask = TVIF_CHILDREN;
        tvi.cChildren = 0;
        TreeView_SetItem (GetDlgItem (hWnd, ID_TREEV), &tvi);
    }
    return i;
}
//======================================================================
// About Dialog procedure
//
BOOL CALLBACK AboutDlgProc (HWND hWnd, UINT wMsg, WPARAM wParam,
                            LPARAM lParam) {
    switch (wMsg) {
        case WM_COMMAND:
            switch (LOWORD (wParam)) {
                case IDOK:
                case IDCANCEL:
                    EndDialog (hWnd, 0);
                    return TRUE;
            }
        break;
    }
    return FALSE;
}
```

The workhorses of this program are the enumeration functions that query what keys and values are under each key. As a key is opened in the tree view control, the control sends a *WM_NOTIFY* message. In response, RegView enumerates the items below that key and fills the tree view with the child keys and the list view control with the values.

The registry provides a central clearinghouse for configuration information for both the operating system and the applications that run on it. Knowing how to use but not abuse the registry is critical for all Windows programmers. Fortunately, the registry structure and interface are quite familiar to Windows programmers and should present no surprises. Now it's time to look at one other type of data that can be stored in the file system, Windows CE databases. The database API is unique to Windows CE. Let's see how it works.

Chapter 11
Windows CE Databases

Windows CE supports a unique database API for storing and organizing data in the system. The database functions provide a simple tool for managing and organizing data. They aren't to be confused with the powerful multilevel SQL databases found on other computers. Even with its modest functionality, however, the database API is convenient for storing and organizing simple groups of data, such as address lists and mail folders.

In this chapter, I'll give you an overview of the database API. The database API is one of the areas that have experienced a fair amount of change as Windows CE has evolved. Essentially, functionality has been added to later versions of Windows CE. Where appropriate, I'll cover the differences between the different versions and show workarounds, where possible, for maintaining a common code base.

The Two Databases

Windows CE has supported native database functionality since its inception. However, in the years since Windows CE was introduced, databases have grown in size and complexity and the original database engine was not able to keep up. Starting with Windows CE 5, Microsoft introduced a new database engine as an option for Windows CE. This new engine is known as the embedded database (EDB) while the old engine, which has been kept for backward compatibility, is referred to as the CE database (CEDB).

The embedded database provides significantly better performance for large datasets, support for transactions, and more flexible data type support. For the most part, the new engine is backward compatible from the API perspective, although there is some breakage due to the characteristics of the implementation. Throughout this discussion, I will refer to the places where a particular feature or characteristic is unique to the embedded database or the old CE database engine. Regardless of the engine, the database implemented by Windows CE is simple, but it serves as an effective tool for organizing uncomplicated data.

Basic Definitions

The structure of a Windows CE database consists of database *volumes* that are typically stored as files on a file system. Each database volume contains one or more *databases*. Each database consists of *records* that contain *properties*. Properties contain data in of the of the predefined datatypes shown in Table 11-1.

TABLE 11-1 Database Data Types Supported by Windows CE

Data type	Database engine	Description
sVal	Both	2-byte signed integer
usVal	Both	2-byte unsigned integer
iVal	Both	4-byte signed integer
uiVal	Both	4-byte unsigned integer
FILETIME	Both	A time and date structure
LPWSTR	Both	Zero-terminated Unicode string
CEBLOB	Both[1]	A collection of bytes
BOOL	Both	Boolean
Float	Both	8-byte floating point value
Stream	EDB only	Binary stream of data
GUID	EDB only	128-bit GUID
Auto iVal	EDB only	Auto-generated 4-byte integer
Auto-Double	EDB only	Auto-generated 8-byte integer

Records can't contain other records. Also, records can reside in only one database. The embedded database engine allows one or more databases within a volume to be locked for the duration of a *transaction*. Transactions can include one or more database reads or writes. Finally, Windows CE does provide a method of notifying a process that another thread has modified a database.

An embedded database can have up to 16 multilevel sort indexes. (In a multilevel sort index, the database sorts by a primary property and then sorts within that property by a second, third, and up to a 16th property.) The sort indexes are defined by a schema that is set when the database is created.

The CEDB engine is more limited, allowing only four multilevel sort indexes. Each sort index is limited to three properties. These indexes are defined when the database is created but can be redefined later, although the restructuring of a database takes a large amount of time. Each sort index by itself results in a fair amount of overhead, so you should limit the number of sort indexes to what you really need.

One other difference between an EDB and a CEDB is that an EDB can be created with a *schema*. That is, a specification for the data stored for each record. CEDBs store records with whatever properties are specified when a record is written.

In short, Windows CE gives you a basic database functionality that helps applications organize simple data structures. Windows Mobile devices use the database API to manage the address book, the task list, and e-mail messages. So if you have a collection of data, this database API might just be the best method of managing that data.

[1] EDB limits blobs to 8 KB while CEDB allows blobs to be up to 64 KB in size.

Designing a Database

Before you can jump in with a call to *CeCreateDatabaseEx2*, you need to think carefully about how the database will be used. While the basic limitations of the Windows CE database structure rule out complex databases, the structure is quite handy for managing collections of related data on a small personal device, which, after all, is one of the target markets for Windows CE.

Each record in a database can have as many properties as you need as long as they don't exceed the basic limits of the database structure. The limits are fairly loose. An individual property can't exceed the constant *CEDB_MAXPROPDATASIZE*, which is set to 8,192 for an embedded database and 65,471 for the CE database. A single record can't exceed *CEDB_MAXRECORDSIZE*, defined as 8,192 for EDB and 131,072 for CEDB. The maximum number of records that can be in a single database is 2,147,483,647 for EDB and 65,535 for CEDB.

Database Volumes

Both EDB volumes and CEDB volumes are stored as files in the file system. CEDBs can also be stored directly in the object store, which in this case acts as the default database volume. When you're working with database volumes, they must be first *mounted* before a database is opened, then *unmounted* after you close the databases within the volume. Essentially, mounting the database creates or opens the file that contains one or more databases along with the transaction data for those databases.

There are disadvantages to database volumes aside from the overhead of mounting and unmounting the volumes. Database volumes are actual files and therefore can be deleted by means of standard file operations. The volumes are, by default, marked as hidden, but that wouldn't deter the intrepid user from finding and deleting a volume in a desperate search for more space on the device. CEDBs created directly within the object store aren't files and therefore are much more difficult for the user to accidentally delete.

The Database API

Once you have planned your database and given the restrictions and considerations necessary to it, the programming can begin.

Mounting a Database Volume

If your database is on external media, such as a CompactFlash card, you'll need to mount the database volume that contains it. To mount a database volume, call

```
BOOL CeMountDBVol (PCEGUID pguid, LPWSTR lpszVol, DWORD dwFlags);
```

This function performs a dual purpose: it can create a new volume or open an existing volume. The first parameter is a pointer to a guid. *CeMountDBVol* returns a guid that's used by most of the database functions to identify the volume. You shouldn't confuse the *CEGUID*-type guid parameter in the database functions with the *GUID* type that is used by OLE and parts of the Windows shell. A *CEGUID* is simply a handle that tracks the opened database volume.

The second parameter in *CeMountDBVol* is the name of the volume to mount. This isn't a database name, but the name of a file that will contain one or more databases. Since the parameter is a file name, you should define it in \path\name.ext format.

The last parameter, *dwFlags*, should be loaded with flags that define how this function acts. The possible flags are the following:

- **CREATE_NEW** Creates a new database volume. If the volume already exists, the function fails.
- **CREATE_ALWAYS** Creates a new database volume. If the volume already exists, it overwrites the old volume.
- **OPEN_EXISTING** Opens a database volume. If the volume doesn't exist, the function fails.
- **OPEN_ALWAYS** Opens a database volume. If the volume doesn't exist, a new database volume is created.
- **TRUNCATE_EXISTING** Opens a database volume and truncates it to 0 bytes. If the volume does not exist, the function fails.

If the flags resemble the action flags for *CreateFile*, they should. The actions of *CeMountDBVol* essentially mirror *CreateFile* except that instead of creating or opening a generic file, *CeMountDBVol* creates or opens a file especially designed to hold databases.

If the function succeeds, it returns *TRUE* and the guid is set to a value that is then passed to the other database functions. If the function fails, a call to *GetLastError* returns an error code indicating the reason for the failure.

An extended mount function, available only to EDBs is

```
BOOL CeMountDBVolEx (PCEGUID pGuid, LPWSTR lpwszDBVol,
                     CEVOLUMEOPTIONS* pOptions, DWORD dwFlags);
```

The difference between this function and *CeMountDBVol* is the addition of the *pOptions* parameter that points to a *CEVOLUMEOPTIONS* structure that fine tunes how the volume is managed by the operating system. The structure is defined as

```
typedef struct _CEVOLUMEOPTIONS {
    WORD        wVersion;
    DWORD       cbBufferPool;
    DWORD       dwAutoShrinkPercent;
    DWORD       dwFlushInterval;
    DWORD       cMaxNotifyChanges;
    DWORD       dwDefaultTimeout;
    WCHAR       wszPassword[CCH_MAX_PASSWORD + 1];
    DWORD       dwFlags;
    DWORD       cMaxSize;
} CEVOLUMEOPTIONS, *PCEVOLUMEOPTIONS;
```

The only fields that must be filled in are the *wVersion* and *dwFlags*. The *wVersion* field must be set to *CEVOLUMEOPTIONS_VERSION* for Windows CE 5 and *CEVOLUMEOPTIONS_VERSIONEX* for Windows CE 6 and later. If the application specifies a *wVersion* of *CEVOLUMEOPTIONS_VERSION* in Windows CE 6, the *cMaxSize* field will be ignored by the operating system. The *dwFlags* field should be set with bit flags indicating which of the other fields contains valid data.

The *cbBufferPool* field can contian the number of bytes in the pool of RAM used to cache the database data. The larger the value, the faster the performance of the database with the penality of using more RAM. The default buffer pool is 640 KB. The *dwAutoShrinkPercent* field can be set to the free percentage that the volume has to fall below before the operating system triggers its shrink thread that reduces the footprint of the volume on the disk. The default auto-shrink percentage is 60. The *dwFlushInterval* field can specify the interval, in seconds, between the times that the operating system will flush modified data to the volume file. The default interval is 10 seconds. The *cMaxNotifyChanges* field specifies how many changes are queued during a transaction before the individual changes are dropped in lieu of a single "volume changed" notification when the transaction commits. The *dwDefaultTimeout* parameter is the default time, in milliseconds, that the pending database change will wait before timing out due to a long transaction. The *wszPassword* field can specifiy up to a 40-character password for the volume. The previously mentioned *dwFlags* field specifies in flags which of the other fields are valid. Finally, the *cMaxSize* field can specify a limit to the size of the database.

Database volumes can be opened by more than one process at a time. The system maintains a reference count for the volume. As the last process unmounts a database volume, the system unmounts the volume.

Enumerating Mounted Database Volumes

You can determine which database volumes are currently mounted by repeatedly calling this function:

```
BOOL CeEnumDBVolumes (PCEGUID pguid, LPWSTR lpBuf, DWORD dwSize);
```

The first time you call *CeEnumDBVolumes*, set the guid pointed to by *pguid* to be invalid. You use the *CREATE_INVALIDGUID* macro to accomplish this. *CeEnumDBVolumes* returns *TRUE* if a mounted volume is found and returns the guid and name of that volume in the variables pointed to by *pguid* and *lpBuff*. The *dwSize* parameter should be loaded with the size of the buffer pointed to by *lpBuff*. To enumerate the next volume, pass the guid returned by the previous call to the function. Repeat this process until *CeEnumDBVolumes* returns *FALSE*. The code below demonstrates this process:

```
CEGUID guid;
TCHAR szVolume[MAX_PATH];
INT nCnt = 0;

CREATE_INVALIDGUID (&guid);
while (CeEnumDBVolumes (&guid, szVolume, sizeof (szVolume))) {
    // guid contains the guid of the mounted volume;
    // szVolume contains the name of the volume.
    nCnt++;   // Count the number of mounted volumes.
}
```

Flushing a Database Volume

To force a flush of changes to the the database volume, call the function

```
BOOL CeFlushDBVol (PCEGUID pguid);
```

The function's only parameter is the guid of a mounted database volume. To cause a flush of all mounted databases, call this function with a *pguid* value of *NULL*. Database writes are cached until the flush interval for the volume is elapsed, the volume is unmounted, or the *CeFlushDBVol* function is called.

While it is important that database data be flushed before a reset or power failure to avoid loss of data, excessive calling of this function will impact system performance. Take care when using this function to balance the needs of data integrity and system performance.

Unmounting a Database Volume

When you have completed using the volume, you should unmount it by calling this function:

```
BOOL CeUnmountDBVol (PCEGUID pguid);
```

The function's only parameter is the guid of a mounted database volume. Calling this function is necessary when you no longer need a database volume and you want to free system resources. Database volumes are unmounted only when all applications that have mounted the volume have called *CeUnmountDBVol*.

Using the Object Store as a Database Volume

Even though you can store databases in volumes on external media, it is possible to treat the object store as a database volume for a CEDB. Because many of the database functions require a *CEGUID* that identifies a database volume, you need a *CEGUID* that references the system object store. Fortunately, one can be created using this macro:

```
CREATE_SYSTEMGUID (PCEGUID pguid);
```

The parameter is, of course, a pointer to a *CEGUID*. The value set in the *CEGUID* by this macro can then be passed to any of the database functions that require a separate volume *CEGUID*.

Creating a Database

The prefered method for creating an EDB is to call the function

```
CEOID CeCreateDatabaseWithProps (PCEGUID pGuid, CEDBASEINFOEX* pInfo,
                                 DWORD cProps, CEPROPSPEC* prgProps);
```

The first parameter is a *pguid* parameter that identifies the mounted database volume where the database is located. The second parameter is a pointer to a *CEDBASEINFOEX* structure, which I will discuss shortly. The *cProps* parameter indicates the number of properties listed in the *prgProps* array. The *prgProps* array specifies the properties for the records to be added in the newly created database. This structure defines the schema of the database being created. The schema is the format for each of the records in the database.

The key to understanding this function are the two rather complex structures: the *CEDBASEINFOEX* and *CEPROPSPEC* structures. I'm going to discuss the second of these two structures first because it is shorter, specific to this function, and introduces some of the basic concepts important to Windows CE databases.

The *CEPROPSPEC* structure is defined as

```
typedef struct _CEPROPSPEC {
   WORD     wVersion;
   CEPROPID propid;
   DWORD    dwFlags;
   LPWSTR   pwszPropName;
   DWORD    cchPropName;
} CEPROPSPEC, *PCEPROPSPEC;
```

The *wVersion* field should be set to *CEPROPSPEC_VERSION*. The *propid* field describes the data type and ID value for the property being specified. A *CEPROPID* or property ID is nothing more than a unique identifier for a property in the database. The property ID is a *DWORD* value with the low 16 bits containing the data type and the upper 16 bits containing an application-defined value. A property ID is defined as a constant and is used by various database functions to identify the property. For example, the property ID for a property that contained the address of a contact might be defined as

```
#define PID_ADDRESS       MAKELONG (CEVT_LPWSTR, 1)
```

The *MAKELONG* macro simply combines two 16-bit values into a *DWORD* or *LONG*. The first parameter is the low word or the result, while the second parameter becomes the high word. In this case, the *CEVT_LPWSTR* constant indicates that the property contains a string, while the second parameter is simply a value that uniquely identifies the *Address* property, distinguishing it from other string properties in the record.

The *dwFlags* field of the *CEPROPSPEC* structure can optionally contain the flags *DB_PROP_NOTNULL,* which indicates that all records in the database contain this property, and *DB_PROP_COMPRESSED,* which indicates that noninteger property types be compressed. The *pwszPropName* field specifies a name for the property while the *cchPropName* field is used to indicate the length of the buffer pointed to by the name field when this structure is used by other functions.

The CEDBASEINFOEX structure is defined as

```
typedef struct _CEDBASEINFOEX {
    WORD      wVersion;
    WORD      wNumSortOrder;
    DWORD     dwFlags;
    WCHAR     szDbaseName[CEDB_MAXDBASENAMELEN];
    DWORD     dwDbaseType;
    DWORD     dwNumRecords;
    DWORD     dwSize;
    FILETIME ftLastModified;
    SORTORDERSPECEX rgSortSpecs[CEDB_MAXSORTORDER];
} CEDBASEINFOEX, *PCEDBASEINFOEX;
```

The first field, *wVersion*, specifies the version of the structure itself. It should be set to *CEDBASEINFOEX_VERSION*. This constant is defined differently for EDBs and CEDBs. The *wNumSortOrder* parameter should be set to the number of sort order structures in *rgSortSpecsArray*. The maximum number of sort indexes that can be specified is 16 for an EDB and 4 for a CEDB.

The *dwFlags* field has two uses. First, it contains flags indicating which fields in the structure are valid. The possible values for the *dwFlags* field are *CEDB_VALIDNAME*, *CEDB_VALIDTYPE*, *CEDB_VALIDSORTSPEC*, and *CEDB_ VALIDDBFLAGS*. When you're creating a database, it's easier to set the *dwFlags* field to *CEDB_VALIDCREATE*, which is a combination of the flags I just listed. An additional flag, *CEDB_VALIDMODTIME*, is used when *CeOidGetInfo* uses this structure.

The other use for the *dwFlags* parameter is to specify the properties of the database. Two flags are currently defined. The first is *CEDB_NOCOMPRESS*, which can be specified if you don't want the database you're creating to be compressed. By default, all databases are compressed, which saves storage space at the expense of speed. By specifying the *CEDB_NOCOMPRESS* flag, the database will be larger but you will be able to read and write to the database faster. The second flag that can be defined is *CEDB_SYSTEMDB*. For versions of Windows CE before 6.0, this flag indicates that the database cannot be deleted by an untrusted application.

The *szDbaseName* field specifies the name of the new database. Unlike file names, the database name is limited to 128 characters for EDBs and 32 for CEDBs, including the terminating zero. The *dwDbaseType* field is a user-defined parameter that can be employed to differentiate families of databases. For example, you might want to use a common type value for all databases that your application creates. This allows them to be easily enumerated. At this point, there are no rules for what type values to use. The fields *wNumRecords*, *dwSize*, and *ftLastModified* are ignored during the call to *CeCreateDatabaseWithProps*. They are used by other database functions that utilize this same structure.

The final field, *rgSortSpecs*, specifies the sort specification for the database. This parameter contains an array of *SORTORDERSPECEX* structures defined as

```
typedef struct _SORTORDERSPECEX {
    WORD wVersion;
    WORD wNumProps;
    WORD wKeyFlags;
    WORD wReserved;
    CEPROPID rgPropID[CEDB_MAXSORTPROP];
    DWORD rgdwFlags[CEDB_MAXSORTPROP];
} SORTORDERSPECEX;
```

The first field in *SORTORDERSPECEX* is the *wVersion* field, which should be set to *SORTORDERSPECEX_VERSION*. The *wNumProps* field specifies the number of sort properties used in this sort specification. The *wKeyFlags* field defines characteristics for the specification. The only flag currently supported is *CEDB_SORT_UNIQUE*, which indicates that each record in the database must have a unique value in this property. The *rgPropID* field is an array of property IDs that indicate which properties are to be used for sorting when this sort order specification is referenced.

The final field in *SORTORDERSPECEX*, *rgdwFlags*, contains an array of flags that define how the sort is to be accomplished. Each entry in the array matches the corresponding entry in the *rgPropID* array. The following flags are defined for this field:

- **CEDB_SORT_DESCENDING** The sort is to be in descending order. By default, properties are sorted in ascending order.
- **CEDB_SORT_CASEINSENSITIVE** The sort should ignore the case of the letters in the string.
- **CEDB_SORT_UNKNOWNFIRST** Records without this property are to be placed at the start of the sort order. By default, these records are placed last.
- **CEDB_SORT_IGNORENONSPACE** The sort should ignore nonspace characters, such as accents, during sorting. This flag is valid only for string properties.
- **CEDB_SORT_IGNORESYMBOLS** The sort should ignore symbols during sorting. This flag is valid only for string properties.
- **CEDB_SORT_IGNOREKANATYPE** The sort should not differentiate between Hiragana and Katakana characters. This flag is valid only for string properties.

- **CEDB_SORT_IGNOREWIDTH** The sort should ignore the difference between single-byte characters and the same character represented by a double-byte value. This flag is valid only for string properties.
- **CEDB_SORT_NONNULL** This flag specifies that this sort property must be present in all records in the database.

A typical database might have a number of sort orders defined. After a database is created, these sort orders can be changed; however, this process is quite resource intensive and can take from seconds up to minutes to execute on large databases.

The value returned by *CeCreateDatabaseWithProps* is a *CEOID.* We have seen this kind of value a couple of times so far in this chapter. It's an ID value that identifies the newly created database. If the value is 0, an error occurred while you were trying to create the database. You can call *GetLastError* to diagnose the reason the database creation failed.

The function *CeCreateDatabaseWithProps* works only for EDBs. To create a CEDB, use *CeCreateDatabaseEx2,* which has similar parameters but does not specify the properties within a database. For CEDBs, the properties are specified by the sort orders and when the records are written.

Opening a Session

How the database is opened depends on whether the database is opened by multiple applications or threads or by a single application or thread. The point is: does the database (or databases) need to contend with multiple reads and writes of the data at the same time? If so, the database reads and writes need to be transacted, which can only be accomplished with an EDB. If only a single application will be accessing the database, then the process is much simpler and either an EDB or CEDB will suffice, and in this case, the portions of the chapter dealing with Sessions and Transactions can be skipped.

Both EDBs and CEDBs are transacted during single operations such as a record read or record write. However, if you want to transact multiple reads and writes, such as a read of one database and a write to another database within a single volume, then you must first create a session with the function

```
HANDLE CeCreateSession (CEGUID* pGuid);
```

The single parameter to the function is the *CEGUID* of a previously mounted database volume. The return value from this function is the handle of the newly created session or *INVALID_HANDLE_VALUE* if an error occurred. When you no longer need the session, the handle should be closed with a call to *CloseHandle.*

Opening a Database

A database can be opened with one of two functions, depending on whether transaction support is needed and the type of database (EDB or CEDB) being opened. If session support isn't needed, the function to call is *CeOpenDatabaseEx2*. I'll discuss it later, because it's functionally a subset of the session-based function

```
HANDLE CeOpenDatabaseInSession (HANDLE hSession, PCEGUID pguid,
                                PCEOID poid, LPWSTR lpszName,
                                SORTORDERSPECEX *pSort,
                                DWORD dwFlags,
                                CENOTIFYREQUEST *pRequest);
```

The first parameter is the session handle previously created. If *hSession* is null, the database manager creates a session handle for the database. This handle can be queried with *CeGetDatabaseSession*. The second parameter is the address of the *CEGUID* that indicates the database volume that contains the database. If this parameter is *CREATE_INVALIDEDBGUID*, all mounted volumes will be searched for the database. A database can be opened either by referencing its *CEOID* value or by referencing its name. To open the database by using its name, set the value pointed to by the *poid* parameter to 0 and specify the name of the database using the *lpszName* parameter. If you already know the *CEOID* of the database, simply put that value in the parameter pointed to by *poid*. If the *CEOID* value isn't 0, the function ignores the *lpszName* parameter.

The *pSort* parameter specifies which of the sort order specifications should be used to sort the database while it's opened. This parameter should point to a *SORTORDERSPECEX* structure that matches one of the entries in the *SORTORDERSPECEX* array that was defined when the database was created. The pointer doesn't have to point to the exact entry used when the database was created. Instead, the data within the *SORTORDERSPECEX* structure must match the data in the original *SORTORDERSPECEX* array entry. A Windows CE database can have only one active sort order. To use a different sort order, you can open a database again, specifying a different sort order.

The *dwFlags* parameter can contain either 0 or *CEDB_AUTOINCREMENT*. If *CEDB_AUTOINCREMENT* is specified, each read of a record in the database results in the database pointer being moved to the next record in the sort order. Opening a database without this flag means that the record pointer must be manually moved to the next record to be read. This flag is helpful if you plan to read the database records in sequential order.

The final parameter points to a structure that specifies how your application will be notified when another process or thread modifies the database. The scheme is a message-based notification that allows you to monitor changes to the database while you have it opened. To specify the window that receives the notification messages, you pass a pointer to a *CENOTIFYREQUEST* structure that you have previously filled in. This structure is defined as

```
typedef struct _CENOTIFYREQUEST {
    DWORD dwSize;
    HWND hWnd;
    DWORD dwFlags;
    HANDLE hHeap;
    DWORD dwParam;
} CENOTIFYREQUEST;
```

The first field must be initialized to the size of the structure. The *hWnd* field should be set to the window that will receive the change notifications. The *dwFlags* field specifies how you want to be notified. For EDBs, put *CEDB_EXNOTIFICATION* in the *dwFlags* field. This notification method passes a structure to the window detailing the change to the database. If you specify a handle to a heap in the *hHeap* field, the structure will be allocated there. If you set *hHeap* to 0, the structure will be allocated in your local heap. The *dwParam* field is a user-defined value that will be passed back to your application in the notification structure.

When a change is detected in the database, your window receives a *WM_DBNOTIFICATION* message. The *lParam* parameter points to a *CENOTIFICATION* structure defined as

```
typedef struct _CENOTIFICATION {
    DWORD dwSize
    DWORD dwParam;
    UINT uType;
    CEGUID guid;
    CEOID oid;
    CEOID oidParent;
} CENOTIFICATION;
```

As expected, the *dwSize* field fills with the size of the structure. The *dwParam* field contains the value passed in the *dwParam* field in the *CENOTIFYREQUEST* structure. This is an application-defined value that can be used for any purpose.

The *uType* field indicates why the *WM_DBNOTIFICATION* message was sent. It will be set to one of the following values:

- **DB_CEOID_CREATED** A new file system object was created.
- **DB_CEOID_DATABASE_DELETED** The database was deleted from a volume.
- **DB_CEOID_RECORD_DELETED** A record was deleted in a database.
- **DB_CEOID_CHANGED** An object was modified.

The *guid* field contains the guid for the database volume that the message relates to, while the *oid* field contains the relevant database record oid. Finally, the *oidParent* field contains the oid of the parent of the oid that the message references.

When you receive a *WM_DBNOTIFICATION* message, the *CENOTIFICATION* structure is placed in a memory block that must be freed. If you specified a handle to a heap in the *hHeap* field of *CENOTIFYREQUEST*, the notification structure will be placed in that heap; otherwise, the system places this structure in your local heap. Regardless of its location, you are responsible for freeing the memory that contains the *CENOTIFICATION* structure. You do this with a call to

```
BOOL CeFreeNotification(PCENOTIFYREQUEST pRequest,
                        PCENOTIFICATION pNotify);
```

The function's two parameters are a pointer to the original *CENOTIFYREQUEST* structure and a pointer to the *CENOTIFICATION* structure to free. You must free the *CENOTIFICATION* structure each time you receive a *WM_DBNOTIFICATION* message.

Seeking (or Searching for) a Record

Now that the database is opened, you can read and write the records. But before you can read a record, you must *seek* to that record. That is, you must move the database pointer to the record you want to read. You accomplish this using

```
CEOID CeSeekDatabaseEx (HANDLE hDatabase, DWORD dwSeekType, DWORD dwValue,
                        WORD wNumVals, LPDWORD lpdwIndex);
```

The first parameter for this function is the handle to the opened database. The *dwSeekType* parameter describes how the seek is to be accomplished. The parameter can have one of the following values:

- **CEDB_SEEK_CEOID** Seek a specific record identified by its object ID. The object ID is specified in the dwValue parameter. This type of seek is particularly efficient in Windows CE databases.
- **CEDB_SEEK_BEGINNING** Seek the nth record in the database. The index is contained in the dwValue parameter.
- **CEDB_SEEK_CURRENT** Seek from the current position n records forward or backward in the database. The offset is contained in the dwValue parameter. Even though dwValue is typed as an unsigned value, for this seek it's interpreted as a signed value.
- **CEDB_SEEK_END** Seek backward from the end of the database n records. The number of records to seek backward from the end is specified in the dwValue parameter.
- **CEDB_SEEK_VALUESMALLER** Seek from the current location until a record is found that contains a property that is the closest to but not equal to or over the value specified. The value is specified by a CEPROPVAL structure pointed to by dwValue.
- **CEDB_SEEK_VALUESMALLEROREQUAL** Seek from the current location until a record is found that contains a property that is the closest to or equal to but not over the value specified. The value is specified by a CEPROPVAL structure pointed to by dwValue.
- **CEDB_SEEK_VALUEFIRSTEQUAL** Starting with the start of the database, seek forward until a record is found that contains the property that's equal to the value specified. The value is specified by a CEPROPVAL structure pointed to by dwValue. The location returned can be the current record.

- **CEDB_SEEK_VALUENEXTEQUAL** Starting with the next location after the record found with CEDB_SEEK_VALUEFIRSTEQUAL, seek until a record is found that contains a property that's equal to the value specified.
- **CEDB_SEEK_VALUEGREATER** Seek from the current location until a record is found that contains a property that is the closest to, but not equal to, the value specified. The value is specified by a CEPROPVAL structure pointed to by dwValue.
- **CEDB_SEEK_VALUEGREATEROREQUAL** Seek from the current location until a record is found that contains a property that is equal to, or the closest to, the value specified. The value is specified by a CEPROPVAL structure pointed to by dwValue.

As you can see from the available flags, seeking in the database is more than just moving a pointer; it also allows you to search the database for a particular record.

As I just mentioned in the descriptions of the seek flags, the *dwValue* parameter can either be loaded with an offset value for the seeks or point to an array of property values for the searches. The values are described in an array of *CEPROPVAL* structures, each defined as

```
typedef struct _CEPROPVAL {
    CEPROPID propid;
    WORD wLenData;
    WORD wFlags;
    CEVALUNION val;
} CEPROPVAL;
```

The *propid* field must match the property ID values of the sort order you specified when the database was opened. Remember that the property ID is a combination of a data type identifier along with an application-specific ID value that uniquely identifies a property in the database. This field identifies the property to examine when seeking. The *wLenData* field is ignored. None of the defined flags for the *wFlags* field are used by *CeSeekDatabase*, so this field should be set to 0. The *val* field is actually a union of the different data types supported in the database.

Following is a short code fragment that demonstrates seeking to the third record in the database.

```
DWORD dwIndex;
CEOID oid;

// Seek to the third record.
oid = CeSeekDatabase (g_hDB, CEDB_SEEK_BEGINNING, 3, &dwIndex);
if (oid == 0) {
    // There is no third item in the database.
}
```

Now say we want to find the first record in the database that has a height property of greater than 100. For this example, assume the size property type is a signed long value.

```
// Define pid for height property as a signed long with ID of 1.
#define PID_HEIGHT     MAKELONG (CEVT_I4, 1)

CEOID oid;
DWORD dwIndex;
CEPROPVAL Property;

// First seek to the start of the database.
oid = CeSeekDatabaseEx (g_hDB, CEDB_SEEK_BEGINNING, 0, 1, &dwIndex);

// Seek the record with height > 100.
Property.propid = PID_HEIGHT;           // Set property to search.
Property.wLenData = 0;                  // Not used but clear anyway.
Property.wFlags = 0;                    // No flags to set
Property.val.lVal = 100;                // Data for property

oid = CeSeekDatabaseEx (g_hDB, CEDB_SEEK_VALUEGREATER, (DWORD)&Property,
                        1, &dwIndex);
if (oid == 0) {
    // No matching property found; db pointer now points to end of db.
} else {
    // oid contains the object ID for the record,
    // dwIndex contains the offset from the start of the database
    // of the matching record.
}
```

Because the search for the property starts at the current location of the database pointer, you first need to seek to the start of the database if you want to find the first record in the database that has the matching property.

Changing the Sort Order

I talked earlier about how *CeDatabaseSeekEx* depends on the sort order of the opened database. If you want to choose one of the predefined sort orders instead, you must close the database and then reopen it specifying the predefined sort order. But what if you need a sort order that isn't one of the four sort orders that were defined when the database was created? You can redefine the sort orders using this function:

```
BOOL CeSetDatabaseInfoEx (PCEGUID pguid,
                          CEOID oidDbase,
                          CEDBASEINFOEX *pNewInfo);
```

The function takes the *CEGUID* of the database volume and the object ID of the database you want to redefine and a pointer to a *CEDBASEINFOEX* structure. This structure is the same one used by *CeCreateDatabaseWithProps*. You can use these functions to rename the database, change its type, or redefine the four sort orders. You shouldn't redefine the sort orders casually. When the database sort orders are redefined, the system has to iterate through every record in the database to rebuild the sort indexes. This can take minutes for large databases. If you must redefine the sort order of a database, you should inform the user of the massive amount of time it might take to perform the operation.

The preceding function *CeSetDatabaseInfoEx* works for EDBs. To change the sort order of a CEDB, the recommended function is *CeSetDatabaseInfoEx2*.

Reading a Record

Once you have the database pointer at the record you're interested in, you can read or write that record. You can read a record in a database by calling the following function:

```
CEOID CeReadRecordPropsEx (HANDLE hDbase, DWORD dwFlags,
                           LPWORD lpcPropID,
                           CEPROPID *rgPropID, LPBYTE *lplpBuffer,
                           LPDWORD lpcbBuffer,
                           HANDLE hHeap);
```

The first parameter in this function is the handle to the opened database. The-*lpcPropID* parameter points to a variable that contains the number of *CEPROPID* structures pointed to by the next parameter, *rgPropID*. These two parameters combine to tell the function which properties of the record you want to read. There are two ways to utilize the *lpcPropID* and *rg-PropID* parameters. If you want only to read a selected few of the properties of a record, you can initialize the array of *CEPROPID* structures with the ID values of the properties you want and set the variable pointed to by *lpcPropID* with the number of these structures. When you call the function, the returned data will be inserted into the *CEPROPID* structures for data types such as integers. For strings and blobs, where the length of the data is variable, the data is returned in the buffer indirectly pointed to by *lplpBuffer*.

Since *CeReadRecordPropsEx* has a significant overhead to read a record, it is always best to read all the properties necessary for a record in one call.[2] To do this, simply set *rgPropID* to *NULL*. When the function returns, the variable pointed to by *lpcPropID* will contain the count of properties returned, and the function will return all the properties for that record in the buffer. The buffer will contain an array of *CEPROPID* structures created by the function, immediately followed by the data for those properties, such as blobs and strings, where the data isn't stored directly in the *CEPROPID* array.

One very handy feature of *CeReadRecordPropsEx* is that if you set *CEDB_ALLOWREALLOC* in the *dwFlags* parameter, the function will enlarge, if necessary, the results buffer to fit the data being returned. Of course, for this to work, the buffer being passed to the function must not be on the stack or in the static data area. Instead, it must be an allocated buffer in the local heap or a separate heap. In fact, if you use the *CEDB_ALLOWREALLOC* flag, you don't even need to pass a buffer to the function; instead, you can set the buffer pointer to 0. In this case, the function will allocate the buffer for you.

Notice that the buffer parameter isn't a pointer to a buffer but the address of a pointer to a buffer. There actually is a method to this pointer madness. Since the resulting buffer can be reallocated by the function, it might be moved if the buffer needs to be reallocated. So the

[2] The exception would be stream properties, which will be discussed below.

pointer to the buffer must be modified by the function. You must always use the pointer to the buffer returned by the function because it might have changed. Also, you're responsible for freeing the buffer after you have used it. Even if the function failed for some reason, the buffer might have moved or even have been freed by the function. You must clean up after the read by freeing the buffer if the pointer returned isn't 0.

As you might have guessed from the preceding paragraphs, the *hHeap* parameter allows *CeReadRecordPropsEx* to use a heap different from the local heap when reallocating the buffer. When you use *CeReadRecordPropsEx* and you want to use the local heap, simply pass a 0 in the *hHeap* parameter.

The following routine reads all the properties for a record and then copies the data into a structure.

```
int ReadDBRecord (HANDLE hDB, DATASTRUCT *pData, HANDLE hHeap) {
    WORD wProps;
    CEOID oid;
    PCEPROPVAL pRecord;
    PBYTE pBuff;
    DWORD dwRecSize;
    int i;

    // Read all properties for the record.
    pBuff = 0;   // Let the function allocate the buffer.
    oid = CeReadRecordPropsEx (hDB, CEDB_ALLOWREALLOC, &wProps, NULL,
                               &(LPBYTE)pBuff, &dwRecSize, hHeap);
    // Failure on read.
    if (oid == 0)
        return 0;

    // Copy the data from the record to the structure. The order
    // of the array is not defined.
    memset (pData, 0 , sizeof (DATASTRUCT));  // Zero return struct
    pRecord = (PCEPROPVAL)pBuff;              // Point to CEPROPVAL
                                              // array.
    for (i = 0; i < wProps; i++) {
        switch (pRecord->propid) {
        case PID_NAME:
            lstrcpy (pData->szName, pRecord->val.lpwstr);
            break;
        case PID_TYPE:
            lstrcpy (pData->szType, pRecord->val.lpwstr);
            break;
        case PID_SIZE:
            pData->nSize = pRecord->val.iVal;
            break;
        }
        pRecord++;
    }
    if (hHeap)
        HeapFree (hHeap, 0, pBuff);
    else
        LocalFree (pBuff);
    return i;
```

```
}
```

Because this function reads all the properties for the record, *CeReadRecordPropsEx* creates the array of *CEPROPVAL* structures. The order of these structures isn't defined, so the function cycles through each one to look for the data to fill in the structure. After all the data has been read, a call to either *HeapFree* or *LocalFree* is made to free the buffer that was returned by *CeReadRecordPropsEx*.

Nothing requires every record to contain all the same properties. You might encounter a situation where you request a specific property from a record by defining the *CEPROPID* array and that property doesn't exist in the record. When this happens, *CeReadRecordPropsEx* will set the *CEDB_PROPNOTFOUND* flag in the *wFlags* field of the *CEPROPID* structure for that property. You should always check for this flag if you call *CeReadRecordPropsEx* and you specify the properties to be read. In the example above, all properties were requested, so if a property didn't exist, no *CEPROPID* structure for that property would have been returned.

Writing a Record

You can write a record to the database using this function:

```
CEOID CeWriteRecordProps (HANDLE hDbase, CEOID oidRecord, WORD cPropID,
                          CEPROPVAL * rgPropVal);
```

The first parameter is the obligatory handle to the opened database. The *oidRecord* parameter is the object ID of the record to be written. To create a new record instead of modifying a record in the database, set *oidRecord* to 0. The *cPropID* parameter should contain the number of items in the array of property ID structures pointed to by *rgPropVal*. The *rgPropVal* array specifies which of the properties in the record to modify and the data to write.

Reading and Writing Stream Properties

The procedures for reading and writing simple property types such as strings and integers are fairly straightforward. However, the methods discussed previously for reading and writing properties don't work as well when dealing with huge amounts of data. EDBs support a database type called a *stream*. The stream data type can be read and written, as the name suggests, as a stream of data instead of a monolithic block of data. To read or write a stream property, the application first seeks the record containing the stream property to be accessed. To access that property, call

```
HANDLE CeOpenStream (HANDLE hDatabase, CEPROPID propid, DWORD dwMode);
```

The first parameter is the handle to the opened database, while the second parameter is the property ID of the stream property to be opened. The *dwMode* parameter indicates the access desired. The two flags allowed are *GENERIC_READ* and *GENERIC_WRITE*.

To read an opened stream, call the function

```
BOOL CeStreamRead (HANDLE hStream, LPBYTE lprgbBuffer, DWORD cbRead,
                   LPDWORD lpcbRead);
```

The parameters start with the handle to the opened stream. The next two parameters are the pointer to the buffer that will receive the data and the size of the data to read. The final parameter is a pointer to a *DWORD* that will receive the number of bytes actually read during the call. The function returns *TRUE* if successful. As always, if the function fails, call *GetLastError* for the reason for failure.

Writing a stream starts with a call to

```
BOOL CeStreamWrite (HANDLE hStream, LPBYTE lprgbBuffer, DWORD cbWrite,
                    LPDWORD lpcbWritten);
```

The parameters mirror the ones for *CeStreamRead*, with the handle to the stream, the pointer to the buffer, the size of the data to write, and a pointer to a *DWORD* that will be filled with the number of bytes actually written. The function returns *TRUE* if successful.

After the data has been written, it must be committed to the database with a call to

```
BOOL CeStreamSaveChanges (HANDLE hStream);
```

The only parameter is the handle to the open stream. If a stream is written to with a call to *CeStreamWrite* or *CeStreamSetSize*, which is discussed below, and the stream is closed before a call is made to *CeStreamSaveChanges*, the changes will be lost.

To truncate or extend a stream's length, a call can be made to

```
BOOL CeStreamSetSize (HANDLE hStream, DWORD cbSize);
```

The first parameter is the stream handle, while the second parameter is the new length of the stream. You must have write access to set the length of a stream. As mentioned above, to commit this change, a subsequent call must be made to *CeStreamSaveChanges*.

You can seek to a different location within the stream with a call to

```
BOOL CeStreamSeek (HANDLE hStream, DWORD cbMove, DWORD dwOrigin,
                   LPDWORD lpcbNewOffset);
```

The first parameter is the stream handle. The second parameter is the number of bytes to move in the stream. As with a file seek operation, how *cbMove is* interpeted depends on the next parameter *dwOrigin*. When *dwOrigin* is set to *STREAM_SEEK_SET, cbMove* is the number of bytes from the start of the stream. When *dwOrigin* is *STREAM_SEEK_CUR, cbMove* is relative from the current stream location. Finally, if *dwOrigin* is *STREAM_SEEK_END, cbMove* is relative from the end of the stream. When the *dwOrigin* flag is *STREAM_SEEK_CUR*, the *cbMove* value is interpeted as a signed value instead of an unsigned value. The final parameter is the address of a *DWORD* that receives the new location within the stream.

When you are finished with the stream property, close the stream handle with a call to *CloseHandle*. Take care not to confuse the handle to a stream property with the handle to the database itself.

Using Transactions

Any single read or write to a Windows CE database is atomic. That is, the read or write will complete before another thread can access the database. However, if you want to perform multiple reads or writes on a database or even multiple databases within a single database volume, you need to use the EDB engine's transaction support. Before using transactions, a session handle needs to be either created with *CeCreateSession* or queried from an open EDB using *CeGetDatabaseSession*. All databases involved in the transaction must be opened with the same session handle.

To start a transaction, call the function

```
BOOL CeBeginTransaction (HANDLE hSession, CEDBISOLATIONLEVEL isoLevel);
```

The parameter is the handle to the session. The *isoLevel* parameter provides the isolation level for the transaction. The possible values are:

- **CEDB_ISOLEVEL_READCOMMITTED** Data being modified by another transaction can't be read by another transaction until the data is committed.
- **CEDB_ISOLEVEL_DEFAULT** Same as CEDB_ISOLEVEL_READCOMMITTED
- **CEDB_ISOLEVEL_REPEATABLEREAD** Data read by a transaction can be read but not modified by another transaction.
- **CEDB_ISOLEVEL_SERIALIZABLE** Data read by a transaction cannot be read or modified by another transaction.

Once the transaction is opened, the database queues up each of the reads and writes to the various databases opened with the same session handle. To commit the changes, make a call to

```
BOOL CeEndTransaction (HANDLE hSession, BOOL fCommit);
```

The first parameter is the handle to the session. The second parameter allows you to either commit the changes made while the transaction was opened or to discard the changes. If the data is committed, the changes will be flushed to the database volume at the next flush interval or after the next call to *CeFlushDBVol*. Although changes to records can be discarded, any change to the structure of the database, such as adding properties or changing sort orders, cannot be discarded.

Deleting Properties, Records, and Entire Databases

You can delete individual properties in a record using *CeWriteRecordProps*. To do this, create a *CEPROPVAL* structure that identifies the property to delete and set *CEDB_PROPDELETE* in the *wFlags* field.

To delete an entire record in a database, call

```
BOOL CeDeleteRecord (HANDLE hDatabase, CEOID oidRecord);
```

The parameters are the handle to the database and the object ID of the record to delete.

You can delete an entire database using this function:

```
BOOL CeDeleteDatabaseEx (PCEGUID pguid, CEOID oid);
```

The two parameters are the *CEGUID* of the database volume and the object ID of the database. Of course, you can't delete a database that is currently open.

Enumerating Databases

Sometimes you must search the system to determine what databases are on the system. Windows CE provides a set of functions to enumerate the databases in a volume. These functions are

```
HANDLE CeFindFirstDatabaseEx (PCEGUID pguid, DWORD dwDbaseType);
```

and

```
CEOID CeFindNextDatabaseEx (HANDLE hEnum, PCEGUID pguid);
```

These functions act like *FindFirstFile* and *FindNextFile,* with the exception that *CeFindFirstDatabaseEx* only opens the search; it doesn't return the first database found. The *PCEGUID* parameter for both functions is the address of the *CEGUID* of the database volume you want to search. You can limit the search by specifying the ID of a specific database type in the *dwDbaseType* parameter. If this parameter is set to 0, all databases are enumerated. *CeFindFirstDatabaseEx* returns a handle that is then passed to *CeFindNextDatabaseEx* to actually enumerate the databases.

Here's how to enumerate the databases in the object store:

```
HANDLE hDBList;
CEOID oidDB;
CEGUID guidVol;

// Enumerate the databases in the object store.
CREATE_SYSTEMGUID(&guidVol);
```

```
hDBList = CeFindFirstDatabaseEx (&guidVol, 0);
if (hDBList != INVALID_HANDLE_VALUE) {

    oidDB = CeFindNextDatabaseEx (hDBList, &guidVol);
    while (oidDB) {
        // Enumerated database identified by object ID.
        MyDisplayDatabaseInfo (hCeDB);

        hCeDB = CeFindNextDatabaseEx (hDBList, &guidVol);
    }
    CloseHandle (hDBList);
}
```

The code first creates the *CEGUID* of the object store using the macro *CREATE_SYSTEMGUID*. That parameter, along with the database type specifier 0, is passed to *CeFindFirstDatabaseEx* to enumerate all the databases in the object store. If the function is successful, the databases are enumerated by repeatedly calling *CeFindNextDatabaseEx*.

Querying Object Information

To query information about a database, use this function:

```
BOOL CeOidGetInfoEx2 (PCEGUID pguid, CEOID oid, CEOIDINFOEX *oidInfo);
```

These functions return information about not just databases, but any object in the object store. This includes files and directories as well as databases and database records. The function is passed the database volume and object ID of the item of interest and a pointer to a *CEOIDINFOEX* structure.

Here's the definition of the *CEOIDINFOEX* structure:

```
typedef struct _CEOIDINFOEX {
    WORD wVersion;
    WORD wObjType;
    union {
        CEFILEINFO infFile;
        CEDIRINFO infDirectory;
        CEDBASEINFOEX infDatabase;
        CERECORDINFO infRecord;
    };
} CEOIDINFOEX;
```

This structure starts with a version field that should be set to *CEOIDINFOEX_VERSION*. The second field indicates the type of the item and a union of four different structures, each detailing information about that type of object. The currently supported flags are *OBJTYPE_FILE*, indicating that the object is a file; *OBJTYPE_DIRECTORY*, for directory objects; *OBJTYPE_DATABASE*, for database objects; and *OBJTYPE_RECORD*, indicating that the object is a record inside a database. The structures in the union are specific to each object type.

The various structures of the union are defined as

```
typedef struct _CEFILEINFO {
    DWORD dwAttributes;
    CEOID oidParent;
    WCHAR szFileName[MAX_PATH];
    FILETIME ftLastChanged;
    DWORD dwLength;
} CEFILEINFO;
```

the *CEDIRINFO* structure is defined as

```
typedef struct _CEDIRINFO {
    DWORD dwAttributes;
    CEOID oidParent;
    WCHAR szDirName[MAX_PATH];
} CEDIRINFO;
```

and the *CERECORDINFO* structure is defined as

```
typedef struct _CERECORDINFO {
    CEOID oidParent;
} CERECORDINFO;
```

You've already seen the *CEDBASEINFOEX* structure used in *CeCreateDatabaseEx2* and *CeSetDatabaseInfoEx2*. As you can see from the preceding structures, *CeGetOidInfoEx2* returns a wealth of information about each object. One of the more powerful bits of information is the object's parent oid, which will allow you to trace the chain of files and directories back to the root. These functions also allow you to convert an object ID to a name of a database, directory, or file.

The object ID method of tracking a file object should not be confused with the PID scheme used by the shell. Object IDs are maintained by the file system and are independent of whatever shell is being used. This would be a minor point under other versions of Windows, but with the ability of Windows CE to be built as components and customized for different targets, it's important to know what parts of the operating system support which functions.

The database API is unique to Windows CE and provides a valuable function for the information-centric devices that Windows CE supports. Although it doesn't have powerful query language like an SQL-based database, its functionality is a handy tool for the Windows CE developer.

In the preceding five chapters, I've covered the basics of the Windows CE kernel from memory to processes and threads to the file system. Now it's time to break from this low-level stuff and start looking outward. In the final chapter of this section, I'll cover the Windows CE notification API. The notification API frees applications from having to keep running in the background to monitor what is going on in the system.

Chapter 12
Notifications

One area in which Microsoft Windows CE exceeds the desktop Windows API is the notification interface. Windows CE applications can register to be launched at a predetermined time or when any of a set of system events occur. Applications can also register a *user notification*. In a user notification, the system notifies the user at a specific time without the application itself being launched at that time. Another type of notification can display message, or *bubble*, windows in plain text and even formatted HTML text.

These are the original notification interface that has been supported since the inception of Windows CE and the "bubble" notification interface that has its orgins in Windows Mobile systems. The original notification interface is based on only a handful of functions, the most important of which is *CeSetUserNotificationEx*. This omnibus function provides all the functionality to schedule any of the three types of notifications: user, system, and timer. Bubble notifications are a bit more complex, with a series of functions that support a powerful user notification interface.

User Notifications

A Windows CE application can schedule the user to be notified at a given time using the *CeSetUserNotificationEx* function. When the time of the notification occurs, the system alerts the user by displaying a dialog box, playing a wave file, vibrating the device, or flashing an external LED. If the system was suspended at the time of the notification, Windows CE turns the system on. Because many Windows CE systems have a suspend-resume style power scheme, suspended systems will quickly turn themselves back on if the notification fires while the system is unattended. Figure 12-1 shows the notification dialog box on an embedded Windows CE device.

Windows CE also displays the icon of the application that set the notification on the taskbar. The user has the option of acknowledging the notification by clicking OK on the notification dialog box, pressing the Notify button on the system case (if one is present), or on some systems, tapping the application's taskbar annunciator icon, which launches the application that registered the notification. After a user notification has been set, you can modify it by making another call to *CeSetUserNotificationEx*.

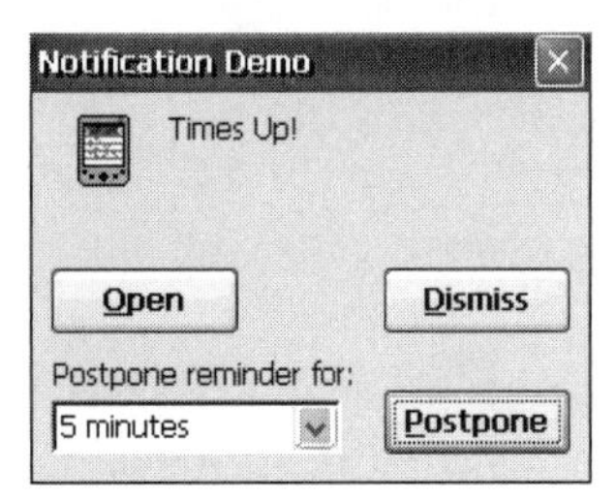

FIGURE 12-1 The notification dialog box on an embedded Windows CE device

Setting a User Notification

CeSetUserNotificationEx is prototyped as

```
HANDLE CeSetUserNotificationEx (HANDLE hNotification,
                                CE_NOTIFICATION_TRIGGER *pcnt,
                                CE_USER_NOTIFICATION *pceun);
```

The *hNotification* parameter is set to 0 to create a new notification. To modify a notification already registered, you should set *hNotification* to the handle of the notification that you want to modify.

The *CE_NOTIFICATION_TRIGGER* structure defines the type and detail of the notification being set. This structure is defined as

```
typedef struct UserNotificationTrigger {
    DWORD dwSize;
    DWORD dwType;
    DWORD dwEvent;
    WCHAR *lpszApplication;
    WCHAR *lpszArguments;
    SYSTEMTIME stStartTime;
    SYSTEMTIME stEndTime;
} CE_NOTIFICATION_TRIGGER, *PCE_NOTIFICATION_TRIGGER;
```

The first field should be set to the size of the structure. The second field, *dwType*, should be filled with a flag indicating the type of notification being set. For user notifications, set this field to either *CNT_PERIOD* or *CNT_TIME*. The *CNT_PERIOD* flag creates a notification that will dismiss itself after a set time, while a *CNT_TIME* notification will not dismiss itself without user action. For user notifications, the *dwEvent* field isn't used. I'll talk about that field when I discuss event notifications.

The next field, *lpszApplication*, specifies the application that will be launched if the user requests more detail from the notification. If the application is launched, its command line is specified by the next field, *lpszArguments*.

Another use for the *lpszApplication* field is to specify an event to be signaled when the notification fires. To specify an event, the field should be formatted as

```
\\.\Notifications\NamedEvents\<Event Name>
```

where *<Event Name>* is any name chosen for the event. Remember that when you specify this string in C, the backslash character must be replicated because it's used as the escape character. So to have a notification trigger an event named Bob, the string pointed to by the *lpszApplication* field would look like this:

```
TEXT ("\\\\.\\Notifications\\NamedEvents\\Bob")
```

To be notified using an event, an application must create a named event with the same name as <Event Name> by using the *CreateEvent* function and wait on the handle returned, as in

```
hEvent = CreateEvent (NULL, FALSE, FALSE, TEXT ("Bob"));
```

The final two fields, *stStartTime* and *stEndTime*, specify the starting time and ending time of the notice. The starting time, of course, is when the system first notifies the user by means of a number of different methods I'll talk about in a moment. You use the ending time only in a *CNT_PERIOD*-style user notification; the *CeSetUserNotificationEx* function ignores the ending time for *CNT_TIME* notifications. *stEndTime* designates the time the system is to remove the notice if the user doesn't acknowledge the notification. This time must be later than the starting time.

How the system notifies the user is specified by the third parameter of *CeSetUserNotificationEx*, which points to a *CE_USER_NOTIFICATION* structure. This structure is defined as

```
typedef struct UserNotificationType {
    DWORD ActionFlags;
    TCHAR *pwszDialogTitle;
    TCHAR *pwszDialogText;
    TCHAR *pwszSound;
    DWORD nMaxSound;
    DWORD dwReserved;
} CE_USER_NOTIFICATION;
```

The *ActionFlags* field of this structure contains a set of flags that define how the user is notified. The flags can be any combination of the following:

- **PUN_LED** Flash the external LED.
- **PUN_VIBRATE** Vibrate the device.
- **PUN_DIALOG** Display a dialog box.
- **PUN_SOUND** Play a wave file.
- **PUN_REPEAT** Repeat the wave file for 10 to 15 seconds.

The fact that these flags are defined doesn't mean that all systems implement all these actions. Most Windows CE devices can't vibrate and many don't even have an external LED. There isn't a defined method for determining the notification capabilities of a device, but as I'll presently show you, the system provides a dialog box that's customized by the OEM for the capabilities of each device.

The remainder of the fields in the structure depend on the flags set in the *ActionFlags* field. If the *PUN_DIALOG* flag is set, the *pwszDialogTitle* and *pwszDialogText* fields specify the title and text of the dialog that's displayed. The *pwszSound* field is loaded with the file name of a wave file to play if the *PUN_SOUND* flag is set. The *nMaxSound* field defines the size of the *pwszSound* field.

Configuring a User Notification

To give you a consistent user interface for choosing the method of notification, Windows CE provides a dialog box to query the user about how he wants to be notified. To display the user configuration dialog box, you call this function:

```
BOOL CeGetUserNotificationPreferences (HWND hWndParent,
                                       PCE_USER_NOTIFICATION lpNotification);
```

This function takes two parameters—the window handle of the parent window for the dialog box and a pointer to a *CE_USER_NOTIFICATION* structure. You can initialize the *CE_USER_NOTIFICATION* structure with default settings for the dialog before *CeGetUserNotification Preferences* is called. When the function returns, this structure is filled with the changes the user made. *CeGetUserNotificationPreferences* returns *TRUE* if the user clicked the OK button to accept the changes and *FALSE* if an error occurred or the user canceled the dialog box. Figure 12-2 shows the notification preferences dialog box opened through the *CeGetUserNotificationPreferences* function on an embedded device.

This function gives you a convenient method for configuring user notifications. The dialog box lets you have check boxes for playing a sound, displaying another dialog box, and flashing the LED. It also contains a combo box that lists the available wave files that the user can choose from if he wants sound. The dialog box doesn't have fields to allow the user to specify the text or title of the dialog box if one is to be displayed. That text must be provided by the application.

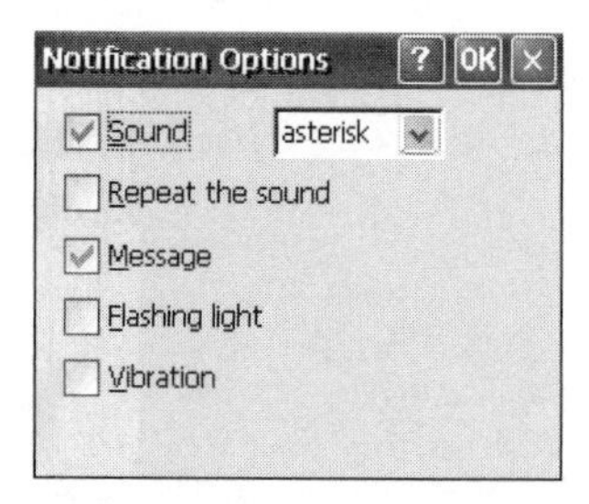

FIGURE 12-2 The dialog box opened by *CeGetUserNotificationPreferences*

Acknowledging a User Notification

A user notification can be cleared by the application before it times out by calling

```
BOOL CeClearUserNotification (HANDLE hNotification);
```

Once a user notification has occurred, it must be acknowledged by the user unless the user notification's end time has passed. The user can tap the Dismiss button on the notification dialog box or press the notification button on the device case. Or the user can tap the Snooze button, which automatically reschedules the notification for a later time. On an embedded Windows CE system, the user can tap the Open button to launch the application specified when the notification was scheduled.

If the user taps the Open button, the notification isn't automatically acknowledged. Instead, an application should programmatically acknowledge the notification by calling this function:

```
BOOL CeHandleAppNotifications (TCHAR *pwszAppName);
```

The one parameter is the name of the application that was launched because the user tapped the Open button. Calling this function removes the dialog box; stops the sound; turns off the flashing LED; and on systems with the Windows CE Explorer shell, removes the application's annunciator icon from the taskbar. This function doesn't affect any notifications that are scheduled but haven't fired.

When the system starts an application because of a notification, it passes a command line argument to indicate why the application was started. For a user notification, this argument is the command line string specified in the *lpszArguments* field of the *CE_NOTIFICATION_TRIGGER* structure. If you scheduled the notification using the *CNT_CLASSICTIME* flag, the command line is the predefined string constant *APP_RUN_TO_HANDLE_NOTIFICATION*. If the event notification method is specified, the application won't be started. Instead, an event of the specified name will be signaled.

As a general rule, an application started by a notification should first check to see whether another instance of the application is running. If so, the application should communicate to the first instance that the notification occurred and terminate. This saves memory because only one instance of the application is running. The following code fragment shows how this can be easily accomplished.

```
INT i;
HWND hWnd;
HANDLE hNotify;
TCHAR szText[128];
TCHAR szFileName[MAX_PATH];

if (*lpCmdLine) {
    pPtr = lpCmdLine;
    // Parse the first word of the command line.
```

```
    for (i = 0; i < dim(szText) && *lpCmdLine > TEXT (' '); i++)
        szText[i] = *pPtr++;
    szText[i] = TEXT ('\0');

    // Check to see if app started due to notification.
    if (lstrcmp (szText, TEXT("My Notification cmdline")) == 0) {
        // Acknowledge the notification.
        GetModuleFileName (hInst, szFileName, sizeof (szFileName));
        CeHandleAppNotifications (szFileName);

        // Get handle off the command line.
        hNotify = (HANDLE)_wtol (pPtr);

        // Look to see if another instance of the app is running.
        hWnd = FindWindow (NULL, szAppName);
        if (hWnd) {
            SendMessage (hWnd, MYMSG_TELLNOTIFY, 0, (LPARAM)hNotify);
            // This app should terminate here.
            return 0;
        }
    }
}
```

This code first looks to see whether a command line parameter exists and, if so, whether the first word is the keyword indicating that the application was launched by the system in response to a user notification. If so, the notification is acknowledged and the application looks for an instance of the application already running, using *FindWindow*. If found, the routine sends an application-defined message to the main window of the first instance and terminates. Otherwise, the application can take actions necessary to respond to the user's tap of the Open button on the alert dialog.

Timer Event Notifications

To run an application at a given time without user intervention, use a *timer event notification*. To schedule a timer event notification, use *CeSetUserNotificationEx* just as you do for the user notification, but pass a *NULL* value in the *pceun* parameter, as you see on the following page.

```
CE_NOTIFICATION_TRIGGER cnt;
TCHAR szArgs[] = TEXT ("This is a timer notification.");
TCHAR szExeName[MAX_PATH];

memset (&nt, 0, sizeof (CE_NOTIFICATION_TRIGGER));
nt.dwSize = sizeof (CE_NOTIFICATION_TRIGGER);
nt.dwType = CNT_TIME;
nt.lpszApplication = szExeName;
nt.lpszArguments = szArgs;
nt.stStartTime = st;
GetModuleFileName (hInst, szExeName, sizeof (szExeName));
hNotify = CeSetUserNotificationEx (0, &nt, NULL);
```

When the timer notification is activated, the system powers on if currently off, and launches the application with a command line parameter specified in the *lpszArguments* field of the notification trigger structure. As with the user notification, if the application is started, it should check to see whether another instance of the application is running and, if so, pass the notification on if one is running. Also, an application should be careful about creating a window and taking control of the machine during a timer event. The user might object to having his game of solitaire interrupted by another application popping up because of a timer notification.

System Event Notifications

Sometimes, you might want an application to be automatically started. Windows CE supports a third type of notification, known as a *system event notification*. This notification starts an application when one of a set of system events occurs, such as after the system has completed synchronizing with its companion PC. To set a system event notification, you again use the omnibus *CeSetUserNotificationEx* function. This time, you specify the type of event you want to monitor in the *dwEvent* field of the notification trigger structure, as in

```
CE_NOTIFICATION_TRIGGER nt;
TCHAR szExeName[MAX_PATH];
TCHAR szArgs[128] = TEXT("This is my event notification string.");

memset (&nt, 0, sizeof (CE_NOTIFICATION_TRIGGER));
nt.dwSize = sizeof (CE_NOTIFICATION_TRIGGER);
nt.dwType = CNT_EVENT;
nt.dwEvent = dwMyEventFlags;
nt.lpszApplication = szExeName;
nt.lpszArguments = szArgs;
GetModuleFileName (hInst, szExeName, sizeof (szExeName));
CeSetUserNotificationEx (0, &nt, NULL);
```

The event flags are the following:

- **NOTIFICATION_EVENT_SYNC_END** Notify when sync is complete.
- **NOTIFICATION_EVENT_DEVICE_CHANGE** Notify when a device driver is loaded or unloaded.
- **NOTIFICATION_EVENT_RS232_DETECTED** Notify when an RS232 connection is detected.
- **NOTIFICATION_EVENT_TIME_CHANGE** Notify when the system time is changed.
- **NOTIFICATION_EVENT_TZ_CHANGE** Notify when time zone is changed.1
- **NOTIFICATION_EVENT_RESTORE_END** Notify when a device restore is complete.
- **NOTIFICATION_EVENT_WAKEUP** Notify when a device wakes up.

---

1 The *NOTIFICATION_EVENT_TZ_CHANGE* notification flag isn't supported on some Windows Mobile devices.

- **NOTIFICATION_EVENT_MACHINE_NAME_CHANGE** Notify when a device name changes.
- **NOTIFICATION_EVENT_RNDIS_FN_DETECTED** Notify when an RNDIS connection is detected.
- **NOTIFICATION_EVENT_INTERNET_PROXY_CHANGE** Notify when proxy server changes.

For each of these events, the application is launched with a specific command line parameter indicating why the application was launched. In the case of a device change notification, the specified command line string is followed by either */ADD* or */REMOVE* and the name of the device being added or removed. For example, if the user inserts a modem card, the command line for the notification would look like this:

```
My event command line string /ADD COM3:
```

A number of additional system events are defined in Notify.h, but OEMs must provide support for these additional notifications, and at this point few, if any, of the additional notification events are supported.

Once an application has registered for a system event notification, Windows CE will start or signal the application again if the event that caused the notification is repeated.

Clearing out system event notifications is best done with what might be thought of as an obsolete function, the old *CeRunAppAtEvent* function, prototyped as

```
BOOL CeRunAppAtEvent (TCHAR *pwszAppName, LONG lWhichEvent);
```

The parameters are the application to run and the event flag for the event of which you want to be notified. While the function has been superseded by *CeSetUserNotificationEx*, it does still have one use—clearing out all the system notifications for a specific application. If you pass your application name along with the flag *NOTIFICATION_EVENT_NONE* in the *lWhichEvent* parameter, Windows CE clears out all event notifications assigned to that application. While you would think you could pass the same flag to *CeSetUserNotificationEx* to clear out the events, it doesn't unless you pass the original handle returned by that function when you originally scheduled the notification.

The NoteDemo Example Program

The following program, NoteDemo, demonstrates each of the notification functions that allow you to set user notifications, system notifications, and timer notifications. The program presents a simple dialog box equipped with five buttons. The first two buttons allow you to configure and set a user notification. The second two buttons let you set system and timer notifications. The last button clears out all the notifications you might have set using NoteDemo. The gap above the buttons is filled with the command line, if any, that was passed when the application started. That space also displays a message when another instance of NoteDemo starts because of a user notification. Figure 12-3 shows two NoteDemo windows. The one in the foreground was launched because of a user notification, with the command-line parameter, "This is my user notification string."

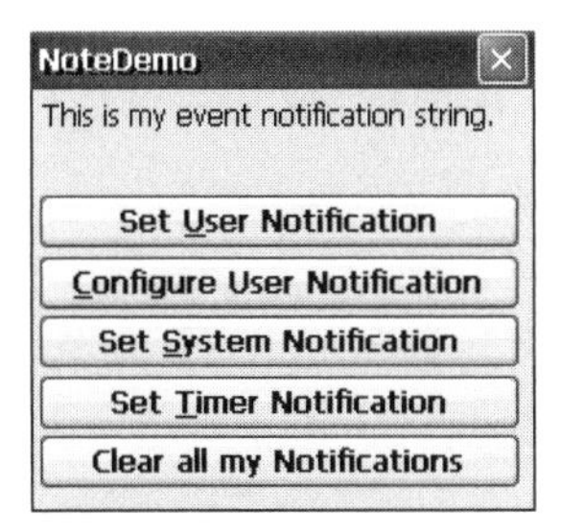

FIGURE 12-3 The NoteDemo window

The source code for NoteDemo appears in Listing 12-1. The notification code is confined to the button handler routines. The code is fairly simple: for each type of notification, the appropriate Windows CE function is called. When asked to configure a user notification, the application calls *CeGetUserNotificationPreferences*. The program gives you one additional dialog box with which to configure the system notifications.

LISTING 12-1

NoteDemo.rc

```
//======================================================================
// Resource file
//
// Written for the book Programming Windows CE
// Copyright (C) 2007 Douglas Boling
//======================================================================
#include "windows.h"
#include "NoteDemo.h"                          // Program-specific stuff

//----------------------------------------------------------------------
// Icons and bitmaps
//
ID_ICON ICON   "NoteDemo.ico"                  // Program icon

//----------------------------------------------------------------------
// Main window dialog template
//
NoteDemo DIALOG discardable  25, 5, 120,  98
STYLE  WS_OVERLAPPED | WS_VISIBLE | WS_CAPTION | WS_SYSMENU |
       DS_CENTER | DS_MODALFRAME
CAPTION "NoteDemo"
BEGIN
    LTEXT "",            IDD_OUTPUT,   2,   2, 115,  21
```

```
     PUSHBUTTON "Set &User Notification",
                         IDD_ADDUSERNOT,   2,  25, 115,  12, WS_TABSTOP
    PUSHBUTTON "&Configure User Notification",
                         IDD_CFGUSERNOT,   2,  39, 115,  12, WS_TABSTOP

    PUSHBUTTON "Set &System Notification",
                         IDD_ADDSYSNOT,    2,  53, 115,  12, WS_TABSTOP
    PUSHBUTTON "Set &Timer Notification",
                         IDD_ADDTIMENOT,   2,  67, 115,  12, WS_TABSTOP
    PUSHBUTTON "Clear all my Notifications",
                         IDD_CLEARNOT,     2,  81, 115,  12, WS_TABSTOP
END
//----------------------------------------------------------------------
// Set system event notification dialog box dialog template.
//
SysNotifyConfig DIALOG DISCARDABLE  0, 0, 130, 125
STYLE DS_MODALFRAME | WS_POPUP | WS_CAPTION | WS_SYSMENU
EXSTYLE WS_EX_CAPTIONOKBTN
CAPTION "Notify On..."
BEGIN
    AUTOCHECKBOX "Sync End",          IDC_SYNC_END,    7,   5, 121,  10,
                                                  WS_TABSTOP
    AUTOCHECKBOX "Device Change",IDC_DEVICE_CHANGE,    7,  17, 121,  10,
                                                  WS_TABSTOP
    AUTOCHECKBOX "Serial Connection Detected",
                                IDC_SERIAL_DETECT,    7,  29, 121,  10,
                                                  WS_TABSTOP
    AUTOCHECKBOX "System Time Change",
                                  IDC_TIME_CHANGE,    7,  41, 121,  10,
                                                  WS_TABSTOP
    AUTOCHECKBOX "Restore End",    IDC_RESTORE_END,    7,  53, 121,  10,
                                                  WS_TABSTOP
    AUTOCHECKBOX "System Wake Up",    IDC_POWER_UP,    7,  65, 121,  10,
                                                  WS_TABSTOP
    AUTOCHECKBOX "Time Zone Change", IDC_TZ_CHANGE,    7,  77, 121,  10,
                                                  WS_TABSTOP
    AUTOCHECKBOX "Name Change",    IDC_NAME_CHANGE,    7,  89, 121,  10,
                                                  WS_TABSTOP
    AUTOCHECKBOX "RNDIS Detected",IDC_RNDIS_CHANGE,    7, 101, 121,  10,
                                                  WS_TABSTOP
    AUTOCHECKBOX "Proxy Change",  IDC_PROXY_CHANGE,    7, 113, 121,  10,
                                                  WS_TABSTOP

END
```

NoteDemo.h

```
//======================================================================
// Header file
//
// Written for the book Programming Windows CE
// Copyright (C) 2007 Douglas Boling
//======================================================================
// Returns number of elements
#define dim(x) (sizeof(x) / sizeof(x[0]))

//----------------------------------------------------------------------
// Generic defines and data types
//
struct decodeUINT {                             // Structure associates
    UINT Code;                                  // messages
                                                // with a function.
    BOOL (*Fxn)(HWND, UINT, WPARAM, LPARAM);
};
struct decodeCMD {                              // Structure associates
    UINT Code;                                  // menu IDs with a
    LRESULT (*Fxn)(HWND, WORD, HWND, WORD);     // function.
};

struct decodeBtn {                              // Structure associates
    DWORD dwID;                                 // btn IDs with
    DWORD dwFlag;                               // notification flags
};

// Define function not supported under Windows CE.
#ifndef IsDlgButtonChecked
#define IsDlgButtonChecked(a, b)\
                        SendDlgItemMessage (a, b, BM_GETCHECK, 0, 0)
#endif
//----------------------------------------------------------------------
// Generic defines used by application

#define  ID_ICON             1

#define  IDD_ADDUSERNOT      10                 // Control IDs
#define  IDD_CFGUSERNOT      11
#define  IDD_ADDSYSNOT       12
#define  IDD_ADDTIMENOT      13
#define  IDD_OUTPUT          14
#define  IDD_CLEARNOT        15

#define  IDC_SYNC_END        20
#define  IDC_DEVICE_CHANGE   21
#define  IDC_SERIAL_DETECT   22
#define  IDC_TIME_CHANGE     23
#define  IDC_RESTORE_END     24
#define  IDC_POWER_UP        25
#define  IDC_TZ_CHANGE       26
#define  IDC_NAME_CHANGE     27
#define  IDC_RNDIS_CHANGE    28
#define  IDC_PROXY_CHANGE    29
```

```
#define MYMSG_TELLNOTIFY     (WM_USER + 100)

//----------------------------------------------------------------------
// Function prototypes
//
void Add2List (HWND hWnd, LPTSTR lpszFormat, ...);
// Window procedures
BOOL CALLBACK MainDlgProc (HWND, UINT, WPARAM, LPARAM);
BOOL CALLBACK SetEventNotifyDlgProc (HWND, UINT, WPARAM, LPARAM);

// Message handlers
BOOL DoInitDialogMain (HWND, UINT, WPARAM, LPARAM);
BOOL DoCommandMain (HWND, UINT, WPARAM, LPARAM);
BOOL DoTellNotifyMain (HWND, UINT, WPARAM, LPARAM);

// Command functions
LPARAM DoMainCommandExit (HWND, WORD, HWND, WORD);
LPARAM DoMainCommandAddUserNotification (HWND, WORD, HWND, WORD);
LPARAM DoMainCommandConfigUserNotification (HWND, WORD, HWND, WORD);
LPARAM DoMainCommandAddSysNotification (HWND, WORD, HWND, WORD);
LPARAM DoMainCommandAddTimerNotification (HWND, WORD, HWND, WORD);
LPARAM DoMainCommandClearNotifications (HWND, WORD, HWND, WORD);
// Thread prototype
DWORD WINAPI MonitorThread (PVOID pArg);
```

NoteDemo.cpp

```
//======================================================================
// NoteDemo - Demonstrates the Windows CE Notification API
//
// Written for the book Programming Windows CE
// Copyright (C) 2007 Douglas Boling
//======================================================================
#include <windows.h>                  // For all that Windows stuff
#include <notify.h>                   // For notification defines
#include "NoteDemo.h"                 // Program-specific stuff

//----------------------------------------------------------------------
// Global data
//
const TCHAR szAppName[] = TEXT ("NoteDemo");
HINSTANCE hInst;                      // Program instance handle
HWND g_hMain;

CE_USER_NOTIFICATION g_ceun;          // User notification structure
TCHAR szDlgTitle[] = TEXT ("Notification Demo");
TCHAR szDlgText[] = TEXT ("Times Up!");
TCHAR szSound[MAX_PATH] = TEXT ("alarm1.wav");

// Used for timer event notification
TCHAR szEventName[] = TEXT ("Bob");
```

```
HANDLE g_hNoteEvent = 0;
BOOL g_fContinue = TRUE;

// Message dispatch table for MainWindowProc
const struct decodeUINT MainMessages[] = {
    WM_INITDIALOG, DoInitDialogMain,
    WM_COMMAND, DoCommandMain,
    MYMSG_TELLNOTIFY, DoTellNotifyMain,
};
// Command Message dispatch for MainWindowProc
const struct decodeCMD MainCommandItems[] = {
    IDOK, DoMainCommandExit,
    IDCANCEL, DoMainCommandExit,
    IDD_ADDUSERNOT, DoMainCommandAddUserNotification,
    IDD_CFGUSERNOT, DoMainCommandConfigUserNotification,
    IDD_ADDSYSNOT, DoMainCommandAddSysNotification,
    IDD_ADDTIMENOT, DoMainCommandAddTimerNotification,
    IDD_CLEARNOT, DoMainCommandClearNotifications,
};
// Used by Set System Notification dialog
const struct decodeBtn SysTypeBtns[] = {
    IDC_SYNC_END       , NOTIFICATION_EVENT_SYNC_END,
    IDC_DEVICE_CHANGE, NOTIFICATION_EVENT_DEVICE_CHANGE,
    IDC_SERIAL_DETECT, NOTIFICATION_EVENT_RS232_DETECTED,
    IDC_TIME_CHANGE  , NOTIFICATION_EVENT_TIME_CHANGE,
    IDC_RESTORE_END  , NOTIFICATION_EVENT_RESTORE_END,
    IDC_POWER_UP     , NOTIFICATION_EVENT_WAKEUP,
    IDC_TZ_CHANGE    , NOTIFICATION_EVENT_TZ_CHANGE,
    IDC_NAME_CHANGE  , NOTIFICATION_EVENT_MACHINE_NAME_CHANGE,
    IDC_RNDIS_CHANGE , NOTIFICATION_EVENT_RNDIS_FN_DETECTED,
    IDC_PROXY_CHANGE , NOTIFICATION_EVENT_INTERNET_PROXY_CHANGE,
};

//======================================================================
// Program entry point
//
int WINAPI WinMain (HINSTANCE hInstance, HINSTANCE hPrevInstance,
                    LPWSTR lpCmdLine, int nCmdShow) {
    INT i;
    TCHAR szText[MAX_PATH];
    WCHAR *pPtr;
    HANDLE hNotify;
    HWND hWnd;
    HANDLE hThread;

    hInst = hInstance;

    if (*lpCmdLine) {
        pPtr = lpCmdLine;
        // Parse the first word of the command line.
        for (i = 0; (i < dim(szText)-1) && (*pPtr > TEXT (' ')); i++)
            szText[i] = *pPtr++;
        szText[i] = TEXT ('\0');
```

```
            // Check to see if app started due to notification.
            if (lstrcmp (szText, APP_RUN_TO_HANDLE_NOTIFICATION) == 0) {
                // Acknowledge the notification.
                GetModuleFileName (hInst, szText, sizeof (szText));
                CeHandleAppNotifications (szText);

                // Get handle of command line.
                hNotify = (HANDLE)_wtol (pPtr);

                // Look to see if another instance of the app is running.
                hWnd = FindWindow (NULL, szAppName);
                if (hWnd) {
                    SendMessage (hWnd, MYMSG_TELLNOTIFY, 0,
                                 (LPARAM)hNotify);
                    // I should terminate this app here, but I don't so you
                    // can see what happens.
                    return 0;
                }
            }
        }
        // Do a little initialization of CE_USER_NOTIFICATION.
        memset (&g_ceun, 0, sizeof (g_ceun));
        g_ceun.ActionFlags = PUN_DIALOG;
        g_ceun.pwszDialogTitle = szDlgTitle;
        g_ceun.pwszDialogText = szDlgText;
        g_ceun.pwszSound = szSound;
        g_ceun.nMaxSound = sizeof (szSound);

        // Create secondary thread for timer event notification.
        g_hNoteEvent = CreateEvent (NULL, FALSE, FALSE, szEventName);
        hThread = CreateThread (NULL, 0, MonitorThread, hWnd, 0, (DWORD *)&i);
        if (hThread == 0)
            return -1;

        // Display dialog box as main window.
        DialogBoxParam (hInstance, szAppName, NULL, MainDlgProc,
                        (LPARAM)lpCmdLine);
        // Signal notification thread to terminate
        g_fContinue = FALSE;
        SetEvent (g_hNoteEvent);
        WaitForSingleObject (hThread, 1000);
        CloseHandle (hThread);
        CloseHandle (g_hNoteEvent);
        return 0;

    }
    //======================================================================
    // Message handling procedures for main window
    //----------------------------------------------------------------------
    // MainDlgProc - Callback function for application window
    //
    BOOL CALLBACK MainDlgProc (HWND hWnd, UINT wMsg, WPARAM wParam,
                               LPARAM lParam) {
```

```
    INT i;
    //
    // Search message list to see if we need to handle this
    // message. If in list, call procedure.
    //
    for (i = 0; i < dim(MainMessages); i++) {
        if (wMsg == MainMessages[i].Code)
            return (*MainMessages[i].Fxn)(hWnd, wMsg, wParam, lParam);
    }
    return FALSE;
}
//----------------------------------------------------------------------
// DoInitDialogMain - Process WM_INITDIALOG message for window.
//
BOOL DoInitDialogMain (HWND hWnd, UINT wMsg, WPARAM wParam,
                       LPARAM lParam) {

    g_hMain = hWnd;
    if (*(LPTSTR)lParam)
        Add2List (hWnd, (LPTSTR)lParam);
    return FALSE;
}
//----------------------------------------------------------------------
// DoCommandMain - Process WM_COMMAND message for window.
//
BOOL DoCommandMain (HWND hWnd, UINT wMsg, WPARAM wParam, LPARAM lParam){
    WORD idItem, wNotifyCode;
    HWND hwndCtl;
    INT  i;

    // Parse the parameters.
    idItem = (WORD) LOWORD (wParam);
    wNotifyCode = (WORD) HIWORD (wParam);
    hwndCtl = (HWND) lParam;

    // Call routine to handle control message.
    for (i = 0; i < dim(MainCommandItems); i++) {
        if (idItem == MainCommandItems[i].Code) {
            (*MainCommandItems[i].Fxn)(hWnd, idItem, hwndCtl,
                                       wNotifyCode);
            return TRUE;
        }
    }
    return FALSE;
}
//----------------------------------------------------------------------
// DoTellNotifyMain - Process MYMSG_TELLNOTIFY message for window.
//
BOOL DoTellNotifyMain (HWND hWnd, UINT wMsg, WPARAM wParam,
                       LPARAM lParam) {
    Add2List (hWnd, TEXT ("Notification %x reported"), lParam);
    SetForegroundWindow ((HWND)((DWORD)hWnd | 0x01));
    return 0;
}
```

```
//======================================================================
// Command handler routines
//----------------------------------------------------------------------
// DoMainCommandExit - Process Program Exit command.
//
LPARAM DoMainCommandExit (HWND hWnd, WORD idItem, HWND hwndCtl,
                          WORD wNotifyCode) {
    EndDialog (hWnd, 0);
    return 0;
}
//----------------------------------------------------------------------
// DoMainCommandAddUserNotification - Process Add User Notify button.
//
LPARAM DoMainCommandAddUserNotification (HWND hWnd, WORD idItem,
                                         HWND hwndCtl, WORD wNotifyCode) {
    SYSTEMTIME st, ste;
    TCHAR szExeName[MAX_PATH], szText[128];
    TCHAR szArgs[128] = TEXT("This is my user notification string.");
    CE_NOTIFICATION_TRIGGER nt;
    HANDLE hNotify;

    // Initialize time structure with local time.
    GetLocalTime (&st);
    // Do a trivial amount of error checking.
    st.wMinute++;
    if (st.wMinute > 59) {
        st.wHour++;
        st.wMinute -= 60;
    }

    // Set end time 10 minutes past start.
    ste = st;
    // Do a trivial amount of error checking.
    ste.wMinute += 10;
    if (ste.wMinute > 59) {
        ste.wHour++;
        ste.wMinute -= 60;
    }

    memset (&nt, 0, sizeof (CE_NOTIFICATION_TRIGGER));
    nt.dwSize = sizeof (CE_NOTIFICATION_TRIGGER);
    nt.dwType = CNT_PERIOD;
    nt.lpszApplication = szExeName;
    nt.lpszArguments = szArgs;
    nt.stStartTime = st;
    nt.stEndTime = ste;
    GetModuleFileName (hInst, szExeName, sizeof (szExeName));

    hNotify = CeSetUserNotificationEx (0, &nt, &g_ceun);
    // Tell the user the notification was set.
    if (hNotify)
        wsprintf (szText, TEXT ("User notification set for %d:%02d:%02d"),
                  st.wHour, st.wMinute, st.wSecond);
```

```
    else
        wsprintf (szText, TEXT ("User notification failed. rc = %d"),
                  GetLastError());

    MessageBox (hWnd, szText, szAppName, MB_OK);
    return 0;
}
//----------------------------------------------------------------------
// DoMainCommandConfigUserNotification - Process Config user
// notification button.
//
LPARAM DoMainCommandConfigUserNotification (HWND hWnd, WORD idItem,
                                            HWND hwndCtl, WORD wNotifyCode) {

    // Display the system-provided configuration dialog.
    CeGetUserNotificationPreferences (hWnd, &g_ceun);
    return 0;
}
//----------------------------------------------------------------------
//  DoMainCommandAddSysNotification - Process Add Sys notify button.
//
LPARAM DoMainCommandAddSysNotification (HWND hWnd, WORD idItem,
                                        HWND hwndCtl, WORD wNotifyCode) {

    DialogBox (hInst, TEXT ("SysNotifyConfig"), hWnd,
               SetEventNotifyDlgProc);
    return 0;
}
//----------------------------------------------------------------------
// DoMainCommandAddTimerNotification - Process add timer notify button.
//
LPARAM DoMainCommandAddTimerNotification (HWND hWnd, WORD idItem,
                                          HWND hwndCtl, WORD wNotifyCode) {
    SYSTEMTIME st;
    HANDLE hNotify;
    CE_NOTIFICATION_TRIGGER nt;
    TCHAR szExeName[MAX_PATH], szText[128];
    TCHAR szArgs[128] = TEXT("This is my timer notification string.");

    // Initialize time structure with local time.
    GetLocalTime (&st);
    // Do a trivial amount of error checking.
    if (st.wMinute == 59) {
        st.wHour++;
        st.wMinute = 0;
    } else
        st.wMinute++;

    memset (&nt, 0, sizeof (CE_NOTIFICATION_TRIGGER));
    nt.dwSize = sizeof (CE_NOTIFICATION_TRIGGER);
    nt.dwType = CNT_TIME;
    nt.lpszApplication = szExeName;
    nt.lpszArguments = szArgs;
    nt.stStartTime = st;
```

```
    StringCchCopy (szExeName, dim(szExeName), NAMED_EVENT_PREFIX_TEXT);
    StringCchCat (szExeName, dim(szExeName), szEventName);
    // Set the notification.
    hNotify = CeSetUserNotificationEx (0, &nt, NULL);
    if (hNotify)
        wsprintf (szText, TEXT ("Timer notification set for %d:%02d:%02d"),
                  st.wHour, st.wMinute, st.wSecond);
    else
        wsprintf (szText, TEXT ("Timer notification failed. rc = %d"),
                  GetLastError());
    MessageBox (hWnd, szText, szAppName, MB_OK);
    return 0;
}
//----------------------------------------------------------------------
// DoMainCommandClearNotifications - Clear all notifications pointing
// to this application.  Note: this is a fairly large stack frame.
//
LPARAM DoMainCommandClearNotifications (HWND hWnd, WORD idItem,
                                        HWND hwndCtl, WORD wNotifyCode) {
    PBYTE pBuff = NULL;
    PCE_NOTIFICATION_INFO_HEADER pnih;
    HANDLE hNotHandles[128];  // Assume this is large enough.
    int rc, nCnt = 0;
    TCHAR szExeName[MAX_PATH], szText[128];
    DWORD i, dwSize, nHandCnt = 0;

    // Get our filename.
    GetModuleFileName (hInst, szExeName, sizeof (szExeName));

    pBuff = (PBYTE)LocalAlloc (LPTR, 8192);
    if (!pBuff) {
        MessageBox (hWnd, TEXT ("Out of memory"), szAppName, MB_OK);
        return 0;
    }
    rc = CeGetUserNotificationHandles (hNotHandles, dim (hNotHandles),
                                       &nHandCnt);
    if (rc) {
        for (i = 0; i < nHandCnt; i++) {
            // Query info on a single handle.
            rc = CeGetUserNotification (hNotHandles[i], 8192,
                                        &dwSize, pBuff);
            if (rc) {
                pnih = (PCE_NOTIFICATION_INFO_HEADER)pBuff;
                if (!lstrcmp (pnih->pcent->lpszApplication, szExeName)){
                    if (CeClearUserNotification (pnih->hNotification))
                        nCnt++;
                }
            }
        }
        wsprintf (szText, TEXT ("Cleared %d notifications"), nCnt);
        MessageBox (hWnd, szText, szAppName, MB_OK);
    } else
       MessageBox (hWnd, TEXT ("Could not query handles"),
                   szAppName, MB_OK);
```

```
    LocalFree (pBuff);
    return 0;
}
//----------------------------------------------------------------------
// MySetEventNotification  - Sets event notifications
//
int MySetEventNotification (HWND hWnd, DWORD dwEvent) {
    TCHAR szArgs[] = TEXT("This is my event notification string.");
    CE_NOTIFICATION_TRIGGER nt;
    HANDLE hNotify;
    TCHAR szExeName[MAX_PATH], szText[128];

    memset (&nt, 0, sizeof (CE_NOTIFICATION_TRIGGER));
    nt.dwSize = sizeof (CE_NOTIFICATION_TRIGGER);
    nt.dwType = CNT_EVENT;
    nt.dwEvent = dwEvent;
    nt.lpszApplication = szExeName;
    nt.lpszArguments = szArgs;
    GetModuleFileName (hInst, szExeName, sizeof (szExeName));

    // Set the notification.
    hNotify = CeSetUserNotificationEx (0, &nt, NULL);
    if (hNotify)
        wsprintf (szText, TEXT ("Event notification set for %08x"),
                  dwEvent);
    else
        wsprintf (szText, TEXT("Set Event notification failed rc: %d"),
                  GetLastError());
    MessageBox (hWnd, szText, szAppName, MB_OK);
    return 0;
}
//----------------------------------------------------------------------
// Add2List - Add string to the report list box.
//
void Add2List (HWND hWnd, LPTSTR lpszFormat, ...) {
    int i, nBuf;
    TCHAR szBuffer[512];

    va_list args;
    va_start(args, lpszFormat);

    nBuf = _vstprintf_s (szBuffer, dim (szBuffer), lpszFormat, args);
    i = SendDlgItemMessage (hWnd, IDD_OUTPUT, WM_SETTEXT, 0,
                            (LPARAM)(LPCTSTR)szBuffer);
    va_end(args);
}

//======================================================================
// SetEventNotifyDlgProc - Callback function for Event dialog box
//
BOOL CALLBACK SetEventNotifyDlgProc (HWND hWnd, UINT wMsg,
                                     WPARAM wParam, LPARAM lParam) {
    DWORD dwEvent;
    int i;
```

```
    switch (wMsg) {
    case WM_COMMAND:
        {
            WORD idItem = LOWORD (wParam);
            switch (idItem) {
            case IDOK:
                dwEvent = 0;
                for (i = 0; i < dim (SysTypeBtns); i++) {
                    if (IsDlgButtonChecked (hWnd,
                                            SysTypeBtns[i].dwID) == 1)
                        dwEvent |= SysTypeBtns[i].dwFlag;
                }
                // Call my set event notification function above.
                MySetEventNotification (hWnd, dwEvent);
                EndDialog (hWnd, 1);
                return TRUE;

            case IDCANCEL:
                EndDialog (hWnd, 0);
                return TRUE;
            }
        }
        break;
    }
    return FALSE;
}
//======================================================================
// MonitorThread - Monitors event for timer notificaiton
//
DWORD WINAPI MonitorThread (PVOID pArg) {
    int rc;

    while (g_fContinue) {
        rc = WaitForSingleObject (g_hNoteEvent, INFINITE);
        if (!g_fContinue)
            break;
        if (rc == WAIT_OBJECT_0)
            SendMessage (g_hMain, MYMSG_TELLNOTIFY, 0, (LPARAM)g_hNoteEvent);
        else
            break;
    }
    return 0;
}
```

When NoteDemo starts, it examines the command line to determine whether it was started by a user notification. If so, the program attempts to find another instance of the application already running. If the program finds one, a message is sent to the first instance, informing it of the user notification. Because this is an example program, the second instance doesn't terminate itself as it would if it were a commercial application.

The timer notification uses a named event as its signal instead of launching a second copy of the application. To monitor the event, NoteDemo creates a second thread before the main window is created. This routine, *MonitorThread*, simply waits on the event handle that was created for the timer notification. When NoteDemo terminates, it sets a quit flag for the thread and signals the event itself. This causes *MonitorThread* to terminate.

The last button that clears all the notifications scheduled for the NoteDemo application has an interesting task. How does it know what is scheduled? Does it keep a record of every notification it has scheduled? Fortunately, that's not necessary. NoteDemo simply queries the notifications scheduled for all applications, finds the ones for itself, and clears them. Let's see how that's done.

Querying Scheduled Notifications

While scheduling the different notifications is often all that applications need, additional functions allow applications to query the notifications currently scheduled in the system. Here's the function that queries the notifications:

```
BOOL CeGetUserNotificationHandles (HANDLE *rghNotifications,
                                   DWORD cHandles, LPDWORD pcHandlesNeeded);
```

This function returns an array filled with handles to all notifications currently scheduled in the system. The first parameter is the pointer to a handle array. The second parameter, *cHandles*, should be filled with the number of entries in the array. The third parameter should contain the address of a *DWORD* that will be filled with the number of entries in the array filled with valid notification handles.

If the array is large enough to hold all the handles, the function returns *TRUE* and provides the number of handles returned in the variable pointed to by *pcHandlesNeeded*. If the array is too small, the function fails. You can query the number of handles the system will return by passing *NULL* in the *rghNotifications* parameter and 0 in the *cHandles* parameter. The function will then return the number of handles in the variable pointed to by *pcHandlesNeeded*.

After you have queried all the handles, you can determine the details of each notification by passing each handle to the function:

```
BOOL CeGetUserNotification (HANDLE hNotification, DWORD cBufferSize,
                            LPDWORD pcBytesNeeded, LPBYTE pBuffer);
```

The first parameter is the handle to the notification in which you're interested. The second parameter is the size of the buffer you're providing the function to return the data about the notification. The third parameter is the address of a *DWORD* that will receive the size of the data returned. The final parameter is the address of a buffer that will receive the details about the notification.

The size of the required buffer changes depending on the notification. The buffer begins with a *CE_NOTIFICATION_INFO_HEADER* structure. The buffer also contains a *CE_NOTIFICATION_TRIGGER* structure and, depending on the type of notification, an optional

CE_USER_NOTIFICATION structure. Because these structures contain pointers to strings for application names and command lines, these strings must also be stored in the buffer.

To determine how big the buffer needs to be, you can call *CeGetUserNotification* with *cBufferSize* set to 0 and *pBuffer* set to *NULL*. The function returns the number of bytes required by the buffer in the variable that *pcBytesNeeded* points to. However, calling the function this way takes just as much time as retrieving the data itself, so it would be better to assume a size for the buffer and call the function. Only if the call fails because the buffer is too small do you then reallocate the buffer so that it's large enough to hold the data.

Now on to the data returned. The *CE_NOTIFICATION_INFO_HEADER* structure is defined this way:

```
typedef struct UserNotificationInfoHeader {
    HANDLE hNotification;
    DWORD dwStatus;
    CE_NOTIFICATION_TRIGGER   *pcent;
    CE_USER_NOTIFICATION   *pceun;
} CE_NOTIFICATION_INFO_HEADER;
```

The first field is the handle of the event you are querying. The second field contains the status of the notification. This field contains 0 if the notification hasn't fired or *CNS_SIGNALLED* if it has. The next two fields are pointers to the same structures discussed earlier in the chapter. The pointer to the *CE_NOTIFICATION_TRIGGER* structure points to an address in the buffer in which that structure is defined. Depending on the type of notification, the pointer to the *CE_USER_NOTIFICATION* structure could be *NULL*.

The combination of the two structures, *CE_NOTIFICATION_TRIGGER* and *CE_USER_NOTIFICATION* along with the status flag, completely describes the notification. By examining the trigger structure, you can determine the application that's scheduled to run as a result of the notification, its command line, and of course, the type of notification itself.

The Notification API is a handy way to monitor events in a Windows CE system. The ability to have the operating system launch your application instead of having to lurk around in memory waiting for the event significantly reduces the memory requirements for a well-designed system. User notifications give you a convenient and uniform way to alert the user of events that need attention.

Bubble Notifications

Originally developed for Windows Mobile devices, bubble notifications provide a method of notifying users with pop-up windows. Bubble notifications can display an icon on the taskbar, optionally display an information bubble with HTML text, and even beep the user as necessary. The user can respond by tapping on hyperlinks or buttons within the bubble. These responses are then sent back to the originating application. Unlike the standard Windows CE notifications, the bubble notifications require the application be running and manually set the notification as needed. After the notification is set, the application can stay running and receive feedback from the notification via window messages or terminate and specify that a COM in-proc server receives the feedback. Figure 12-4 shows the desktop with a notification bubble being displayed.

FIGURE 12-4 A notification bubble

The bubble is anchored to the application-defined icon on the taskbar. Notice that the look of the "bubble" isn't that appealing. The code in the operating system that displays bubble notifications, along with other user interface elements taken from Windows Mobile systems, is intentially "uglyfied" on embedded systems by default to differentiate them from Windows Mobile systems. Fortunately, the code that displays bubble notifications is available to OEMs for modification to change the look and feel of the bubble notifications. While Figure 12-4 shows what the unmodified code presents, you might expect that embedded systems and, of course, Windows Mobile systems, will look much better.

Adding a Notification

To display a notification, the *SHNotificationAdd* function is used. Its rather simple prototype is

```
LRESULT SHNotificationAdd (SHNOTIFICATIONDATA * pndAdd);
```

The single parameter is a pointer to a not-so-simple *SHNOTIFICATIONDATA* structure defined as

```
typedef struct _SHNOTIFICATIONDATA {
    DWORD cbStruct;
    DWORD dwID;
    SHNP npPriority;
    DWORD csDuration;
    HICON hicon;
    DWORD grfFlags;
    CLSID clsid;
    HWND hwndSink;
    LPCTSTR pszHTML;
    LPCTSTR pszTitle;
    LPARAM lParam;
} SHNOTIFICATIONDATA;
```

The initial field, *cbStruct*, is the obligatory size field that must be initialized to the size of the structure. The *dwID* field will be the ID value for the notification. The ID value will be used to identify any user responses to the notification. The *npPriority* field is set to either *SHNP_ICONIC* to have the notification simply display an icon on the navigation bar or to *SHNP_INFORM* if the notification is to display the bubble text immediately. In the case of *SHNP_ICONIC*, if the user taps the icon, the bubble text is then displayed. The *csDuration* field specifies how long the notification should be displayed before the system automatically removes the icon and bubble. Unlike almost every other time parameter in Windows, this *csDuration* is measured in seconds, not milliseconds. The *hIcon* field should be set to a 16-by-16 icon that will be displayed on the taskbar during the notification.

The *grfFlags* flags field can be set with a series of flags that configure the notification. The *SHNF_CRITICAL* flag changes the color of the title and border of the bubble. The *SHNF_FORCEMESSAGE* flag displays the bubble even if the registry settings of the device are configured to not display notification bubbles. The *SHNF_DISPLAYON* flag turns on the display if it's off when the notification is displayed.

The *clsid* field has two uses. First, it's an identifier for the notification. It should be set to a *GUID* defined by the application. The second use is to identify a COM in-proc server. The in-proc server is one way the shell can provide feedback to the application. The *hwndSink* field can also be used in the feedback mechanism. If the *hwndSink* field is set to a valid window handle, the shell will provide feedback via *WM_NOTIFY* messages to that window. Feedback is sent when the text bubble is displayed, when it is closed, and when the user taps on any hyperlinks in the HTML text in the bubble. If the *clsid* field is set to the CLSID of a COM in-proc server that exposes an *IShellNotificationCallback* interface, the feedback is delivered using calls to the interface's *OnShow*, *OnDismiss*, *OnCommandSelected*, and *OnLinkSelected* methods. The difference between *OnCommandSelected* and *OnLinkSelected* will be explained momentarily.

The *pszHTML* field can be *NULL*, in the case of an icon-only notification or either unformatted Unicode text or HTML Unicode text. The HTML text allows for surprisingly elaborate formatting of the text in the bubble. Paragraph breaks, links, and even simple controls can be displayed in the bubble. The following HTML was used to display the bubble shown in Figure 12-5:

```
<html><body><p>This is a list</p>
<ul>
  <li>Item 1</li>
  <li>Item 2</li>
  <li>Item 3</li>
</ul>
  <input type=\"button\" value=\"Yes\" name=\"cmd:200\">
  <input type=\"button\" value=\"No\" name=\"cmd:201\">
  <input type=\"button\" value=\"Cancel\" name=\"cmd:202\"></p>
<p> </p>
<p>Click <a href=\"http://www.msnbc.com\">here</a> to follow a link.</p>
</body></html>"; </html>
```

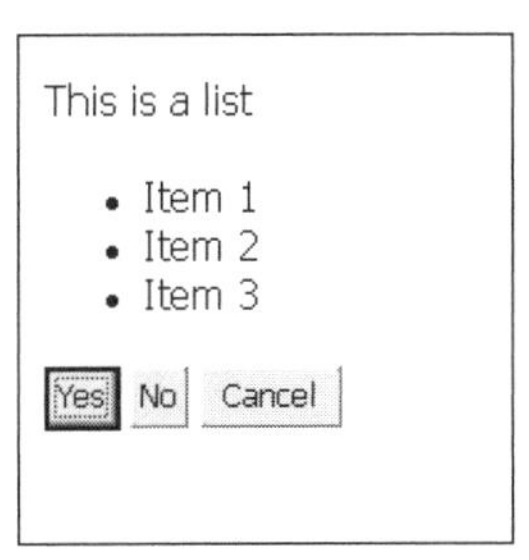

FIGURE 12-5 Complex HTML displayed in a notification bubble

The *pszTitle* field should point to a text string that will be the title of the bubble. The final field, *lParam*, is an application-defined value that will be passed back in the feedback *WM_NOTIFY* messages or in the callback to the in-proc server.

The feedback received by the application depends on how the user responds to the notification. When the user clicks on the notification icon, the system sends a *WM_NOTIFY* to the window specified in the *hwndSink* field. If the application returns a zero, the text bubble will be displayed. If the application returns a nonzero value, the bubble will not be displayed. In this case, the application needs to provide whatever feedback it deems necessary to the user.

The HTML text can contain two types of feedback elements. The first is the standard hyperlink, as shown below.

```
Click <a href="http://www.msnbc.com\">here</a> to go to MSNBC
```

If the user clicks on a hyperlink, the notification system sends a *WM_NOTIFY* message to the window with a notification code of *SHNN_LINKSEL*. The notification structure provides the text of the URL as well as the data defined in the *lParam* field of *SHNOTIFICATIONDATA*. If the HREF is in the format CMD:n, as in

```
Click <a href=\"cmd:205\">here</a> to go to MSNBC
```

the system sends a *WM_COMMAND* message instead of a *WM_NOTIFY* to the window. In this case, the value *n* is the ID value of the message, and the ID of the notification is returned in *lParam*. For the in-proc server, clicking the standard hyperlink results in a call to the interface's *OnLinkSelected* method while clicking on links with the CMD:n format results in the *OnCommandSelected* method being called. The CMD value 0 is reserved, a value of 1 sends a notification, but does not dismiss the bubble; and a command value of 2 does not dismiss the bubble, nor does it result in a *WM_COMMAND* message being sent. Applications should generally use CMD values greater than 2.

When the user dismisses the bubble either by clicking a hyperlink or by clicking on the bubble itself, a final notification that the bubble is being dismissed is sent either by message or to the in-proc server.

Modifying a Notification

Configuration data can be queried from a notification by calling the *SHNotificationGetData* function. Its prototype is shown here:

```
LRESULT SHNotificationGetData (const CLSID * pclsid,
                               DWORD dwID, SHNOTIFICATIONDATA * pndBuffer);
```

The first two parameters are *pclsid*, which points to the CLSID of the notification, and *dwID*, which specifies the ID of the notification. The function fills in the *SHNOTIFICATIONDATA* structure pointed to by the third parameter, *pndBuffer*.

The notification can then be modified by changing the relevant data in the *SHNOTIFICATIONDATA* structure and calling *SHNotificationUpdate*, prototyped as

```
LRESULT SHNotificationUpdate (DWORD grnumUpdateMask,
                              SHNOTIFICATIONDATA *pndNew);
```

The *grnumUpdateMask* parameter is a set of flags that indicate which of the fields in the *SHNOTIFICATIONDATA* structure pointed to by *pndNew* should be used to update the notification. The flags are *SHNUM_PRIORITY* to change the priority of the notification, *SHNUM_DURATION* to change the duration, *SHNUM_ICON* to change the icon, *SHNUM_HTML* to change the bubble text, and *SHNUM_TITLE* to change the bubble title text.

Removing a Notification

If the notification is simply an icon, it will be automatically removed when the notification times out. However, if the notification displays a bubble, the timeout value of the notification is used to automatically dismiss the bubble, not the icon. If the bubble text doesn't have a link or command, the user can dismiss the text bubble, but the icon remains. In this case and in the case where the timeout is set to infinite, there needs to be a way for the application to remove the notification. Removing the notification is accomplished with the aptly named *SHNotificationRemove* function defined as

```
LRESULT SHNotificationRemove (const CLSID * pclsid, DWORD dwID);
```

The two parameters are the CLSID and ID value of the notification.

Now that we've looked at the Notification API, we've covered the basics of Windows CE applications. The next section of this book turns from the basics to the advanced areas of Windows CE programming. This next section covers everything from networking to Bluetooth and even device drivers.

Part III
Advanced Windows CE

Chapter 13

Windows CE Networking

Networks are at the heart of modern computer systems. Over the years, Microsoft Windows has supported a variety of networks and networking APIs. The evolving nature of networking APIs, along with the need to keep systems backward compatible, have resulted in a huge array of overlapping functions and parallel APIs. As in many places in Windows CE, the networking API is a subset of the vast array of networking functions supported under the desktop versions of Windows. This chapter covers the networking from two perspectives: first, the Windows Networking API that supports basic network connections so that a Windows CE device can access disks and printers on a network; then TCP/IP networking through a presentation of WinSock,Windows's socket API.

Windows Networking Support

The WNet API is a provider-independent interface that allows Windows applications to access network resources without regard for the network implementation. The Windows CE version of the WNet API has fewer functions but provides the basics so that a Windows CE application can gain access to shared network resources, such as disks and printers. The WNet API is implemented by a "redirector" DLL that translates the WNet functions into network commands for a specific network protocol.

By default, the only network supported by the WNet API is Windows Networking. Support, for even this network is limited by the fact that redirector files that implement Windows Networking aren't bundled with some Windows CE devices. For the WNet API to work, the redirector DLLs must be installed in the \windows directory. In addition, the network control panel, also a supplementary component on some systems, must be used to configure the network card so that it can access the network. If the redirector DLLs aren't installed, or an error occurs when you're configuring or initializing the network adapter, the WNet functions return the error code *ERROR_NO_NETWORK*.

WNet Functions

As with other areas in Windows CE, the WNet implementation under Windows CE is a subset of the same API on the desktop, but support is provided for the critical functions, while the overlapping and obsolete functions are eliminated. For example, the standard WNet API contains four different and overlapping *WNetAddConnection* functions, while Windows CE supports only one, *WNetAddConnection3*.

Conventions of UNC

Network drives can be accessed in one of two ways. The first method is to explicitly name the resource using the *Universal Naming Convention* (UNC) naming syntax, which is a combination of the name of the server and the shared resource. An example of this is *\\BIGSRVR\DRVC*, where the server name is BIGSRVR and the resource on the server is named DRVC. The leading double backslashes immediately indicate that the name is a UNC name. Directories and file names can be included in the UNC name, as in *\\bigsrvr\drvc\dir2\file1.ext*. Notice that I changed case in the two names. That doesn't matter because UNC paths are case insensitive.

As long as the WNet redirector is installed, you can use UNC names wherever you use standard file names in the Windows CE API. You'll have problems, though, with some programs, which might not understand UNC syntax.

Mapping a Remote Drive

To get around applications that don't understand UNC names, you can map a network drive to a local name. When a network drive is mapped on a Windows CE system, the remote drive appears as a folder in the \network folder in the file system. The \network folder isn't a standard folder; in fact, in early versions of Windows CE, it didn't even show up in the Explorer. (For current systems, the visibility of the \network folder depends on a registry setting that's usually enabled.) Instead, it's a placeholder name by which the local names of the mapped network drives can be addressed. For example, the network drive *\\BigSrvr\DrvC* could be mapped to the local name JoeBob. Files and directories on *\\BigSrvr\DrvC* would appear under the folder \network\joebob. The local name can't be represented as a drive letter, such as G:, because Windows CE doesn't support drive letters.

I mentioned that the \network folder is a virtual folder; this needs further explanation. If you use the *FindFirstFile/FindNextFile* process to enumerate the directories in the root directory, the \network directory might not be enumerated. However, *FindFirstFile/ FindNextFile* enumerates the mapped resources contained in the \network folder. So if the search string is *.* to enumerate the root directory, the \network folder might not be enumerated, but if you use *\network**.* as the search string, any mapped drives will be enumerated.

In Windows CE, the visibility of the \network folder is controlled by a registry setting. The \network folder is visible if the *DWORD* value *RegisterFSRoot* under the key *[HKEY_LOCAL_MACHINE]\comm\redir* exists and is set to a nonzero value. Deleting this value or setting it to 0 hides the \network folder.

The most direct way to map a remote resource is to call this function:

```
DWORD WNetAddConnection3 (HWND hwndOwner, LPNETRESOURCE lpNetResource,
                          LPTSTR lpPassword, LPTSTR lpUserName,
                          DWORD dwFlags);
```

The first parameter is a handle to a window that owns any network support dialogs that might need to be displayed to complete the connection. The window handle can be *NULL* if you don't want to specify an owner window. This effectively turns the *WNetAddConnection3* function into the *WNetAddConnection2* function supported under other versions of Windows.

The second parameter, *lpNetResource*, should point to a *NETRESOURCE* structure that defines the remote resource being connected. The structure is defined as

```
typedef struct _NETRESOURCE {
    DWORD  dwScope;
    DWORD  dwType;
    DWORD  dwDisplayType;
    DWORD  dwUsage;
    LPTSTR lpLocalName;
    LPTSTR lpRemoteName;
    LPTSTR lpComment;
    LPTSTR lpProvider;
} NETRESOURCE;
```

Most of these fields aren't used for the *WNetAddConnection3* function and should be set to 0. All you need to do is specify the UNC name of the remote resource in a string pointed to by *lpRemoteName* and the local name in a string pointed to by *lpLocalName*. The local name is limited to 99 characters in length. The other fields in this structure are used by the WNet enumeration functions that I'll describe shortly.

You use the next two parameters in *WNetAddConnection3*, *lpPassword* and *lpUserName*, when requesting access from the server to the remote device. If you don't specify a user name and Windows CE can't find user information for network access already defined in the registry, the system displays a dialog box requesting the user name and password. Finally, the *dwFlags* parameter can be either 0 or the flag *CONNECT_UPDATE_PROFILE*. When this flag is set, the connection is dubbed *persistent*. Windows CE stores the connection data for persistent connections in the registry. Unlike other versions of Windows, Windows CE doesn't restore persistent connections when the user logs on. Instead, the local name to remote name mapping is tracked only in the registry. If the local folder is later accessed after the original connection was dropped, a reconnection is automatically attempted when the local folder is accessed.

If the call to *WNetAddConnection3* is successful, it returns *NO_ERROR*. Unlike most Win32 functions, *WNetAddConnection3* returns an error code in the return value if an error occurs. This is a nod to compatibility that stretches back to the Windows 3.1 days. You can also call *GetLastError* to return the error information. As an aside, the function *WNetGetLastError* is supported under Windows CE, but it's just an alias for *GetLastError*, so you can call that function if compatibility with other platforms is important.

The other function you can use under Windows CE to connect a remote resource is *WNetConnectionDialog1*. This function presents a dialog box to the user requesting the remote and local names for the connection. The function is prototyped as

```
DWORD WNetConnectionDialog1 (LPCONNECTDLGSTRUCT lpConnectDlgStruc);
```

The one parameter is a pointer to a *CONNECTDLGSTRUCT* structure defined as the following:

```
typedef struct {
    DWORD cbStructure;
    HWND hwndOwner;
    LPNETRESOURCE lpConnRes;
    DWORD dwFlags;
    DWORD dwDevNum;
} CONNECTDLGSTRUCT;
```

The first field in the structure is the size field and must be set with the size of the *CONNECTDLGSTRUCT* structure before you call *WNetConnectionDialog1*. The *hwndOwner* field should be filled with the handle of the owner window for the dialog box. The *lpConnRes* field should point to a *NETRESOURCE* structure. This structure should be filled with zeros except for the *lpRemoteName* field, which may be filled to specify the default remote name in the dialog. You can leave the *lpRemoteName* field 0 if you don't want to specify a suggested remote path.

The *dwFlags* field can either be 0 or be set to the flag *CONNDLG_RO_PATH*. When this flag is specified, the user can't change the remote name field in the dialog box. Of course, this requirement means that the *lpRemoteName* field in the *NETRESOURCE* structure must contain a valid remote name. Windows CE ignores the *dwDevNum* field in the *CONNECTDLGSTRUCT* structure.

When the function is called, it displays a dialog box that allows the user to specify a local name and, if not invoked with the *CONNDLG_RO_PATH* flag, the remote name as well. If the user taps on the OK button, Windows attempts to make the connection specified. The connection, if successful, is recorded as a persistent connection in the registry.

If the connection is successful, the function returns *NO_ERROR*. If the user presses the Cancel button in the dialog box, the function returns -1. Other return codes indicate errors processing the function.

If you are running software specifically on Windows Embedded CE 6, be aware that there is a bug in the initial versions of CE 6 that causes this function to fail. Microsoft will release a fix for this problem, but for systems released without the fix you will need to programatically create your own dialog box and use *WNetAddConnection3* to make the network connection. I've added just such a dialog in the ListNet example later in this chapter.

Disconnecting a Remote Resource

You can choose from three ways to disconnect a connected resource. The first method is to delete the connection with this function:

```
DWORD WNetCancelConnection2 (LPTSTR lpName, DWORD dwFlags,
                             BOOL fForce);
```

The *lpName* parameter points to either the local name or the remote network name of the connection you want to remove. The *dwFlags* parameter should be set to 0 or *CONNECT_UPDATE_PROFILE*. If *CONNECT_UPDATE_PROFILE* is set, the entry in the registry that references the connection is removed; otherwise, the call won't change that information. Finally, the *fForce* parameter indicates whether the system should continue with the disconnect, even if there are open files or print jobs on the remote device. If the function is successful, it returns *NO_ERROR*.

You can prompt the user to specify a network resource to delete using this function:

```
DWORD WNetDisconnectDialog (HWND hwnd, DWORD dwType);
```

This function brings up a system-provided dialog box that lists all connections currently defined. The user can select one from the list and tap on the OK button to disconnect that resource. The two parameters for this function are a handle to the window that owns the dialog box and *dwType*, which is supposed to define the type of resources—printer (*RESOURCETYPE_PRINT*) or disk (*RESOURCETYPE_DISK*)—enumerated in the dialog box. However, some systems ignore this parameter and enumerate both disk and print devices. This dialog, displayed by *WNetDisconnectDialog*, is actually implemented by the network driver. So it's up to each OEM to get this dialog to work correctly.

A more specific method to disconnect a network resource is to call

```
DWORD WNetDisconnectDialog1 (LPDISCDLGSTRUCT lpDiscDlgStruc);
```

This function is misleadingly named in that it won't display a dialog box if all the parameters in *DISCDLGSTRUCT* are correct and point to a resource not currently being used. The dialog part of this function appears when the resource is being used.

DISCDLGSTRUCT is defined as

```
typedef struct {
    DWORD cbStructure;
    HWND hwndOwner;
    LPTSTR lpLocalName;
    LPTSTR lpRemoteName;
    DWORD dwFlags;
} DISCDLGSTRUCT;
```

As usual, the *cbStructure* field should be set to the size of the structure. The *hwndOwner* field should be set to the window that owns any dialog box displayed. The *lpLocalName* and *lpRemoteName* fields should be set to the local and remote names of the resource that's to be disconnected. Under current implementations, *lpLocalName* is optional, while the *lpRemoteName* field must be set for the function to work correctly. The *dwFlags* parameter can be either 0 or *DISC_NO_FORCE*. If this flag is set and the network resource is currently being used, the system simply fails the function. Otherwise, a dialog appears asking the user if he or she wants to disconnect the resource even though the resource is being used. Under the current implementations, the *DISC_NO_FORCE* flag is ignored.

Enumerating Network Resources

It's all very well and good to connect to a network resource, but it helps if you know what resources are available to connect to. Windows CE supports three WNet functions used to enumerate network resources: *WNetOpenEnum*, *WNetEnumResource*, and *WNetCloseEnum*. The process is similar to enumerating files with *FileFindFirst*, *FileFindNext*, and *FileFindClose*.

To start the process of enumerating network resources, first call the function

```
DWORD WNetOpenEnum (DWORD dwScope, DWORD dwType, DWORD dwUsage,
                    LPNETRESOURCE lpNetResource,
                    LPHANDLE lphEnum);
```

The first parameter, *dwScope*, specifies the scope of the enumeration. It can be one of the following flags:

- **RESOURCE_CONNECTED** Enumerate the connected resources.
- **RESOURCE_REMEMBERED** Enumerate the persistent network connections.
- **RESOURCE_GLOBALNET** Enumerate all resources on the network.

The first two flags, *RESOURCE_CONNECTED* and *RESOURCE_REMEMBERED*, simply enumerate the resources already connected on your machine. The difference is that *RESOURCE_CONNECTED* returns the network resources that are connected at the time of the call, while *RESOURCE_REMEMBERED* returns those that are persistent regardless of whether they're currently connected. When either of these flags is used, the *dwUsage* parameter is ignored and the *lpNetResource* parameters must be *NULL*.

The third flag, *RESOURCE_GLOBALNET*, allows you to enumerate resources—such as servers, shared drives, or printers out on the network—that aren't connected. The *dwType* parameter specifies what you're attempting to enumerate—shared disks (*RESOURCETYPE_DISK*), shared printers (*RESOURCETYPE_PRINT*), or both (*RESOURCETYPE_ANY*).

You use the third and fourth parameters only if the *dwScope* parameter is set to *RESOURCE_GLOBALNET*. The *dwUsage* parameter specifies the usage of the resource and can be 0 to enumerate any resource, *RESOURCEUSAGE_CONNECTABLE* to enumerate only connectable resources, or *RESOURCEUSAGE_CONTAINER* to enumerate only containers such as servers.

If the *dwScope* parameter is set to RESOURCE_GLOBALNET, the fourth parameter, *lpNetResource*, must point to a *NETRESOURCE* structure; otherwise, the parameter must be *NULL*. The *NETRESOURCE* structure should be initialized to specify the starting point on the network for the enumeration. The starting point is specified by a UNC name in the *lpRemoteName* field of *NETRESOURCE*. The *dwUsage* field of the *NETRESOURCE* structure must be set to *RESOURCETYPE_CONTAINER*. For example, to enumerate the shared resources on the server BIGSERV, the *lpRemoteName* field would point to the string *\\BIGSERV*. To enumerate all servers in a domain, *lpRemoteName* should simply specify the domain name. For the domain EntireNet, the *lpRemoteName* field should point to the string *EntireNet*. Because Windows CE doesn't allow you to pass a *NULL* into *lpRemoteName* when you use the RESOURCE_GLOBALNET flag, you can't enumerate all resources in the network namespace as you can under other versions of Windows. This restriction exists because Windows CE doesn't support the concept of a Windows CE device belonging to a specific network context.

The final parameter of *WNetOpenEnum*, *lphEnum*, is a pointer to an enumeration handle that will be passed to the other functions in the enumeration process. *WNetOpenEnum* returns a value of *NO_ERROR* if successful. If the function isn't successful, you can call *GetLastError* to query the extended error information.

Once you have successfully started the enumeration process, you actually query data by calling this function:

```
DWORD WNetEnumResource (HANDLE hEnum, LPDWORD lpcCount,
                        LPVOID lpBuffer,
                        LPDWORD lpBufferSize);
```

The function takes the handle returned by *WNetOpenEnum* as its first parameter. The second parameter is a pointer to a variable that should be initialized with the number of resources you want to enumerate in each call to *WNetEnumResource*. You can specify -1 in this variable if you want *WNetEnumResource* to return the data for as many resources as will fit in the return buffer specified by the *lpBuffer* parameter. The final parameter is a pointer to a *DWORD* that should be initialized with the size of the buffer pointed to by *lpBuffer*. If the buffer is too small to hold the data for even one resource, *WNetEnumResource* sets this variable to the required size for the buffer.

The information about the shared resources returned by data is returned in the form of an array of *NETRESOURCE* structures. While this is the same structure I described when I talked about the *WNetAddConnection3* function, I'll list the elements of the structure here again for convenience:

```
typedef struct _NETRESOURCE {
    DWORD  dwScope;
    DWORD  dwType;
    DWORD  dwDisplayType;
    DWORD  dwUsage;
    LPTSTR lpLocalName;
    LPTSTR lpRemoteName;
    LPTSTR lpComment;
    LPTSTR lpProvider;
} NETRESOURCE;
```

The interesting fields in the context of enumeration start with the *dwType* field, which indicates the type of resource that was enumerated. The value can be *RESOURCETYPE_DISK* or *RESOURCETYPE_PRINT*. The *dwDisplayType* field provides even more information about the resource, demarcating domains (*RESOURCEDISPLAYTYPE_DOMAIN*) from servers (*RESOURCEDISPLAYTYPE_SERVER*) and from shared disks and printers (*RESOURCEDISPLAYTYPE_SHARE*). A fourth flag, *RESOURCEDISPLAYTYPE_GENERIC*, is returned if the display type doesn't matter.

The *lpLocalName* field points to a string containing the local name of the resource if the resource is currently connected or is a persistent connection. The *lpRemoteName* field points to the UNC name of the resource. The *lpComment* field contains the comment line describing the resource that's provided by some servers.

WNetEnumResource either returns *NO_ERROR*, indicating that the function succeeded but you need to call it again to enumerate more resources, or *ERROR_NO_MORE_ITEMS*, indicating that you have enumerated all resources matching the specification passed in *WNetOpenEnum*. With any other return code, you should call *GetLastError* to further diagnose the problem.

You have few strategies when enumerating the network resources. You can specify a huge buffer and pass -1 in the variable pointed to by *lpcCount*, telling *WNetEnumResource* to return as much information as possible in one shot. Or you can specify a smaller buffer, and ask for only one or two resources for each call to *WNetEnumResource*. The one caveat on the small buffer approach is that the strings that contain the local and remote names are also placed in the specified buffer. The name pointers inside the *NETRESOURCE* structure then point to those strings. This means that you can't specify the size of the buffer to be exactly the size of the *NETRESOURCE* structure and expect to get any data back. A third possibility is to call *WNetEnumResource* twice, the first time with the *lpBuffer* parameter 0, and have Windows CE tell you the size necessary for the buffer. Then you allocate the buffer and call *WNetEnumResource* again to actually query the data. However you use *WNetEnumResource*, you'll need to check the return code to see whether it needs to be called again to enumerate more resources.

When you have enumerated all the resources, you must make one final call to the function:

```
DWORD WNetCloseEnum (HANDLE hEnum);
```

The only parameter to this function is the enumeration handle first returned by *WNetOpenEnum*. This function cleans up the system resources used by the enumeration process.

Following is a short routine that uses the enumeration functions to query the network for available resources. You pass to a function a UNC name to use as the root of the search. The function returns a buffer of zero-delimited strings that designate the local name, if any, and the UNC name of each shared resource found.

```
/// Helper routine
int AddToList (LPTSTR *pPtr, INT *pnListSize, LPTSTR pszStr) {
               int nLen = lstrlen (pszStr) + 1;

    if (FAILED(StringCchCopy (*pPtr, *pnListSize, pszStr)))
        return -1;
    *pPtr += nLen;
    *pnListSize -= nLen;
    return 0;
}
//----------------------------------------------------------------------
// EnumNetDisks - Produces a list of shared disks on a network
//
int EnumNetDisks (LPTSTR pszRoot, LPTSTR pszNetList, int nNetSize){
    int i = 0, rc, nBuffSize = 1024;
    DWORD dwCnt, dwSize;
    HANDLE hEnum;
    NETRESOURCE nr;
    LPNETRESOURCE pnr;
    PBYTE pPtr, pNew;

    // Allocate buffer for enumeration data.
    pPtr = (PBYTE) LocalAlloc (LPTR, nBuffSize);
    if (!pPtr)
        return -1;

    // Initialize specification for search root.
    memset (&nr, 0, sizeof (nr));
    nr.lpRemoteName = pszRoot;
    nr.dwUsage = RESOURCEUSAGE_CONTAINER;

    // Start enumeration.
    rc = WNetOpenEnum (RESOURCE_GLOBALNET, RESOURCETYPE_DISK, 0, &nr,
                       &hEnum);
    if (rc != NO_ERROR)
        return -1;

    // Enumerate one item per loop.
    do {
        dwCnt = 1;
        dwSize = nBuffSize;
        rc = WNetEnumResource (hEnum, &dwCnt, pPtr, &dwSize);

        // Process returned data.
        if (rc == NO_ERROR) {
            pnr = (NETRESOURCE *)pPtr;
            if (pnr->lpRemoteName)
                rc = AddToList (&pszNetList, &nNetSize,
                                pnr->lpRemoteName);
```

```
        // If our buffer was too small, try again.
        } else if (rc == ERROR_MORE_DATA) {
            pNew = LocalReAlloc (pPtr, dwSize, LMEM_MOVEABLE);
            if (pNew) {
                pPtr = pNew;
                nBuffSize = LocalSize (pPtr);
                rc = 0;
            }
        }
    } while (rc == 0);

    // If the loop was successful, add extra zero to list.
    if (rc == ERROR_NO_MORE_ITEMS) {
        rc = AddToList (&pszNetList, &nNetSize, TEXT (""));
        rc = 0;
    }

    // Clean up.
    WNetCloseEnum (hEnum);
    LocalFree (pPtr);
    return rc;
}
```

Although the enumeration functions work well for querying what's available on the net, you can use another strategy for determining the current connected resources. At the simplest level, you can use *FileFindFirst* and *FileFindNext* to enumerate the locally-connected network disks by searching the folders in the \network directory. Once you have the local name, a few functions are available to you for querying just what that local name is connected to.

Querying Connections and Resources

The folders in the \network directory represent the local names of network-shared disks that are persistently connected to network resources. To determine which of the folders are currently connected, you can use the function

```
DWORD WNetGetConnection (LPCTSTR lpLocalName,
                         LPTSTR lpRemoteName,
                         LPDWORD lpnLength);
```

WNetGetConnection returns the UNC name of the network resource associated with a local device or folder. The *lpLocalName* parameter is filled with the local name of a shared folder or printer. The *lpRemoteName* parameter should point to a buffer that can receive the UNC name for the device. The *lpnLength* parameter points to a *DWORD* value that initially contains the length in characters of the remote name buffer. If the buffer is too small to receive the name, the length value is loaded with the number of characters required to hold the UNC name.

One feature (or problem, depending on how you look at it) of *WNetGetConnection* is that it fails unless the local folder or device has a current connection to the remote shared device. This allows us an easy way to determine which local folders are currently connected and which are just placeholders for persistent connections that aren't currently connected.

Sometimes you need to transfer a file name from one system to another and you need a common format for the file name that would be understood by both systems. The *WNetGetUniversalName* function translates a file name that contains a local network name into one using the UNC name of the connected resource. The prototype for *WNetGetUniversalName* is the following:

```
DWORD WNetGetUniversalName (LPCTSTR lpLocalPath, DWORD dwInfoLevel,
                            LPVOID lpBuffer, LPDWORD lpBufferSize);
```

Like *WNetGetConnection*, this function returns a UNC name for a local name. There are two main differences between *WNetGetConnection* and *WNetGetUniversalName*. First, *WNetGetUniversalName* works even if the remote resource isn't currently connected. Second, you can pass a complete file name to *WNetGetUniversalName* instead of simply the local name of the shared resource, which is all that is accepted by *WNetGetConnection*.

WNetGetUniversalName returns the remote information in two different formats. If the *dwInfoLevel* parameter is set to *UNIVERSAL_NAME_INFO_LEVEL*, the buffer pointed to by *lpBuffer* is loaded with the following structure:

```
typedef struct _UNIVERSAL_NAME_INFO {
    LPTSTR  lpUniversalName;
} UNIVERSAL_NAME_INFO;
```

The only field in the structure is a pointer to the UNC name for the shared resource. The string is returned in the buffer immediately following the structure. So if a server *\\BigServ\DriveC* was attached as *LocC* and you pass *WNetGetUniversalName* the file name *\Network\LocC\Win32\Filename.ext*, the function returns the UNC name *\\BigServ\DriveC\win32\filename.ext*.

If the *dwInfoLevel* parameter is set to *REMOTE_NAME_INFO_LEVEL*, the buffer is filled with the following structure:

```
typedef struct _REMOTE_NAME_INFO
    LPTSTR  lpUniversalName;
    LPTSTR  lpConnectionName;
    LPTSTR  lpRemainingPath;
} REMOTE_NAME_INFO;
```

This structure not only returns the UNC name but also parses the UNC name into the share name and the remaining path. So, using the same file name as in the previous example, *\network\LocC\win32\filename.ext*, the *REMOTE_NAME_INFO* fields would point to the following strings:

lpUniversalName: \\BigServ\DriveC\win32\filename.ext

lpConnectionName: \\BigServ\DriveC

lpRemainingPath: \win32\filename.ext

One more thing: you don't have to prefix the local share name with \network. In the preceding example, the file name *\LocC\Win32\filename.ext* would have produced the same results.

One final WNet function supported by Windows CE is

```
DWORD WNetGetUser (LPCTSTR lpName, LPTSTR lpUserName,
                   LPDWORD lpnLength);
```

This function returns the name the system used to connect to the remote resource. *WNetGetUser* is passed the local name of the shared resource and returns the user name the system used when connecting to the remote resource in the buffer pointed to by *lpUser-Name*. The *lpnLength* parameter should point to a variable that contains the size of the buffer. If the buffer isn't big enough to contain the user name, the variable pointed to by *lpn-Length* is filled with the required size for the buffer.

The ListNet Example Program

ListNet is a short program that lists the persistent network connections on a Windows CE machine. The program's window is a dialog box with three controls: a list box that displays the network connections, a Connect button that lets you add a new persistent connection, and a Disconnect button that lets you delete one of the connections. Double-clicking on a connection in the list box opens an Explorer window to display the contents of that network resource. Figure 13-1 shows the ListNet window, while Listing 13-1 shows the ListNet source code.

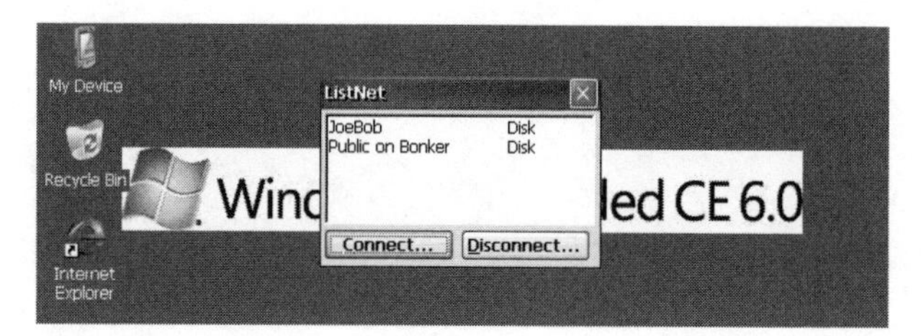

FIGURE 13-1 The ListNet window containing a few network folders

LISTING 13-1

ListNet.rc

```
//======================================================================
// Resource file
//
// Written for the book Programming Windows CE
// Copyright (C) 2007 Douglas Boling
//======================================================================
#include "windows.h"
#include "ListNet.h"                        // Program-specific stuff

//----------------------------------------------------------------------
// Icons and bitmaps
//
ID_ICON ICON   "ListNet.ico"                // Program icon

//----------------------------------------------------------------------
// Main window dialog template
//
ListNet DIALOG discardable 10, 10, 120, 65
STYLE  WS_OVERLAPPED | WS_VISIBLE | WS_CAPTION | WS_SYSMENU |
       DS_CENTER | DS_MODALFRAME
CAPTION "ListNet"
BEGIN
    LISTBOX                  IDD_NETLIST,   2,   2, 116,  46,
                             WS_TABSTOP | WS_VSCROLL |
                             LBS_NOINTEGRALHEIGHT | LBS_USETABSTOPS
    PUSHBUTTON "&Connect...",   IDD_CNCT,   2,  50,  55,  12, WS_TABSTOP
    PUSHBUTTON "&Disconnect...",
                               IDD_DCNCT,  61,  50,  55,  12, WS_TABSTOP
END

//----------------------------------------------------------------------
// Custom Add Connection dialog
//
MyConnDlg DIALOG discardable 10, 10, 140, 69
STYLE  WS_OVERLAPPED | WS_VISIBLE | WS_CAPTION | WS_SYSMENU |
       DS_CENTER | DS_MODALFRAME
EXSTYLE  WS_EX_CAPTIONOKBTN

CAPTION "Connect To Share"
BEGIN
    LTEXT "Remote path:",        -1,   7,   7, 128,   8
    EDITTEXT         IDD_SHARENAME,   7,  18, 128,  14,
                         WS_TABSTOP | ES_AUTOHSCROLL

    LTEXT "Local Name",          -1,   7,  37, 128,   8
    EDITTEXT         IDD_LOCALNAME,   7,  48, 128,  14,
                         WS_TABSTOP | ES_AUTOHSCROLL
END
```

ListNet.h

```
//======================================================================
// Header file
//
// Written for the book Programming Windows CE
// Copyright (C) 2007 Douglas Boling
//======================================================================
// Returns number of elements
#define dim(x) (sizeof(x) / sizeof(x[0]))

//----------------------------------------------------------------------
// Generic defines and data types
//
struct decodeUINT {                             // Structure associates
    UINT Code;                                  // messages
                                                // with a function.
    LRESULT (*Fxn)(HWND, UINT, WPARAM, LPARAM);
};
struct decodeCMD {                              // Structure associates
    UINT Code;                                  // menu IDs with a
    LRESULT (*Fxn)(HWND, WORD, HWND, WORD);     // function.
};
//----------------------------------------------------------------------
// Generic defines used by application

#define  ID_ICON             1

#define  IDD_NETLIST         100                // Control IDs
#define  IDD_CNCT            101
#define  IDD_DCNCT           102

#define  IDD_SHARENAME       200
#define  IDD_LOCALNAME       201

//----------------------------------------------------------------------
// Function prototypes
//
INT RefreshLocalNetDrives (HWND hWnd);
int CheckErrorCode (HWND hWnd, int rc, LPTSTR lpText);
DWORD MyWNetConnectionDialog1 (LPCONNECTDLGSTRUCTW lpConnDlgStruct);

// Dialog window procedure
BOOL CALLBACK MainWndProc (HWND, UINT, WPARAM, LPARAM);

// Dialog window Message handlers
BOOL DoCommandMain (HWND, UINT, WPARAM, LPARAM);
// Command functions
LPARAM DoMainCommandExit (HWND, WORD, HWND, WORD);
LPARAM DoMainCommandViewDrive (HWND, WORD, HWND, WORD);
LPARAM DoMainCommandMapDrive (HWND, WORD, HWND, WORD);
LPARAM DoMainCommandFreeDrive  (HWND, WORD, HWND, WORD);
```

ListNet.cpp

```
//======================================================================
// ListNet - A network demo application for Windows CE
//
// Written for the book Programming Windows CE
// Copyright (C) 2007 Douglas Boling
//======================================================================
#include <windows.h>                 // For all that Windows stuff
#include <winnetwk.h>                // Network includes
#include "ListNet.h"                 // Program-specific stuff

#if defined(WIN32_PLATFORM_PSPC)
#include <aygshell.h>                // Add new shell includes.
#pragma comment( lib, "aygshell" )   // Link new shell lib for menu bar.
#endif

// Work around bug in initial version of CE 6
#if _WIN32_WCE == 0x600
#define CE6_BUGFIX
#endif
//----------------------------------------------------------------------
// Global data
//
const TCHAR szAppName[] = TEXT ("ListNet");
HINSTANCE hInst;                     // Program instance handle
BOOL fFirst = TRUE;

// Command Message dispatch for MainWindowProc
const struct decodeCMD MainCommandItems[] = {
    IDOK, DoMainCommandExit,
    IDCANCEL, DoMainCommandExit,
    IDD_NETLIST, DoMainCommandViewDrive,
    IDD_CNCT, DoMainCommandMapDrive,
    IDD_DCNCT, DoMainCommandFreeDrive,
};
//======================================================================
//
// Program entry point
//
int WINAPI WinMain (HINSTANCE hInstance, HINSTANCE hPrevInstance,
                    LPWSTR lpCmdLine, int nCmdShow) {
    // Save program instance handle in global variable.
    hInst = hInstance;
    // Create main window.
    DialogBox (hInst, szAppName, NULL, MainWndProc);
    return 0;
}
//======================================================================
// Message handling procedures for main window
//----------------------------------------------------------------------
// MainWndProc - Callback function for application window
//
```

```
BOOL CALLBACK MainWndProc (HWND hWnd, UINT wMsg, WPARAM wParam,
                           LPARAM lParam) {
    INT i;
    // With only two messages, do it the old-fashioned way.
    switch (wMsg) {
    case WM_INITDIALOG:
#if defined(WIN32_PLATFORM_PSPC) || defined(WIN32_PLATFORM_WFSP)
        // For Windows Mobile devices, allow only one instance of the app

        SHINITDLGINFO di;
        SHMENUBARINFO mbi;                        // For Win Mobile, create
        memset(&mbi, 0, sizeof(SHMENUBARINFO)); // menu bar so that we
        mbi.cbSize = sizeof(SHMENUBARINFO);     // have a sip button.
        mbi.hwndParent = hWnd;
        mbi.dwFlags = SHCMBF_EMPTYBAR;
        SHCreateMenuBar(&mbi);

        di.dwMask = SHIDIM_FLAGS;
        di.hDlg = hWnd;
        di.dwFlags = SHIDIF_DONEBUTTON | SHIDIF_SIZEDLG;
        SHInitDialog (&di);

#endif
        i = 75;
        SendDlgItemMessage (hWnd, IDD_NETLIST, LB_SETTABSTOPS, 1,
                            (LPARAM)&i);
        RefreshLocalNetDrives (hWnd);
        break;

    case WM_COMMAND:
        return DoCommandMain (hWnd, wMsg, wParam, lParam);
    }
    return FALSE;
}
//----------------------------------------------------------------------
// DoCommandMain - Process WM_COMMAND message for window.
//
BOOL DoCommandMain (HWND hWnd, UINT wMsg, WPARAM wParam, LPARAM lParam){
    WORD idItem, wNotifyCode;
    HWND hwndCtl;
    INT  i;

    // Parse the parameters.
    idItem = (WORD) LOWORD (wParam);
    wNotifyCode = (WORD) HIWORD (wParam);
    hwndCtl = (HWND) lParam;

    // Call routine to handle control message.
    for (i = 0; i < dim(MainCommandItems); i++) {
        if (idItem == MainCommandItems[i].Code) {
            (*MainCommandItems[i].Fxn)(hWnd, idItem, hwndCtl,
                                       wNotifyCode);
            return TRUE;
        }
```

```
    }
    return FALSE;
}
//======================================================================
// Command handler routines
//----------------------------------------------------------------------
// DoMainCommandExit - Process Program Exit command.
//
LPARAM DoMainCommandExit (HWND hWnd, WORD idItem, HWND hwndCtl,
                          WORD wNotifyCode) {
    EndDialog (hWnd, 0);
    return 0;
}
//----------------------------------------------------------------------
// DoMainCommandViewDrive - Process list box double clicks.
//
LPARAM DoMainCommandViewDrive (HWND hWnd, WORD idItem, HWND hwndCtl,
                               WORD wNotifyCode) {
    TCHAR szCmdLine[128], szFolder[MAX_PATH];
    PROCESS_INFORMATION pi;
    HCURSOR hOld;
    INT i, rc, nLen;

    // We're interested only in list box double-clicks.
    if (wNotifyCode != LBN_DBLCLK)
        return 0;

    i = SendMessage (hwndCtl, LB_GETCURSEL, 0, 0);
    if (i == LB_ERR) return 0;
    nLen = SendMessage (hwndCtl, LB_GETTEXT, i, (LPARAM)szFolder);
    if (nLen == LB_ERR)
        return 0;
    // Trim off description of share.
    for (i = 0; i < nLen; i++)
        if (szFolder[i] == TEXT ('\t'))
            break;
    szFolder[i] = TEXT ('\0');

    hOld = SetCursor (LoadCursor (NULL, IDC_WAIT));
    wsprintf (szCmdLine, TEXT("\\network\\%s"), szFolder);

    rc = CreateProcess (TEXT ("Explorer"), szCmdLine, NULL, NULL,
                        FALSE, 0, NULL, NULL, NULL, &pi);
    if (rc) {
        CloseHandle (pi.hProcess);
        CloseHandle (pi.hThread);
    }
    SetCursor (hOld);
    return TRUE;
}
//----------------------------------------------------------------------
// DoMainCommandMapDrive - Process map network drive command.
//
```

```
LPARAM DoMainCommandMapDrive (HWND hWnd, WORD idItem, HWND hwndCtl,
                              WORD wNotifyCode) {
    DWORD rc = WS_EX_CONTEXTHELP;
    CONNECTDLGSTRUCT cds;
    NETRESOURCE nr;
    TCHAR szRmt[256];

    memset (&nr, 0, sizeof (nr));
    nr.dwType = RESOURCETYPE_DISK;
    memset (szRmt, 0, sizeof (szRmt));

    memset (&cds, 0, sizeof (cds));
    cds.cbStructure = sizeof (cds);
    cds.hwndOwner = hWnd;
    cds.lpConnRes = &nr;
    cds.dwFlags = CONNDLG_PERSIST;

    // Display dialog box.
#ifdef CE6_BUGFIX
    rc = MyWNetConnectionDialog1 (&cds);
#else
    rc = WNetConnectionDialog1 (&cds);
#endif
    if (rc == NO_ERROR)
        RefreshLocalNetDrives (hWnd);
    else
        CheckErrorCode (hWnd, rc, TEXT ("WNetConnectionDialog1"));
    return 0;
}
//----------------------------------------------------------------------
// DoMainCommandFreeDrive - Process disconnect network drive command.
//
LPARAM DoMainCommandFreeDrive (HWND hWnd, WORD idItem, HWND hwndCtl,
                               WORD wNotifyCode) {
    int rc = WNetDisconnectDialog (hWnd, RESOURCETYPE_DISK);
    if (rc == NO_ERROR)
        RefreshLocalNetDrives (hWnd);
    else
        CheckErrorCode (hWnd, rc, TEXT ("WnetDisconnectDialog"));
    return 0;
}
//======================================================================
// Network browsing functions
//----------------------------------------------------------------------
// EnumerateLocalNetDrives - Add an item to the list view control.
//
INT RefreshLocalNetDrives (HWND hWnd) {
    HWND hwndCtl = GetDlgItem (hWnd, IDD_NETLIST);
    INT rc, nBuffSize = 1024;
    DWORD dwCnt, dwSize;
    HANDLE hEnum;
    LPNETRESOURCE pnr;
    PBYTE pPtr, pNew;
    TCHAR szText[256];
```

```
    SendMessage (hwndCtl, LB_RESETCONTENT, 0, 0);

    // Allocate buffer for enumeration data.
    pPtr = (PBYTE) LocalAlloc (LPTR, nBuffSize);
    if (!pPtr)
        return -1;

    // Start enumeration.
    rc = WNetOpenEnum (RESOURCE_REMEMBERED, RESOURCETYPE_ANY, 0, 0,
                       &hEnum);
    if (rc != NO_ERROR) return -1;

    // Enumerate one item per loop.
    do {
        dwCnt = 1;
        dwSize = nBuffSize;
        rc = WNetEnumResource (hEnum, &dwCnt, pPtr, &dwSize);
        if (rc == NO_ERROR) {
            pnr = (NETRESOURCE *)pPtr;
            StringCchCopy (szText, dim (szText), pnr->lpLocalName);
            // Process returned data.
            if (rc == NO_ERROR) {
                switch (pnr->dwType) {
                case RESOURCETYPE_ANY:
                    StringCchCat (szText, dim (szText), TEXT ("\t Share"));
                    break;
                case RESOURCETYPE_PRINT:
                    StringCchCat (szText, dim (szText),
                                  TEXT ("\t Printer"));
                    break;
                case RESOURCETYPE_DISK:
                    StringCchCat (szText, dim (szText), TEXT ("\t Disk"));
                    break;
                }
                SendMessage (hwndCtl, LB_ADDSTRING, 0, (LPARAM)szText);

            // If our buffer was too small, try again.
            } else if (rc == ERROR_MORE_DATA) {
                pNew = (PBYTE)LocalReAlloc (pPtr, dwSize, LMEM_MOVEABLE);
                if (pNew) {
                    pPtr = pNew;
                    nBuffSize = LocalSize (pPtr);
                    rc = 0;
                } else
                    break;
            }
        }
    } while (rc == 0);
    // Clean up.
    WNetCloseEnum (hEnum);
    LocalFree (pPtr);
    return 0;
}
//----------------------------------------------------------------------
```

```
// CheckErrorCode - Print error messages as necessary.
//
int CheckErrorCode (HWND hWnd, int rc, LPTSTR lpText) {
    TCHAR szTxt[128];

    // If good or dialog canceled, just return.
    if ((rc == NO_ERROR) || (rc == -1))
        return rc;
    if (rc == ERROR_NO_NETWORK)
        StringCchCat (szTxt, dim (szTxt), TEXT ("No network detected."));
    else
        wsprintf (szTxt, TEXT ("%s failed rc = %d"), lpText, rc);

    MessageBox (hWnd, szTxt, szAppName, MB_OK);
    return rc;
}
//======================================================================
// My Network Connection Dialog procedure
//
BOOL CALLBACK MyNetConnDlgProc(HWND hWnd, UINT wMsg, WPARAM wParam,
                               LPARAM lParam) {
    LPCONNECTDLGSTRUCT lpCDS;
    LPNETRESOURCE lpNR;
    BOOL bReadOnly = FALSE;

    switch (wMsg) {
        case WM_INITDIALOG:
            if (!lParam) {
                EndDialog (hWnd, -2);
                return 0;
            }
            // Save the structure ptr
            SetWindowLong (hWnd, GWL_USERDATA, lParam);

            // Get what we need from the structure
            bReadOnly = ((LPCONNECTDLGSTRUCT)lParam)->dwFlags &
                                                  CONNDLG_RO_PATH;
            lpNR = ((LPCONNECTDLGSTRUCT)lParam)->lpConnRes;

            // Init the fields in the dialog box
            SetDlgItemText (hWnd, IDD_SHARENAME, lpNR->lpRemoteName);
            SetDlgItemText (hWnd, IDD_LOCALNAME, lpNR->lpLocalName);

            // If remote name specified, make that field read-only
            if (lpNR->lpRemoteName[0] && bReadOnly) {
                SendDlgItemMessage (hWnd, IDD_SHARENAME, EM_SETREADONLY,
                                    1, 0);
                SetFocus (GetDlgItem (hWnd, IDD_LOCALNAME));
            }
            else
                SetFocus (GetDlgItem (hWnd, IDD_SHARENAME));
            return FALSE;
```

```
        case WM_COMMAND:
            switch (LOWORD (wParam)) {
                case IDOK:
                    lpCDS = (LPCONNECTDLGSTRUCT)GetWindowLong (hWnd,
                                                               GWL_USERDATA);
                    lpNR = lpCDS->lpConnRes;
                    GetDlgItemText (hWnd, IDD_SHARENAME,
                                    lpNR->lpRemoteName, MAX_PATH);

                    GetDlgItemText (hWnd, IDD_LOCALNAME,
                                    lpNR->lpLocalName, MAX_PATH);

                    // Unlike CE's version, I don't auto-create a
                    // local share name.
                    if ((lpNR->lpLocalName[0] == TEXT('\0')) ||
                        (lpNR->lpLocalName[0] == TEXT('*'))) {

                        MessageBox (hWnd, TEXT("Enter a local name"),
                                    TEXT("Network"), MB_OK);
                        return TRUE;
                    }
                    EndDialog (hWnd, 0);
                    return TRUE;

                case IDCANCEL:
                    EndDialog (hWnd, -1);
                    return TRUE;
            }
        break;
    }
    return FALSE;
}
//----------------------------------------------------------------------
// MyWNetConnectionDialog1 - My version of the network connection dlg
//
DWORD MyWNetConnectionDialog1 (LPCONNECTDLGSTRUCT lpConnDlgStruct) {
    DWORD rc, dwFlags = 0;
    HWND hParent = NULL;
    TCHAR szLocal[MAX_PATH];
    TCHAR szRmt[MAX_PATH];

    // Parameter checking
    if ((lpConnDlgStruct == 0) ||
        (lpConnDlgStruct->cbStructure != sizeof (CONNECTDLGSTRUCT)) ||
        (lpConnDlgStruct->lpConnRes == 0) ||
        (lpConnDlgStruct->lpConnRes->dwType != RESOURCETYPE_DISK) ||
         // can't have both persist and non-persist flags set
        (((lpConnDlgStruct->dwFlags & CONNDLG_PERSIST) &&
          (lpConnDlgStruct->dwFlags & CONNDLG_NOT_PERSIST)))) {
        return ERROR_INVALID_PARAMETER;
    }
    szLocal[0] = TEXT('\0');
    szRmt[0] = TEXT('\0');
```

```
    lpConnDlgStruct->lpConnRes->lpRemoteName = szRmt;
    lpConnDlgStruct->lpConnRes->lpLocalName = szLocal;

    // If specified, copy over strings
    if ((lpConnDlgStruct->lpConnRes->lpRemoteName != 0) &&
        (lpConnDlgStruct->lpConnRes->lpRemoteName[0] != TEXT('\0')))
        StringCchCopy (szRmt, dim (szRmt),
                       lpConnDlgStruct->lpConnRes->lpRemoteName);

    if ((lpConnDlgStruct->lpConnRes->lpLocalName != 0) &&
        (lpConnDlgStruct->lpConnRes->lpLocalName[0] != TEXT('\0')))
        StringCchCopy (szLocal, dim (szLocal),
                       lpConnDlgStruct->lpConnRes->lpLocalName);

    // Display the dialog box
    rc = DialogBoxParam (hInst, TEXT("MyConnDlg"), hParent,
                         MyNetConnDlgProc, (LPARAM)lpConnDlgStruct);
    if (rc == 0) {
        // The 'real' function always persists the link
        if (lpConnDlgStruct->dwFlags & CONNDLG_PERSIST)
            dwFlags = CONNECT_UPDATE_PROFILE;

        // Make the connection
        rc = WNetAddConnection3 (lpConnDlgStruct->hwndOwner,
                             lpConnDlgStruct->lpConnRes, NULL, NULL,
                             dwFlags);
    }
    return rc;
}
```

The heart of the networking code is at the end of ListNet, in the routine *RefreshLocalNetDrives*. This routine uses the WNet enumerate functions to determine the persistent network resources mapped to the system. Network connections and disconnections are accomplished with calls to *WNetConnectionDialog1* and *WNetDisconnectDialog* respectively. You open an Explorer window containing the shared network disk by launching Explorer.exe with a command line that's the path of the folder to open.

For Windows Embedded CE 6 systems where *WNetConnectionDialog1 is failing, ListNet provides a replacement routine that displays a dialog to query the connection parameters and then uses WNetAddConnection3 to make the connection.*

TCP/IP Programming

As with all modern operating systems, Windows CE uses TCP/IP as its basic networking protocol. Also, like other operating systems, the programming interface to the TCP/IP network is the "socket" application programming interface. In the case of Windows, the name of the TCP/IP networking stack and the socket API is Winsock. The Windows CE implementation of

Winsock doesn't support everything provided on the desktop, but what it does support provides plenty of functionality to create robust network applications.

Windows CE supports two different Winsock stacks, one based on Winsock 1.1 and the other based on Winsock 2.0. The Winsock 2 stack is more functional, closely matching the functionality of the desktop winsock stack but also much larger than its Winsock 1.1 counterpart. Most new devices will support the Winsock 2.0 stack, although some designers might choose the size advantage of the smaller Winsock 1.1 stack over the greater functionality of the Winsock 2.0 stack.

Socket Programming

Like all socket implementations, Winsock under Windows CE supports both stream and datagram connections. In a stream connection, a socket is basically a data pipe. Once two points are connected, data is sent back and forth without the need for additional addressing. In a datagram connection, the socket is more like a mailslot, with discrete packets of data being sent to specific addresses. In describing the Winsock functions, I'm going to cover the process of creating a *stream* connection (sometimes called a *connection-oriented* connection) between a client application and a server application. I'll leave the explanation of the datagram connection to other, more network-specific, books.

The life of a stream socket is fairly straightforward: it's created, bound, or connected to an address; read from or written to; and finally closed. A few extra steps along the way, however, complicate the story slightly. Sockets work in a client/server model. A client initiates a conversation with a known server. The server, on the other hand, waits around until a client requests data. When setting up a socket, you have to approach the process from either the client side or the server side. This decision determines which functions you call to configure a socket. Table 13-1 illustrates the process from both the client and the server side. For each step in the process, the corresponding Winsock function is shown.

TABLE 13-1 Process for Producing a Connection-Oriented Socket Connection

Server	Function	Client	Function
Create socket	*socket*	Create socket	*socket*
Bind socket to an address	*bind*	Find desired server	(many functions)
Listen for client connections	*listen*	Connect to server	*connect*
Accept client's connection	*accept*		
Receive data from client	*recv*	Send data to server	*send*
Send data to client	*send*	Receive data from server	*recv*

Both the client and the server must first create a socket. After that, the process diverges. The server must attach or, to use the function name, *bind*, the socket to an address so that another computer or even a local process can connect to the socket. Once an address has been bound, the server configures the socket to listen for a connection from a client. The server then waits to accept a connection from a client. Finally, after all this, the server is ready to converse.

The client's job is simpler: the client creates the socket, connects the socket to a remote address, and then sends and receives data. This procedure, of course, ignores the sometimes not-so-simple process of determining the address to connect to. I'll leave that problem for a few moments while I talk about the functions behind this process.

ASCII versus Unicode One issue that you'll have to be careful of is that almost all the string fields used in the socket structures are char fields, not Unicode. Because of this, you'll find yourself using the functions

```
int WideCharToMultiByte(UINT CodePage, DWORD dwFlags,
                        LPCWSTR lpWideCharStr, int cchWideChar,
                        LPSTR lpMultiByteStr, int cchMultiByte,
                        LPCSTR lpDefaultChar, LPBOOL lpUsedDefaultChar);
```

to convert Unicode strings to multibyte strings and

```
int MultiByteToWideChar (UINT CodePage, DWORD dwFlags,
                         LPCSTR lpMultiByteStr, int cchMultiByte,
                         LPWSTR lpWideCharStr, int cchWideChar);
```

to convert multibyte characters to Unicode. The functions refer to multibyte characters instead of ASCII because on double-byte coded systems, they convert double-byte characters to Unicode. As with all string-related functions, take care to size the buffers approperriately.

Initializing the Winsock DLL

Like other versions of Winsock, the Windows CE version should be initialized before you use it. You accomplish this by calling *WSAStartup*, which initializes the Winsock DLL. It's prototyped as

```
int WSAStartup (WORD wVersionRequested, LPWSADATA lpWSAData);
```

The first parameter is the version of Winsock you're requesting to open. For all current versions of Windows CE, you should indicate version 2.0. An easy way to do this is to use the *MAKEWORD* macro, as in *MAKEWORD (2,0)*. The second parameter must point to a *WSAData* structure.

```
struct WSAData {
    WORD wVersion;
    WORD wHighVersion;
    char szDescription[WSADESCRIPTION_LEN+1];
    char szSystemStatus[WSASYSSTATUS_LEN+1];
    unsigned short iMaxSockets;
    unsigned short iMaxUdpDg;
    char FAR * lpVendorInfo;
};
```

This structure is filled in by *WSAStartup*, providing information about the specific implementation of this version of Winsock. Currently the first two fields return either 0x0101, indicating support for version 1.1, or 0x0202, indicating that the system supports the Winsock 2.0 stack. The *szDescription* and *szSystemStatus* fields can be used by Winsock to return information about itself. In the current Windows CE version of Winsock, these fields aren't used. The *iMaxSockets* parameter suggests a maximum number of sockets that an application should be able to open. This number isn't a hard maximum, but rather a suggested maximum. The *iMaxUdpDg* field indicates the maximum size of a datagram packet. A 0 indicates no maximum size for this version of Winsock. Finally, *lpVendorInfo* points to optional vendor-specific information.

WSAStartup returns 0 if successful; otherwise, the return value is the error code for the function. Don't call *WSAGetLastError* in this situation because the failure of this function indicates that Winsock, which provides *WSAGetLastError*, wasn't initialized correctly.

Windows CE also supports *WSACleanup*, which is traditionally called when an application has finished using the Winsock DLL. The prototype is

```
int WSACleanup ();
```

For Windows CE, this function performs no action but is provided for compatibility.

Creating a Socket You create a socket with the function

```
SOCKET socket (int af, int type, int protocol);
```

The first parameter, *af*, specifies the addressing family for the socket. Windows CE supports three addressing formats: *AF_INET*, *AF_IRDA*, and *AF_BT*. You use the *AF_BT* constant when you're creating a socket for Bluetooth use, *AF_IRDA* for an IrDA socket, and *AF_INET* for TCP/IP communication. The *type* parameter specifies the type of socket being created. For a TCP/IP socket, this can be either *SOCK_STREAM* for a stream socket or *SOCK_DGRAM* for a datagram socket or *SOCK_RAW* for a raw socket. Raw sockets are sockets that allow you to interact with the IP layer of the TCP/IP. Raw sockets are used to send an echo request to other servers, in the process known as pinging. Windows CE provides another method of sending an Internet Control Message Protocol (ICMP) echo request through the IP Helper API. Windows CE supports raw sockets for only the IPv4 network stack. Raw sockets are not supported on the IPv6 stack.

The *protocol* parameter specifies the protocol used by the address family specified by the *af* parameter. The function returns a handle to the newly created socket. If an error occurs, the socket returns *INVALID_SOCKET*. You can call *WSAGetLastError* to query the extended error code.

Server Side: Binding a Socket to an Address

For the server, the next step is to bind the socket to an address. You accomplish this with the function

```
int bind (SOCKET s, const struct sockaddr FAR *addr, int namelen);
```

The first parameter is the handle to the newly created socket. The second parameter is dependent on whether you're dealing with a TCP/IP socket, an IrDA socket, or a Bluetooth socket. For a standard TCP/IP socket, the structure pointed to by *addr* should be *SOCKADDR_IN*, which is defined as

```
struct sockaddr_in {
    short sin_family;
    unsigned short sin_port;
    IN_ADDR sin_addr;
    char sin_zero[8];
};
```

The first field, *sin_family*, must be set to *AF_INET*. The second field is the IP port, while the third field specifies the IP address. The last field is simply padding to fit the standard *SOCKADDR* structure. The last parameter of bind, *namelen*, should be set to the size of the *SOCKADDR_IN* structure.

```
Listening for a Connection
```

Once a socket has been bound to an address, the server places the socket in listen mode so that it will accept incoming communication attempts. You place the socket in listen mode by using the aptly named function

```
int listen (SOCKET s, int backlog);
```

The two parameters are the handle to the socket and the size of the queue that you're creating to hold the pending connection attempts. This size value can be set to *SOMAXCONN* to set the queue to the maximum supported by the socket implementation.

Accepting a Connection

When a server is ready to accept a connection to a socket in listen mode, it calls this function:

```
SOCKET accept (SOCKET s, struct sockaddr FAR *addr,
               int FAR *addrlen);
```

The first parameter is the socket that has already been placed in listen mode. The next parameter should point to a buffer that receives the address of the client socket that has initiated a connection. The format of this address is dependent on the protocol used by the socket. For Windows CE, this is a *SOCKADDR_IN*, a *SOCKADDR_IRDA*, or a *SOCKADDR_BTH* structure. The final parameter is a pointer to a variable that contains the size of the buffer.

This variable is updated with the size of the structure returned in the address buffer when the function returns.

The *accept* function returns the handle to a new socket that's used to communicate with the client. The socket that was originally created by the call to *socket* will remain in listen mode and can potentially accept other connections. If *accept* detects an error, it returns *INVALID_SOCKET*. In this case, you can call *WSAGetLastError* to get the error code.

The *accept* function is the first function I've talked about so far that blocks. That is, it won't return until a remote client requests a connection. You can set the socket in nonblocking mode so that, if no request for connection is queued, *accept* will return *INVALID_SOCKET* with the extended error code *WSAEWOULDBLOCK*. I'll talk about blocking vs. nonblocking sockets shortly.

Client Side: Connecting a Socket to a Server

On the client side, things are different. Instead of calling the *bind* and *accept* functions, the client simply connects to a known server. I said simply, but as with most things, we must note a few complications. The primary one is addressing—knowing the address of the server you want to connect to. I'll put that topic aside and assume the client knows the address of the server.

To connect a newly created socket to a server, the client uses the function

```
int connect (SOCKET s, const struct sockaddr FAR *name,
             int namelen);
```

The first parameter is the socket handle that the client created with a call to *socket*. The other two parameters are the address and address length values we've seen in the *bind* and *accept* functions.

If connect is successful, it returns 0. Otherwise, it returns *SOCKET_ERROR*, and you should call *WSAGetLastError* to get the reason for the failure.

Sending and Receiving Data

At this point, both the server and the client have socket handles they can use to communicate with one another. The client uses the socket originally created with the call to *socket*, while the server uses the socket handle returned by the *accept* function.

All that remains is data transfer. You write data to a socket this way:

```
int send (SOCKET s, const char FAR *buf, int len, int flags);
```

The first parameter is the socket handle to send the data. You specify the data you want to send in the buffer pointed to by the *buf* parameter, while the length of that data is specified in *len*. The *flags* parameter must be 0.

You receive data by using the function

```
int recv (SOCKET s, char FAR *buf, int len, int flags);
```

The first parameter is the socket handle. The second parameter points to the buffer that receives the data, while the third parameter should be set to the size of the buffer. The flags parameter can be 0, or it can be *MSG_PEEK* if you want to have the current data copied into the receive buffer but not removed from the input queue or, if this is a TCP/IP socket (*MSG_OOB*), for receiving any out-of-band data that has been sent.

Two other functions can send and receive data; they are the following:

```
int sendto (SOCKET s, const char FAR *buf, int len, int flags,
            const struct sockaddr FAR *to, int token);
```

and

```
int recvfrom (SOCKET s, char FAR *buf, int len, int flags,
              struct sockaddr FAR *from, int FAR *fromlen);
```

These functions enable you to direct individual packets of data using the address parameters provided in the functions. They're used for connectionless sockets, but I mention them now for completeness. When used with connection-oriented sockets such as those I've just described, the addresses in *sendto* and *recvfrom* are ignored and the functions act like their simpler counterparts, *send* and *recv*.

Closing a Socket

When you have finished using the sockets, call this function:

```
int shutdown (SOCKET s, int how);
```

The *shutdown* function takes the handle to the socket and a flag indicating the part of the connection you want to shut down. The *how* parameter can be *SD_RECEIVE* to prevent any further *recv* calls from being processed, *SD_SEND* to prevent any further *send* calls from being processed, or *SD_BOTH* to prevent either *send* or *recv* calls from being processed. The *shutdown* function affects the higher-level functions *send* and *recv* but doesn't prevent data previously queued from being processed. Once you have shut down a socket, it can't be used again. It should be closed and a new socket created to restart a session.

After a connection has been shut down, you should close the socket with a call to this function:

```
int closesocket (SOCKET s);
```

The action of *closesocket* depends on how the socket is configured. If you've properly shut down the socket with a call to *shutdown*, no more events will be pending and *closesocket* should return without blocking. If the socket has been configured into linger mode and configured with a timeout value, *closesocket* will block until any data in the send queue has been sent or the timeout expires.

A Simple Example

The following code demonstrates a simple client-server connection. The code is divided into three routines: the server routine, the receive routine, and the transmit routine. The first code fragment is the server code.

```
//
// ServerThread - Waits for a client to connect. Spins a new thread
//
BOOL fCont = TRUE;
DWORD WINAPI ServerThread (PVOID pArg) {
    INT rc, nSize;
    HANDLE hTh;
    SOCKET t_sock, s_sock;
    SOCKADDR_IN sadr, t_sadr;
    WORD wPort = LOWORD(pArg);

    // Open a socket.
    s_sock = socket (AF_INET, SOCK_STREAM, 0);
    if (s_sock == INVALID_SOCKET)
        return -1;

    // Fill in socket address structure.
    memset (&sadr, 0, sizeof (sadr));
    sadr.sin_family = AF_INET;
    sadr.sin_port = htons(wPort);

    __try {
        // Bind address to socket.
        rc = bind (s_sock, (struct sockaddr *)&sadr, sizeof(sadr));
        if (rc == SOCKET_ERROR) __leave;

        // Set socket into listen mode.
        rc = listen (s_sock, SOMAXCONN);
        if (rc == SOCKET_ERROR) __leave;

        // Block on accept.
        while (fCont) {
            nSize = sizeof (t_sadr);
            t_sock = accept(s_sock, (struct sockaddr *)&t_sadr, &nSize);
            if (t_sock == INVALID_SOCKET)
                break;

            hTh = CreateThread (NULL, 0, ReceiveThread,
                                (PVOID)t_sock, 0, NULL);
            CloseHandle (hTh);
        }
```

```
    }
    __finally {
        closesocket (s_sock);
    }
    return rc;
}
```

The previous code is presented as thread routine because it can't be on the main thread of the application because of the call to accept blocks. The routine starts by opening a socket and binding an address. In this case, the *bind* call binds to whatever port number was passed in the argument to the thread. Next, the thread sets the socket to listen mode and calls *accept*. The accept call only returns when there is a connection made from a client. The code then starts yet another thread to handle the conversation between the client and the server. Meanwhile, the server thread loops back and calls *accept* again to wait for another connection.

The conversation the server has with the client is handled by the following routine. Here again, the routine is presented as a thread because it was created by the previous server thread.

```
//
// ReceiveThread - Receives a string and send another back
//
DWORD WINAPI ReceiveThread (PVOID pArg) {
    SOCKET t_sock = (SOCKET)pArg;
    int nCnt, rc, rcResp;
    char szString[256];
     char szSend[] = "A response string";

    __try {
        // Read the number of bytes in the string.
        rc = recv (t_sock, (LPSTR)&nCnt, sizeof (nCnt), 0);
        if (rc != SOCKET_ERROR)
            rc = 0;

        // Check for buffer overrun
        if (nCnt > sizeof (szString))
            rc = ERROR_INSUFFICIENT_BUFFER;
        if (rc) __leave;

        // Send response
        rc = send (t_sock, (char *)&rc, sizeof (rc), 0);
        if (rc == SOCKET_ERROR) __leave;

        // Read the string.
        rc = recv (t_sock, szString, nCnt, 0);
        if (rc == SOCKET_ERROR)
            __leave;

        // Send response
```

```
        rc = send (t_sock, (char *)&rc, sizeof (rc), 0);
        if (rc == SOCKET_ERROR)
            __leave;

        // Send our string length
        nCnt = strlen (szSend) + 1;
        rc = send (t_sock, (char *)&nCnt, sizeof (nCnt), 0);
        if (rc == SOCKET_ERROR)
            __leave;

        // Recv response code
        rc = recv (t_sock, (char *)&rcResp, sizeof (rcResp), 0);
        if ((rc == SOCKET_ERROR) || (rcResp != 0))
            __leave;

        // Send our string
        rc = send (t_sock, szSend, nCnt, 0);
        if (rc == SOCKET_ERROR)
            __leave;

        // Recv response code
        rc = recv (t_sock, (char *)&rcResp, sizeof (rcResp), 0);
    }
    __finally {
        if (rc == SOCKET_ERROR)
            rc = WSAGetLastError ();
        send (t_sock, (char *)&rc, sizeof (rc), 0);
        closesocket (t_sock);
    }
    return 0;
}
```

Although the server code is generic, this code is specific to the example because the data sent and received by the client and server is application specific. The previous code, which is still part of the server, demonstrates sending and receiving data by receiving a string from the client and responding by sending a string back. It's not quite that simple, because there is some handshaking involved to insure that both client and server stay coordinated. Still, the previous code demonstrates the sending and receving of data.

The final section of code, which follows, would be the client code.

```
//
// Client code.
//
int Client (char *szIPAddr, WORD wPort) {
    SOCKET sock;
    SOCKADDR_IN dest_sin;
    int nCnt, rc, rcResp;
    char szString[256];
     char szSend[] = "A string to Send";
```

```
// Create socket
 sock = socket( AF_INET, SOCK_STREAM, 0);
 if (sock == INVALID_SOCKET)
    return INVALID_SOCKET;

__try {
    // Set up IP address to access
    memset (&dest_sin, 0, sizeof (dest_sin));
    dest_sin.sin_family = AF_INET;
    dest_sin.sin_addr.S_un.S_addr = inet_addr (szIPAddr);
    dest_sin.sin_port = htons(wPort);

    // Connect to the device
    rc = connect(sock, (PSOCKADDR) &dest_sin, sizeof( dest_sin));
    if (rc == SOCKET_ERROR) {
        printf («Err in connect. %d\r\n», WSAGetLastError());
        closesocket( sock );
        __leave;
    }

    // Send our string length
    nCnt = strlen (szSend) + 1;
    rc = send (sock, (char *)&nCnt, sizeof (nCnt), 0);
    if (rc == SOCKET_ERROR)
        __leave;

    // Recv response code
    rc = recv (sock, (char *)&rcResp, sizeof (rcResp), 0);
    if ((rc == SOCKET_ERROR) || (rcResp != 0))
        __leave;

    // Send our string
    rc = send (sock, szSend, nCnt, 0);
    if (rc == SOCKET_ERROR)
        __leave;

    // Recv response code
    rc = recv (sock, (char *)&rcResp, sizeof (rcResp), 0);
    if (rc == SOCKET_ERROR) __leave;

    // Now read the string back...

    // Read the number of bytes in the string.
    rc = recv (sock, (LPSTR)&nCnt, sizeof (nCnt), 0);
    if (rc != SOCKET_ERROR)
        rc = 0;

    // Check for buffer overrun
    if (nCnt > sizeof (szString))
        rc = ERROR_INSUFFICIENT_BUFFER;
    if (rc) __leave;

    // Send response
```

```
        rc = send (sock, (char *)&rc, sizeof (rc), 0);
        if (rc == SOCKET_ERROR) __leave;

        // Read the string.
        rc = recv (sock, szString, nCnt, 0);
        if (rc == SOCKET_ERROR)
            __leave;

        // Send response
        rc = send (sock, (char *)&rc, sizeof (rc), 0);
        if (rc == SOCKET_ERROR)
            __leave;
    }
    __finally {
        if (rc == SOCKET_ERROR)
            rc = WSAGetLastError ();
        send (sock, (char *)&rc, sizeof (rc), 0);
        closesocket (sock);
    }
    Add2List (hwndMain, TEXT(«client thread exit»));
    return 0;
}
```

The previous code creates a socket, but instead of binding the socket like the server, attempts to connect to the server. The IP address of the server and the port to connect to are passed to the routine. After the call to connect, the remainder of the routine is the complement of the *ReceiveThread* routine. In this case, a string is first sent and then one is received. After completing the work, each of the previous routines closes its respective sockets. This is ensured by using a *__try __finally* block with the *__finally* block containing the call to *closesocket.*

Blocking versus Nonblocking Sockets

One issue I briefly touched on as I was introducing sockets is blocking. Windows programmers are used to the quite handy asynchronous socket calls that are an extension of the standard Berkeley socket API. By default, a socket is in blocking mode so that, for example, if you call *recv* to read data from a socket and no data is available, the call blocks until some data can be read. This isn't the type of call you want to be making with a thread that's servicing the message loop for your application.

The *WSAAsync* calls that provide asynchronious socket convenience aren't available on Windows CE systems using the Winsock 1.1 stack. All is not lost, however, because you can switch a standard socket from its default blocking mode to nonblocking mode. In nonblocking mode, any socket call that might need to wait to successfully perform its function instead returns immediately with the error code *WSAEWOULDBLOCK*. You are then responsible for calling the would-have-blocked function again at a later time to complete the task.

To set a socket into blocking mode, use this function:

```
int ioctlsocket (SOCKET s, long cmd, u_long *argp);
```

The parameters are the socket handle, a command, and a pointer to a variable that either contains data or receives data depending on the value in *cmd*. The allowable commands for *ioctlsocket* depend on the type of socket. However, a couple of typical commands are *FIONBIO,* which sets or clears a socket's blocking mode, and *FIONREAD, which r*eturns the number of bytes that can be read from the socket with one call to the *recv* function.

So to set a socket in nonblocking mode, you should make a call like this one:

```
fBlocking = FALSE;
rc = ioctlsocket (sock, FIONBIO, &fBlocking);
```

Of course, after you have a socket in nonblocking mode, the worst thing you can do is continually poll the socket to see whether the nonblocked event occurred. On a battery-powered system, this can dramatically lower battery life. Instead of polling, you can use the *select* function to inform you when a socket or set of sockets is in a nonblocking state. The prototype for this function is

```
int select (int nfds, fd_set FAR *readfds, fd_set FAR *writefds,
            fd_set FAR *exceptfds,
            const struct timeval FAR *timeout);
```

The parameters for the *select* function look somewhat complex, which, in fact, they are. Just to throw a curve, the function ignores the first parameter. The reason it exists at all is for compatibility with the Berkeley version of the *select* function. The next three parameters are pointers to sets of socket handles. The first set should contain the sockets that you want to be monitored for a nonblocking read state. The second set contains socket handles of sockets that you want checked for a nonblocking write state. Finally, the third set, pointed to by *exceptfds*, contains the handles of sockets that you want monitored for error conditions in that socket.

The final parameter is a timeout value. In keeping with the rather interesting parameter formats for the *select* function, the timeout value isn't a simple millisecond count. Rather, it's a pointer to a *TIMEVAL* structure defined as

```
struct timeval {
    long    tv_sec;
    long    tv_usec;
};
```

If the two fields in *TIMEVAL* are 0, the *select* call returns immediately, even if none of the sockets has had an event occur. If the pointer, *timeout*, is *NULL* instead of pointing to a *TIMEVAL* structure, the select call won't time out and returns only when an event occurs in one of the sockets. Otherwise, the timeout value is specified in seconds and microseconds in the two fields provided.

The function returns the total number of sockets for which the appropriate events occur—0 if the function times out or *SOCKET_ERROR* if an error occurs. If an error does occur, you can call *WSAGetLastError* to get the error code. The function modifies the contents of the sets so that, on returning from the function, the sets contain only the socket handles of sockets for which events occur.

The sets that contain the events should be considered opaque. The format of the sets doesn't match their Berkeley socket counterparts. Each of the sets is manipulated by four macros defined in WINSOCK.H. These are the four macros:

- **FD_CLR** Removes the specified socket handle from the set
- **FD_ISSET** Returns TRUE if the socket handle is part of the set
- **FD_SET** Adds the specified socket handle to the set
- **FD_ZERO** Initializes the set to 0

To use a set, you have to declare a set of type *fd_set*, then initialize the set with a call to *FD_ZERO,* and add the socket handles you want with *FD_SET.* An example would be

```
fd_set fdReadSocks;

FD_ZERO (&fdReadSocks);
FD_SET (hSock1, &fdReadSocks);
FD_SET (hSock2, &fdReadSocks);

rc = select (0, &fdReadSocks, NULL, NULL, NULL);
if (rc != SOCKET_ERROR) {
    if (FD_ISSET (hSock1, &fdReadSocks))
        // A read event occurred in socket 1.
    if (FD_ISSET (hSock2, &fdReadSocks))
        // A read event occurred in socket 2.
}
```

In this example, the *select* call waits on read events from two sockets with the handles *hSock1* and *hSock2.* The write and error sets are *NULL*, as is the pointer to the *timeout* structure, so the call to *select* won't return until a read event occurs in one of the two sockets. When the function returns, the code checks to see whether the socket handles are in the returned set. If so, that socket has a nonblocking read condition.

The last little subtlety concerning the *select* function is just what qualifies as a read, write, and error condition. A socket in the read set is signaled when one of the following events occurs:

- There is data in the input queue, so *recv* can be called without blocking.
- The socket is in listen mode and a connection has been attempted, so a call to *accept* won't block.

- The connection has been closed, reset, or terminated. If the connection was gracefully closed, *recv* returns with 0 bytes read; otherwise, the *recv* call returns *SOCKET_ERROR*. If the socket has been reset, the *recv* function returns the error *WSACONNRESET*.

A socket in the write set is signaled under the following conditions:

- Data can be written to the socket. A call to send still might block if you attempt to write more data than can be held in the outgoing queue.
- A socket is processing a *connect* and the connect has been accepted by the server.
- A socket in the exception set is signaled under the following condition:
- A socket is processing a *connect* and the connect failed.

This chapter has given you a basic introduction to some of the networking features of Windows CE. Next on our plate is networking from a different angle: peer-to-peer communication. In Chapter 14, we look at how a Windows CE device can communicate with another Windows CE device using infrared and Bluetooth communication. Let's take a look.

Chapter 14

Device-to-Device Communication

The personal nature of mobile devices requires that a new type of network be supported by these systems. Embedded systems also are increasingly in need of communication services for data transfer and diagnostic queries. Wide area and local area networks supported by Windows CE devices must share time with personal area networks—those networks that link devices over a short distance perhaps for only a short time. Windows CE supports personal area networking (PAN) over two transport technologies: infrared and radio frequency. The infrared transport conforms to the Infrared Data Association (IrDA) standard, while Windows CE uses the Bluetooth standard for radio-frequency networking.

Applications interact with both the IrDA communications stack and the Bluetooth stack using the Winsock API. The basics of Winsock were covered in Chapter 13. In this chapter, I'll refer to Winsock in relation to how you need to program it differently for IrDA and Bluetooth. Let's start by diving into the specifics of IrDA.

Infrared Communication

Like all systems today, Windows CE supports the IrDA standard. As mentioned earlier, both Windows desktop and Windows CE use Winsock as the programming interface for IrDA communcation. The extensions to the standard Winsock programming model involve two items: publication of a service and discovery of that service by another device. These additions, along with the accompanying limitations of the IR communication medium, are collectively known as IrSock.

Some of the major differences between IrSock and Winsock are that IrSock doesn't support datagrams, it doesn't support security, and the method used for addressing it is completely different from that used for Winsock. What IrSock does provide is a method to query the devices ready to talk across the infrared port, as well as arbitration and collision detection and control.

IR Basics

From the programming perspective, communicating over IR is very similar to communicating over a TCP/IP network. The server creates a socket, binds to an address, sets the socket to listen mode and calls *accept*. On the client side, the client creates a socket and connects to the server. The major differences are the extensions that allow the server to publish the fact that the device is ready to receive IR communication and how the client device descovers the server. Before all that can happen, though, a socket has to be created. Creating an IR socket is accomplished through a call to *socket*, but with a few different parameters. First, the address format needs to be *AF_IRDA*. Second, the socket type must be *SOCK_STREAM*. Finally, the protocol needs to be null. This results in a call that looks like this:

```
SOCKET irSoc = socket (AF_IRDA, SOCK_STREAM, 0);
```

As with any socket call, the function returns a handle to the newly created socket. If an error occurs, the socket returns *INVALID_SOCKET*. You can call *WSAGetLastError* to query the extended error code.

Discovery

Now that we have a socket, we need to find other devices that we might want to connect to. This is a process called discovery. Discovering a device that is expecting IR communication is accomplished using Winsock's *getsockopt* function. prototyped as

```
int getsockopt (SOCKET s, int level, int optname,
                char FAR* optval, int FAR* optlen);
```

The first parameter is the socket created by a call to *socket*. The *level* parameter indicates the socket protocol you wish to work with. For IrDA discovery, the *level* parameter should be *SOL_IRLMP*. The *optname* parameter is the specific option to query. For an IR device discovery, this parameter should be set to *IRLMP_ENUMDEVICES*. The *optval* and *optlen* parameters specify the location and size of the buffer to receive the information. For our discovery call, this buffer will be filled with a *DEVICELIST* structure. So, for IR device discovery, the call would look like the following:

```
dwBuffSize = sizeof (buffer);
rc = getsockopt (hIrSock, SOL_IRLMP, IRLMP_ENUMDEVICES,
                 buffer, &dwBuffSize);
The resulting DEVICELIST structure is defined as
typedef struct _DEVICELIST {
    ULONG numDevice;
    IRDA_DEVICE_INFO Device[1];
} DEVICELIST;
```

The *DEVICELIST* structure is simply a count followed by an array of *IRDA_DEVICE_INFO* structures, one for each device found. The *IRDA_DEVICE_INFO* structure is defined as

```
typedef struct _IRDA_DEVICE_INFO {
    u_char irdaDeviceID[4];
    char irdaDeviceName[22];
    u_char Reserved[2];
} IRDA_DEVICE_INFO;
```

The two fields in the *IRDA_DEVICE_INFO* structure are a device ID and a string that can be used to identify the remote device.

Following is a routine that opens an IR socket and uses *getsockopt* to query the remote devices that are in range. If any devices are found, their names and IDs are printed to the debug port.

```
//
// Poll for IR devices.
//
DWORD WINAPI IrPoll (HWND hWnd) {
    INT rc, nSize, i, j;
    char cDevice[256];
    TCHAR szName[32], szOut[256];
    DEVICELIST *pDL;
    SOCKET irsock;

    // Open an infrared socket.
    irsock = socket (AF_IRDA, SOCK_STREAM, 0);
    if (irsock == INVALID_SOCKET)
        return -1;

    // Search for someone to talk to; try 10 times over 5 seconds.
    for (i = 0; i < 10; i++) {

        // Call getsockopt to query devices.
        memset (cDevice, 0, sizeof (cDevice));
        nSize = sizeof (cDevice);
        rc = getsockopt (irsock, SOL_IRLMP, IRLMP_ENUMDEVICES,
                         cDevice, &nSize);
        if (rc)
            break;

        pDL = (DEVICELIST *) cDevice;
        if (pDL->numDevice) {
            for (j = 0; j < (int)pDL->numDevice; j++) {
                // Convert device ID.
                wsprintf (szOut,
                          TEXT ("DeviceID \t%02X.%02X.%02X.%02X"),
                          pDL->Device[j].irdaDeviceID[0],
                          pDL->Device[j].irdaDeviceID[1],
                          pDL->Device[j].irdaDeviceID[2],
                          pDL->Device[j].irdaDeviceID[3]);
                OutputDebugString (szOut);

                // Print the ASCII device name.
                wsprintf (szOut, TEXT («irdaDeviceName \t%s»),
                          pDL->Device[j].irdaDeviceName);
                OutputDebugString (szOut);
            }
        }
        Sleep(500);
    }
    closesocket (irsock);
    return 0;
}
```

Just having a device with an IR port in range isn't enough; the remote device must have an application running that has opened an IR socket, bound it, and placed it into listen mode. This requirement is appropriate because these are the steps any server using the socket API would perform to configure a socket to accept communication.

Publishing an IR Service

I just talked about the client, but what about the server? How does the serving device publish the fact that it wants IR communication? Publishing an IR service is actually quite simple and is implicit in the call to bind. Let's look into it.

The call to bind for an IR socket differs in the *sockaddr* structure passed to the function. When you're using *IrSock*, the address structure pointed to by *sockaddr* is *SOCKADDR_IRDA*, which is defined as

```
struct sockaddr_irda {
    u_short irdaAddressFamily;
    u_char irdaDeviceID[4];
    char irdaServiceName[25];
};
```

The first field, *irdaAddressFamily*, should be set to *AF_IRDA* to identify the structure. The second field, *irdaDeviceID*, is a 4-byte array that defines the address for this IR socket. This can be set to 0 for an IrSock server. The last field should be set to a string to identify the server.

You can also use a special predefined name in the *irdaServiceName* field to bypass the IrDA address resolution features. If you specify the name *LSAP-SELxxx*, where *xxx* is a value from 001 through 127, the socket will be bound directly to the Logical Service Access Point (LSAP) selector defined by the value. Applications should not, unless absolutely required, bind directly to a specific LSAP selector. Instead, by specifying a generic string, the IrDA address resolution code determines a free LSAP selector and uses it.

The code that follows demonstrates a server thread that publishes an IR service. Notice that aside from the different address formats and sockaddr structure, the code is quite similar to the standard TCP/IP server code shown in Chapter 13.

```
DWORD WINAPI ServerThread (PVOID pArg) {
    int rc, nSize;
    SOCKADDR_IRDA iraddr, t_iraddr;
    SOCKET t_sock, s_sock;
    char SOCKET t_sock, s_sock;
    char chzAppName[] = "My IR service name";
    // Open an infrared socket.
    s_sock = socket (AF_IRDA, SOCK_STREAM, 0);
    if (s_sock == INVALID_SOCKET)
        return -1;
    __try {
        // Fill in irda socket address structure.
```

```
        memset (&iraddr, 0, sizeof (iraddr));
        iraddr.irdaAddressFamily = AF_IRDA;
        memcpy (iraddr.irdaServiceName, chzServiceName,
                sizeof (chzAppName) + 1);

        // Bind address to socket.
        rc = bind (s_sock, (struct sockaddr *)&iraddr, sizeof (iraddr));
        if (rc) __leave;

        // Set socket into listen mode.
        rc = listen (s_sock, SOMAXCONN);
        if (rc) __leave;

        // Wait for remote requests.
        while (fContinue) {
            nSize = sizeof (t_iraddr);
            t_sock = accept (s_sock, (struct sockaddr *)&t_iraddr, &nSize);
            if (t_sock == INVALID_SOCKET)
                __leave;
            CreateThread (NULL, 0, ReceiveThread, (PVOID)t_sock, 0, NULL);
        }
        rc = 0;
    }
    __finally {
        closesocket (s_sock);
    }
    return rc;
}
```

The preceding code creates a socket with the *AF_IRDA* address format. It then initializes a *SOCKADDR_IDRA* structure identifying the address format and the name of the service. Aside from that, the code has nothing special, with subsequent calls to bind, listen, and accept. As with other server loops like this, the code spins a separate thread when a connection is detected.

Querying and Setting IR Socket Options

IrSock supports the *getsockopt* and *setsockopt* functions for getting and setting the socket options, but the options supported have little overlap with the socket options supported for a standard TCP/IP socket. To query socket options, use this function:

```
int getsockopt (SOCKET s, int level, int optname,
                char FAR *optval, int FAR *optlen);
```

The first parameter is the handle to the socket, while the second parameter is the level in the communications stack for the specific option. The level can be at the socket level, *SOL_SOCKET*, or a level unique to IrSock, *SOL_IRLMP*. The options supported for IrSock are shown in the following lists.

For the *SOL_SOCKET* level, your option is

- **SO_LINGER** Queries the linger mode

For the *SOL_IRLMP* level, your options are

- **IRLMP_ENUMDEVICES** Enumerates remote IrDA devices
- **IRLMP_IAS_QUERY** Queries IAS attributes
- **IRLMP_SEND_PDU_LEN** Queries the maximum size of send packet for IrLPT mode

The corresponding function with which to set the options is

```
int setsockopt (SOCKET s, int level, int optname,
                const char FAR *optval, int optlen);
```

The parameters are similar to *getsockopt*. A list of the allowable options follows.

For the *SOL_SOCKET* level, your single option is

- **SO_LINGER** Delays the close of a socket if unsent data remains in the outgoing queue

For the *SOL_IRLMP* level, your options are

- **IRLMP_IAS_SET** Sets IAS attributes
- **IRLMP_IRLPT_MODE** Sets the IrDA protocol to IrLPT
- **IRLMP_9WIRE_MODE** Sets the IrDA protocol to 9-wire serial mode
- **IRLMP_SHARP_MODE** Sets the IrDA protocol to Sharp mode

The MySquirt Example Program

To demonstrate IrSock, the following program, MySquirt, shows how to transfer files from one Windows system to another. It's similar to the IrSquirt program provided with the Windows Mobile devices. The difference is that this program is designed to be compiled for and run on Windows CE and desktop Windows systems.[1] So by running the program on these systems, you can send, that is, *squirt*, files from one system to another. MySquirt has a window that displays a list of status messages as the handshaking takes place between the two Windows systems. To use MySquirt, you'll need to have it running on two Windows systems. To transfer a file, enter the name of the file you want to send and press the Send button. The system transmits the name and size of the file to the receiving system, and, if it's accepted, the file data is subsequently sent. Figure 14-1 shows MySquirt after it has sent a file. The source code for the example is shown in Listing 14-1.

---

1 To build MySquirt for Windows XP or Windows Vista, useMicrosoft Visual Studio with a project target of Win32 application.

FIGURE 14-1 The MySquirt window after a file has been sent

LISTING 14-1

MySquirt.rc

```
//======================================================================
// Resource file
//
// Written for the book Programming Windows CE
// Copyright (C) 2007 Douglas Boling
//======================================================================
#include "windows.h"
#include "MySquirt.h"                          // Program-specific stuff

//----------------------------------------------------------------------
// Icons and bitmaps
//
ID_ICON ICON   "MySquirt.ico"                  // Program icon

//----------------------------------------------------------------------
// Main window dialog template
//
MySquirt DIALOG discardable 10, 10, 135, 110
STYLE  WS_OVERLAPPED | WS_VISIBLE | WS_CAPTION | WS_SYSMENU |
       DS_CENTER | DS_MODALFRAME
CAPTION "MySquirt"
CLASS "MySquirt"
BEGIN
    LTEXT "&File:"                    -1,   2,  11,  15,  12
    EDITTEXT                IDD_OUTTEXT,  17,  10,  71,  12,
                            WS_TABSTOP | ES_AUTOHSCROLL
    PUSHBUTTON "&Send File" IDD_SENDFILE,  92,  10,  38,  12, WS_TABSTOP

    LISTBOX                 IDD_INTEXT,   2,  25, 128,  80,
                            WS_TABSTOP | WS_VSCROLL
END
```

MySquirt.h

```
//======================================================================
// Header file
//
// Written for the book Programming Windows CE
// Copyright (C) 2007 Douglas Boling
//======================================================================
// Returns number of elements
#define dim(x) (sizeof(x) / sizeof(x[0]))
// Defines that are different between Windows CE and Desktop Windows
#ifdef _WIN32_WCE
// Windows CE-specific defines
#define LPCMDLINE LPWSTR
// On Windows CE, we call begin thread directly.
#define MyCreateThread CreateThread

// Desktop Windows defines
#else
#define LPCMDLINE LPSTR
// This macro calls beginthreadex when this program is compiled
// for the desktop.
typedef unsigned (__stdcall *PTHREAD_START)(void *);
#define MyCreateThread(psa, cbStack, pfnStartAddr, pvParam, fdwCreate,\
    pdwThreadID)((HANDLE) _beginthreadex ((void *)(psa), \
    (unsigned)(cbStack), (PTHREAD_START)(pfnStartAddr),\
    (void *)(pvParam), (unsigned)(fdwCreate), (unsigned *)(pdwThreadID)))

#define StringCchVPrintf vswprintf_s
#define StringCchCopy wcscpy_s
#endif

//----------------------------------------------------------------------
// Generic defines and data types
//
struct decodeUINT {                             // Structure associates
    UINT Code;                                  // messages
                                                // with a function.
    LRESULT (*Fxn)(HWND, UINT, WPARAM, LPARAM);
};
struct decodeCMD {                              // Structure associates
    UINT Code;                                  // menu IDs with a
    LRESULT (*Fxn)(HWND, WORD, HWND, WORD);     // function.
};

//----------------------------------------------------------------------
// Generic defines used by application

#define  ID_ICON            1

#define  IDD_INTEXT         10                  // Control IDs
#define  IDD_SENDFILE       11
#define  IDD_OUTTEXT        12
```

```
// Error codes used by transfer protocol
#define GOOD_XFER           0
#define BAD_FILEOPEN       -1
#define BAD_FILEMEM        -2
#define BAD_FILEREAD       -3
#define BAD_FILEWRITE      -3
#define BAD_SOCKET         -4
#define BAD_SOCKETRECV     -5
#define BAD_FILESIZE       -6
#define BAD_MEMORY         -7

#define BLKSIZE          8192                 // Transfer block size

//----------------------------------------------------------------------
// Function prototypes
//
HWND InitInstance (HINSTANCE, LPCMDLINE, int);
int TermInstance (HINSTANCE, int);

// Window procedures
LRESULT CALLBACK MainWndProc (HWND, UINT, WPARAM, LPARAM);

// Message handlers
LRESULT DoCreateMain (HWND, UINT, WPARAM, LPARAM);
LRESULT DoSizeMain (HWND, UINT, WPARAM, LPARAM);
LRESULT DoCommandMain (HWND, UINT, WPARAM, LPARAM);
LRESULT DoPocketPCShell (HWND, UINT, WPARAM, LPARAM);
LRESULT DoDestroyMain (HWND, UINT, WPARAM, LPARAM);

// Command functions
LPARAM DoMainCommandSend (HWND, WORD, HWND, WORD);
LPARAM DoMainCommandExit (HWND, WORD, HWND, WORD);

// Thread functions
DWORD WINAPI MonitorThread (PVOID pArg);
DWORD WINAPI ReceiveThread (PVOID pArg);
DWORD WINAPI SendFileThread (PVOID pArg);
```

MySquirt.cpp

```
//======================================================================
// MySquirt - A simple IrSock application for Windows CE
//
// Written for the book Programming Windows CE
// Copyright (C) 2007 Douglas Boling
//======================================================================
#ifndef _WIN32_WCE
#define _UNICODE                    // Force Unicode compile on desktop
#define UNICODE
#endif
#include <windows.h>                      // For all that Windows stuff
```

```
#include <stdlib.h>
#include <stdio.h>
#include <af_irda.h>                    // IrDA includes
#include <winsock.h>                    // Socket includes
#include «MySquirt.h»                   // Program-specific stuff
#ifndef _WIN32_WCE
#include <process.h>                    // Desktop multithread includes
#include <tchar.h>
#endif
#if defined(WIN32_PLATFORM_PSPC)
#include <aygshell.h>                   // Add Pocket PC includes.
#pragma comment( lib, «aygshell» )      // Link Pocket PC lib for menu bar.
#endif

#ifdef _WIN32_WCE
#pragma comment( lib, «Winsock.lib» )   // Winsock lib for CE
#else
#pragma comment( lib, «Ws2_32.lib» )    // Winsock lib for desktop
#endif
//----------------------------------------------------------------------
// Global data
//
const TCHAR szAppName[] = TEXT («MySquirt»);
const char chzAppName[] = «MySquirt»;
HINSTANCE hInst;                        // Program instance handle
HWND hMain;                             // Main window handle
BOOL fContinue = TRUE;                  // Server thread continue flag
BOOL fFirstSize = TRUE;                 // First WM_SIZE flag
#if defined(WIN32_PLATFORM_PSPC) && (_WIN32_WCE >= 300)
SHACTIVATEINFO sai;                     // Needed for P/PC helper functions
#endif
wchar_t bob;
// Message dispatch table for MainWindowProc
const struct decodeUINT MainMessages[] = {
    WM_CREATE, DoCreateMain,
    WM_SIZE, DoSizeMain,
    WM_COMMAND, DoCommandMain,
    WM_SETTINGCHANGE, DoPocketPCShell,
    WM_ACTIVATE, DoPocketPCShell,
    WM_DESTROY, DoDestroyMain,
};
// Command Message dispatch for MainWindowProc
const struct decodeCMD MainCommandItems[] = {
#if defined(WIN32_PLATFORM_PSPC) && (_WIN32_WCE >= 300)
    IDOK, DoMainCommandExit,
#else
    IDOK, DoMainCommandSend,
#endif
    IDCANCEL, DoMainCommandExit,
    IDD_SENDFILE, DoMainCommandSend,
};
//======================================================================
// Program entry point
//
```

```
int WINAPI WinMain (HINSTANCE hInstance, HINSTANCE hPrevInstance,
                    LPCMDLINE lpCmdLine, int nCmdShow) {
    MSG msg;
    int rc = 0;

    // Initialize application.
    hMain = InitInstance (hInstance, lpCmdLine, nCmdShow);
    if (hMain == 0)
        return TermInstance (hInstance, 0x10);

    // Application message loop
    while (GetMessage (&msg, NULL, 0, 0)) {
        if ((hMain == 0) || !IsDialogMessage (hMain, &msg)) {
            TranslateMessage (&msg);
            DispatchMessage (&msg);
        }
    }
    // Instance cleanup
    return TermInstance (hInstance, (int)msg.wParam);
}
//----------------------------------------------------------------------
// InitInstance - Instance initialization
//
HWND InitInstance (HINSTANCE hInstance, LPCMDLINE lpCmdLine,
                   int nCmdShow){
    HWND hWnd;
    HANDLE hThread;
    WNDCLASS wc;
    WSADATA wsaData;
    int rc;

    hInst = hInstance;                // Save program instance handle.

    // For all systems, if previous instance exists, activate it instead
    // of starting a new one.
    hWnd = FindWindow (szAppName, NULL);
    if (hWnd) {
        SetForegroundWindow ((HWND)((DWORD)hWnd | 0x01));
        return 0;
    }
    // Init Winsock
    rc = WSAStartup (1, &wsaData);
    if (rc) {
        MessageBox (NULL, TEXT(«Error in WSAStartup»), szAppName, MB_OK);
        return 0;
    }
    // Register application main window class.
    wc.style = 0;                             // Window style
    wc.lpfnWndProc = MainWndProc;             // Callback function
    wc.cbClsExtra = 0;                        // Extra class data
    wc.cbWndExtra = DLGWINDOWEXTRA;           // Extra window data
    wc.hInstance = hInstance;                 // Owner handle
    wc.hIcon = NULL;                          // Application icon
    wc.hCursor = LoadCursor (NULL, IDC_ARROW);// Default cursor
```

```
    wc.hbrBackground = (HBRUSH) GetStockObject (LTGRAY_BRUSH);
    wc.lpszMenuName = NULL;                     // Menu name
    wc.lpszClassName = szAppName;               // Window class name
    if (RegisterClass (&wc) == 0) return 0;

    // Create main window.
    hWnd = CreateDialog (hInst, szAppName, NULL, NULL);
    // Return 0 if window not created.
    if (!IsWindow (hWnd)) return 0;

    // Create secondary threads for interprocess communication.
    hThread = MyCreateThread (NULL, 0, MonitorThread, hWnd, 0, 0);
    if (hThread == 0) {
        DestroyWindow (hWnd);
        return 0;
    }
    CloseHandle (hThread);

    ShowWindow (hWnd, nCmdShow);        // Standard show and update calls
    UpdateWindow (hWnd);
    SetFocus (GetDlgItem (hWnd, IDD_OUTTEXT));
    return hWnd;
}
//----------------------------------------------------------------------
// TermInstance - Program cleanup
//
int TermInstance (HINSTANCE hInstance, int nDefRC) {
    return nDefRC;
}
//======================================================================
// Message handling procedures for main window
TCHAR szTitle[128];
//----------------------------------------------------------------------
// MainWndProc - Callback function for application window
//
LRESULT CALLBACK MainWndProc (HWND hWnd, UINT wMsg, WPARAM wParam,
                              LPARAM lParam) {
    INT i;
    //
    // Search message list to see if we need to handle this
    // message. If in list, call procedure.
    //
    for (i = 0; i < dim(MainMessages); i++) {
        if (wMsg == MainMessages[i].Code)
            return (*MainMessages[i].Fxn)(hWnd, wMsg, wParam, lParam);
    }
    return DefWindowProc (hWnd, wMsg, wParam, lParam);
}
//----------------------------------------------------------------------
// DoCreateMain - Process WM_CREATE message for window.
//
LRESULT DoCreateMain (HWND hWnd, UINT wMsg, WPARAM wParam,
                      LPARAM lParam) {
```

```
#if defined(WIN32_PLATFORM_PSPC)
    SHINITDLGINFO shidi;
    SHMENUBARINFO mbi;                        // For Pocket PC, create
    memset(&mbi, 0, sizeof(SHMENUBARINFO)); // menu bar so that we
    mbi.cbSize = sizeof(SHMENUBARINFO);      // have a sip button.
    mbi.dwFlags = SHCMBF_EMPTYBAR;
    mbi.hwndParent = hWnd;
    SHCreateMenuBar(&mbi);
    SendMessage(mbi.hwndMB, SHCMBM_GETSUBMENU, 0, 100);

    // For WinMobile, make dialog box full screen.
    shidi.dwMask = SHIDIM_FLAGS;
    shidi.dwFlags = SHIDIF_DONEBUTTON | SHIDIF_SIZEDLG | SHIDIF_SIPDOWN;
    shidi.hDlg = hWnd;
    SHInitDialog(&shidi);

    sai.cbSize = sizeof (sai);
    SHHandleWMSettingChange(hWnd, wParam, lParam, &sai);
#endif
    GetWindowText (hWnd, szTitle, dim (szTitle));
    return 0;
}
//----------------------------------------------------------------------
// DoSizeMain - Process WM_SIZE message for window.
//
LRESULT DoSizeMain (HWND hWnd, UINT wMsg, WPARAM wParam,
                    LPARAM lParam) {
#if defined(WIN32_PLATFORM_PSPC)
    static RECT rectListbox;
    RECT rect;

    GetClientRect (hWnd, &rect);
    if (fFirstSize) {
        // First time through, get the position of the list box for
        // resizing later. Store the distance from the sides of
        // the list box control to the side of the parent window.
        if (IsWindow (GetDlgItem (hWnd, IDD_INTEXT))) {
            fFirstSize = FALSE;
            GetWindowRect (GetDlgItem (hWnd, IDD_INTEXT), &rectListbox);
            MapWindowPoints (HWND_DESKTOP, hWnd, (LPPOINT)&rectListbox, 2);
            rectListbox.right = rect.right - rectListbox.right;
            rectListbox.bottom = rect.bottom - rectListbox.bottom;
        }
    }
    SetWindowPos (GetDlgItem (hWnd, IDD_INTEXT), 0, rect.left + 5,
                  rectListbox.top, rect.right - 10,
                  rect.bottom - rectListbox.top - 5,
                  SWP_NOZORDER);
#endif
    return 0;
}
//----------------------------------------------------------------------
// DoCommandMain - Process WM_COMMAND message for window.
//
```

```
LRESULT DoCommandMain (HWND hWnd, UINT wMsg, WPARAM wParam,
                       LPARAM lParam) {
    WORD idItem, wNotifyCode;
    HWND hwndCtl;
    INT i;

    // Parse the parameters.
    idItem = (WORD) LOWORD (wParam);
    wNotifyCode = (WORD) HIWORD (wParam);
    hwndCtl = (HWND) lParam;

    // Call routine to handle control message.
    for (i = 0; i < dim(MainCommandItems); i++) {
        if (idItem == MainCommandItems[i].Code)
            return (*MainCommandItems[i].Fxn)(hWnd, idItem, hwndCtl,
                                              wNotifyCode);
    }
    return 0;
}
//----------------------------------------------------------------------
// DoPocketPCShell - Process Pocket PC-required messages.
//
LRESULT DoPocketPCShell (HWND hWnd, UINT wMsg, WPARAM wParam,
                         LPARAM lParam) {
#if defined(WIN32_PLATFORM_PSPC)
    if (wMsg == WM_SETTINGCHANGE)
        return SHHandleWMSettingChange(hWnd, wParam, lParam, &sai);
    if (wMsg == WM_ACTIVATE)
        return SHHandleWMActivate(hWnd, wParam, lParam, &sai, 0);
#endif
    return 0;
}
//----------------------------------------------------------------------
// DoDestroyMain - Process WM_DESTROY message for window.
//
LRESULT DoDestroyMain (HWND hWnd, UINT wMsg, WPARAM wParam,
                       LPARAM lParam) {
    fContinue = FALSE;                      // Shut down server thread.
    Sleep (0);                              // Pass on timeslice.
    PostQuitMessage (0);
    return 0;
}
//======================================================================
// Command handler routines
//----------------------------------------------------------------------
// DoMainCommandExit - Process Program Exit command.
//
LPARAM DoMainCommandExit (HWND hWnd, WORD idItem, HWND hwndCtl,
                          WORD wNotifyCode) {

    SendMessage (hWnd, WM_CLOSE, 0, 0);
    return 0;
}
//----------------------------------------------------------------------
```

```
// DoMainCommandSend - Process Program Send File command.
//
LPARAM DoMainCommandSend (HWND hWnd, WORD idItem, HWND hwndCtl,
                          WORD wNotifyCode) {
    HANDLE hTh;
    static TCHAR szName[MAX_PATH];

    GetDlgItemText (hWnd, IDD_OUTTEXT, szName, dim(szName));
    hTh = MyCreateThread (NULL, 0, SendFileThread, (PVOID)szName, 0,
                          NULL);
    CloseHandle (hTh);
    return 0;
}
//----------------------------------------------------------------------
// Add2List - Add string to the report list box.
//
void Add2List (HWND hWnd, LPTSTR lpszFormat, ...) {
    int i, nBuf;
    wchar_t szBuffer[512];

    va_list args;
    va_start(args, lpszFormat);

    nBuf = StringCchVPrintf(szBuffer, dim (szBuffer),
                            (wchar_t *)lpszFormat, args);

    i = (int)SendDlgItemMessage (hWnd, IDD_INTEXT, LB_ADDSTRING, 0,
                            (LPARAM)(LPCTSTR)szBuffer);
    if (i != LB_ERR)
        SendDlgItemMessage (hWnd, IDD_INTEXT, LB_SETTOPINDEX, i,
                            (LPARAM)(LPCTSTR)szBuffer);
    va_end(args);
}
//----------------------------------------------------------------------
// MySetWindowText - Set window title to passed printf style string.
//
void MySetWindowText (HWND hWnd, LPTSTR lpszFormat, ...) {
    int nBuf;
    wchar_t szBuffer[512];

    va_list args;
    va_start(args, lpszFormat);

    nBuf = StringCchVPrintf(szBuffer, dim (szBuffer),
                            (wchar_t *)lpszFormat, args);

    SetWindowText (hWnd, (LPCWSTR)szBuffer);
    va_end(args);
}
//======================================================================
// MonitorThread - Monitors for connections; connects and notifies
// user when a connection occurs.
//
```

```
DWORD WINAPI MonitorThread (PVOID pArg) {
    HWND hWnd = (HWND)pArg;
    INT rc, nSize, i;
    SOCKADDR_IRDA iraddr, t_iraddr;
    SOCKET t_sock, s_sock;

    Add2List (hWnd, TEXT(«Monitor thread entered»));

    // Open an infrared socket.
    s_sock = socket (AF_IRDA, SOCK_STREAM, 0);
    if (s_sock == INVALID_SOCKET) {
        Add2List (hWnd, TEXT(«Socket failed. rc %d»), WSAGetLastError());
        return 0;
    }
    // Fill in irda socket address structure.
    iraddr.irdaAddressFamily = AF_IRDA;
    for (i = 0; i < dim (iraddr.irdaDeviceID); i++)
        iraddr.irdaDeviceID[i] = 0;
    memcpy (iraddr.irdaServiceName, chzAppName, sizeof (chzAppName) + 1);

    // Bind address to socket.
    rc = bind (s_sock, (struct sockaddr *)&iraddr, sizeof (iraddr));
    if (rc) {
        Add2List (hWnd, TEXT(« bind failed»));
        closesocket (s_sock);
        return 0;
    }
    // Set socket into listen mode.
    rc = listen (s_sock, SOMAXCONN);
    if (rc == SOCKET_ERROR) {
        Add2List (hWnd, TEXT(« listen failed %d»), GetLastError());
        closesocket (s_sock);
        return 0;
    }
    // Wait for remote requests.
    // Block on accept.
    while (fContinue) {
        nSize = sizeof (t_iraddr);
        t_sock = accept (s_sock, (struct sockaddr *)&t_iraddr, &nSize);
        if (t_sock == INVALID_SOCKET) {
            Add2List (hWnd, TEXT(« accept failed %d»), GetLastError());
        }
        Add2List (hWnd, TEXT(«sock accept...»));
        HANDLE hTh = MyCreateThread (NULL, 0, ReceiveThread,
                                     (PVOID)t_sock, 0, NULL);
        CloseHandle (hTh);
    }
    closesocket (s_sock);
    Add2List (hWnd, TEXT(«Monitor thread exit»));
    return 0;
}
//======================================================================
// ReceiveThread - Receives the file requested by the remote device
//
```

```
DWORD WINAPI ReceiveThread (PVOID pArg) {
    SOCKET t_sock = (SOCKET)pArg;
    HWND hWnd = hMain; // I'm cheating here.
    int nCnt, nFileSize, rc;
    TCHAR szFileName[MAX_PATH];
    PBYTE pBuff;
    int i, nSize, nTotal;
    DWORD dwBytes;
    HANDLE hFile;
    Add2List (hWnd, TEXT(«receive thread entered»));
    SetThreadPriority (GetCurrentThread (), THREAD_PRIORITY_ABOVE_NORMAL);

    // Read the number of bytes in the filename.
    rc = recv (t_sock, (LPSTR)&nCnt, sizeof (nCnt), 0);
    if ((rc == SOCKET_ERROR) || (nCnt > MAX_PATH)) {
        Add2List (hWnd, TEXT(«failed receiving name size»));
        closesocket (t_sock);
        return 0;
    }
    // Read the filename. If Win Mobile, put file in my documents.
#if defined(WIN32_PLATFORM_PSPC)
    StringCchCopy (szFileName, dim (szFileName), L»\\my documents\\»);
#else
    StringCchCopy (szFileName, dim (szFileName), L»\\»);
#endif //defined(WIN32_PLATFORM_PSPC)
    i = (int) wcslen (szFileName);
    rc = recv (t_sock, (LPSTR)&szFileName[i], nCnt, 0);
    if (rc == SOCKET_ERROR) {
        Add2List (hWnd, TEXT(«failed receiving name»));
        closesocket (t_sock);
        return 0;
    }
    Add2List (hWnd, TEXT(«name: %s»), szFileName);

    pBuff = (PBYTE)LocalAlloc (LPTR, BLKSIZE); //Create buff for file.
    //
    // Receive file size.
    //
    rc = recv (t_sock, (LPSTR)&nFileSize, sizeof (nFileSize), 0);
    Add2List (hWnd, TEXT(«received file size of %d bytes»), nFileSize);

    if ((rc != SOCKET_ERROR) && (nFileSize > 0)) {
        // We should really check here to see if there is enough
        // free space to receive the file.

        // Create the file. Overwrite if user says so.
        rc = 0;
        hFile = CreateFile (szFileName, GENERIC_WRITE, 0, NULL,
                            CREATE_ALWAYS, FILE_ATTRIBUTE_NORMAL, NULL);
        if (hFile == INVALID_HANDLE_VALUE) {
            Add2List (hWnd, TEXT(«File Open failed. rc %d»),
                      GetLastError());
            rc = BAD_FILEWRITE;
        }
```

```
        // Send ack code.
        Add2List (hWnd, TEXT(«Sending size ack.»));
        send (t_sock, (LPSTR)&rc, sizeof (rc), 0);
        //
        // Receive file.
        //
        nTotal = nFileSize;
        while ((!rc) && (nFileSize > 0)) {

            MySetWindowText (hWnd, TEXT («%02d%% received»),
                             (nTotal-nFileSize)*100/nTotal);
            nCnt = min (BLKSIZE, nFileSize);
            for (nSize = 0; nSize < nCnt;) {
                i = recv (t_sock, (LPSTR)pBuff+nSize, nCnt-nSize, 0);
                if (i == SOCKET_ERROR) {
                    Add2List (hWnd, TEXT(«recv socket err %d»),
                              GetLastError());
                    rc = BAD_SOCKETRECV;
                    break;
                }
                nSize += i;
            }
            Add2List (hWnd, TEXT(«recv'd %d bytes.»), nSize);
            if (i) {
                if (!WriteFile (hFile, pBuff, nSize, &dwBytes, 0))
                    rc = BAD_FILEWRITE;
                nFileSize -= dwBytes;
            } else
                Sleep(50);
            // Send ack of packet.
            send (t_sock, (LPSTR)&rc, sizeof (rc), 0);
        }
    } else if (rc == BAD_FILEOPEN)
        Add2List (hWnd, TEXT(«File not found.»));
    Add2List (hWnd, TEXT(«receive finished»));
    SetWindowText (hWnd, szTitle);
    LocalFree (pBuff);
    CloseHandle (hFile);
    Add2List (hWnd, TEXT(«receive thread exit»));
    return 0;
}
//----------------------------------------------------------------------
// SendFile - Sends a file to the remote device
//
DWORD WINAPI SendFileThread (PVOID pArg) {
    TCHAR *szFileName = (LPTSTR)pArg;
    HWND hWnd = hMain;
    SOCKET c_sock;
    HANDLE hFile;
    INT rc, nSize, i, nFileSize, nTotal, nCnt;
    char cDevice[256];
    SOCKADDR_IRDA iraddr;
    DEVICELIST *pDL;
    LPSTR pPtr;
```

```
    PBYTE pBuff;

    // Open the file.
    hFile = CreateFile (szFileName, GENERIC_READ, FILE_SHARE_READ,
                        NULL, OPEN_EXISTING, 0, NULL);
    if (hFile == INVALID_HANDLE_VALUE) {
        Add2List (hWnd, TEXT("File open failed. rc %d"),
                  GetLastError());
        return -1;
    }

    // Open an infrared socket.
    c_sock = socket (AF_IRDA, SOCK_STREAM, 0);
    if (c_sock == INVALID_SOCKET) {
        Add2List (hWnd, TEXT("Sock failed. rc %d"), WSAGetLastError());
        CloseHandle (hFile);
        return 0;
    }
    // Search for someone to talk to.
    for (i = 0; i < 5; i++) {
        memset (cDevice, 0, sizeof (cDevice));
        nSize = sizeof (cDevice);
        rc = getsockopt (c_sock, SOL_IRLMP, IRLMP_ENUMDEVICES,
                         cDevice, &nSize);
        if (rc)
            Add2List (hWnd, TEXT("Getsockopt failed. rc %d"),
                      WSAGetLastError());

        pDL = (DEVICELIST *) cDevice;
        if (pDL->numDevice) {
            Add2List (hWnd, TEXT("%d devices found."), pDL->numDevice);
            break;
        }
        Sleep(500);
    }
    // If no device found, exit.
    if (pDL->numDevice == 0) {
        closesocket (c_sock);
        CloseHandle (hFile);
        Add2List (hWnd, TEXT("No infrared devices found in range."));
        return -2;
    }

    //
    // Copy address of found device.
    //
    memset (&iraddr, 0, sizeof (iraddr));
    iraddr.irdaAddressFamily = AF_IRDA;
    memcpy (iraddr.irdaDeviceID, pDL->Device[0].irdaDeviceID, 4);
    //
    // Now initialize the specific socket we're interested in.
    //
    memcpy (iraddr.irdaServiceName, chzAppName, sizeof (chzAppName)+1);
    Add2List (hWnd, TEXT("Found: %hs"), pDL->Device[0].irdaDeviceName);
```

```
//
// Connect to remote socket.
//
rc = connect (c_sock, (struct sockaddr *)&iraddr, sizeof (iraddr));
if (rc) {
    Add2List (hWnd, TEXT("Connect failed. rc %d"), WSAGetLastError());
    closesocket (c_sock);
    return -4;
}
Add2List (hWnd, TEXT("connected..."));

rc = 0;
nFileSize = GetFileSize (hFile, NULL);

// Allocate buffer and read file.
pBuff = (LPBYTE)LocalAlloc (LPTR, nFileSize);
if (pBuff) {
    ReadFile (hFile, pBuff, nFileSize, (DWORD *)&nCnt, NULL);
    if (nCnt != nFileSize)
        rc = BAD_FILEREAD;
} else
    rc = BAD_MEMORY;

if (rc) {
    closesocket (c_sock);
    CloseHandle (hFile);
    Add2List (hWnd, TEXT("Error allocating buffer or reading file."));
    return rc;
}
// Start transfer. First send size and get ack.

// Strip off any leading path, assume len > 1 since we've opened file.
for (i = lstrlen (szFileName)-1; (i > 0) &&
                                 (szFileName[i] != TEXT ('\\')) ; i--);
if (szFileName[i] == TEXT ('\\')) i++;
// Send name size.
nCnt = ((lstrlen (&szFileName[i]) + 1) * sizeof (WCHAR));
rc = send (c_sock, (LPSTR)&nCnt, sizeof (nCnt), 0);

// Send filename.
if (rc != SOCKET_ERROR)
    rc = send (c_sock, (LPSTR)szFileName, nCnt, 0);

if (rc != SOCKET_ERROR)  {
    // Send file size. Size will always be < 2 gig.
    rc = send (c_sock, (LPSTR)&nFileSize, sizeof (nFileSize), 0);
    if (rc == SOCKET_ERROR)
        rc = BAD_SOCKET;
    else
        // Recv ack of file size.
        recv (c_sock, (LPSTR)&rc, sizeof (rc), 0);

    // Send the file.
    nTotal = nFileSize;
```

```
        pPtr = (LPSTR)pBuff;
        while ((!rc) && nFileSize) {

            MySetWindowText (hWnd, TEXT ("%02d%% sent"),
                             (nTotal-nFileSize)*100/nTotal);
            // Send up to the block size.
            nCnt = min (BLKSIZE, nFileSize);
            rc = send (c_sock, pPtr, nCnt, 0);
            if (rc == SOCKET_ERROR) {
                Add2List (hWnd, TEXT("send error %d "), GetLastError());
                rc = BAD_SOCKET;
            } else
                Add2List (hWnd, TEXT("sent %d bytes"), rc);
            pPtr += rc;
            nFileSize -= rc;

            // Receive ack.
            recv (c_sock, (LPSTR)&rc, sizeof (rc), 0);
        }
        SetWindowText (hWnd, szTitle);
    }
    // Send close code.
    if (rc != BAD_SOCKET)
        send (c_sock, (LPSTR)&rc, sizeof (rc), 0);

    closesocket (c_sock);
    // Clean up.
    CloseHandle (hFile);
    LocalFree (pBuff);
    if (rc)
        Add2List (hWnd, TEXT("SendFile Exit rc = %d"), rc);
    else
        Add2List (hWnd, TEXT("File sent successfully."));
    return 0;
}
```

From a Windows standpoint, MySquirt is a simple program. It uses a dialog box as its main window. When the program is first launched, it creates a thread to monitor for other devices that creates an infrared socket, binds it to a service name, puts the socket into listen mode, and blocks on a call to *accept*. When a remote device connects, the monitor thread creates another thread to handle the actual receiving of the file while it loops back and waits for another connection.

A transmission is initiated when another device running MySquirt sends a file. This process begins when the user on the sending device presses the Send button. If text exists in the edit box, the application reads it and calls the *SendFile* routine. In this routine, a socket is created, and any remote devices are enumerated using repeated calls to *getsockopt*. If a device is found, a connection is attempted with a call to *connect*. *Connect* succeeds only if the remote device has bound an IR socket using the same service name, which happens to be defined as the string contained in *chzAppName*, an ASCII representation of the program name. This addressing scheme ensures that if a connection is made, the remote device is running MySquirt. Once a connection is made, the sending device sends over the filename, which it does in two steps: first it sends the byte length of the filename and then the name itself. This process allows the server to know how many characters to receive before continuing. The device then sends the file size. If the file sent by the server device fits in the object store, the routine creates the file on the client side, notifying the user if the file already exists. If all has gone well to this point, the data is received and written to the file. The application closes the socket and frees the buffer created to read the data into.

On the receiving side, a transmission is initiated when the monitor thread's call to *accept* returns. The monitor thread creates a receiving thread and loops back looking for other sending devices. The receiving thread receives the name and size of the file and determines whether the file is acceptable. If so, it sends an acknowledgment back to the sending device. From then on, the receiving thread reads the data from the socket and writes it to the newly created file. When the transmission is complete, the receiving thread closes the file, closes the receiving socket, and terminates.

The other interesting aspect of MySquirt is that I wrote the program to be compiled on both Windows CE and the desktop. There are a few adjustments to the program to handle the different declarations for the *lpCmdLine* parameter of *WinMain* and a macro to hide the differences between calling *CreateThread* in Windows CE and *beginthreadex* on the desktop. The example on this book's companion Web site has two projects within the Visual Studio solution. One targets Windows CE, and the other project compiles for the desktop. Both projects use the same source files.

Bluetooth

Bluetooth is the name of a wireless interface standard that uses radio frequency (RF) as its medium instead of infrared frequency, as is used with IrDA. Bluetooth is designed to be a successor to IrDA, providing the file transfer capabilities of IrDA along with a number of other capabilities centering on cableless connections.

Bluetooth is named for Harald Blåtand (Bluetooth), who was king of Denmark from 940 to 985. Harald was the grandson of King Ethelred of England and the grandfather of King Canute, famous for demonstrating the limits of kingly power by commanding the tide not to come in.[2] Harald's claim to fame is the unification of Denmark and Norway during his rule. One thousand, ten years later, following an Ericsson-initiated feasibility study of using a low-power radio frequency network to link peripherals, a special interest group (SIG) was formed with Ericsson, IBM, Toshiba, Nokia, and Intel to organize and form a standard under

[2] For those wondering, the tide came in anyway.

the code name Bluetooth. That catchy code name was soon chosen as the actual name of the standard.

Although it took longer than expected for Bluetooth-enabled devices to reach the mainstream, the number of devices supporting Bluetooth has grown. Following this trend, most Windows Mobile devices and a number of other Windows CE devices now include support for Bluetooth. Windows CE has supported Bluetooth since 4.0 and Windows Mobile systems have supported it since the Pocket PC 2003. Some Windows Mobile OEMs use third-party Bluetooth software on their devices instead of the Windows CE stack. This Bluetooth discussion covers only the Windows CE Bluetooth API. To program third-party Bluetooth stacks, developers should contact the device manufacturers for information.

Bluetooth functionality is centered on profiles that define services provided to the user. Profiles include Cordless Telephony, Intercom, Headset, Fax, Dial-Up Networking, LAN Access, Object Push, Synchronization, and File Transfer. Not all profiles are supported by all devices. In fact, most devices support only a very few profiles relevant to the device.

Windows CE provides the Dial-up Networking, LAN Access, Object Push and File Transfer profiles out of the box, although OEMs are free to add support for other profiles in their products. Windows Mobile devices typically provide support for Object Push, File Transfer profiles, and, of course, hands-free or headset profiles for wireless headsets.

The applications, such as Pocket Inbox and Pocket Outlook, that are bundled with the devices support Bluetooth for file transfer, business card exchange, and synchronization. Working with these applications is preferable to writing code to work directly with the Bluetooth API because of the complexity of that API.

For those who are interested in working directly with the Bluetooth API, the task isn't easy, clean, or quick. Part of the problem is the flexibility of the Bluetooth standard and the complexity of the discovery protocol that communicates which services are available from a device. Before we can dive into this code, a bit of background is necessary.

Stack

A diagram of the Bluetooth stack is shown in Figure 14-2. The lower three layers—Baseband, Link Manager Protocol, and the first Host Controller Interface (HCI) layer—are implemented in the Bluetooth hardware. The layers above the hardware and below the application are provided by Windows CE, although it's possible for third parties to extend the Bluetooth stack by providing additional profiles above the HCI layer.

Applications interact with the Bluetooth stack through one of two interfaces. The preferred method is for applications to use the Winsock API to access the Bluetooth stack. Just as with IrDA, applications use standard Winsock functions to open sockets associated with the Bluetooth stack. Control is accomplished through various *WSAxxx* functions. Data transfer is accomplished through the standard socket *send* and *recv* functions.

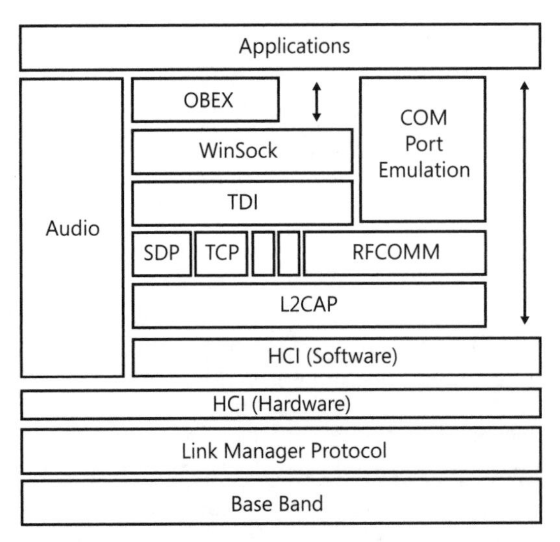

FIGURE 14-2 A diagram of the Bluetooth stack on Windows CE

Winsock support for Bluetooth depends on the Winsock stack installed on the device. If the system has Winsock 2.0 installed, such as Windows Mobile devices, Bluetooth functionality is accessed directly through Winsock calls such as *setsockopt*. For systems with Winsock 1.1 installed, the Bluetooth stack needs to be configured through a dedicated Bluetooth API. For example, to query the current mode of an asynchronous connection, an application can use the dedicated function *BthGetCurrentMode* or, if Winsock 2.0 is on the system, a call to *getsockopt* with the option name *SO_BTH_GET_MODE*.

The other way applications can work with Bluetooth is through *virtual serial ports*. With this method, applications load a Bluetooth-dedicated serial driver. Control of the stack is accomplished through *DeviceIoControl* calls to the COM driver. Calling *WriteFile* and *ReadFile* to write and read the COM port sends and receives data across the Bluetooth connection.

Discovery

Before devices can communicate across a Bluetooth connection, devices and the services those devices provide must be discovered. The discovery process is quite complex because of the flexible nature of the Bluetooth feature set. Devices and services on particular devices can be queried in a general way—all printers, for example—or they can be specifically queried—for example, whether a particular device supports a particular service, such as the Headset profile-Audio-Gateway service.

Both device discovery and service discovery are accomplished through the same series of functions, albeit with significantly different parameters. The discovery process is accomplished through a series of three functions: *WSALookupServiceBegin*, *WSALookupServiceNext*, and *WSALookupServiceEnd*. These functions aren't specific to Winsock 2.0, but in the discussion that follows, I'm providing information only about using them in Bluetooth applications. A parallel series of functions—*BthNsLookupServiceBegin*, *BthNsLookupServiceNext*, and *BthNsLookupServiceEnd*—are functionally identical and can be used for systems with Winsock 1.1. Although the function names imply a simple iterative search, the parameters required for the search are daunting.

Device Discovery

To find local devices, an application first calls *WSALookupServiceBegin*, which is prototyped as

```
INT WSALookupServiceBegin (LPWSAQUERYSET pQuerySet, DWORD dwFlags,
                           LPHANDLE lphLookup);
```

The first parameter is a pointer to a *WSAQUERYSET* structure, which I'll discuss shortly. For device searches, the *dwFlags* parameter should contain the flag *LUP_CONTAINERS*. The other allowable flags for this parameter will be covered in the upcoming discussion about service queries. The final parameter should point to a handle value that will be filled in with a search handle; this search handle will be used for the other calls in the search. The return value is an *HRESULT* with 0, indicating success.

The *WSAQUERYSET* structure is defined as

```
typedef struct _WSAQuerySet {
    DWORD           dwSize;
    LPTSTR          lpszServiceInstanceName;
    LPGUID          lpServiceClassId;
    LPWSAVERSION    lpVersion;
    LPTSTR          lpszComment;
    DWORD           dwNameSpace;
    LPGUID          lpNSProviderId;
    LPTSTR          lpszContext;
    DWORD           dwNumberOfProtocols;
    LPAFPROTOCOLS   lpafpProtocols;
    LPTSTR          lpszQueryString;
    DWORD           dwNumberOfCsAddrs;
    LPCSADDR_INFO   lpcsaBuffer;
    DWORD           dwOutputFlags;
    LPBLOB          lpBlob;
} WSAQUERYSET, *PWSAQUERYSET;
```

The *dwSize* field should be set to the size of the structure. For device queries, the only other fields that need to be used are the *dwNameSpace* field, which must be set to *NS_BT*, and the *lpBlob* field, which should point to a *BLOB* structure. The remaining fields should be set to 0.

The *BLOB* structure pointed to by the *lpBlob* field is actually optional for the initial device query call, but it's recommended so that the time the Bluetooth stack spends looking for devices can be defined. If the query time isn't specified, the Bluetooth stack defaults to a rather long 15 to 20 seconds waiting for devices to respond. To define the query time, *lpBlob* points to a *container BLOB* structure that, in turn, points to a blob of a specific type. The container *BLOB* structure is defined as

```
typedef struct _BLOB {
    ULONG cbSize;
    BYTE* pBlobData;
} BLOB, LPBLOB;
```

The two fields are the size of the specific *BLOB* structure being pointed to the specific *BLOB* data. For device queries, the blob we're interested in is an *inquiry* blob defined as

```
typedef struct _BTHNS_INQUIRYBLOB {
    ULONG LAP;
    unsigned char length;
    unsigned char num_responses;
} BTHNS_INQUIRYBLOB, *PBTHNS_INQUIRYBLOB;
```

The first field should be set to BT_ADDR_GIAC, which is the general inquiry access code (GIAC), defined as 0x9e8b33. The *length* field should be set to the time the stack should wait for devices to respond. The unit of time for this field is 1.28 seconds,[3] so if you want to wait approximately 5 seconds, the value 4 in the field will produce a wait of 4 × 1.28, or 5.12, seconds. The final field, *num_responses*, specifies the maximum number of devices that need to respond to end the query before the timeout value.

So before a call to *WSALookupServiceBegin* is made to query the available devices, the *WSAQUERYSET*, *BLOB*, and *BTHNS_INQUIRYBLOB* structures should be initialized with the *WSAQUERYSET* structure's *lpBlob* field pointing to the *BLOB* structure. The *BLOB* structure should be initialized so that the *cbSize* field contains the size of the *BTHNS_INQUIRYBLOB* structure and the *pBlobData* field points to the *BTHNS_INQUIRYBLOB* structure. The *BTHNS_INQUIRYBLOB* structure should be filled in with the search criteria.

When the call to *WSALookupServiceBegin* returns successfully, a call to *WSALookupServiceNext* is made. Whereas the *WSALookupServiceBegin* call can take a number of seconds, the *WSALookupServiceNext* call can return immediately as long as the data being requested has been cached in the stack by the *WSALookupServiceBegin* call. The *WSALookupServiceNext* call is defined as

```
INT WSALookupServiceNext (HANDLE hLookup, DWORD dwFlags,
                          LPDWORD lpdwBufferLength,
                          LPWSAQUERYSET pResults);
```

[3] 1.28 seconds is the polling interval used by discoverable devices.

The first parameter is the handle returned by *WSALookupServiceBegin*. The *dwFlags* parameter contains a number of different flags that define the data returned by the function. The possible flags are

- **LUP_RETURN_NAME** Return the name of the remote device.
- **LUP_RETURN_ADDRESS** Return the address of the remote device.
- **LUP_RETURN_BLOB** Return *BTHINQUIRYRESULT* structure with information about the remote device.
- **BTHNS_LUP_RESET_ITERATOR** Reset the enumeration so that the next call to *WSALookupServiceNext* will return information about the first device in the list.
- **BTHNS_LUP_NO_ADVANCE** Return information about a device but don't increment the device index so that the next call to *WSALookupServiceNext* returns information about the same device.

The final two parameters are the address of a variable that contains the size of the output buffer and a pointer to the output buffer. Although the output buffer pointer is cast as a pointer to a *WSAQUERYSET* structure, the buffer passed to *WSALookupServiceNext* should be significantly larger than the structure so that the function can marshal any strings into the buffer beyond the end of the structure itself.

When the function returns without error, the *WSAQUERYSET* structure pointed to by *pResults* contains information about a Bluetooth device. The name of the device, if requested with the *LUP_RETURN_NAME* flag, is pointed to by the *lpszServiceInstanceName* field. The address of the remote device is contained in the *CSADDR_INFO* structure pointed to by *lpcsaBuffer*. *CSADDR_INFO* provides information about the local and remote device addresses and is defined as

```
typedef struct _CSADDR_INFO {
    SOCKET_ADDRESS LocalAddr;
    SOCKET_ADDRESS RemoteAddr;
    INT iSocketType;
    INT iProtocol;
} CSADDR_INFO;
```

The *SOCKET_ADDRESS* fields are filled in with Bluetooth-specific *SOCKADDR_BTH* addresses, so to get the remote address, the *RemoteAddr* field should be properly cast, as in

```
bt = ((SOCKADDR_BTH *)
    pQueryResult->lpcsaBuffer->RemoteAddr.lpSockaddr)->btAddr;
```

Each call to *WSALookupServiceNext* returns information about a single device. The function should be called repeatedly until it returns *SOCKET_ERROR*. If *GetLastError* returns *WSA_E_NO_MORE*, there was no error; there are simply no more devices to be found.

After completing the *WSALookupServiceNext* loop, the program should call *WSALookupServiceEnd* to clean up any resources the Winsock stack has maintained during the search. The function is prototyped as

```
INT WSALookupServiceEnd (HANDLE hLookup);
```

The single parameter is the handle returned by *WSALookupServiceBegin*.

The following routine queries the Bluetooth devices that are in range and returns their names and addresses in an array.

```
#define MYBUFFSIZE 16384
typedef struct {
    TCHAR szName[256];
    BT_ADDR btaddr;
} MYBTDEVICE, *PMYBTDEVICE;
//
// FindDevices - Find devices in range.
//
int FindDevices (PMYBTDEVICE pbtDev, int *pnDevs) {
    DWORD dwFlags, dwLen;
    HANDLE hLookup;
    int i, rc;

    // Create inquiry blob to limit time of search
    BTHNS_INQUIRYBLOB inqblob;
    memset (&inqblob, 0, sizeof (inqblob));
    inqblob.LAP = BT_ADDR_GIAC;  // Default GIAC
    inqblob.length = 4;          // 4 * 1.28 = 5 seconds
    inqblob.num_responses = *pnDevs;

    // Create blob to point to inquiry blob
    BLOB blob;
    blob.cbSize = sizeof (BTHNS_INQUIRYBLOB);
    blob.pBlobData = (PBYTE)&inqblob;

    // Init query
    WSAQUERYSET QuerySet;
    memset (&QuerySet,0,sizeof (WSAQUERYSET));
    QuerySet.dwSize = sizeof (WSAQUERYSET);
    QuerySet.dwNameSpace = NS_BTH;
    QuerySet.lpBlob = &blob;

    // Start query for devices
    rc = WSALookupServiceBegin (&QuerySet, LUP_CONTAINERS, &hLookup);
    if (rc) return rc;

    // Allocate output buffer
    PBYTE pOut = (PBYTE)LocalAlloc (LPTR, MYBUFFSIZE);
    if (!pOut) return -1;
    WSAQUERYSET *pQueryResult = (WSAQUERYSET *)pOut;

    // Loop through the devices by repeatedly calling WSALookupServiceNext
    for (i = 0; i < *pnDevs; i++) {
```

```
        dwLen = MYBUFFSIZE;
        dwFlags = LUP_RETURN_NAME | LUP_RETURN_ADDR;
        rc = WSALookupServiceNext (hLookup, dwFlags, &dwLen, pQueryResult);
        if (rc == SOCKET_ERROR) {
            rc = GetLastError();
            break;
        }
        // Copy device name
        StringCchCopy (pbtDev[i].szName, dim(pbtDev[i].szName),
                     pQueryResult->lpszServiceInstanceName);
        // Copy Bluetooth device address
        SOCKADDR_BTH *pbta;
        pbta = (SOCKADDR_BTH *)
            pQueryResult->lpcsaBuffer->RemoteAddr.lpSockaddr;
        pbtDev[i].btaddr = pbta->btAddr;
    }
    // See if we left the loop simply because there were no more devices
    if (rc == WSA_E_NO_MORE) rc = 0;

    // Return the number of devices found
    *pnDevs = i;

    // Clean up
    WSALookupServiceEnd (hLookup);
    LocalFree (pOut);
    return rc;
}
```

The preceding routine uses *WSALookupServiceBegin*, *WSALookupServiceNext*, and *WSALookupServiceEnd* to iterate through the Bluetooth devices in range. The routine could query other information about the remote devices by passing the *LUP_RETURN_BLOB* flag in *WSALookupServiceNext*, but the information returned isn't needed to connect to the device.

Service Discovery

Once the device of interest is found, the next task is to discover whether that device supplies the service needed. Services are identified in a multilevel fashion. The service can publish itself under a generic service, such as printer or fax service, or publish itself under a specific unique identifier, or GUID.

If you know the specific service as well as its documented GUID, there is no need for service discovery. Simply connect a Bluetooth socket to the specific service as discussed in the "Bluetooth Communication with Winsock" section on page 504. If, however, you don't know the exact service GUID, you must take on the task of service discovery.

Querying services is accomplished through the same *WSALookupServiceBegin*, *WSALookupServiceNext*, and *WSALookupServiceEnd* functions discussed earlier in the device discovery section. As with device discovery, the initial query is accomplished with a call to *WSALookupServiceBegin*. To query the services on a remote device, set the *dwFlags* parameter to 0 instead of using the *LUP_CONTAINERS* flag. To query the service provided by the local system instead of remote devices, set the *LUP_RES_SERVICE* flag in the *dwFlags* parameter.

When you're querying the services of another device, the *WSAQUERYSET* structure needs to specify the target device that's being queried. This is accomplished by referencing a restriction blob in the *WSAQUERYSET* structure. The restriction blob is defined as

```
typedef struct _BTHNS_RESTRICTIONBLOB {
    ULONG type;
    ULONG serviceHandle;
    SdpQueryUuid uuids[12];
    ULONG numRange;
    SdpAttributeRange pRange[1];
} BTHNS_RESTRICTIONBLOB;
```

The *type* field specifies whether the query should check for services, attributes of the services, or both attributes and services by specifying the flags *SDP_SERVICE_SEARCH_REQUEST*, *SDP_SERVICE_ATTRIBUTE_REQUEST*, and *SDP_SERVICE_SEARCH_ATTRIBUTE_REQUEST*, respectively. The *serviceHandle* parameter is used in attribute-only searches to specify the service being queried. If the services are being queried, the *uuids* array contains up to 12 service IDs to check. The service IDs are specified in an *SdpQueryUuid* structure defined as

```
typedef struct _SdpQueryUuid {
    SdpQueryUuidUnion u;
    USHORT uuidType;
} SdpQueryUuid;
```

The *SdpQueryUuid* structure allows the service IDs to be specified as 16-, 32-, or 128-bit ID values. The ID values for documented services provided in the Bluetooth include file Bt_sdp.h in the SDK.

When you're querying attributes for a service or services, the *pRange* array can specify the minimum and maximum attribute range to query. The size of the *pRange* array is specified in the *numRange* parameter. In the following code, a specific service is queried to see whether it exists on the device. If it does, the query also returns the attributes associated with the service.

```
int QueryService (HWND hWnd, BT_ADDR bta, GUID *pguid) {
    DWORD dwFlags, dwLen;
    HANDLE hLookup;
    TCHAR szDeviceName[256];
    LPWSAQUERYSET pQuerySet;
    PBYTE pQuery;
    int i, rc;

    pQuery = (PBYTE)LocalAlloc (LPTR, MYBUFFSIZE);
    if (!pQuery) return 0;

    pQuerySet = (LPWSAQUERYSET)pQuery;
    memset (pQuerySet, 0, MYBUFFSIZE);
```

```
pQuerySet->dwSize = sizeof (WSAQUERYSET);
pQuerySet->dwNameSpace = NS_BTH;

// Specify device
CSADDR_INFO csi;
memset (&csi, 0, sizeof (csi));

SOCKADDR_BTH sa;
memset (&sa, 0, sizeof (sa));
sa.btAddr = bta;
sa.addressFamily = AF_BT;

// Specify the remote device address
csi.RemoteAddr.lpSockaddr = (LPSOCKADDR) &sa;
csi.RemoteAddr.iSockaddrLength = sizeof(SOCKADDR_BTH);
pQuerySet->lpcsaBuffer = &csi;
pQuerySet->dwNumberOfCsAddrs = 1;

// Form query based on service class being checked
BTHNS_RESTRICTIONBLOB btrblb;
memset (&btrblb, 0, sizeof (btrblb));
btrblb.type = SDP_SERVICE_SEARCH_ATTRIBUTE_REQUEST;
btrblb.numRange = 1;
btrblb.pRange[0].minAttribute = 0;
btrblb.pRange[0].maxAttribute = 0xffff;
btrblb.uuids[0].uuidType = SDP_ST_UUID128; //Define search type
memcpy (&btrblb.uuids[0].u.uuid128, pguid, sizeof (GUID));

// Create blob to point to restriction blob
BLOB blob;
blob.cbSize = sizeof (BTHNS_RESTRICTIONBLOB);
blob.pBlobData = (PBYTE)&btrblb;
pQuerySet->lpBlob = &blob;
dwFlags = 0;

rc = WSALookupServiceBegin (pQuerySet, dwFlags, &hLookup);
if (rc) return rc;

// Setup query set for ServiceNext call
pQuerySet->dwNumberOfCsAddrs = 1;
pQuerySet->lpszServiceInstanceName = szDeviceName;
memset (szDeviceName, 0, sizeof (szDeviceName));

dwFlags = LUP_RETURN_NAME | LUP_RETURN_ADDR;
dwLen = MYBUFFSIZE;
while ((rc = WSALookupServiceNext (hLookup, dwFlags, &dwLen,
                                   pQuerySet)) == 0) {
    ISdpRecord **pRecordArg;
    int cRecordArg = 0;

    // Setup attribute query
    HRESULT hr = ParseBlobToRecs (pQuerySet->lpBlob->pBlobData,
                                  pQuerySet->lpBlob->cbSize,
                                  &pRecordArg, (ULONG *)&cRecordArg);
    if (hr == ERROR_SUCCESS) {
        // Parse the records
```

```
            // Clean up records
            for (i = 0; i < cRecordArg; i++)
                pRecordArg[i]->Release();
            CoTaskMemFree(pRecordArg);
        }
        dwLen = MYBUFFSIZE;
        i++;
    }
    rc = WSALookupServiceEnd (hLookup);
    LocalFree (pQuery);
    return rc;
}
```

Notice that in this code, the Service Discovery Protocol (SDP) data for the service is returned in the buffer pointed to by the *lpBlob* structure. This data isn't parsed in the routine. Instead, a routine named *ParseBlobToRecs* is called to parse the data. The routine *ParseBlobToRecs*, shown here, returns a series of *ISdpRecord* interface pointers, one for each record in the SDP data.

```
//
// ParseBlobToRecs - Use ISdpStream object to parse the response
// from the SDP server.
//
HRESULT ParseBlobToRecs (UCHAR *pbData, DWORD cbStream,
                         ISdpRecord ***pppSdpRecords, ULONG *pcbRec) {
    HRESULT hr;
    ULONG ulError;
    ISdpStream *pIStream = NULL;
    *pppSdpRecords = NULL;
    *pcbRec = 0;

    hr = CoCreateInstance (__uuidof(SdpStream), NULL,
                           CLSCTX_INPROC_SERVER, __uuidof(ISdpStream),
                           (LPVOID *)&pIStream);
    if (FAILED(hr)) return hr;
    // Validate SDP data blob
    hr = pIStream->Validate (pbData, cbStream, &ulError);

    if (SUCCEEDED(hr)) {
        hr = pIStream->VerifySequenceOf (pbData, cbStream,
                                         SDP_TYPE_SEQUENCE, NULL, pcbRec);
        if (SUCCEEDED(hr) && *pcbRec > 0) {
            *pppSdpRecords = (ISdpRecord **)CoTaskMemAlloc (
                                             sizeof (ISdpRecord*) *
                                            (*pcbRec));
            if (pppSdpRecords != NULL) {
                hr = pIStream->RetrieveRecords (pbData, cbStream,
                                                *pppSdpRecords, pcbRec);
                if (!SUCCEEDED(hr)) {
                    CoTaskMemFree (*pppSdpRecords);
                    *pppSdpRecords = NULL;
                    *pcbRec = 0;
                }
            }
```

```
            else
                hr = E_OUTOFMEMORY;
        }
    }
    if (pIStream != NULL) {
        pIStream->Release();
        pIStream = NULL;
    }
    return hr;
}
```

The routine returns the data in an array of *ISdpRecord* pointers. It's left to the reader to parse the record data using the other interfaces provided in the Bluetooth API.

Publishing a Service

The other side of service discovery is service publication. Bluetooth applications that want to provide a service to other applications must do more than simply create a Bluetooth socket, bind the socket, and call *accept* as would an IrDA service. In addition to the socket work, the service must publish the details of the service through the SDP API.

The actual publication of a service is actually quite simple. All that's necessary is to call *WSASetService*, which is prototyped as

```
INT WSASetService (LPWSAQUERYSET lpqsRegInfo,
                   WSAESETSERVICEOP essoperation,
                   DWORD dwControlFlags);
```

The three parameters are a pointer to a *WSAQUERYSET* structure; a service operation flag, which needs to be set to *RNRSERVICE_REGISTER*; and a *dwControlFlags* parameter set to 0.

If only registration were that simple. The problem isn't calling the function; it's composing the SDP data that's placed in the *WSAQUERYSET* structure. The *dwNameSpace* field should be set to *NS_BTH*. And, as with the discovery process, the blobs are involved. The blob used in setting the service is a *BTHNS_SETBLOB* structure defined as

```
typedef struct _BTHNS_SETBLOB {
    ULONG* pRecordHandle;
    ULONG fSecurity;
    ULONG fOptions;
    ULONG ulRecordLength;
    UCHAR pRecord[1];
} BTHNS_SETBLOB, *PBTHNS_SETBLOB;
```

The first parameter points to a *ULONG* that will receive a handle for the SDP record being created. The *fSecurity* and *fOptions* fields are reserved and should be set to 0. The *ulRecord-Length* parameter should be set to the length of the SDP record to publish, whereas *pRecord* is the starting byte of the byte array that is the SDP record to publish.

The following code demonstrates publishing an SDP record. The routine is passed an SDP record and its size. It then initializes the proper structures and calls *WSASetService* to publish the record.

```
int PublishRecord (HWND hWnd, PBYTE pSDPRec, int nRecSize,
                   ULONG *pRecord) {
    BTHNS_SETBLOB *pSetBlob;
    ULONG ulSdpVersion = BTH_SDP_VERSION;
    int rc;

    // Zero out the record handle that will be returned by the call
    *pRecord = 0;

    // Allocate and init the SetBlob
    pSetBlob = (BTHNS_SETBLOB *)LocalAlloc (LPTR,
                                sizeof (BTHNS_SETBLOB) + nRecSize);
    if (!pSetBlob) return -1;

    pSetBlob->pRecordHandle = pRecord;
    pSetBlob->pSdpVersion = &ulSdpVersion;
    pSetBlob->fSecurity = 0;
    pSetBlob->fOptions = 0;
    pSetBlob->ulRecordLength = nRecSize;
    memcpy (pSetBlob->pRecord, pSDPRec, nRecSize);

    // Init the container blob
    BLOB blob;
    blob.cbSize = sizeof(BTHNS_SETBLOB) + SDP_RECORD_SIZE - 1;
    blob.pBlobData = (PBYTE) pSetBlob;

    // Init the WSAQuerySet struct
    WSAQUERYSET Service;
    memset (&Service, 0, sizeof(Service));
    Service.dwSize = sizeof(Service);
    Service.lpBlob = &blob;
    Service.dwNameSpace = NS_BTH;

    // Publish the service
    rc = WSASetService(&Service, RNRSERVICE_REGISTER, 0);
    if (rc == SOCKET_ERROR) rc = GetLastError();
    // Clean up
    LocalFree ((PBYTE)pSetBlob);
    return rc;
}
```

When the application no longer wants to support the service, it needs to remove the record from the SDP database. Removing the record is accomplished by using *WSASetService*, specifying the record handle of the service and the flag *RNRSERVICE_DELETE*. The record handle is passed in the *BTHNS_SETBLOB* structure. The other fields of this structure are ignored. The following code shows a routine that unregisters a service.

```
int UnpublishRecord (ULONG hRecord) {
    ULONG ulSdpVersion = BTH_SDP_VERSION;
    int rc;
```

```
    BTHNS_SETBLOB SetBlob;
    memset (&SetBlob, 0, sizeof (SetBlob));
    SetBlob.pRecordHandle = &hRecord;
    SetBlob.pSdpVersion = &ulSdpVersion;

    // Init the container blob
    BLOB blob;
    blob.cbSize = sizeof(BTHNS_SETBLOB);
    blob.pBlobData = (PBYTE) &SetBlob;

    // Init the WSAQuerySet struct
    WSAQUERYSET Service;
    memset (&Service, 0, sizeof(Service));
    Service.dwSize = sizeof(Service);
    Service.lpBlob = &blob;
    Service.dwNameSpace = NS_BTH;

    // Unpublish the service
    rc = WSASetService(&Service, RNRSERVICE_DELETE, 0);
    return rc;
}
```

SDP Records

The format of the SDP information that's published is so complex that Windows CE provides a special COM control to construct and deconstruct SDP records. Even with the control, parsing SDP records isn't easy. The first problem is knowing what's required in the SDP record. The information in the SDP record is defined by the Bluetooth specification, and a complete explanation of this data far exceeds the space available in this book for such an explanation.

As a shortcut, many Bluetooth applications compose a generic record, either hand-assembling the record or using an example tool named *BthNsCreate* that's provided in the Platform Builder. These hand-generated records are saved as a byte array in the application. The known offsets where the GUID and the RFCOMM channel are stored are known and are updated in the array at run time. The record is then published using *WSASetService*, as shown earlier.

The following code shows a routine that uses a canned SDP record with the GUID of the service and the channel stuffed into the appropriate places in the record.

```
int RegisterService (HWND hWnd, GUID *pguid, byte bChannel,
                     ULONG *pRecord) {
    // SDP dummy record
    // GUID goes at offset 8
    // Channel goes in last byte of record.
    static BYTE bSDPRecord[] = {
    0x35, 0x27, 0x09, 0x00, 0x01, 0x35, 0x11, 0x1C, 0x00, 0x00, 0x00,
    0x00, 0x00, 0x00, 0x00, 0x00, 0x00, 0x00, 0x00, 0x00, 0x00, 0x00,
    0x00, 0x00, 0x09, 0x00, 0x04, 0x35, 0x0C, 0x35, 0x03, 0x19, 0x01,
    0x00, 0x35, 0x05, 0x19, 0x00, 0x03, 0x08, 0x00};
```

```
    // Translate guid into net byte order for SDP record
    GUID *p = (GUID *)&bSDPRecord[8];
    p->Data1 = htonl (pguid->Data1);
    p->Data2 = htons (pguid->Data2);
    p->Data3 = htons (pguid->Data3);
    memcpy (p->Data4, pguid->Data4, sizeof (pguid->Data4));

    // Copy channel value into record
    bSDPRecord[sizeof (bSDPRecord)-1] = bChannel;

    return PublishRecord (hWnd, bSDPRecord, sizeof (bSDPRecord), pRecord);
}
```

Bluetooth Communication with Winsock

The hard part of Bluetooth communication is the setup. Once a service is published, the communication with remote devices is simple regardless of the method, Winsock or virtual COM port, used by the application.

As with IrDA, using Winsock to communicate over Bluetooth consists of implementing a client/server design with the server creating a socket that's bound to an address and a client that connects to the server socket by specifying the address and port of the server.

Server Side

A Bluetooth application providing a service first must set up a server routine that creates a socket and performs all the necessary calls to support the server side of a socket communication. The task starts with creating a socket with the standard socket call. The address format of the socket should be set to *AF_BT*, indicating a socket bound to the Bluetooth transport.

Once created, the socket needs to be bound with a call to bind. The following code shows a socket being created followed by a call to bind the socket. The address the socket is bound to is left blank, indicating that the system will provide the proper settings. The address format for the Bluetooth address used in the bind call is set to *AF_BT*.

```
// Open a bluetooth socket
s_sock = socket (AF_BT, SOCK_STREAM, BTHPROTO_RFCOMM);
if (s_sock == INVALID_SOCKET)
    return -1;

// Fill in address stuff
memset (&btaddr, 0, sizeof (btaddr));
btaddr.addressFamily = AF_BT;
btaddr.port = 0;    // Let driver assign a channel

// Bind to socket
rc = bind (s_sock, (struct sockaddr *)&btaddr, sizeof (btaddr));
if (rc) {
    closesocket (s_sock);
    return -2;
```

```
}
// Get information on the port assigned
len = sizeof (btaddr);
rc = getsockname (s_sock, (SOCKADDR *)&btaddr, &len);
if (rc) {
    closesocket (s_sock);
    return 0;
}
// Tell the world what we've bound to.
printf ("Addr %04x.%08x, port %d", GET_NAP(btaddr.btAddr),
    GET_SAP(btaddr.btAddr), btaddr.port)
```

Once the call to bind succeeds, the code calls *getsockname*, which fills in the details of the address of the device and, more important, the Bluetooth RFCOMM channel the socket was bound to. This RFCOMM channel is important since it will need to be published with the SDP record so that other devices will know which port to connect to when connecting to the service. The macros in the *printf* statement in the preceding code demonstrate the division of the Bluetooth device address into its two parts: the NAP, or nonsignificant address portion, and the SAP, or significant address portion.

Once the RFCOMM channel is known, the SDP record can be constructed and published as shown earlier in this section. The socket is then placed in listen mode, and a call to accept is made, which blocks until a client application socket connects to the address. When the client does connect, the accept call returns with the handle of a new socket that's connected with the client. This new socket is then used to communicate with the client device.

Client Side

On the client side, the task of connecting starts with device discovery. Once the Bluetooth address of the client is discovered, the client can create a thread that will communicate with the server. The process mirrors any socket-based client with calls to create the socket, and the client connects the socket to the remote server by specifying the address of the server. In the case of a Bluetooth client, the address of the server must include either the RFCOMM channel or the GUID of the service being connected to. In the following code, a client connects to a remote service knowing the remote device's Bluetooth address and the GUID of the client.

```
// Open a bluetooth socket
t_sock = socket (AF_BT, SOCK_STREAM, BTHPROTO_RFCOMM);
if (t_sock == INVALID_SOCKET)
    return 0;

// Fill in address stuff
memset (&btaddr, 0, sizeof (btaddr));
btaddr.btAddr = btaddrTarget;
btaddr.addressFamily = AF_BT;
btaddr.port = 0;   // Let driver assign a channel
memcpy (&btaddr.serviceClassId, &guidbthello, sizeof (GUID));
```

```
// Connect to remote socket
rc = connect (t_sock, (struct sockaddr *)&btaddr, sizeof (btaddr));
if (rc) {
    closesocket (t_sock);
    return -4;
}
// Connected...
```

After the client is connected, data can be exchanged with the server with the standard socket routines *send* and *recv.* When the conversation is concluded, both client and server should close their respective sockets with a call to *closesocket.*

Bluetooth Communication with Virtual COM Ports

If using Winsock for communication isn't to your liking, the Windows CE Bluetooth stack can also be accessed by using a serial driver that can be loaded. This method has a number of shortcomings, but some developers prefer it to using Winsock because of the familiarity of using a simple serial port compared with the complexity of Winsock. In any case, before I show you how to use the virtual serial port method, a few of the problems should be discussed.

The first problem is that the Bluetooth driver name is already the most used driver name in Windows CE. The Windows CE stream driver architecture is such that the operating system is limited to 10 instances of a given driver name in the standard namespace, such as COM or WAV. Since typically 2 to 4 instances of serial drivers are already in a Windows CE system, the available number of virtual COM ports is limited. Also, since the Bluetooth stack typically exposes some of its profiles through COM ports, the 2 to 4 number quickly increases to 6 to 8 ports, leaving only 2 to 4 *available* COM driver instances for Bluetooth applications that want to use virtual COM ports. An intrepid programmer could register the Bluetooth driver under a different name, such as BTC for Bluetooth COM, but this nonstandard name wouldn't be expected if it were to be passed on to other applications. Another option would be to use the bus driver-style driver naming, but here again this is unusual and wouldn't be expected.

The second problem is that although the virtual COM port method is used on a number of platforms, the implementation on Windows CE is unique. At least with the Winsock method, an application can be written to be fairly source-code compatible with the desktop. That isn't the case with the virtual COM port method.

Finally, creating COM ports using this method is accomplished using the *RegisterDevice* function. Although perfectly functional, this function has been deprecated for quite a while under newer versions of Windows CE. Drivers loaded with *RegisterDevice* aren't listed in the active device list maintained in the registry by the system. *RegisterDevice* requires that the application provide the index value for the driver being loaded. Because there's no simple method for determining which instance values are in use, the application must try all 10 instance values until one doesn't fail because it's used by another COM driver. Still, in some circumstances—when legacy support is needed, for example—using a virtual COM port is necessary.

Creating a virtual COM port is accomplished with the function *RegisterDevice*, which is prototyped as

```
HANDLE RegisterDevice (LPCWSTR lpszType, DWORD dwIndex, LPCWSTR lpszLib,
                       DWORD dwInfo);
```

The first parameter is a three-character name of the driver, such as COM or WAV. The second parameter is the instance value from 1 through 9, or 0 for instance 10. This value can't already be in use by another driver of the same name. The third parameter is the name of the DLL that implements the driver. The final parameter is a *DWORD* that's passed to the *Init* entry point of the driver.[4]

When used to load a Bluetooth virtual COM port, *RegisterDevice* is used as follows:

```
hDev = RegisterDevice (TEXT("COM"), dwIndex, TEXT("btd.dll"),
                       (DWORD) &pp);
```

where *pp* is the address of a *PORTEMUPortParams* structure defined as

```
typedef struct _portemu_port_params {
    int channel;
    int flocal;
    BD_ADDR device;
    int imtu;
    int iminmtu;
    int imaxmtu;
    int isendquota;
    int irecvquota;
    GUID uuidService;
    unsigned int uiportflags;
} PORTEMUPortParams;
```

The first field is the RFCOMM channel to be used for this port. If the channel is to be assigned automatically, the field can be set to *RFCOMM_CHANNEL_MULTIPLE*. The *fLocal* field should be set to *TRUE* for the server application and *FALSE* for the client application. The *device* field is used by client applications to specify the Bluetooth address of the remote server. This field must be 0 for server applications.

The next three parameters allow the application to specify the maximum transaction unit (MTU). The first field in this series, *imtu*, is the suggested value, while *iminmtu* is the minimum acceptable MTU and *imaxmtu* is the maximum acceptable MTU. If all three of these fields are 0, the driver uses default values for the MTU. The *isendquota* and *irecvquota* fields set the buffer sizes for send and receive operations. Setting these fields to 0 indicates that the driver should use the default values.

---

[4] *RegisterDevice* is a deprecated function but quite useful in this situation. In almost all other cases, an application would use *ActivateDevice* to load a driver.

The *uuidService* field is used by the client application to specify the service being connected to on the server. If the *channel* field is 0, this field must be set. If the *uuidService* is nonzero, the Bluetooth stack will perform an SDP search to determine the proper channel for the service. The actual SDP search will take place when the COM port is opened, not when it's loaded with *RegisterDevice*.

The *upportflags* field can contain a combination of the following flags:

- **RFCOMM_PORT_FLAGS_AUTHENTICATE** Perform authentication with the remote device when connecting.
- **RFCOMM_PORT_FLAGS_ENCRYPT** Encrypt the stream.
- **RFCOMM_PORT_FLAGS_REMOTE_DCB** When this flag is specified, changing the DCB settings of the port results in a negation with the peer device DCB settings.
- **RFCOMM_PORT_FLAGS_KEEP_DCD** If this flag is set, the emulated DCD line will always be set.

Server Side

As when using Winsock to talk to the Bluetooth stack, using virtual COM ports requires that one device be the server and the other the client. The server's responsibility includes loading the driver, opening the driver, determining the RFCOMM channel assigned to the port, and advertising the port using the SDP process discussed earlier.

The following code fragment demonstrates a server registering a virtual COM port driver. Notice that the routine makes multiple attempts at registering the driver, starting with instance value 9 and going down. Because the upper instance values are typically less used, this results in a quicker registration process. Notice that as soon as the registration loop completes, the code saves the instance value because that value forms the name of the driver. The driver name is then used to open the driver with *CreateFile*. Once the driver is opened, the server uses one of the two special I/O Control (IOCTL) commands available on a virtual COM port to query the RFCOMM channel. The server then calls its *RegisterService* routine to advertise the service through an SDP record.

```
//
// Server process for opening a virtual COM port
//
int i, rc;
PORTEMUPortParams pp;
TCHAR szDrvName[6];

memset (&pp, 0, sizeof (pp));
pp.channel = RFCOMM_CHANNEL_MULTIPLE;
pp.flocal = TRUE;
pp.uiportflags = 0;
```

```
// Find free instance number and load Bluetooth virt serial driver
for (i = 9; i >= 0; i--) {
    hDev = RegisterDevice (L"COM", i, L"btd.dll", (DWORD)&pp);
    if (hDev)
        break;
}
// See if driver registered
if (hDev == 0) return -1;

// Form the driver name and save it.
wsprintf (szDrvName, TEXT("COM%d:"), i);

// Open the driver
hDevOpen = CreateFile (szDrvName, GENERIC_READ | GENERIC_WRITE, 0,
                       NULL, OPEN_ALWAYS, 0, 0);
if (hDevOpen == INVALID_HANDLE_VALUE) {
    DeregisterDevice (hDev);
    return -2;
}
DWORD port = 0;
DWORD dwSizeOut;
rc = DeviceIoControl (hDevOpen, IOCTL_BLUETOOTH_GET_RFCOMM_CHANNEL,
                      NULL, 0, &port, sizeof(port), &dwSizeOut, NULL);
printf ("rc = %d Port value is %d", rc, port);

rc = RegisterService (hWnd, &guidbthello, (unsigned char) port, &hService);
```

The IOCTL command used in the preceding code, *IOCTL_BLUETOOTH_GET_RFCOMM_CHANNEL*, returns the RFCOMM channel of the COM port. For the call to *DeviceIoControl*, the output buffer points to a *DWORD* value that will receive the port number. The output buffer size must be set to the size of a *DWORD*. Once the port is determined, the routine simply calls the *RegisterService* routine, shown earlier in this chapter.

Client Side

The client side of the process is similar to the server side, with the exception that the client needs to know the Bluetooth address of the server and the GUID of the service on the server. Both of these parameters are specified in the *PORTEMUPortParams* structure when the device is registered. The following code shows the COM port initialization process from the client perspective.

```
//
// Client side
//
int i, rc;
PORTEMUPortParams pp;
TCHAR szDrvName[6];

int nDevs2 = MAX_DEVICES;
MYBTDEVICE btd2[MAX_DEVICES];
```

```
// Find the server's Bluetooth address
rc = FindDevices (btaServ);
if (rc) return -1;

memset (&pp, 0, sizeof (pp));
pp.channel = 0;
pp.flocal = FALSE;
pp.device = btaServ;
pp.uuidService = guidbtService;
pp.uiportflags = 0;

// Find free instance number and load Bluetooth virt serial driver
for (i = 9; i >= 0; i--) {
    hDev = RegisterDevice (L"COM", i, L"btd.dll", (DWORD)&pp);
    if (hDev)
        break;
}
// See if driver registered
if (hDev == 0) return -1;

// Form the driver name and save it.
wsprintf (szDrvName, TEXT("COM%d:"), i);

// Open the driver
hDevOpen = CreateFile (szDrvName, GENERIC_READ | GENERIC_WRITE, 0,
                       NULL, OPEN_ALWAYS, 0, 0);
if (hDevOpen == INVALID_HANDLE_VALUE) {
    DeregisterDevice (hDev);
    return -2;
}
BT_ADDR bt;
DWORD dwSizeOut;
rc = DeviceIoControl (hDevOpen, IOCTL_BLUETOOTH_GET_PEER_DEVICE,
                      NULL, 0, &bt, sizeof(bt), &dwSizeOut, NULL);
printf ("Connection detected with %04x%08x\r\n", GET_NAP(bt), GET_SAP(bt));
```

Notice the use of the second IOCTL command provided for Bluetooth support, *IOCTL_BLUETOOTH_GET_PEER_DEVICE*. This command returns the Bluetooth address of the device on the other end of the connected virtual serial port.

Communication between the client and the server is accomplished through the standard Win32 file functions *ReadFile* and *WriteFile*. When the conversation has been concluded, the driver should be closed with a call to *CloseHandle* and the driver unloaded with a call to *DeregisterDevice*, prototyped here:

```
BOOL DeregisterDevice (HANDLE hDevice);
```

The only parameter is the handle returned by *RegisterDevice*.

The BtSquirt Example Program

The BtSquirt example demonstrates a fairly complete Bluetooth application that can act as both a client and a server. *BtSquirt* must be running on two Windows CE devices that use the Windows CE Bluetooth stack for it to work. When started, BtSquirt searches for other Bluetooth devices in the area and lists them in the device list. The user can then select a destination device and send a file to it by clicking Send. BtSquirt connects to the *BtSquirt* service on the other device. Once connected, the client sends filename, file size, and then the file data. After the file transfer is complete, *BtSquirt* closes the connection. The server reads the file information and saves the file in the root directory of the device. Figure 14-3 shows the BtSquirt example after it has received the message from the other device.

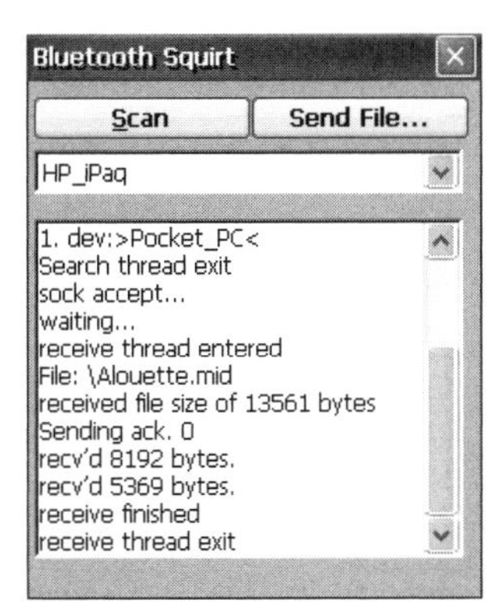

FIGURE 14-3 The BtSquirt example after it has received a message from another device

The source code for BtSquirt is shown in Listing 14-2. The application is a simple dialog-based application. The source code is divided into two .cpp files and their associated include files: BtSquirt.cpp, which contains the majority of the source code; and MyBtUtil.cpp, which contains handy Bluetooth routines for finding devices and for registering service GUIDs with the SDP service.

LISTING 14-2

MyBtUtil.rc

```
//======================================================================
// Resource file
//
// Written for the book Programming Windows CE
// Copyright (C) 2007 Douglas Boling
//======================================================================

#include "windows.h"
#include "BtSquirt.h"                        // Program-specific stuff

//----------------------------------------------------------------------
```

```
// Icons and bitmaps
//
ID_ICON ICON   "BtSquirt.ico"                  // Program icon

//----------------------------------------------------------------------
// Main window dialog template
//
btsquirt DIALOG discardable 10, 10, 135, 150
STYLE  WS_OVERLAPPED | WS_VISIBLE | WS_CAPTION | WS_SYSMENU |
       DS_CENTER | DS_MODALFRAME
CAPTION "Bluetooth Squirt"
CLASS "btsquirt"
BEGIN
    PUSHBUTTON "Send File..."IDD_SENDFILE, 67,   5,  65,  12, WS_TABSTOP
    PUSHBUTTON "&Scan"          IDD_SCAN,   2,   5,  65,  12, WS_TABSTOP

    COMBOBOX                 IDD_DEVICES,   2,  20, 128, 100,
                                            WS_TABSTOP | WS_VSCROLL

    LISTBOX                   IDD_INTEXT,   2,  40, 128, 100,
                                            WS_TABSTOP | WS_VSCROLL
END
```

MyBtUtil.h

```
//======================================================================
// Header file
//
// Written for the book Programming Windows CE
// Copyright (C) 2007 Douglas Boling
//======================================================================

#ifndef _MYBTUTIL_H_
#define _MYBTUTIL_H_

#if defined (__cplusplus)
extern "C" {
#endif

typedef struct {
    TCHAR szName[256];
    BT_ADDR btaddr;
} MYBTDEVICE, *PMYBTDEVICE;

// Finds Bluetooth devices
int FindDevices (PMYBTDEVICE pbtDev, int *pnDevs);

// Registers a BT service
int RegisterBtService (GUID *pguid, byte bChannel,
                       ULONG *pRecord);
```

```
// Clears a BT service from the SDP database
int UnregisterBtService (HWND hWnd, ULONG hRecord);

#if defined (__cplusplus)
}
#endif

#endif // _MYBTUTIL_H_
```

MyBtUtil.cpp

```
//======================================================================
// MyBtUtil - Handy Bluetooth routines
//
// Written for the book Programming Windows CE
// Copyright (C) 2007 Douglas Boling
//======================================================================
#include <windows.h>
#include <winsock2.h>
#include <ws2bth.h>
#include <bthapi.h>

#include "MyBtUtil.h"

// Returns number of elements
#define dim(x) (sizeof(x) / sizeof(x[0]))

#define MYBUFFSIZE      16384
//----------------------------------------------------------------------
// FindDevices - Find devices in range.
//
int FindDevices (PMYBTDEVICE pbtDev, int *pnDevs) {
    DWORD dwFlags, dwLen;
    HANDLE hLookup;
    int i, rc, nMax = *pnDevs;
    *pnDevs = 0;

    // Create inquiry blob to limit time of search
    BTHNS_INQUIRYBLOB inqblob;
    memset (&inqblob, 0, sizeof (inqblob));
    inqblob.LAP = BT_ADDR_GIAC;  // Default GIAC
    inqblob.length = 4;          // 4 * 1.28 = 5 seconds
    inqblob.num_responses = nMax;

    // Create blob to point to inquiry blob
    BLOB blob;
    blob.cbSize = sizeof (BTHNS_INQUIRYBLOB);
    blob.pBlobData = (PBYTE)&inqblob;

    // Init query
    WSAQUERYSET QuerySet;
```

```
    memset(&QuerySet,0,sizeof(WSAQUERYSET));
    QuerySet.dwSize      = sizeof(WSAQUERYSET);
    QuerySet.dwNameSpace = NS_BTH;
    QuerySet.lpBlob      = &blob;

    // Start query for devices
    rc = WSALookupServiceBegin (&QuerySet, LUP_CONTAINERS, &hLookup);
    if (rc) return rc;

    PBYTE pOut = (PBYTE)LocalAlloc (LPTR, MYBUFFSIZE);
    if (!pOut) return -1;
    WSAQUERYSET *pQueryResult = (WSAQUERYSET *)pOut;

    for (i = 0; i < nMax; i++) {
        dwLen = MYBUFFSIZE;
        dwFlags = LUP_RETURN_NAME | LUP_RETURN_ADDR;
        rc = WSALookupServiceNext (hLookup, dwFlags, &dwLen, pQueryResult);
        if (rc == SOCKET_ERROR) {
            rc = GetLastError();
            break;
        }
        // Copy device name
      if (pQueryResult->lpszServiceInstanceName)
         StringCchCopy (pbtDev[i].szName, dim (pbtDev[i].szName),
                        pQueryResult->lpszServiceInstanceName);
      else
         pbtDev[i].szName[0] = TEXT('\0');
        // Copy bluetooth device address
        SOCKADDR_BTH *pbta;
        pbta = (SOCKADDR_BTH *)
                   pQueryResult->lpcsaBuffer->RemoteAddr.lpSockaddr;
        pbtDev[i].btaddr = pbta->btAddr;
    }
    if (rc == WSA_E_NO_MORE) rc = 0;
    *pnDevs = i;
    WSALookupServiceEnd (hLookup);
    LocalFree (pOut);
    return rc;
}
//----------------------------------------------------------------------
// PublishRecord - Helper routine that actually does the registering
// of the SDP record.
//
int PublishRecord (PBYTE pSDPRec, int nRecSize, ULONG *pRecord) {
    BTHNS_SETBLOB *pSetBlob;
    ULONG ulSdpVersion = BTH_SDP_VERSION;
    int rc;

    // Zero out the record handle that will be returned by the call
    *pRecord = 0;

    // Allocate and init the SetBlob
    pSetBlob = (BTHNS_SETBLOB *)LocalAlloc (LPTR,
                                    sizeof (BTHNS_SETBLOB) + nRecSize-1);
```

```
    if (!pSetBlob) return -1;

    pSetBlob->pRecordHandle = pRecord;
    pSetBlob->pSdpVersion = &ulSdpVersion;
    pSetBlob->fSecurity = 0;
    pSetBlob->fOptions = 0;
    pSetBlob->ulRecordLength = nRecSize;
    memcpy (pSetBlob->pRecord, pSDPRec, nRecSize);

    // Init the container blob
    BLOB blob;
    blob.cbSize    = sizeof(BTHNS_SETBLOB) + nRecSize - 1;
    blob.pBlobData = (PBYTE) pSetBlob;

    // Init the WSAQuerySet struct
    WSAQUERYSET Service;
    memset (&Service, 0, sizeof(Service));
    Service.dwSize = sizeof(Service);
    Service.lpBlob = &blob;
    Service.dwNameSpace = NS_BTH;

    // Publish the service
    rc = WSASetService(&Service, RNRSERVICE_REGISTER, 0);
    if (rc == SOCKET_ERROR)
        rc = GetLastError();

    // Clean up
    LocalFree ((PBYTE)pSetBlob);
    return rc;
}
//----------------------------------------------------------------------
// UnregisterBtService - Remove service from SDP database
//
int UnregisterBtService (HWND hWnd, ULONG hRecord) {
    ULONG ulSdpVersion = BTH_SDP_VERSION;
    int rc;

    BTHNS_SETBLOB SetBlob;
    memset (&SetBlob, 0, sizeof (SetBlob));
    SetBlob.pRecordHandle = &hRecord;
    SetBlob.pSdpVersion = &ulSdpVersion;

    // Init the container blob
    BLOB blob;
    blob.cbSize = sizeof(BTHNS_SETBLOB);
    blob.pBlobData = (PBYTE) &SetBlob;

    // Init the WSAQuerySet struct
    WSAQUERYSET Service;
    memset (&Service, 0, sizeof(Service));
    Service.dwSize = sizeof(Service);
    Service.lpBlob = &blob;
    Service.dwNameSpace = NS_BTH;
```

```
    // Unpublish the service
    rc = WSASetService(&Service, RNRSERVICE_DELETE, 0);
    if (rc == SOCKET_ERROR)
        rc = GetLastError();
    return rc;
}
//----------------------------------------------------------------------
// RegisterBtService - Registers a service with a guid and RFChannel
//
int RegisterBtService (GUID *pguid, byte bChannel, ULONG *pRecord) {

    // SDP dummy record
    // GUID goes at offset 8
    // Channel goes in last byte of record.
    static BYTE bSDPRecord[] = {
    0x35, 0x27, 0x09, 0x00, 0x01, 0x35, 0x11, 0x1C, 0x00, 0x00, 0x00,
    0x00, 0x00, 0x00, 0x00, 0x00, 0x00, 0x00, 0x00, 0x00, 0x00, 0x00,
    0x00, 0x00, 0x09, 0x00, 0x04, 0x35, 0x0C, 0x35, 0x03, 0x19, 0x01,
    0x00, 0x35, 0x05, 0x19, 0x00, 0x03, 0x08, 0x00};

    // Update the SDP record

    // Translate guid into net byte order for SDP record
    GUID *p = (GUID *)&bSDPRecord[8];
    p->Data1 = htonl (pguid->Data1);
    p->Data2 = htons (pguid->Data2);
    p->Data3 = htons (pguid->Data3);
    memcpy (p->Data4, pguid->Data4, sizeof (pguid->Data4));

    // Copy channel value into record
    bSDPRecord[sizeof (bSDPRecord)-1] = bChannel;

    return PublishRecord (bSDPRecord, sizeof (bSDPRecord), pRecord);
}
```

BtSquirt.h

```
//======================================================================
// Header file
//
// Written for the book Programming Windows CE
// Copyright (C) 2007 Douglas Boling
//======================================================================
// Returns number of elements
#define dim(x) (sizeof(x) / sizeof(x[0]))

// Windows CE Specific defines
#define LPCMDLINE LPWSTR

//----------------------------------------------------------------------
```

```
// Generic defines and data types
//
struct decodeUINT {                               // Structure associates
    UINT Code;                                    // messages
                                                  // with a function.
    LRESULT (*Fxn)(HWND, UINT, WPARAM, LPARAM);
};
struct decodeCMD {                                // Structure associates
    UINT Code;                                    // menu IDs with a
    LRESULT (*Fxn)(HWND, WORD, HWND, WORD);       // function.
};

//----------------------------------------------------------------------
// Defines used by application

typedef struct {
   HANDLE hFile;
   int nDevice;
   TCHAR szName[MAX_PATH];
} SENDTHSTRUCT, *PSENDTHSTRUCT;

#define  ID_ICON            1

#define  IDD_INTEXT         10                    // Control IDs
#define  IDD_SENDFILE       11
#define  IDD_SCAN           12
#define  IDD_DEVICES        13

// Error codes used by transfer protocol
#define BAD_TEXTLEN         -1
#define BAD_SOCKET          -2

#define MYMSG_ENABLESEND    (WM_USER+1000)
#define MYMSG_PRINTF        (WM_USER+1001)
#define MYMSG_NEWDEV        (WM_USER+1002)

// Error codes used by transfer protocol
#define GOOD_XFER       0
#define BAD_FILEOPEN    -1
#define BAD_FILEMEM     -2
#define BAD_FILEREAD    -3
#define BAD_FILEWRITE   -3
#define BAD_SOCKETRECV  -5
#define BAD_FILESIZE    -6
#define BAD_MEMORY      -7

#define BLKSIZE         8192                      // Transfer block size
#define BUFFSIZE        8192                      // Buff size (>=BLKSIZE)

//----------------------------------------------------------------------
// Function prototypes
//
HWND InitInstance (HINSTANCE, LPCMDLINE, int);
int TermInstance (HINSTANCE, int);
```

```
void Add2List (HWND hWnd, LPTSTR lpszFormat, ...);

// Window procedures
LRESULT CALLBACK MainWndProc (HWND, UINT, WPARAM, LPARAM);

// Message handlers
LRESULT DoCreateMain (HWND, UINT, WPARAM, LPARAM);
LRESULT DoSizeMain (HWND, UINT, WPARAM, LPARAM);
LRESULT DoCharMain (HWND, UINT, WPARAM, LPARAM);
LRESULT DoCommandMain (HWND, UINT, WPARAM, LPARAM);
LRESULT DoPocketPCShell (HWND, UINT, WPARAM, LPARAM);
LRESULT DoDestroyMain (HWND, UINT, WPARAM, LPARAM);
LRESULT DoEnableSendMain (HWND, UINT, WPARAM, LPARAM);
LRESULT DoPrintfNotifyMain (HWND, UINT, WPARAM, LPARAM);
LRESULT DoAddDeviceMain (HWND, UINT, WPARAM, LPARAM);

// Command functions
LPARAM DoMainCommandSend (HWND, WORD, HWND, WORD);
LPARAM DoMainCommandExit (HWND, WORD, HWND, WORD);
LPARAM DoMainCommandScan (HWND, WORD, HWND, WORD);

// Thread functions
DWORD WINAPI SearchThread (PVOID pArg);
DWORD WINAPI ServerThread (PVOID pArg);
DWORD WINAPI ReceiveThread (PVOID pArg);
DWORD WINAPI SendFileThread (PVOID pArg);
```

BtSquirt.cpp

```
//======================================================================
// BtSquirt - A demonstration of a Bluetooth application
//
// Written for the book Programming Windows CE
// Copyright (C) 2007 Douglas Boling
//======================================================================
#include <windows.h>                 // For all that Windows stuff
#include <commdlg.h>                 // For common dialogs
#include <winsock2.h>                // Socket functions
#include <ws2bth.h>                  // Bluetooth extensions
#include <Msgqueue.h>
#include <aygshell.h>                // Add WinMobile includes

#include "BtSquirt.h"                // Program-specific stuff
#include "MyBTUtil.h"                // My Bluetooth routines

#pragma comment( lib, "aygshell" )   // Link WinMobile lib for menubar
#pragma comment( lib, "ws2" )        // Link WinSock 2.0 lib
#if defined(WIN32_PLATFORM_PSPC) || defined(WIN32_PLATFORM_WFSP)
#include <bthutil.h>                 // Bluetooth Util API
#pragma comment( lib, "bthutil")     // Link BT util lib
#endif
```

```
//----------------------------------------------------------------------
// Global data
//
const TCHAR szAppName[] = TEXT ("BtSquirt");
TCHAR szTitleText[128];

// Be sure to create your own GUID with GuidGen!
// {23EABC54-6923-480c-AC59-CDD83C154D87}
static GUID guidBtSquirt =
{ 0x23eabc54, 0x6923, 0x480c, { 0xac, 0x59, 0xcd, 0xd8,
                                0x3c, 0x15, 0x4d, 0x87 } };

HINSTANCE hInst;                     // Program instance handle
HWND hMain;                          // Main window handle
BOOL fContinue = TRUE;               // Server thread cont. flag
BOOL fFirstSize = TRUE;              // First WM_SIZE flag after lb
BOOL fFirstTime = TRUE;              // First WM_SIZE flag
SOCKET s_sock;

#if defined(WIN32_PLATFORM_PSPC) && (_WIN32_WCE >= 300)
SHACTIVATEINFO sai;                  // Needed for PPC helper funcs
#endif

HANDLE hQRead = 0;                   // Used for thread safe print
HANDLE hQWrite = 0;
CRITICAL_SECTION csPrintf;

#define MAX_DEVICES  32
MYBTDEVICE btd[MAX_DEVICES];         // List of BT devices
int nDevs = 0;                       // Count of BT devices

// Message dispatch table for MainWindowProc
const struct decodeUINT MainMessages[] = {
    WM_CREATE, DoCreateMain,
    WM_SIZE, DoSizeMain,
    WM_CHAR, DoCharMain,
    WM_COMMAND, DoCommandMain,
    MYMSG_ENABLESEND, DoEnableSendMain,
    MYMSG_PRINTF, DoPrintfNotifyMain,
    MYMSG_NEWDEV, DoAddDeviceMain,
    WM_SETTINGCHANGE, DoPocketPCShell,
    WM_ACTIVATE, DoPocketPCShell,
    WM_DESTROY, DoDestroyMain,
};
// Command Message dispatch for MainWindowProc
const struct decodeCMD MainCommandItems[] = {
#if defined(WIN32_PLATFORM_PSPC) || defined(WIN32_PLATFORM_WFSP)
    IDOK, DoMainCommandExit,
#else
    IDOK, DoMainCommandSend,
#endif
    IDCANCEL, DoMainCommandExit,
    IDD_SENDFILE, DoMainCommandSend,
    IDD_SCAN, DoMainCommandScan,
```

```
};
//======================================================================
// Program entry point
//
int WINAPI WinMain (HINSTANCE hInstance, HINSTANCE hPrevInstance,
                    LPCMDLINE lpCmdLine, int nCmdShow) {
    MSG msg;
    int rc = 0;

    // Initialize this instance.
    hMain = InitInstance (hInstance, lpCmdLine, nCmdShow);
    if (hMain == 0)
        return TermInstance (hInstance, 0x10);

    // Application message loop
    while (GetMessage (&msg, NULL, 0, 0)) {
        if ((hMain == 0) || !IsDialogMessage (hMain, &msg)) {
            TranslateMessage (&msg);
            DispatchMessage (&msg);
        }
    }
    // Instance cleanup
    return TermInstance (hInstance, msg.wParam);
}
//----------------------------------------------------------------------
// InitInstance - Instance initialization
//
HWND InitInstance (HINSTANCE hInstance, LPCMDLINE lpCmdLine,
                   int nCmdShow){
    WNDCLASS wc;
    HWND hWnd;
    HANDLE hThread;
    int rc;

    hInst = hInstance;                // Save program instance handle.

    // For all systems, if previous instance, activate it instead of us.
    hWnd = FindWindow (szAppName, NULL);
    if (hWnd) {
        SetForegroundWindow ((HWND)((DWORD)hWnd | 0x01));
        return 0;
    }
    // Init Winsock
    WSADATA wsaData;
    rc = WSAStartup (0x0202, &wsaData);
    if (rc) {
        MessageBox (NULL,TEXT("Error in WSAStartup"), szAppName, MB_OK);
        return 0;
    }
    InitializeCriticalSection (&csPrintf);

    // Create message queue.  First for read access
    MSGQUEUEOPTIONS mqo;
    mqo.dwSize = sizeof (mqo);
```

```
    mqo.dwFlags = MSGQUEUE_ALLOW_BROKEN;
    mqo.dwMaxMessages = 16;
    mqo.cbMaxMessage = 512;
    mqo.bReadAccess = TRUE;
    hQRead = CreateMsgQueue (NULL, &mqo);
    // Open it again for write access
    mqo.bReadAccess = FALSE;
    hQWrite = OpenMsgQueue (GetCurrentProcess(), hQRead, &mqo);

    // Register application main window class.
    wc.style = 0;                                // Window style
    wc.lpfnWndProc = MainWndProc;                // Callback function
    wc.cbClsExtra = 0;                           // Extra class data
    wc.cbWndExtra = DLGWINDOWEXTRA;              // Extra window data
    wc.hInstance = hInstance;                    // Owner handle
    wc.hIcon = NULL;                             // Application icon
    wc.hCursor = LoadCursor (NULL, IDC_ARROW);// Default cursor
    wc.hbrBackground = (HBRUSH) GetStockObject (LTGRAY_BRUSH);
    wc.lpszMenuName =  NULL;                     // Menu name
    wc.lpszClassName = szAppName;                // Window class name

    if (RegisterClass (&wc) == 0) return 0;

    // Create main window.
    hWnd = CreateDialog (hInst, szAppName, NULL, NULL);

    // Return fail code if window not created.
    if (!IsWindow (hWnd)) return 0;

    GetWindowText (hWnd, szTitleText, dim (szTitleText));

#if defined(WIN32_PLATFORM_PSPC) || defined(WIN32_PLATFORM_WFSP)
    // See if Bluetooth radio on.
    DWORD dwBTStatus;
    rc = BthGetMode (&dwBTStatus);
    if (rc != ERROR_SUCCESS)
        Add2List (hWnd, TEXT("Error querying BT radio status %d"),
                  GetLastError());
    else {
        if (dwBTStatus == BTH_POWER_OFF) {
            rc = MessageBox (hWnd,
                         TEXT("The Bluetooth radio is currently off. ")
                         TEXT("do you want to turn it on?"), szAppName,
                         MB_YESNO);
            if (rc == IDYES) {
                BthSetMode (BTH_DISCOVERABLE);  // Make discoverable
                BthGetMode (&dwBTStatus);       // Update status
            }
        }
        if (dwBTStatus == BTH_POWER_OFF)
            Add2List (hWnd, TEXT("Bluetooth radio *** off ***"));
        else if (dwBTStatus == BTH_CONNECTABLE)
            Add2List (hWnd, TEXT("Bluetooth radio on, not discoverable!"));
```

```
        else if (dwBTStatus == BTH_DISCOVERABLE)
            Add2List (hWnd, TEXT("Bluetooth radio on and discoverable"));

    }
#endif
    // Create secondary thread for server function.
    hThread = CreateThread (NULL, 0, ServerThread, hWnd, 0, 0);
    if (hThread == 0) {
        DestroyWindow (hWnd);
        return 0;
    }
    CloseHandle (hThread);

    // Post a message to have device discovery start
    PostMessage (hWnd, WM_COMMAND, MAKEWPARAM (IDD_SCAN, BN_CLICKED),0);

    ShowWindow (hWnd, nCmdShow);      // Standard show and update calls
    UpdateWindow (hWnd);
    SetFocus (GetDlgItem (hWnd, IDD_SENDFILE));
    return hWnd;
}
//----------------------------------------------------------------------
// TermInstance - Program cleanup
//
int TermInstance (HINSTANCE hInstance, int nDefRC) {
    WSACleanup ();
    Sleep (0);
    CloseMsgQueue (hQRead);
    CloseMsgQueue (hQWrite);
    return nDefRC;
}
//======================================================================
// Message handling procedures for main window
//----------------------------------------------------------------------
// MainWndProc - Callback function for application window
//
LRESULT CALLBACK MainWndProc (HWND hWnd, UINT wMsg, WPARAM wParam,
                              LPARAM lParam) {
    INT i;
    //
    // Search message list to see if we need to handle this
    // message.  If in list, call procedure.
    //
    for (i = 0; i < dim(MainMessages); i++) {
        if (wMsg == MainMessages[i].Code)
            return (*MainMessages[i].Fxn)(hWnd, wMsg, wParam, lParam);
    }
    return DefWindowProc (hWnd, wMsg, wParam, lParam);
}
//----------------------------------------------------------------------
// DoCreateMain - Process WM_CREATE message for window.
//
LRESULT DoCreateMain (HWND hWnd, UINT wMsg, WPARAM wParam,
                      LPARAM lParam) {
```

```
#if defined(WIN32_PLATFORM_PSPC) || defined(WIN32_PLATFORM_WFSP)
    SHINITDLGINFO shidi;
    SHMENUBARINFO mbi;                      // For Pocket PC, create
    memset(&mbi, 0, sizeof(SHMENUBARINFO)); // menu bar so that we
    mbi.cbSize = sizeof(SHMENUBARINFO);     // have a sip button
    mbi.dwFlags = SHCMBF_EMPTYBAR;
    mbi.hwndParent = hWnd;
    SHCreateMenuBar(&mbi);
    SendMessage(mbi.hwndMB, SHCMBM_GETSUBMENU, 0, 100);

    // For Pocket PC, make dialog box full screen with PPC
    // specific call.
    shidi.dwMask = SHIDIM_FLAGS;
    shidi.dwFlags = SHIDIF_DONEBUTTON | SHIDIF_SIZEDLG | SHIDIF_SIPDOWN;
    shidi.hDlg = hWnd;
    SHInitDialog(&shidi);

    sai.cbSize = sizeof (sai);
    SHHandleWMSettingChange(hWnd, wParam, lParam, &sai);
#endif
    return 0;
}
//----------------------------------------------------------------------
// DoCharMain - Process WM_CHAR message for window.
//
LRESULT DoCharMain (HWND hWnd, UINT wMsg, WPARAM wParam,
                    LPARAM lParam) {

    if (wParam == '1')
        PostMessage (hWnd, WM_COMMAND, MAKELONG (IDD_SCAN, 0),
                     (LPARAM)GetDlgItem (hWnd, IDD_SCAN));
    else if (wParam == '2')
        PostMessage (hWnd, WM_COMMAND, MAKELONG (IDD_SENDFILE, 0),
                     (LPARAM)GetDlgItem (hWnd, IDD_SENDFILE));
    else if (wParam == '9')
        PostMessage (hWnd, WM_COMMAND, MAKELONG (IDCANCEL, 0),
                     (LPARAM)GetDlgItem (hWnd, IDCANCEL));
    return 0;
}
//----------------------------------------------------------------------
// DoSizeMain - Process WM_SIZE message for window.
//
LRESULT DoSizeMain (HWND hWnd, UINT wMsg, WPARAM wParam,
                    LPARAM lParam) {

#if defined(WIN32_PLATFORM_PSPC)
    static RECT rectListbox;
    RECT rect;

    GetClientRect (hWnd, &rect);
    if (fFirstTime) {
        // First time through, get the position of the listbox for
        // resizeing later.  Store the distance from the sides of
        // the listbox control to the side of the parent window
```

```
            if (IsWindow (GetDlgItem (hWnd, IDD_INTEXT))) {
                GetWindowRect (GetDlgItem (hWnd, IDD_INTEXT), &rectListbox);
                MapWindowPoints (HWND_DESKTOP, hWnd, (LPPOINT)&rectListbox,2);
                rectListbox.right = rect.right - rectListbox.right;
                rectListbox.bottom = rect.bottom - rectListbox.bottom;

                SetWindowPos (GetDlgItem (hWnd, IDD_INTEXT), 0, rect.left+5,
                              rectListbox.top, rect.right-10,
                              rect.bottom - rectListbox.top - 5,
                              SWP_NOZORDER);
                fFirstTime = FALSE;
            }
        }
#endif
    if (fFirstSize) {
        EnableWindow (GetDlgItem (hWnd, IDD_SENDFILE), FALSE);
        EnableWindow (GetDlgItem (hWnd, IDD_SCAN), FALSE);
        fFirstSize = FALSE;
    }
    //SetFocus (hWnd);
    return 0;
}
//----------------------------------------------------------------------
// DoCommandMain - Process WM_COMMAND message for window.
//
LRESULT DoCommandMain (HWND hWnd, UINT wMsg, WPARAM wParam,
                       LPARAM lParam) {
    WORD idItem, wNotifyCode;
    HWND hwndCtl;
    INT i;

    // Parse the parameters.
    idItem = (WORD) LOWORD (wParam);
    wNotifyCode = (WORD) HIWORD (wParam);
    hwndCtl = (HWND) lParam;

    // Call routine to handle control message.
    for (i = 0; i < dim(MainCommandItems); i++) {
        if (idItem == MainCommandItems[i].Code)
            return (*MainCommandItems[i].Fxn)(hWnd, idItem, hwndCtl,
                                              wNotifyCode);
    }
    return 0;
}
//----------------------------------------------------------------------
// DoEnableSendMain - Process user message to enable send button
//
LRESULT DoEnableSendMain (HWND hWnd, UINT wMsg, WPARAM wParam,
                          LPARAM lParam) {
    int i;
    EnableWindow (GetDlgItem (hWnd, IDD_SENDFILE), lParam);
    EnableWindow (GetDlgItem (hWnd, IDD_SCAN), TRUE);
    i = (int)SendDlgItemMessage (hWnd, IDD_DEVICES, CB_GETCURSEL, 0, 0);
```

```
    if (i == -1)
        SendDlgItemMessage (hWnd, IDD_DEVICES, CB_SETCURSEL, 0, 0);
    SetWindowText (hWnd, szTitleText);
    return 0;
}
//----------------------------------------------------------------------
// DoAddDeviceMain - Process user message to add to device list
//
LRESULT DoAddDeviceMain (HWND hWnd, UINT wMsg, WPARAM wParam,
                         LPARAM lParam) {
    SendDlgItemMessage (hWnd, IDD_DEVICES, CB_ADDSTRING, 0, lParam);
    return 0;
}
//----------------------------------------------------------------------
// DoPrintfNotifyMain - Process printf notify message
//
LRESULT DoPrintfNotifyMain (HWND hWnd, UINT wMsg, WPARAM wParam,
                            LPARAM lParam) {
    TCHAR szBuffer[512];
    int rc;
    DWORD dwLen = 0;
    DWORD dwFlags = 0;

    memset (szBuffer, 0, sizeof (szBuffer));
    rc = ReadMsgQueue (hQRead, (LPBYTE)szBuffer, sizeof (szBuffer),
                       &dwLen, 0, &dwFlags);
    if (rc) {
        if (dwFlags & MSGQUEUE_MSGALERT)
            SetWindowText (hWnd, szBuffer);
        else {
            rc = SendDlgItemMessage (hWnd, IDD_INTEXT, LB_ADDSTRING, 0,
                                     (LPARAM)(LPCTSTR)szBuffer);
            if (rc != LB_ERR)
                SendDlgItemMessage (hWnd, IDD_INTEXT, LB_SETTOPINDEX,rc,
                                     (LPARAM)(LPCTSTR)szBuffer);
        }
    }
    return 0;
}
//----------------------------------------------------------------------
// DoPocketPCShell - Process Pocket PC required messages
//
LRESULT DoPocketPCShell (HWND hWnd, UINT wMsg, WPARAM wParam,
                         LPARAM lParam) {
#if defined(WIN32_PLATFORM_PSPC)
    if (wMsg == WM_SETTINGCHANGE)
        return SHHandleWMSettingChange(hWnd, wParam, lParam, &sai);
    if (wMsg == WM_ACTIVATE)
        return SHHandleWMActivate(hWnd, wParam, lParam, &sai, 0);
#endif
    return 0;
}
//----------------------------------------------------------------------
// DoDestroyMain - Process WM_DESTROY message for window.
```

```
//
LRESULT DoDestroyMain (HWND hWnd, UINT wMsg, WPARAM wParam,
                       LPARAM lParam) {
    fContinue = FALSE;                          // Shut down server thread.
    closesocket (s_sock);
    Sleep (0);                                  // Pass on timeslice.
    PostQuitMessage (0);
    return 0;
}
//======================================================================
// Command handler routines
//----------------------------------------------------------------------
// DoMainCommandExit - Process Program Exit command.
//
LPARAM DoMainCommandExit (HWND hWnd, WORD idItem, HWND hwndCtl,
                          WORD wNotifyCode) {

    SendMessage (hWnd, WM_CLOSE, 0, 0);
    return 0;
}
//----------------------------------------------------------------------
// DoMainCommandSend - Process Program Send File command.
//
LPARAM DoMainCommandSend (HWND hWnd, WORD idItem, HWND hwndCtl,
                          WORD wNotifyCode) {
    const LPTSTR pszOpenFilter = TEXT ("All Documents (*.*)\0*.*\0\0");
    OPENFILENAME of;
    HANDLE hTh;

    PSENDTHSTRUCT psfs = (PSENDTHSTRUCT) malloc (sizeof (SENDTHSTRUCT));
    if (psfs == 0) {
        Add2List (hWnd, TEXT("Out of memory."));
        return 0;
    }

    memset (&of, 0, sizeof (of));
    of.lStructSize = sizeof (of);
    of.lpstrTitle = TEXT("Select file to send");
    of.lpstrFile = psfs->szName;
    of.nMaxFile = dim (psfs->szName);
    of.lpstrFilter = pszOpenFilter;
    if (!GetOpenFileName (&of))
        return 0;

    // Open the file.
    psfs->hFile = CreateFile (psfs->szName, GENERIC_READ,
                              FILE_SHARE_READ, NULL, OPEN_EXISTING,
                              0, NULL);
    if (psfs->hFile == INVALID_HANDLE_VALUE) {
        Add2List (hWnd, TEXT("File open failed. rc %d"),
                  GetLastError());
        return -1;
    }
```

```
    psfs->nDevice = (int)SendDlgItemMessage (hWnd, IDD_DEVICES,
                                             CB_GETCURSEL, 0, 0);
    // Send the file on another thread.
    hTh = CreateThread (NULL, 0, SendFileThread, (PVOID)psfs, 0, NULL);
    CloseHandle (hTh);
    return 0;
}
//----------------------------------------------------------------------
// DoMainCommandScan - Process Device Scan command.
//
LPARAM DoMainCommandScan (HWND hWnd, WORD idItem, HWND hwndCtl,
                          WORD wNotifyCode) {
    HANDLE hTh;
    SetWindowText (hWnd, TEXT("Scanning..."));
    EnableWindow (GetDlgItem (hWnd, IDD_SENDFILE), FALSE);
    EnableWindow (GetDlgItem (hWnd, IDD_SCAN), FALSE);
    SendDlgItemMessage (hWnd, IDD_DEVICES, CB_RESETCONTENT, 0, 0);
    hTh = CreateThread (NULL, 0, SearchThread, (PVOID)hWnd, 0, NULL);
    CloseHandle (hTh);
    return 0;
}
//----------------------------------------------------------------------
// Add2List - Add string to the report list box.
//
void Add2List (HWND hWnd, LPTSTR lpszFormat, ...) {
    int nBuf, nLen;
    TCHAR szBuffer[512];
    va_list args;
    if (hWnd == 0)
        hWnd = hMain;

    EnterCriticalSection (&csPrintf);
    va_start(args, lpszFormat);
    nBuf = StringCchVPrintf (szBuffer, dim(szBuffer), lpszFormat, args);
    va_end(args);

    nLen = (lstrlen (szBuffer)+1) * sizeof (TCHAR);
    WriteMsgQueue (hQWrite, (LPBYTE)szBuffer, nLen, 0, 0);
    PostMessage (hWnd, MYMSG_PRINTF, 0, 0);
    LeaveCriticalSection (&csPrintf);
}
//----------------------------------------------------------------------
// MySetWindowText - Set Window title to passed printf style string.
//
void MySetWindowText (HWND hWnd, LPTSTR lpszFormat, ...) {
    int nBuf, nLen;
    TCHAR szBuffer[512];
    va_list args;

    EnterCriticalSection (&csPrintf);
    va_start(args, lpszFormat);
    nBuf = StringCchVPrintf (szBuffer, dim (szBuffer), lpszFormat, args);
    va_end(args);
```

```
    nLen = (lstrlen (szBuffer)+1) * sizeof (TCHAR);
    WriteMsgQueue (hQWrite, (LPBYTE)szBuffer, nLen, 0,MSGQUEUE_MSGALERT);
    PostMessage (hWnd, MYMSG_PRINTF, 0, 0);
    LeaveCriticalSection (&csPrintf);
}
//======================================================================
// SearchThread - Monitors for other devices.
//
DWORD WINAPI SearchThread (PVOID pArg) {
    HWND hWnd = (HWND)pArg;
    int i, rc, Channel = 0;

    Add2List (hWnd, TEXT("Search thread entered"));

    // Init COM for the thread.
    CoInitializeEx(NULL,COINIT_MULTITHREADED);

    // Find the Bluetooth devices
    nDevs = MAX_DEVICES;
    rc = FindDevices (btd, &nDevs);

    // List them.
    for (i = 0; i < nDevs; i++) {
        PostMessage (hWnd, MYMSG_NEWDEV, i, (LPARAM)btd[i].szName);
        Add2List (hWnd, TEXT(«%d. dev:>%s<  «), i, btd[i].szName);
    }
    PostMessage (hWnd, MYMSG_ENABLESEND, 0, 1);
    CoUninitialize();
    Add2List (hWnd, TEXT(«Search thread exit»));
    return 0;
}
//======================================================================
// ServerThread - Monitors for connections, connnects and notifies
// user when a connection occurs.
//
DWORD WINAPI ServerThread (PVOID pArg) {
    HWND hWnd = (HWND)pArg;
    INT rc, len, nSize;
    SOCKADDR_BTH btaddr, t_btaddr;
    SOCKET r_sock;
    ULONG RecordHandle;
    HRESULT hr;

    Add2List (hWnd, TEXT(«Server thread entered»));
    CoInitializeEx(NULL,COINIT_MULTITHREADED);

    // Print out our name
    char sz[256];
    gethostname (sz, 256);
    Add2List (hWnd, TEXT(«This device name: %S»), sz);

    // Open a bluetooth socket
    s_sock = socket (AF_BT, SOCK_STREAM, BTHPROTO_RFCOMM);
    if (s_sock == INVALID_SOCKET) {
```

```
        Add2List (hWnd, TEXT(«socket failed. rc %d»),WSAGetLastError());
        return 0;
    }
    // Fill in address stuff
    memset (&btaddr, 0, sizeof (btaddr));
    btaddr.addressFamily = AF_BT;
    btaddr.port = 0;   // Let driver assign a channel

    // Bind to socket
    rc = bind (s_sock, (struct sockaddr *)&btaddr, sizeof (btaddr));
    if (rc) {
        Add2List (hWnd, TEXT(«bind failed»));
        closesocket (s_sock);
        return 0;
    }
    // Get information on the port assigned
    len = sizeof (btaddr);
    rc = getsockname (s_sock, (SOCKADDR *)&btaddr, &len);
    if (rc) {
        Add2List (hWnd, TEXT(«getsockname failed»));
        closesocket (s_sock);
        return 0;
    }
    Add2List (hWnd, TEXT(«Addr %04x.%08x, port %d»),
          GET_NAP(btaddr.btAddr), GET_SAP(btaddr.btAddr), btaddr.port);

    // Register our service
    rc = RegisterBtService (&guidBtSquirt, (unsigned char) btaddr.port,
                            &RecordHandle);
    if (rc) {
        Add2List (hWnd, TEXT(«RegisterService fail %d %d»), rc,
                  GetLastError());
        closesocket (s_sock);
        return 0;
    }

    // Set socket into listen mode
    rc = listen (s_sock, SOMAXCONN);
    if (rc == SOCKET_ERROR) {
        Add2List (hWnd, TEXT(« listen failed %d»), GetLastError());
        closesocket (s_sock);
        return 0;
    }
    // Wait for remote requests
    while (fContinue) {
        Add2List (hWnd, TEXT(«waiting...»));
        nSize = sizeof (t_btaddr);
        // Block on accept
        r_sock = accept (s_sock, (struct sockaddr *)&t_btaddr, &nSize);
        if (r_sock == INVALID_SOCKET) {
            Add2List (hWnd, TEXT(« accept failed %d»), GetLastError());
            break;
        }
        Add2List (hWnd, TEXT(«sock accept...»));
```

```
        HANDLE h = CreateThread (NULL, 0, ReceiveThread, (PVOID)r_sock,
                                 0, NULL);
        CloseHandle (h);
    }
    closesocket (s_sock);

    // Deregister the service
    hr = UnregisterBtService (hWnd, RecordHandle);
    CoUninitialize();
    Add2List (hWnd, TEXT(«Server thread exit»));
    return 0;
}
//======================================================================
// ReceiveThread - Receives the file requested by the remote device
//
DWORD WINAPI ReceiveThread (PVOID pArg) {
    SOCKET t_sock = (SOCKET)pArg;
    HWND hWnd = hMain; // I'm cheating here.
    int nCnt, nFileSize, rc;
    TCHAR szFileName[MAX_PATH];
    PBYTE pBuff;
    int i, nSize, nTotal;
    DWORD dwBytes;
    HANDLE hFile;
    Add2List (hWnd, TEXT(«receive thread entered»));
    SetThreadPriority (GetCurrentThread (), THREAD_PRIORITY_ABOVE_NORMAL);

    // Read the number of bytes in the filename.
    rc = recv (t_sock, (LPSTR)&nCnt, sizeof (nCnt), 0);
    if ((rc == SOCKET_ERROR) || (nCnt > MAX_PATH)) {
        Add2List (hWnd, TEXT(«failed receiving name size»));
        closesocket (t_sock);
        return 0;
    }
    // Read the filename. Place the file in the root of the file system
    StringCchCopy (szFileName, dim (szFileName), L»\\»);
    i = (int) wcslen (szFileName);
    rc = recv (t_sock, (LPSTR)&szFileName[i], nCnt, 0);
    if (rc == SOCKET_ERROR) {
        Add2List (hWnd, TEXT(«failed receiving name»));
        closesocket (t_sock);
        return 0;
    }
    Add2List (hWnd, TEXT(«File: %s»), szFileName);

    pBuff = (PBYTE)LocalAlloc (LPTR, BLKSIZE); //Create buff for file.
    //
    // Receive file size.
    //
    rc = recv (t_sock, (LPSTR)&nFileSize, sizeof (nFileSize), 0);
    Add2List (hWnd, TEXT(«received file size of %d bytes»), nFileSize);

    if ((rc != SOCKET_ERROR) && (nFileSize > 0)) {
        // Create the file. Overwrite if user says so.
```

```
        rc = 0;
        hFile = CreateFile (szFileName, GENERIC_WRITE, 0, NULL,
                            CREATE_ALWAYS, FILE_ATTRIBUTE_NORMAL, NULL);
        if (hFile == INVALID_HANDLE_VALUE) {
            Add2List (hWnd, TEXT(«File Open failed. rc %d»),
                      GetLastError());
            rc = BAD_FILEWRITE;
        }
        // Send ack code.
        Add2List (hWnd, TEXT(«Sending ack. %d»), rc);
        send (t_sock, (LPSTR)&rc, sizeof (rc), 0);
        //
        // Receive file.
        //
        nTotal = nFileSize;
        while ((!rc) && (nFileSize > 0)) {

            MySetWindowText (hWnd, TEXT («%02d%% received»),
                      (nTotal-nFileSize)*100/nTotal);
            nCnt = min (BLKSIZE, nFileSize);
            for (nSize = 0; nSize < nCnt;) {
                i = recv (t_sock, (LPSTR)pBuff+nSize, nCnt-nSize, 0);
                if (i == SOCKET_ERROR) {
                    Add2List (hWnd, TEXT(«recv socket err %d»),
                              GetLastError());
                    rc = BAD_SOCKETRECV;
                    break;
                }
                nSize += i;
            }
            Add2List (hWnd, TEXT(«recv'd %d bytes.»), nSize);
            if (i) {
                if (!WriteFile (hFile, pBuff, nSize, &dwBytes, 0))
                    rc = BAD_FILEWRITE;
                nFileSize -= dwBytes;
            } else
                Sleep(50);
            // Send ack of packet.
            send (t_sock, (LPSTR)&rc, sizeof (rc), 0);
        }
    } else if (rc == BAD_FILEOPEN)
        Add2List (hWnd, TEXT(«File not found.»));
    Add2List (hWnd, TEXT(«receive finished»));
    LocalFree (pBuff);
    CloseHandle (hFile);
    SetWindowText (hWnd, szTitleText);
    Add2List (hWnd, TEXT(«receive thread exit»));
    return 0;
}

//----------------------------------------------------------------------
// SendThread - Sends a file to the remote device
//
```

```
DWORD WINAPI SendFileThread (PVOID pArg) {
    PSENDTHSTRUCT psfs = (PSENDTHSTRUCT) pArg;
    HWND hWnd = hMain;
    SOCKET t_sock;
    int i, rc, nCnt, nBytes, nTotal = 0;
    SOCKADDR_BTH btaddr;
    BOOL fSuccess = FALSE;
    char *pBuff;

    // Open a bluetooth socket
    t_sock = socket (AF_BT, SOCK_STREAM, BTHPROTO_RFCOMM);
    if (t_sock == INVALID_SOCKET) {
        Add2List (hWnd, TEXT(«socket failed. rc %d»),WSAGetLastError());
        return 0;
    }
    Add2List (hWnd, TEXT(«Trying device %s»), btd[psfs->nDevice].szName);

    // Fill in address stuff
    memset (&btaddr, 0, sizeof (btaddr));
    btaddr.btAddr = btd[psfs->nDevice].btaddr;
    btaddr.addressFamily = AF_BT;
    btaddr.port = 0;                  // Let driver find the channel
    memcpy (&btaddr.serviceClassId, &guidBtSquirt, sizeof (GUID));
    //
    // Connect to remote socket
    //
    rc = connect (t_sock, (struct sockaddr *)&btaddr, sizeof (btaddr));
    if (rc) {
        Add2List (hWnd, TEXT(«Connected failed %d»), rc);
        closesocket (t_sock);
        return 0;
    }
    Add2List (hWnd, TEXT(«connected...»));

    // Allocate a buffer
    pBuff = (char *)LocalAlloc (LPTR, BUFFSIZE);

    // Send the file name
    // Strip off any leading path, assume len > 1 since we've opened file.
    for (i = lstrlen (psfs->szName)-1;
         (i > 0) && (psfs->szName[i] != TEXT ('\\')) ; i--);
    if (psfs->szName[i] == TEXT ('\\')) i++;
    LPTSTR pszNameOnly = &psfs->szName[i];
    // Send name size.
    nCnt = ((lstrlen (pszNameOnly) + 1) * sizeof (WCHAR));
    rc = send (t_sock, (LPSTR)&nCnt, sizeof (nCnt), 0);

    // Send filename.
    if (rc != SOCKET_ERROR)
        rc = send (t_sock, (LPSTR)pszNameOnly, nCnt, 0);

    if (rc != SOCKET_ERROR)  {
        int nFileSize = GetFileSize (psfs->hFile, NULL);
```

```
        // Send file size. Size will always be < 2 gig.
        rc = send (t_sock, (LPSTR)&nFileSize, sizeof (nFileSize), 0);
        if (rc == SOCKET_ERROR)
            rc = BAD_SOCKET;
        else
            // Recv ack of file size.
            recv (t_sock, (LPSTR)&rc, sizeof (rc), 0);

        // Send the file.
        nTotal = nFileSize;
        while ((!rc) && nFileSize) {

            MySetWindowText (hWnd, TEXT («%02d%% sent»),
                             (nTotal-nFileSize)*100/nTotal);
            // Read up to the block size.
            nCnt = min (BLKSIZE, nFileSize);
            ReadFile (psfs->hFile, pBuff, nCnt, (DWORD *)&nBytes, NULL);
            if (nCnt != nBytes) {
                rc = BAD_FILEREAD;
                break;
            }

            // Send the block
            rc = send (t_sock, pBuff, nCnt, 0);
            if (rc == SOCKET_ERROR) {
                Add2List (hWnd, TEXT(«send error %d «), GetLastError());
                rc = BAD_SOCKET;
            } else
                Add2List (hWnd, TEXT(«sent %d bytes»), rc);
            nFileSize -= rc;

            // Receive ack.
            recv (t_sock, (LPSTR)&rc, sizeof (rc), 0);
        }
        SetWindowText (hWnd, szTitleText);
    }
    // Send close code.
    if (rc != BAD_SOCKET)
        send (t_sock, (LPSTR)&rc, sizeof (rc), 0);

    // Clean up.
    closesocket (t_sock);
    CloseHandle (psfs->hFile);
    LocalFree (pBuff);
    LocalFree (psfs);
    if (rc)
        Add2List (hWnd, TEXT(«SendFile Exit rc = %d»), rc);
    else
        Add2List (hWnd, TEXT(«File sent successfully.»));
    return 0;
}
```

The interesting routines are the search thread routine *SearchThread* and the server thread routine *ServerThread*. The *SearchThread* calls the *FindDevice* routine to enumerate the Bluetooth devices in the immediate area. The search is set to take approximately 5 seconds. Once found, the device names are listed in the device list combo box. The names and the addresses of all the devices are saved in an array.

The server routine, *ServerThread*, creates a socket and binds it to an address. The routine then queries Winsock for the RFCOMM channel assigned to the socket. The *RegisterBtService* routine is then called to advertise the *bthelloBtSquirt* service. The *RegisterBtService* routine uses a prebuilt SDP record and inserts the GUID for the service and the RFCOMM channel in the appropriate parts of the record. Once constructed, the SDP packet is registered in the *PublishRecord* routine.

When the user taps Send, *BtSquirt* displays a File Open dialog box so the user can select a file. Once the file is selected, the program attempts to connect to the device currently selected in the combo box. If the connection is successful, the file is sent to the other device.

Accessing Bluetooth through either Winsock or virtual COM ports provides the most flexible way to wirelessly communicate with another device. The problem is that with either of these methods, the custom application, such as BtSquirt, has to be on both machines unless the application communicates through one of the public services. Public services are handy, but for linking two machines with a custom stream, sometimes you have to bite the bullet and write a custom Bluetooth application.

This chapter has given you a basic introduction to some of the ways Windows CE devices can communicate with other devices. In the next chapter, we look at the the Windows CE from a systems perspective, diving into such topics as the how the system manages memory and power management.

Chapter 15

System Programming

This chapter takes a slightly different tack from the previous chapters of the book. Instead of touring the API of a particular section of Windows CE, I'll show you Windows CE from a systems perspective.

Windows CE presents standard Windows programmers with some unique challenges. First, because Windows CE supports a variety of different microprocessors and system architectures, you can't count on the tried and true IBM/Intel PC–compatible design that can be directly traced to the IBM PC/AT released in 1984. Windows CE runs on devices that are more different than alike. Different CPUs use different memory layouts, and while the sets of peripherals are similar, they have totally different designs.

In addition to using different hardware, Windows CE itself changes, depending on how it's ported to a specific platform. While all Windows Mobile devices of a particular version have the same set of functions, that set is slightly different from the functions provided by different configurations of Windows CE. In addition, Windows CE is designed as a collection of components so that OEMs using Windows CE in embedded devices can remove unneeded sections of the operating system, such as the Fiber API.

All of these conditions make programming Windows CE unique and, I might add, fun. This chapter describes some of these cross-platform programming issues. I'll begin the chapter by describing the system memory architecture.

The Windows CE Memory Architecture

In operating system circles, much is made of the extent to which the operating system goes to protect one application's memory from other applications. The old Microsoft Windows Me used a single address space that provides minimal protection between applications and the Windows operating system code. Windows XP and Windows Vista, on the other hand, implement completely separate address spaces for each Win32 application.

From its inception in 1996 until the relase of Windows Embedded CE 6.0 in November 2006, Windows CE implemented a single 2-GB virtual address space for all applications. Even with the single address space, the memory space of an application was protected so that it couldn't be accessed by another application. This architecture served Windows CE well, but the design imposed the famous (or infamous) 32/32 limts of 32 MB per virtual machine and 32 concurrent processes.

The release of Windows CE 6 brought a completely redesigned kernel and operating system architecture to Windows CE. Gone was the single address space, replaced by separate virtual address spaces for each application. Each application address space ranges from virtual address zero to the 2-GB boundary. The upper half of the address space from 2 GB to the top at 4 GB is addressable only in kernel mode and therefore only addressable by the kernel and the other parts of the operating system running in kernel mode. Figure 15-1 illustrates this memory architecture. When a thread in an application is executing, the application that the thread is executing in is enabled by the operating system. This user address space is mated to a common kernel address space. Of course, the application doesn't know that the kernel address space is consistent across applications because application threads that run in *user mode* threads can't access any address above the 2-GB boundary.[1]

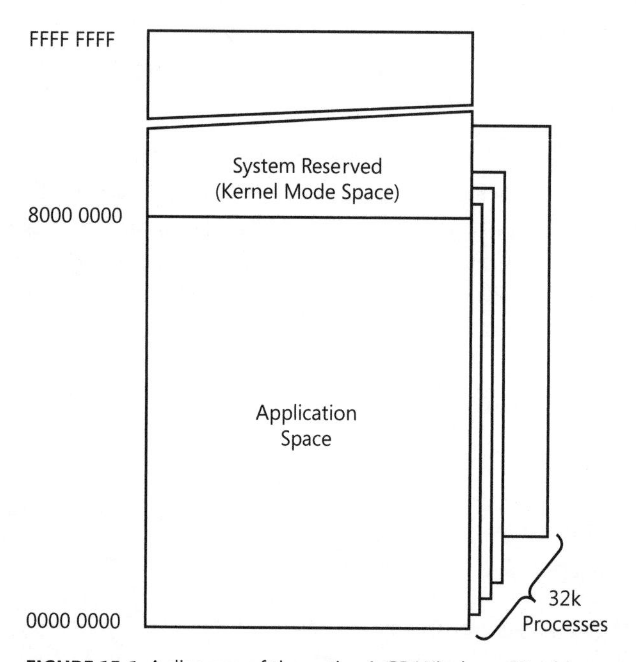

FIGURE 15-1 A diagram of the entire 4-GB Windows CE address space

Application Space

The application address space is shown in Figure 15-2. This address space is divided into a number of regions, each with a specific purpose. The first region is the lower gigabyte of the address space that contains the application code and all memory allocations. As with other versions of Windows, the application code is loaded at a base address of 0001 0000 and is loaded upward. Above the code, the operating system places the static data areas for the application,

1 Unlike earlier versions of Windows CE, this new architecture does not support a "kernel mode only" configuration where every thread in the system runs in kernel mode.

the resource data for the application, and the local heap. There is at least one stack, which is the stack for the main thread of the application, and there are subsequent stacks for all other threads created by the application. All memory allocations, whether they be stack, heap, or direct virtual allocations, will be placed in this first gigabyte of the application's address space.

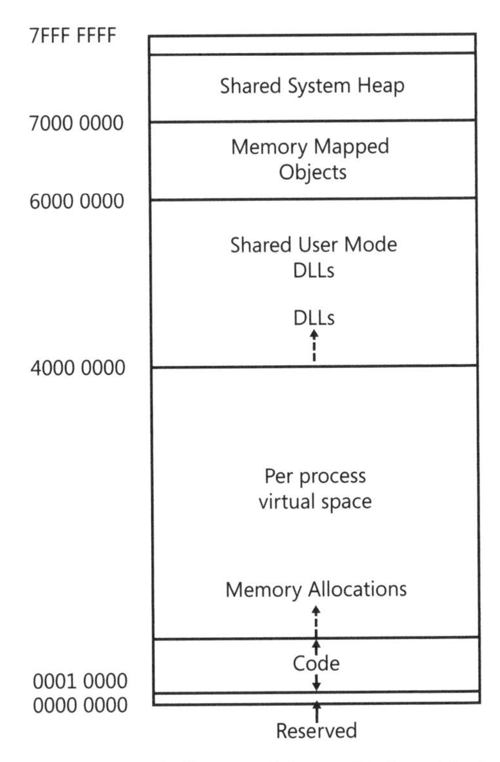

FIGURE 15-2 A diagram of the application virtual memory space

The 512-MB region from address 4000 0000 to 5FFF FFFF is reserved for the code and data for DLLs loaded by the various applications. When an application loads a DLL, either because it was loaded when the application was loaded or by a call to *LoadLibrary*, Windows CE will map the DLL to this region. Each DLL in the system is loaded at a unique address within this region. For a given DLL, the address of that DLL is consistent across all applications. So for example, if application "A" loaded BOB.DLL and application "B" also loaded Bob, the base address for the DLL would be the same in the virtual address spaces for both applications "A" and "B". To application "C", which hadn't loaded Bob, the virtual address where Bob was loaded in the other applications would appear as an unallocated region. Departing from the methodology used in earlier versions of Windows CE, DLLs in this region are loaded "bottom up" with the first DLL loaded at 4000 0000 and subsequent DLLs loaded at successively higher addresses.

The region from 6000 0000 to 6FFF FFFF is reserved for memory-mapped objects, sometimes called RAM-based memory mapped files. As mentioned in Chapter 7, these memory mapped "files" don't have any real files behind them. Instead, they are temporary memory buffers that are primarily used for interprocess communication. The reason for this special region for RAM-based memory mapped files is to allow the operating system the ability to map the same object at the same address for each appliation that opens that object. This allows the backward compatibility with earlier versions of Windows CE that allocated memory-mapped files in the shared Large Memory Area, which doesn't exist in the new design. While the operating system places memory mapped objects in this region, if an application opens an actual file for memory mapped access, that mapping will occur in the bottom 1 GB of the application's address space.

The region from 7000 0000 to 7FFF 0000 is called the shared system heap. This region is used by the operating system to pass data down to the applications. Applications can only read the region, while operating system components running in kernel mode can both read and write the region. At the very top of the application space is a 1-MB region that is a "guard" region. Any access to this region by the application or by components in the operating system will result in an exception.

Kernel Space

The address space above the 2-GB boundary, addresses 8000 0000 through FFFF FFFF, is reserved for the operating system and isn't accessible to applications and drivers running in user mode. This address space is used by the operating system and the kernel mode drivers loaded by the operating system. A diagram of the kernel mode address space is shown in figure 15-3.

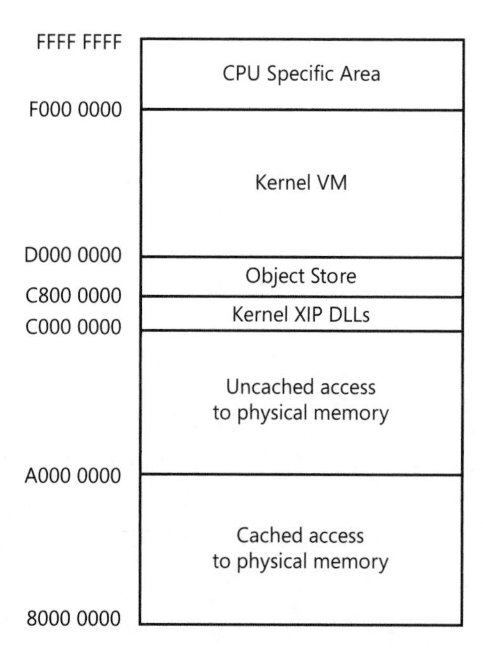

FIGURE 15-3 A diagram of the upper half of the Windows CE memory map

Like the application space, the upper 2 GB of kernel space are divided into a number of regions. The first 512-MB memory region, from addresses 8000 0000 to 9FFF FFFF, is mapped to the physical address space. On some CPUs, this region is a linear map to the first 512 MB of the physical address space. On other CPUs, there is a table created by the OEM when the system is designed that maps this region to various areas in the physical address space. This table is read when the system boots and does not change. Memory accesses through this window are cached in the CPU's data cache to improve performance.

The second 512-MB region, from A000 0000 through BFFF to the window starting at 8000 0000. The difference between this window and the window at 8000 0000 is that accesses through the A000 0000 window are not cached. While the performance is slower through this window, the noncached access is necessary when you read registers in devices that might change independently of the execution of the CPU.

The area between C000 0000 and C7FF FFFF is used for the kernel execute-in-place DLLs. This generally includes almost all of the operating system code as well as the kernel mode device drivers. The area between C800 0000 and CFFF FFFF is used for the object store.

The region from D000 0000 to EFFF FFFF is used by the kernel for virtual allocations and other memory needs. All but SHx CPUs can utilize this entire region. The SHx is limited to the bottom half of the region ending at DFFF FFFFF. Finally, the region from F000 0000 to the top of the memory space at FFFF FFFF is used by the kernel for system-related functions.

Writing Cross-Platform Windows CE Applications

Over the years, Windows programmers have had to deal concurrently with different versions of the operating system. Part of the solution to the problem this situation posed was to call *GetVersion* or *GetVersionEx* and to act differently depending on the version of the operating system you were working with. You can't do that under Windows CE. Because of the flexible nature of Windows CE, two builds of the same version of Windows CE can have different APIs. The questions remain, though. How do you support multiple platforms with a common code base? How does the operating system version relate to the different platforms?

Platforms and Operating System Versions

To understand how the different platforms relate to the different versions of Windows CE, it helps to know how the Windows CE development team is organized within Microsoft. Windows CE is supported by a core operating system group within Microsoft. This team is responsible for developing the operating system, including the file system and the various communication stacks.

Coordinating efforts with the operating system team are the various platform teams, working on Windows Mobile devices, the Microsoft Zune media player, and many other platforms.

Each team is responsible for defining a suggested hardware platform, defining applications that will be bundled with the platform, and deciding which version of the operating system the platform will use. Because the operating system team works continually to enhance Windows CE, planning new versions over time, each platform team generally looks to see what version of Windows CE will be ready when that team's platform ships.

The individual platform teams also develop the shells for their platforms. Because each team develops its own shell, many new functions or platform-specific functions first appear as part of the shell of a specific platform. Then if the newly introduced functions have a more general applicability, they're moved to the base operating system in a later version. You can see this process in both the Notification API and the Cellcore driver. Both these sets of features started in their specific platform group and have now been moved out of the shell and into the base operating system.

Table 15-1 shows some of the different platforms that have been released and the version of Windows CE that each platform uses.

TABLE 15-1 Versions for Windows CE Platforms

Platform	Windows CE version
Original Handheld PC	1.00
Japanese release of H/PC	1.01
Handheld PC 2.0	2.00
Original Palm-size PC	2.01
Handheld PC Pro 3.0	2.11
Palm-size PC 1.2	2.11
Pocket PC	3.0
Handheld PC Pro 2000	3.0
Pocket PC 2002	3.0
Smartphone 2002	3.0
Smart Display 1.0	4.1
Pocket PC 2003	4.2
Smartphone 2003	4.2
Pocket PC 2003 2nd Ed.	4.21
Smartphone 2003 2nd Ed.	4.21
WM 5 Pocket PC	5.01
WM 5 Smartphone	5.01
WM 6 Professional	5.02
WM 6 Standard	5.02
WM 6 Classic	5.02

You can choose from a number of ways to deal with the problem of different platforms and different versions of Windows CE. Let's look at a few.

Compile-Time Versioning

The version problem can be tackled in a couple of places in the development process of an application. At compile time, you can use the preprocessor definition *_WIN32_WCE* to determine the version of the operating system you're currently building for. By enclosing code in a *#if* preprocessor block, you can cause code to be compiled for specific versions of Windows CE.

Following is an example of a routine that's tuned to use the AlphaBlend API on Windows CE 6, but a simple *StretchBlt* call on earlier versions of Windows CE.

```
int DrawBackground (HWND hWnd, HDC hdcDest, int cx, int cy)
{
   RECT rt;
   GetClientRect (hWnd, &rt);
#if (_WIN32_WCE >= 0x600)
   BLENDFUNCTION blend;
   blend.BlendOp = AC_SRC_OVER;
   blend.BlendFlags = 0;
   blend.AlphaFormat = 0;
   blend.SourceConstantAlpha = 200;
   AlphaBlend (hdcDest, 0, 0, rt.right, rt.bottom,
               m_hSrcDc, 0, 0, rt.right, rt.bottom, blend);
#else
   StretchBlt (hdcDest, 0, 0, rt.right, rt.bottom,
               m_hSrcDc, 0, 0, rt.right, rt.bottom, SRCCOPY);
#endif
   return 0;
}
```

A virtue of this code is that the linker links the appropriate function for the appropriate platform. Without this sort of compile-time code, you couldn't simply put a run-time *if* statement around the call to *AlphaBlend* because the program would never load on anything running versions of Windows CE before 6.0. The loader wouldn't be able to find the exported function *AlphaBlend* in Coredll.dll because it's not present on earlier versions of Windows CE.

The SDKs Windows Mobile systems have additional defines. Windows Mobile Classic and Windows Mobile Professional (Pocket PC) SDKs set a defined named *WIN32_PLATFORM_PSPC*. Windows Mobile Standard (Smartphone) SDKs define *WIN32_PLATFORM_WFSP*. So you can block Pocket PC–specific code in the following way:

```
#ifdef WIN32_PLATFORM_PSPC
    // Insert Pocket PC code here.
#endif
```

There are platform-specific defines for other Windows CE platforms. Table 15-2 shows some of these defines.

TABLE 15-2 Defines for Windows CE Platforms

Platform	Define
Windows Mobile 6 Standard	*WIN32_PLATFORM_WFSP* (= 1)
Windows Mobile 6 Professional/Classic	*WIN32_PLATFORM_PSPC* (= 1)
Windows Mobile 5 Smartphone	*WIN32_PLATFORM_WFSP* (= 1)
Windows Mobile 5 Pocket PC	*WIN32_PLATFORM_PSPC* (= 1)
Smartphone 2003 Second Edition	*WIN32_PLATFORM_WFSP* (= 1)
Pocket PC 2003 Second Edition	*WIN32_PLATFORM_PSPC* (= 1)
Pocket PC 2003	*WIN32_PLATFORM_PSPC* (= 400)
Smartphone 2003	*WIN32_PLATFORM_WFSP* (= 200)
Pocket PC 2002	*WIN32_PLATFORM_PSPC* (= 310)
Smartphone 2002	*WIN32_PLATFORM_WFSP* (= 100)
Handheld PC 2000	*WIN32_PLATFORM_HPC2000*
Pocket PC 2000	*WIN32_PLATFORM_PSPC*
Palm-size PC	*WIN32_PLATFORM_PSPC*
Handheld PC Professional	*WIN32_PLATFORM_HPCPRO*

Early Pocket PCs could be detected using the value assigned to *WIN32_PLATFORM_PSPC*, but lately Microsoft has simply defined the value to 1. To distinguish between the different versions of the Pocket PC, you must now provide a check of the target Windows CE version using the *_WIN32_WCE* definition, as in

```
#if defined(WIN32_PLATFORM_PSPC)
#if (_WIN32_WCE == 0x502)
    // Windows Mobile 6 Professional / Classic
#elif (_WIN32_WCE == 0x501)
    // Windows Mobile 5 Pocket PC
#elif (_WIN32_WCE == 0x421)
    // Pocket PC 2003 Second Edition
#elif (_WIN32_WCE == 0x420)
    // Pocket PC 2003
#else
    // Earlier Pocket PC
#endif
#endif  // ifdef WIN32_PLATFORM_PSPC
```

The only issue with using conditional compilation is that while you still have a common source file, the resulting executable will be different for each platform.

Explicit Linking

You can tackle the version problem other ways. Sometimes one platform requires that you call a function different from one you need for another platform you're working with, but you want the same executable file for both platforms. A way to accomplish this is to explicitly link to a DLL using *LoadLibrary*, *GetProcAddress*, and *FreeLibrary*. These functions were covered in Chapter 8.

Run-Time Version Checking

When you're determining the version of the Windows CE operating system at run time, you use the same function as under other versions of Windows—*GetVersionEx*, which fills in an *OSVERSIONINFO* structure defined as

```
typedef struct _OSVERSIONINFO{
    DWORD dwOSVersionInfoSize;
    DWORD dwMajorVersion;
    DWORD dwMinorVersion;
    DWORD dwBuildNumber;
    DWORD dwPlatformId;
    TCHAR szCSDVersion[ 128 ];
} OSVERSIONINFO;
```

Upon return from *GetVersionEx*, the major and minor version fields are filled with the Windows CE version. This means, of course, that you can't simply copy desktop Windows code that branches on classic version numbers like 3.5 or 5.0. The *dwPlatformId* field contains the constant *VER_PLATFORM_WIN32_CE* under Windows CE.

Although you can differentiate platforms by means of their unique Windows CE version numbers, you shouldn't. For example, you can identify a Windows Mobile 6 platform by its unique Windows CE version, 5.02; but to test for any Windows Mobile Classic (Pocket PC) system, you should call *SystemParametersInfo* with the *SPI_GETPLATFORMTYPE* constant, as in

```
TCHAR szPlat[256];
INT rc;

rc = SystemParametersInfo (SPI_GETPLATFORMTYPE, sizeof (szPlat),
                           szPlat, 0);
if (lstrcmp (szPlat, TEXT ("PocketPC")) == 0) {
    // Running on a Pocket PC
}
```

Aside from the differences in their shells, though, the platform differences aren't really that important. The base operating system is identical in all but some fringe cases. The best strategy for writing cross-platform Windows CE software is to avoid differentiating among the platforms at all—or at least differentiate among them as little as possible.

For the most part, discrepancies among the user interfaces for the different consumer Windows CE devices can be illustrated by the issue of screen dimension and input methods. A portrait-mode screen requires a completely different layout for most windows compared with landscape-mode screens. So instead of looking at the platform type to determine what screen layout to use, you'd do better to simply check the screen dimensions using *GetDeviceCaps*. Also remember that many Windows CE devices can rotate the screen, so applications need to detect this and respond correctly. Different input methodologies also drive the user interface. Systems with touch screens require different designs from systems with mice or systems with no pointer-style input.

Power Management

Managing power is critical to almost all Windows CE systems. Even systems that are not battery driven still must deal with power consumption and heat-generation issues that are driven by power consumption.

Most Windows CE systems use the optional Power Manager component for this task. When the power manager isn't used, GWES takes over and performs some rudimentary power management tasks. Because power management is so important, I'll cover power management from both perspectives, first using the power manager and then using the older GWES methodology. However, before I discuss how to manage the power, we need to agree on one seemingly straightforward question: "What is off?"

Defining the Meaning of "Off"

When the user powers down a battery-powered Windows CE device, the power system may not turn off the way a PC powers off. Instead, the system may be placed in a *suspended* state. When the system is suspended and the user powers up the device, the device doesn't reboot like a PC; it resumes, returning to the same state it was in before it was suspended. As a result, an application running before the system was suspended is still running when the system resumes. In fact, on systems that support suspend/resume, the application won't know that it was suspended at all unless it explicitly requested to be notified when the system was suspended.

Other Windows CE systems truly turn off, shutting down the system completely. These systems reboot the operating system when powered on. On these systems, all the applications were either asked to close nicely or were terminated during shutdown and need to be restarted after the system boots.

The OEM, when designing the system, decides whether a system is designed to suspend/resume or shutdown/reboot.[2] Windows CE has complete support for both methodologies. For good or bad, there is no documented method for an application to know if a device is designed for suspend/resume or shutdown/reboot. However, the applcation can monitor the power state and can control that state. Let's look at power management from three perspectives: querying the power state, changing the power state, and preventing the power state from changing.

[2] The suspend vs. power off decision is made by Microsoft for Windows Mobile systems.

Querying the Power State

Regardless of whether the power manager is supported on a particular device, applications can always query the current power state of the system by calling

```
DWORD GetSystemPowerStatusEx2 (
                            PSYSTEM_POWER_STATUS_EX2 pSystemPowerStatusEx2,
                            DWORD dwLen, BOOL fUpdate);
```

This function takes three parameters: a pointer to a *SYSTEM_POWER_STATUS_EX2* structure, the length of that structure, and a Boolean value that tells the operating system if it should query the battery driver during the call to get the latest information or to return the cached battery information. The system queries the battery approximately every 5 seconds, so if this third parameter is *FALSE*, the data is still not too stale. The *SYSTEM_POWER_STATUS_EX2* structure is defined as

```
typedef struct _SYSTEM_POWER_STATUS_EX2 {
    BYTE ACLineStatus;
    BYTE BatteryFlag;
    BYTE BatteryLifePercent;
    BYTE Reserved1;
    DWORD BatteryLifeTime;
    DWORD BatteryFullLifeTime;
    BYTE Reserved2;
    BYTE BackupBatteryFlag;
    BYTE BackupBatteryLifePercent;
    BYTE Reserved3;
    DWORD BackupBatteryLifeTime;
    DWORD BackupBatteryFullLifeTime;
    WORD BatteryVoltage;
    DWORD BatteryCurrent;
    DWORD BatteryAverageCurrent;
    DWORD BatteryAverageInterval;
    DWORD BatterymAHourConsumed;
    DWORD BatteryTemperature;
    DWORD BackupBatteryVoltage;
    BYTE  BatteryChemistry;
} SYSTEM_POWER_STATUS_EX2;
```

Before I describe this rather large structure, I must warn you that the data returned in this structure is only as accurate as the system's battery driver. This same structure is passed to the battery driver to query its status. Windows CE doesn't validate the data returned by the battery driver. The data returned by this function depends on the battery driver and therefore varies across different systems. For example, many systems won't report an accurate value for the battery level when the system is on AC power; other systems will. Applications using *GetSystemPowerStatusEx2* should program defensively and test on all systems that might run the application.

The first field, *ACLineStatus*, contains a flag indicating whether the system is connected to AC power. The possible values are *AC_LINE_OFFLINE*, indicating that the system isn't on AC power;

AC_LINE_ONLINE, indicating that the system is on AC power; *AC_LINE_BACKUP_POWER*; and *AC_LINE_UNKNOWN*. The *BatteryFlag* field, which provides a gross indication of the current state of the battery, can have one of the following values:

- **BATTERY_FLAG_HIGH** The battery is fully or close to fully charged.
- **BATTERY_FLAG_LOW** The battery has little charge left.
- **BATTERY_FLAG_CRITICAL** The battery charge is at a critical state.
- **BATTERY_FLAG_CHARGING** The battery is currently being charged.
- **BATTERY_FLAG_NO_BATTERY** The system has no battery.
- **BATTERY_FLAG_UNKNOWN** The battery state is unknown.

The *BatteryLifePercent* field contains the estimated percentage of charge remaining in the battery. Either the value will be between 0 and 100 or it will be 255, indicating that the percentage is unknown. The *BatteryLifeTime* field contains the estimated number of seconds remaining before the battery is exhausted. If this value can't be estimated, the field contains *BATTERY_LIFE_UNKNOWN*. The *BatteryFullLifeTime* field contains the estimated life in seconds of the battery when it is fully charged. If this value can't be estimated, the field contains *BATTERY_LIFE_UNKNOWN*. Note that on many systems, these lifetime values are difficult, if not impossible, to accurately measure. Many OEMs simply fill in *BATTERY_LIFE_UNKNOWN* for both fields.

The next four fields (not counting the reserved fields) replicate the fields previously described except that they contain values for the system's backup battery. Again, because many of these values are difficult to measure, many systems simply return an "unknown" value for these fields.

The remaining fields describe the electrical state of the battery and backup battery. Because many systems lack the capacity to measure these values, these fields are simply filled with the default "unknown" values. The final field, *BatteryChemistry*, contains a flag indicating the type of battery in the system. The currently defined self-describing values are

- BATTERY_CHEMISTRY_ALKALINE
- BATTERY_CHEMISTRY_NICD
- BATTERY_CHEMISTRY_NIMH
- BATTERY_CHEMISTRY_LION
- BATTERY_CHEMISTRY_LIPOLY
- BATTERY_CHEMISTRY_UNKNOWN

The Power Manager

The Power Manager component provides a central clearinghouse for all things related to power. It notifies the system when power conditions change, it can be told to change the power state, and applications can request it not to automatically change power states. The power manager can even control the power states of individual drivers.

The power manager is quite flexible. In fact, OEMs can redesign it from the ground up or simply modify the default power state definitions. By default, Windows CE provides a series of power states and then maps them to typical use conditions. All of this ends up meaning that it's almost imposible to define the power manager because it is so flexible. So in this section I'm going to define the default power management API with the hope that you will be able to use this knowledge with whatever Windows CE–based system you have.

The Power Manager defines a series of power states as D0, D1, D2, and D3. These rather cryptic names are then mapped to more friendly names at the system level. For embedded systems, OEMs define the system power states. Examples of power states might be something like On, Idle, and Suspend. Other power states can be defined, such as ScreenOff, InCradle, and OnBattery.

From an application perspective, the Power Manager provides the ability to be notified when the power state changes as well as a uniform method of changing the power state of the system through a series of functions.

The power states for the system are defined in the registry. The SDK defines *PWRMGR_REG_KEY* so that you don't have to know the registry string, but for the times when the constant isn't defined, the Power Manager's registry data is kept at HKEY_LOCAL_MACHINE\System\CurrentControlSet\Control\Power. The power states are then defined as subkeys under the key *State*.

Power Notifications

One of the nice features of the Power Manager is its ability to notify an application when the power state of the system changes. This ability frees the application from polling the battery state manually to monitor the power. An application can request that the Power Manager send a notification to the application when the power state of the system changes by calling *RequestPowerNotifications*. The Power Manager then sends the notifications through a message queue that has been previously created by the application.

RequestPowerNotifications is prototyped as

```
HANDLE RequestPowerNotifications (HANDLE hMsgQ, DWORD Flags);
```

The first parameter is the handle to a message queue that the application has previously created. The second parameter is a series of flags indicating which notifications the application wants to receive. The flags, which can be ORed together, are as follows:

- **PBT_TRANSITION** Receive notifications when the power state changes—for example, when the system goes from On to Suspend.
- **PBT_RESUME** Receive notifications when the system resumes.
- **PBT_POWERSTATUSCHANGE** Receive notifications when the system transitions between AC and battery power.
- **PBT_POWERINFOCHANGE** Receive notifications when the power information, such as the battery level, changes.
- **POWER_NOTIFY_ALL** Receive all power notifications.

The *RequestPowerNotifications* function returns a handle to the power notification, or *NULL* if the function fails. The message queue should be created with read access by the application, since it will be reading the power notifications from the queue.

To receive the notifications, an application should block on the queue handle by using *WaitForSingleObject*. As discussed in Chapter 8, the handle will be signaled when a notification is placed in the queue. The actual notification is received in the form of a *POWER_BROADCAST* structure defined as follows:

```
typedef struct _POWER_BROADCAST {
    DWORD Message;
    DWORD Flags;
    DWORD Length;
    WCHAR SystemPowerState[1];
} POWER_BROADCAST, *PPOWER_BROADCAST;
```

First, note that this structure is a variable-length structure. The last field, *SystemPowerState*, is defined as an array of *WCHAR*s but can be filled with other, nonstring, data. The first field is the identifier of the notification itself. This field is filled with one of the *PBT_* flags listed earlier. The *Flags* field can contain the following flags, depending on the notification being received.

- **POWER_STATE_ON** The system is on.
- **POWER_STATE_OFF** The system is off.
- **POWER_STATE_CRITICAL** The system is performing a critical off.
- **POWER_STATE_BOOT** The system is booting.
- **POWER_STATE_IDLE** The system is idle.
- **POWER_STATE_SUSPEND** The system is suspended.
- **POWER_STATE_RESET** The system is starting after a reset.

The final two parameters are related. The *Length* field is the length of the data in the *SystemPowerState* field. The data contained in the *SystemPowerState* field depends on the notification being sent. For the *PBT_TRANSITION* notification, the *SystemPowerState* field contains a string that identifies the new power state. This string is not zero terminated. To terminate the string, use the *Length* field to determine the length of the string. Note that the *Length* field is in bytes, while the characters are 2-byte Unicode characters, so to obtain the length of the string in characters, divide the *Length* field by the size of *TCHAR*.

For the *PBT_POWERINFOCHANGE* notification, the *SystemPowerState* field contains a *PPOWER_BROADCAST_POWER_INFO* structure defined as follows:

```
typedef struct _POWER_BROADCAST_POWER_INFO {
    DWORD        dwNumLevels;
    DWORD        dwBatteryLifeTime;
    DWORD        dwBatteryFullLifeTime;
    DWORD        dwBackupBatteryLifeTime;
    DWORD        dwBackupBatteryFullLifeTime;
    BYTE         bACLineStatus;
    BYTE         bBatteryFlag;
    BYTE         bBatteryLifePercent;
    BYTE         bBackupBatteryFlag;
    BYTE         bBackupBatteryLifePercent;
} POWER_BROADCAST_POWER_INFO, *PPOWER_BROADCAST_POWER_INFO;
```

Notice that the fields are similar in name and function to many of the fields previously discussed in the *SYSTEM_POWER_STATUS_EX2* structure.

Setting the Power State

Functions provided by the Power Manager also allow applications to control the power state. There are two methods for controlling the power. The first method has the application demand a given power setting. The second method has the application request that the power not drop below a given level.

An application can request a specific power state by calling the function *SetSystemPowerState*. This function is prototyped as

```
DWORD SetSystemPowerState (LPCWSTR psState, DWORD StateFlags,
                           DWORD Options);
```

The power state being requested can be specified in either the first or the second parameter of the function. If the first parameter is nonzero, it points to a string that identifies the state being requested. The string should match one of the power states enumerated in the registry.

If *psState* is *NULL*, the second parameter, *StateFlags*, defines the requested power state. This parameter is one of the same power states, from *POWER_STATE_ON* to *POWER_STATE_RESET*, that were described in the *POWER_BROADCAST* structure earlier.

Of particular interest is the flag *POWER_STATE_RESET*. This flag requests that the system reset. This method of resetting the system using *SetSystemPowerState* is much better than directly calling *KernelIoControl* with the IOCTL command *IOCTL_HAL_REBOOT*, since using *SetSystemPowerState* will cause the system to flush any buffered data to the file system before the function resets the device.

Although calling *SetSystemPowerState* is a direct method of changing the power state, a more subtle method is to request that the system maintain the minimal power state needed by the application by calling *SetPowerRequirement*. Using *SetSystemPowerState* assumes the application knows best, while calling *SetPowerRequirement* allows the system to optimize the power settings while still meeting the needs of the application. An example of a situation in which *SetPowerRequirement* is handy occurs when an application is using a serial port and needs the port to stay powered while communication is active. *SetPowerRequirement* is defined as

```
HANDLE SetPowerRequirement (PVOID pvDevice,
                            CEDEVICE_POWER_STATE DeviceState,
                            ULONG DeviceFlags, PVOID pvSystemState,
                            ULONG StateFlags);
```

The first parameter specifies the device that the application needs to remain at a given power state. The *DeviceState* parameter defines the power state for the device. The enumeration *CEDEVICE_POWER_STATE* specifies the state, ranging from D0 (meaning that the device must remain fully powered) to D4 (meaning that the device is powered off). The *DeviceFlags* parameter can be a combination of two flags: *POWER_NAME*, indicating that the device name is valid; and *POWER_FORCE*, indicating that the device should remain in that state even if the system suspends. If the *pvSystemState* is not *NULL*, it indicates that the power requirement is valid only for the power state named in *pvSystemState*. The device might not be able to change to the requested state.

As soon as possible, the application should remove the power requirement with a call to *ReleasePowerRequirement*, prototyped as

```
DWORD ReleasePowerRequirement (HANDLE hPowerReq);
```

The only parameter is the handle returned from *SetPowerRequirement*.

Managing Power without the Power Manager

Even without the power manager, there is rudimentary power management support provided by Windows CE. GWES provides a method of powering down or suspending the system and a way to automatically power down the system after a time of no user input. The following techniques, while quite useful, should be employed only on systems without the power manager. If the system supports the power manager, use it. The power manager coordinates your request with those of the other applications, and frankly, it's typically easier.

Powering Down

An application can power down the system by calling the little-documented *GwesPowerOffSystem* function. This function has been available for many versions of Windows CE but is little known. In fact, many SDKs don't include the prototype for the function, so you might have to provide the prototype. The function is defined as

```
void GwesPowerOffSystem(void);
```

The use of *GwesPowerOffSystem* is simple: simply call, and the system suspends.

If you prefer to avoid little-documented functions, you can also power off the system by simulating the action of a user pressing the Off button. You can easily enable your application to suspend the system by using the *keybd_event* function, as in

```
keybd_event (VK_OFF, 0, KEYEVENTF_SILENT, 0);
keybd_event (VK_OFF, 0, KEYEVENTF_SILENT | KEYEVENTF_KEYUP, 0);
```

The two calls to *keybd_event* simulate the press and release of the power button, which has the virtual key code of *VK_OFF*. Executing the preceding two lines of code will suspend the system. Because the virtual key code has to be seen and acted on by GWES, the two functions probably will both return, and a few more statements will be executed before the system actually suspends. If it is important that your program stop work after calling the *keybd_event* functions, add a call to *Sleep* to cause the application to pause for a number of milliseconds, allowing time for GWES to truly suspend the system.

Turning Off the Screen

On systems with color backlit displays, the main power drain on the system isn't the CPU—it's the backlight. In some situations, an application needs to run, but doesn't need the screen. An example of this might be a music player application when the user is listening to the music, not watching the screen. In these situations, the ability to turn off the backlight can significantly improve battery life.

Of course, any application that turns off the backlight needs to have a simple and user-friendly way of reenabling the screen when the user wants to look at the screen. Also, remember that users typically think the unit is off if the screen is black, so plan accordingly. For example, a user might attempt to power on the system when it is already running, and in doing so, accidentally turn off the device. Also, when the system powers down the display in this fashion, it also disables the touch screen. This means that you can't tell the user to tap the screen to turn it back on. Instead, you need to use some other event such as a set time, the completion of a task, or the user pressing a button. Finally, the method discussed here has been superseded by the method provided by the Power Manager. Before using this method, check to see whether the Power Manager is available, and control the screen through it. If that fails, the *ExtEscape* method might work.

On Windows CE, the control of the display is exposed through the *ExtEscape* function, which is a back door to the display and printer device drivers. Windows CE display drivers support a number of device escape codes, which are documented in the Platform Builder. For our purposes, only two escape codes are needed: *SETPOWERMANAGEMENT* to set the power state of the display and *QUERYESCSUPPORT* to query if the *SETPOWERMANAGEMENT* escape is supported by the driver. The following routine turns the display on or off on systems with display drivers that support the proper escape codes.

```
//
// Defines and structures taken from pwingdi.h in the Platform Builder
//
#define QUERYESCSUPPORT              8
#define SETPOWERMANAGEMENT           6147
#define GETPOWERMANAGEMENT           6148

typedef enum _VIDEO_POWER_STATE {
    VideoPowerOn = 1,
    VideoPowerStandBy,
    VideoPowerSuspend,
    VideoPowerOff
} VIDEO_POWER_STATE, *PVIDEO_POWER_STATE;

typedef struct _VIDEO_POWER_MANAGEMENT {
    ULONG Length;
    ULONG DPMSVersion;
    ULONG PowerState;
} VIDEO_POWER_MANAGEMENT, *PVIDEO_POWER_MANAGEMENT;

//----------------------------------------------------------------------
// SetVideoPower - Turns on or off the display
//
int SetVideoPower (BOOL fOn) {
    VIDEO_POWER_MANAGEMENT vpm;
    int rc, fQueryEsc;
    HDC hdc;

    // Get the display dc.
    hdc = GetDC (NULL);
    // See if supported.
    fQueryEsc = SETPOWERMANAGEMENT;
    rc = ExtEscape (hdc, QUERYESCSUPPORT, sizeof (fQueryEsc),
                    (LPSTR)&fQueryEsc, 0, 0);
    if (rc == 0) {
        // No support, fail.
        ReleaseDC (NULL, hdc);
        return -1;
    }
    // Fill in the power management structure.
    vpm.Length = sizeof (vpm);
    vpm.DPMSVersion = 1;
    if (fOn)
        vpm.PowerState = VideoPowerOn;
```

```
    else
        vpm.PowerState = VideoPowerOff;

    // Tell the driver to turn on or off the display.
    rc = ExtEscape (hdc, SETPOWERMANAGEMENT, sizeof (vpm),
                    (LPSTR)&vpm, 0, 0);

    // Always release what you get.
    ReleaseDC (NULL, hdc);
    return 0;
}
```

The preceding code queries to see whether the escape is supported by calling *ExtEscape* with the command *QUERYESCSUPPORT*. The command being queried is passed in the input buffer. If the *SETPOWERMANAGEMENT* command is supported, the routine fills in the *VIDEO_POWER_MANAGEMENT* structure and calls *ExtEscape* again to set the power state.

Although these escape codes allow applications to turn the display on and off, Windows CE has no uniform method to control the brightness of the backlight. Each system has its own OEM-unique method of backlight brightness control. If there's a standard method of brightness control in the future, it will probably be exposed through the power manager.

Powering Up the System

If the system is suspended, applications aren't running, so it seems that an application would have no control on when the system resumes. However, there are a few methods for waking a suspended device. First, an application can schedule the system to resume at a given time by using the Notification API discussed in Chapter 12. In addition, OEMs can assign some interrupt conditions so that they power up (or in power management talk, resume) the system. An example of this behavior is a system that resumes when it is placed in a synchronization cradle.

Preventing the System from Powering Down

The opposite problem—preventing the system from suspending—can also be an issue. Windows CE systems are usually configured to automatically suspend after some period of no user input. To prevent this automatic suspension, an application can periodically call the following function:

```
void WINAPI SystemIdleTimerReset (void);
```

This function resets the timer that Windows CE maintains to monitor user input. If the timer reaches a predefined interval without user input, the system automatically suspends itself. Because the suspend timeout value can be changed, an application needs to know the timeout value so that it can call *SystemIdleTimerReset* slightly more often. The system maintains three timeout values, all of which can be queried using the *SystemParametersInfo* function.

The different values, represented by the constant passed to *SystemParametersInfo*, are shown here:

- **SPI_GETBATTERYIDLETIMEOUT** Time from the last user input when the system is running on battery power
- **SPI_GETEXTERNALIDLETIMEOUT** Time from the last user input when the system is running on AC power
- **SPI_GETWAKEUPIDLETIMEOUT** Time from the system auto-powering before the system suspends again

To prevent the system from suspending automatically, you need to query these three values and call *SystemIdleTimerReset* before the shortest time returned. If any timeout value is 0, that specific timeout is disabled.

In the next chapter, I'll take a swing back into communication with a discussion of serial ports. Many devices in the embedded world communicate with serial communication, so knowing how to use Windows CE's serial API is quite handy at times. Let's see how it's done.

Chapter 16
Serial Communications

If there's one area of the Win32 API where Windows CE doesn't skimp, it's in communication. It makes sense. Either systems running Windows CE are mobile, requiring extensive communication functionality, or they're devices generally employed to communicate with remote servers or as remote servers. In this chapter, I introduce the low-level serial communication APIs.

Talking to a serial port involves opening and conversing with a serial device driver. Talking to a device driver isn't a complicated process. In fact, in the tradition of most modern operating systems, applications in Windows CE access device drivers through the file system API, using functions such as *CreateFile*, *ReadFile*, *WriteFile*, and *CloseHandle*. In addition, there are times, and the serial driver occasions one of those times, when an application needs to talk to the device, not just send data through the device. To do this, use the *DeviceIoControl* function. We'll use all these functions in this chapter.

Basic Serial Communication

The interface for a serial device is a combination of generic driver I/O calls and specific communication-related functions. The serial device is treated as a generic, installable stream device for opening, closing, reading from, and writing to the serial port. For configuring the port, the Win32 API supports a set of Comm functions. Windows CE supports most of the Comm functions supported on the desktop.

A word of warning: programming a serial port under Windows CE isn't like programming one under MS-DOS. You can't simply find the base address of the serial port and program the registers directly. While there are ways for a program to gain access to the physical memory space, every Windows CE device has a different physical memory map. Even if you solved the access problem by knowing exactly where the serial hardware resided in the memory map, there's no guarantee the serial hardware is going to be compatible with the 16550-compatible serial interface we've all come to know and love in the PC world. In fact, the implementation of the serial port on some Windows CE devices looks nothing like a 16550.

But even if you know where to go in the memory map and the implementation of the serial hardware, you still don't need to "hack down to the hardware." The serial port drivers in Windows CE are interrupt-driven designs and are written to support its specific serial hardware. If you have any special needs not provided by the base serial driver, you can purchase the Microsoft Windows CE Platform Builder and write a serial driver yourself. Aside from that extreme case, there's just no reason not to use the published Win32 serial interface under Windows CE.

Opening and Closing a Serial Port

As with all stream device drivers, a serial port device is opened using *CreateFile*. The name used needs to follow a specific format: the three letters *COM* followed by the number of the COM port to open and then a colon. The colon is required under Windows CE and is a departure from the naming convention used for device driver names used on the desktop versions of Windows.

The traditional driver naming convention allowed only 10 instances of a COM port. Windows CE also supports an extended naming convention that allows instance values other than 0 to 9. This convention prefixes the string "\$device\" in front of the driver name and omits the trailing colon. A driver name in this format would look like "\$device\COM1" or "\$device\COM24".

The following line opens COM port 1 for reading and writing:

```
hSer = CreateFile (TEXT ("COM1:"), GENERIC_READ | GENERIC_WRITE,
                   0, NULL, OPEN_EXISTING, 0, NULL);
```

You must pass a 0 in the sharing parameter as well as in the security attributes and the template file parameters of *CreateFile*. Windows CE doesn't support overlapped I/O for devices, so you can't pass the *FILE_FLAG_OVERLAPPED* flag in the *dwFlagsAndAttributes* parameter. The handle returned is either the handle to the opened serial port or *INVALID_HANDLE_VALUE*. Remember that unlike many of the Windows functions, *CreateFile* doesn't return a 0 for a failed open.

You close a serial port by calling *CloseHandle*, as in the following:

```
CloseHandle (hSer);
```

You don't do anything differently when using *CloseHandle* to close a serial device than when you use it to close a file handle.

Reading from and Writing to a Serial Port

Just as you use the *CreateFile* function to open a serial port, you use the functions *ReadFile* and *WriteFile* to read and write to that serial port. Reading data from a serial port is as simple as making this call to *ReadFile*:

```
INT rc;
DWORD cBytes;
BYTE ch;

rc = ReadFile(hSer, &ch, 1, &cBytes, NULL);
```

This call assumes the serial port has been successfully opened with a call to *CreateFile*. If the call is successful, one byte is read into the variable *ch*, and *cBytes* is set to the number of bytes read.

Writing to a serial port is just as simple. The call would look something like the following:

```
INT rc;
DWORD cBytes;
BYTE ch;

ch = TEXT ('a');
rc = WriteFile(hSer, &ch, 1, &cBytes, NULL);
```

This code writes the character *a* to the serial port previously opened. As you may remember from Chapter 9, both *ReadFile* and *WriteFile* return *TRUE* if successful.

Because overlapped I/O isn't supported under Windows CE, you should be careful not to attempt to read or write a large amount of serial data from your primary thread or from any thread that has created a window. Because those threads are also responsible for handling the message queues for their windows, they can't be blocked waiting on a relatively slow serial read or write. Instead, you should use separate threads for reading from and writing to the serial port.

You can also transmit a single character using this function:

```
BOOL TransmitCommChar (HANDLE hFile, char cChar);
```

The difference between the *TransmitCommChar* and *WriteFile* functions is that *TransmitCommChar* puts the character to be transmitted at the front of the transmit queue. When you call *WriteFile*, the characters are queued up after any characters that haven't yet been transmitted by the serial driver. *TransmitCommChar* allows you to insert control characters quickly in the stream without having to wait for the queue to empty.

Asynchronous Serial I/O

While Windows CE doesn't support overlapped I/O, there's no reason why you can't use multiple threads to implement the same type of overlapped operation. All that's required is that you launch separate threads to handle the synchronous I/O operations while your primary thread goes about its business. In addition to using separate threads for reading and writing, Windows CE supports the Win32 *WaitCommEvent* function that blocks a thread until one of a group of preselected serial events occurs. I'll demonstrate how to use separate threads for reading and writing a serial port in the CeChat example program later in this chapter.

You can make a thread wait on serial driver events by means of the following three functions:

```
BOOL SetCommMask (HANDLE hFile, DWORD dwEvtMask);
BOOL GetCommMask (HANDLE hFile, LPDWORD lpEvtMask);
```

and

```
BOOL WaitCommEvent (HANDLE hFile, LPDWORD lpEvtMask,
                    LPOVERLAPPED lpOverlapped);
```

To wait on an event, you first set the event mask using *SetCommMask*. The parameters for this function are the handle to the serial device and a combination of the following event flags:

- **EV_BREAK** A break was detected.
- **EV_CTS** The Clear to Send (CTS) signal changed state.
- **EV_DSR** The Data Set Ready (DSR) signal changed state.
- **EV_ERR** An error was detected by the serial driver.
- **EV_RLSD** The Receive Line Signal Detect (RLSD) line changed state.
- **EV_RXCHAR** A character was received.
- **EV_RXFLAG** An event character was received.
- **EV_TXEMPTY** The transmit buffer is empty.

You can set any or all of the flags in this list at the same time using *SetCommMask*. You can query the current event mask using *GetCommMask*.

To wait on the events specified by *SetCommMask*, you call *WaitCommEvent*. The parameters for this call are the handle to the device; a pointer to a *DWORD* that will receive the reason the call returned; and *lpOverlapped*, which under Windows CE must be set to *NULL*. The code fragment that follows waits on a character being received or an error. The code assumes that the serial port has already been opened and that the handle is contained in *hComPort*.

```
DWORD dwMask;
// Set mask and wait.
SetCommMask (hComPort, EV_RXCHAR | EV_ERR);
if (WaitCommEvent (hComPort, &dwMask, 0) {

    // Use the flags returned in dwMask to determine the reason
    // for returning.
    Switch (dwMask) {
    case EV_RXCHAR:
        //Read character.
        break;
    case EV_ERR:
        // Process error.
        break;
    }
}
```

Configuring the Serial Port

Reading from and writing to a serial port is fairly straightforward, but you also must configure the port for the proper baud rate, character size, and so forth. The masochist could configure the serial driver through device I/O control (IOCTL) calls, but the *IoCtl* codes necessary for this are exposed only in the Platform Builder, not the Software Development Kit. Besides, there's a simpler method.

You can go a long way in configuring the serial port using two functions, *GetCommState* and *SetCommState*, prototyped here:

```
BOOL SetCommState (HANDLE hFile, LPDCB lpDCB);
BOOL GetCommState (HANDLE hFile, LPDCB lpDCB);
```

Both these functions take two parameters: the handle to the opened serial port and a pointer to a *DCB* structure. The extensive *DCB* structure is defined as follows:

```
typedef struct _DCB {
    DWORD DCBlength;
    DWORD BaudRate;
    DWORD fBinary: 1;
    DWORD fParity: 1;
    DWORD fOutxCtsFlow:1;
    DWORD fOutxDsrFlow:1;
    DWORD fDtrControl:2;
    DWORD fDsrSensitivity:1;
    DWORD fTXContinueOnXoff:1;
    DWORD fOutX: 1;
    DWORD fInX: 1;
    DWORD fErrorChar: 1;
    DWORD fNull: 1;
    DWORD fRtsControl:2;
    DWORD fAbortOnError:1;
    DWORD fDummy2:17;
    WORD wReserved;
    WORD XonLim;
    WORD XoffLim;
    BYTE ByteSize;
    BYTE Parity;
    BYTE StopBits;
    char XonChar;
    char XoffChar;
    char ErrorChar;
    char EofChar;
    char EvtChar;
    WORD wReserved1;
} DCB;
```

As you can see from the structure, *SetCommState* can set a fair number of states. Instead of attempting to fill out the entire structure from scratch, you should use the best method of modifying a serial port, which is to call *GetCommState* to fill in a *DCB* structure, modify the fields necessary, and then call *SetCommState* to configure the serial port.

The first field in the *DCB* structure, *DCBlength*, should be set to the size of the structure. This field should be initialized before the call to either *GetCommState* or *SetCommState*. The *BaudRate* field should be set to one of the baud rate constants defined in Winbase.h. The baud rate constants range from *CBR_110* for 110 bits per second to *CBR_256000* for 256 kilobits per second (Kbps). Just because constants are defined for speeds up to 256 Kbps doesn't mean that all serial ports support that speed. To determine what baud rates a serial port supports, you can call *GetCommProperties*, which I'll describe later. Windows CE devices generally support speeds up to 115 Kbps, although some support faster speeds. The *fBinary* field must be set to *TRUE* because no Win32 operating system currently supports a nonbinary serial transmit mode familiar to MS-DOS programmers. The *fParity* field can be set to *TRUE* to enable parity checking.

The *fOutxCtsFlow* field should be set to *TRUE* if the output of the serial port should be controlled by the port CTS line. The *fOutxDsrFlow* field should be set to *TRUE* if the output of the serial port should be controlled by the DSR line of the serial port. The *fDtrControl* field can be set to one of three values: *DTR_CONTROL_DISABLE*, which disables the DTR (Data Terminal Ready) line and leaves it disabled; *DTR_CONTROL_ENABLE*, which enables the DTR line; or *DTR_CONTROL_HANDSHAKE*, which tells the serial driver to toggle the DTR line in response to how much data is in the receive buffer.

The *fDsrSensitivity* field is set to *TRUE*, and the serial port ignores any incoming bytes unless the port DSR line is enabled. Setting the *fTXContinueOnXoff* field to *TRUE* tells the driver to stop transmitting characters if its receive buffer has reached its limit and the driver has transmitted an XOFF character. Setting the *fOutX* field to *TRUE* specifies that the XON/XOFF control is used to control the serial output. Setting the *fInX* field to *TRUE* specifies that the XON/XOFF control is used for the input serial stream.

The *fErrorChar* and *ErrorChar* fields are ignored by the default implementation of the Windows CE serial driver, although some drivers might support these fields. Likewise, the *fAbortOnError* field is also ignored. Setting the *fNull* field to *TRUE* tells the serial driver to discard null bytes received.

The *fRtsControl* field specifies the operation of the RTS (Request to Send) line. The field can be set to one of the following: *RTS_CONTROL_DISABLE*, indicating that the RTS line is set to the disabled state while the port is open; *RTS_CONTROL_ENABLE*, indicating that the RTS line is set to the enabled state while the port is open; or *RTS_CONTROL_HANDSHAKE*, indicating that the RTS line is controlled by the driver. In this mode, the RTS line is enabled if the serial input buffer is less than half full; it's disabled otherwise. Finally, *RTS_CONTROL_TOGGLE* indicates that the driver enables the RTS line if there are bytes in the output buffer ready to be transmitted and disables the line otherwise.

The *XonLim* field specifies the minimum number of bytes in the input buffer before an XON character is automatically sent. The *XoffLim* field specifies the maximum number of bytes in the input buffer before the XOFF character is sent. This limit value is computed by taking the size of the input buffer and subtracting the value in *XoffLim*. In the sample Windows CE implementation of the serial driver provided in the Platform Builder, the *XonLim* field is ignored and XON and XOFF characters are sent based on the value in *XoffLim*. However, this behavior might differ in some systems.

The next three fields, *ByteSize*, *Parity*, and *StopBits*, define the format of the serial data word transmitted. The *ByteSize* field specifies the number of bits per byte, usually a value of 7 or 8, but in some older modes the number of bits per byte can be as small as 5. The *Parity* field can be set to the self-explanatory constant *EVENPARITY*, *MARKPARITY*, *NOPARITY*, *ODDPARITY*, or *SPACEPARITY*. The *StopBits* field should be set to *ONESTOPBIT*, *ONE5STOPBITS*, or *TWOSTOPBITS*, depending on whether you want one, one and a half, or two stop bits per byte.

The next two fields, *XonChar* and *XoffChar*, let you specify the XON and XOFF characters. Likewise, the *EvtChar* field lets you specify the character used to signal an event. If an event character is received, an *EV_RXFLAG* event is signaled by the driver. This "event" is what triggers the *WaitCommEvent* function to return if the *EV_RXFLAG* bit is set in the event mask.

Setting the Port Timeout Values

As you can see, *SetCommState* can fine-tune, to almost the smallest detail, the operation of the serial driver. However, one more step is necessary—setting the timeout values for the port. The timeout is the length of time Windows CE waits on a read or write operation before *ReadFile* or *WriteFile* automatically returns. The functions that control the serial timeouts are the following:

```
BOOL GetCommTimeouts (HANDLE hFile, LPCOMMTIMEOUTS lpCommTimeouts);
```

and

```
BOOL SetCommTimeouts (HANDLE hFile, LPCOMMTIMEOUTS lpCommTimeouts);
```

Both functions take the handle to the open serial device and a pointer to a *COMMTIMEOUTS* structure, defined as the following:

```
typedef struct _COMMTIMEOUTS {
    DWORD ReadIntervalTimeout;
    DWORD ReadTotalTimeoutMultiplier;
    DWORD ReadTotalTimeoutConstant;
    DWORD WriteTotalTimeoutMultiplier;
    DWORD WriteTotalTimeoutConstant;
} COMMTIMEOUTS;
```

The *COMMTIMEOUTS* structure provides for a set of timeout parameters that time both the interval between characters and the total time to read and write a block of characters. Timeouts are computed in two ways. First, *ReadIntervalTimeout* specifies the maximum interval between characters received. If this time is exceeded, the *ReadFile* call returns immediately.

The other timeout is based on the number of characters you're waiting to receive. The value in *ReadTotalTimeoutMultiplier* is multiplied by the number of characters requested in the call to *ReadFile* and is added to *ReadTotalTimeoutConstant* to compute a total timeout for a call to *ReadFile*.

The write timeout can be specified only for the total time spent during the *WriteFile* call. This timeout is computed the same way as the total read timeout: by specifying a multiplier value, the time in *WriteTotalTimeoutMultiplier*, and a constant value in *WriteTotalTimeoutConstant*. All of the times in this structure are specified in milliseconds.

In addition to the basic timeouts that I just described, you can set values in the *COMMTIMEOUTS* structure to control whether and exactly how timeouts are used in calls to *ReadFile* and *WriteFile*. You can configure the timeouts in the following ways:

- Timeouts for reading and writing as well as an interval timeout: set the fields in the *COMMTIMEOUTS* structure for the appropriate timeout values.
- Timeouts for reading and writing with no interval timeout: set *ReadIntervalTimeout* to 0. Set the other fields for the appropriate timeout values.
- The *ReadFile* function returns immediately regardless of whether there is data to be read. Set *ReadIntervalTimeout* to *MAXDWORD*. Set *ReadTotalTimeoutMultiplier* and *ReadTotalTimeoutConstant* to 0.
- *ReadFile* doesn't have a timeout. The function doesn't return until the proper number of bytes is returned or an error occurs. Set the *ReadIntervalTimeout*, *ReadTotalTimeoutMultiplier*, and *ReadTotalTimeoutConstant* fields to 0.
- *WriteFile* doesn't have a timeout. Set *WriteTotalTimeoutMultiplier* and *WriteTotalTimeoutConstant* to 0.

The timeout values are important because the worst thing you can do is to spin in a loop waiting on characters from the serial port. While the calls to *ReadFile* and *WriteFile* are waiting on the serial port, the calling threads are efficiently blocked on an event object internal to the driver. This saves precious CPU and battery power during the serial transmit and receive operations. Of course, to block on *ReadFile* and *WriteFile*, you'll have to create secondary threads because you can't have your primary thread blocked waiting on the serial port.

Another call isn't quite as useful—*SetupComm*, prototyped this way:

```
BOOL SetupComm (HANDLE hFile, DWORD dwInQueue, DWORD dwOutQueue);
```

This function lets you specify the size of the input and output buffers for the driver. However, the sizes passed in *SetupComm* are only recommendations, not requirements to the serial driver. For example, the example implementation of the serial driver in the Platform Builder ignores these recommended buffer sizes.

Querying the Capabilities of the Serial Driver

The configuration functions enable you to configure the serial driver, but with varied implementations of serial ports, you need to know just what features a serial port supports before you configure it. The function *GetCommProperties* provides just this service. The function is prototyped this way:

```
BOOL GetCommProperties (HANDLE hFile, LPCOMMPROP lpCommProp);
```

GetCommProperties takes two parameters: the handle to the opened serial driver and a pointer to a *COMMPROP* structure defined as

```
typedef struct _COMMPROP {
    WORD wPacketLength;
    WORD wPacketVersion;
    DWORD dwServiceMask;
    DWORD dwReserved1;
    DWORD dwMaxTxQueue;
    DWORD dwMaxRxQueue;
    DWORD dwMaxBaud;
    DWORD dwProvSubType;
    DWORD dwProvCapabilities;
    DWORD dwSettableParams;
    DWORD dwSettableBaud;
    WORD wSettableData;
    WORD wSettableStopParity;
    DWORD dwCurrentTxQueue;
    DWORD dwCurrentRxQueue;
    DWORD dwProvSpec1;
    DWORD dwProvSpec2;
    WCHAR wcProvChar[1];
} COMMPROP;
```

As you can see from the fields of the *COMMPROP* structure, *GetCommProperties* returns generally enough information to determine the capabilities of the device. Of immediate interest to speed demons is the *dwMaxBaud* field that indicates the maximum baud rate of the serial port. The *dwSettableBaud* field contains bit flags that indicate the allowable baud rates for the port. Both these fields use bit flags that are defined in WinBase.h. These constants are expressed as *BAUD_xxxx*, as in *BAUD_19200*, which indicates that the port is capable of a speed of 19.2 kbps. Note that these constants are *not* the constants used to set the speed of the serial port in the *DCB* structure. Those constants are numbers, not bit flags. To set the speed of a COM port in the *DCB* structure to 19.2 kbps, you would use the constant *CBR_19200* in the *BaudRate* field of the *DCB* structure.

Starting back at the top of the structure are the *wPacketLength* and *wPacketVersion* fields. These fields allow you to request more information from the driver than is supported by the generic call. The *dwServiceMask* field indicates what services the port supports. The only service currently supported is *SP_SERIALCOMM*, indicating that the port is a serial communication port.

The *dwMaxTxQueue* and *dwMaxRxQueue* fields indicate the maximum size of the output and input buffers internal to the driver. The value 0 in these fields indicates that you'll encounter no limit in the size of the internal queues. The *dwCurrentTxQueue* and *dwCurrentRxQueue* fields indicate the current size for the queues. These fields are 0 if the queue size can't be determined.

The *dwProvSubType* field contains flags that indicate the type of serial port supported by the driver. Values here include *PST_RS232*, *PST_RS422*, and *PST_RS423*, indicating the physical layer protocol of the port. *PST_MODEM* indicates a modem device, and *PST_FAX* tells you the port is a fax device. Other *PST_* flags are defined as well. This field reports what the driver thinks the port is, not what device is attached to the port. For example, if an external modem is attached to a standard RS-232 serial port, the driver returns the *PST_RS232* flag, not the *PST_MODEM* flag.

The *dwProvCapabilities* field contains flags indicating the handshaking the port supports, such as XON/XOFF, RTS/CTS, and DTR/DSR. This field also shows you whether the port supports setting the characters used for XON/XOFF, parity checking, and so forth. The *dwSettableParams*, *dwSettableData*, and *dwSettableStopParity* fields give you information about how the serial data stream can be configured. Finally, the fields *dwProvSpec1*, *dwProvSpec2*, and *wcProvChar* are used by the driver to return driver-specific data.

Controlling the Serial Port

You can stop and start a serial stream using the following functions:

```
BOOL SetCommBreak (HANDLE hFile);
```

and

```
BOOL ClearCommBreak (HANDLE hFile);
```

The only parameter for both these functions is the handle to the opened COM port. When *SetCommBreak* is called, the COM port stops transmitting characters and places the port in a break state. Communication is resumed with the *ClearCommBreak* function.

You can clear out any characters in either the transmit or the receive queue internal to the serial driver using this function:

```
BOOL PurgeComm (HANDLE hFile, DWORD dwFlags);
```

The *dwFlags* parameter can be a combination of the flags *PURGE_TXCLEAR* and *PURGE_RXCLEAR*. These flags terminate any pending writes and reads and reset the queues. In the case of *PURGE_RXCLEAR*, the driver also clears any receive holds due to any flow control states, transmitting an XON character if necessary, and setting RTS and DTR if those flow control methods are enabled. Because Windows CE doesn't support overlapped I/O, the flags

PURGE_TXABORT and *PURGE_RXABORT*, used under the desktop versions of Windows, are ignored.

The *EscapeCommFunction* provides a more general method of controlling the serial driver. It allows you to set and clear the state of specific signals on the port. On Windows CE devices, it's also used to control serial hardware that's shared between the serial port and the IrDA port. The function is prototyped as

```
BOOL EscapeCommFunction (HANDLE hFile, DWORD dwFunc);
```

The function takes two parameters: the handle to the device and a set of flags in *dwFunc*. The flags can be one of the following values:

- **SETDTR** Sets the DTR signal
- **CLRDTR** Clears the DTR signal
- **SETRTS** Sets the RTS signal
- **CLRRTS** Clears the RTS signal
- **SETXOFF** Tells the driver to act as if an XOFF character has been received
- **SETXON** Tells the driver to act as if an XON character has been received
- **SETBREAK** Suspends serial transmission and sets the port in a break state
- **CLRBREAK** Resumes serial transmission from a break state
- **SETIR** Tells the serial port to transmit and receive through the infrared transceiver
- **CLRIR** Tells the serial port to transmit and receive through the standard serial transceiver

The *SETBREAK* and *CLRBREAK* commands act identically to *SetCommBreak* and *ClearCommBreak* and can be used interchangeably. For example, you can use *EscapeCommFunction* to put the port in a break state and *ClearCommBreak* to restore communication.

Clearing Errors and Querying Status

The function

```
BOOL ClearCommError (HANDLE hFile, LPDWORD lpErrors, LPCOMSTAT lpStat);
```

performs two functions. As you might expect from the name, it clears any error states within the driver so that I/O can continue. The serial device driver is responsible for reporting the errors. The default serial driver returns the following flags in the variable pointed to by *lpErrors*: *CE_OVERRUN*, *CE_RXPARITY*, *CE_FRAME*, and *CE_TXFULL*. *ClearCommError* also returns the status of the port. The third parameter of *ClearCommError* is a pointer to a *COMSTAT* structure defined as

```
typedef struct _COMSTAT {
    DWORD fCtsHold : 1;
    DWORD fDsrHold : 1;
    DWORD fRlsdHold : 1;
    DWORD fXoffHold : 1;
    DWORD fXoffSent : 1;
    DWORD fEof : 1;
    DWORD fTxim : 1;
    DWORD fReserved : 25;
    DWORD cbInQue;
    DWORD cbOutQue;
} COMSTAT;
```

The first five fields indicate that serial transmission is waiting for one of the following reasons; it's waiting for a CTS signal, waiting for a DSR signal, waiting for a Receive Line Signal Detect (also known as a Carrier Detect), waiting because an XOFF character was received, or waiting because an XOFF character was sent by the driver. The *fEor* field indicates that an end-of-file character has been received. The *fTxim* field is *TRUE* if a character placed in the queue by the *TransmitCommChar* function (instead of a call to *WriteFile*) is queued for transmission. The final two fields, *cbInQue* and *cbOutQue*, return the number of characters in the input and output queues of the serial driver.

The function

```
BOOL GetCommModemStatus (HANDLE hFile, LPDWORD lpModemStat);
```

returns the status of the modem control signals in the variable pointed to by *lpModemStat*. The flags returned can be any of the following:

- **MS_CTS_ON** Clear to Send (CTS) is active.
- **MS_DSR_ON** Data Set Ready (DSR) is active.
- **MS_RING_ON** Ring Indicate (RI) is active.
- **MS_RLSD_ON** Receive Line Signal Detect (RLSD) is active.

Stayin' Alive

One of the issues with serial communication is preventing the system from powering down while a serial link is active. A Windows CE system has a power management scheme that may automatically suspend the system if the user hasn't interacted with the device within a predetermined time. Because a communication program can run unattended, the program might need to prevent the auto-suspend feature of Windows CE from suspending the system. I covered this topic in the "Preventing the System from Powering Down" section in Chapter 15.

The CeChat Example Program

The CeChat program is a simple point-to-point chat program that connects two Windows CE devices using any of the available serial ports on the device. The CeChat window is shown in Figure 16-1. Most of the window is taken up by the receive text window. Text received from the other device is displayed here. Along the bottom of the screen is the send text window. If you type characters here and either hit the Enter key or tap the Send button, the text is sent to the other device. The combo box on the command bar selects the serial port to use.

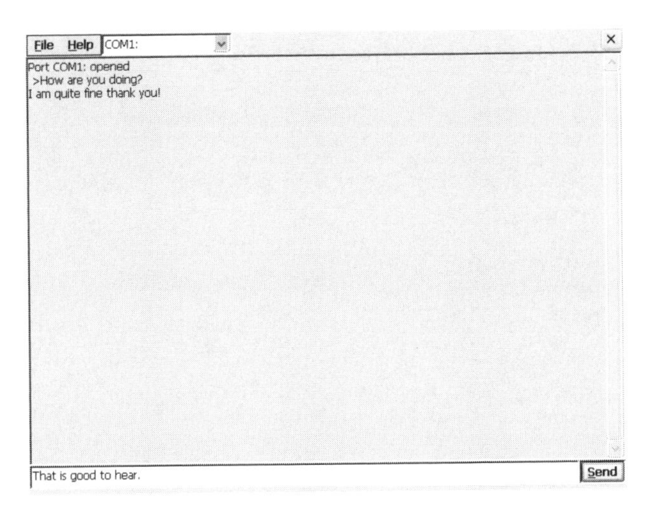

FIGURE 16-1 The CeChat window

The source code for CeChat is shown in Listing 16-1. CeChat uses three threads to accomplish its work. The primary thread manages the window and the message loop. The two secondary threads handle reading from and writing to the appropriate serial port.

LISTING 16-1

CeChat.rc

```
//======================================================================
// Resource file
//
// Written for the book Programming Windows CE
// Copyright (C) 2007 Douglas Boling
//======================================================================
#include "windows.h"
#include "CeChat.h"                              // Program-specific stuff
//----------------------------------------------------------------------
// Icons and bitmaps
//
ID_ICON ICON   "CeChat.ico"                      // Program icon
```

```
//----------------------------------------------------------------------
// Menu
//
ID_MENU MENU DISCARDABLE
BEGIN
    POPUP "&File"
    BEGIN
        MENUITEM "E&xit",                       IDM_EXIT
    END
    POPUP "&Help"
    BEGIN
        MENUITEM "&About...",                   IDM_ABOUT
    END
END
//----------------------------------------------------------------------
// Accelerator table
//
ID_ACCEL ACCELERATORS DISCARDABLE
BEGIN
    "Q",       IDM_EXIT,   VIRTKEY, CONTROL, NOINVERT
    "S",       ID_SENDBTN, VIRTKEY, ALT
    VK_RETURN, ID_SENDBTN, VIRTKEY
END

///---------------------------------------------------------------------
// About box dialog template
//
aboutbox DIALOG discardable 10, 10, 135, 40
STYLE  WS_POPUP | WS_VISIBLE | WS_CAPTION | WS_SYSMENU | DS_CENTER |
       DS_MODALFRAME
CAPTION "About"
BEGIN
    ICON  ID_ICON,                    -1,   3,   5,  10,  10
    LTEXT "CeChat - Written for the book Programming Windows \
           CE Copyright 2007 Douglas Boling"
                                      -1,  30,   5, 102,  37
END
```

CeChat.h

```
/ //====================================================================
// Header file
//
// Written for the book Programming Windows CE
// Copyright (C) 2007 Douglas Boling
//======================================================================
// Returns number of elements
#define dim(x) (sizeof(x) / sizeof(x[0]))

//----------------------------------------------------------------------
// Generic defines and data types
```

```
//
struct decodeUINT {                             // Structure associates
    UINT Code;                                  // messages
                                                // with a function.
    LRESULT (*Fxn)(HWND, UINT, WPARAM, LPARAM);
};
struct decodeCMD {                              // Structure associates
    UINT Code;                                  // menu IDs with a
    LRESULT (*Fxn)(HWND, WORD, HWND, WORD);     // function.
};
//----------------------------------------------------------------------
// Generic defines used by application
#define  ID_ICON            1                   // App icon resource ID
#define  ID_MENU            2                   // Menu resource ID
#define  ID_ACCEL           3                   // Accel table ID
#define  IDC_CMDBAR         4                   // Command band ID
#define  ID_RCVTEXT         5                   // Receive text box
#define  ID_SENDTEXT        6                   // Send text box
#define  ID_SENDBTN         7                   // Send button
// Menu item IDs
#define  IDM_EXIT           1

#define  IDM_USECOM         110                 // Use COM.
#define  IDM_ABOUT          120                 // Help menu

// Command bar IDs
#define  IDC_COMPORT        150                 // COM port combo box
#define  IDC_BAUDRATE       151                 // Baud rate combo box

#define TEXTSIZE 256
//----------------------------------------------------------------------
// Function prototypes
//
DWORD WINAPI ReadThread (PVOID pArg);
DWORD WINAPI SendThread (PVOID pArg);
HANDLE InitCommunication (HWND, LPTSTR);
int FillComComboBox (HWND);

HWND InitInstance (HINSTANCE, LPWSTR, int);
int TermInstance (HINSTANCE, int);

// Window procedures
LRESULT CALLBACK MainWndProc (HWND, UINT, WPARAM, LPARAM);

// Message handlers
LRESULT DoCreateMain (HWND, UINT, WPARAM, LPARAM);
LRESULT DoSizeMain (HWND, UINT, WPARAM, LPARAM);
LRESULT DoSetFocusMain (HWND, UINT, WPARAM, LPARAM);
LRESULT DoPocketPCShell (HWND, UINT, WPARAM, LPARAM);
LRESULT DoCommandMain (HWND, UINT, WPARAM, LPARAM);
LRESULT DoDestroyMain (HWND, UINT, WPARAM, LPARAM);
// Command functions
LPARAM DoMainCommandExit (HWND, WORD, HWND, WORD);
LPARAM DoMainCommandComPort (HWND, WORD, HWND, WORD);
```

```
LPARAM DoMainCommandSendText (HWND, WORD, HWND, WORD);
LPARAM DoMainCommandAbout (HWND, WORD, HWND, WORD);

// Dialog procedures
BOOL CALLBACK AboutDlgProc (HWND, UINT, WPARAM, LPARAM);
BOOL CALLBACK EditAlbumDlgProc (HWND, UINT, WPARAM, LPARAM);
```

CeChat.cpp

```
//======================================================================
// CeChat - A Windows CE communication demo
//
// Written for the book Programming Windows CE
// Copyright (C) 2007 Douglas Boling
//======================================================================
#include <windows.h>                 // For all that Windows stuff
#include <commctrl.h>                // Command bar includes
#include "CeChat.h"                  // Program-specific stuff

#if defined(WIN32_PLATFORM_PSPC)
#include <aygshell.h>                // Add Pocket PC includes.
#pragma comment( lib, "aygshell" )   // Link Pocket PC lib for menu bar.
#endif
//----------------------------------------------------------------------
// Global data
//
const TCHAR szAppName[] = TEXT ("CeChat");
HINSTANCE hInst;                     // Program instance handle.

BOOL fContinue = TRUE;
HANDLE hComPort = INVALID_HANDLE_VALUE;
int nSpeed = CBR_19200;
int nLastDev = -1;

#if defined(WIN32_PLATFORM_PSPC) && (_WIN32_WCE >= 300)
SHACTIVATEINFO sai;
#endif

HANDLE g_hSendEvent = INVALID_HANDLE_VALUE;
HANDLE hReadThread = INVALID_HANDLE_VALUE;

// Message dispatch table for MainWindowProc
const struct decodeUINT MainMessages[] = {
    WM_CREATE, DoCreateMain,
    WM_SIZE, DoSizeMain,
    WM_COMMAND, DoCommandMain,
    WM_SETTINGCHANGE, DoPocketPCShell,
    WM_ACTIVATE, DoPocketPCShell,
    WM_SETFOCUS, DoSetFocusMain,
    WM_DESTROY, DoDestroyMain,
};
```

```
// Command Message dispatch for MainWindowProc
const struct decodeCMD MainCommandItems[] = {
    IDC_COMPORT, DoMainCommandComPort,
    ID_SENDBTN, DoMainCommandSendText,
    IDM_EXIT, DoMainCommandExit,
    IDM_ABOUT, DoMainCommandAbout,
};
//======================================================================
// Program entry point
//
int WINAPI WinMain (HINSTANCE hInstance, HINSTANCE hPrevInstance,
                    LPWSTR lpCmdLine, int nCmdShow) {
    HWND hwndMain;
    HACCEL hAccel;
    MSG msg;
    int rc = 0;

    // Initialize this instance.
    hwndMain = InitInstance (hInstance, lpCmdLine, nCmdShow);
    if (hwndMain == 0)
        return 0x10;

    // Load accelerator table.
    hAccel = LoadAccelerators (hInst, MAKEINTRESOURCE (ID_ACCEL));

    // Application message loop
    while (GetMessage (&msg, NULL, 0, 0)) {
        if (!TranslateAccelerator (hwndMain, hAccel, &msg)) {
            TranslateMessage (&msg);
            DispatchMessage (&msg);
        }
    }
    // Instance cleanup
    return TermInstance (hInstance, msg.wParam);
}
//----------------------------------------------------------------------
// InitInstance - Instance initialization
//
HWND InitInstance (HINSTANCE hInstance, LPWSTR lpCmdLine, int nCmdShow){
    HWND hWnd;
    HANDLE hThread;
    WNDCLASS wc;
    INITCOMMONCONTROLSEX icex;

    // Save program instance handle in global variable.
    hInst = hInstance;

#if defined(WIN32_PLATFORM_PSPC)
    // If Win Mobile, allow only one instance of the application.
    hWnd = FindWindow (szAppName, NULL);
    if (hWnd) {
        SetForegroundWindow ((HWND)(((DWORD)hWnd) | 0x01));
        return 0;
    }
```

```
#endif
// Register application main window class.
    wc.style = 0;                               // Window style
    wc.lpfnWndProc = MainWndProc;               // Callback function
    wc.cbClsExtra = 0;                          // Extra class data
    wc.cbWndExtra = 0;                          // Extra window data
    wc.hInstance = hInstance;                   // Owner handle
    wc.hIcon = NULL;                            // Application icon
    wc.hCursor = LoadCursor (NULL, IDC_ARROW);// Default cursor
    wc.hbrBackground = (HBRUSH) GetStockObject (WHITE_BRUSH);
    wc.lpszMenuName =  NULL;                    // Menu name
    wc.lpszClassName = szAppName;               // Window class name

    if (RegisterClass (&wc) == 0) return 0;

    // Load the command bar common control class.
    icex.dwSize = sizeof (INITCOMMONCONTROLSEX);
    icex.dwICC = ICC_BAR_CLASSES;
    InitCommonControlsEx (&icex);

    // Create unnamed auto-reset event initially false.
    g_hSendEvent = CreateEvent (NULL, FALSE, FALSE, NULL);

    // Create main window.
    hWnd = CreateWindow (szAppName, TEXT ("CeChat"),
                         WS_VISIBLE, CW_USEDEFAULT, CW_USEDEFAULT,
                         CW_USEDEFAULT, CW_USEDEFAULT, NULL,
                         NULL, hInstance, NULL);
    // Return fail code if window not created.
    if (!IsWindow (hWnd)) return 0;

    // Create write thread. Read thread created when port opened.
    hThread = CreateThread (NULL, 0, SendThread, hWnd, 0, NULL);
    if (hThread)
        CloseHandle (hThread);
    else {
        DestroyWindow (hWnd);
        return 0;
    }
    // Standard show and update calls
    ShowWindow (hWnd, nCmdShow);
    UpdateWindow (hWnd);
    return hWnd;
}
//----------------------------------------------------------------------
// TermInstance - Program cleanup
//
int TermInstance (HINSTANCE hInstance, int nDefRC) {
    HANDLE hPort = hComPort;

    fContinue = FALSE;

    hComPort = INVALID_HANDLE_VALUE;
```

```
    if (hPort != INVALID_HANDLE_VALUE)
        CloseHandle (hPort);

    if (g_hSendEvent != INVALID_HANDLE_VALUE) {
        PulseEvent (g_hSendEvent);
        Sleep(100);
        CloseHandle (g_hSendEvent);
    }
    return nDefRC;
}
//======================================================================
// Message handling procedures for MainWindow
//----------------------------------------------------------------------
// MainWndProc - Callback function for application window
//
LRESULT CALLBACK MainWndProc (HWND hWnd, UINT wMsg, WPARAM wParam,
                              LPARAM lParam) {
    int i;
    //
    // Search message list to see if we need to handle this
    // message.  If in list, call procedure.
    //
    for (i = 0; i < dim(MainMessages); i++) {
        if (wMsg == MainMessages[i].Code)
            return (*MainMessages[i].Fxn)(hWnd, wMsg, wParam, lParam);
    }
    return DefWindowProc (hWnd, wMsg, wParam, lParam);
}
//----------------------------------------------------------------------
// DoCreateMain - Process WM_CREATE message for window.
//
LRESULT DoCreateMain (HWND hWnd, UINT wMsg, WPARAM wParam,
                      LPARAM lParam) {
    HWND hwndCB, hC1, hC2, hC3;
    int  i;
    TCHAR szFirstDev[32];
    LPCREATESTRUCT lpcs = (LPCREATESTRUCT) lParam;

#if defined(WIN32_PLATFORM_PSPC)
    memset (&sai, 0, sizeof (sai));
    sai.cbSize = sizeof (sai);
    {
    SHMENUBARINFO mbi;                        // For WinMobile, create
    memset(&mbi, 0, sizeof(SHMENUBARINFO)); // menu bar so that we
    mbi.cbSize = sizeof(SHMENUBARINFO);     // have a sip button.
    mbi.hwndParent = hWnd;
    mbi.dwFlags = SHCMBF_EMPTYBAR;
    SHCreateMenuBar(&mbi);
    SetWindowPos (hWnd, 0, 0, 0, lpcs->cx, lpcs->cy-26,
                  SWP_NOZORDER | SWP_NOMOVE);
    }
#endif

    // Create a command bar.
```

```
    hwndCB = CommandBar_Create (hInst, hWnd, IDC_CMDBAR);
    CommandBar_InsertMenubar (hwndCB, hInst, ID_MENU, 0);

    // Insert the COM port combo box.
    CommandBar_InsertComboBox (hwndCB, hInst, 140, CBS_DROPDOWNLIST,
                               IDC_COMPORT, 1);
    FillComComboBox (hWnd);

    // Add exit button to command bar.
    CommandBar_AddAdornments (hwndCB, 0, 0);

    // Create child windows. They will be positioned in WM_SIZE.
    // Create receive text window.
    hC1 = CreateWindowEx (WS_EX_CLIENTEDGE, TEXT ("edit"),
                          TEXT (""), WS_VISIBLE | WS_CHILD |
                          WS_VSCROLL | ES_MULTILINE | ES_AUTOHSCROLL |
                          ES_READONLY, 0, 0, 10, 10, hWnd,
                          (HMENU)ID_RCVTEXT, hInst, NULL);
    // Create send text window.
    hC2 = CreateWindowEx (WS_EX_CLIENTEDGE, TEXT ("edit"),
                          TEXT (""), WS_VISIBLE | WS_CHILD,
                          0, 0, 10, 10,  hWnd, (HMENU)ID_SENDTEXT,
                            hInst, NULL);
    // Create send text window.
    hC3 = CreateWindowEx (WS_EX_CLIENTEDGE, TEXT ("button"),
                          TEXT ("&Send"), WS_VISIBLE | WS_CHILD |
                          BS_DEFPUSHBUTTON, 0, 0, 10, 10,
                          hWnd, (HMENU)ID_SENDBTN, hInst, NULL);
    // Destroy frame if window not created.
    if (!IsWindow (hC1) || !IsWindow (hC2) || !IsWindow (hC3)) {
        DestroyWindow (hWnd);
        return 0;
    }
    // Open a COM port.
    for (i = 0; i < 10; i++) {
        if (SendDlgItemMessage (hwndCB, IDC_COMPORT, CB_GETLBTEXT, i,
                           (LPARAM)szFirstDev) == CB_ERR)
            break;
        if (InitCommunication (hWnd, szFirstDev) !=
            INVALID_HANDLE_VALUE) {
            SendDlgItemMessage (hwndCB, IDC_COMPORT, CB_SETCURSEL, i,
                                (LPARAM)szFirstDev);
            break;
        }
    }
    return 0;
}
//----------------------------------------------------------------------
// DoSizeMain - Process WM_SIZE message for window.
//
LRESULT DoSizeMain (HWND hWnd, UINT wMsg, WPARAM wParam, LPARAM lParam){
    RECT rect;

    // Adjust the size of the client rect to take into account
```

```
    // the command bar height.
    GetClientRect (hWnd, &rect);
    rect.top += CommandBar_Height (GetDlgItem (hWnd, IDC_CMDBAR));

    SetWindowPos (GetDlgItem (hWnd, ID_RCVTEXT), NULL, rect.left,
                  rect.top, (rect.right - rect.left),
                  rect.bottom - rect.top - 25, SWP_NOZORDER);
    SetWindowPos (GetDlgItem (hWnd, ID_SENDTEXT), NULL, rect.left,
                  rect.bottom - 25, (rect.right - rect.left) - 50,
                  25, SWP_NOZORDER);
    SetWindowPos (GetDlgItem (hWnd, ID_SENDBTN), NULL,
                  (rect.right - rect.left) - 50, rect.bottom - 25,
                  50, 25, SWP_NOZORDER);
    return 0;
}
//----------------------------------------------------------------------
// DoPocketPCShell - Process Pocket PC required messages.
//
LRESULT DoPocketPCShell (HWND hWnd, UINT wMsg, WPARAM wParam,
                         LPARAM lParam) {
#if defined(WIN32_PLATFORM_PSPC)
    if (wMsg == WM_SETTINGCHANGE)
        return SHHandleWMSettingChange(hWnd, wParam, lParam, &sai);
    if (wMsg == WM_ACTIVATE)
        return SHHandleWMActivate(hWnd, wParam, lParam, &sai, 0);
#endif
    return 0;
}
//----------------------------------------------------------------------
// DoFocusMain - Process WM_SETFOCUS message for window.
//
LRESULT DoSetFocusMain (HWND hWnd, UINT wMsg, WPARAM wParam,
                        LPARAM lParam) {
    SetFocus (GetDlgItem (hWnd, ID_SENDTEXT));
    return 0;
}
//----------------------------------------------------------------------
// DoCommandMain - Process WM_COMMAND message for window.
//
LRESULT DoCommandMain (HWND hWnd, UINT wMsg, WPARAM wParam,
                       LPARAM lParam) {
    WORD    idItem, wNotifyCode;
    HWND hwndCtl;
    int  i;

    // Parse the parameters.
    idItem = (WORD) LOWORD (wParam);
    wNotifyCode = (WORD) HIWORD (wParam);
    hwndCtl = (HWND) lParam;

    // Call routine to handle control message.
    for (i = 0; i < dim(MainCommandItems); i++) {
        if (idItem == MainCommandItems[i].Code)
```

```
            return (*MainCommandItems[i].Fxn)(hWnd, idItem, hwndCtl,
                                              wNotifyCode);
    }
    return 0;
}
//----------------------------------------------------------------------
// DoDestroyMain - Process WM_DESTROY message for window.
//
LRESULT DoDestroyMain (HWND hWnd, UINT wMsg, WPARAM wParam,
                       LPARAM lParam) {
    PostQuitMessage (0);
    return 0;
}
//======================================================================
// Command handler routines
//----------------------------------------------------------------------
// DoMainCommandExit - Process Program Exit command.
//
LPARAM DoMainCommandExit (HWND hWnd, WORD idItem, HWND hwndCtl,
                          WORD wNotifyCode) {
    SendMessage (hWnd, WM_CLOSE, 0, 0);
    return 0;
}
//----------------------------------------------------------------------
// DoMainCommandComPort - Process the COM port combo box commands.
//
LPARAM DoMainCommandComPort (HWND hWnd, WORD idItem, HWND hwndCtl,
                             WORD wNotifyCode) {
    int i;
    TCHAR szDev[32];

    if (wNotifyCode == CBN_SELCHANGE) {
        i = SendMessage (hwndCtl, CB_GETCURSEL, 0, 0);
        if (i != nLastDev) {
            SendMessage (hwndCtl, CB_GETLBTEXT, i, (LPARAM)szDev);
            InitCommunication (hWnd, szDev);
            SetFocus (GetDlgItem (hWnd, ID_SENDTEXT));
        }
    }
    return 0;
}
//----------------------------------------------------------------------
// DoMainCommandSendText - Process the Send text button.
//
LPARAM DoMainCommandSendText (HWND hWnd, WORD idItem, HWND hwndCtl,
                              WORD wNotifyCode) {

    // Set event so that sender thread will send the text.
    SetEvent (g_hSendEvent);
    SetFocus (GetDlgItem (hWnd, ID_SENDTEXT));
    return 0;
}
//----------------------------------------------------------------------
// DoMainCommandAbout - Process the Help | About menu command.
```

```
//
LPARAM DoMainCommandAbout(HWND hWnd, WORD idItem, HWND hwndCtl,
                          WORD wNotifyCode) {
    // Use DialogBox to create modal dialog.
    DialogBox (hInst, TEXT ("aboutbox"), hWnd, AboutDlgProc);
    return 0;
}
//======================================================================
// About Dialog procedure
//
BOOL CALLBACK AboutDlgProc (HWND hWnd, UINT wMsg, WPARAM wParam,
                            LPARAM lParam) {
    switch (wMsg) {
        case WM_COMMAND:
            switch (LOWORD (wParam)) {
                case IDOK:
                case IDCANCEL:
                    EndDialog (hWnd, 0);
                    return TRUE;
}
        break;
    }
    return FALSE;
}
//----------------------------------------------------------------------
// FillComComboBox - Fills the COM port combo box
//
int FillComComboBox (HWND hWnd) {
    int rc;
    WIN32_FIND_DATA fd;
    HANDLE hFind;

    hFind = FindFirstFileEx (TEXT ("COM?:"), FindExInfoStandard, &fd,
                             FindExSearchLimitToDevices, NULL, 0);
    if (hFind != INVALID_HANDLE_VALUE) {
        do {
            SendDlgItemMessage (GetDlgItem (hWnd, IDC_CMDBAR),
                                IDC_COMPORT, CB_INSERTSTRING,
                                -1, (LPARAM)fd.cFileName);
            rc = FindNextFile (hFind, &fd);
        } while (rc);

        rc = FindClose (hFind);
    }
    SendDlgItemMessage (GetDlgItem (hWnd, IDC_CMDBAR), IDC_COMPORT,
                        CB_SETCURSEL, 0, 0);
    return 0;
}
//----------------------------------------------------------------------
// InitCommunication - Open and initialize selected COM port.
//
HANDLE InitCommunication (HWND hWnd, LPTSTR pszDevName) {
    DCB dcb;
    TCHAR szDbg[128];
```

```
    COMMTIMEOUTS cto;
    HANDLE hLocal;
    DWORD dwTStat;
    hLocal = hComPort;
    hComPort = INVALID_HANDLE_VALUE;

    if (hLocal != INVALID_HANDLE_VALUE)
        CloseHandle (hLocal);  // This causes WaitCommEvent to return.

    hLocal = CreateFile (pszDevName, GENERIC_READ | GENERIC_WRITE,
                         0, NULL, OPEN_EXISTING, 0, NULL);

    if (hLocal != INVALID_HANDLE_VALUE) {
        // Configure port.
        dcb.DCBlength = sizeof (dcb);
        GetCommState (hLocal, &dcb);
        dcb.BaudRate = nSpeed;
        dcb.fParity = FALSE;
        dcb.fNull = FALSE;
        dcb.StopBits = ONESTOPBIT;
        dcb.Parity = NOPARITY;
        dcb.ByteSize = 8;
        SetCommState (hLocal, &dcb);

        // Set the timeouts. Set infinite read timeout.
        cto.ReadIntervalTimeout = 0;
        cto.ReadTotalTimeoutMultiplier = 0;
        cto.ReadTotalTimeoutConstant = 0;
        cto.WriteTotalTimeoutMultiplier = 0;
        cto.WriteTotalTimeoutConstant = 0;
        SetCommTimeouts (hLocal, &cto);

        wsprintf (szDbg, TEXT ("Port %s opened\r\n"), pszDevName);
        SendDlgItemMessage (hWnd, ID_RCVTEXT, EM_REPLACESEL, 0,
                            (LPARAM)szDbg);

        // Start read thread if not already started.
        hComPort = hLocal;
        if (!GetExitCodeThread (hReadThread, &dwTStat) ||
            (dwTStat != STILL_ACTIVE)) {
            hReadThread = CreateThread (NULL, 0, ReadThread, hWnd,
                                        0, &dwTStat);
            if (hReadThread)
                CloseHandle (hReadThread);
        }
    } else {
        wsprintf (szDbg, TEXT ("Couldn\'t open port %s. rc=%d\r\n"),
                  pszDevName, GetLastError());
        SendDlgItemMessage (hWnd, ID_RCVTEXT, EM_REPLACESEL,
                            0, (LPARAM)szDbg);
    }
    return hComPort;
}
//======================================================================
```

```
// SendThread - Sends characters to the serial port
//
DWORD WINAPI SendThread (PVOID pArg) {
    HWND hWnd, hwndSText;
    int rc;
    DWORD cBytes;
    WCHAR szText[TEXTSIZE];
    char szAnsi[TEXTSIZE];
    size_t siz;

    hWnd = (HWND)pArg;
    hwndSText = GetDlgItem (hWnd, ID_SENDTEXT);
    while (1) {
        rc = WaitForSingleObject (g_hSendEvent, INFINITE);
        if (rc == WAIT_OBJECT_0) {
            if (!fContinue)
                break;
            // Disable send button while sending.
            EnableWindow (GetDlgItem (hWnd, ID_SENDBTN), FALSE);

            // Get the text, terminate the line and convert to ansi
            GetWindowText (hwndSText, szText, dim(szText));
            StringCchCat (szText, dim(szText), TEXT ("\r\n"));
            wcstombs_s (&siz, szAnsi, sizeof (szAnsi), szText, _TRUNCATE);

            // Write to the serial port
            rc = WriteFile (hComPort, szText,
                       lstrlen (szText)*sizeof (TCHAR),&cBytes, 0);
            if (rc) {
                // Copy sent text to output window.
                SendDlgItemMessage (hWnd, ID_RCVTEXT, EM_REPLACESEL, 0,
                                    (LPARAM)TEXT (" >"));
                SetWindowText (hwndSText, TEXT ("")); // Clear text box
            } else {
                // Else, print error message.
                wsprintf (szText, TEXT ("Send failed rc=%d\r\n"),
                          GetLastError());
                DWORD dwErr = 0;
                COMSTAT Stat;

                if (ClearCommError (hComPort, &dwErr, &Stat)) {
                    printf ("fail\n");
                }
            }
            // Put text in receive text box.
            SendDlgItemMessage (hWnd, ID_RCVTEXT, EM_REPLACESEL, 0,
                                (LPARAM)szText);
            EnableWindow (GetDlgItem (hWnd, ID_SENDBTN), TRUE);
        } else
            break;
    }
    return 0;
}
//======================================================================
```

```
// ReadThread - Receives characters from the serial port
//
DWORD WINAPI ReadThread (PVOID pArg) {
    HWND hWnd;
    DWORD cBytes, i;
    WCHAR szText[TEXTSIZE];
    char szAnsi[TEXTSIZE];
    size_t siz;

    hWnd = (HWND)pArg;
    while (fContinue) {
        for (i = 0; i < sizeof (szAnsi)-1; i++) {

            while (!ReadFile (hComPort, &szAnsi[i], 1, &cBytes, 0))
                if (hComPort == INVALID_HANDLE_VALUE)
                    return 0;

            if (szAnsi[i] == '\n') {
                szAnsi[i+1] = '\0';
                break;
            }
        }
        // Convert to Unicode
        mbstowcs_s (&siz, szText, dim (szText), szAnsi, _TRUNCATE);

        SendDlgItemMessage (hWnd, ID_RCVTEXT, EM_REPLACESEL, 0,
                            (LPARAM)szText);
    }
    return 0;
}
```

When the CeChat window is created, it sniffs out the COM port names using *FindFileEx*. The combo box is then filled, and an attempt is made to open each of the COM ports. The process stops when the first COM port is opened. Once a port is opened, the read thread is created to wait on characters.

The send thread is actually quite simple. All it does is block on an event that was created when CeChat was started. When the event is signaled, it reads the text from the send text edit control and calls *WriteFile*. Once that has completed, the send thread clears the text from the edit control and loops back to where it blocks again.

The serial API provides applications with a hardware agnostic method of accessing the serial hardware. But how does the operating system know how to talk to the serial hardware? It doesn't. Instead, the operating system talks to a device driver that hides the specifics of the serial port implementation. Perhaps it's time to look at how a driver is implemented. In the final chapter of this book, we will look at how to write a Windows CE device driver and a Windows CE service. Writing a service or even a driver isn't that hard in Windows CE. Let's dive in and check it out.

Chapter 17
Device Drivers and Services

Device drivers are modules that provide the interface between the operating system and the hardware. Device drivers take on an air of mystery because they're a mix of operating system–specific code and hardware customization. Most application developers are quite happy to let the real operating system junkies handle writing device drivers. This chapter shows you that while dealing with hardware can be a pain, the basic structure of a Windows CE driver is actually quite simple. An application developer might even have reason to write a driver every now and then.

Real operating system junkies also know about services. On the desktop, a service is a background application that typically runs in the background. Services can be automatically started when the operating system boots, or they can be manually started. They can also be stopped and restarted as needed. Windows CE supports services, although not with the same architecture as Windows XP and Vista services. Instead, Windows CE services are quite similar to Windows CE drivers, as we will see. In this chapter, I'll first introduce drivers, because the basics of that discussion are important to both drivers and services, and then I'll dive into how to write a Windows CE service.

Basic Drivers

Before I dive into how to write a device driver, we must take a brief look at how Windows CE handles drivers in general. Before Windows CE 6, most Windows CE drivers were loaded by the device manager process. Three drivers—the display, keyboard, and touch panel drivers—were loaded by the Graphics, Windowing, and Event Subsytem (GWES) process. Starting with CE 5, the file system process (FileSys) could directly load block mode disk drivers. All drivers, regardless of the process that loaded them, ran in user mode.

The kernel redesign of Windows CE 6 dramatically changed the management of device drivers. Drivers can be loaded in either kernel mode, with the other parts of the operating system, or in user mode by what is known as the User Mode Device Manager. Device drivers loaded by the kernel (*kernel mode drivers*) provide the best performance, while drivers loaded by the User Mode Device Manager (*user mode drivers*) are more secure because they can't corrupt the operating system either accidentally or intentionally.

Most drivers expose a *stream interface* to the operating system. These drivers, appropriately known as *stream drivers*, provide the same entry points to the driver regardless of their underlying hardware. There are a few nonstream drivers in the operating system. The display driver, keyboard, and touch screen drivers have different operating system interfaces and are sometimes referred to as *native drivers*.

Stream interface device drivers can be supplied by third-party manufacturers to support hardware added to the system. Although some Windows CE systems have a PCI bus for extra cards, the additional hardware is usually installed via a Personal Computer Memory Card International Association (PCMCIA), a CompactFlash, or a Secure Digital I/O (SDIO) slot. In this case, the device driver would use functions provided by the bus driver to access the hardware.

Bus drivers manage the system buses such as a PCI bus. PCMCIA, CompactFlash, and SDIO slots are also considered buses. Bus drivers are in charge of interrogating the hardware on the bus to determine what hardware is installed and allocating resources. The bus driver also asks the Device Manager to load the proper drivers for the hardware on the bus and provides a system-independent method of accessing the hardware registers without the device drivers having to know the physical memory map of the system.

In addition, a device driver might be written to extend the functionality of an existing driver. For example, you might write a driver to provide a compressed or encrypted data stream over a serial link. In this case, an application would access the encryption driver, which would in turn use the serial driver to access the serial hardware.

Driver Names

Historically, stream interface device drivers have been identified by a three-character name followed by a single digit, as in COM2. This scheme allows for 10 device drivers of one name to be installed on a Windows CE device at any one time. Instance values are numbered from one to nine, with the tenth instance having an instance number of zero. When referencing a stream interface driver, an application uses the three-character name, followed by the single digit, followed by a colon (:). The colon is required under Windows CE for the system to recognize the driver name.

Drivers can also be referenced through an extended namespace. In this form, the driver name begins with \$device\. For example, a driver normally referenced as COM3: would be referenced as \$device\COM3. The advantage of this scheme is that the instance value isn't limited to a single digit. So, in this naming scheme, the driver could be COM15, as in \$device\COM15. Note that in this naming method, the trailing colon is not used.

A third naming method involves referencing the driver in relation to the bus driver that loads it. The name begins with \$bus\ followed by the bus name, its bus number, device number, and function number as in \$bus\PCMCA_1_2_3.

Regardless of the naming scheme, stream drivers are always referenced by their three-character name. Here are a few examples of some names currently in use:

- **COM** Serial driver
- **ACM** Audio compression manager
- **WAV** Audio wave driver
- **CON** Console driver

The Device Driver Load Process

When the device manager loads, it looks in the registry under [HKEY_LOCAL_ MACHINE]\Drivers for a string value named *RootKey*. This value points to the registry key that lists the drivers that should be loaded when the system boots. Traditionally, this key is named *BuiltIn*. In addition, an optional key named *DLL* can be present listing the bus enumerator, the DLL that actually reads and interprets the registry structure. If no *DLL* key is found, the default enumerator BusEnum.dll is used.

The Device Manager then uses the bus enumerator to read the key specified by *RootKey* for the list of the drivers it must load when it initializes. This list is contained in a series of keys. The names of the keys don't matter—it's the values contained in the keys that define which drivers to load and the order in which to load them. Figure 17-1 shows the contents of the *WaveDev* key. The Wave driver is the audio driver.

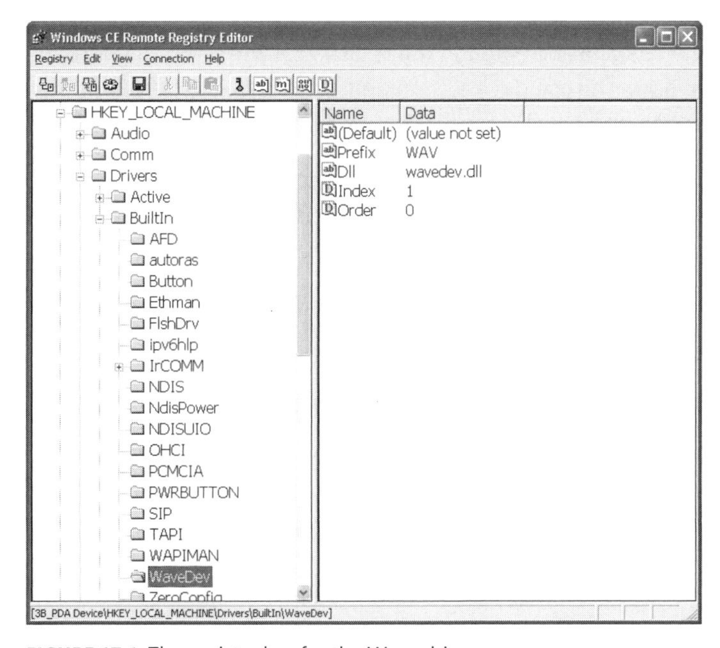

FIGURE 17-1 The registry key for the Wave driver

The four values under this key are the basic four entries used by a device driver under Windows CE. The *DLL* key specifies the name of the DLL that implements the driver. This is the DLL that the registry enumerator loads. The *Order* value ranges from 0 through 255 and specifies the order in which the drivers are loaded. The registry enumerator loads drivers with lower *Order* values before drivers with higher *Order* values in the registry.

The *Prefix* value defines the three-letter name of the driver. This value is mandatory for stream drivers but typically not used for bus drivers. Applications that want to open this driver use the three-letter key with the number that Windows CE appends to create the device name. The *Index* value is the number that will be appended to the device name.

As the bus enumerator reads each of the registry keys, it calls *ActivateDeviceEx* to have the device manager load the driver listed in that key. *ActivateDeviceEx* creates a new key under [HKEY_LOCAL_MACHINE\Drivers\Active and initializes it. It then finds a free index for the driver if one wasn't specified in the original registry key. *ActivateDeviceEx* then loads the driver in memory using the *LoadDevice* function.[1] *LoadDevice* is similar to *LoadLibrary* but loads the entire DLL into memory and locks the pages so they can't be discarded. Next, the DLL is queried to get function pointers to the 12 external entry points in the driver. For named, stream, drivers, the entry points *Init*, *Deinit*, *Open*, *Close*, and at least one of the *Read*, *Write*, *Seek*, or *IOControl* entry points must exist or the driver load fails. If the driver exports a *PreClose* entry point, it must also export a *PreDeinit* entry point. For unnamed drivers, *ActivateDeviceEx* tries to get all 12 entry points, but fails only if the *Init* and *Deinit* functions can't be found.

Once the entry points have been saved, the device manager calls the driver's *Init* function, passing the name of the Active key created in the registry for the driver. If *Init* returns a nonzero value, the driver is added to the device chain and *ActivateDeviceEx* returns. If *Init* returns zero, the driver is unloaded and the driver initialization fails.

Although this is the standard load procedure, another registry value can modify the load process. If the driver key contains a *Flags* value, the load process can change in a number of ways. The following values are currently valid for the *Flags* value:

- **DEVFLAGS_UNLOAD** Unload the driver after the call to Init returns.
- **DEVFLAGS_LOADLIBRARY** Use LoadLibrary to load the driver instead of LoadDriver.
- **DEVFLAGS_NOLOAD** Don't load the driver at all.
- **DEVFLAGS_NAKEDENTRIES** The driver entry points aren't prefixed by the driver name.
- **DEVFLAGS_LOAD_AS_USERPROC** The driver is loaded in user mode instead of kernel mode.

[1] Depending on the registry setting for the driver, the device manager may load the DLL with the *LoadLibrary* function.

- **DEVFLAGS_NOUNLOAD** The driver cannot be unloaded.
- **DEVFLAGS_BOOTPHASE_1** The driver is only loaded during boot phase 1.
- **DEVFLAGS_IRQ_EXCLUSIVE** The driver loads only if it has exclusive access to an interrupt.

Another way the driver load process can be modified depends on the now-deprecated registry value named *Entry*. If this value is found, the DLL is loaded, and then, instead of calling *ActivateDeviceEx*, the system calls the entry point in the driver named in *Entry*. The driver itself is then responsible for calling the *ActivateDeviceEx* function if it's to be registered as a driver with the system.

If the *Entry* value is present, another value, *Keep*, can also be specified. Specifying the *Keep* value tells the system not to unload the driver after it calls the driver's entry point. This arrangement allows the driver DLL to avoid calling *ActiveDeviceEx* and thereby avoid being a driver at all. Instead, the DLL is simply loaded into the process space of Device.exe.

Device drivers can also be loaded manually by applications. The preferred function for loading a device driver is *ActivateDeviceEx*, prototyped as

```
HANDLE ActivateDeviceEx (LPCWSTR lpszDevKey, LPCVOID lpRegEnts,
                         DWORD cRegEnts, LPVOID lpvParam);
```

The first parameter is the name of a registry key under [HKEY_LOCAL_ MACHINE] where the driver information is saved. The format of the registry key is identical to the format discussed earlier. The next two parameters, *lpRegEnts* and *cRegEnts*, describe an array of *REGINI* structures that define a series of registry values that will be added to the device's *Active* key. Generally, adding values is done only for bus drivers. The final parameter is a pointer that is passed to the device driver's *Init* function when the driver is loaded. This pointer can point to any device-specific information.

The return value from *ActivateDeviceEx* is the handle to the instance of the device. If the return value is zero, the load failed. In this case, use *GetLastError* to determine why the function failed. The returned handle can't be used to read or write to the device; instead, the driver should be opened with *CreateFile*. The handle should be saved in case the driver needs to be unloaded in the future.

An older method of loading a driver is *RegisterDevice*. *RegisterDevice* is dangerous because drivers loaded with this function will not have an *Active* key associated with the driver. The only reason for discussing the function at all is that it doesn't require a registry key to load the driver, which can be handy when writing a quick and simple test program that loads and later unloads the driver.

RegisterDevice is prototyped as

```
HANDLE RegisterDevice (LPCWSTR lpszType, DWORD dwIndex,
                       LPCWSTR lpszLib, DWORD dwInfo);
```

The first two parameters are the three-character prefix of the driver and the instance number of the device. To load COM3, for example, *lpszType* would point to the string COM and *dwIndex* would have a value of 3. If an instance of the driver is already loaded, the function will fail, so it's important to check the return value to see whether the function fails and determine why the failure occurred.

The *lpszLib* parameter identifies the name of the DLL that implements the driver. The final parameter, *dwInfo*, is passed to the driver in the *Init* call in the *dwContext* value. Because most drivers expect the *dwContext* value to point to a string naming a registry key, this value should at least point to a zero-terminated null string. *RegisterDevice* returns the handle to the instance of the driver if the load was successful and zero otherwise.

A driver can be unloaded with

```
BOOL DeactivateDevice (Handle hDevice);
```

The only parameter is the handle that was returned with *ActivateDeviceEx* or *RegisterDevice*.

Loading a Driver in User Mode

A device driver is loaded in user mode using the same process that is used to load a kernel mode driver. The only difference is setting the DEVFLAGS_LOAD_AS_USERPROC flag in the driver's registry entry. This entry alone will cause the operating system to launch a new instance of the user mode driver manager, which will then load the driver.

If you want to load a number of drivers in the same user mode driver manager, you can tell Windows CE to load a driver in a specific instance of the user mode driver manager. To do this, specify a ProcGroup by creating a registry key under HKEY_LOCAL_MACHINE\Drivers named ProcGroup_xxxx where xxxx is a unique number. For example, the following registry entry declares a ProcGroup.

```
[HKEY_LOCAL_MACHINE\Drivers\ProcGroup_0003]
        "ProcName"="udevice.exe
        "ProcVolPrefix"="$udevice"
```

In the entry for the drivers you want to be loaded by this instance of the user mode driver manager, specify the registry key *UserProcGroup* and set it to the number specified in the declaration of the ProcGroup. For the previous example, the process group name is ProcGroup_0003, so the registry value would be set to 3. The following example shows the registry entry to load a driver into the user mode driver manager instance 3.

```
[HKEY_LOCAL_MACHINE\Drivers\BuiltIn\MyDriver]
        "DLL"="MyDriver.DLL"
        "Prefix"="DRV"
        "Flags"=dword:10
        "Index"=dword:1
        "ProcGroup"=dword:3
```

In the previous example, the flags value of 10 specifies the DEVFLAGS_LOAD_AS_USERPROC flag telling Windows CE to load the driver in user mode and the ProcGroup value set to 3 indicates the instance of the user mode driver manager to use.

Enumerating the Active Drivers

The most reliable way to find a device driver is to use *FindFirstFileEx* and set the *fSearchOp* parameter to *FindExSearchLimitToDevices*. Using the search string * and repeatedly calling *FindNextFile* results in a list of the stream drivers loaded.

The more general method for determining what drivers are loaded onto a Windows CE system is to look in the registry under the key \Drivers\Active under HKEY_LOCAL_MACHINE. The Device Manager dynamically updates the subkeys contained here as drivers are loaded and unloaded from the system. Contained in this key is a list of subkeys, one for each active driver loaded with *ActivateDevice*. The contents of these subkeys might change in future versions of Windows CE, but knowing what these subkeys contain can be helpful in some situations.

The name of the key is simply a placeholder; the values inside the keys are what indicate the active drivers. Figure 17-2 shows the registry key for the COM1 serial driver.

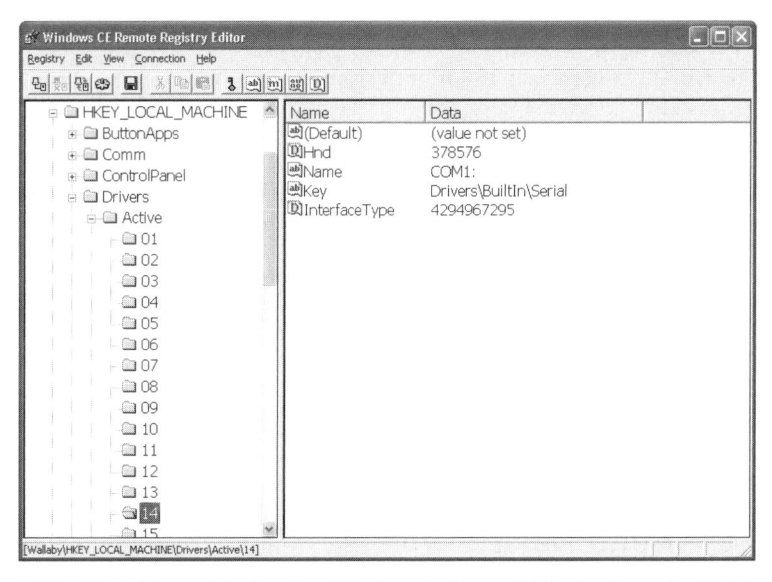

FIGURE 17-2 The registry's active list values for the serial device driver for COM1

In Figure 17-2, the *Name* value contains the official five-character name (four characters plus a colon) of the device. The *Hnd* value is a handle used internally by Windows CE. The interesting entry is the *Key* value. This value points to the registry key where the device driver stores its configuration information. This second key is necessary because the active list is dynamic, changing whenever a device is installed. Instead, the driver should open the registry key specified by the *Key* value in the active list to determine the driver's permanent configuration data. The configuration data for the serial driver is shown in Figure 17-3.

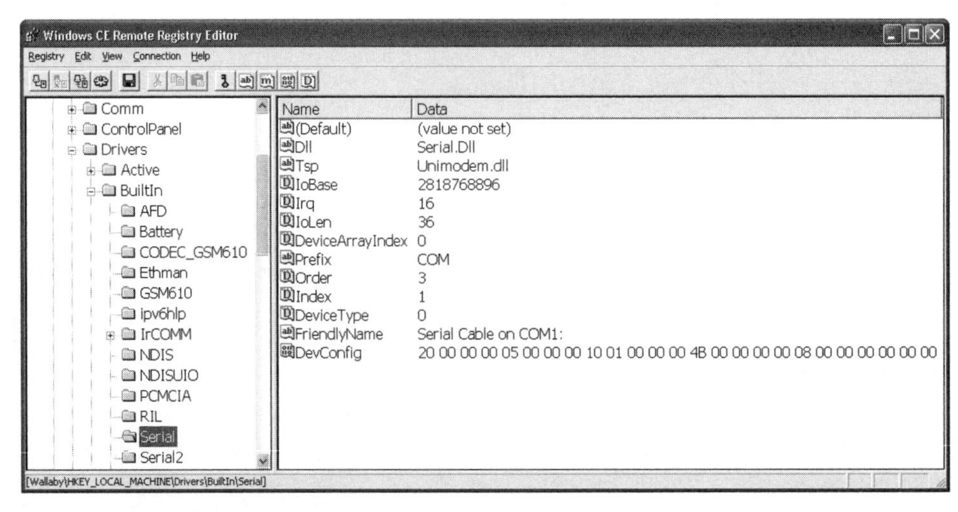

FIGURE 17-3 The registry entry for the serial driver

You can look in the serial driver registry key for such information as the name of the DLL that actually implements the driver, the three-letter prefix defining the driver name; the order in which the driver wants to be loaded; and something handy for user interfaces, the *friendly name* of the driver. Not all drivers have this friendly name, but when they do, it's a much more descriptive name than COM2 or NDS1.

Drivers for PCMCIA or CompactFlash cards have an additional value in their active list key. The *PnpId* value contains the Plug and Play ID string that was created from the card's ID string. Some PCMCIA and CompactFlash cards have their *PnpId* strings registered in the system if they use a specific device driver. If so, a registry key for the *PnpId* value is located in the *Drivers\PCMCIA* key under HKEY_LOCAL_MACHINE. For example, a PCMCIA card that had a *PnpId* string *This_is_a_pc_card* would be registered under the key *\Drivers\PCMCIA\This_is_a_pc_card*. That key may contain a *FriendlyName* string for the driver. Other PCMCIA cards use generic drivers. For example, most CompactFlash storage cards use the ATADISK driver registered under \Drivers\PCMCIA\ATADISK.

Reading and Writing Device Drivers

Applications access device drivers under Windows CE through the file I/O functions, *CreateFile*, *ReadFile*, *WriteFile*, and *CloseHandle*. The application opens the device using *CreateFile*, with the name of the device being the five-character (three characters plus digit plus colon) name of the driver. Drivers can be opened with all the varied access rights: read only, write only, read/write, or neither read nor write access.

Once a device is open, data can be sent to it using *WriteFile* and can read from the device using *ReadFile*. As is the case with file operations, overlapped I/O isn't supported for devices under Windows CE. The driver can be sent control characters using the function *DeviceIoControl*. The function is prototyped this way:

```
BOOL DeviceIoControl (HANDLE hDevice, DWORD dwIoControlCode,
                      LPVOID lpInBuffer, DWORD nInBufferSize,
                      LPVOID lpOutBuffer, DWORD nOutBufferSize,
                      LPDWORD lpBytesReturned,
                      LPOVERLAPPED lpOverlapped);
```

The first parameter is the handle to the opened device. The second parameter, *dwIoControl-Code*, is the IOCTL (pronounced eye-OC-tal) code. This value defines the operation of the call to the driver. The next series of parameters are generic input and output buffers and their sizes. The use of these buffers is dependent on the IOCTL code passed in *dwIoControlCode*. The *lpBytesReturned* parameter must point to a *DWORD* value that will receive the number of bytes returned by the driver in the buffer pointed to by *lpOutBuffer*.

Each driver has its own set of IOCTL codes. If you look in the source code for the example serial driver provided in the Platform Builder, you'll see that the following IOCTL codes are defined for the COM driver. Note that these codes aren't defined in the Windows CE SDK because an application doesn't need to directly call *DeviceIoControl* using these codes.

IOCTL_SERIAL_SET_BREAK_O N	*IOCTL_SERIAL_SET_BREAK_O FF*
IOCTL_SERIAL_SET_DTR	*IOCTL_SERIAL_CLR_DTR*
IOCTL_SERIAL_SET_RTS	*IOCTL_SERIAL_CLR_RTS*
IOCTL_SERIAL_SET_XOFF	*IOCTL_SERIAL_SET_XON*
IOCTL_SERIAL_GET_WAIT_MA SK	*IOCTL_SERIAL_SET_WAIT_MA SK*
IOCTL_SERIAL_WAIT_ON_MAS K	*IOCTL_SERIAL_GET_COMMST ATUS*
IOCTL_SERIAL_GET_MODEMS TATUS	*IOCTL_SERIAL_GET_PROPERT IES*
IOCTL_SERIAL_SET_TIMEOUT S	*IOCTL_SERIAL_GET_TIMEOUT S*
IOCTL_SERIAL_PURGE	*IOCTL_SERIAL_SET_QUEUE_S IZE*
IOCTL_SERIAL_IMMEDIATE_C HAR	*IOCTL_SERIAL_GET_DCB*
IOCTL_SERIAL_SET_DCB	*IOCTL_SERIAL_ENABLE_IR*
IOCTL_SERIAL_DISABLE_IR	

As you can see from the fairly self-descriptive names, the serial driver IOCTL functions expose significant function to the calling process. Windows uses these IOCTL codes to control some of the specific features of a serial port, such as the handshaking lines and timeouts. Each driver has its own set of IOCTL codes. I've shown the preceding ones simply as an example of how the *DeviceIoControl* function is typically used. Under most circumstances, an application has no reason to use the *DeviceIoControl* function with the serial driver. Windows provides its own set of functions that then call down to the serial driver using *DeviceIoControl*.

Okay, we've talked enough about generic drivers. It's time to sit down to the meat of the chapter—writing a driver.

Writing a Windows CE Stream Device Driver

As I mentioned earlier, Windows CE device drivers are simply DLLs. So on the surface, writing a device driver would seem to be a simple matter of writing a Windows CE DLL with specific exported entry points. For the most part, this is true. You have only a few issues to deal with when writing a Windows CE device driver.

A device driver isn't loaded by the application communicating with the driver. Instead, the Device Manager loads most drivers, including all stream drivers. This state of affairs affects the driver in two ways. First, an application can't simply call private entry points in a driver as it can in a DLL. The only way an application could directly call an entry point would be if it called *LoadLibrary* and *GetProcAddress* to get the address of the entry point so the entry point could be called. This situation would result in the DLL (notice I'm not calling it a driver anymore) that implemented the driver being loaded in the process space of the application, not in the process space of the Kernel or User Mode Device Manager. The problem is that this second copy of the DLL isn't the driver—it's the DLL that implemented the driver. The difference is that the first copy of the DLL (the driver)—when properly loaded by the Device Manager—has some state data associated with it that isn't present in the second copy of the DLL loaded by the application. Perversely, the calls to *LoadLibrary* and *GetProcAddress* will succeed because the driver is a DLL. In addition, calling the entry points in the driver results in calling the correct code. The problem is that the code will be acting on data present only in the second copy of the DLL, not in the proper data maintained by the driver. This situation can, and usually does, result in subtle bugs that can confuse and even lock up the hardware the driver is managing. In short, never interact with a driver by calling *LoadLibrary* and *GetProcAddress*.

The second effect of the driver being loaded by the Device Manager is that if the driver is loaded as a kernel mode driver and a driver DLL is used for more than one instance of a piece of hardware; for example, on a serial driver being used for both COM1 and COM2, the Device Manager will load the DLL only once. When the driver is "loaded" a second time, the driver's initialization entry point, *COM_Init*, is simply called again.

The reason for this dual use of the same DLL instance is that under Windows CE a DLL is never loaded twice by the same process. Instead, if an application asks to load a DLL again, the original DLL is used and a call is made to *DllMain* to indicate that a second thread has attached to the DLL. So if the Device Manager, which is simply a DLL loaded by the kernel, loads the same driver for two different pieces of hardware, the same DLL is used for both instances of the hardware.

It is possible to load a driver DLL twice, but only if it is loaded in user mode. If the driver DLL is loaded by more than one User Mode Device Manger, the DLL will be loaded in each process seperately.

Drivers written to handle multiple instances of themselves must not store data in global variables because the second instance of the driver would overwrite the data from the first instance. Instead, a multi-instance driver must store its state data in a structure allocated in memory. If multiple instances of the driver are loaded, the driver will allocate a separate state data structure for each instance. The driver can keep track of which instance data structure to use by passing the pointer to the instance data structure back to the Device Manager as its "handle," which is returned by the device driver's *Init* function.

One final issue with Windows CE device drivers is that they can be re-entered by the operating system, which means that a driver must be written in a totally thread-safe manner. References to state data must be protected by critical sections, interlock functions, or other thread-safe methods.

The Stream Driver Entry Points

A stream driver exposes 12 external entry points—summarized in the following list—that the Device Manager calls to talk to the driver. I'll describe each entry point in detail in the following sections.

- **xxx_Init** Called when an instance of the driver is loaded.
- **xxx_PreDeinit** Called just before a driver is unloaded. At this point, the driver is still considered a loaded driver by the operating system.
- **xxx_Deinit** Called when an instance of the driver is unloaded.
- **xxx_Open** Called when a driver is opened by an application with CreateFile.
- **xxx_PreClose** Called just before a driver's xxx_Close entry point is called. At this point, the driver is technically still open.
- **xxx_Close** Called when a driver is closed by the application with Closehandle.
- **xxx_Read** Called when the application calls ReadFile.
- **xxx_Write** Called when the application calls WriteFile.
- **xxx_Seek** Called when the application calls SetFilePointer.
- **xxx_IOControl** Called when the application calls DeviceIoControl.
- **xxx_PowerDown** Called just before the system suspends.
- **xxx_PowerUp** Called just before the system resumes.

The *xxx* preceding each function name is the three-character name of the driver, if the driver has a name. For example, if the driver is a COM driver, the functions are named *COM_Init*, *COM_Deinit*, and so on. For unnamed drivers (those without a prefix value specified in the registry), the entry points are the name without the leading *xxx*, as in *Init* and *Deinit*. Also, although the preceding list describes applications talking to the driver, there's no reason one driver can't open another driver by calling *CreateFile* and communicate with it just as an application can.

xxx_Init

When the Device Manager first loads an instance of the driver, the Device Manager calls the driver's *Init* function. The prototype is

```
DWORD XXX_Init (LPCTSTR pContext, LPCVOID lpvBusContext);
```

The first parameter, *pContext*, typically contains a pointer to a string identifying the *Active* key created by the Device Manager for the driver. I say *typically* because an application using *RegisterDevice* can load the device to pass any value, including 0, in this parameter. The moral of the story is to look for a string but plan for the *dwContext* value to point to anything. The second parameter is a pointer to driver specific data structure. This pointer is actually the fourth parameter to *ActivateDeviceEx,* so it can be used for whatever data needs to be passed from the caller of *ActivateDeviceEx* to the driver.

Drivers may use a legacy prototype of the *Init* function, which is prototyped as

```
DWORD XXX_Init (DWORD dwContext);
```

Here again, the first, and this time only, parameter almost always contains a pointer to the name of the *Active* key in the registry. Although the newer function prototype is recommended, drivers using the old *Init* prototype work just as well.

The driver should respond to the *Init* call by verifying that any hardware that the driver accesses functions correctly. The driver should initialize the hardware, initialize its state, and return a nonzero value. If the driver detects an error during its initialization, it should set the proper error code with *SetLastError* and return 0 from the *Init* function. If the Device Manager sees a 0 return value from the *Init* function, it unloads the driver and removes the *Active* key for the driver from the registry.

The device driver can pass any nonzero value back to the Device Manager. The typical use of this value, which is referred to as the *device context handle*, is to pass the address of a structure that contains the driver's state data. For drivers that can be multi-instanced (loaded more than once to support more than one instance of a hardware device), the state data of the driver must be independently maintained for each instance of the driver.

xxx_PreDeinit

The *PreDeinit* entry point is called just before the driver is removed from the list of loaded drivers kept by the operating system. This means that during the call, the driver is still considered a "driver" by the operating system. This entry point must be prototyped as

```
BOOL XXX_PreDeinit (DWORD hDeviceContext);
```

The single parameter is the device-context value the driver returned from the *Init* call. This value allows the driver to determine which instance of the driver is about to be unloaded. The driver can use this call to notify other drivers that it is about to be unloaded and to signal other threads within the driver that it is about to be unloaded.

xxx_Deinit

The *Deinit* entry point is called when the driver is unloaded. This entry point must be prototyped as

```
BOOL XXX_Deinit (DWORD hDeviceContext);
```

The single parameter is the device-context value the driver returned from the *Init* call. This value allows the driver to determine which instance of the driver is being unloaded. The driver should respond to this call by powering down any hardware it controls and freeing any memory and resources it owns. The driver will be unloaded following this call.

xxx_Open

The *Open* entry point to the driver is called when an application or another driver calls *CreateFile* to open the driver. The entry point is prototyped as

```
DWORD XXX_Open (DWORD hDeviceContext, DWORD AccessCode, DWORD ShareMode);
```

The first parameter is the device context value returned by the *Init* call. The *AccessCode* and *ShareMode* parameters are taken directly from *CreateFile*'s *dwDesiredAccess* and *dwShare-Mode* parameters and indicate how the application wants to access (read/write or read only) and share (*FILE_SHARE_READ* or *FILE_SHARE_WRITE*) the device. The device driver can refuse the open for any reason by simply returning 0 from the function. If the driver accepts the open call, it returns a nonzero value.

The return value is traditionally used, like the device context value returned by the *Init* call, as a pointer to an open context data structure. If the driver allows only one application to open it at a time, the return value is usually the device context value passed in the first parameter. This arrangement allows all the functions to access the device context structure directly, because one of these two values—the device context or the open context value—is passed in every call to the driver. The open context value returned by the *Open* function is *not* the handle returned to the application when the *CreateFile* function returns.

Windows CE typically runs on hardware that's designed so that individual components in the system can be separately powered. Windows CE drivers that are designed to work without the Power Manager typically power the hardware they control only when the device is opened. The driver then removes power when the *Close* notification is made. This means that the device will be powered on only when an application or another driver is actually using the device.

xxx_PreClose

The *PreClose* entry point is called when an application or driver that has previously opened the driver closes it by calling *CloseHandle* but before the operating system actually removes the driver from the list of opened drivers. The entry point is prototyped as

```
BOOL XXX_PreClose (DWORD hOpenContext);
```

The single parameter is the open context value that the driver returned from the Open call. The driver can use this call to notify other threads in the driver that is is about to be closed so that they can exit before this call returns. Upon return of this call, the device manager will call the xxx_Close entry point.

xxx_Close

The *Close* entry point is called after xxx_Close, or for drivers that don't implement xxx_PreClose, when the driver is closed with a call to *CloseHandle*. The entry point is prototyped as

```
BOOL XXX_Close (DWORD hOpenContext);
```

The single parameter is the open context value that the driver returned from the *Open* call. The driver should power down any hardware and free any memory or open context data associated with the open state.

xxx_Read

The *Read* entry point is called when an application or another driver calls *ReadFile* on the device. This entry point is prototyped as

```
DWORD XXX_Read (DWORD hOpenContext, LPVOID pBuffer, DWORD Count);
```

The first parameter is the open context value returned by the *Open* call. The second parameter is a pointer to the calling application's buffer, where the read data is to be copied. The final parameter is the size of the buffer. The driver should return the number of bytes read into the buffer. If an error occurs, the driver should set the proper error code using *SetLastError* and return –1. A return code of 0 is valid and indicates that the driver read no data.

A device driver should program defensively when using any passed pointer. The following series of functions tests the validity of a pointer:

```
BOOL IsBadWritePtr (LPVOID lp, UINT ucb);
BOOL IsBadReadPtr (const void *lp, UINT ucb);
BOOL IsBadCodePtr (FARPROC lpfn);
```

The parameters are the pointer to be tested and, for the *Read* and *Write* tests, the size of the buffer pointed to by the pointer. Each of these functions verifies that the pointer passed is valid for the use tested. However, the access rights of a page can change during the processing of the call. For this reason, always couch any use of the *pBuffer* pointer in a *__try, __except* block. This will prevent the driver from causing an exception when the application passes a bad pointer. For example, you could use the following code:

```
DWORD xxx_Read (DWORD dwOpen, LPVOID pBuffer, DWORD dwCount) {
    DWORD dwBytesRead;

    // Test the pointer.
    if (IsBadReadPtr (pBuffer, dwCount)) {
        SetLastError (ERROR_INVALID_PARAMETER);
        return -1;
    }
    __try {
        dwBytesRead = InternalRead (pBuffer, dwCount);
    }
    __except (EXCEPTION_EXECUTE_HANDLER) {
        SetLastError (ERROR_INVALID_PARAMETER);
        return -1;
    }
    return dwBytesRead;
}
```

In the preceding code, the pointer is initially tested by using *IsBadReadPtr* to see whether it's a valid pointer. The code that actually performs the read is hidden in an internal routine named *InternalRead*. If that function throws an exception, presumably because of a bad *pBuffer* pointer or an invalid *dwCount* value, the function sets the error code to *ERROR_INVALID_PARAMETER* and returns –1 to indicate that an error occurred.

xxx_Write

The *Write* entry point is called when the application that has opened the device calls *WriteFile*. The entry point is prototyped as

```
DWORD XXX_Write (DWORD hOpenContext, LPCVOID pBuffer, DWORD Count);
```

As with the *Read* entry point, the three parameters are the open context value returned by the *Open* call, the pointer to the data buffer containing the data, and the size of the buffer. The function should return the number of bytes written to the device or –1 to indicate an error.

xxx_Seek

The *Seek* entry point is called when an application or driver that has opened the driver calls *SetFilePointer* on the device handle. The entry point is prototyped as

```
DWORD XXX_Seek (DWORD hOpenContext, long Amount, WORD Type);
```

The parameters are what you would expect: the open context value returned from the *Open* call, the absolute offset value that is passed from the *SetFilePointer* call, and the type of seek.

There are three types of seek: *FILE_BEGIN* seeks from the start of the device, *FILE_CURRENT* seeks from the current position, and *FILE_END* seeks from the end of the device. The *Seek* function has limited use in a device driver but it is provided for completeness.

xxx_PowerDown

The *PowerDown* entry point is called when the system is about to suspend. For legacy drivers without a power management interface, the device driver should power down any hardware it controls and save any necessary hardware state. The entry point is prototyped as

```
void XXX_PowerDown (DWORD hDeviceContext);
```

The single parameter is the device context handle returned by the *Init* call. The driver, if it supports the legacy power management scheme, should prepare its hardware for the system's suspend state.

xxx_PowerUp

The *PowerUp* entry point is called when the system resumes. Legacy drivers without a power management interface can use this notification to know when to power up and restore the state to the hardware it controls. The *PowerUp* notification is prototyped as

```
void XXX_PowerUp (DWORD hDeviceContext);
```

The *hDeviceContext* parameter is the device context handle returned by the *Init* call.

Although the *PowerUp* notification allows the driver to restore power to the hardware it manages, well-written drivers restore only the minimal power necessary for the device. Typically, the driver will power the hardware only on instruction from the Power Manager.

xxx_IOControl

Because many device drivers don't use the *Read, Write, Seek* metaphor for their interface, the *IOControl* entry point becomes the primary entry point for interfacing with the driver. The *IOControl* entry point is called when a device or application calls the *DeviceIOControl* function. The entry point is prototyped as

```
BOOL XXX_IOControl (DWORD hOpenContext, DWORD dwCode, PBYTE pBufIn,
                    DWORD dwLenIn, PBYTE pBufOut, DWORD dwLenOut,
                    PDWORD pdwActualOut);
```

The first parameter is the open context value returned by the *Open* call. The second parameter, *dwCode*, is a device-defined value passed by the application to indicate why the call is being made. Unlike the desktop versions of Windows, Windows CE does very little processing before the IOCTL code is passed to the driver. This means that the device driver developer ought to be able to pick any values for the codes. However, this behavior might change in the future so it's prudent to define IOCTL codes that conform to the format used by the desktop versions of Windows. Basically, this means that the IOCTL codes are created with the *CTL_CODE* macro, which is defined identically in the Windows Driver Development Kit and the Windows CE Platform Builder. The problem with application developers creating conforming IOCTL code values is that the *CTL_CODE* macro might not be defined in some SDKs. So, developers are sometimes forced to define *CTL_CODE* manually to create conforming IOCTL codes.

The next two parameters describe the buffer that contains the data being passed to the device. The *pBufIn* parameter points to the input buffer that contains the data being passed to the driver; the *dwLenIn* parameter contains the length of the data. The next two parameters are *pBufOut* and *dwLenOut*. The parameter *pBufOut* contains a pointer to the output buffer, and *dwLenOut* contains the length of that buffer. These parameters aren't required to point to valid buffers. The application calling *DeviceIoControl* might possibly pass 0s for the buffer pointer parameters. It's up to the device driver to validate the buffer parameters given the IOCTL code being passed.

The final parameter is the address of a *DWORD* value that receives the number of bytes written to the output buffer. The device driver should return *TRUE* if the function was successful and *FALSE* otherwise. If an error occurs, the device driver should return an error code using *SetLastError.*

The input and output buffers of *DeviceIoControl* calls allow for any type of data to be sent to the device and returned to the calling application. Typically, the data is formatted using a structure with fields containing the parameters for the specific call.

The serial driver makes extensive use of *DeviceIoControl* calls to configure the serial hardware. For example, one of the many IOCTL calls is one to set the serial timeout values. To do this, an application allocates a buffer, casts the buffer pointer to a pointer to a *COMMTIMEOUTS* structure, fills in the structure, and passes the buffer pointer as the input buffer when it calls *DeviceIoControl.* The driver then receives an *IOControl* call with the input buffer pointing to the *COMMTIMEOUTS* structure. I've taken the serial driver's code for processing this IOCTL call and shown a modified version here:

```
BOOL COM_IOControl (PHW_OPEN_INFO pOpenHead,  DWORD dwCode,
                    PBYTE pBufIn, DWORD dwLenIn,
                    PBYTE pBufOut, DWORD dwLenOut,
                    PDWORD pdwActualOut) {
    BOOL RetVal = TRUE;      // assume success
    COMMTIMEOUTS *pComTO;

    switch (dwCode) {
    case IOCTL_SERIAL_SET_TIMEOUTS :
        if ((dwLenIn < sizeof(COMMTIMEOUTS)) || (NULL == pBufIn)) {
            SetLastError (ERROR_INVALID_PARAMETER);
            RetVal = FALSE;
            break;
        }
```

```
        pComTO = (COMMTIMEOUTS *)pBufIn;
        ReadIntervalTimeout = pComTO->ReadIntervalTimeout;
        ReadTotalTimeoutMultiplier = pComTO->ReadTotalTimeoutMultiplier;
        ReadTotalTimeoutConstant = pComTO->ReadTotalTimeoutConstant;
        WriteTotalTimeoutMultiplier = pComTO->WriteTotalTimeoutMultiplier;
        WriteTotalTimeoutConstant = pComTO->WriteTotalTimeoutConstant;
        break;
    }
    return RetVal;
}
```

Notice how the serial driver first verifies that the input buffer is at least the size of the timeout structure and that the input pointer is nonzero. If either of these tests fails, the driver sets the error code to *ERROR_INVALID_PARAMETER* and returns *FALSE*. Otherwise, the driver assumes that the input buffer points to a *COMMTIMEOUTS* structure and uses the data in that structure to set the timeout values. Although the preceding example doesn't enclose the pointer access in *__try, __except* blocks, a more robust driver might.

The preceding scheme works fine as long as the data being passed to or from the driver is all contained within the structure. However, if you pass a pointer in the structure and the driver attempts to use the pointer, an exception will occur. To understand why, you have to remember how Windows CE manages memory protection across processes. (At this point, you might want to review the first part of Chapter 15.)

Managing Buffers

The biggest difference between Windows Embedded CE 6.0 and the earlier versions of Windows CE is the way the operating system manages memory. As I discussed in Chapter 15, gone is the old *slot* model, with its eccentric 32-MB divisions of virtual space. Now the operating system places applications in their own 2-GB address spaces and places the kernel in the top 2 GB of the address space. This change to memory management has its greatest impact on developers in the device driver area. What is interesting is that for drivers loaded in kernel mode, the changes to memory management scheme actually make things easier for the developer.

Figure 17-4 illustrates that when an application is running, the application's address space is in the lower 2 GB of the address space while the kernel mode address space remains inaccessible. When the application calls a kernel mode device driver, the calling thread transitions into kernel mode and calls the device driver code. During the life of the call, the right side of the code in the device driver has access to the kernel mode address space and the calling processes' address space. This means that any buffers in the application that are referenced by pointers passed to the driver are visible to the driver. This is a change to earlier versions of Windows CE where any pointer not passed as a parameter needed to be mapped back to the calling processes' slot.

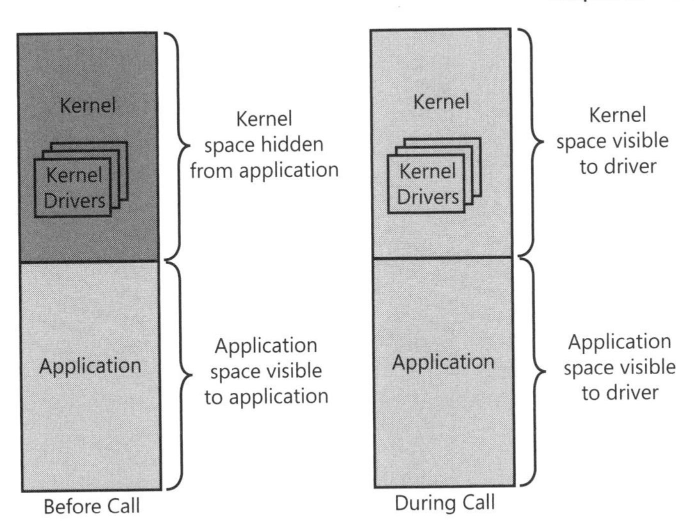

FIGURE 17-4 The memory configuration when calling a kernel mode driver

While managing buffers for kernel mode drivers is simpler in Windows CE 6 than earlier versions, managing buffers for user mode drivers is much more complex. The problem is illustrated in Figure 17-5. This shows the address space when an application calls a user mode driver. Notice that when the device driver code is executing, the calling application's address space isn't accessible because the user mode driver manager is now in the lower 2 GB of the address space instead of the calling process.

To manage this issue, Windows CE 6.0 has new functions that device drivers can use to marshal data across process boundaries. These functions are designed to "do the right thing" for a given situation so that calling them won't hurt performance when there is no marshalling necessary. These functions come in pairs: one for marshalling a buffer, and a matching one for freeing the marshalled buffer. This is a change from earlier versions of Windows CE where drivers only had to map a pointer but didn't have to "unmap" it. There are a number of reasons, aside from the needs of user mode drivers, to use these marshalling functions.

Just like in earlier versions of the operating system, any buffer pointed to by a pointer passed in the parameter list is marshalled by the operating system, so no other action is necessary. This means that the buffers pointed to by *pBufIn* and *pBufOut* in the *DeviceIoControl* call are marshalled automatically by Windows CE, while any buffers referenced from within a structure passed to the driver must be marshalled by the driver.

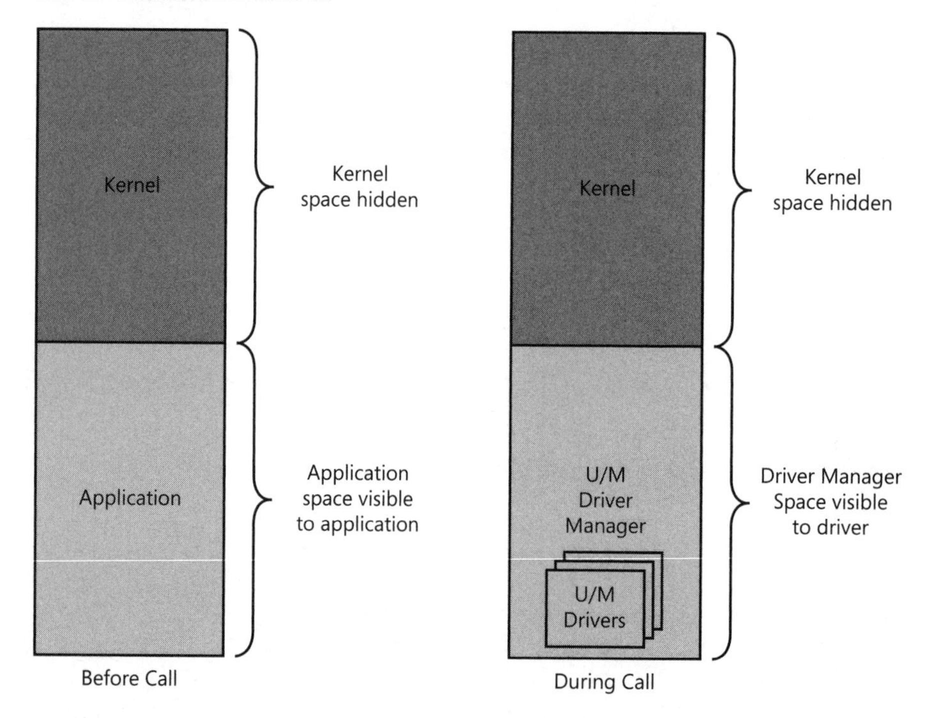

FIGURE 17-5 The memory configuration when calling a user mode driver

As just mentioned, the operating system provides the marshalling for buffers referenced by function parameters. However, if the driver is going to reference the buffers asynchronously after the original call to the driver returns, they must be marshalled by the driver even for kernel mode drivers. The mapping scheme shown earlier in Figure 17-4 is only valid while the original call is being processed by the driver. Once the driver call returns to the application, the memory map will change depending on the thread currently running.

Finally, sometimes it is useful to marshal a buffer not because it is technically necessary, but because it is more secure to work with data inaccessable to the application. If a driver directly accesses a buffer that is in the application's address space, there is nothing to prevent another thread from within the application from modifying the buffer during the driver call. This can happen unintentionally due to a programming mistake or intentionally due to malicious code. So, if you are worried about security or bad application code, it is sometimes wise to marshal buffers for kernel mode drivers even though they don't absolutely require it.

To marshal a buffer passed to a driver, the function to use is

```
HRESULT CeOpenCallerBuffer (PVOID * ppDestMarshalled,
                            PVOID pSrcUnmarshalled, DWORD cbSrc,
                            DWORD ArgumentDescriptor, BOOL ForceDuplicate);
```

The first parameter is the address of a pointer that will be set to point to the newly marshalled buffer. The second paramter is the pointer to the original buffer. The third parameter is the size of the buffer being marshalled.

The *ArgumentDescriptor* parameter is interesting in that this parameter is used to describe the data being passed in the buffer. This information is useful to the operating system to optimize the marshalling. For example, if the application is passing down a string that is only 20 characters long in a buffer; only the first 20 characters plus the terminating zero need to be copied. The allowable values for the *ArgumentDescriptor* parameters are

- **ARG_I_PTR** Input only pointer to binary data
- **ARG_I_WSTR** Input only pointer to a Unicode string
- **ARG_I_ASTR** Input only pointer to a ANSI string
- **ARG_O_PTR** Output only pointer to binary data
- **ARG_O_PI64** Output only pointer to a 64-bit value
- **ARG_IO_PTR** Input and output only pointer to binary data
- **ARG_IO_PI64** Input and output only pointer to a 64-bit value

The final parameter to *CeOpenCallerBuffer* is *ForceDuplicate*, which tells the operating system to duplicate the buffer in the driver's protected address space even if it isn't technically necessary. This allows the marshalled buffer to be accessed only by the driver. Of course, unless you need this for security or other reasons, you should not force buffers to be duplicated because there is a performance hit to copying the data. The return code from *CeOpenCallerBuffer* is an HRESULT that should be checked for success before working with the marshalled data.

When the driver has completed work on the marshalled data and before the driver returns, it should call

```
HRESULT CeCloseCallerBuffer (PVOID pDestMarshalled,
                             PVOID pSrcUnmarshalled, DWORD cbSrc,
                             DWORD ArgumentDescriptor);
```

The parameters closely follow the parmaters of *CeOpenCallerBuffer* with pointers to the marshalled and original unmarshalled buffers followed by the size of the buffer and the argument descriptor parameter. Here, too, you should check the return code to ensure that the function succeeded.

One limitation of *CeOpenCallerBuffer* is that it should not be called on pointers passed in the parmeter list of a function. For example, the call to a drivers XXX_Write function contains the paramter *pBuffer*, which points to the data to be written to the device. Because this pointer is passed in the parameter list, the buffer has already been marshalled by the operating system.

However, what if you want that buffer to be duplicated for security reasons? In this specific case, use the function

```
HRESULT CeAllocDuplicateBuffer (PVOID *ppDestDuplicate,
                                PVOID pSrcMarshalled, DWORD cbSrc,
                                DWORD ArgumentDescriptor);
```

Here again, the parameters closely follow the parmaters of *CeOpenCallerBuffer*. The difference is that this function can be called on buffers referenced by function parameters. Don't call this function unless you need to duplicate a buffer. Nor should you call this function for buffers referenced by pointers embedded in structures. Those buffers should be marshalled by *CeOpenCallerBuffer* with the *ForceDuplicate* flag set to TRUE.

If you do use *CeAllocDuplicateBuffer*, the buffer should be freed with a call to

```
HRESULT CeFreeDuplicateBuffer (PVOID pDestDuplicate,
                               PVOID pSrcMarshalled, DWORD cbSrc,
                               DWORD ArgumentDescriptor);
```

Any data in the copy of the buffer will be written back to the original buffer if the *ArgumentDescriptor* parameters indicate that the data is an output or input/output parameter.

While *CeOpenCallerBuffer* and *CeCloseCallerBuffer* are required for user mode drivers, they are also required for kernel mode drivers if the driver needs asynchronous access to the buffer after the original driver call returns. To access buffers asynchronously, another set of functions must be called on the marshalled buffer. This second set starts with the function

```
HRESULT CeAllocAsynchronousBuffer (PVOID *ppDestAsyncMarshalled,
                                   PVOID pSrcSyncMarshalled, DWORD cbSrc,
                                   DWORD ArgumentDescriptor);
```

The parameters should now be quite familiar to you as they closely follow the *CeOpenCallerBuffer* and *CeAllocDuplicateBuffer*. This function can only be called on buffers previously marshalled by *CeOpenCallerBuffer*.

To free an asynchronous buffer, call the function

```
HRESULT CeFreeAsynchronousBuffer (PVOID pDestAsyncMarshalled,
                                  PVOID pSrcSyncMarshalled, DWORD cbSrc,
                                  DWORD ArgumentDescriptor);
```

As before, the parameter list is similar to the other calls.

All these functions are used in slightly different ways for sightly different reasons depending on whether the driver is operating in kernel mode or user mode, whether the buffer is to be accessed synchronously or asynchronously, and whether the pointer is passed on the parameter list or embedded in a structure that is passed to the driver. Table 17-1 summarizes the various situations and the appropriate functions to use.

TABLE 17-1 Table showing the proper buffer mapping calls for a given situation

	Kernel Mode Driver		User Mode Driver	
	Synchronous	Asynchronous	Synchronous	Asynchronous
Pointer in parameter list	No action necessary	CeAllocDuplicateBuffer CeFreeDuplicateBuffer	No action necessary	CeAllocDuplicateBuffer CeFreeDuplicateBuffer
Pointer embedded in structure	No action required	CeOpenCallerBuffer CeAllocAsynchronousBuffer CeFreeAsynchronousBuffer CeCloseCallerBuffer	CeOpenCaller-Buffer CeCloseCaller-Buffer	CeOpenCallerBuffer CeAllocAsynchronousBuffer CeFreeAsynchronousBuffer CeCloseCallerBuffer

For some conditions, such as kernel mode drivers asynchronously accessing a buffer referenced in a structure, there are multiple functions that must be called. In these cases, the functions are listed in the order they need to be called.

While the table is helpful, the best illustration is an example. Assume a driver has an IOCTL function to checksum a series of buffers. Because the buffers are disjointed, the pointers to the buffers are passed to the driver in a structure. The driver must map each pointer in the structure, checksum the data in the buffers, and return the result, as in the following code:

```
#define IOCTL_CHECKSUM 2
#define MAX_BUFFS 5
typedef struct {
    int nSize;
    PBYTE pData;
} BUFDAT, *PBUFDAT;

typedef struct {
    int nBuffs;
    BUFDAT bd[MAX_BUFFS];
} CHKSUMSTRUCT, *PCHKSUMSTRUCT;

DWORD xxx_IOControl (DWORD dwOpen, DWORD dwCode, PBYTE pIn, DWORD dwIn,
                     PBYTE pOut, DWORD dwOut, DWORD *pdwBytesWritten) {

    switch (dwCode) {

    case IOCTL_CHECKSUM:
        {
            PCHKSUMSTRUCT pchs;
            DWORD dwSum = 0;
            HRESULT hr;
            PBYTE pData;
            int i, j;

            // Verify the input parameters.
            if (!pIn || (dwIn < sizeof (CHKSUMSTRUCT)) ||
                !pOut || (dwOut < sizeof (DWORD))) {
                SetLastError (ERROR_INVALID_PARAMETER);
                return FALSE;
```

```
            }
            // Perform the checksum.  Protect against bad pointers.
            pchs = (PCHKSUMSTRUCT)pIn;
            __try {
                for (i = 0; (i < pchs->nBuffs) && (i < MAX_BUFFS); i++) {

                    // Marshal the buffer
                    hr = CeOpenCallerBuffer ((PVOID *)&pData,
                                             pchs->bd[i].pData,
                                             pchs->bd[i].nSize,
                                             ARG_I_PTR, FALSE);
                    if (SUCCEEDED (hr)) {
                        // Checksum the buffer.
                        for (j = 0; j < pchs->bd[i].nSize; j++)
                            dwSum += *pData++;

                        CeCloseCallerBuffer (pData, pchs->bd[i].pData,
                                             pchs->bd[i].nSize, ARG_I_PTR);
                    }
                }
                // Write out the result.
                *(DWORD *)pOut = dwSum;
                *pdwBytesWritten = sizeof (DWORD);
            }
            __except (EXCEPTION_EXECUTE_HANDLER) {
                SetLastError (ERROR_INVALID_PARAMETER);
                return FALSE;
            }
        }
        SetLastError (0);
        break;

        default:
            SetLastError (ERROR_INVALID_PARAMETER);
            return FALSE;
    }
    return TRUE;
}
```

In the preceding code, the driver has one IOCTL command, *IOCTL_CHECKSUM*. When this command is received, the driver uses the structures passed in the input buffer to locate the data buffers. Each of the buffers needs to be marshalled if the driver is loaded as a user mode driver. Once marshalled with *CeOpenCallerBuffer*, the driver can perform the checksum on the buffers. Then the buffers are closed using *CeCloseCallerBuffer*. Note that the *ArgumentDescriptor* parameter is *ARG_I_PTR* indicating that the data is only read and not written. This allows Windows CE to optimize the marshalling of the data.

Device Interface Classes

In a generic sense, the driver is free to define any set of commands to respond to in the *IOControl* function. However, it would be nice if drivers that implement similar functions agreed on a set of common IOCTL commands that would be implemented by all the common drivers. In addition, there is additional functionality that all drivers may optionally implement. For drivers that implement this common functionality, it would be convenient if they all responded to the same set of IOCTL commands.

Driver interface classes are a way to organize and describe these common IOCTL commands. For example, Windows CE defines a set of IOCTL commands that are used by the Power Manager to control the power use of a driver. Drivers that respond to these power management IOCTLs are said to support the power management interface class. The list of driver interface classes grows with each release of Windows CE, but here is a short summary:

- Power Management interface
- Block Driver interface
- Card services interface
- Keyboard interface
- Camera and Camera Pin interfaces
- Battery interface
- NDIS miniport interface
- Generic Stream interface

In addition to grouping like sets of IOCTL commands, device drivers can advertise their support of one or more interfaces. Other drivers, or even applications, can be informed when a driver is loaded that supports a given interface. Interface classes are uniquely identified with a GUID defined in the Platform Builder include files. Unfortunately, the GUID definitions are distributed across the different include files relevant to the different driver types related to the specific interface, so finding them can be a challenge.

Advertising an Interface

Drivers that support a given interface need to tell the system that they support it. Advertising support for an interface can be accomplished in a couple of ways. First, the registry key specifying the driver can contain an *IClass* value that specifies one or more GUIDs identifying the interface classes the driver supports. For drivers that support a single interface, the *IClass* value is a string. For drivers that support multiple interfaces, the *IClass* value is a multi-z string with each individual string containing a GUID.

A driver can manually advertise an interface by calling *AdvertiseInterface* defined as

```
BOOL AdvertiseInterface (const GUID* devclass, LPCWSTR name, BOOL fAdd);
```

The first parameter is the GUID for the interface being advertised. The second parameter is a string that uniquely identifies the name of the driver. The easiest way to do this is to provide the name of the driver, such as DSK1:. Recall that the name of a driver can be found in its *Active* key. The last parameter, *fAdd*, should be *TRUE* if the interface is now available and *FALSE* if the interface is no longer available. It is important to advertise the removal of the interface if the driver is being removed. Otherwise the Device Manager won't free the memory used to track the interface.

Monitoring for an Interface

Applications or drivers can ask to be notified when a driver advertises an interface being either created or removed. To be notified, a message queue should be created with read access. Set the maximum message length to *MAX_DEVCLASS_NAMELEN*. The message queue handle is then passed to the *RequestDeviceNotifications* function defined as

```
HANDLE RequestDeviceNotifications (const GUID* devclass, HANDLE hMsgQ,
                                   BOOL fAll);
```

The first parameter is a string representing the GUID of the interface that the application or driver wants to monitor. The string *PMCLASS_GENERIC_DEVICE* provides a method for being notified when any power-managed stream device is loaded or unloaded. This parameter can be set to *NULL* to receive all notifications. However, monitoring all interfaces isn't recommended for performance reasons. The second parameter is the handle to the previously created message queue. The final parameter is a Boolean that should be set to *TRUE* to receive all past notifications or *FALSE* to receive notifications only from the time of the call forward.

After the call, the application or driver should create a thread to block on the message queue handle that will be signaled when a message is inserted in the queue. The message format depends on the specific notification being sent.

To stop the notifications, call the function *StopDeviceNotifications* prototyped as

```
BOOL StopDeviceNotifications (HANDLE h);
```

The only parameter is the handle returned by *RequestDeviceNotifications*.

The interface class scheme provides a handy way for a developer to know what IOCTL commands to support for a given driver. The classic example of this system is power management. The power management methodology was radically redesigned with the release of Windows CE 4.0. However, the stream interface couldn't be changed without causing all the drivers to be redesigned. Instead, the new power management support was exposed through a newly defined power management interface class.

Device Driver Power Management

The basics of this power manager are discussed in Chapter 15. Device drivers support the Power Manager by exposing a power management interface that allows the Power Manager to query the power capabilities of the device and to control its state. The control of the Power Manager is tempered by the actual response of the driver, which might not be in position to change its power state at the time of the request.

Power Management Functions for Devices

The power state of a device is defined to be one of the following:

- **D0** Device is fully powered. All devices are fully powered and running.
- **D1** Device is fully functional, but in a power-saving mode.
- **D2** Device is in standby.
- **D3** Device is in sleep mode.
- **D4** Device is unpowered.

These power states are defined in *CEDEVICE_POWER_STATE* enumeration, which also defines additional values for *PwrDeviceUnspecified* and *PwrDeviceMaximum*.

When a device wants to set its own power state, it should call the *DevicePowerNotify* function defined as

```
DWORD DevicePowerNotify (PVOID pvDevice, CEDEVICE_POWER_STATE DeviceState,
                         DWORD Flags);
```

The *pvDevice* parameter points to a string naming the device driver to change. The second parameter is *CEDEVICE_POWER_STATE* enumeration. The *dwDeviceFlags* parameter should be set to *POWER_NAME*.

When changing its own power state, the device should not immediately change to the state requested in the *SetDevicePower* call. Instead, the device should wait until it is instructed to change its power state through an IOCTL command sent by the Power Manager. The driver should not assume that just because it requests a given state that the Power Manager will set the device to that state. There might be system reasons for leaving the device in a higher power state.

Now let's look at the IOCTL commands that are sent to a device driver that supports the power management interface class.

IOCTL_POWER_CAPABILITIES

This IOCTL command is sent to query the power capabilities of the device. The input buffer of the *IoControl* function is filled with a *POWER_RELATIONSHIP* structure that describes any parent-child relationships between the driver and a bus driver. The output buffer contains a

POWER_CAPABILITIES structure that should be filled in by the driver. The structure is defined as

```
typedef struct _POWER_CAPABILITIES {
    UCHAR DeviceDx;
    UCHAR WakeFromDx;
    UCHAR InrushDx;
    DWORD Power[5];
    DWORD Latency[5];
    DWORD Flags;
} POWER_CAPABILITIES, *PPOWER_CAPABILITIES;
```

The *DeviceDx* field is a bitmask that indicates which of the power states, from D0 to D*n*, the device driver supports. The *WakeFromDx* field is also a bitmask. This field indicates which of the device states the hardware can wake from if an external signal is detected by the device. The *InrunshDx* field indicates which entries of the *Power* array are valid. The *Power* array contains entries that specify the amount of power used by the device, in milliwatts, for each given power state. The *Latency* array describes the amount of time, in milliseconds, that it takes the device to return to the D0 state from each of the other power states. Finally, the *Flags* field should be set to *TRUE* if the driver wants to receive an *IOCTL_REGISTER_POWER_RELATIONSHIP* command to manage other *child* devices.

The level of detail involved in filling out the *POWER_CAPABILITIES* structure can be intimidating. Many drivers only fill out the first field, *DeviceDx*, to at least indicate to the system which power levels the device supports and set the remaining fields to zero.

IOCTL_REGISTER_POWER_RELATIONSHIP

This command is sent to a driver that wants to control the power management of any *child* drivers. During this call, the parent driver can inform the Power Manager of any devices it controls.

IOCTL_POWER_GET

This command is sent to the device to query the current power state of the device. The output buffer points to a *DWORD* that should be set to one of the *CEDEVICE_POWER_STATE* enumeration values.

IOCTL_POWER_QUERY

This command is sent to ask the device whether it will change to a given power state. The input buffer points to a *POWER_RELATIONSHIP* structure while the output buffer contains a *CEDEVICE_POWER_STATE* enumeration containing the power state that the Power Manager wants the device to enter. If the device wishes to reject the request, it should set the *CEDEVICE_POWER_STATE* enumeration to *PwrDeviceUnspecified*. Otherwise, the Power Manager assumes the driver is willing to enter the requested power state. The driver shouldn't enter the state on this command. Instead it should wait until it receives an *IOCTL_POWER_SET* command. Be warned that the simple implementation of the Power Manager in Windows CE doesn't call this IOCTL, so a driver shouldn't depend on receiving this command before an *IOCTL_POWER_SET* command is received.

IOCTL_POWER_SET

This command is sent to instruct the device to change to a given power state. The input buffer points to a *POWER_RELATIONSHIP* structure whereas the output buffer contains a *CEDEVICE_POWER_STATE* enumeration containing the power state that the device should enter. The device should respond by configuring its hardware to match the requested power state.

Building a Device Driver

Building a device driver is as simple as building a DLL. Although you can use the Platform Builder and its more extensive set of tools, you can easily build stream drivers by using Visual Studio, even if you don't have Platform Builder. All you need to do is create a Smart Device DLL project, export the proper entry points, and write the code. The most frequently made mistake I see is in not declaring the entry points as *extern C* so that the C++ compiler doesn't mangle the exported function names.

Debug Zones

Debug zones allow a programmer or tester to manipulate debug messages from any module, EXE or DLL, in a Windows CE system. Debug zones are typically used by developers who use Platform Builder because debug zones allow developers to access the debug shell that allows them to interactively enable and disable specific groups, or *zones*, of debug messages. Another feature of debug zone messages is that the macros that are used to declare the messages insert the messages only when compiling a debug build of the module. When a release build is made, the macros resolve to 0 and don't insert any space-hogging Unicode strings. The value of debug zones isn't just that developers can use them; it's that all the modules that make up Windows CE have debug builds that are packed full of debug messages that can be enabled.

Using debug zones in applications or DLLs is a fairly straightforward process. First, up to 16 zones can be assigned to group all the debug messages in the module. The zones are declared using the *DEBUGZONE* macro, as in

```
#define ZONE_ERROR        DEBUGZONE(0)
#define ZONE_WARNING      DEBUGZONE(1)
#define ZONE_INIT         DEBUGZONE(2)
```

Then debug messages are inserted in the code. Instead of directly calling *OutputDebugString*, which was the old way of sending strings to a debug port, the messages should be enclosed in a *DEBUGZONE* macro, defined as

```
DEBUGMSG (zone, (printf expression));
```

The zone parameter is one of the 16 zones declared. The *printf expression* can be any *printf* style string plus the parameters. Note the additional parentheses around the *printf* expression. These are needed because *DEBUGMSG* is a macro and requires a fixed number of parameters. The following is an example of using *DEBUGMSG*:

```
DEBUGMSG (ZONE_ERROR, (TEXT("Read failed. rc=%d\r\n"), GetLastError()));
```

In addition to inserting the debug messages, a module must declare a structure named *dpCurSettings* of type *DBGPARAM*, defined as

```
typedef struct _DBGPARAM {
    WCHAR lpszName[32];
    WCHAR rglpszZones[16][32];
    ULONG ulZoneMask;
} DBGPARAM, *LPDBGPARAM;
```

The first field is the debug name of the module. Typically, but not always, this is the name of the file. The second field is an array of strings. Each string identifies a particular zone. These names can be queried by the system to tell the programmer what zones are in a module. The final field, *ulZoneMask*, is a bitmask that sets the zones that are enabled by default. Although this field is a 32-bit value, only the first 16 bits are used.

The only action a module must take at run time to enable debug zones is to initialize the zones with the following macro:

```
DEBUGREGISTER(HANDLE hInstance);
```

The only parameter is the instance handle of the EXE or DLL. Typically this call is made early in WinMain for applications and in the process attach call to *LibMain* for DLLs. The GenDriver example shown in Listing 17-1 demonstrates the use of debug zones.

Unfortunately for application developers, the debug messages produced by debug zones are sent to the debug port, which is generally not available on shipping systems. Some systems, however, do allow the primary serial port on the system to be redirected so that it's used as a debug port, instead of as COM1. Because each OEM will have a different method of enabling this redirection, you will need to contact the specific OEM for information on how to redirect the serial port. Nonetheless, debug zones are a powerful tool for debugging Windows CE systems.

The Generic Driver Example

The following example, GenDriver, is a simple stream driver. Although it doesn't talk to any hardware, it exports the proper 12 entry points and can be loaded by any Windows CE system. To have a system load GenDriver, you can add an entry under [HKEY_LOCAL_MACHINE]\Drivers\Builtin to have the driver loaded when the system boots, or you can write an application that creates the proper driver keys elsewhere and calls *ActivateDevice*.

LISTING 17-1 The GenDriver example

GenDriver.h

```
//======================================================================
// Header file
//
// Written for the book Programming Windows CE
// Copyright (C) 2007 Douglas Boling
//======================================================================

//
// Declare the external entry points here. Use declspec so we don't
// need a .def file. Bracketed with extern C to avoid mangling in C++.
//
#ifdef __cplusplus
extern "C" {
#endif //__cplusplus
__declspec(dllexport) DWORD GEN_Init (DWORD dwContext);
__declspec(dllexport) BOOL  GEN_PreDeinit (DWORD dwContext);
__declspec(dllexport) BOOL  GEN_Deinit (DWORD dwContext);
__declspec(dllexport) DWORD GEN_Open (DWORD dwContext, DWORD dwAccess,
                                      DWORD dwShare);
__declspec(dllexport) BOOL  GEN_PreClose (DWORD dwOpen);
__declspec(dllexport) BOOL  GEN_Close (DWORD dwOpen);
__declspec(dllexport) DWORD GEN_Read (DWORD dwOpen, LPVOID pBuffer,
                                      DWORD dwCount);
__declspec(dllexport) DWORD GEN_Write (DWORD dwOpen, LPVOID pBuffer,
                                       DWORD dwCount);
__declspec(dllexport) DWORD GEN_Seek (DWORD dwOpen, long lDelta,
                                      WORD wType);
__declspec(dllexport) DWORD GEN_IOControl (DWORD dwOpen, DWORD dwCode,
                                           PBYTE pIn, DWORD dwIn,
                                           PBYTE pOut, DWORD dwOut,
                                           DWORD *pdwBytesWritten);
__declspec(dllexport) void GEN_PowerDown (DWORD dwContext);
__declspec(dllexport) void GEN_PowerUp (DWORD dwContext);
#ifdef __cplusplus
} // extern "C"
#endif //__cplusplus

// Suppress warnings by declaring the undeclared.
```

```
DWORD GetConfigData (DWORD);
//
// Driver instance structure
//
typedef struct {
    DWORD dwSize;
    INT nNumOpens;
} DRVCONTEXT, *PDRVCONTEXT;""""
```

GenDriver.cpp

```
//======================================================================
// GenDriver - Generic stream device driver for Windows CE
//
// Written for the book Programming Windows CE
// Copyright (C) 2007 Douglas Boling
//======================================================================
#include <windows.h>                     // For all that Windows stuff
#include "GenDriver.h"                   // Local program includes

//
// Globals
//
HINSTANCE hInst;                         // DLL instance handle

//
// Debug zone support
//
#ifdef DEBUG
// Used as a prefix string for all debug zone messages.
#define DTAG        TEXT ("GENDrv: ")

// Debug zone constants
#define ZONE_ERROR      DEBUGZONE(0)
#define ZONE_WARNING    DEBUGZONE(1)
#define ZONE_FUNC       DEBUGZONE(2)
#define ZONE_INIT       DEBUGZONE(3)
#define ZONE_DRVCALLS   DEBUGZONE(4)
#define ZONE_EXENTRY  (ZONE_FUNC | ZONE_DRVCALLS)
// Debug zone structure
DBGPARAM dpCurSettings = {
    TEXT("GenDriver"), {
    TEXT("Errors"),TEXT("Warnings"),TEXT("Functions"),
    TEXT("Init"),TEXT("Driver Calls"),TEXT("Undefined"),
    TEXT("Undefined"),TEXT("Undefined"), TEXT("Undefined"),
    TEXT("Undefined"),TEXT("Undefined"),TEXT("Undefined"),
    TEXT("Undefined"),TEXT("Undefined"),TEXT("Undefined"),
    TEXT("Undefined") },
    0x0003
};
#endif //DEBUG
```

```
//======================================================================
// DllMain - DLL initialization entry point
//
BOOL WINAPI DllMain (HANDLE hinstDLL, DWORD dwReason,
                     LPVOID lpvReserved) {
    hInst = (HINSTANCE)hinstDLL;

    switch (dwReason) {
        case DLL_PROCESS_ATTACH:
            DEBUGREGISTER(hInst);
            // Improve performance by passing on thread attach calls
            DisableThreadLibraryCalls (hInst);
        break;

        case DLL_PROCESS_DETACH:
            DEBUGMSG(ZONE_INIT, (DTAG TEXT("DLL_PROCESS_DETACH\r\n")));
            break;
    }
    return TRUE;
}
//======================================================================
// GEN_Init - Driver initialization function
//
DWORD GEN_Init (DWORD dwContext, LPCVOID lpvBusContext) {
    PDRVCONTEXT pDrv;

    DEBUGMSG (ZONE_INIT | ZONE_EXENTRY,
              (DTAG TEXT("GEN_Init++ dwContex:%x\r\n"), dwContext));

    // Allocate a device instance structure.
    pDrv = (PDRVCONTEXT)LocalAlloc (LPTR, sizeof (DRVCONTEXT));
    if (pDrv) {
        // Initialize structure.
        memset ((PBYTE) pDrv, 0, sizeof (DRVCONTEXT));
        pDrv->dwSize = sizeof (DRVCONTEXT);

        // Read registry to determine the size of the disk.
        GetConfigData (dwContext);
    } else
        DEBUGMSG (ZONE_INIT | ZONE_ERROR,
                  (DTAG TEXT("GEN_Init failure. Out of memory\r\n")));
    DEBUGMSG (ZONE_FUNC, (DTAG TEXT("GEN_Init-- pDrv: %x\r\n"), pDrv));
    return (DWORD)pDrv;
}
//======================================================================
// GEN_PreDeinit - Driver de-initialization notification function
//
BOOL GEN_PreDeinit (DWORD dwContext) {

    DEBUGMSG (ZONE_EXENTRY,
              (DTAG TEXT("GEN_PreDeinit++ dwContex:%x\r\n"), dwContext));

    DEBUGMSG (ZONE_FUNC, (DTAG TEXT("GEN_PreDeinit--\r\n")));
    return TRUE;
```

```
}
//======================================================================
// GEN_Deinit - Driver de-initialization function
//
BOOL GEN_Deinit (DWORD dwContext) {
    PDRVCONTEXT pDrv = (PDRVCONTEXT) dwContext;

    DEBUGMSG (ZONE_EXENTRY,
              (DTAG TEXT("GEN_Deinit++ dwContex:%x\r\n"), dwContext));

    if (pDrv && (pDrv->dwSize == sizeof (DRVCONTEXT))) {

        // Free the driver state buffer.
        LocalFree ((PBYTE)pDrv);
    }
    DEBUGMSG (ZONE_FUNC, (DTAG TEXT("GEN_Deinit--\r\n")));
    return TRUE;
}
//======================================================================
// GEN_Open - Called when driver opened
//
DWORD GEN_Open (DWORD dwContext, DWORD dwAccess, DWORD dwShare) {
    PDRVCONTEXT pDrv = (PDRVCONTEXT) dwContext;

    DEBUGMSG (ZONE_EXENTRY,
              (DTAG TEXT("GEN_Open++ dwContext: %x\r\n"), dwContext));

    // Verify that the context handle is valid.
    if (pDrv && (pDrv->dwSize != sizeof (DRVCONTEXT))) {
        DEBUGMSG (ZONE_ERROR, (DTAG TEXT("GEN_Open failed\r\n")));
        return 0;
    }
    // Count the number of opens.
    InterlockedIncrement ((long *)&pDrv->nNumOpens);
    DEBUGMSG (ZONE_FUNC, (DTAG TEXT("GEN_Open--\r\n")));
    return (DWORD)pDrv;
}
//======================================================================
// GEN_PreClose - Called when the driver is about to be closed
//
BOOL GEN_PreClose (DWORD dwOpen) {

    DEBUGMSG (ZONE_EXENTRY,
              (DTAG TEXT("GEN_PreClose++ dwOpen: %x\r\n"), dwOpen));

    DEBUGMSG (ZONE_FUNC, (DTAG TEXT("GEN_PreClose--\r\n")));
    return TRUE;
}
//======================================================================
// GEN_Close - Called when driver closed
//
```

```
BOOL GEN_Close (DWORD dwOpen) {
    PDRVCONTEXT pDrv = (PDRVCONTEXT) dwOpen;

    DEBUGMSG (ZONE_EXENTRY,
              (DTAG TEXT("GEN_Close++ dwOpen: %x\r\n"), dwOpen));

    if (pDrv && (pDrv->dwSize != sizeof (DRVCONTEXT))) {
        DEBUGMSG (ZONE_FUNC | ZONE_ERROR,
                  (DTAG TEXT("GEN_Close failed\r\n")));
        return 0;
    }
    if (pDrv->nNumOpens)
        pDrv->nNumOpens--;

    DEBUGMSG (ZONE_FUNC, (DTAG TEXT("GEN_Close--\r\n")));
    return TRUE;
}
//======================================================================
// GEN_Read - Called when driver read
//
DWORD GEN_Read (DWORD dwOpen, LPVOID pBuffer, DWORD dwCount) {
    DWORD dwBytesRead = 0;
    DEBUGMSG (ZONE_EXENTRY,
              (DTAG TEXT("GEN_Read++ dwOpen: %x\r\n"), dwOpen));

    DEBUGMSG (ZONE_FUNC, (DTAG TEXT("GEN_Read--\r\n")));
    return dwBytesRead;
}
//======================================================================
// GEN_Write - Called when driver written
//
DWORD GEN_Write (DWORD dwOpen, LPVOID pBuffer, DWORD dwCount) {
    DWORD dwBytesWritten = 0;
    DEBUGMSG (ZONE_EXENTRY,
              (DTAG TEXT("GEN_Write++ dwOpen: %x\r\n"), dwOpen));

    DEBUGMSG (ZONE_FUNC, (DTAG TEXT("GEN_Write--\r\n")));
    return dwBytesWritten;
}
//======================================================================
// GEN_Seek - Called when SetFilePtr called
//
DWORD GEN_Seek (DWORD dwOpen, long lDelta, WORD wType) {
    DEBUGMSG (ZONE_EXENTRY,(DTAG TEXT("GEN_Seek++ dwOpen:%x %d %d\r\n"),
              dwOpen, lDelta, wType));

    DEBUGMSG (ZONE_EXENTRY, (DTAG TEXT("GEN_Seek--\r\n")));
    return 0;
}
//======================================================================
// GEN_IOControl - Called when DeviceIOControl called
//
```

```
DWORD GEN_IOControl (DWORD dwOpen, DWORD dwCode, PBYTE pIn, DWORD dwIn,
                     PBYTE pOut, DWORD dwOut, DWORD *pdwBytesWritten) {
    PDRVCONTEXT pState;
    DWORD err = ERROR_INVALID_PARAMETER;

    DEBUGMSG (ZONE_EXENTRY,
             (DTAG TEXT("GEN_IOControl++ dwOpen: %x  dwCode: %x\r\n"),
             dwOpen, dwCode));

    pState = (PDRVCONTEXT) dwOpen;
    switch (dwCode) {
        // Insert IOCTL codes here.

        default:
            DEBUGMSG (ZONE_ERROR,
             (DTAG TEXT("GEN_IOControl: unknown code %x\r\n"), dwCode));
            return FALSE;
    }
    SetLastError (err);
    DEBUGMSG (ZONE_FUNC, (DTAG TEXT("GEN_IOControl--\r\n")));
    return TRUE;
}
//======================================================================
// GEN_PowerDown - Called when system suspends
//
void GEN_PowerDown (DWORD dwContext) {
    return;
}
//======================================================================
// GEN_PowerUp - Called when resumes
//
void GEN_PowerUp (DWORD dwContext) {
    return;
}
//----------------------------------------------------------------------
// GetConfigData - Get the configuration data from the registry.
//
DWORD GetConfigData (DWORD dwContext) {
    int nLen, rc;
    DWORD dwLen, dwType, dwSize = 0;
    HKEY hKey;
    TCHAR szKeyName[256], szPrefix[8];

    DEBUGMSG (ZONE_FUNC, (DTAG TEXT("GetConfigData++\r\n")));
    nLen = 0;
    // If ptr < 65K, it's a value, not a pointer.
    if (dwContext < 0x10000) {
        return -1;
    } else {
        __try {
            nLen = lstrlen ((LPTSTR)dwContext);
        }
        __except (EXCEPTION_EXECUTE_HANDLER) {
            nLen = 0;
        }
```

```
    }
    if (!nLen) {
        DEBUGMSG (ZONE_ERROR, (DTAG TEXT("dwContext not a ptr\r\n")));
        return -2;
    }
    // Open the Active key for the driver.
    rc = RegOpenKeyEx(HKEY_LOCAL_MACHINE,(LPTSTR)dwContext,0, 0, &hKey);

    if (rc == ERROR_SUCCESS) {
        // Read the key value.
        dwLen = sizeof(szKeyName);
        rc = RegQueryValueEx (hKey, TEXT("Key"), NULL, &dwType,
                                   (PBYTE)szKeyName, &dwLen);

        RegCloseKey(hKey);
        if (rc == ERROR_SUCCESS)
            rc = RegOpenKeyEx (HKEY_LOCAL_MACHINE, (LPTSTR)
                                   dwContext, 0, 0, &hKey);
        if (rc == ERROR_SUCCESS) {
            // This driver doesn't need any data from the key, so as
            // an example, it just reads the Prefix value, which
            // identifies the three-char prefix (GEN) of this driver.
            dwLen = sizeof (szPrefix);
            rc = RegQueryValueEx (hKey, TEXT("Prefix"), NULL,
                                  &dwType, (PBYTE)szPrefix, &dwLen);
            RegCloseKey(hKey);
        } else
            DEBUGMSG (ZONE_ERROR, (TEXT("Error opening key\r\n")));
    } else
        DEBUGMSG (ZONE_ERROR, (TEXT("Error opening Active key\r\n")));

    DEBUGMSG (ZONE_FUNC, (DTAG TEXT("GetConfigData--\r\n")));
    return 0;
}""""""""""""""""""""""""""""""""""""""""""""""""""""""""""""""""""""""""""""""""""""""""""""""""""""""""""""""""
""""""""""
```

The majority of the lines of code in GenDriver are *DEBUGZONE* macros. The messages are handy for learning exactly when and how the different entry points of the driver are called. The *GetConfigData* routine at the end of the code shows how to test the *Context* value to determine whether the value passed to the *Init* function was a pointer to a string or merely a number.

The preceding driver template is a good starting point for any stream driver you want to write. Simply change the three-character name GEN to whatever your driver is named and go from there.

Services

Before Windows CE 4.0, Windows CE did not have the concept of a service. To make up for the lack of service support, so-called *device drivers* were written, not to interface with hardware, but rather to manage some software interface such as a telnet server. The problem with this design was that these services ran in the same process as most of the other device drivers. If there was a bug in the service code, the service could corrupt a device driver, some of which are critical to the operation of the system. To solve this problem, the Services Manager was added in Windows CE 4.0.

The Services Manager is quite similar in design to the User Mode Device Manager; it loads services when the operating system boots by looking at a list in the registry. The manager can also load services upon request from an application, and finally, it expects the service to be implemented as a DLL with the 8 of the 12 external entry points expected of a Windows CE device driver.[2]

In addition to the similarities, the Services Manager has a quite convenient capability beyond the Device Manager. The Services Manager implements a *super service* that monitors, upon request connections to TCP/IP ports on the device. Because many of the services implemented for Windows CE are server related, such as a telnet server or Web server, the super service alleviates the need for a number of services to create a thread and open a socket just to monitor a port. Instead, the super service does this and notifies the service that has requested monitoring when the port is connected.

Service Architecture

The architecture of a Windows CE service belies the history of using device drivers as service providers under Windows CE. A Windows CE service is a DLL that is constructed almost identically to a stream device driver. Like a stream driver, a Windows CE service exports most of the same entry points, from *xxx_Init* to *xxx_IoControl*. Also, like a stream driver, a service has a three-character prefix that, along with an instance number, is used to identify the loaded service.

One convenient characteristic of a service is that the Services Manager doesn't require that all the stream functions be exported from a service. If the service isn't intended to be exposed as an interface by the standard stream functions, the service only needs to export *xxx_Init*, *xxx_Deinit*, *xxx_Open*, *xxx_Close*, and *xxx_IOControl*. Although this arrangement generally just saves writing and exporting a handful of null functions, it's still a handy feature.

[2] The entry points not in a service are PowerUp, PowerDown, PreDeinit and PreClose.

The Life of a Service

Services are always in one of two basic states, started or stopped, or transitioning between these two states. When stopped, the service should not respond to net connections or perform any local processing that the service was designed to support. The service can be programmatically started and stopped by applications with an IOCTL command.

Services can be loaded on reset or manually loaded by an application. To load a service automatically on reset, add a registry key under the key [HKEY_LOCAL_MACHINE]\Services. The name of the key created is used by the Services Manager to identify the service. The contents of the key are quite similar to the contents of a device driver key for a user mode driver. Most of the same values used in device keys—*DLL*, *Prefix*, *Index*, and so forth—are used in the *Services* key. One change for Windows CE 6 is that the registry value *ServiceContext* replaces the old *Context* value. In fact, if a legacy service uses the *Context* value in the registry, Windows CE 6.0 will not load that service. Figure 17-6 shows the registry key for the Bluetooth service.

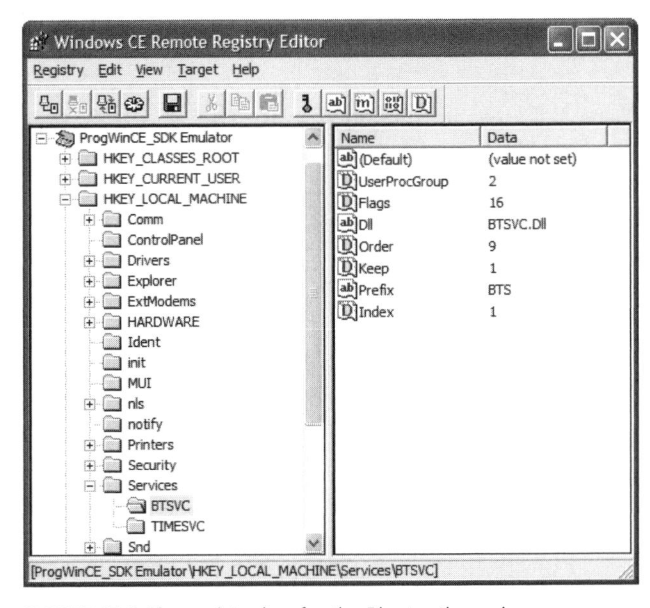

FIGURE 17-6 The registry key for the Bluetooth service

There are a few differences between a registry entry for a device and a service. The service entry must contain the *Index* value that is optional for a device. Also, the *ServiceContext* value in the registry has a defined use. It's used to determine what state the service is in when it loads. *ServiceContext* can be one of the following values:

- 0 Indicates that the service should auto-start itself.
- 1 Indicates that the service is initially stopped. If a Super Service key is present, the super service is automatically started.

These values correspond to the values *SERVICE_INIT_STARTED, SERVICE_INIT_STOPPED* discussed in the service *Init* routine later in this chapter.

However the service is loaded, the Services Manager will load the DLL implementing the service into its process space. Using the information gathered from the registry or the *RegisterService* function, the Services Manager uses the prefix to generate the names of the entry points to the service and uses *GetProcAddress* to get their addresses. Aside from the required *Init*, *Deinit*, and *IOControl* entry points, pointers to any of the other entry points that aren't found are simply redirected to a dummy routine that returns the error code *ERROR_NOT_SUPPORTED*.

Once the DLL is loaded, the service's *Init* function is called. The single parameter is the *Context* value either read from the registry or passed in the *RegisterService* function. If the service returns a nonzero value, the *Init* call is deemed to be a success and the service is then added to the chain of active services.

The service can be started and stopped by sending it IOCTL commands using *DeviceIoControl*. If the service receives a start command and it's currently stopped, it should start any processing that is the task of the service. If running, the service can be stopped by another IOCTL command. A stopped service isn't unloaded. Instead, it waits in memory until restarted or unloaded. Aside from stopping super service support, the Services Manager doesn't prevent a stopped service from performing any action. It's up to the service to heed the start and stop commands.

When the service is requested to be unloaded, the Services Manager calls the *Deinit* function of the service, and the DLL is unloaded from the process space of the Services Manager.

Application Control of a Service

Applications can load, unload, and communicate to a service using a series of dedicated functions. An application can load a service using one of two calls. If the service has a registry key defined, the function *ActivateService* function can be used. *ActivateService* is defined as

```
HANDLE ActivateService (LPCWSTR lpszDevKey, DWORD dwClientInfo);
```

The first parameter is the name of the registry key that provides load information on the service. The registry key must be located under [HKEY_LOCAL_ MACHINE]\Services. The format of the key must be the same as mentioned earlier for service registry keys. The second parameter is reserved and must be set to zero.

An application can also load a service with the function *RegisterService*. Like *RegisterDevice*, *RegisterService* doesn't require a registry entry for the service to load. The function is defined as

```
HANDLE RegisterService (LPCWSTR lpszType, DWORD dwIndex, LPCWSTR lpszLib,
                        DWORD dwInfo);
```

The parameters are quite similar to *RegisterDevice*: the prefix string of the service is passed in the first parameter; the index value in the second; the name of the DLL implementing the service in the third; and the context value, passed to the *Init* function, in the fourth parameter.

The return value for *RegisterService* as well as *ActivateService* is the handle to the instance of the service. This value can be used later to unload the service.

To communicate to with the service, an application uses the standard file I/O functions just as if the application were talking to a device driver. The application should call *CreateFile* indicating the name of the service, as in BTH1, and the type of access: read or read/write. Once the service is opened, the application can call *ReadFile*, *WriteFile*, and *DeviceIoControl* to talk to the service. When the conversation is complete, the application should call *CloseHandle* to close the service handle returned by *CreateFile*.

A list of the currently running services can be obtained with the *EnumServices* function. *EnumServices* is defined as

```
BOOL EnumServices (PBYTE pBuffer, DWORD *pdwServiceEntries,
                   DWORD *pdwBufferLen);
```

The *pBuffer* parameter points to a buffer that will be filled with an array of *ServiceEnumInfo* structures combined with a series of strings containing the names of the DLLs implementing the services. The function places one *ServiceEnumInfo* structure for each service managed by the Services Manager. The *pdwServiceEntries* parameter points to a *DWORD* that will be filled with the number of *ServiceEnumInfo* structures placed in the buffer by the function. The *pdwBufferLen* parameter points to a *DWORD* that should be initialized with the size of the buffer pointed to by *pBuffer*. When the function returns, the value is set to the number of bytes placed in the buffer.

The *ServiceEnumInfo* structure is defined as

```
typedef struct_ServiceEnumInfo {
    WCHAR szPrefix[6];
    WCHAR szDllName;
    HANDLE hServiceHandle;
    DWORD dwServiceState;
} ServiceEnumInfo;
```

Each instance of the structure describes one service. The somewhat misnamed *szPrefix* field contains the complete name of the service, as in *SRV0:*, which is a combination of the three-character service prefix along with its instance number and a trailing colon. The *szDllName* field points to a string naming the DLL implementing the service. The *hServiceHandle* field contains the handle of the service, whereas the *dwServiceState* field contains the current state (running, stopped, and so forth) of the service.

A service can be unloaded with the function *DeregisterService* defined as

```
BOOL DeregisterService (HANDLE hDevice);
```

The only parameter is the handle to the service. The Services Manager will first ask the service if it can be unloaded. If the service assents, the service will be unloaded; otherwise, the function will fail.

The Service DLL Entry Points

Because the architecture of the services is so similar to a device driver, I'm only going to discuss the differences between the service and the driver. The first difference is in how the service is initialized, so let's look at the *Init* function.

xxx_Init

The *Init* function follows the legacy *Init* prototype as in

```
DWORD xxx_Init (DWORD dwData);
```

The only parameter is a flag indicating the initial state of the service. The parameter can contain one of the following flags: *SERVICE_INIT_STARTED* indicates the service should provide its own initialization to start the service and *SERVICE_INIT_STOPPED* indicates that the service is currently stopped but may be started by the super service.

Like a device driver, a service should perform any necessary initialization during the call to the *Init* function. If an error is discovered, the *Init* function should return a zero indicating that the service should fail to load. The Services Manager will then unload the DLL implementing the service. The Services Manager interprets any nonzero value as a successful initialization. Also, as with a driver, the service isn't really a service until the *Init* function returns. This means that the *Init* function can't make any call that expects the service to be up and running.

xxx_Deinit

The *Deinit* function is called when the service is unloaded. The prototype of *Deinit* shown here matches the device driver *Deinit* function.

```
DWORD xxx_Deinit (DWORD dwContext);
```

The only parameter is the value that was returned from the *Init* function.

xxx_Open

The *Open* entry point to the service is called when an application or the services manager opens the service by calling *CreateFile*. The entry point is prototyped as

```
DWORD XXX_Open (DWORD hDeviceContext, DWORD AccessCode, DWORD ShareMode);
```

The first parameter is the device context value returned by the *Init* call. The *AccessCode* and *ShareMode* parameters are taken directly from *CreateFile*'s *dwDesiredAccess* and *dwShareMode* parameters and indicate how the application wants to access (read/write or read only) and share (*FILE_SHARE_READ* or *FILE_SHARE_WRITE*) the device. The services can refuse to open for any reason by simply returning 0 from the function.

xxx_Close

The *Close* function is called when the service is closed. The prototype of *Close* is

```
DWORD xxx_Deinit (DWORD dwContext);
```

The only parameter is the value that was returned from the *Open* function.

xxx_IOControl

The *IOControl* function is much more structured than the similarly named counterpart in a device driver. Instead of being a generic call that the driver can use as it pleases, in a service the *IOControl* call must support a series of commands used by both the Services Manager and by applications communicating with the service.

The prototype of the *IOControl* entry point is shown here.

```
DWORD xxx_IOControl (DWORD dwData, DWORD dwCode, PBYTE pBufIn, DWORD dwLenIn,
                     PBYTE pBufOut, DWORD dwLenOut, PDWORD pdwActualOut);
```

The parameters are the same as the ones used in *xxx_IOControl* for the device driver. The *dwData* parameter can either contain the value returned by the service's *Open* function or the value returned by the *Init* function. The service must be written to accept the value returned by *Init* or the values returned by both *Init* and *Open* if it implements an *Open* function. Because there is an extensive list of commands, they are discussed individually in the following section. The other entry points to the driver, *Read*, *Write*, and *Seek*, are optional.

The Service IOCTL Commands

A Windows CE service must field a series of IOCTL commands sent through the *IOControl* function. These commands can be grouped into a series of categories such as commands used to control the service, those used to query the state of the service, those commands used to help debug the service, and those commands used for super service support.

For each of the following commands, the service should return *TRUE* if the command was successful and *FALSE* if an error occurred. Extended error information should be sent by calling *SetLastError* before returning.

IOCTL_SERVICE_START

The first command, *IOCTL_SERVICE_START*, is sent to the service to start it. This command isn't sent by the system when the service is loaded. Instead, it's only sent by an application that wants to start a stopped service. If not already running, the service should make any connections or perform any initialization necessary to provide the service for which it was designed.

If the service has registry entries that tell the super service to automatically start port monitoring, the super service will start and bind to the specified ports if this IOCTL command returns a nonzero value.

IOCTL_SERVICE_STOP

The *IOCTL_SERVICE_STOP* command is sent by applications to stop a currently running service. The service won't be unloaded from memory just because it was stopped.

If the service has a super service running and the registry entry for the service is configured to auto-start a super service, the super service will be shut down if the service returns a nonzero value from this command.

IOCTL_SERVICE_REFRESH

The *IOCTL_SERVICE_REFRESH* command is sent by an application or the Services Manager to tell the service to reread its configuration data from the registry. Any changes in the configuration read should immediately be reflected in the service.

IOCTL_SERVICE_INSTALL

This optional command is sent to have the service modify the registry so that the service automatically starts on reset. This command is similar in action to the *DllRegisterServer* function of a COM in-proc server. Although optional, the command is convenient to have because any installation program for the service will not have to have knowledge of the registry entries required by the service. The registry entries needed for auto-load are described later in the "Super Service" section.

IOCTL_SERVICE_UNINSTALL

The complement to the *IOCTL_SERVICE_INSTALL* command, also optional, is the *IOCTL_SERVICE_UNINSTALL* command, which removes the registry entries that cause the driver to load on boot. An install/remove application can use this command to make a service remove its own registry entries so that the application need not enumerate the registry to find the installation entries.

This completes the list of IOCTL commands sent by applications; now let's look at the queries that are sent by both applications and the Services Manager to query the state of the service.

IOCTL_SERVICE_STATUS

The *IOCTL_SERVICE_STATUS* command is sent to query the state of the service. The state is returned in the output buffer pointed to by the *pOut* parameter of the *IOControl* call. The service should verify that *pOut* is nonzero and that *dwOut* indicates the buffer is large enough to hold a *DWORD*.

The service state can be one of the following, rather self-explanatory, values.

- SERVICE_STATE_OFF
- SERVICE_STATE_ON
- SERVICE_STATE_STARTING_UP
- SERVICE_STATE_SHUTTING_DOWN
- SERVICE_STATE_UNLOADING
- SERVICE_STATE_UNINITIALIZED
- SERVICE_STATE_UNKNOWN

IOCTL_SERVICE_CONSOLE

This optional command is sent to have the service display a service console. A service does not have to implement this command, but it can be handy in some situations.

The command is sent with a string in the input buffer. If the string is "On", or if the input buffer pointer is *NULL*, the service should display a service console. If the input buffer contains the string "Off", the service should remove the service console.

IOCTL_SERVICE_CONTROL

This command is basically the IOCTL of the IOCTL commands. That is, it's a generic command that can be used by the applications to communicate custom commands to the service. The format of the input and output buffers is defined by the service-defined command.

IOCTL_SERVICE_DEBUG

This command is sent to set the debug zone bitmask for the service. The first *DWORD* of the input buffer contains the new state for the zone bitmap. The service should verify that the input buffer exists and is at least a *DWORD* in size.

Because the debug zone structure *dpCurrParams* is typically only defined for debug builds of the service, the code fielding this command is typically couched in an *#ifdef* block to prevent it from being compiled in a nondebug build.

There are examples of where this command has been extended to perform debug duties beyond the settings of the zone mask. To extend the functionality, the service can use the size of the input buffer, specified in *dwIn*, to determine the meaning of the input buffer data. To be compatible, the service should default to setting the debug zone mask if *dwIn* is set to the size of a *DWORD*.

IOCTL_SERVICE_SUPPORTED_OPTIONS

This command queries the currently supported options of the service. The option flags are returned in a *DWORD* in the output buffer.

Super Service

The super service provides all services with a convenient method for monitoring TCP/IP ports without requiring customized code to monitor the port inside the service. The super service can either work automatically, if the proper registry settings are in place for the service, or manually through a series of function calls. It's more convenient to use the registry method for configuring the super service, so I will cover that method first.

If the service wants the super service to start automatically when the service is loaded, a subkey, named *Accept*, must be present under the service's key. Under the *Accept* key, there should be one or more subkeys each providing the IP address of a port to monitor. The Services Manager doesn't use the name of the subkey under the *Accept* key, although the key is traditionally named TCP-*xxx*, where *xxx* is the port number to be monitored. Each subkey should contain a binary value named *SockAddr*. The data in *SockAddr* should comprise bytes that make up a *SOCKADDR* structure that describes the port being monitored. The subkey can optionally contain a *Protocol* value that specifies the protocol for the socket. If this value isn't present, the protocol value is assumed to be zero. The following code initializes a *SOCKADDR* structure and then writes it to the registry.

```
int AddRegSuperServ (HKEY hKey, WORD wPort, DWORD dwProtocol) {
    SOCKADDR_IN sa;
    HKEY hSubKey;
    TCHAR szKeyName[128];
    DWORD dw;
    int rc;

    memset (&sa, 0, sizeof (sa));
    sa.sin_family = AF_INET;
    sa.sin_port = htons(wPort);
    sa.sin_addr.s_addr = INADDR_ANY;
```

```
    // Create accept key for this service
    wsprintf (szKeyName, TEXT("Accept\\TCP-%d"), wPort);
    rc = RegCreateKeyEx (hKey, szKeyName, 0, NULL, 0, NULL,
                         NULL, &hSubKey, &dw);
    if (rc == ERROR_SUCCESS)
        rc = RegSetValueEx (hSubKey, TEXT("SockAddr"), 0, REG_BINARY,
                            (PBYTE)&sa, sizeof (sa));
        rc = RegSetValueEx (hSubKey, TEXT("Protocol"), 0, REG_DWORD,
                            (PBYTE)&dwProtocol, sizeof (DWORD));
    return rc;
}
```

As we will soon see, the *ServiceAddPort* function has the capability to create this registry key as well. It's still handy to be able to write the key manually in the case in which the service doesn't want to start the super service when it's writing the key.

In addition to the *Accept* keys, the registry entry for the service must have a *ServiceContext* value of 1. If the *ServiceContext* value is 0, the super service will not start, nor will it start if the service is loaded in a standalone copy of the Services Manager.

When a service is started, either during system startup or with the *ActivateService* function, the service is loaded, its *Init* function is called, and then, if the *ServiceContext* value is 1, the super service queries the service through an IOCTL command to determine whether it wants super service support. If so, the super service enumerates the *Accept* keys and creates sockets to monitor the ports described in the keys. As each socket is opened and bound to the appropriate address, the service is notified, through an IOCTL command, that the socket is being monitored. Then, once all sockets are opened, and if the service is first being loaded, it sends a final IOCTL indicating that all the sockets are listening.

When a connection is made to one of the listening sockets, another IOCTL command is sent to the service along with the socket handle of the connection. The service then must create a new thread to handle the communication with the socket. The IOCTL call must return quickly because the calling thread is necessary for monitoring other ports. After the communication is complete, the service should close the socket handle passed during the connection notification. When the service shuts down, IOCTL commands are sent to the service notifying it that the sockets monitoring the ports have been closed.

Programmatically Controlling the Super Service

It's possible to have super service support without entries in the registry, but it's more complicated. In this scheme, the service must tell the super service about each port to be monitored. This can be done with the function *ServiceAddPort*, defined as

```
ServiceAddPort (HANDLE hService, SOCKADDR pSockAddr, INT cbSockAddr,
                INT iProtocol, WCHAR szRegWritePath);
```

The first parameter is the handle to the service, which, ironically, is somewhat difficult for the service to get. The *SOCKADDR* structure should be initialized with the address information for the listening socket. The *iProtocol* value should contain the protocol to be used by the socket. The *szRegWritePath* parameter can optionally specify a registry key name where this information will be written so that the next time the service is started, the super service will start automatically.

The issue with a service getting its own handle is that *GetServiceHandle* requires not just the three-character prefix of the service but also the instance number of the service. If the service was loaded with *RegisterService*, determining the service instance isn't easy. If, however, the service was loaded because of a registry key entry, the instance value is specified in the registry. Of course, if the service was loaded due to a registry entry, it's just as convenient to have the registry key also specify that the super service automatically start.

A specific port can be closed for monitoring by calling the *ServiceClosePort* function. Its prototype is

```
BOOL ServiceClosePort (HANDLE hService, SOCKADDR* pSockAddr,
                       int cbSockAddr, int iProtocol, BOOL fRemoveFromRegistry);
```

The parameters are identical to the *ServiceAddPort* function with the exception of the last parameter, *fRemoveFromRegistry*, which is a Boolean flag that tells the function whether the corresponding registry entry should be removed for the port.

To close all the ports being monitored by a service, *ServiceUnbindPorts* can be used.

```
BOOL ServiceUnbindPorts (HANDLE hService);
```

The only parameter is the handle to the service.

SuperService IOCTLs

Services that use the super service must respond to a series of additional IOCTL commands. These commands are either queries to check for support or are notifications indicating an event has occurred within the super service.

IOCTL_SERVICE_REGISTER_SOCKADDR

This command is sent at least twice during the initialization of the super service. The super service first sends this command to query whether the service will accept super service support. In this case, the input buffer pointer, *pIn*, is *NULL*.

The super service next sends this command again, once for each port the service is monitoring to verify the socket has been created to monitor the requested address. During these subsequent calls to verify the individual addresses, *pIn* points to a *SOCKADDR* structure that describes the socket address being monitored.

IOCTL_SERVICE_STARTED

This notification is sent when the super service completes its initialization after the service is first loaded. When this notification has been received, the service can assume that the super service is listening on all the ports requested. This notification isn't sent when the service is restarted after it has been stopped.

IOCTL_SERVICE_DEREGISTER_SOCKADDR

This notification is sent after the super service has closed the socket monitoring a given socket address. The *pIn* parameter points to the *SOCKADDR* structure that describes the socket address. This notification can be sent if the service is being stopped or because the service is being unloaded.

IOCTL_SERVICE_CONNECTION

The *IOCTL_SERVICE_CONNECTION* notification is sent when another application connects to the socket address being monitored by the super service. The input parameter *pIn* points to a socket handle for the connected socket. It's the responsibility of the service to spawn a thread to handle communication on this socket. The service must also close the socket when communication is complete.

IOCTL_SERVICE_NOTIFY_ADDR_CHANGE

This notification is sent if the system's IP address changes. The input buffer is filled with an *IP_ADAPTER_ INFO* structure defined as

```
typedef struct _IP_ADAPTER_INFO {
    struct _IP_ADAPTER_INFO* Next;
    DWORD ComboIndex;
    Char AdapterName[MAX_ADAPTER_NAME_LENGTH + 4];
    char Description[MAX_ADAPTER_DESCRIPTION_LENGTH + 4];
    UINT AddressLength;
    BYTE Address[MAX_ADAPTER_ADDRESS_LENGTH];
    DWORD Index;
    UINT Type;
    UINT DhcpEnabled;
    PIP_ADDR_STRING CurrentIpAddress;
    IP_ADDR_STRING IpAddressList;
    IP_ADDR_STRING GatewayList;
    IP_ADDR_STRING DhcpServer;
    BOOL HaveWins;
    IP_ADDR_STRING PrimaryWinsServer;
    IP_ADDR_STRING SecondaryWinsServer;
    time_t LeaseObtained;
    time_t LeaseExpires;
} IP_ADAPTER_INFO, *PIP_ADAPTER_INFO;
```

The fairly self-explanatory *IP_ADDRESS_INFO* structure contains everything from the IP address of the system to gateway, Dynamic Host Configuration Protocol (DHCP), and Windows Internet Naming Service (WINS) information.

Services.exe Command Line

In addition to being the Services Manager for the system, the application services.exe also has a command-line interface. For systems with a console, simply type

```
services help
```

This command produces a list of the available commands. Services can list the current services, start them and stop them, load them and unload them, and even add and remove them from from the registry.

For systems without console support, services can be launched with an *–f* command-line switch and the name of a file to send the output to, as in

```
services -f Outfile.txt
```

Other command-line parameters include *–d* to send the output to the debug serial port and *– q* to suppress output entirely.

TickSrv Example Service

The TickSrv example demonstrates a service that uses the super service. TickSrv monitors port 1000 on a Windows CE device and, for any application that connects, provides the current tick count and the number of milliseconds the system has been running since it was reset. TickSrv is implemented as a standard Windows CE service. Because there is no reason for a local application to use the service, it doesn't implement the standard stream exports, *Read*, *Write*, or *Seek*. The source code for TickSrv is shown in Listing 17-2.

LISTING 17-2 The TickSrv example

TickSrv.h

```
//======================================================================
// Header file
//
// Written for the book Programming Windows CE
// Copyright (C) 2007 Douglas Boling
//======================================================================
#define dim(a)  (sizeof (a)/sizeof(a[0]))
//
```

```
// Declare the external entry points here. Use declspec so we don't
// need a .def file. Bracketed with extern C to avoid mangling in C++.
//
#ifdef __cplusplus
extern "C" {
#endif //__cplusplus
__declspec(dllexport) DWORD TCK_Init (DWORD dwContext);
__declspec(dllexport) BOOL  TCK_Deinit (DWORD dwContext);
__declspec(dllexport) DWORD TCK_Open (DWORD dwContext, DWORD dwAccess,
                                      DWORD dwShare);
__declspec(dllexport) BOOL  TCK_Close (DWORD dwOpen);
__declspec(dllexport) DWORD TCK_IOControl (DWORD dwOpen, DWORD dwCode,
                                           PBYTE pIn, DWORD dwIn,
                                           PBYTE pOut, DWORD dwOut,
                                           DWORD *pdwBytesWritten);
#ifdef __cplusplus
} // extern "C"
#endif //__cplusplus

int RegisterService (void);
int DeregisterService (void);
DWORD WINAPI AcceptThread (PVOID pArg);
//
// Service state structure
//
typedef struct {
    DWORD dwSize;                  // Size of structure
    CRITICAL_SECTION csData;       // Crit Section protecting this struct
    int servState;                 // Service state
} SRVCONTEXT, *PSRVCONTEXT;
```

TickSrv.cpp

```
//======================================================================
// TickSrv - Simple example service for Windows CE
//
// Written for the book Programming Windows CE
// Copyright (C) 2007 Douglas Boling
//======================================================================
#include <windows.h>                 // For all that Windows stuff
#include <winsock.h>                 // Socket support
#include "service.h"                 // Service includes

#include "TickSrv.h"                 // Local program includes

// This links in the Winsock library without having to adjust the
// project settings.
#pragma comment( lib, "ws2" )        // Link WinSock 2.0 lib
```

```
#define REGNAME      TEXT("TickSrv")  // Reg name under services key
#define PORTNUM      1000             // Port number to monitor

//
// Globals
//
HINSTANCE hInst;                      // DLL instance handle

//
// Debug zone support
//
#ifdef DEBUG
// Used as a prefix string for all debug zone messages.
#define DTAG         TEXT ("TickSrv: ")

// Debug zone constants
#define ZONE_ERROR      DEBUGZONE(0)
#define ZONE_WARNING    DEBUGZONE(1)
#define ZONE_FUNC       DEBUGZONE(2)
#define ZONE_INIT       DEBUGZONE(3)
#define ZONE_DRVCALLS   DEBUGZONE(4)
#define ZONE_IOCTLS     DEBUGZONE(5)
#define ZONE_THREAD     DEBUGZONE(6)
#define ZONE_EXENTRY    (ZONE_FUNC | ZONE_DRVCALLS)
// Debug zone structure
DBGPARAM dpCurSettings = {
    TEXT("TickSrv"), {
    TEXT("Errors"),TEXT("Warnings"),TEXT("Functions"),
    TEXT("Init"),TEXT("Service Calls"),TEXT("Undefined"),
    TEXT("IOCtls"),TEXT("Thread"), TEXT("Undefined"),
    TEXT("Undefined"),TEXT("Undefined"),TEXT("Undefined"),
    TEXT("Undefined"),TEXT("Undefined"),TEXT("Undefined"),
    TEXT("Undefined") },
    0x0003
};
#endif //DEBUG

//======================================================================
// DllMain - DLL initialization entry point
//
BOOL WINAPI DllMain (HANDLE hinstDLL, DWORD dwReason,
                     LPVOID lpvReserved) {
    hInst = (HINSTANCE)hinstDLL;

    switch (dwReason) {
        case DLL_PROCESS_ATTACH:
            DEBUGREGISTER(hInst);
            // Improve performance by passing on thread attach calls
            DisableThreadLibraryCalls (hInst);
        break;
```

```
        case DLL_PROCESS_DETACH:
            DEBUGMSG(ZONE_INIT, (DTAG TEXT("DLL_PROCESS_DETACH\r\n")));
            break;
    }
    return TRUE;
}
//======================================================================
// TCK_Init - Service initialization function
//
DWORD TCK_Init (DWORD dwContext) {
    PSRVCONTEXT pSrv;

    DEBUGMSG (ZONE_INIT | ZONE_EXENTRY,
              (DTAG TEXT("TCK_Init++ dwContext:%x\r\n"), dwContext));

    // Init WinSock
    WSADATA wsaData;
    WSAStartup(0x101,&wsaData);

    // Allocate a drive instance structure.
    pSrv = (PSRVCONTEXT)LocalAlloc (LPTR, sizeof (SRVCONTEXT));
    if (pSrv) {
        // Initialize structure.
        memset ((PBYTE) pSrv, 0, sizeof (SRVCONTEXT));
        pSrv->dwSize = sizeof (SRVCONTEXT);
        pSrv->servState = SERVICE_STATE_UNKNOWN;
        InitializeCriticalSection (&pSrv->csData);

        switch (dwContext) {
        case SERVICE_INIT_STARTED:
            pSrv->servState = SERVICE_STATE_ON;
            break;

        case SERVICE_INIT_STOPPED:
            pSrv->servState = SERVICE_STATE_OFF;
            break;
        default:
            break;
        }
    } else
        DEBUGMSG (ZONE_INIT | ZONE_ERROR,
                  (DTAG TEXT("TCK_Init failure. Out of memory\r\n")));
    DEBUGMSG (ZONE_FUNC, (DTAG TEXT("TCK_Init-- pSrv: %x\r\n"), pSrv));
    return (DWORD)pSrv;
}
//======================================================================
// TCK_Deinit - Service de-initialization function
//
```

```
BOOL TCK_Deinit (DWORD dwContext) {
    PSRVCONTEXT pSrv = (PSRVCONTEXT) dwContext;

    DEBUGMSG (ZONE_EXENTRY,
              (DTAG TEXT("TCK_Deinit++ dwContex:%x\r\n"), dwContext));

    if (pSrv && (pSrv->dwSize == sizeof (SRVCONTEXT))) {
        // Free the Service state buffer.
        LocalFree ((PBYTE)pSrv);
    }
    DEBUGMSG (ZONE_FUNC, (DTAG TEXT("TCK_Deinit--\r\n")));
    return TRUE;
}
//======================================================================
// TCK_Open - Service Open function
//
DWORD TCK_Open (DWORD dwContext, DWORD dwAccess, DWORD dwShare) {
    PSRVCONTEXT pSrv = (PSRVCONTEXT) dwContext;

    DEBUGMSG (ZONE_EXENTRY,
              (DTAG TEXT("TCK_Open++ dwContex:%x\r\n"), dwContext));

    DEBUGMSG (ZONE_FUNC, (DTAG TEXT("TCK_Open--\r\n")));
    return (DWORD)pSrv;
}
//======================================================================
// TCK_Close - Service Close function
//
BOOL TCK_Close (DWORD dwContext) {
    PSRVCONTEXT pSrv = (PSRVCONTEXT) dwContext;

    DEBUGMSG (ZONE_EXENTRY,
              (DTAG TEXT("TCK_Close++ dwContex:%x\r\n"), dwContext));

    DEBUGMSG (ZONE_FUNC, (DTAG TEXT("TCK_Close--\r\n")));
    return 0;
}
//======================================================================
// TCK_IOControl - Called when DeviceIOControl called
// ServiceEnumInfo
DWORD TCK_IOControl (DWORD dwOpen, DWORD dwCode, PBYTE pIn, DWORD dwIn,
                     PBYTE pOut, DWORD dwOut, DWORD *pdwBytesWritten) {
    PSRVCONTEXT pSrv;
    DWORD err = ERROR_INVALID_PARAMETER;
    HANDLE hThrd;
    pSrv = (PSRVCONTEXT) dwOpen;

    DEBUGMSG (ZONE_EXENTRY,
              (DTAG TEXT("TCK_IOControl++ dwOpen: %x  dwCode: %x %d\r\n"),
              dwOpen, dwCode, pSrv->servState));
```

```
switch (dwCode) {
// -------------
// Commands
// -------------

// Cmd to start service
case IOCTL_SERVICE_START:
    DEBUGMSG (ZONE_IOCTLS, (DTAG TEXT("IOCTL_SERVICE_START\r\n")));
    EnterCriticalSection (&pSrv->csData);
    if ((pSrv->servState == SERVICE_STATE_OFF) |
        (pSrv->servState == SERVICE_STATE_UNKNOWN)) {

        pSrv->servState = SERVICE_STATE_ON;
        err = 0;
    } else
        err = ERROR_SERVICE_ALREADY_RUNNING;
    LeaveCriticalSection (&pSrv->csData);
    break;

// Cmd to stop service
case IOCTL_SERVICE_STOP:
    DEBUGMSG (ZONE_IOCTLS, (DTAG TEXT("IOCTL_SERVICE_STOP\r\n")));
    EnterCriticalSection (&pSrv->csData);
    if ((pSrv->servState == SERVICE_STATE_ON)) {

        pSrv->servState = SERVICE_STATE_SHUTTING_DOWN;
    } else
        err = ERROR_SERVICE_NOT_ACTIVE;
    LeaveCriticalSection (&pSrv->csData);
    break;

//Reread service reg setting
case IOCTL_SERVICE_REFRESH:
    DEBUGMSG (ZONE_IOCTLS, (DTAG TEXT("IOCTL_SERVICE_REFRESH\r\n")));
    // No settings in example service to read
    break;

//Config registry for auto load on boot
case IOCTL_SERVICE_INSTALL:
    DEBUGMSG (ZONE_IOCTLS, (DTAG TEXT("IOCTL_SERVICE_INSTALL\r\n")));
    err = RegisterService();
    break;

//Clear registry of auto load stuff
case IOCTL_SERVICE_UNINSTALL:
    DEBUGMSG (ZONE_IOCTLS, (DTAG TEXT("IOCTL_SERVICE_UNINSTALL\r\n")));
    err = DeregisterService();
    break;

//Clear registry of auto load stuff
case IOCTL_SERVICE_CONTROL:
    DEBUGMSG (ZONE_IOCTLS, (DTAG TEXT("IOCTL_SERVICE_CONTROL\r\n")));
    err = 0;
    break;
```

```
#ifdef DEBUG
    // Set debug zones
    case IOCTL_SERVICE_DEBUG:
        DEBUGMSG (ZONE_IOCTLS, (DTAG TEXT("IOCTL_SERVICE_DEBUG\r\n")));
        if (!pIn || (dwIn < sizeof (DWORD)))
            break;
        __try {
            dpCurSettings.ulZoneMask = *(DWORD *)pIn;
            err = 0;
        }
        __except (EXCEPTION_EXECUTE_HANDLER) {
            ;
        }
#endif
    // -------------
    // Queries
    // -------------

    // Query for current service state
    case IOCTL_SERVICE_STATUS:
        DEBUGMSG (ZONE_IOCTLS, (DTAG TEXT("IOCTL_SERVICE_STATUS\r\n")));
        if (!pOut || (dwOut < sizeof (DWORD)))
            break;
        __try {
            *(DWORD *)pOut = pSrv->servState;
            if (pdwBytesWritten)
                *pdwBytesWritten = sizeof (DWORD);
            err = 0;
        }
        __except (EXCEPTION_EXECUTE_HANDLER) {
            ;
        }
        break;

// IOCTL_SERVICE_QUERY_CAN_DEINIT was depricated for CE 6. To
// prevent unload, use DEVFLAGS_NOUNLOAD in Flags val in registry
#if (_WIN32_WCE < 0x600)
    // Query for unload.
    case IOCTL_SERVICE_QUERY_CAN_DEINIT:
        DEBUGMSG (ZONE_IOCTLS,
                  (DTAG TEXT("IOCTL_SERVICE_QUERY_CAN_DEINIT\r\n")));
        if (!pOut || (dwOut < sizeof (DWORD)))
            break;
        __try {
            *(DWORD *)pOut = 1; // non-zero == Yes, can be unloaded.
            if (pdwBytesWritten)
                *pdwBytesWritten = sizeof (DWORD);
            err = 0;
        }
        __except (EXCEPTION_EXECUTE_HANDLER) {
            ;
        }
        break;
```

```
#endif
    // Query to see if sock address okay for monitoring
    case IOCTL_SERVICE_REGISTER_SOCKADDR:
        DEBUGMSG (ZONE_IOCTLS,
                  (DTAG TEXT("IOCTL_SERVICE_REGISTER_SOCKADDR\r\n")));
        // Calling to see if service can accept super service help
        if (!pIn || (dwIn < sizeof (DWORD))) {

            if ((pSrv->servState == SERVICE_STATE_OFF) |
                (pSrv->servState == SERVICE_STATE_UNKNOWN))
                    pSrv->servState = SERVICE_STATE_STARTING_UP;
            err = 0;
            break;
        }
        // Confirming a specific sock address
        DEBUGMSG (ZONE_IOCTLS, (DTAG TEXT("Socket:%x\r\n"), *pIn));
        err = 0;
        break;

    // -------------
    // Notifications
    // -------------

    // Notify that sock address going away
    case IOCTL_SERVICE_DEREGISTER_SOCKADDR:
        DEBUGMSG (ZONE_IOCTLS,
                  (DTAG TEXT("IOCTL_SERVICE_DEREGISTER_SOCKADDR\r\n")));
        EnterCriticalSection (&pSrv->csData);
        if (pSrv->servState == SERVICE_STATE_SHUTTING_DOWN)
            pSrv->servState = SERVICE_STATE_OFF;

        LeaveCriticalSection (&pSrv->csData);
        err = 0;
        break;

    // All super service ports open
    case IOCTL_SERVICE_STARTED:
        DEBUGMSG (ZONE_IOCTLS, (DTAG TEXT("IOCTL_SERVICE_STARTED\r\n")));
        EnterCriticalSection (&pSrv->csData);
        if ((pSrv->servState == SERVICE_STATE_STARTING_UP) |
            (pSrv->servState == SERVICE_STATE_UNKNOWN))
            pSrv->servState = SERVICE_STATE_ON;

        LeaveCriticalSection (&pSrv->csData);
        err = 0;
        break;

    // Notification that connect has occurred
    case IOCTL_SERVICE_CONNECTION:
        DEBUGMSG (ZONE_IOCTLS,
                  (DTAG TEXT("IOCTL_SERVICE_CONNECTION\r\n")));
        if (!pIn || (dwIn < sizeof (DWORD)))
            break;
```

```
        // Create thread to handle the socket
        hThrd = CreateThread (NULL, 0, AcceptThread, (PVOID)*(DWORD*)pIn, 0,
                              NULL);
        if (hThrd) {
            CloseHandle (hThrd);
            err = 0;
        }
        else
            err = GetLastError();
        break;

    default:
        DEBUGMSG (ZONE_ERROR | ZONE_IOCTLS,
                  (DTAG TEXT("Unsupported IOCTL code %x (%d)\r\n"),
                  dwCode, (dwCode & 0x00ff) / 4));
            return FALSE;
    }
    SetLastError (err);
    DEBUGMSG (ZONE_FUNC, (DTAG TEXT("TCK_IOControl-- %d\r\n"), err));
    return (err == 0) ? TRUE : FALSE;
}
//======================================================================
// External entry point to make it easy to init the registry
//======================================================================
int ExternRegisterServer () {

    return RegisterService();
}
//----------------------------------------------------------------------
// AddRegString - Helper routine
//
int AddRegString (HKEY hKey, LPTSTR lpName, LPTSTR lpStr) {

    return RegSetValueEx (hKey, lpName, 0, REG_SZ, (PBYTE)lpStr,
                          (lstrlen (lpStr) + 1) * sizeof (TCHAR));
}
//----------------------------------------------------------------------
// AddRegDW - Helper routine
//
int AddRegDW (HKEY hKey, LPTSTR lpName, DWORD dw) {
    return RegSetValueEx (hKey, lpName, 0, REG_DWORD, (PBYTE)&dw, 4);
}
//----------------------------------------------------------------------
// AddRegSuperServ - Helper routine
//
int AddRegSuperServ (HKEY hKey, WORD wPort) {
    SOCKADDR_IN sa;
    HKEY hSubKey;
    TCHAR szKeyName[128];
    DWORD dw;
    int rc;
```

```
    DEBUGMSG (ZONE_FUNC, (DTAG TEXT("AddRegSuperServ++ %d\r\n"), wPort));

    memset (&sa, 0, sizeof (sa));
    sa.sin_family = AF_INET;
    sa.sin_port = htons(wPort);
    sa.sin_addr.s_addr = INADDR_ANY;

    // Create key for this service
    wsprintf (szKeyName, TEXT("Accept\\TCP-%d"), wPort);
    rc = RegCreateKeyEx (hKey, szKeyName, 0, NULL, 0, NULL,
                         NULL, &hSubKey, &dw);
    DEBUGMSG (1, (TEXT("RegCreateKeyEx %d %d\r\n"), rc, GetLastError()));
    if (rc == ERROR_SUCCESS)
        rc = RegSetValueEx (hSubKey, TEXT("SockAddr"), 0, REG_BINARY,
                        (PBYTE)&sa, sizeof (sa));

    DEBUGMSG (ZONE_FUNC, (DTAG TEXT("AddRegSuperServ-- %d\r\n"),rc));
    return rc;
}
//----------------------------------------------------------------------
// RegisterService - Add registry settings for auto load
//
int RegisterService () {
    HKEY hKey, hSubKey;
    TCHAR szModName[MAX_PATH], *pName;
    DWORD dw;
    int rc;

    // Open the Services key
    rc = RegOpenKeyEx(HKEY_LOCAL_MACHINE,TEXT("Services"),0, 0, &hKey);
    if (rc == ERROR_SUCCESS) {
        // Create key for this service
        rc = RegCreateKeyEx (hKey, REGNAME, 0, NULL, 0, NULL,
                             NULL, &hSubKey, &dw);
        if (rc == ERROR_SUCCESS) {

            GetModuleFileName (hInst, szModName, dim (szModName));
            // Scan to filename
            pName = szModName + lstrlen (szModName);
            while ((pName > szModName) && (*pName != TEXT('\\')))
                pName--;
            if (*pName == TEXT('\\')) pName++;
            AddRegString (hSubKey, TEXT ("DLL"),  pName);

            AddRegString (hSubKey, TEXT ("Prefix"),  TEXT("TCK"));

            AddRegDW (hSubKey, TEXT("Index"), 0);
#if (_WIN32_WCE >= 0x600)
            AddRegDW (hSubKey, TEXT("ServiceContext"), SERVICE_INIT_STOPPED);
#else
            AddRegDW (hSubKey, TEXT("Context"), SERVICE_INIT_STOPPED);
```

```
#endif
            AddRegString (hSubKey, TEXT("DisplayName"),
                          TEXT("Tick Service"));

            AddRegString (hSubKey, TEXT("Description"),
                          TEXT("Returns system tick cnt on Port 1000"));

            AddRegSuperServ (hSubKey, PORTNUM);

        } else
            DEBUGMSG (ZONE_ERROR, (TEXT("Error creating key\r\n")));

        RegCloseKey(hKey);
    } else
        DEBUGMSG (ZONE_ERROR, (TEXT("Error opening key\r\n")));

    return (rc == ERROR_SUCCESS) ? 0 : -1;
}
//----------------------------------------------------------------------
// DeregisterService - Remove auto load settings from registry
//
int DeregisterService () {
    HKEY hKey;
    int rc;

    // Open the Services key
    rc = RegOpenKeyEx(HKEY_LOCAL_MACHINE,TEXT("Services"),0, 0, &hKey);
    if (rc == ERROR_SUCCESS) {
        // Delete key for this service
        rc = RegDeleteKey (hKey, REGNAME);
        if (rc != ERROR_SUCCESS)
            DEBUGMSG(ZONE_ERROR, (DTAG TEXT("Error deleting key %d\r\n"),
                     GetLastError()));
        RegCloseKey(hKey);
    } else
        DEBUGMSG (ZONE_ERROR, (TEXT("Error opening key\r\n")));
    return (rc == ERROR_SUCCESS) ? 0 : -1;
}
//======================================================================
// AcceptThread - Thread for managing connected sockets
//
DWORD WINAPI AcceptThread (PVOID pArg) {
    SOCKET sock;
    int rc;
    DWORD dwCmd, dwTicks;

    sock = (SOCKET)pArg;

    DEBUGMSG (ZONE_THREAD, (TEXT("AcceptThread++ %x\r\n"), pArg));

    // Simple task, for any nonzero received byte, sent tick count back
    rc = recv (sock, (char *)&dwCmd, sizeof (DWORD), 0);
```

```
    while ((rc != SOCKET_ERROR) && (dwCmd != 0)) {
        DEBUGMSG (ZONE_THREAD, (TEXT("Recv cmd %x\r\n"), dwCmd));

        dwTicks = GetTickCount ();
        DEBUGMSG (ZONE_THREAD, (TEXT("sending %d\r\n"), dwTicks));
        rc = send (sock, (char *)&dwTicks, 4, 0);

        // Read next cmd
        rc = recv (sock, (char *)&dwCmd, sizeof (DWORD), 0);
    }
    closesocket (sock);
    DEBUGMSG (ZONE_THREAD, (TEXT("AcceptThread-- %d %d\r\n"),rc, GetLastError()));
    return 0;
}
```

The service interface is quite simple. Applications can query the tick count of the device by sending a nonzero *DWORD* to the device. The service will disconnect when the *DWORD* received is zero.

To make it easy to initialize the registry for *TickSrv*, the service exports an additional function, *ExternRegisterServer*. The trivial program, shown following this paragraph, will load *TickSrv* as a DLL, find the entry point and call it.

```
#include "stdafx.h"
int WINAPI WinMain( HINSTANCE hInstance, HINSTANCE hPrevInstance,
                   LPTSTR lpCmdLine, int nCmdShow) {
    HINSTANCE hLib;
    FARPROC lpfn;
    hLib = LoadLibrary (TEXT("TickSrv.DLL"));
    if (hLib == 0) {
        printf ("Error loading TickSrv. rc = %d\r\n", GetLastError());
        return -1;
    }
    lpfn = GetProcAddress (hLib, TEXT("ExternRegisterServer"));
    if (lpfn == 0) {
        printf ("Error finding entry point. rc = %d\r\n", GetLastError());
        return -2;
    }
    // Call the install routine
    (*lpfn)();
    return 0;
}
```

The install application uses *LoadLibrary* and *GetProcAddress* to have TickSrv update the registry. TickSrv will load on the next system reset, but it can also be loaded manually using the Services Manager. Run the following command line to load TickSrv manually:

```
services load TickSrv
```

Listing 17-3 is a simple PC-based client that will open port 1000 on a specified device, send it a command to receive the tick count, wait a few milliseconds, ask again, and then terminate the connection and quit.

LISTING 17-3 The PCClient example

PCClient.cpp

```
//======================================================================
// PCClient.cpp : Simple client for the tick server example
//
// Written for the book Programming Windows CE
// Copyright (C) 2007 Douglas Boling
//======================================================================
#include "stdafx.h"

int _tmain(int argc, _TCHAR* argv[])
{
    SOCKET sock;
    SOCKADDR_IN dest_sin;
    WORD wPort = 1000;
    int rc;

    if (argc < 2) {
        printf ("Syntax: %s <IP Addr> %d\r\n", argv[0], argc);
        return 0;
    }
    // Init winsock
    WSADATA wsaData;
    if ((rc = WSAStartup(0x101,&wsaData)) != 0) {
        printf ("WSAStartup failed\r\n");
        WSACleanup();
        return 0;
    }
    // Create socket
    sock = socket( AF_INET, SOCK_STREAM, 0);
    if (sock == INVALID_SOCKET) {
        return INVALID_SOCKET;
    }

    // Set up IP address to access
    memset (&dest_sin, 0, sizeof (dest_sin));
    dest_sin.sin_family = AF_INET;
    dest_sin.sin_addr.S_un.S_addr = inet_addr (argv[1]);
    dest_sin.sin_port = htons(wPort);

    printf ("Connecting to %s  Port %d\r\n",
            inet_ntoa (dest_sin.sin_addr), wPort);
```

```
    // Connect to the device
    rc == connect( sock, (PSOCKADDR) &dest_sin, sizeof( dest_sin));
    if (rc == SOCKET_ERROR) {
        printf ("Err in connect. %d\r\n", WSAGetLastError());
        closesocket( sock );
        return INVALID_SOCKET;
    }
    DWORD dwCmd = 1, dwTicks = 0;

    // Ask for ticks
    send (sock, (char *)&dwCmd, 4, 0);
    recv (sock, (char *)&dwTicks, 4, 0);
    printf ("Ticks: %d\r\n", dwTicks);

    // Wait 1/4 second and ask again
    Sleep(250);
    send (sock, (char *)&dwCmd, 4, 0);
    recv (sock, (char *)&dwTicks, 4, 0);
    printf ("Ticks: %d\r\n", dwTicks);

    // Terminate connection and close socket
    dwCmd = 0;
    send (sock, (char *)&dwCmd, 4, 0);
    Sleep(100);
    closesocket (sock);
    return 0;
}
```

The Services Manager is quite useful. It provides support for those background tasks that are so often needed in embedded systems. Using a service instead of writing a standalone application also reduces the memory used by the system. In addition, a service can be talked to by applications simply by using the File API.

In this book I have attempted to guide you through the many features of Windows CE, from its base threading API to the peer-to-peer support of the operating system. The componentized design of Windows CE, coupled with a Win32-standard API, provides a unique combination of flexibility and familiarity that is unmatched among today's operating systems. All in all, it's not a bad operating system. Have fun programming Windows CE. I do.

Index

Symbols

A

B

C

D

E

F

G

H

K

L

M

N

O

P

Q

R

S

T

U

V

W

Z

Douglas Boling

Kathleen Atkins

Douglas Boling has been working with small computers since hanging out after school at the Byte Shop in Knoxville, Tennessee, in the mid-1970s. After graduating from single-board computers to Apples to IBM PCs, he has now returned to his roots in embedded systems. He conceived the idea of Vadem Clio and worked on its core design team. Doug teaches classes on Microsoft Windows CE application development and OAL and driver development and has taught many of the leading companies in the Windows CE market. His consulting service assists companies developing Windows CE products. Both his teaching and consulting are done through his company, Boling Consulting (*www.bolingconsulting.com*). Doug has degrees in electrical engineering from the University of Tennessee and the Georgia Institute of Technology. When not sitting in front of a computer monitor or speaking, Doug likes to play with his children, go out on dates with his wife, and drive his convertible on a sunny day.